Divine Love

Islamic Literature and the Path to God

William C. Chittick

Foreword by Seyyed Hossein Nasr

Yale
UNIVERSITY
PRESS
New Haven & London

Published with assistance from the foundation established in memory of Philip Hamilton McMillan of the Class of 1894, Yale College.

Set in Postscript Electra type by Westchester Book Group.
Printed in the United States of America.

Library of Congress Cataloging-in-Publication Data

Chittick, William C.
Divine love : Islamic literature and the path to god / William C. Chittick.
pages cm
Includes bibliographical references and index.
ISBN 978-0-300-18595-9 (alk. paper)
1. Sufism. 2. Sufi literature—History and criticism. I. Title.
BP189.C527 2013
297.2'11—dc23

2012044733

A catalogue record for this book is available from the British Library.

This paper meets the requirements of ANSI/NISO Z39.48–1992 (Permanence of Paper).

10 9 8 7 6 5 4 3 2 1

Contents

FOREWORD

The musician of love, what wondrous musical instrument and playing it possesses,
For whatever melody it plays has a path to some Abode.
May the world be never empty of the moaning of lovers,
For it bears a sweetly melodious and heart-wrenching song.

—(Ḥāfiẓ)

Can one who has not loved write of love? To this question one can respond by asking, Has there ever been someone who has not loved? Indeed, no one can write of love effectively who has not loved, but in order for such writing to convey something of the reality of love, the person must have been able to go beyond that first stage of love, which is love for oneself. Human beings begin to love themselves as soon as they become aware of their own selves as distinct from others. Even men and women who "hate themselves" for one reason or another are attached to and "love" that element within themselves that "hates their selves." For the spiritual person, however, this hating of themselves—or more precisely, lower selves, or *nafs*—is the first stage toward the love of that which lies beyond themselves and ultimately the love of God, which resides already in the heart of His creatures, whether they are aware of it or not. The process of realization in Islamic spirituality involves becoming aware of the ever-expanding circle of what one loves until that ever-widening circle reaches the shore of Divinity and one realizes the love of God and, moreover, becomes aware that this love is the only real love (*al-ʿishq al-ḥaqīqī*), while all other love is metaphorical love (*al-ʿishq al-majāzī*) and a reflection of that one real love that, in the words of Dante at the end of his *Divine Comedy*, "moves the sun and the stars."

Not everyone whose love has reached the other "shore of existence" and who has experienced the love of God has written about it. But those who have done so have set out to express that love because of their love for God's creatures, whom God loves. It has been the vocation of such authors to write of supreme love in order to guide others to the abode of the Beloved, not for any worldly end. And since in the principial domain, love and beauty are combined, a wedding that we experience on the human plane also, their exposition of love has usually been combined with great beauty of expression, whether in poetry or prose.

Islamic spirituality is impregnated with love combined with principial knowledge, as we already see in the Qur'an and the Hadith. The *fedeli d'amore* of Islam have emphasized over and over that love and knowledge complement each other on the spiritual plane. To love God is to know Him, for how can one love that which one does not know? And God is also the Ultimate Reality, one of whose names is *al-Wadūd*, or Love, and so one cannot know Him without loving Him. He is Love and the source of all love. The Sufis often distinguish between real love and metaphorical love, but even metaphorical love is but a ladder that can lead those who yearn for God to the supreme Love that is His alone. The supreme commandment of Christ to love God and to love one's neighbor refers, from the Sufi point of view, not to two loves but to a single Love that pervades all reality. As the famous sacred tradition (*ḥadīth qudsī*) asserts, God was a hidden treasure (*kanz makhfī*) who *loved* to be known, *aḥbabtu an uʿraf*, that is, "I loved to be known," and created the world so that He would be known. This hadith, quoted so often in Sufi texts, not only reveals the principial intertwining of knowledge and love, but also asserts that Divine Love (*al-ḥubb*), combined with knowledge, is the cause of the creation of the world.

Moreover, since God is the Ultimate Cause of all things, His Love for us precedes and is the cause that allows us to love Him. One of the greatest expositors in Islam of the meaning of love, Aḥmad Ghazālī, writes in his *Sawāniḥ* that the greatest distinction of human beings is that God loved them before they could love Him, according to the well-known Qur'anic verse *yuḥibbuhum wa yuḥibbūnah*, "He loves them and [therefore] they love Him." The *wa* in Arabic, which usually means "and," implies implicitly in this verse "therefore." The verse does not say that they love God and therefore God loves them, but asserts that Love begins from the Divine side. Of course, from a human point of view we must exert our will to love God. Metaphysically, however, we cannot love God unless He loves us. The person whom God does not love because of his or her rebellion against Him or disobedience to His commands will not find the love of God in his or her heart, although this love exists in the heart of all human beings by virtue of their being human, even if in many cases it remains hidden and latent, unbeknown to one whose heart has hardened.

One may wonder why so many Western and modern writings on Islam neglect the central reality of love in Islamic piety and spirituality and refuse to consider the relation between Islam and the unparalleled richness of Islamic literature devoted to love, not to speak of the role of love in everyday Islamic devotion. There are many reasons for this myopia, including the centuries-old Christian polemic that seeks to present Christianity as the religion based on love, in contrast to Islam, which, according to them, has the concept of the Divine only as the God of judgment and retribution. They speak as if there were no hell or purgatory in Christianity, and no forgiveness, compassion, or love in Islam.

A thorough discussion of this important issue is not possible in this foreword, but suffice it to say that as a complete religion, Islam of necessity emphasizes also the importance of the fear of God in man's religious life in addition to love and knowledge. It was not a Muslim but the Bible that said, "The fear of the Lord is the beginning of wisdom," a saying that is repeated almost word for word in a well-known hadith of the Prophet. To know God, we must love Him, and to love Him, we must fear Him. The fear of God must not be confused with the ordinary meaning of fear as a negative emotive state. As Abū Ḥāmid Muḥammad Ghazālī said, when a person fears a creature, he runs away from it, but when that person fears the Creator, he runs toward Him. There is something in the soul of man that prevents him from attaining spiritual perfection. That something has to shrivel through fear of the Majesty of God and His Justice so that the higher elements of the soul can be freed to love God. From the human point of view there is the hierarchy of fear, love, and knowledge that the soul marching toward perfection must experience successively.

The present book is one of the most perceptive and authentic works written in English on the theme of love in Islamic spirituality. Some might criticize the book as incomplete because it deals with sources only up to the sixth/twelfth century, but that quibble would be irrelevant, based as it is on unawareness of the nature of the historical unfolding of the tradition of Islamic spirituality. Yes, many Muslim authors after the sixth/twelfth century have written important works on love in both prose and poetry, but the sixth/twelfth century served as a watershed for what was to follow, and limiting oneself to earlier centuries does not mean neglecting any of the central teachings of Islamic spirituality on love.

Moreover, the present work deals solely with prose works in Arabic and Persian. The reader might ask why, in light of there being so many masterpieces in poetry dealing with love, poetic works have not been included. The answer is that there are already numerous studies and translations of the poetic tradition, including Chittick's own well-known work *The Sufi Path of Love,* which deals with the poetry of one of the greatest Sufi masters who sang constantly of love, namely, Jalāl al-Dīn Rūmī. By contrast, the very rich tradition of works on love in prose is hardly known in the West. The author's careful translations of writings by figures such as Maybudī and Samʿānī open the door to a whole literary world of great significance practically unknown to readers of English until now. One has to commend the author for his judicious choice of works treated as well as his meticulous translations and penetrating analyses.

The Sufi authors whose writings are treated here described love not on the basis of the descriptions of others but from their own experience of Divine Love. As for the author of the present volume, when one reads his treatment, one feels that he not only combines the finest scholarship with love for the works he is treating, but also loves the subject with which these texts are concerned. The result is a major work of scholarship in the field of Sufism as well as a valuable treatise on Islamic spirituality in general, from which emanates something of the perfume and light of the *baraka,* or grace, of the reality of Sufism, a reality that is always imbued with love for the One and also for the many in light of the One.

Seyyed Hossein Nasr
July 2012
Ramadan 1433 (A.H.)

Preface

Not too long ago I exchanged e-mails with an old friend, a professor of religious studies who specializes in Hinduism. I happened to mention that I was writing a book on love, and he asked whether I was doing another study of Rūmī. Here we have a well-informed scholar who has taught Islam in his survey courses and guesses that someone writing about the Islamic understanding of love would be talking about Rūmī. Those who know little or nothing about Rūmī's historical context but have been exposed to the popular translations of his poetry may well be surprised to hear that he was a Muslim. In any case, my point is simply that few people associate love with Islam.

In contrast, those familiar with the histories and literatures of the Islamic peoples know that love has been the preoccupation of thousands of Muslim scholars and saints. It is so central to the overall ethos of the religion that if any single word can sum up Islamic spirituality—by which I mean the very heart of the Qur'anic message—it should surely be *love*. I used to think that *knowledge* deserved this honor and that the Orientalist Franz Rosenthal had it right in the title of his book *Knowledge Triumphant*. Now I think that *love* does a better job of conveying the nature of the quest for God that lies at the tradition's heart.

When readers in the West come to appreciate poets like Rūmī, ʿAṭṭār, Ibn al-Fāriḍ, Yūnus Emre, and Ḥāfiẓ, part of the reason is that their poetry conveys the mercy and compassion that inspire the human search for meaning and fulfillment. Some of these poets, most notably Rūmī, taught explicitly that true and real love can be found only in the ultimate source of mercy and compassion. As he puts it in a typical passage:

> Count it a grace that loss comes from the lane of love:
> Let go of metaphorical love, the goal is love for the Real.

The warrior gives a wooden sword to his son
  so that he may become a champion in battle.
Love for a human being is that wooden sword.
  When the trial comes to its end, you will love the All-Merciful.
(*Kulliyyāt* 336–38)

Most poets were not so direct. They did not bother explaining the distinction between true and metaphorical love, because, in the end, lovers will indeed know who it is that they truly love. The task of the poet is rather to stimulate love, fall where it may.

We should keep in mind that the Muslim poets lived in a vibrant culture. They were familiar with an extensive Arabic literature in many fields of learning, a good portion of which talked about love. The Persians among them were proud heirs of an ancient civilization, the language of which had been transformed and invigorated under the influence of Arabic. Given the prominence of Persian sources in the present book, it is worth recalling that the language, which has hardly changed over the past one thousand years, belongs to the Indo-European family, so its grammar is closer to that of English than of Arabic (a sister of Hebrew in the Semitic family). Linguists call it New Persian to distinguish it from Middle Persian and Old Persian. Nowadays, many English speakers call it *Farsi*, but this is like calling German *Deutsch* or Japanese *Nihongo*. New Persian differs from Middle Persian in various ways, most notably in that it takes half its vocabulary from Arabic and uses the Arabic script.

There is something magical about the Persian that appeared in Islamic times. It is as if the language itself invited its speakers to express themselves poetically. I rather doubt whether any native speaker of Persian can be found, even today, who has never tried his or her hand at composing verse. Somewhere I heard a saying that Arabic is the language of God, and Persian the language of the angels. Arabic has its own extraordinary beauty and, especially in the Qur'an, a majestic awesomeness. But talking about God in Arabic keeps Him rather distant, more on the transcendent than immanent side. In contrast, Persian pulls God's beauty into the world on the wings of angels. Persian poetry, which began its great flowering in the eleventh century, shines forth with this angelic presence. The same attention to love and beauty is found also in languages influenced by Persian literary traditions, such as Turkish and Urdu.

Beginning in the late tenth century, there was an upsurge of Persian writing, much of it addressing religious teachings taken from Arabic sources. A good portion was poetry, such as the epic saga of the ancient kings by Firdawsī (d. 1020), which can be enjoyed by any Persian speaker today. During the eleventh and early twelfth centuries, prose came into its own, and several major authors devoted chapters or books to the significance of love for human life. Much of this material has been ignored by Western scholarship, so we get a rather truncated view of how the themes of love developed in Persian poetry.

At the time, Arabic had already seen a good deal of writing devoted to love. The topic was not neglected in the Qur'an, the Hadith (the sayings of Muḥammad), or early Arabic literature, but explanations of love's transformative power came to the fore only gradually. It was as if, at a certain point, scholars and saints felt that the spiritual vibrancy of the original message was becoming obscured, so they set out to make the heart of the message as explicit as possible. This is what I see happening in the love poetry of the newly flowering Persian language.

Love's universality was very much a concern of those who wrote about it. By this I mean they insisted that no one can escape love's call. Religious affiliation or lack thereof is of no account. Many, even most, of those who gave it prominence understood it to be one of God's greatest gifts to His creation.

I was first struck by the notion of love's universal call when, as an undergraduate. I discovered Rūmī, long before anyone other than specialists had heard his name. I devoted two semesters to a careful reading of R. A. Nicholson's translation of Rūmī's *Mathnawī*, and that led me to the study of Persian and Arabic so that I could get at the original sources. By the time I had finished my PhD in Persian literature, I had come to see Rūmī as one wave in a great sea—a large wave to be sure. The first book I published on love, *Divine Flashes* (1981), was a study and translation of a Persian prose classic devoted to love, the *Lamaʿāt* of Fakhr al-Dīn ʿIrāqī (d. 1281). He would have crossed paths with Rūmī in Konya, where he studied with Rūmī's friend Ṣadr al-Dīn Qūnawī (d. 1274), the foremost disciple of Ibn al-ʿArabī (d. 1240). Ibn al-ʿArabī, the great sage from Andalusia, was in turn one of the most prolific and profound authors in Islamic history, not least on the topic of love. It was his unsurpassed ability to bring out the secrets lurking just beneath the surface of the three great books—the universe, the human soul, and the revealed Word—that led me to put aside my exploration of the riches of Persian and to devote many years to a careful study of his writings. Having translated ʿIrāqī's classic on love, I turned to Rūmī with the thought of writing the book I wished I had had as an undergraduate when I was stumbling in the underbrush of the *Mathnawī*, trying to make sense of the forest. That book was published as *The Sufi Path of Love: The Spiritual Teachings of Rumi* (1983). I designed it to be a gradual, systematic introduction to Rūmī's key terminology and concepts, but presented in his words rather than mine.

Despite my forays into many other authors and topics over the years, I remained fascinated by the manner in which Muslim authors were able to employ the language of love to contextualize the yearnings of the human soul in an overall theological vision. I also continued to be a bit puzzled by the insistence of various learned acquaintances that love is the key to Islam, not knowledge, as I had always assumed. It was my wish to understand the exact role that love plays in Islam's theological vision that gave me the idea of preparing a wide-ranging thematic study of love's theological and literary dimensions. The plan was to do what I had done in several previous books: explain the basic teachings and support my explanations by copious quotations from primary sources. Too often the secondary literature has supported its analyses of Islamic thought by brief selections or the say-so of a scholarly expert.

At I first I thought I would draw from Arabic and Persian literature dealing with divine love from the Qur'an down to the nineteenth century. I limited myself to those two languages for the simple reason that I am ignorant of the other Islamic languages and unable to take direct advantage of their rich contributions. Hoping to find time to carry out the project, I submitted a proposal to the National Endowment for the Humanities, and in November 2009 was notified that it had been approved. Needless to say, I am extremely grateful for this assistance, without which I could not have taken leave from teaching and devoted my energies to the research and writing that led to this book.

After receiving the fellowship, I began reading books on love and translating anything that might prove useful. I had planned to include the views of Muslim philosophers, and to this end I translated much of the writing on love by the Ikhwān al-Ṣafāʾ (tenth century), Avicenna (d. 1037), Suhrawardī (d. 1191), and Mullā Ṣadrā (d. 1640). I was planning to include Ibn al-ʿArabī's school of thought also, so I translated many discussions of love from his thirteenth-century followers. These, like the philosophical texts, are presented in abstruse language with logical rigor. When I finally sat down to put the book together, I decided that the more rarefied and speculative approaches deserve a separate study, not least because their complexity would clash with the lightness of the other material.

With some regret, I also decided that the texts I had prepared from the thirteenth century onward would have to be dropped because I had more than enough early material to bring out and contextualize the theology of love. If I had attempted to include the abundant later sources, that would have added a great diversity of voices, but it also would have diluted the remarkable writings of the earlier and less well-known figures. Looking back at this point, I feel fairly confident that the book covers the main theoretical issues addressed by writings on love from the Qur'an down to recent times, even if the vast majority of those who wrote on the topic are not mentioned by name. I hope that other scholars will bring out the still relatively unexplored riches of Islamic love literature in the later period, not only in Arabic and Persian, but also in the other Islamic languages, which came into their own during this time.

Let me come back to the universality of love's call, which attracted me to Rūmī when I was an undergraduate. By this I mean Rūmī's ability to express the ache of every human soul for fulfillment, an ache that he and others understood as an essential component of love. It gradually became clear to me that authors like Rūmī were not floating in the clouds of universal love, detached from the world and the suffering of their fellow human beings. Quite the contrary, the particularity of human existence was as much a part of their message as love's universality, which is to say that they never ignored their own human embodiment and their specifically Islamic foundations, not least the obligations imposed on them by the Prophet's Sunnah. Nonetheless, for many of them the word *islām* was simply a Qur'anic designation for the submission to divine love that is a precondition for attaining full human stature. Therefore, it can be applied to all religions sent by God (as the Qur'an itself makes clear). At the same time, the attention paid by these authors to the particularities of the Islamic tradition presupposes a kind of universal particularism, that is, the recognition that there exists a multiplicity of particularistic divine messages. I mention this point at the outset in order to make clear that this book is not addressed to any specific group of people. Or rather, I wrote it for lovers, whoever they may be and from wherever they may come. At the same time, I have observed the norms of careful scholarship, so perhaps my colleagues in academia will not be too hard on me for ignoring the social and political contexts of the times.

This book can be considered an anthology of Persian and Arabic texts on divine love from the eleventh and twelfth centuries. The book's main thrust, however, is to show that those authors (and their fellow scholars) were rooted in a theological vision that gave love the unique role of bridging the gap between the divine and the human. The texts show how this vision was presented to readers, most of whom—especially the Persian speakers among them—would not have been scholars, but rather ordinary people, searching, like the rest of us, for meaning in their lives.

The book covers a wide range of Islamic theological and philosophical teachings, but the authors of the texts do not present their ideas in the dry and abstract manner of those who are typically presented in the secondary literature as Muslim authorities in these fields. The language of most of the authors I quote is immersed in the mythic imagination, with its concrete imagery and appeal to the immediate concerns of human souls. What I have translated is mainly prose, but a great deal of it is highly poetical. Those familiar with the Persian poetical tradition will recognize much of the imagery and symbolism that was carried over into the still more beautiful and enticing literary forms by poets such as Rūmī, Niẓāmī, Saʿdī, and Ḥāfiẓ.

Once I had the promise of free time for this project, I set out to study a book that I had always wanted to read carefully, though its length prevented me from doing so. Called *The Unveiling of the Secrets and the Provision of the Pious* (*Kashf al-asrār wa ʿuddat al-abrār*), it is one of the earliest and longest commentaries on the Qur'an in the Persian language, though a good portion of it is in Arabic. It was written by Rashīd al-Dīn Maybudī (from the town of Maybud, near Yazd in central Iran), who began the final draft in 1126. Until publication of Annabel Keeler's recent monograph, Maybudī had been largely ignored by Western scholarship. Twenty-some years ago, an erudite and prolific European scholar of Sufism was visiting our home. Noticing the ten volumes of Maybudī's *Unveiling of the Secrets* displayed prominently on our shelves, the scholar asked what sort of book it was. When I replied that it was the most detailed and important twelfth-century source for Sufi teachings in the Persian language, the statement was met with suitable skepticism. I would not make exactly the same judgment today, but I hope that I have been able to illustrate that Maybudī's book deserves much more recognition than it has received.

Maybudī comments on the entire Qur'an in batches of ten or twenty verses and in three stages. In Stage One, he translates the verses literally into Persian, offering no explanation other than the translation itself. In the second and by far the longest stage, he summarizes explanations provided by the Prophet, his companions, and various scholars and commentators, though he seldom mentions his written sources. In Stage Three, which amounts to 1,500 pages, he takes at most a third of the verses and explains their allusions (*ishāra*), by which he means the manner in which the words and imagery can be understood as pointing to various dimensions of the soul's relationship with God.

In the third stage, Maybudī often cites Arabic sayings from earlier figures, many of whom by his time were called Sufis. Usually, but not always, he translates these sayings into Persian and offers explanations and elaborations. In his time, the word *Sufi* was not used as it usually is nowadays, that is, as a generic term for spiritual teachers and their followers (indeed, as Carl Ernst has shown in his *Shambhala Guide to Sufism*, today's meaning of the word is largely a modern coinage laden with political baggage). The word *Sufi* referred rather to certain outstanding individuals who had reached the highest degrees of proximity to God by following in the Prophet's footsteps. In any case, there is no doubt that Stage Three addresses what we can rightly call Islamic spirituality, even if *spirituality* is an academically suspect word. By using this expression, we can single out an approach to Islamic teachings that is radically different from those of jurisprudence (Islamic law) or Kalam (dogmatic and dialectical theology). We can call this approach Sufism, but most of the authors quoted in this book would not have considered themselves Sufis, nor would their contemporaries have referred to them as such. Moreover, philosophers such as the Ikhwān al-Ṣafāʾ and Avicenna say much the same thing about love's reality (as will be seen in Chapter 7), but no one has suggested that they should be called Sufis.

We need to keep in mind that the various approaches to Islamic learning were frequently combined in a single individual, just as they were implicit in the Qur'an and the person of the Prophet. Maybudī provides a fine example of an accomplished scholar who freely shifts from issues in Kalam and jurisprudence—both of which he discusses extensively in Stage Two—to those of spirituality, in each case offering plausible explanations that might help his readers in their own quests for understanding and self-realization. Maybudī's contemporaries would hardly have called him a Sufi. Rather, he was an accomplished master of the various fields of Islamic learning. The title of Keeler's study of Maybudī, *Sufi Hermeneutics*, is thus suggestive but rather misleading, since he is nothing if not eclectic in his approach.

According to the subtitle of the published edition of Maybudī's *Unveiling of the Secrets*, his book was *Known as the Qur'an Commentary of Master ʿAbdallāh Anṣārī*. It came to be called by this name because Maybudī, as he tells us in the introduction, wrote it after having studied the Qur'an commentary of Anṣārī (d. 1088), a famous scholar from Herat. He found it profound and eloquent, but far too short to be of much help to seekers of knowledge and spiritual guidance. Hence, he decided to expand on it so that everyone could benefit. Historians have wondered whether Anṣārī actually wrote a commentary, given that no such book has survived. Keeler, among others, thinks that Maybudī is referring to oral teachings received from Anṣārī's students, since it is unlikely that Maybudī could have studied with him. In the text itself, Maybudī often cites Anṣārī, but on the whole those quotations make up less than 10 percent of Stage Three and little of Stage Two.

After reading through Maybudī and translating several hundred pages, I turned to my favorite Persian text of the twelfth century, *Repose of the Spirits: Explaining the Names of the All-Opening King* (*Rawḥ al-arwāḥ fī sharḥ asmāʾ al-malik al-fattāḥ*), by Aḥmad ibn Manṣūr Samʿānī, who died at the age of forty-six in 1140. I had skimmed through this book in the past and published a study of some of it as "The Myth of Adam's Fall" (by many accounts, the favorite chapter of my little book *Sufism: A Beginner's Guide*). Samʿānī's book seems to be the earliest Persian example of a common theological genre: an explanation of the meaning of the ninety-nine, or most beautiful, names of God (not everyone counts them as ninety-nine, though Samʿānī does). After providing a quick and more or less standard linguistic analysis of the name in question and citing one or two Qur'anic verses in which the name is mentioned, Samʿānī ruminates on the name's implications for human existence. In almost every case, he ties the name back to God's love and compassion. His prose is interspersed with Persian poetry, some of it his own. He quotes Arabic poetry and includes Arabic prose passages that may or may not be quotations. He mentions no sources, though he cites many sayings from early teachers. The final result is one of the longest expositions of love ever written in Arabic or Persian, and perhaps the most profound and enticing. If it has not been recognized as a book on love in the secondary literature, the neglect may be because modern scholars have not read it with care. It was published relatively recently, and the title gives no hint as to its real content. Moreover, its approach is allusive and indirect (as most authors on love thought the topic deserved to be treated), and the prose often dense and convoluted.

The little we know about Samʿānī's life is provided by his nephew, ʿAbd al-Karīm Samʿānī (d. 1167), author of *The Lineages* (*al-Ansāb*), a well-known biographical dictionary. The two were members of a scholarly family from the cosmopolitan city of Merv (in today's Turkmenistan). ʿAbd al-Karīm says that his uncle was an eloquent preacher, but he does not mention any books by him. He describes him as a master of Islamic learning, but in no way does he suggest that he was a Sufi. ʿAbd al-Karīm tells us that his grandfather, Aḥmad's father Manṣūr (d. 1096), wrote books on the Hadith and jurisprudence as well as a commentary on the Qur'an. Samʿānī sometimes cites sayings from his father in *Repose of the Spirits*, but he must have received them through an intermediary, since, according to his nephew at least, he was only two years old when his father died.

When I first looked at Samʿānī's book twenty-some years ago, I noticed a few passages similar to Maybudī's commentary. Keeler mentions that an Iranian scholar pointed this out in an article. Samʿānī and Maybudī were contemporaries, and it was not clear to me or to anyone else who was reading whom, or whether the two were drawing from the same source. In the course of studying the two books, I was able to determine that Maybudī drew from Samʿānī. He must have received a copy of *Repose of the Spirits* around the time he finished his explanation of Surah 16 (about halfway through his book). From the beginning of the commentary on Surah 17 to the end of the book, Maybudī frequently draws from *Repose*, sometimes verbatim. As often as not, he revises and simplifies Samʿānī's complicated prose.

On the whole Maybudī uses at least as much material from Samʿānī as he does from Anṣārī, and indeed, the tone and style of the second half of Stage Three shifts noticeably under Samʿānī's influence. In the case of Anṣārī, however, Maybudī usually mentions his name or refers to him by the epithet Pir of the Tariqah (*pīr-i ṭarīqat*). *Pīr*, the Persian translation of the Arabic *shaykh*, means elder or teacher, and the *ṭarīqat* is the narrow path to God, that followed by those who were called Sufis as well as by countless other Muslims who would have seemed unremarkable to their contemporaries. Pir of the Tariqah was a title given to those who guided disciples on this path. Maybudī uses the expression in reference to other teachers as well, but in those cases he also mentions their names. Almost invariably, when he ascribes a passage simply to the Pir of the Tariqah, he means Anṣārī.

When Maybudī borrows from Samʿānī, he rarely indicates that he is quoting. When he does, he gives no hint of the speaker's identity. Failure to mention sources was common in Islamic texts before modern times, since there was little sense of personal ownership of ideas or their expression. In any case, Maybudī does not identify any sources other than Anṣārī, so we should not imagine that he was singling Samʿānī out for neglect. For example, in Stage Three, Maybudī makes extensive use of *Subtle Allusions* (*Laṭāʾif al-ishārāt*), a Qur'an commentary by Abu'l-Qāsim al-Qushayrī (d. 1072). Qushayrī is the author of the famous *Treatise* (*Risāla*), a standard Arabic teaching text concerning the path to God, wholly or partly translated into English three times. Despite frequent verbatim borrowings, Maybudī never mentions the book or its author by name.

When I began my research, I knew that Anṣārī himself would have important things to say about love, but I was pleasantly surprised to see how rich a source he turned out to be. He wrote in both Arabic and Persian on theology, jurisprudence, and the spiritual path. Historians have pointed out that many of his works were compiled by disciples. However that may be, the texts I used are consistent in style and content, a fact that helped me find several passages that Maybudī cites from him without saying so. Among the books that were likely compiled after his death is the first Persian account of the lives of the great masters of Islamic spirituality, *The Generations of the Sufis* (*Ṭabaqāt al-ṣūfiyya*). This was a major source for ʿAṭṭār's well-known *Memorial of the Friends* (*Tadhkirat al-awliyāʾ*). Anṣārī is considered an authority in Hanbalite theology, a school that in the fourteenth century famously produced Ibn Taymiyya and Ibn Qayyim al-Jawziyya, both of whom—it is often forgotten—wrote extensively on love (as Joseph Norment Bell has shown in *Love Theory in Later Hanbalite Islam*).

Anṣārī's best-known Arabic book is *Way Stations of the Travelers* (*Manāzil al-sā'irīn*), the classic description of the path to God, depicted as one hundred stages, each of which is subdivided into three levels. The text provides a dense description of the soul's transformation as it gains ever-greater proximity to the divine reality. Anṣārī had already written a similar book in Persian called *One Hundred Fields* (*Ṣad maydān*). The word *field* is used for battlefields, polo grounds, and city squares. Here he seems to have in mind the battlefields in which the seeker of God engages in struggle (*jihād*) against his own self. The Arabic book, composed about thirty years after the Persian, is similar in structure but by no means based upon it.

Anṣārī wrote beautifully in both Arabic and Persian. He is one of the first authors who can be cited to demonstrate the truth of the saying "Persian is sugar" (*pārsī shikar ast*). The sweetness of his language is especially obvious in his most famous Persian compositions, his whispered prayers (*munājāt*). This Arabic word, derived from *najwā*, "to whisper," means to talk secretly with someone or to hold a private conversation. According to the Prophet, "The person saying the ritual prayer [*ṣalāt*] is whispering [*munājāt*] with his Lord." The word gradually came to designate an especially intimate form of addressing God, and Anṣārī was the first and greatest master of the art in the Persian language. He probably never wrote the prayers down as a separate work, and there are different collections of them in manuscript. Some of his writings, such as *Forty-Two Chapters* (*Chihil u daw faṣl*), have passages that were later cited among the prayers. Maybudī frequently quotes the prayers, some of them several times, but it is fairly clear, not least because of variants of the same prayer, that he was drawing from memory, not a written text. Anṣārī also wrote what may be the first independent Persian treatise on love, *The Book of Love* (*Maḥabbat-nāma*). In twenty-eight chapters and thirty-some pages, it describes various qualities that the soul may come to acquire by loving God. It is an exquisite text, even more aphoristic and allusive than is usual in books on love.

Maybudī and Samʿānī were younger contemporaries of the Ghazālī brothers, though I found little evidence that either was familiar with their works. Muḥammad Ghazālī (d. 1111) is universally regarded as one of the greatest scholars of the Islamic tradition, and has been the object of numerous studies in Western languages. He wrote outstanding books on the important Islamic sciences, not least jurisprudence, principles of jurisprudence, Kalam, philosophy, and the spiritual path. What sets him apart from most other early authors is how he integrated various perspectives and schools of thought. His most famous book in Arabic, *Giving Life to the Sciences of the Religion* (*Iḥyā' ʿulūm al-dīn*), in four volumes of ten chapters each, addresses all the concerns of those who aspire to understand God and to act as He wants them to. Ghazālī begins each chapter by citing the Qur'an, the Hadith, and the sayings of great Muslims, and then explains the ideas in a fluent, systematic, and logical fashion. Many of the chapters of *Giving Life* have been translated into English, in each case as an independent book; the chapter on love appeared in 2011. Ghazālī's abbreviated Persian version of that chapter has been translated as part of the book in which it is found, *The Alchemy of Felicity* (*Kīmiyā-yi sa'ādat*). Given Ghazālī's fame in the Western literature and the availability of his two chapters on love, I have mostly ignored him, despite his great importance.

As for Muḥammad's younger brother Aḥmad (d. 1126), he is the author of several prose treatises in Arabic and Persian, by far the most famous of which is *Apparitions* (*Sawāniḥ*), which has often been considered the classic Persian text on love. Historians have written that the book was highly influential in the tradition of writing on love, though my sense is that they might have demoted it if they had been familiar with Maybudī and Samʿānī. Keeler follows in the usual line when she says that aside from Anṣārī, the two works that had the most influence on Maybudī were Qushayrī's *Subtle Allusions* and Aḥmad's *Apparitions*, though she offers no more evidence for the latter than a single short passage. She does speak of stylistic similarities, but given Maybudī's propensity to quote without ascription or alteration, the lack of any other citations from *Apparitions* is surprising. Aḥmad's book has been translated into English with little attention to its poetic quality, so I hope that the few examples I have provided here will show why it has proved attractive over the centuries, much more so than his brother's Persian writings.

I cite passages from other authors, about whom I will say something in the text. These include the Ikhwān al-Ṣafā', Avicenna, Abū Ibrāhīm Bukhārī, Hujwīrī, Manṣūr ʿAbbādī, and Rūzbihān Baqlī. I have not drawn from the love poets, not least because their verse demands contextualization and commentary, whereas prose is relatively self-explanatory. Moreover, the poets have been studied extensively in the secondary literature. The most important single poem on divine love in the Arabic language, the 760-verse *Poem of Wayfaring* (*Naẓm al-sulūk*) by Ibn al-Fāriḍ (d. 1235), would have been a bit late for my final draft, but in any case it has been translated into English three times by important scholars.

The first in the line of great Persian love poets, Sanā'ī of Ghazna (d. 1131), has attracted a good deal of attention, though not nearly as much as he deserves. A contemporary of Maybudī and Samʿānī, Sanā'ī wrote dense and difficult verse, so it is not without reason that he was given the title *ḥakīm*, sage or philosopher. His poetry is rich with allusions to the Qur'an, the Hadith, philosophy, theology, Arabic poetry, and so on. A thorough analysis of any of his great *qaṣīdas* could occupy a lengthy monograph. It is worth noting that he was Maybudī's favorite poet. When citing him, Maybudī typically quotes one or two lines from "that chevalier." In the twelfth century, the word *chevalier* (Persian *jawānmard*, translation of Arabic *fatā*, literally, "young man") was used to designate the ideal lover of God. Maybudī, Samʿānī, and Aḥmad Ghazālī, among others, sometimes address their readers with it, indicating not who the readers are, but what they should be striving to become, namely, people of perfect virtue, wisdom, generosity, kindness, and compassion.

As for the other great Persian love poet before Rūmī, ʿAṭṭār of Nishapur (d. 1221), author of the famous *Language of the Birds* (*Manṭiq al-ṭayr*), he was the object of the massive study of Helmut Ritter, *The Ocean of the Soul: Man, the World, and God in the Stories of Farīd al-Dīn ʿAṭṭār.* The book was published in German in 1955 and translated into English in 2003 (with an updated bibliography and apparatus). The pages devoted specifically to love (360–614) provide a rich survey of the literature. Ritter wrote as a historian and a classifier, analyzing ʿAṭṭār's concepts and themes by reducing them to statements, providing summaries or translations of the illustrative stories, and cross-referencing with a wealth of earlier and later sources, both Arabic and Persian (and sometimes Turkish). Despite his vast knowledge of Arabic and Persian manuscripts, Ritter apparently had not come across the books of Samʿānī and Maybudī, the two richest Persian sources for teachings on love before ʿAṭṭār.

When I first began collecting material, I thought that I would make use of the earliest-known full-length Arabic book on love for God, written by Ḥasan al-Daylamī (d. ca. 1000). This is an excellent example of a transitional work between early Sufi writings, which are mainly compilations of sayings from the Qur'an, the Hadith, and the great spiritual teachers, and later, theoretical works, such as those of Muḥammad Ghazālī, which provide extensive elaborations on the same sayings. What distinguishes Daylamī's book from chapters on love in the Sufi literature of the same period—like the *Treatise* by Qushayrī or *Food of the Hearts* (*Qūt al-qulūb*) by Abū Ṭālib Makkī (d. 996)—is its length and its attention to Kalam, philosophy, and belles lettres. In the end, I decided that the fine English translation of this book by Joseph Norment Bell and Hassan Al Shafie made it unnecessary for me to cite from it (with one exception).

It is worth remarking that Bell and Al Shafie call their translation of Daylamī's book *A Treatise on Mystical Love. Mystical* here should be understood as the counterpart of *profane*, which is the expression chosen by Lois Giffen for her survey of the literary genre that addresses interpersonal or romantic love,

Theory of Profane Love Among the Arabs. What makes Daylamī's book mystical is that it talks of the mysteries of the relationship between the soul and God, and what makes the other genre profane is that it does not specifically address this issue. As a general rule, however, authors of books in both genres drew from the same stock of Arabic poetry and sometimes the same anecdotes, such as those handed down about the famous lovers Laylā and Majnūn. In one case, the authors read the verses or anecdotes as referring to the soul's love for God, and in the other to interpersonal human love. In Islamic thought, generally there is no essential difference between the two sorts of love, for love is a divine reality wherever it appears (Avicenna sets the tone on this point in the treatise cited in Chapter 7).

Although I set out to give equal weight to Arabic and Persian, the book ended up heavily slanted toward the latter. From the beginning, I knew that Maybudī and Samʿānī would provide excellent material, but I had hoped that I would find as much in Arabic (indeed, I easily could have had I gone into the thirteenth century; Ibn al-ʿArabī's teachings alone could fill a lengthy volume). In the short amount of time at my disposal, it would have been impossible to find and read every book on love in Arabic that I had not yet seen, but I did my best to review what I had in hand and to look closely at other books mentioned in the secondary literature. I do not think I missed too much of the published material. In the final push and shove of writing, I chose sweetness of expression over precision of argument. That decision helps explain why I included Aḥmad Ghazālī's Persian *Apparitions* and ignored his brother's chapters on love. If we were looking simply at the theological and doctrinal dimensions of love, Muḥammad Ghazālī's treatment is far more thorough and complete than Aḥmad's. But if we want to bring out the mysteries of the interpenetration of divine and human love, *Apparitions* does a better job, and without the abstract language.

Generally speaking, Persian texts on religious issues are more accessible than Arabic books on the same topics. This is often because they were written as summaries of or commentaries on Arabic originals. The authors intended them for those who did not have the training to look at the Arabic sources or the wherewithal to find teachers. Many Persian authors went to great lengths to write clearly, and if anything, they tended to become long-winded in drawing out the implications of a brief Arabic statement. That sort of writing is relatively easy to follow in English translation because it does not assume a great deal of knowledge, in contrast to the original Arabic passages. Moreover, the Persian authors tended to employ rich, concrete imagery, whereas the parallel Arabic discussions preferred abstract, technical terms.

Maybudī provides a good example of the advantage of Persian over Arabic, at least for nonspecialists. As noted, he often draws from Qushayrī's *Subtle Allusions*, a dense and aphoristic text. In explaining a single Qur'anic verse, Qushayrī will sometimes offer five or ten brief interpretations drawn from usually unnamed authors. On occasion, Maybudī will quote all or part of Qushayrī's text and leave it at that. Often, after quoting Qushayrī, he will provide an interpretive translation, at which point an aphorism becomes a long paragraph, much clearer than the original. Frequently, Maybudī does not bother citing the Arabic, but takes inspiration and goes off on his own. Much of his popularity over the centuries has been due to his ability to bring the abstruse sayings of the early Sufis into everyday language.

I began writing this book by classifying well over a thousand pages of newly translated texts according to theme. It gradually became obvious that the authors were answering three basic questions: Where does love come from? How can people live up to love in their everyday lives? Where will love take them in the end? Hence, I arranged the selections under three general headings: the origin of love, the life of love, and the goal of love. Having made a final choice about which texts to include and which to drop, I set out to provide the necessary theological contextualization. Nowhere do I try to define love, for the authors insist that it cannot be defined or explained, even if its symptoms can be described. Love's reality can be understood only by embracing and living it. As Rūmī puts it:

> Someone asked, "What is love?" I said,
> "Don't ask about these meanings
> When you become like me, you'll know.
> When He calls you, you'll recite its tale."
>
> (*Kulliyyāt* 29050–51)

At this point I should say something about the words used for love in Arabic and Persian. Early discussions typically used the Qur'anic words *ḥubb* and *maḥabba*, two gerunds from a root that is found in the Qur'an eighty times. The Qur'an talks about love also in terms of a second root, whose gerunds are *wudd* and *mawadda*, about thirty times. From this root is derived the divine name Loving, *wadūd*. The Qur'an uses a third term, *hawā*, "caprice" or "whim," to designate misguided love, but the later literature frequently uses it without a negative connotation.

The most important extra-Qur'anic word for love is *ʿishq*, which is often taken to mean intense or passionate love. In the early philosophical literature, it is typically used as the generic word. Most authors agree that *ʿishq* designates the intense and passionate love that can appear in a human relationship. Some cite with approval the saying, traceable to Plato's *Phaedrus*, that ʿishq is a divine madness (*junūn ilāhī*). Many would contrast it with the long-term, deeply rooted love of two spouses, which can better be called maḥabba or mawadda. The Kalam experts held that the word *ʿishq* could not be applied to God's love for man or man's love for God, but scholars in other disciplines seldom paid much attention to their objections (Bell and Al Shafie provide a good summary of the theological debates in their introduction to *A Treatise on Mystical Love*). In Persian poetry, *ʿishq* is the preferred term.

From early times, scholars writing in Arabic analyzed a great variety of words that are used in talking about love. In *Theory of Profane Love Among the Arabs*, Giffen says that those who attempted to be comprehensive provided from sixty to eighty "names and kinds" of love. In *Love Theory in Later Hanbalite Islam*, Bell points out that Ibn Qayyim al-Jawziyya provided definitions of fifty-one words referring to love at the beginning of his theological tract *The Garden of Lovers* (*Rawḍat al-muḥibbīn*). In the meticulous study *Love in the Holy Qur'an*, the contemporary Jordanian scholar Ghazi bin Muhammad finds thirty-eight Qur'anic terms designating various kinds of love.

By the time authors started writing about love in Persian, they used the same Arabic terms, often treating *maḥabba* and *ʿishq* as synonyms. The most common approach to the debates over whether *ʿishq* can be applied to divine love came to be that voiced by ʿIrāqī in the introduction to *Lamaʿāt*: "Call it maḥabba or ʿishq—let us not quarrel over words." In addition, authors often used two Persian words. One is *mihr*, which is the New Persian descendent of the Avestan *mithra*, the name of one of the twelve Zoroastrian archangels and the object of worship in the Greco-Roman Mithraic mysteries. The second, used much more commonly, is *dūstī*, a noun derived from *dūst*, meaning "friend," "lover," or "beloved." In today's Persian, *dūstī* means friendship, not love. Even so, in order to say, "I love you," you need to say, "*Dūstat dāram*," literally, "I have you as friend." As a synonym for the Arabic *ḥubb*, the compound verb *dūst dāshtan*, "to have as friend," goes back to the beginning of New Persian, as is shown by, among other things, the fact that Maybudī translates Qur'anic verses using *ḥubb* with this verb. Anṣārī used *dūstī* interchangeably with *maḥabba* and *mihr*. It should be noted also that in Arabic, *ḥubb* is one of the most common words for friendship, so the distinction between friendship and love is often made by translators.

When Persian authors wrote about friendship, they used *dūstī* or *maḥabba* rather than *ʿishq*, which is reserved for intense or romantic love. When the word *dūst* is used in Persian poetry, translators commonly render it as "friend," though one could also translate it as "lover," in the sense of someone you love and who loves you. When the word *dūst* refers to God, I translate it as "the Friend."

Another terminological complication arises with the Arabic word *walī*, "friend," an important Qur'anic word and one of the divine names. When translating it into Persian, Maybudī and others use *dūst*, but they use *dūst* to translate *ḥabīb* and *maḥbūb* also (both derived from *ḥubb*). *Friendship* is then *walāʾ* and *walāya* (or *wilāya*). The root meaning of *walī* is "closeness," along with "activity appropriate for closeness." Thus we have *wālī*, which means "governor" or "ruler," that is, someone who, because of closeness to the king, is given rulership (walāya) over a province (walāya). In Shi'ism, the specific authority handed over to the Imams by the Prophet is called walāya. In today's Iran, this word has been given a political twist with the expression *walāyat-i faqīh*, the "rulership of the jurist."

The Qur'an uses the word *awliyāʾ*, the plural of *walī*, to designate the friends of God, and a great discussion arose over the centuries as to their identity. They are not simply the prophets, though the prophets are certainly friends of God, nor do they seem to be the same as the faithful, even though "*God is the friend of those who have faith*" (Qur'an 2:257). They are usually understood as a third category, standing between the ordinary faithful and the prophets. Moreover, throughout the Islamic world from early times, Muslims have recognized certain deceased individuals as God's friends and, as a result, have venerated their memory and their tombs. Scholars often translate the term in this sense as "saint," but the English word is problematic, given its strong Christian connotations and the fact that Christian saints are designated by the church. In Islam, God's friends are determined by the consensus of a community, often local. Moreover, the Qur'an makes clear that Satan has awliyāʾ, and they are surely not saints. In any case, in our texts here, when authors use the word *walī*, they follow Qur'anic usage, understanding God's friends as those who are exceptionally close to Him and thus objects of His love.

In what follows I translate *ḥubb* and its derivatives as "love," *wudd* (rarely used outside the Qur'anic context) as "love" or "affection," *ʿishq* as "passion," *mihr* as "love," and *dūstī* as "friendship." It needs to be kept in mind, however, that these words are often used interchangeably, which is to say that love, passion, and friendship are frequently the same notion. Nonetheless, there are passages in which authors make distinctions among the meanings of the words, and those familiar with the languages may want to know which word is being used in any given case.

Abbreviations

Chihil.	Anṣārī, *Chihil u daw faṣl.*
Iḥyā'.	Ghazālī, *Iḥyā' 'ulūm al-dīn.*
Kashf.	Maybudī, *Kashf al-asrār.*
Laṭā'if.	Qushayrī, *Laṭā'if* al-*ishārāt*
Maḥabbat.	Anṣārī, *Maḥabbat-nāma.*
Manāzil.	Anṣārī, *Manāzil al-sā'irīn.*
Maydān.	Anṣārī, *Ṣad maydān.*
Rawḥ.	Sam'ānī, *Rawḥ al-arwāḥ.*
Sawāniḥ.	Aḥmad Ghazālī, *Sawāniḥ.*
Taṣfiya.	'Abbādī, *al-Taṣfiya fī aḥwāl al-ṣūfiyya.*

A Note on Format

I have avoided endnotes as much as I could. Citations from the Qur'an are italicized, with chapter and verse in brackets. Hadiths that are quoted in translated passages without explicit ascription to the Prophet are indicated by an asterisk. Unascribed quotations usually mean that an Arabic proverb or saying is being mentioned in the midst of a Persian discussion, or that the author of the passage is putting words into someone's mouth. Proper names are identified in the index of names and terms. Transliteration follows the standard, modified system of *The Encyclopedia of Islam*. Capital letters are used for pronouns referring to God both to avoid ambiguity and to maintain consistency.

Part One

The Origin of Love

1

The Theological Context

By *theology,* I mean discussion of the divine reality and its relationship with the universe. During the formative period of Islamic thought, up until around the eleventh century, theologians could be classified into three broad schools of thought, which historians have typically called Kalam (dogmatic, scholastic, or dialectical theology), Sufism or mysticism, and philosophy. At least from the time of Muḥammad Ghazālī, the categories started to break down as authors tended more and more to combine the approaches.

Those theologians who addressed the issue of love did so in the context of various terminological givens, such as the notion of unity; the depiction of God as Essence, attributes (or names), and acts; and the complementarity of divine attributes. Part of what distinguishes the approach of those with Sufi leanings from that of the Kalam experts is the stress on the human side of the divine-human relationship.

Generally speaking, experts in Kalam insisted on God's utter transcendence and downplayed any suggestion of immanence. By doing so, they obscured the fact that the human perception and reception of God are intimately bound up with human nature. Trying to avoid anthropomorphism, they sought refuge in the abstrusities of rational thought and avoided the imagery and symbolism of the Qur'an and the Hadith, especially when these depicted God in blatantly human terms. A good portion of the writing of Ibn al-ʿArabī addresses this allergy of Kalam to taking the Qur'an at face value. He advises the Kalam experts to stop explaining away the apparent meaning of the verses and to open up their souls to God's disclosure of Himself in forms and symbols. He does not deny the necessity of the abstracting power of rationality (reason, in his view, is one of the two eyes of the heart), but he wants people to give equal time to imagination and symbolism.[1]

Theologians who stressed the centrality of love in the human-divine relationship often talked about dry issues of theological discourse, but tended to avoid the abstractions and tedious argumentation favored by Kalam and philosophy and instead tied the discussion back to Qur'anic symbolism and the everyday experience of the human soul. The fact that they focused on love shows that they were writing with the goal of bringing humans and God together, not keeping them apart. Rational analysis, as Ibn al-ʿArabī never tires of reminding his readers, drives God from the soul and leaves seekers bereft of the object they should be seeking. Kalam experts advised those who would like to love God that He is far, far beyond pitiful human attempts to grasp Him in their embrace. Ibn al-ʿArabī and others like him never forgot that it is God's very otherness, the fact that He utterly transcends every notion of transcendence, that puts Him in the midst of the human soul and opens it up to love.

In one of my favorite passages contrasting the abstract theorizing of the rational thinkers with the scriptural imagery and symbolism embraced by lovers, Ibn al-ʿArabī offers the following observation. Notice that he is referring to a famous divine saying about the creation of the universe. In its most common version, it reads: "I was a hidden treasure and I loved to be recognized, so I created the creatures so that they might recognize Me." He is also referring to the Hadith of Gabriel, in which the Prophet defines *iḥsān*, "doing the beautiful," as "worshiping God *as if* you see Him." As we will see, this definition of *iḥsān* is central to the general understanding of the path to God. Notice also that Ibn al-ʿArabī uses the word *Shariah* (*sharīʿa*) in its broadest sense, that is, revealed religion. This becomes clear when he pluralizes it in the first paragraph, meaning all the religions sent by God.[2]

> By God, were it not for the Shariah that came with the divine report-giving, no one would recognize God! Had we remained with our rational proofs—which, in the opinion of the rational thinkers, demonstrate the knowledge that God's Essence is "not like this" and "not like that"—no created thing would ever have loved Him. But the divine reports have come in the tongues of the Shariahs, saying that "He is like this" and "He is like that" and mentioning things whose outward meanings are contradicted by rational proofs.
>
> He made us love Him through these positive attributes. Then, having set down the relationships and established the causes and kinship that bring about love, He said, "*Nothing is as His likeness*" [42:11].
>
> Thus He affirmed the causes that bring about love, even if rational proofs deny them. This is the meaning of His words, "I created the creatures and made Myself recognized to them, so they came to recognize Me." They rec-

ognize God only by means of what He reported about Himself: His love for us, His mercy toward us, His clemency, His tenderness, His loving-kindness, His descent into limitation so that we may conceive of Him in images and place Him before our eyes in our hearts, our kiblah, and our imagination, such that it is "as if" we see Him. Or rather, we do indeed see Him within ourselves, for we have come to recognize Him by His making Himself recognized, not by our own rational consideration.

(*al-Futūḥāt al-makkiyya* 2:326)

THE ISLAMIC WORLDVIEW

A good deal of the secondary literature on love in Islamic civilization investigates writings on profane love, which make relatively little reference to the Qur'an and the Hadith, preferring instead to address the trials and tribulations of human lovers, especially as they were celebrated in Arabic poetry from earliest times. In contrast, books on divine love are rooted explicitly or implicitly in the Qur'anic worldview (though in the case of early philosophers, that basis may not be obvious). Failure to grasp the givens of the discussion will make it difficult to see the ground on which the authors were standing. Let me then summarize the basic standpoint of the texts.

The most concise expression of the Islamic worldview is found in the Shahadah (*shahāda*), the formula of bearing witness: "I bear witness that there is no god but God and I bear witness that Muḥammad is God's messenger." This statement gives us three primary issues, each of which is discussed throughout the Qur'an: First, there are those who bear witness to the message, that is, human beings. Second, there is God, who sends the message. Third, there are the Messenger and the message, the intermediaries between God and man. More simply, we have human beings, Ultimate Reality, and the tie that binds them together; or lovers, the Beloved, and love.

These three issues are the foundation upon which most religious traditions are built, whatever the language used to express them. They become Islamic when those who speak of them take the truth of the Qur'an for granted and pose the issues in its terms. To say that they take the Qur'an as true, however, does not mean that they think its meaning is always clear. Any survey of Islamic literature will show that the question of how to interpret the message has always been hotly debated. I have already alluded to the fact that Qur'an commentators like Maybudī and Qushayrī, not to mention the great Fakhr al-Dīn Rāzī (d. 1209), frequently offer several interpretations for any given verse. The plethora of Qur'an commentaries throughout history provides a great variety of readings and standpoints. Ibn al-ʿArabī goes so far as to assert that every interpretation of the Qur'an for which a case can be made on the basis of the Arabic language was in fact intended by God, who knew from the outset every possible interpretation of His speech.[3]

The Shahadah acknowledges the existence of man, asserts that God is the reality beyond all, and adds that this reality communicates itself by means of the Messenger. But who exactly is man, what exactly is God, and what precisely does the message say? Uttering the Shahadah before two witnesses is the minimal definition of being a Muslim. The act provides orientation, but it is simply the first step in a lifelong process. Understanding the implications of the utterance is the goal of Islamic scholarship.

Theologians often speak of God's message as having three basic principles: *tawḥīd*, or the assertion of God's unity; prophecy (*nubuwwa*), or the explication of the nature of the intermediaries between God and man; and the Return (*maʿād*), or the final encounter, when human beings go back to their Origin (*mabda*'). The relationship between Origin and Return became a vital discussion in both philosophy and Sufism, though the experts in Kalam paid relatively little attention to it. Many scholars described the two together as "the circle of existence" (*dā'irat al-wujūd*), beginning with God, descending into creation and manifestation, and ascending back to God. The force that drives this process was frequently called love. Most discussions of divine love look at the universe as love's fruit, and the human return to God as its final goal.

The first formula of the Shahadah, "(There is) no god but God," is called *kalimat al-tawḥīd*, the sentence voicing (God's) unity. The basic meaning of the word *tawḥīd* is to say one. Islamic theology in all forms makes tawḥīd the foundational axiom for discussion of God, the universe, and man. Implications of tawḥīd can quickly be discerned with the help of the formula. It means that there is no true god but the Eternal God, nothing truly one but the Eternal One, nothing truly alive but the Living, nothing truly knowing but the Omniscient, nothing truly powerful but the Omnipotent, nothing truly loving but the Loving. Each of God's most beautiful names (*al-asmā' al-ḥusnā*) can be inserted into the formula to throw light on the Divine Reality.

Tawḥīd is a statement about God per se, the Ultimate Reality as such, without regard to the universe, time, or history. At first glance, it provides a static picture: the one God is the true reality, and all positive qualities of existence—life, love, creativity, consciousness, compassion, forgiveness, justice—are true and real in Him alone. At second glance, it contains an implicit dynamism, for the True Reality brings the universe into existence, sustains all things moment by moment, and takes each of them back to its final home. Everything comes from God, is constantly supported by Him, and returns to Him. Things come and go, originate and return, descend and ascend. All are driven by love.

The second formula of the Shahadah, "Muḥammad is God's messenger," brings up the issue of the human role in creation. Given our innate intelligence, awareness, and moral sense, what should we do with ourselves? The brief answer: God in His love and mercy recognizes our inability to figure out who we are and what we should be doing about it, so He provides guidance to show us how to live in conformity with our true selves. We will return to God whether we want to or not, so the wisest course is to prepare for the encounter. As Plato pointed out, philosophy—love of wisdom—is preparing oneself for death, and the Muslim philosophers, like Muslims generally, took wisdom to heart. There is none truly wise, after all, but God. To love God is to love wisdom, and wisdom demands activity appropriate for returning to the Origin.

In His gentleness and kindness, God would like us to return in a manner congenial to our natures. So He sends messengers with good news and warning. The good news is that if we follow God's guidance, we will put ourselves in harmony with His mercy. The bad news is that if we do not follow His guidance, we will diverge from what is required by mercy and expose ourselves to mercy's complement, wrath.

In sum, the two formulae of the Shahadah have clear implications on two basic levels: The first formula points to the way things actually are (that is, tawḥīd), and the second to the way human beings ought to be (that is, in harmony with God's mercy and wisdom).

From the standpoint of tawḥīd, everything is exactly as it must be, so good and evil do not enter the picture. There is no reality but the True Reality, and all things come into being to be precisely what they are.

From the standpoint of those who receive the revealed messages, some things are good and some bad, some better and some worse. Left to ourselves, we do not have sufficient resources to sort things out—hence, the need for merciful guidance. The whole enterprise of modernity, of course, rejects this principle out of hand. It is claimed that we do indeed have the resources, in the form of science, technology, ideology, and so on, and that we can and must reconfigure the world in keeping with our own understanding of how things ought to be.

The obvious distinction between the way things are and the way things ought to be, or the ontological imperative and the moral imperative, has always been discussed by religionists, philosophers, politicians, and theoreticians of all sorts. It lies behind all human endeavor, all attempts to understand and to change. It props up theories of evolution, progress, and every sort of ideology. In the Abrahamic traditions, it has appeared in the endless debates over predestination and free will, in the Indian traditions in analyses of the workings of karma, and in China in the vexing issue of the human ability to upset the mandate of Heaven. In modern times, we tend rather to talk of natural laws as opposed to moral laws, or nature versus nurture.

Muslim thinkers conceptualized the distinction between what is and what ought to be in many different ways. Commonly, they distinguished between two divine commands (*amr*).[4] The first command expresses the truth of tawḥīd—there is no reality but the True Reality, so all apparent reality is utterly subservient to the True Reality. Everything follows this command, which is called the creative command (*al-amr al-khalqī*) or the engendering command (*al-amr al-takwīnī*). Its most salient characteristic is that it cannot be disobeyed. Many Qur'anic verses are cited in support, such as "*His only command, when He desires a thing, is to say to it 'Be!,' and it comes to be*" (36:82).

God desires the universe to be what it is, and the proof is that the universe is what it is. He said *Be!* and it has come to be. *Be!* is His eternal word, which is to say that it is outside time. It has temporal repercussions as soon as it brings the universe into existence. From the standpoint of our own immersion in the constantly changing realm of time, God is uttering *Be!* without beginning and end. All things other than God—whatever these may be, in this world or the next, in any world whatsoever—come into existence in obedience and subservience to this command: "*None is there in the heavens and the earth that comes not to the All-Merciful as a servant*" (19:93). Notice that this verse associates all things with the All-Merciful (*raḥmān*), one of the quasi-synonyms of the name Loving (wadūd). Without the motherly quality of love and mercy, there would be no creation.

When we switch our focus to the second formula of the Shahadah, we see that it allows for human freedom. God issues a whole series of commands by means of prophets (*nabī*) and messengers (*rasūl*). These Qur'anic terms are broad enough to embrace avatars, buddhas, and sages, for "*Every community has a messenger*" (10:47). The salient characteristic of prophetic commands is that people are free to obey or disobey them. Thus, God commands Muslims to perform the ritual prayers, fast during Ramadan, pay the alms tax, avoid pork, act with charity, deal with people justly, and so on, but He does not coerce them to do so. If He did, they would be angels, not humans.

Viewed as a whole, God's commands and prohibitions are called the religious command (*al-amr al-dīnī*), since they establish religion (*dīn*), one example of which came to be known as Islam. They are also called the prescriptive command (*al-amr al-taklīfī*), because they prescribe guidelines for activity and life.

If we acknowledge the universality of prophecy as taught by the Qur'an, it is clear that there have been many religious commands. What remained debatable for Muslim scholars is who exactly was a prophet and to what extent any given prophecy remained valid at that point, or at any point, in human history. There has never been any consensus on these issues.

In short, the two commands—creative and religious—are clear corollaries of the two formulae of the Shahadah. First, God does as He wills, because there is no god but He, and no one can say a word about it. Second, He sends prophets to address whatever measure of freedom people do in fact have. They can choose among alternatives, and their choices will have repercussions. The way they live their lives will shape their destinies, not only in this world but also in the next.

TWO VERSES ON LOVE

When God is the subject of the verb *love* in the Qur'an, the only object of His love is human beings. When human beings are the subject, their object can be any number of things, but the point of mentioning love is always that people *ought* to love God and what He loves. In any case, this is not the place to analyze the Qur'anic passages; our authors do so. Here I want to stress that two Qur'anic verses are taken as the starting points for all discussions of divine and human love. One of these can be read as an application of tawḥīd, the other as expressing the necessity of prophetic intermediaries between God and man. Thus, in the first and obvious meaning of the verses, one expresses the creative command and the other the religious command. Both verses use the word *ḥubb* for love.

The first verse, the most commonly cited Qur'anic passage on love, reads: "*He loves them, and they love Him*" (5:54). These two clauses are part of a longer verse. When authors quote the whole verse, the clauses need to be translated differently: "*O you who have faith, should any of you turn back on your religion, God will bring a people whom He loves, and who love Him*." Although every Qur'an commentary discusses this verse as a whole, texts focusing on love frequently cite the two clauses without reference to the rest. Authors were perfectly aware of the context, of course, because any scholar worth his salt knew the Qur'an by heart. They felt free to ignore the rest of the verse because they understood the two clauses as having a universal application.

Authors read this verse as an expression of tawḥīd because they understood it as a simple statement of fact (though they also read the second half as explaining what ought to be). What is the human situation in the universe? God loves them, and they love God.

First, the verse tells us that God loves. This is to say that God is a lover. In light of the formula of tawḥīd, this is to say that there is no true lover but God. Then the verse tells us that God is beloved, for *they love Him.* In light of tawḥīd, there is no true beloved but God. Moreover, the verse says that God loves human beings specifically (and the Qur'an never mentions that God loves anything else). Given the eternity of God's attributes, this means that God loves human beings always and forever. Finally, the verse tells us that human beings love God; since human nature does not change, human beings always love God, whether they know it or not.

In short, read in terms of tawḥīd and the creative command, the verse of mutual love expresses four themes that reverberate throughout the literature: God's eternally loving nature, humans as the specific object of God's love, human beings' innate loving nature, and God as the true object of human love. These facts of existence are put into effect by the creative command. God says *Be!* to all things precisely because of His eternal love for human beings. In saying *Be!* He brings people into existence as lovers of Himself. They cannot avoid loving Him because they cannot avoid coming to be.

The second key verse on love points to the role of prophecy, and specifically to the role of Muḥammad in the Islamic universe: "*Say [O Muḥammad!]: 'If you love God, follow me; God will love you'*" (3:31). The role of prophets is to bring guidance. Human beings were created to love God. We all know that we love, desire, want, crave, and so on, but most of us are never quite sure what it is that we really love. We often see that we (or others) fall in love, with people or things, and then the love disappears, so we switch the focus of love to someone or something else. This verse addresses those who have reached the point of understanding that what they really ought to love is God. What should they do next? They should put their love into practice by following divine guidance. Then they will find that God loves them, and they will live in the presence of their true beloved.

In short, by following divine guidance as embodied in Muḥammad, people can complete the circle of existence, which began when God created the universe because *He loves them.* They came into existence as objects of His love, and they are infused with love and desire because of the creative command, which demands that *they love Him.* They cannot disobey this command, but they can lose sight of their true object of love. In yearning to reach their beloved, they may choose to follow a guide sent by God. The function of the guide is to take them back to God, and God in His love will then embrace them.

According to a sound hadith that the texts frequently quote, God says that once His servant has approached Him with good deeds—that is, by following in the footsteps of Muḥammad—"Then I will love him. When I love him, I am the hearing with which he hears, the eyesight with which he sees, the hand with which he holds, and the foot with which he walks." This is the final goal of love, the point at which people return to God, when lover and beloved become one. In the literature of love, it is commonly called proximity (*qurb*) or union (*wiṣāl*), and sometimes unification (*ittiḥād*). It is the full and final realization of tawḥīd.

TAWḤĪD

As noted, the basic meaning of the word *tawḥīd* is to say (that God is) one. In technical language, its first meaning is to utter the formula "(There is) no god but God." Maybudī explains some of tawḥīd's implications while commenting on the first of the thirty-six instances in which this formula (in a number of variants) occurs in the Qur'an: "*And your God is one God. There is no god but He, the All-Merciful, the Ever-Merciful*" (2:163). First, he points out that God is one in every respect, and then he suggests why this One God refers to Himself as both the All-Merciful and the Ever-Merciful.

> This is the description of the One Lord, the One Creator and King. He is one in magnanimity and governance, one in forbearance and beautiful-doing, one in generosity and peerlessness, one in loving-kindness and servant-caressing. Every magnificence is the mantle of His majesty, and in that He is one. Every tremendousness and invincibility is the shawl of His lordhood, and in that He is one. He is one in Essence, one in attributes, one in deed and mark, one in loyalty and compact, one in gentleness and caressing, one in love and friendship.
>
> On the day of apportioning, who was there but He, the One? Before the day of apportioning who was there? That same One. After the day of apportioning, who handed over those portions? That same One. Who shows? That same One. Who adorns? That same One.
>
> He is more apparent than everything in the world of apparentness, and in this apparentness He is one. He is more hidden than anything in the world of hiddenness, and in this hiddenness He is one.
>
> O You who are more visible than all that is visible!
> You are more hidden than the world's most hidden thing.
> O You who are more distant than all the servants imagine!
> You are closer to the servants than the jugular vein.

How disloyal the Adamite who does not know the worth of this declaration and the exaltedness of this ascription! God says, *"And your God is one God."* The wonder is not that He ascribed the servants to Himself, joined them to Himself, and said, *"Surely My servants"* [15:42]. The wonder is that He ascribed Himself to the servants and joined His name to their name, saying, *"Your God."* This is not because His lordhood must be joined to the servant's servanthood, or that the servants are deserving of that. Rather, in generosity and loving-kindness He Himself is unique and one. In magnanimity He is worthy of every generous bestowal and every gift.

In the place of our Heart-taker's beauty and loveliness,
we are not suited for Him—He is suited for us.

And your God is one God. There was no world and no Adam. There were no tracks and no traces, there was no one in the house. He was the caretaking and loving Lord, writing out your good fortune and accepting you to be His friend while you were still in nonexistence.

O You who were there for me
when I was not there for You!

On the night of the Prophet's ascent to God, when secrets were told to the Master of the world, one of them was this: "Belong to Me as you always were, and I will belong to you as I have always been." Belong totally to Me and be nothing, just as you were; then I will be for you as I was in the Beginningless.

Shaykh al-Islām Anṣārī said in his whispered prayers, "I am happy that You were there at first and I was not. Your work took effect and mine did not. You put forth Your worth and You sent Your Messenger.

"O God! Whatever You have given us without our seeking—do not ruin it with what we deserve! Whatever good You have done for us—do not cut it off because of our defects! Whatever You have made without our worthiness—do not separate it from us by our unworthiness!

"O God! Do not bring to fruit what we ourselves have planted! Keep blights away from what You planted for us!"

There is no god but He, the All-Merciful, the Ever-Merciful. Other than He there is no Lord, and other than He there is none worthy of worship, for no one caresses and bestows bounty like Him. He is the All-Merciful who gives when they ask of Him, and He is the Ever-Merciful who becomes angry when they do not ask. A report has come, "When someone does not ask from God, God becomes wrathful toward him."

He is the All-Merciful who accepts the servants' obedience, even if it is little, and He is the Ever-Merciful who forgives their disobedient acts even if

> they are great. He is the All-Merciful who adorns outwardness and sculpts the form, and He is the Ever-Merciful who makes inwardness flourish and guards the hearts in His grasp. He is the All-Merciful who makes subtle lights appear in your face, and He is the Ever-Merciful who places secret deposits in your heart.
>
> (*Kashf* 1:439–41)

Love aims to bridge the gap between man and God. If this connection is ever to be achieved, the nature of the gap must become clear. This is why Islamic theology places great stress on God's transcendence or "incomparability" (*tanzīh*), His absolute otherness. The formula of tawḥīd establishes this quickly and clearly: "There is no god but God" means that there is no knowledge but the divine knowledge, no life but the divine life, no desire but the divine desire, no mercy but the divine mercy, no love but the divine love. In short, there is nothing real but the Real (*ḥaqq*)—a Qur'anic divine name that also means "true," "right," "worthy," and "appropriate," as well as the corresponding nouns (truth, rightness, worthiness). Everything other than God is *bāṭil*—unreal, untrue, inappropriate. Authors commonly quote a verse by Labīd (d. 661) that the Prophet called "the truest verse sung by the Arabs":

> Is not everything less than God unreal,
> and every bliss inescapably passing?

Despite the unreality of things, they are sufficiently real for God to know all of them for all eternity. Their unreality means that they have no existence of their own; they gain a semblance of reality when God says *Be!* to them. The universe, which can be defined as everything other than God, is not absolutely unreal; rather, it is unreal when compared to the Real. The reality that things acquire once they have been addressed by the creative command does not belong to them but to their Creator. The true reality of things is their nonexistence (*ʿadam*), their nonbeing (*nīstī*). The theme of the essential nonbeing of everything other than God is common, and was given its most sophisticated expression by Ibn al-ʿArabī.[5] We will encounter it repeatedly.

One of the several explanations that Samʿānī offers for the meaning of the divine name Gentle (*laṭīf*) is that God's greatest gentleness toward the creatures was to create them. This was the utmost kindness, one to which they had no claim whatsoever.

> Laṭīf means knowing and it also means beautiful-doer. God says, "*God is gentle to His servants*" [42:19]. Which beautiful-doing is beyond the fact that you were in the concealment of nonexistence, and He was taking care of your

> work with bounty and generosity? You were in the concealment of nonexistence, and He chose you out from the whole world. You were in the concealment of nonexistence, and He was taking care of your work without any precedent intercession, without any subsequent benefit, without taking any trouble in the present state, and without making anything incumbent in the future. He was tossing the secret hook of *He loves them* into the ocean of *they love Him* [5:54].
>
> (*Rawḥ* 241)

One of the theological presuppositions of Islamic texts is the eternity of the divine word, which is to say that God is always and forever speaking, outside of time. He is the Speaker, so there is no speaker but He. His speech takes a variety of forms, such as *Be!* and it also appears as scripture. What He says in His speech about Himself pertains to His eternal nature. It is of course true, as Samʿānī puts it, that once speech and other divine qualities reach our domain, they are sullied by us. He tells us that God says to us, "O fools! Our decree has the color of Our lordhood. When it turns in your direction, it takes on your color" (*Rawḥ* 522). But when God says something about Himself in the Qur'an, we should not imagine that His words apply simply to the temporal situation. Thus, when He says, "*O My servants!*" (39:53), He is asserting the eternal truth of our servanthood, whether or not we happen to exist in the world. Hence Samʿānī: "May a thousand spirits be sacrificed to the time when we were not, and our hearing was not, and He was talking to us!" (*Rawḥ* 370).

In one passage, Samʿānī applies the principle of the nonexistence of things to the question of how people can know God. They cannot in fact know God until He gives them knowledge, for they are essentially nonbeing and have nothing of their own. Even the Prophet, the greatest of human beings, could not know God without God's bestowal of knowledge.

> It is the consensus of the folk of the Real and the Reality that the proof of God is God: *And to whomsoever God assigns no light, no light has he* [24:40]. The one who shows the road to God is God Himself.
>
> After coming into existence the creatures are just as captive to His power as they were before existence. When they are in nonexistence, they are captive to power. If He wants, He brings them into existence, and if He does not want, He does not. Once they exist, they are still captive to power. If He wants to keep them, He does, and if He does not want, He does not. After their existence they will be exactly what they were in the state of nonexistence. And He, having bestowed existence, is exactly what He was before bestowing existence.

So, the existence of creatures right now is similar to nonexistence, and their subsistence has the constitution of annihilation. It is impossible for an annihilated and nonexistent thing to find the road or to be shown the road. This is why Abū Bakr said, "By God, if not for God, we would not have been guided" and so on. The Prophet said, "I was sent as an inviter, and nothing of guidance goes back to me." In reality, the road-shower is God, and intellect is an instrument, not a cause.

(*Rawḥ* 415)

ESSENCE AND ATTRIBUTES

In the language of theology, the Essence (*dhāt*) is God in His utter unity, unknown to any but Himself. The word is used in conjunction with "names" (*asmā'*) and "attributes" (*ṣifāt*), two terms that are more or less synonymous. *Dhāt* means literally "possessor," for the Essence is the possessor of the attributes (*dhāt al-ṣifāt*). It is also called the Named (*musammā*), that is, that which is designated by the names. No name is adequate for the Essence per se, but every name points in Its direction. As for the name God (*allāh*), it designates the Essence along with all the names and attributes that belong to It. The names themselves, however, are not beyond comprehension, even if we can understand them only in our measure, not in God's measure.

The universe in its infinite diversity provides the means to understand the names while simultaneously showing that God is utterly different from the traces of the names in created things. In Maybudī's commentary on the verse "*Of everything We created a pair*" (51:49), he explains that God's unity demands that all things be dualistic and diverse. Note that "newly arrived" (*ḥādith*) is the opposite of "eternal" (*qadīm*). The newly arrived things are everything other than God, for the universe and all it contains come into being at His creative, engendering command.

In this verse there is an affirmation of the Lord's solitariness and unity. When God creates newly arrived and engendered things, He creates them as pairs, whether linked to each other or opposed to each other. For example: male and female, day and night, light and darkness, heaven and earth, land and sea, sun and moon, jinn and mankind, obedience and disobedience, felicity and wretchedness, guidance and misguidance, exaltation and abasement, power and incapacity, strength and weakness, knowledge and ignorance, life and death.

He created the creatures' attributes in this manner—paired with each other or opposed to each other—so that they would not resemble the attributes of the Creator. Thus His unity and solitariness would become manifest to them, for His exaltation has no abasement, His power no incapacity, His strength no weakness, His knowledge no ignorance, His life no death, His joy no sorrow, His subsistence no annihilation.

The uniquely one God is one in Essence and attributes, unique in worthiness. He is incomparable with everyone and separate from everything. *Nothing is as His likeness* [42:11]. No one is like Him and nothing is similar to or resembles Him. Resemblance derives from partnership, and God has no associate or partner. He is without equal and without need.

The door of His withholding is shut and the door of His munificence open. He forgives sins and caresses the faulty. He makes His love apparent by caressing servants. He loves His servants, though He has no needs. He brings about love between Himself and the servants without association or partnership. Thus the servants, no matter what their states—whether wounded by the arrow of trial or drowned in gentleness and bestowal—should seize hold of His generosity and seek shelter in Him, fleeing to Him from the creatures. This is why He issues the command "*So flee to God!*" [51:50].

(*Kashf* 9:325)

Toward the beginning of his commentary on the divine name Tremendous (*ʿaẓīm*), Samʿānī explains that God's utter unity demands that things have no existence of their own. The fact that they have some sort of existence derives from God's gentleness and grace.

Before He created "how" and "why," He was the Lord. "How" and "why" do not reach the majesty of His pure Essence. He is He, and there is no He but He. He was solitary before all, He is solitary when He brings all into existence, and He will be solitary when they go. He makes them all appear so that they may come to be, and He makes them all cease to be so that He alone may be.

Know that all existent things are nonbeing itself. Count all nonexistent things as coming to be through His power. He acted, spoke, adorned, disclosed, and honored in the Beginningless, and He is in the Endless.

He did the work in the Beginningless, and today He shows you what He did. He spoke the words in the Beginningless, and today He lets you hear the spoken words. He adorned in the Beginningless, and today He discloses what was adorned in the Beginningless. He honored in the Beginningless, and today He conveys the honor: *Each day He is upon some task* [55:29]. He drives the predetermined things to their appointed times—beings and nonexistent things in known moments through recognized causes. Resistance is frivolity.

"Today you know Me—I am not of today. Your knowing is newly arrived, but My Being has the description of eternity. Your taking belongs to now, but My giving is eternal.

"For some time I have been speaking to you of the mysteries, but you hear now. In the Beginningless, the beginningless hearing was your deputy in listening to the beginningless speech. In the Beginningless, the beginningless knowledge was your deputy in knowing the beginningless attributes.

"When a guardian has a child's property, he has it as the child's deputy. When the infant reaches adulthood, he gives it back to him. You were the infants of nonexistence, and the eternal gentleness took care of your work. What is left that I did not do for you?

"I conveyed the Law's prescription to your hearing, I conveyed the decree to your heart, I spoke of mysteries to your spirit, I inscribed obedience on your limbs. At every moment I sent a new gift. I made you anticipate arrivals from the Unseen—at every moment an honor, at every instant a gift, at every new breath a bestowal.

"If I were to be gentle because of your worthiness, I would not be gentle, because you have no worthiness. If I were to bestow because of your gratitude, I would not bestow, because your gratitude is not worthy of My bestowal. If I were to send gifts because of your seeking, I would not send them, because you do not have the ability to seek. O you who await the arrival of My gentleness! O you who look for marks bearing witness to My Unseen!"

(*Rawḥ* 304–5)

Among the divine names that express God's transcendence and difference is *ghanī*—"wealthy," "independent," "unneedy." The Arabic word is typically translated into Persian as *bī-niyāz*, "without need." Maybudī speaks of God's utter lack of need in his commentary on the verse, "*Say: 'Have faith in it, or do not have faith'*" (17:107).

The side of Unity, the exalted Majesty, is alluding to the fact that He has never had and will never have any need for an obedience that was not and then came into being. He is saying, "You have no worth, for nothing is worthy of Me. If you want, have faith, and if you do not want, do not. I have no need for your faith. Beginningless majesty and beauty gain no adornment from the obedience of newly arrived things. I had still not written out existence for any existent thing when My majesty was contemplating My beauty and I was pleased with Myself in Myself. Today that I have created the creatures, I am what I was. I have no need in Myself for any causes and no need in My perfection for any seeking."

(*Kashf* 5:636–37)

Why then did God create the universe? One of the many ways in which authors address this issue is simply to meditate on the divine names. Remember that the names are not arbitrary designations that either we or scripture places on God. Rather, they are God's own designations for His reality in our language. Moreover, the names signify various attributes whose presence cannot be denied, though we can certainly deny, if we like, that they belong essentially to God and metaphorically to us. They cannot be denied because they designate the qualities of our own experience—life, knowledge, desire, power, speech, generosity, justice. Everyone talks about such things all the time, but what many or most fail to see is that there is no reality but the Real, no life but the divine life, no power but the divine power, no justice but God's.

In contrast, Muslim theologians begin with the axiom of tawḥīd. They take it for granted that God is the Real Being and that we are but His shadows or pale reflections. Once tawḥīd is acknowledged, it is obvious that all attributes and qualities must be traced back to the One, directly or indirectly. Then the question of why God created the universe practically answers itself. The universe is demanded by the very nature of things, a nature designated by the divine names.

From about the time of Ibn al-ʿArabī, a common way to address the question was to cite the hadith of the Hidden Treasure, which tells of a conversation between David and God. This "hadith" is not in fact found in the standard collections of the Prophet's sayings. Early authors do not suggest that it came from the Prophet's mouth, but attribute it rather to the corpus of stories handed down about the prophet David.[6] Maybudī cites it in his commentary on the verse "*What, did you reckon that We created you for frivolity?*" (23:115).

> Abū Bakr Wāsiṭī recited this verse and said, "The majestic and perfectly powerful Lord, in His majestic exaltation and His perfect power, brought the beings into existence. Thereby they would know His Being, recognize His lordhood, and deduce His perfect knowledge and power from His artisanry. Just as His knowledge reached them, so also He made apparent the mark of His friendship on the friends and inscribed enmity on the enemies."
>
> He brought them from the concealment of nonexistence into existence in keeping with His knowledge in the Beginningless that He would create creation. He wanted to make His creation come to be in exact correspondence with His knowledge.
>
> David the prophet said in his whispered prayer, "O God, O endless Majesty described by the attribute of perfection and qualified by the description of unneediness! You have no need for anything and You subsist in Your own

description. You require nobody and You take help and aid from no one. Why did You create these creatures? What wisdom is there in their existence?"

The answer came, "I was a hidden treasure, and I loved to be recognized": I was a concealed treasure and no one knew or recognized Me. I wanted to be known and I loved to be recognized.

"I loved to be recognized" is an allusion to the fact that recognition is built on love. Wherever there is love, there is recognition, and wherever there is no love, there is no recognition. The great ones of the religion and the Tariqah have said, "No one recognizes Him save those to whom He has made Himself recognized, no one voices His unity save those to whom He has shown His unity, and no one describes Him save those to whose secret cores He has disclosed Himself."

(*Kashf* 6:477)

Maybudī's only other mention of the Hidden Treasure comes in his commentary on the verse "*We created you from one soul*" (39:6). His explanation of the meaning of the saying is drawn from a passage by Samʿānī (*Rawḥ* 464).

He created heaven and earth and day and night to show the creatures the attribute of His power. Thus they come to know that He is perfectly powerful, an artisan without contrivance, and they take His artisanry as evidence of His unity. He created Adam and the Adamites to make them the treasury of the secrets of Eternity and the target of the gentle favors of generosity. "I was a hidden treasure, so I loved to be recognized."

"I had an incomparable Essence and attributes, so there had to be a recognizer. I had infinite majesty and beauty, so there had to be a lover. I was an ocean of mercy and forgiveness beating its waves, so there had to be an object of mercy."

The other created things had nothing to do with love, for they never saw in themselves a high aspiration. The one with high aspiration is you. The angels have straight and orderly work because there was no talk of love with them. The treasures and intimations put into the Adamic makeup were not placed in them. The ups and downs of the Adamites, their bewilderment and confoundedness, contraction and expansion, sorrow and joy, absence and presence, togetherness and dispersion; the drafts mixed with poison in their hands, the swords hanging over their necks—they have all these because a whiff of love's rose reached their nostrils.

(*Kashf* 8:387)

COMPLEMENTARY NAMES

Samʿānī frequently expands on the complementarity of two sorts of divine names, a common theme in Islamic theology. One sort of name emphasizes God's distance and transcendence, the other His nearness and immanence. The two are called names of majesty (*jalāl*) and beauty (*jamāl*), or severity (*qahr*) and gentleness (*luṭf*), or mercy (*raḥma*) and wrath (*ghaḍab*), or bounty (*faḍl*) and justice (*ʿadl*).

When the basis of judging the world is the lordly unneediness and the perfection of the kingly beauty, then, in reality, the existence of creation is a useless bother. However, He created us so that we would benefit from Him, not so that He would benefit from us. He brought us into existence for the sake of our portions and shares, even though His exalted and majestic Presence is pure of portions and shares.

The attribute of bounty rose up seeking the obedient, the attribute of severity rose up seeking the disobedient, and the attribute of majesty and beauty rose up seeking the lovers.

O chevalier! It is incumbent upon a rich man to give alms to the poor. Supposing that the deserving person does not sit and seek at the door of the rich man's house, then it is incumbent on the rich man to take the alms to the door of the poor man's hut.

The unneedy in reality is the Real, and the poor in reality are we. Alms are of two sorts: secret alms and open alms. Openly He sends the alms of invitation on the hands of the prophets and messengers, and secretly He sends the alms of guidance to secret cores.

O dervish! He had a gentleness and a severity to perfection, a majesty and a beauty to perfection. He wanted to distribute these treasures. On one person's head He placed the crown of gentleness in the garden of bounty. On another person's liver He placed the brand of severity in the prison of justice. He melted one in the fire of majesty, He caressed another in the light of beauty. He lit up a candle of invitation on the bench of the court of *And God invites to the abode of peace* [10:25], and a thousand thousand of the helpless and suffering threw themselves like moths against the candle and were burned, and not a speck was diminished from the candle nor added to it.

(*Rawḥ* 16–17)

O dervish! His majesty displays His exaltedness, and His beauty discloses His gentleness. His majesty makes all speakers dumb, and His beauty brings all the dumb to speech. Wherever in the world there is someone dumb, he is made dumb by His majesty. Wherever in the world there is someone talking, he was brought into words by His beauty. When someone contemplates His majesty, his sorrows are drawn out. When someone contemplates His beauty, his sorrows disappear.

(531)

O chevalier! A lioness has the tenderness of a mother, but she also has sharp claws. When ants come after a lion cub, in her tenderness she wants to pick out the ants, but what will she do about her sharp claws? If she did not have sharp claws, she would not be a lion, and if she did not have tenderness, she would not be a mother. She has the love of a mother, but she is also a lion. Tenderness is born from the mother's love, and awe is born from the lion's attributes. He is the Most Generous of the Generous, but He is also the Invincible, the Severe.

(607)

It is said that a rooster had a debate with a falcon. The falcon said to the rooster, "You are such a disloyal animal!"

The rooster said, "How so?"

He said, "Because the Adamites nurture and feed you with their own hands. But if they ever come after you, your cries reach the whole world and in no way do you give yourself up. As for me, they catch me in the desert, they sew up my eyes with severity's needle, and they afflict me with all sorts of trials. I become accustomed to them, get along with them, and mix with them."

The rooster said, "You have an excuse, for you're far from the source. No one has ever seen a falcon on a spit. I've seen plenty of chickens stuck on spits and put into intense fire."

"O angels, you move over to the side and watch from a distance. It is the Adamites who have tasted the blows of Our severity and are caressed by Our gentleness. Sometimes We slice them up with the sword of severity, sometimes We put balm on them with the gaze of gentleness."

O chevalier! In a place where there is a wedding and a party, people go and watch. In a place where they mete out punishment, they also go and watch: *Let a group of the faithful witness their chastisement* [24:2].

"We have brought a group from the abode of trial and testing into the abode of recompense and favor. We have dressed them in the robe of good fortune and sat them on the chair of joy and elevation. We have pulled another group into the prison of anger and the abode of distance with the shackles of abasement and the chains of contempt. The stipulation is that you angels watch both groups. You who are the glorifiers and the hallowers, watch in your stations of honor and see what We will do to this handful of dust."

(292)

At the beginning of his commentary on the meaning of the divine name *ḥakīm*, the Wise, Samʿānī explains that when God created the universe, He put wisdom in charge of power. Wisdom pulled back on the reins of majesty and severity, giving the names of beauty and gentleness the freedom to attend to the creatures' well-being.

The Wise is He who does every deed appropriately and puts everything in its place. He is wise, not miserly. Whenever He puts something, He puts it in its proper place. Whatever He gives, He gives it to its own folk. He had the power to create a world compared to which this world would be a mosquito's wing, but He did not do so because of wisdom. He is the wise who does not do whatever He can do. He has a power whose reins are in the hands of wisdom, a wisdom that receives power in a mutual embrace. Thus lordhood displays itself rightly.

In this world, He did not create an ant's leg or a mosquito's wing except by the requirement of power and the requisite of wisdom and in conformity with His will and desire. Wisdom had to take the reins of power's authority so that the work would go forward well ordered. If we suppose that wisdom had let go of power's reins, the universe would have been thrown into tumult.

He has attributes that are the antagonists of the existence of the creatures and their acts, and He has attributes that are the interceders for the existence of the creatures and their states. Exaltedness, unneediness, severity, invincibility, magnificence, and exaltation are the creatures' antagonists. Wisdom, mercy, gentleness, clemency, munificence, and generosity are their interceders.

The interceders hold back the reins of the antagonists so that this handful of hapless creatures may live out their brief spans in the shadow of the interceders' existence. Otherwise, if they let the antagonists loose, in one instant everything—from the Throne and the Footstool down to the ant's leg and the mosquito's wing—would cease to be. In the world He gave out one word about His unneediness, and it will come before the unbelievers on the Day of Separation: "*And as for those who are unbelievers—surely God is unneedy toward the worlds*" [3:97].

When He wanted to make this creation appear, He pulled back on the reins of the attribute of unneediness. He said to power and wisdom, "Bring a world into existence!"

As a consequence of power and an effect of wisdom, the world appeared. In each mote of the world there was a power whose hand was around wisdom's neck, and wisdom's head was on power's pillow. Many in the world see the power, but few see the wisdom. A hundred thousand see the power, but no one sees the wisdom.

When the world has been there for a while and the secret of this work and the quintessence of this affair have been gained, He will say to the attribute of munificence, "Let go of the reins of unneediness." As soon as the attribute of munificence lets go, the resurrection will appear and the existent things will go back to the attribute of nonexistence.

What is this? It is the army of the attribute of independence and unneediness attacking from the ambuscade of exaltedness and severity. He will deliver the address "*Whose is the kingdom today? God's, the One, the Severe*" [40:16]. He will step forth in the attribute of unneediness, and the ruling power will belong to severity. The first address that He had given, "*Am I not your Lord?*" [7:172], had gone forth from the attribute of munificence, for the ruling power was the ruling power of gentleness and munificence.

Then, when some time passes, He will once again give the reins over to the hands of munificence. Power and wisdom will be put to work along with the attributes of bounty and justice. Then it will be said, "O unbelievers! O you who belong to Our attribute of power and wisdom! Go with the escort of justice to hell. O pious! O you who belong to Our power and wisdom. Go with the escort of bounty to paradise." *Surely the pious shall be in bliss* [82:13].

(*Rawḥ* 398–99)

MERCY AND COMPASSION

Authors talk of the Hidden Treasure to show that God created the universe generally and human beings specifically because of love: "I was a Hidden Treasure, and I *loved* to be recognized." Instead of "I loved" (*aḥbabtu*), some versions of the saying have "I desired" (*aradtu*), but the point is the same. God desired, wanted, wished, loved to create, so He did. The word *desire*, moreover, is used in similar contexts in the Qur'an, as in the verse "*Our only word to a thing, when We desire it, is to say to it 'Be!', and it comes to be*" (16:40).

A third attribute that is commonly discussed as God's motivation for creating the universe is mercy, which might be defined as God's creative and sustaining love for all that exists. The Arabic word *raḥma*, meaning "mercy," is an abstract noun derived from the concrete noun *raḥim*, "womb." Mercy is a mother's love for her children.

If there is a difference between God's mercy and His love, it lies in the fact that His love comes to be redirected toward Him in the form of human love. In contrast, human beings cannot be merciful toward God. They can only extend His mercy to other creatures. The Qur'an says, *He loves them, and they love Him*, but it would be absurd to say that He has mercy on them and they have mercy on Him. Rather, they can—and they must if they are to be truly human—have mercy on other human beings and on God's creation generally. A number of hadiths make the point: "God has mercy only on His merciful servants"; "God has no mercy on those who are not merciful toward the people."

One might object to this line of reasoning by citing the saying of Jesus, "Inasmuch as ye did it not to one of the least of these, ye did it not to me" (Matthew 25:45). In fact, a version of this saying appears in the hadith literature. God will rebuke people on the Day of Judgment and say to them, "I was hungry, but you did not feed Me; I was ill but you did not visit Me." When they protest that He cannot possibly have been hungry or ill, He will respond, "So-and-so was ill. If you had visited him, you would have found Me with him. So-and-so was hungry. If you had fed him, you would have found Me with Him." This does not mean, however, that God is in need of creaturely mercy and compassion. It means rather that, having created us with love and mercy, He expects us to act in the same way toward others. "*He is with you wherever you are*" (57:4) and with all creatures wherever they may be, so we should act beautifully (iḥsān), as if we see Him there.

There is of course a strain of theological thinking, especially strong in early Kalam, that denies the mutual love of God and man. To square this view with the plain Qur'anic text, Kalam experts claimed that the word *love* means one thing when applied to God, and something quite different when applied to human beings. However true this may be when we look at God in His transcendence, the picture changes as soon as we take into account His immanence and omnipresence. One of the major points our authors make is that love bridges gaps. Once the shining light of love effaces human limitations, the line between divine and human love becomes ever more difficult to draw.

The Qur'an uses the word *mercy* and its derivatives far more than the two basic words for love (325 times as opposed to 110). In only a handful of instances does it ascribe mercy to creatures, typically as a divine gift. One of these verses reads: "*And among His signs is that He created spouses for you from yourselves, that you may rest in them, and He placed between you love* [mawadda] *and mercy*" (30:21). Another speaks of the faithful as ever-merciful (*raḥīm*) toward one another (48:29), and still others of the Prophet as "*a mercy to the worlds*" (21:107) and as "*ever-merciful toward the faithful*" (9:128). In almost all the 320 remaining verses, mercy is strictly a divine attribute.

The Qur'an employs the formula of consecration—"In the name of God, the All-Merciful, the Ever-Merciful"—at the beginning of every chapter except one, though most authorities do not consider these instances actual parts of the revelation (except in the case of the first surah). The net result is that no one can read the Qur'an without noticing the constant references to divine mercy. The theme is much more obvious than that of divine love, and certainly much more prominent than that of God's wrath and severity.

Both Qushayrī and Maybudī offer a different interpretation for every one of the 113 instances in which the formula of consecration occurs at the beginning of the chapters. The general thrust of their explanations is that the name All-Merciful refers to God's universal mercy, which *"embraces everything"* (7:156), and the name Ever-Merciful refers to God's particular mercy, which reaches people in the next world, especially in paradise. Here are two examples of Maybudī's explanations of the formula:

> *In the name of God, the All-Merciful, the Ever-Merciful* [1:1]. As for the wisdom in beginning with *God*, then *the All-Merciful*, then *the Ever-Merciful*, it is this: He sent this down in keeping with the states of the servants, who have three states: first creation, then nurturing, and finally forgiveness. *God* alludes to creation at the beginning through power, *the All-Merciful* alludes to nurturing through continuity of blessings, and *the Ever-Merciful* alludes to forgiveness at the end through mercy. It is as if God said, "First I created through power, then I nurtured through blessings, and at last I will forgive through mercy."
>
> (*Kashf* 1:29)
>
> *In the name of God, the All-Merciful, the Ever-Merciful* [Surah 54]. It is *God* who brings the lost back to the road. From Him kings take greatness and position, and He is powerful over everything, king of every king. He is the hand-taker of all the helpless, and a fine shelter for the incapable. When someone does not call upon Him, he is lost and his work spoiled. This is why the Lord of the Worlds says, *"Misguided are those upon whom you call except Him"* [17:67].
>
> It is *the All-Merciful* who assigns daily bread and nourishes enemies. He is the creator of good and evil, the originator of each thing itself and its traces, the sculptor of Adam from neither father nor mother. You see someone in this world with rank and gravity, his breast unaware of the Real. You see someone else in whose heart is the tree of faith and whose liver is burnt by familiarity, without shoes on his feet or scarf on his head. This is what the Exalted Lord says: *"Surely We created everything according to a measure"* [54:49].
>
> It is *the Ever-Merciful* who bestows faith and healthy hearts and who delivers the faithful from the fire of Gehenna. He sent a noble messenger to the people, He praised him for his *magnificent character* [68:4], and said about

> him, "*who is eagerly desirous for you, and clement and ever-merciful toward the faithful*" [9:128].
>
> (9:397)

The Qur'an takes a polemical stance against the Christian notion of God as father and likewise avoids any notion of God as mother. Nothing could be clearer in Islamic theology than that God stands beyond gender. He/She/It created male and female but is one in every respect. Nonetheless, every noun in Arabic is assigned gender. Translators typically follow the lead of the text in using *she* or *he*, and they also observe English usage. In contrast, Persian has no gender, so *he*, *she*, and *it* are the same word. If translators choose to assign gender to pronouns in translating Persian, it is because English demands it. Otherwise, God is not He, She, or It, but all of the above and none of the above.

Despite God's transcendence of gender, a number of prophetic sayings make the connection between womb, mercy, and motherhood—a connection that is blatantly obvious in the Arabic language, even if many theologians would like to ignore it by employing abstract, nonfigurative language. For example, the Prophet said, "God is more merciful toward His servant than a mother toward her child." In the midst of his commentary on 11:37, a verse that mentions God's commandment to Noah to build the Ark, Maybudī writes,

> In the reports it is mentioned that God's mercy toward the servant is more than a mother's mercy toward her child. Suppose that a child's foot gets caught in the mud a thousand times. Every time the mother will say, "Rise up, O soul of your mother!" Every time she will be even more tender and lovingly kind toward the child.
>
> The Pir of the Tariqah said, "O God, as soon as Your love appeared, all loves became disloyalty. As soon as Your kindness appeared, all disloyalties became loyalty. O God, it was not that we had worth, and then You chose us, nor that we were worthless and then You chose wrongly. Rather, You gave us worth from Yourself when You chose us, and You concealed the defects that You saw."
>
> (*Kashf* 4:395)

In *Forty-Two Chapters*, Anṣārī cites another hadith making the connection between mercy and motherhood: "God made mercy in one hundred parts, and He kept ninety-nine parts at Himself. He sent one part into the earth, and with this part the creatures have mercy on each other. Even the mare lifts her hoof from her colt in fear of harming it." In explaining the meaning of this hadith, Anṣārī begins by talking about the return to the divine at-ness (*ʿindiyya*), where the ninety-nine mercies are waiting, since God has kept them "at Himself."

Wait until you reach the station of at-ness. Then you will see the other ninety-nine mercies pouring down upon you. From every mercy, what opening, what elevation, what generosity, what good fortune, what proximity!

In other words, look at this one part of mercy that He has apportioned to all of creation. In the heart of every mother and father, what hope, love, and passion for their children! Read how it is described in the story of Jacob and Joseph, and see your own incapacity to perceive its quality. Then you will know that unless this one mercy that is turned toward creation enters the heart, the servant will not be able to know those ninety-nine mercies.

Look what love of children has reached every mother and father and what passion and hope has reached every friend toward his friend! Look at the unsettledness at separation from the friend!

The remaining ninety-nine mercies will turn toward bestowing upon you, forgiving and absolving you, caressing and rewarding you, honoring and respecting you. Look at what appears between you and His Presence today! When you reach the station of at-ness, you will taste its flavor.

Unsettledness in this work will set you aside from all others. If, for example, you were to put into this work all the striving and effort that you use in keeping yourself heedless, then at every moment you would find yourself more present with and closer to that Presence; more unsettled, more yearning, and more hopeful. And if you want to become heedless of this work for a moment, the flood of His mercy will come and throw you into the ocean of presence and togetherness. He will make the two worlds wander like straw on the surface of this ocean, as if the whole world has been taken away by a storm and drowned in the water of His mercy and caresses.

There will reach your ears a hundred thousand thousand glorifications and hallowings from every leaf of every tree, every mote of every being, even stones, clods, and dust. They will be saying, "Look at My mercy when you flee from Me, look at My mercy when you flee toward Me, look at My mercy when you cling to obeying and worshiping Me, look at My mercy when you come to Me, look at My mercy when you look at inanimate things, look at My mercy when you look at trees and rivers, look at My mercy when you look at yourself!"

When He takes you away from all and keeps you with Himself, snatching you from you, He will not let your eyes fall on you, for that is poison; He will not let your eyes fall on anyone, for that is fire; He will not let you join with yourself, for that is a whirlpool; and He will not let you have intimacy or joining with anyone, for that is ashes.

It is clear how little of that one part of mercy may have reached a loving mother, yet she will not allow any harm to reach her child. Where there are a hundred mercies, or rather all mercy and generosity—how can anyone try to explain that? Intellect is bewildered in one part. If one iota of what is in the station of at-ness should appear, how could intellect perceive it?

O you who have faith! This world is the locus of trial, affliction, tribulation, and trouble. By means of the one mercy that God in His generosity has bestowed on the faithful, He has given the blessings of faith, submission, tawḥīd, the Qur'an, the straight road, and the many thousands of other outward and inward blessings that we have. In the afterworld, the abode of settledness and recompense, He will combine those ninety-nine mercies with this one that He had sent into this world. What blessings, what bounties, what generosities by which He will ennoble His servants and friends! For intellect is incapable of perceiving and explaining even the finding of this one mercy.

O servant! You should know that His forgiveness and mercy have no limit and end. From a hundred treasuries of mercy He apportioned one mercy for the entire cosmos. Whatever sympathy, gentleness, mercy, and tenderness appear in the world—justice from sultans, kindness and generosity from the rich and wealthy, words of truth from scholars, taking the hand of a neighbor and coming to the aid of those suffering injustice, raising up a hospice or a mosque or a drinking fountain, digging a well, repairing a bridge, commanding the approved, and prohibiting the reprehensible—all are traces of this one mercy. The influence of this one mercy in this abode of annihilation is like this. Tomorrow at the resurrection ninety-nine treasuries of limitless and endless mercy will be apportioned, especially for the folk of tawḥīd and recognition. Look at what will be the share of every tawḥīd-voicing person of faith!

To make the story short: you will know the story of those mercies by tasting these. The further you go from yourself, the closer you will come to this talk and the more you will be immersed in this mercy. Act like a man! Come quickly so that you may see endless mercy in the unveiling of *Surely the final end is unto thy Lord* [53:42].

(*Chihil* 174–76)

Probably the most commonly cited hadith about mercy tells us that the inscription on God's Throne reads, "My mercy takes precedence over My wrath." Mercy is the creative love that brings the universe into existence, but things that come into being display the signs of the contrasting attributes of majesty and beauty, severity and gentleness, mercy and wrath. In the end, all will be taken back to mercy, for the point of return is identical with the point of origin. Maybudī often speaks of the precedent mercy, as in his commentary on the verse "*And an inscribed book*" (52:2).

In the tongue of allusion and according to the tasting of the Folk of the Reality, the Inscribed Book is what He wrote against Himself in the Beginningless Covenant: "My mercy takes precedence over My wrath." May a thousand dear spirits be sacrificed to that heart-caressing moment when He gave us a place of seclusion without us and opened for us the door of His infinite acts of gentleness! With beginningless solicitude and precedent, endless gentleness He was saying to us, "My mercy takes precedence over My wrath."

O chevalier! Give thanks to the God who, before you asked, gave you something that you would not have reached even if He had left you with yourself and you had thought for a thousand thousand years under your own control. He called you when you were heedless, He taught you when you were ignorant, He created you when you were *not a thing remembered* [76:1], and He *will pour* for you from the cup of His kindness in the sitting place of His secret *a pure drink* [76:21]. All these are the traces of the precedence of mercy of which He spoke: "My mercy takes precedence over My wrath."

The Pir of the Tariqah said, "O God, You planted the seed of guidance with beginningless solicitude, You watered it with the messages of the prophets, You cultivated it with help and success-giving, and You nurtured it with Your own gaze. Now it will be fitting if You do not let the wind of justice blow, if You do not stir up the poisons of severity, and if You help with endless kind favor what You planted with beginningless solicitude."

(*Kashf* 9:345)

One of the many implications of the mercy and creative love that take precedence over God's wrath and severity is the omnipresent beauty of the natural world. "Why is the world so full of ugliness, evil, and suffering?" people ask. Here is one of Anṣārī's answers, from *Forty-Two Chapters*. He is commenting on a hadith in which God says, "The children of Adam curse the times, but I am the times: in My hands are night and day." He takes this as a commandment to observe courtesy (*adab*) toward God. Courtesy is a broad-ranging term whose meaning embraces both proper activity and refined behavior. For teachers of love, it is perfect imitation of the Prophet both outwardly and inwardly, in keeping with the hadith "God taught me courtesy, so He made my courtesy beautiful."

In other words, "Night and everything that appears at night, day and everything that appears in daytime—it is I who make them appear and give them being. What makes all appear is My Presence. I bring them into manifestation."

It follows that the servants must preserve courtesy. They must strive to see the beauty of His artisanry in both good and evil. Then they will praise Him alone, saying, "How beautiful is Your doing!"

You should not take up residence in the ugliness of your own ignorance. When you inspect His work with your own incomplete intellect and you count the incompleteness of your own intelligence to be His work, then you protest. In place of saying in praise "How beautiful!" you begin to be disloyal and turn His work over to others. Thus you will associate others with God and become a misfortunate, ignorant wrongdoer. Everything is beautiful and complete within its own limits, but you, in your ignorance, see it as bad and consider it bad.

So, once this hadith has shown its face, you must strive to repel this ignorance and wrongdoing. You must leave behind this lack of intelligence and keep back the tongue of protest, lest you give your faith to the wind—to discourtesy, lack of intelligence, disrespect, and foolishness.

Do not be deluded by His clemency, lest you start asking about His work, "Why? For what?" It is He who knows the work and will always make it happen as it should. Then the pretenders start wagging their beards. Whatever He does, He does with knowledge and wisdom.

(*Chihil* 198–99)

Ibn al-ʿArabī commonly says that mercy per se is identical with *al-wujūd al-ḥaqq*, the Real Existence that is God Himself. Then the mercy of the All-Merciful (*al-raḥmat al-raḥmāniyya*) is the fruit of the creative command, the being that is showered on everything that comes to exist. In contrast, the mercy of the Ever-Merciful (*al-raḥmat al-raḥīmiyya*) embraces some creatures but not others and becomes manifest in the special kindness that God shows to those who follow His guidance. In other words, it is achieved as a result of observing the religious command. Ibn al-ʿArabī sees a reference to both sorts of mercy in the verse "*And My mercy embraces everything, and I shall write it for those who are wary of Me, pay the alms-tax, and have faith in Our signs*" (7:156).[7]

Among scholars who took the same position as Ibn al-ʿArabī was his older contemporary Rūzbihān Baqlī of Shiraz (d. 1209), author of several books in both Arabic and Persian. Rūzbihān has become rather well known as a representative of the religion of love, even if love is only one side to his writings. His Persian work, *The Jasmine of the Passionate* (*ʿAbhar al-ʿāshiqīn*), is a highly poetic and allusive exposition of divine and human love. In his Arabic Qur'an commentary, *The Brides of Explication* (*ʿArāʾis al-bayān*), Rūzbihān frequently cites the aphorisms of early Sufis but also provides his own essays on important topics. In his remarks on the verse of the two mercies, he explains that the general mercy of existence reaches things in the measure of their capacities—hence, the distinctions we draw among inanimate objects, plants, animals, and rational beings, not to speak of the different sorts of human beings. As for the specific mercy, that is reserved for those who achieve tawḥīd by making themselves one for God. The verse of the two mercies begins, "*My chastisement, I strike with it whomsoever I will.*" Rūzbihān writes:

> *Chastisement* is to be separate from Him, when hearts and spirits are prevented from observing the attribute of everlastingness. He conveys His chastisement to whomsoever He will among the recognizers and the lovers, to train them and test them in servanthood. His chastisement arrives by means of His will, and that is a place of both hope and fear for those who have faith.
>
> Then He includes all in His all-embracing, beginningless mercy, which envelops every dust mote, with His words, "*And My mercy embraces everything.*" All creatures are immersed in the oceans of His mercy, for when the Real gives existence to them, no matter what description they may have, that is nothing but His mercy. Wherever they may have been placed, they are under His gaze, His ruling authority, His lordhood, and the application of His power.
>
> Then, however, the creatures are disparate in mercy. Inanimate things are immersed in the light of His act, which is active mercy. Animals are immersed in the light of His attributes, which is attributive mercy. Intelligent beings—jinn, mankind, and angels—are immersed in the light of His Essence, which is essential, eternal mercy; this is so inasmuch as they are given recognition of His lordhood and His unity.
>
> In respect of their bodies and what happens to them, they are in the general mercy; and in respect of their spirits and what happens to them, they are in the specific mercy, and here they are disparate. Some of them melt in the vision of tremendousness, some wander in the vision of eternity and subsistence, and some fall into passion and recklessness in the vision of beauty and majesty.
>
> Those who emerge from the station of mercy into the root of the attribute, and from the attribute to the root of the Essence, are immersed in the All-Merciful Himself and annihilated from mercy. They become *a mercy to the worlds*. This is the description of our Prophet, for he reached the all in the all. Hence God described him with mercy toward the all: "*We sent thee only as a mercy to the worlds*" [21:107].
>
> Then He singled out the specific, attributive mercy—after He had included everything in His general mercy—for those who have become solitary for God without any others, those who are annihilated through His tremendousness in His tremendousness, those who have freely given up their existence because of the rightful due of His lordhood. He says, "*I shall write it for those who are wary of Me, pay the alms-tax, and have faith in Our signs*" [7:156]. In other words, in their love for contemplating Him, they are wary of

> everything familiar and gratifying other than God. They *pay the alms-tax* seeking proximity to Him by sacrificing themselves before Him. *They have faith in Our signs:* they contemplate the loci of witnessing when seeing His signs.
>
> (*ʿArāʾis al-bayān,* 1:480–81)

BEGINNINGLESS LOVE

God's love for human beings has no beginning or end. This is a constant theme and a straightforward application of tawḥīd to the words *"He loves them."* If He does love them, this cannot be a temporary love, because God is eternal, so His love for them is unaffected by their entrance into temporal existence. He loves them now just as He loved them in the Beginningless (*azal*) and just as He will love them in the Endless (*abad*). Though His love never changes, their awareness of His love has ups and downs. As for their love for Him—*They love Him*—that has a beginning but no end. For the moment, people are mostly unaware that He is what they love.

Maybudī offers a typical explanation of God's beginningless attributes in his commentary on the verse *"Ḥā' Mīm"* (41:1), that is, "Ḥ, M." This is one of several instances of so-called disconnected letters at the beginning of some surahs. Commentators came up with a variety of interpretations, often several for any given instance. In this case, Maybudī says that we should read the letters as attached rather than disconnected. Then we will have (among other possibilities), the word *ḥumm,* which means "it has been decreed, decided, done."

> In other words, all beings have been decreed. God is saying: "Whatever is be-able has come to be, whatever is doable I have done, whatever is runable I have run, whatever is choosable I have chosen, whatever is acceptable I have accepted, whatever is liftable I have lifted, whatever is throwable I have thrown. Whatever I wanted, I did; whatever I want, I do. When I have accepted someone, I do not look at the disloyalty I see from him. Rather, I pardon and pass over. I do not turn away from what I have said. *The word does not change with Me* [50:29]."
>
> The Pir of the Tariqah said, "O God, the whole world wants You. What does the work is what You want. Happy is the one whom You want, for even if he turns away, You will be waiting in his road."
>
> (*Kashf* 8:518)

In his commentary on the verse, *"Remind them of the days of God"* (14:5), Maybudī tells us that *the days of God* are situated outside time in the precreational realm, where God always loves us.

> These are the days when the servants were in the concealment of nonexistence and the Real was saying with beginningless speech, "My servants!"
>
> "O Muḥammad, remind them of the days when you were not and I was there for you. Without you I took care of your work. I bound the compact of love and I wrote mercy against myself: *Your Lord has written mercy against Himself* [6:54].' "
>
> This is what the Pir of the Tariqah intimated in his whispered prayer: "O God, where will I find again the day when You belonged to me, and I was not. Until I reach that day, I will be in the midst of fire and smoke. If I find that day again in the two worlds, I will profit. If I find Your Being for myself, I will be pleased with my own nonbeing.
>
> "O God, where was I when You called me? I am not I when You remain for me.
>
> "O God, when You call someone, do not make manifest the offenses that You have concealed!
>
> "O God, You lifted us up and no one said, 'Lift up!' Now that You have lifted up, don't put down! Keep us in the shadow of Your gentleness! Entrust us to none but Your bounty and mercy!"
>
> (*Kashf* 5:232)

Many of Anṣārī's whispered prayers speak of beginningless love and mercy. Here is another, mentioned by Maybudī in his commentary on 2:285:

> The Pir of the Tariqah said, "O Lord, it is You who made an oath of allegiance between Yourself and the servant without the servant. You gave witness to the servant's faith without the servant. You wrote mercy against Yourself for the servant without the servant. You made a pact of friendship between Yourself and the servant without the servant. It is fitting for the believing servant to be delighted that You have made a pact of friendship with him, for the stuff of friendship's treasure is all light, and the fruit of friendship's tree is all joy. The field of friendship is a spacious heart, and the kingdom of paradise is one branch of friendship's tree."
>
> (*Kashf* 1:788)

Maybudī refers again to God's beginningless love in his explanation of the verse, "*Already Our word has preceded to the envoys*" (37:171):

> *Word* here comprises three roots: knowledge, desire, and wisdom. First is the precedence of knowledge: Before the doing, He knew what He must do. Second is the precedence of desire: What He knew He must do, He wanted to do. Third is the precedence of wisdom: What He did, He did rightly and properly.

Know also that God has no need of duration, for duration is a cause, and His doing has no cause. For Him the not-yet-come is hard cash and the past is retained. It is you who must think about the not-yet-come, you who must remember what is past, and you who must preserve what is present.

He has no need to remember the past, for it is in His knowledge. He has no need to think about the not-yet-come, for it is in His decree. He has no need to preserve what it is present, for it is in His kingdom. For Him, from the Beginningless to the Endless is less than one breath, and one hundred years is less than one instant. With Him there is neither yesterday nor tomorrow. He is constant in exaltedness and abides in His measure. This is the secret of the words of ʿAbdallāh ibn Masʿūd, "With your Lord is neither day nor night."

For the equivalent of this verse, recite "*to whom the most beautiful preceded from Us*" [21:101]: "My servant, before you said that you are My servant, I said that I am your Lord: *Your god is only God, other than whom there is no god* [20:98]. Before you said that you are My friend, I said that I am your friend: *He loves them, and they love Him* [5:54]. My servant, you were not, and I was there for you. I was there for Myself in exaltedness, and I was there for you in mercy. 'Belong to Me as you always were, and I will belong to you as I have always been.'*"

(*Kashf* 8:315–16)

Samʿānī often talks of God's beginningless love as the source of all that we are and all that we will be. These passages are typical:

In terms of sonship, our lineage goes back to Adam, but in terms of love, it goes back to beginningless gentleness. God cannot have children, but He can have those whom He loves. When this verse came, "*He does not give birth, nor was He given birth to*" [112:3], it cut off every sort of child. When this verse came, "*He loves them, and they love Him*" [5:54], it established every sort of love.

(*Rawḥ* 204)

"He loved you before you loved Him, He sought you before you sought Him, He remembered you before you remembered Him, He bestowed upon you before you asked from Him and thanked Him, He responded to you before you called upon Him, and He desired you before you desired Him."

Before water and clay reached the degree of love, it never occurred to its mind that it has the station of servanthood. In the Beginningless, He talked first to Himself about you, then He talked to you about you.

Shiblī was once asked, "What is it toward which the hearts of the folk of recognition incline?"

He replied, "Toward what happened to them at first, in the Beginningless, in the Presence when they were absent from It."

(157)

My father said, "God's love in '*He loves them*' does not attach to dust. His love is attached to His own beginningless gaze. After all, if the cause of love were dust, there is plenty of dust in the world."

O dervish! When He looks at you, He looks at the property of the Beginningless, not the property of dust. If He were to look at the property of dust, He would take back your capital goods. If each of your hairs were to turn into an Iblis, every bodily member a Pharaoh, every iota a Nimrod, and every side a hell, once He called you, no one would have a thing to say.

(425–26)

THE PRIMORDIAL MUḤAMMAD

It was pointed out that the Qur'anic verse "*Say: 'If you love God, follow me; God will love you'* " provides the key to the prophetic function in the Islamic worldview. The clear meaning is, "If you love God, then you must follow me, the supreme example of a perfect lover of God and a perfect beloved of God."

Just as people return to God by following Muḥammad, so also they came into existence in his footsteps. This is the Islamic version of the Logos doctrine, developed in its most sophisticated forms by Ibn al-ʿArabī and his followers. Its seeds go back to the Qur'an and the Hadith, and many early Sufis, such as Sahl Tustarī (d. 896), spoke or wrote about it. By the eleventh century, it was being taken for granted, and authors such as Samʿānī and Maybudī discussed it extensively. Among the several hadiths that are taken as references to Muḥammad's exalted station before creation, one is "I was a prophet when Adam was between water and clay." Maybudī alludes to it in explaining the verse "*Trust in the Exalted, the Ever-Merciful!*" (26:217).

"O Muḥammad, O unique pearl! I brought you out from the depths of the ocean of power and displayed you to the world's folk so that the whole world would take on the color of your being's beauty. I created all for your sake, and I created you for My sake. Support yourself with Me and entrust yourself totally to Me. O Muḥammad, Adam was still between caresses and torment when I inscribed gentleness in your heart and, with the hand of generosity, poured the wine of contentment for you to taste. I lifted up the curtain between Myself and you, and I showed Myself to your spirit."

(*Kashf* 7:174)

Texts commonly refer to the Prophet by the title *ḥabīb*, a passive and active participle from *ḥubb*, meaning both "beloved" and "lover." From the standpoint of the creative command, the title indicates that Muḥammad is God's supreme beloved and the final goal of creation, as suggested by a divine saying often mentioned by Maybudī: "But for thee, I would not have created the spheres."

> Were it not for his beauty and exaltation, the compass of power would not have drawn the circle of existence, and neither Adam nor his descendants would have name or mark. "But for thee, I would not have created the two worlds."
>
> (*Kashf* 1:682, on verse 2:253)
>
> "O Muḥammad, the goal in the engendered things and the center-point of the circle of the newly arrived things is you yourself. 'But for thee, I would not have created the engendered universe.' Were it not for your rank and majesty, I would never have created the universe"
>
> (5:208, on verse 13:30).
>
> *Did We not expand thy breast for thee?* [94:1]: "O paragon of the universe! O honored chosen one! O foremost messenger! O ennobled eminent one! Did We not brighten your heart with the light of recognition, give it courtesy and rectification with the subtleties of contemplation and unveiling, give it goodliness and proximity with the generous gifts of exaltedness and elevation, and give your clay the cape of adornment and the robe of elevation?
>
> "O master, the goal of creation was to unveil the sign of your perfection, the flag of your majesty, and the form of your beauty. 'But for thee, I would not have created the spheres. But for thee, the world would have neither bottom nor top.'
>
> "O Master, you were the first in prophethood and the last in being sent out. You are the manifest in union and the nonmanifest in blessings. You are the first of all creatures in nearness and familiarity and the last in judgment and felicity. You are the manifest in sinlessness and greatness and the nonmanifest in the majesty of state."
>
> (10:537–38)

In one of his many discussions of the Prophet's cosmic role, Samʿānī refers to a Prophetic saying, "We are the last, the foremost," and explains it by means of a well-known Aristotelian formula:

> The philosophers say, "The first in thought is the last in act, and the last in act is the first in thought." Whatever is prior in thought is posterior in act,

and whatever is posterior in act is prior in thought. A man says, "I want a house to keep the cold and heat away from me." First he lays down a foundation and raises the walls. Then he puts up the roof. That roof was prior in thought but posterior in act.

(*Rawḥ* 616–17)

In one of the two Qur'anic passages that are typically cited as references to the Prophet's ascent to God, the *miʿrāj*, the text says that he reached a point "*two bows' length away, or closer*" (53:9). Many authors explained this extreme nearness in cosmic terms. Ibn al-ʿArabī and his followers took the word *bow* to mean arc of a circle (like the Latin *arcus*, Arabic *qaws* means both "bow" and "arc"). Then the two bows are the descending and ascending arcs of the Circle of Existence, and the verse alludes to the Prophet's supreme perfection in embracing the entire cosmos. In his commentary on this verse, Maybudī alludes to the Muhammadan Reality, the Logos that becomes manifest through each and every one of the prophets, reaching its most perfect external form in Muḥammad's historical actuality.

Then he drew close, so He came down, until he was two bows' length away, or closer [53:8–9]. Among all the creatures in the World of the Realities, none was greater than Muḥammad Muṣṭafā. The root desire of the divine decree in accordance with the beginningless knowledge was to bring about the state of that paragon and make manifest his majesty.

The first substance that received a robe from the command *Be!* and upon which shone the sun of the Real's gentleness was his pure spirit. There was still no Throne or Carpet, no nighttime intrusion or daytime mercy, when God's artisanry brought his spirit from the repository of beginningless knowledge to the lodging place of endless splendor. He put it on display in the meadow of good pleasure and the station of contemplation. Whatever came into existence afterward rode on the coattails of his spirit's existence. Whatever people imagine of familiarity, nearness, clemency, mercy, leadership, and felicity, He sprinkled over his spirit's essence and attributes. Then He placed it inside the frame of Adam the Chosen and made it pass over the degrees of variegation and the trails of stability. Then He sat it down in the seat of messengerhood, commanding it to call the people to the presence of the religion, to bring the lost back to the road, and to invite the travelers to the Threshold.

You might say that this paragon was a falcon trained on the hand of bounty, nurtured on the carpet of proximity and nearness, and brought forth from the togetherness of contemplation to the dispersion of invitation so that he could hunt a world and place everyone before the gentleness and severity of the Real. Today he makes everyone his prey with the Shariah, and tomorrow, in the station of intercession, he will entrust them all to the Real.

(*Kashf* 9:375)

Maybudī summarizes the notion of the Muhammadan Light, one of the common designations for the Logos, in his commentary on the verses "*Alif Lām Mīm. The sending down of the Book, wherein is no doubt, from the Lord of the Worlds*" (32:1–2):

> It is said that when He created the light of Muḥammad's innate disposition, the Exalted Lord kept it in the Presence of His exaltedness as long as He wanted. It remained before God one hundred thousand years. It is said that for two thousand years He was gazing upon it 70,000 times a day, and with each gaze He would drape it with a new light and a new generosity.
>
> He kept the light of this disposition in His Presence for thousands of years, and each day He would look upon it with the attribute of favor. With each gaze it would gain another secret and mystery, another caress and gentleness, another knowledge and understanding.
>
> In those gazes, the secret core of his disposition was told that the level of the Qur'an's exaltedness would preserve the level of his sinlessness, and this awareness became firmly rooted in his disposition. When his very clay along with the secret core of his disposition was brought into this world, the revelation sent down from the Exalted Threshold turned toward him. He was saying, "I hope that this is the realization of the promise given to me at that time."
>
> In order to soothe his heart and confirm this thought, the Lord of the Worlds sent down this verse: "*Alif Lām Mīm.*" *Alif* alludes to God, *Lām* alludes to Gabriel, and *Mīm* alludes to Muḥammad. He is saying, "By My divinity, Gabriel's holiness, and your splendor, O Muḥammad, this revelation is the Qur'an that We promised would be the keeper of your prophecy's level and the miracle of your good fortune.
>
> "*Wherein is no doubt, from the Lord of the Worlds.* There is no doubt that it is Our missive to Our servants, Our address to Our friends. In every corner We have someone burning in hope of seeing Us, in every nook someone distracted, his heart tied to Our love and his tongue busy with Our mention and remembrance. The poor are needy for Our threshold, the yearners anxious for Our vision."
>
> (*Kashf* 7:525)

Samʿānī describes the universality of Muḥammad's mission, embracing that of all prophets from the time of Adam, in the following passage:

Because of the greatness of that paragon, all existent things, from the era of Adam to the dissolution of the world, live under his shadow. Do you suppose that we alone seek refuge in his shadow?

"On the plain of the resurrection, when I come and set up my lofty banner and noble signpost along with the tent of my leadership and the pavilion of felicity, Adam and his progeny will seek the provisions of the Endless and the supplies of the Everlasting from the pavilion of my majesty.

"When Adam received the garment of chosen-ness, he received it from my greatness. When Idris found the elevated place, he found it because of my good fortune. When Noah's prayer was answered and he received the title 'elder of the prophets,' he received it from my rank. When Abraham received the robe of bosom friendship and found *coolness and peace* [21:69], he found them from my degree. When Moses heard the unmediated Speech at Mount Sinai and was made the foremost of the 600,000 children of Israel, he received it from my leadership." And so on.

Muṣṭafā came with the custom of the Turks: He tied the Throne and the Footstool to his saddle-straps. Because of his aspiration, however, he was detached from both.

A sultan needs a throne, and the throne must have a place and location. The place and location need a courtyard. The world with all this spaciousness is the courtyard for the throne of Muḥammad, God's messenger. He is the center-point of the circle drawn by the compass.

When someone has a compass, it has two legs. When he wants to draw a circle, first he makes one leg firm. The firmer it is, the more beautifully it turns. "All beauty is the trace of my center-point."

"I placed one leg of the compass of power at the Muhammadan Center, and I turned the other around the spheres."

Adam was seated on one side, Noah on another, and so also Abraham and Moses. But the front seat of kingship had been turned over to Muḥammad, God's messenger. At the moment the point was marked, the circle had not yet appeared. He set down the point and made the center appear, but there was no trace of the circle:

"When were you a prophet?"

He said, "I was a prophet when Adam was between water and clay."

It was said to him, "When was prophethood written for you?"

He said, "Before the creation of Adam and the blowing of the spirit into him."

"Adam had still not stretched out his legs in the cradle of creation when I stretched out my hand in the cradle of prophethood's covenant and seized the teat of gentleness. On the day when my prophethood came into existence,

Adam's creation was not yet complete. The existence of creation was the beginning, and the existence of prophethood the end. I had drunk the wine of the end when Adam had not yet finished drinking the draft of the beginning."

(*Rawḥ* 542–43)

2

The Story of Love

Like any worldview, Islam offers a myth, a grand narrative of the human situation as viewed under the aspect of eternity. Like premodern myths generally, the Islamic version begins before creation, dips into time, and eventually takes everything back to its original home. As told by the Qur'an, the events are similar to those recounted in the Hebrew Bible: the creation of Adam and Eve, the Fall, the toil and turmoil of this world, ultimate salvation or damnation. But the details are not the same, so the overall picture looks skewed to Jews and Christians, not least because of the intrusion of Muḥammad on the scene.

Authors who wrote about love looked at the Qur'anic narrative as episodes in a love affair between God and man. This explains why Rūmī's famous companion and teacher, Shams-i Tabrīzī, called the Qur'an "the Book of Passion" (*ʿishq-nāma*).[1] If people do not understand that the Qur'an is a book about love, Shams said, it is because they read the book with the eyes of jurisprudence, or theology, or philosophy (or history, or sociology, or critical theory, and so on). Only a lover recognizes love. Over a hundred years earlier, Maybudī had made a similar point while explaining the meaning of the verse "*When there came to them a book from God*" (2:89):

> A book came to them—and what a book! For it was the Lord's reminder to His lovers. It was a book whose title was "The Eternal Love," a book whose purport is the story of love and lovers. It was a book that provides security from being cut off, the remedy for unsettled breasts, health for ailing hearts, and ease for grieving spirits—a mercy from God to the folk of the world.
>
> (*Kashf* 1:278–79)

The story of love tells of the trials and tribulations of God's lovers in their quest to reach the Beloved. Much of it centers on Adam, the first lover, so it is important to have a sense of the events surrounding his creation. In briefest terms, the tale goes like this: God created the heavens and the earth and told the angels that He would be placing a vicegerent on the earth. They protested, saying that such a creature, in contrast to themselves, would work corruption and shed blood. God told the angels that He knew something that they did not. He created Adam from clay and taught him all the names. He then asked the angels to recite the names, but they could not do so, so He had Adam tell them the names. Next He commanded the angels to prostrate themselves before Adam, which they did. Iblis, though a jinn and not an angel, was present among them, and he refused to obey the command. When God asked why, he replied that he was better than Adam, since he was created of fire and Adam of clay. God sent him out of paradise and agreed not to call him to account until the Day of Resurrection. Iblis declared that he would busy himself with misguiding Adam and his children.

God told Adam to settle down in paradise and then created Eve as his mate. He issued the first religious command, telling the two of them not to approach the tree. Satan (Iblis) whispered to them that if they ate the fruit, they would become immortal. They forgot the command, ate the fruit, and began stitching leaves together to cover themselves. God questioned them, and they asked His pardon for their disobedience. God forgave them and sent them down into the earth, appointing Adam His vicegerent and a prophet to the human race. God continued sending prophets one after another, the traditional number being 124,000. Finally, He sent Muḥammad with a culminating, all-embracing message, confirming the previous messages, but warning of the imminent Last Day, when everyone would be called to account. Once Muḥammad received the Qur'an and embodied its guidance, he was given an exclusive foretaste of the goal of all guidance, which is the encounter with God. He was taken up to meet God in an event known as the miʿrāj, literally, the "ladder" or "ascending stairs."

Gabriel came one night, mounted Muḥammad on an angelic steed called Burāq (from the same root as *barq*, "lightning"), and took him first to Jerusalem, where he led all 124,000 prophets in the ritual prayer. Then Gabriel took him up through the seven celestial spheres, in each of which he met the resident prophet and attendant angels. He was then given a tour of hell and paradise. On the outermost edge of paradise, at the Lote Tree of the Final End, Gabriel told him to go on to encounter God alone, for the angel could go no farther without his wings burning off. Muḥammad went, met God, and "what happened, happened," as the texts like to say. Gabriel was waiting for Muḥammad when he returned to the Lote Tree, and he escorted him back down through the spheres to Jerusalem and then to Mecca, where his bed was still warm. Was Dante familiar with this story? Many historians think he was.

The goal of lovers is to come together. The consummation of God's love for man and man's love for God is achieved in their encounter. Having reached the goal, Muḥammad become the model to be emulated: "*Say: 'If you love God, follow me; God will love you'*" (3:31).

In short, the story of love focuses on two main actors in the mythic universe: Adam, who is the father of all the characters and who slipped once but then went on to reach perfection; and Muḥammad, who demonstrated through his own embodiment of the Qur'an and his ascent to God that love takes the lover to an encounter with the Beloved. As retold by our authors, the story began long before God announced to the angels that He would be creating a vicegerent. Two mythic events mark the origin of love: the Covenant and the Trust.

THE COVENANT

Exegetes and commentators have had their hands full with the verse that speaks of the Covenant of Alast (*alast* means "Am I not?"): "*And when thy Lord took from the Children of Adam, from their loins, their progeny and made them bear witness against their own souls: 'Am I not your Lord?' They said, 'Yes indeed, we bear witness*'" (7:172). All sorts of questions can be raised about this verse, and countless answers have been offered. Here is Maybudi's explanation of its inner meaning.

> In terms of understanding in the tongue of the Reality, this verse has another intimation and another tasting. It alludes to the beginning of the states of the friends and the binding of the compact and covenant of love with them on the first day in the era of the Beginningless, when the Real was present and the Reality was there.
>
> How blessed were Laylā and those nights
> when we were meeting with Laylā!
>
> What a fine day was the day of laying the foundation of love! What an exalted time was the time of making the compact of love! Those who desired on the first day will never forget their desire. Those who yearned at the time of union with the Beloved know the crown of life and the kiblah of the days.
>
> How blessed was the time of Your covenant—without that
> my heart would have had no place for ardor!

The command came, "O Master, *Remind them of the days of God* [14:5]. These servants of Ours have forgotten Our covenant and have busied themselves with others. Remind them of the day when their pure spirits made the covenant of love with Us, and We were anointing their yearning eyes with this collyrium: '*Am I not your Lord?*'

"O indigent man! Remember the day when the spirits and the very persons of the lovers were drinking the wine of passion for Me from the cup of love in the assembly of intimacy. The proximate angels of the Higher Plenum were saying, 'These indeed are a people with high aspiration! As for us, we have never tasted this wine, nor have we found a scent of it. But the roaring and shouting of these beggars has risen to Capella: "*Is there any more?*" [50:30].' "

Of that wine not forbidden by my religion
  my lips will not stay dry till I'm back in nonexistence.

One day that paragon of the world and master of the children of Adam was saying, "This is a mountain that loves me and that I love."

They said, "O Master, you talk like this about a mountain? What is the intimation here?"

He said, "Yes, there I drank the wine of love from the cup of remembrance."

In the beginning of the work, when the traces of prophecy and the marks of revelation were appearing to him, he used to spend days in the Mountain of Ḥirā, and the pain of this talk overtook him in that place of seclusion. That mountain was like his sympathizer.

Your ache knows only to circle round my heart—
  in its wonders Your ache is like You.
Though it put me into the fire,
  how I will ache if Your ache ever leaves me!

For a time he was in contraction, for a time expansion, for a time intoxication, for a time sobriety, for a while affirmation, for a while effacement. Anyone aware of the beginning of the desirer's desire knows what his state was, and what his pain! It was as they say:

Now at least I have the hard cash of pain—
  I won't let it go for a hundred thousand remedies.

The Pir of the Tariqah said in whispered prayer, "O God, what sweet days they are—the days of Your lovers with You! What a sweet bazaar it is—the bazaar of the recognizers in Your work! How fiery are their breaths in mentioning and remembering You! What sweet pain—the pain of those yearning in the fire of passion and love for You! How beautiful is their voicing Your names and marks!"

"Am I not your Lord?" They said, "Yes indeed." On the Day of the Compact, He disclosed Himself to their hearts in the majesty of His exaltation and the perfection of His gentleness—one group with the attributes of exaltedness and dominance, another group in respect of gentleness and generosity. Those who were the folk of dominance were inundated by the oceans of awesomeness and the waves of confoundedness. Upon them was placed the burning brand of deprivation: *Those are like cattle. No, they are farther astray* [7:179]. Those who were fit for caresses and generosity were specified for the redoublings of proximity and the election of love. The proclamation of generosity was placed on the edict of their faith: *Those—they are the rightly guided* [49:7].

Am I not your Lord? Here a beautiful and subtle point is made. He said, "*Am I not your Lord?*" He did not say, "Are you not My servants?" He connected His joining with the servant to His own Godhood, not to the servant's servanthood. Had He connected it to the servant's servanthood, then, when the servant did not comply with servanthood, the joining would be defective. Rather, He connected it to His own Godhood. Given that His Godhood is forever perfect without any defect, it must be that the servant's joining with Him is never broken.

Also, He did not say, "Who am I?" Had He done so, the servant would have been bewildered.

He did not say, "Who are you?" lest the servant become proud of himself or fall into despair.

He did not say, "Who is your God?" lest the servant be helpless.

On the contrary, He asked while inculcating the answer. He said, "Am I not your God?" This is extreme generosity and utmost gentleness.

Shaykh al-Islām Anṣārī said, "Generosity said, '*Am I not your Lord?*' Kindness said, '*Yes indeed.*' Given that the caller and the responder are one, what is the meaning of the two sides? The King called the servant to Himself. The servant listened to Him through Him, and He responded without him, bestowing the response on the servant."

This is just like what He said about Muṣṭafā: "*You did not throw when you threw*" [8:17]. In this verse, He burnt away claims and caressed his meaning, so that whenever he came back to himself, he would recognize Him. He assigned the flood of lordhood to the dust of mortal nature and snatched him away from himself, then made him a deputy.

(*Kashf* 3:793–96)

In explaining the meaning of the verse *"And We honored the children of Adam"* (17:70), Maybudī connects the specific excellence through which God honored human beings with the love that was made manifest at the Covenant.

> It was a great felicitation, a complete bestowal of eminence, and a tremendous honor that God gave to the faithful children of Adam. On the Day of the Compact, at the outset of the work and the commencement of existence, He gave them a place in the grasp of His attributes and addressed them with the quality of gentleness, binding them to love's covenant and compact.
>
> Then, when they came into this world, He gave them a beautiful form, a lovely shape, and a complete robe of honor, adorning them with knowledge, intellect, speech, understanding, and excellence. He did not hold them back from the outward success of struggle or the inner realization of contemplation and recognition. He opened the door of His mercy and generosity to them, and He kept them on the carpet of whispered prayer. Whenever they want, they call upon Him, ask from Him, and tell Him their secrets.
>
> Part of that honoring is that He bestowed before they asked and He forgave before they begged forgiveness, as has come in the report: "I bestowed on you before you asked from Me and I forgave you before you asked Me to forgive you."
>
> Part of that honoring is that among all the created things, He specified them for affection and love. That which He did not bestow on the angels and did not say about the cherubim and the spirituals of heaven, He said about them: *"He loves them, and they love Him"* [5:54]. *"God is well pleased with them and they are well pleased with Him"* [5:119]. *"Those who have faith love God more intensely"* [2:165]. *"So remember Me, and I will remember you"* [2:152].
>
> (*Kashf* 5:597–98)

Samʿānī frequently speaks of the Covenant of Love as the foundation of human existence. Like Maybudī, he usually locates the Day of Alast in beginningless eternity rather than, as is common, in the period between Adam's creation and his entrance into this world.

> May a thousand thousand exalted souls be sacrificed to that heart-caressing moment when we had a private place without us! The door to infinite kindness was opened to us and He was addressing ears that had no control over listening. He asked questions on the part of Knowledge and answered on the part of Will. He made Knowledge like a questioner and Will the respondent. In the chamber of togetherness He fed us the milk of chosen-ness. In the

> cradle of the Covenant, before exertion and effort, He provided the food of kindness. In the bond of the Contract, He took care of our business and made it ready. In the pure desert of listening, He made us hear *"Am I not your Lord?"* It was He who asked and He who inculcated the answer.
>
> Suppose He had said, "Who am I?" All would have been mute and effaced. They would have halted right there in bewilderment. He said, *"Am I not your Lord?"* because of His beginningless gentleness, so that half would be the question, and half the inculcation of the answer.
>
> (*Rawḥ* 84)

In another passage, Samʿānī compares God's love to a veiled virgin and explains that the virgin's father would never give his daughter in marriage to a servant. Although human beings should serve God, servanthood per se is the job description of the angels. Human beings were created for love, not service. They alone were created in God's image, manifesting the names of both majesty and beauty, severity and gentleness. They alone possessed readiness for love, for it demands separation and union, suffering and joy, trial and triumph.

> We are the ones lifted up by His knowledge, we are the ones given eminence by His decree. No one came to the angels asking them to marry the veiled virgin of the Unseen, the daughter of nobility. They did not have the worthiness to speak to her, for they were mere servants. It would be shameful for a master to give his daughter to his own serving boy. Those worthy to marry this veiled virgin were the Adamites, for they were friends, and a man gives his daughter to a friend, not a serving boy. When the angels acquired a lineage, that was through the Spirit, but when the Adamites acquired a lineage, that was through divine opening: "Every tie will be cut, save My tie and My lineage."*
>
> On the day He said, *"I blew into him of My spirit"* [15:29], He set in place the Adamites' qualification. In the Beginningless, He had decreed that sheer servanthood would contract a marriage with utter lordhood: *"Am I not your Lord?"* That contract could be made only with someone qualified. In Adam's dust He prepared a subtlety from the pure realm of the Unseen, and that subtlety was the tie of qualification, for that subtlety received a lineage from the gentleness of the Presence. *He confirmed them with a spirit from Him* [58:22] is an allusion to this subtlety.
>
> Although outwardly He said, *"Am I not your Lord?"* He also addressed them inwardly. That was the words *"He loves them, and they love Him"* [5:54]. He was saying, "I am your friend—by day I am the sultan, by night we are brothers." During the day, He opens up the pavilion of the kingdom and sits on the royal throne, the elect and the commoners standing before Him.

> When night comes again, He comes down from the throne and sits in the midst like a brother.
>
> (*Rawḥ* 512)

Once a covenant has been made between two parties, they need to be loyal (*wafāʾ*) to its stipulations. The Covenant of Alast was made between a Lord (*rabb*) and His servants (*ʿabd*). *"Am I not your Lord?" They said, "Yes indeed."* The duty of a lord is to nurture, sustain, support, and guide. The duty of servants is to obey. Being loyal to the covenant is a virtue pertaining to both sides. God is loyal by continuing to act as a Lord, and man is loyal by performing the duties of servanthood (*ʿubūdiyya*), a word that comes from the same root as *worship* (*ʿibāda*). Failure to live up to the covenant is commonly called disloyalty (*jafāʾ*).

Servanthood demands appropriate response to the commands of the Lord, so it exists in two basic ways, in keeping with the two sorts of divine command. On one hand, all creatures are servants by definition, for they obey the creative command simply by existing. On the other, human beings have the option of obeying or disobeying the religious command. By obeying it, they stay loyal to the Covenant and become worthy servants, and by disobeying it, they become disloyal. Samʿānī points out, however, that even if human beings fail to act as proper servants, God will never fail to act as a proper Lord. The passage belongs to his commentary on the divine name Generous (*karīm*).

> O dervish! Someone is called generous when he gives to the unworthy, not when he gives to the worthy. This is because worthiness is a necessitating cause. Whenever there is a necessitating cause, there is a debt. One does not discharge debts because of generosity.
>
> On the day that He created Adam, He called out to the world, "Wherever there is someone unworthy, let him come to My Presence so that I may give him a robe of honor."
>
> When a sultan appoints someone as the heir apparent, the least he does is bestow robes of honor on all the deputies. "Heaven and earth, the Throne, paradise and hell, the angels, the spheres—all are your deputies."
>
> *And We made covenant with Adam before, but he forgot* [20:115]. *Did We not make covenant with you, O children of Adam?* [36:60]. He made a covenant with us, and He made a covenant with Himself. He made a covenant with Himself for us, and He made a covenant with us for Him. Then He said, "*And be loyal to My covenant, and I shall be loyal to your covenant*" [2:40].
>
> When He made that covenant, Adam had not yet stepped into paradise, yet the call went out from all over paradise, "*Adam disobeyed*" [20:121].

"Lord God, disloyalty finds no room in You, and loyalty finds no room in our attributes."

"Now that loyalty does not come from you, *Who is more loyal to his covenant than God? So rejoice!* [9:111]. If you do not have enough capital to be loyal to Our covenant, you do have enough capital to be happy in Our loyalty. If you do not show the face of beauty, well then, be happy in the beauty of Our Presence."

(*Rawḥ* 576)

THE TRUST

The Covenant is commonly understood along with the verse "*We offered the Trust to the heavens and the earth and the mountains, but they refused to carry it and feared it, and man carried it. Surely he was a great wrongdoer, deeply ignorant*" (33:72). In his commentary on this verse, Maybudī agrees with Samʿānī that the Trust is love (a good deal of this passage is drawn from *Rawḥ* 597–99, 203–5).

For a time Adam the Chosen—that first wayfarer, that wellspring of beginningless gentleness, that coffer of the wonders of omnipotence, that jewel box of the gentleness of the Reality, that shoot in the garden of generosity—was kept between Mecca and Ta'if in the cradle of the covenant of recognitions. The ill-fortuned, ill-eyed Iblis passed by. With the hand of envy he shook Adam's frame and found it empty. He said, "This creature will not be self-possessed. He is empty, and nothing comes forth from something empty."

Beginningless good fortune replied on behalf of Adam: "Wait a few days until the falcon of his mystery takes flight! The first prey it hunts will be you."

The abandoned and accursed Iblis saw Adam's clay but did not see his heart. He saw the form but did not see the attribute. He saw his outwardness but did not see his inwardness.

No one can put a seal on fire. You can put a seal on dust, because dust is receptive to seals. "When We brought Adam into existence from dust and clay, the wisdom was to place the seal of the Trust on the clay of his heart, for *We offered the Trust to the heavens and the earth.*"

He brought a handful of dust into existence and burned it with the fire of love. He gave it a place on the carpet of expansiveness. Then He offered the Trust to the world of form. The heavens, the earths, and the mountains refused. Adam came forth like a man and put out his hand. It was said, "O Adam, it is not being offered to you. Why do you want to receive it?"

He said, "Because I am burnt, and someone burnt can only receive."

On the day when fire was deposited in stone, the stone was made to promise not to submit its head until it saw someone burnt. Do you imagine that this fire is going to come out into the open with the strength of your forearm? No, no, don't think that. It will only come out with the intercession of someone burnt.

We offered the Trust: O chevalier! Strive to preserve that first covenant with that first seal. Then the angels will praise you: *The angels will descend upon them saying, "Fear not! Grieve not!"* [41:30].

It is people's custom when they leave a precious trust with someone to put a seal on it. On the day they want it back, they examine the seal. If the seal is in place, they praise him.

A trust was placed with you at the Covenant of Lordhood—*Am I not your Lord?* Upon that was put the seal of *Yes indeed.* When your life reaches its end, you will be taken to the domicile of dust. The angel will come and say, "Who is your Lord?" This is an examination to see whether the seal of the First Day is in place.

"O poor man! A seal was put on you, from the top of your head to your feet. That was the seal [*muhr*] of love [*mihr*]. A seal was put on the place of love. O Riḍwān, paradise is yours! O Mālik, hell is yours! O cherubim, the Throne is yours! O burnt heart upon which is the seal of love, you are Mine, and I am yours."

We offered the Trust. The mountains did not have the capacity for this burden of the Trust, nor did the earth, the Throne, or the Footstool. Do you not see that the Exalted Lord reports about the incapacity of the mountains? *"If We had sent this Qur'an down on a mountain, you would have seen it humbled, split apart by the fear of God"* [59:21]. You see an angel, one of whose wings spread out would bring the two horizons beneath it, but it does not have the capacity to carry this meaning. Then you see the poor wretch of an Adamite, skin stretched across bones. Like a fearless warrior he drinks down the wine of trial in the goblet of friendship, and no change appears in him. Why is that? Because he is the possessor of the heart, and the heart carries what the body does not.

When Adam the Chosen, who was the marvel of creation and unique in the Desire, saw that the heaven and the earth would not carry the burden of the Trust, he came forth like a man and lifted that burden. He said, "They looked at the tremendousness of the burden and refused it. I looked at the generosity of Him who was placing the Trust."

The burden of the Trust of the Generous is carried by aspiration, not strength. When Adam lifted the burden, he was addressed with the words *"We carried them on land and sea"* [17:70]. *"Is the recompense of beautiful-doing anything but beautiful-doing?"* [55:60].

There is a likeness for this in the outward realm. When trees have sturdier roots and more branches, their fruit is smaller and lighter. Trees that are weaker and softer have thicker and larger fruit, like melon and squash. Here, however, there is a subtle point: when a tree's fruit is thicker and larger and it does not have the capacity to carry it, they say to it, "Take the heavy burden from your shoulders and put it on top of the earth." This is so that the world's folk will know that wherever there is someone frail, he is being nurtured by the gentleness of the Exalted Presence. This is the secret of *We carried them in the land and the sea.*

(*Kashf* 8:100–2)

In one of his several retellings of the events surrounding the Trust, Samʿānī explains that Adam was enjoying himself in paradise, but he sensed that something was missing. The love in his heart drove him to embrace the full wealth of the divine attributes, not just the gentleness of proximity and union. This is why the verse of the Trust concludes by saying that he was "*a great wrongdoer, deeply ignorant*": Adam knew that he could not become a lover without pain and suffering.

That paragon was at rest in the world of repose and ease. Like a king, he was leaning back on the chair of exaltation and nobility. He wandered like a prince according to his own wishes and desires in the orchards of the Highest Paradise. All at once and unexpectedly, the petitioner of passion, the deputy of love, was banging the knocker on his heart's door: "Get up! Go like a lover into the field of severity, the realm of not reaching your desires! Then the beauty of what you seek will be unveiled to your heart. O Adam, you are standing still in good fortune. Move into the world of passion and love!"

Adam's manliness took him by the skirt and sought its own rightful due. Severity's army took his crown in plunder and pulled off his robe. Riḍwān came and said, "Adam, step out of paradise, for this is the house of ease, and there is no ease in the lane and quarter of lovers—only trial upon trial. Settle down in the house of tribulation inside the circle of love. Then the ruling power of passion will take from you everything rightfully due to it."

At that point the Exalted Lord offered the Trust to heaven and earth. The goal was not that heaven and earth should accept it, but rather that the offer would shake the chain of Adam's love. Then bewilderment would stand in the station of jealousy. The exaltedness of Adam's acceptance became manifest because of their refusal and unwillingness, and his courage appeared because of their cowardice. If no one in the world were timid and fainthearted, how would the courage of the courageous appear? In the days of security, everyone wears a weapon. The manly man is he who appears on the day of war. How is it that just the other day the angels were saying, "*We glorify Thy praise*" [2:30], and today they put on the belt of apprehension?

O chevalier! The strength of a sword and its blow lies not in the sword's sharpness but in the arm. The sword of ʿAmr Maʿdī Karib was famous among the Arabs. One day someone came and wanted to borrow his sword, so he lent it. The man was not able to use the sword like ʿAmr. He said, "ʿAmr, your sword doesn't work."

He said, "I lent you my sword, not my arm."

First He offered the Trust to heaven and earth so that they would refuse and Adam's love would appear. Things are offered first to the unworthy so that the worthy will get moving. Adam started moving because of his love.

The address was coming, "*Surely he was a great wrongdoer, deeply ignorant.*" What is this? Adam's incense against the evil eye.

At the first way station, the caravan was attacked and his capital taken as plunder. He was sent as an indigent into this world and shown that if he wanted to reach someplace, he could not do so with his own capital. Once a servant's capital goods are thrown to the wind and his master wants to send him for another transaction, he has to give him new capital.

Know that in verified truth, the foundation of love became firmly established because man carried the burden of the Trust. To carry the Trust of lordhood, man must step outside the limits of mortal nature: *And man carried it.* When Adam carried the Trust, the foundation of the work was firmly established, for once there is carrying, the foundation is firm.

A man buys a slave girl from the bazaar. Whenever he wants, he can sell her. As soon as he takes her in companionship and she carries [his child], they say, "You are not permitted to sell her, for she has your trust."

On the day man carried the Trust, he firmed up the foundation of love. If he now brings into existence a hundred thousand betrayals, sins, disobedient acts, and offenses, the foundation will not be destroyed.

In the firm text of the revelation, the Exalted Lord said, "*Surely We created man of dried clay*" [15:26]. The ascription is to dust, but the attribute is proximity. When fire dies down, nothing is left but ashes, which are not good for anything. If clay breaks, it can be fixed with a few drops of water.

Such was the enemy Iblis. When the lamp of obedience that had been shining upon him was extinguished, he became useless and could not be repaired. But, when Adam stumbled, He repaired him with the water of solicitude: *Then His Lord chose him* [20:122].

"On the first day, We had a gentleness and a gaze for you. We honored you with that gentleness and gaze. If a slip occurs from you, no one will have the gall to start talking. *Who will intercede with Him except by His leave?* [2:255].

When the sultan of the world rebukes his favorite boon companion in an intimate session, who can say anything to either of them?"

It is that first gaze that must come to intercede and scour away the dust of deeds from the mirror of days with the polish of gentleness. He will call us to the Presence and take us to account, mote by mote, so that the knowledge of certainty may become the eye of certainty, for He knows what happened to us. Then He will let that exalted gaze—which He presented to us at first and through which He honored us—intercede. In reality, the only interceder for the sins of the beloveds is their beauty.

When He lets Muḥammad and the other great ones intercede, He will do so to honor them. Nothing new will happen to you because of their words. He will bring that eternal gaze that He had for us, free from any causality, and make it intercede for offenses and sins. Then He will say, "I brought you into existence with that pure gaze, and there was no cause whatsoever. I forgive you with My own pure gaze, and there is no cause whatsoever." Peace!

(*Rawḥ* 276–78)

THE CREATION OF ADAM

Samʿānī frequently describes Adam's creation and the subsequent events, each time throwing a different light on the divine-human relationship. In the following, he explains that Adam—the primordial human being who is each and every one of us—was created by a diversity of divine attributes. All else was created to serve his needs. In effect, Samʿānī is elaborating on a divine saying, said to be derived from one of the scriptures, "I created the whole world for you, and I created you for Me."

The robe of honor on dust and clay is not trivial. We are the ones given eminence by Him. We are the ones pulled up by His remembrance, adorned by His gentleness, made present by His desire, lifted up by His will, made apparent by His artisanry, put here by His bounty. He placed within us what He placed. Our work is not a game, nor is our story a metaphor. The nose of our affair will never be lopped off. Our work came forth from Knowledge, was displayed by Predetermination, has the mark of Desire, and carries the proclamation of Wisdom.

He created the Throne but sent it no message. He gave existence to the Footstool but gave it no mission. Then He brought forth a handful of dust, whose drink was the limpidness of knowledge and whose food was the kernels of the meanings. This dust did not come uninvited. Rather, He sent a hundred thousand requests and entreaties, requesters and seekers, to the door of the hut of his secret core: *messengers bringing good news and warning* [4:165]. And he, with sweet disdain, adopted the amorous glances of the beloveds and the coquetry of the sweethearts.

There were many existent things and countless artifacts, but the work He had with you He did not have with any other existent thing. If causality had been involved, well, He had luminous persons and celestial figures, all of them wearing the garment of sinlessness and the shirt of reverence, standing in the station of service on the feet of obedience. *Who do not disobey God in what He commands them* [66:6] was the edict of their state. *Nay, but they are honored servants* [21:26] was the parasol of their pomp and authority. But not everyone who is worthy for service is also worthy for love. Not everyone who is worthy for the edge of the carpet is also worthy for the station of expansiveness. Not every ornament of the threshold is like the beauty of the gate. Nothing created not to see Him is like the one created to see Him.

"At the beginning of the work, Our knowledge requested that We bring into existence heaven and earth, the Throne and the Footstool. We gave existence to daytime as a white-faced servitor and to night as a black-cheeked maid, and We sent them to serve the house of your dealings. It was the sun of your good fortune that rose over heaven and earth so that We could dress them in the shirt of their existence. We gave forth this overflowing cup: *We offered the Trust to the heavens and the earth and the mountains* [33:72].

"It was the ray of your state's majesty that shone on the Throne so that We could adorn it with the attribute of tremendousness and make it the kiblah for supplication. It was the lightning of your greatness and nobility that struck the Footstool so that We could give it eminence with this declaration: *His Footstool embraces the heavens and the earth* [2:255]. It was the sun of your status that shone on Mount Sinai and dressed it in this robe of elevation: *Then, when his Lord disclosed Himself to the mountain, He made it crumble to dust, and Moses fell down thunderstruck* [7:143]. It was your burning that shone upon a dog and turned it into a saint. It was your pain that shone upon a saint and turned him into a dog.[2]

"It was for the sake of your disobedience that We made apparent the attribute of severity. It was by virtue of your frailty and incapacity that We put bounty to use. It was because of the heat of your desire that We called out, '*He loves them, and they love Him*' [5:54]. It was because of the bounty of Our eternity toward this handful of dust that We said, 'My mercy takes precedence over My wrath.' It was by the kind favor of Our own Beginninglessness that We said concerning this impudent handful, '*Your Lord has written mercy against Himself*' [6:54]."

O dervish! If you gather a large amount of copper and iron and toss a speck of the elixir on it, it will all turn into pure gold. Copper and iron are such that they have no trace of the mystery of the elixir, but once the elixir has acted upon them, they become pure gold.

You and I were a handful of dust, and Adam a handful of clay. Adam had not seen the mold of Power and had not yet come out from behind the curtain of the subtle artisanry. The secret of knowledge had not yet shone its light upon him, and coming down had not yet become his specific attribute. The oyster of the decree had not yet become the container for the pearl of his secret, and the sun of majesty had not yet risen over his days from the constellation of beauty. The mystery of union, the reality of meaning, and the subtlety of love had not yet shown their faces to him. But once these meanings became manifest and the pearls of these realities were deposited in his spirit and heart, if you say that Adam is dust, you will have wronged him. If you say that he is *fetid mud* [15:26], you will have scorned him.

The elixir is an artifact of creatures. If it is suitable for turning iron into gold, how could love, which is the attribute of the Real, not purify dust of its opacity and make it the crown on top of the celestial spheres? If the clay that you knead yields roses, why are you surprised that the clay He kneads yields a heart? Yes, it was dust, but then the gentleness of the Real came and overwhelmed the earth. Had it been nothing but dust, all of it would have been *Adam disobeyed* [20:121]. Had it been nothing but gentleness, all of it would have been *Surely God chose Adam* [3:33].

O chevalier! When a Muslim judge makes a ruling, he does so on the basis of just witnesses and truthful testimony. Dust testifies with the tongue of *Adam disobeyed*. The gentleness of the Real then comes forth and testifies with the tongue of *Then his Lord chose him* [20:122]. What do you say? Which one gives a more just testimony? Dust, which was not and which, once again, will not be, or gentleness, which is the attribute of the Real?

(*Rawḥ* 233–34)

What distinguishes Adam from all other creatures is the fact that he was created to be a lover. The Qur'an repeatedly issues commandments to be obeyed—the religious command. If excellence could be achieved by obeying commandments, the angels would be the most excellent of creatures, because they are pure servants. The first thing Adam did with the religious command was to disobey it. He ate the forbidden fruit, which, in Islamic texts, is identified as wheat.

Preachers in the mosques tell their flocks that they must obey the divine command. They warn of hell and promise paradise, defining good and evil in terms of obedience and disobedience. But this is only the surface of the story.

Not that obedience is unimportant, but God's love and mercy are more important than anything else. Much of the discussion of the angels' role in the saga of Adam's creation and subsequent fall has in view the background noise of obedience and disobedience. This is the standpoint of the Shariah, and Maybudī, for example, discusses its importance extensively, especially in Stage Two of his commentary. As for the lovers of God, the chevaliers and dervishes, they keep their eyes on the Beloved, not on good and evil.

In retelling the story of Adam's creation, our authors often describe the self-centeredness of the angels, their pride in their own piety and worship. As pure servants, the angels could not understand why God would create a creature who would be disobedient. Here is Maybudī's account of what happened as soon as God told the angels that He would be placing a vicegerent in the earth.

> *When thy Lord said to the angels, "I am setting in the earth a vicegerent"* [2:30]. There was a world at ease. No heart burned with passion and no breast was deluded by mad fervor. Then the ocean of mercy began to boil. The treasuries of obedient deeds were full, and no dust of lassitude had settled on the foreheads of the obedient in their obedience. The banner of their boastful claim "*We glorify Thy praise*" [2:30] was raised to Capella.
>
> All those in the cosmos who had any subtle substance began craving for their own selves. The majestic Throne was looking at its tremendousness and saying, "Perhaps the script of these words is written for me." The Footstool was looking at its own amplitude—"Perhaps this sermon is being read in my name." The eight paradises gazed on their own beauty—"Maybe this rulership will be given to us." None wanted anything to do with dust. Each fell into delusion, each caught by mad fervor.
>
> Suddenly, from the Presence of Exaltation and Majesty, this report was given to the world of the angels: "*I am setting in the earth a vicegerent.*" It was not that He was consulting with the angels. Rather, He was laying the foundation of Adam's exaltation and tremendousness. He was not asking for help, but spreading the carpet of Adam's dignity. He was saying, "The ruling property of My severity has acted. I have commanded the pen of generosity to write out a script from the beginning of the world's ledger to its end. This resolution is written for the inhabitants of both worlds, from the top of the Throne to the bottom of the Carpet: 'The dust-dwelling Adam is granted chieftainship over all the empires. His exalted breast will be bright with the light of recognition. In him the subtleties of My generosity and the artifacts of My bounteousness will become apparent.'"
>
> This exalted declaration caused the hearts of the proximate angels to quake with awe. They said, "What is this all about? He has not yet been created."

The exalted Qur'an was beating the drum of his vicegerency at the threshold of his beauty even though he had not yet entered into the bonds of creation. The majesty of predetermination was reporting on the basis of the hidden affairs of the Unseen: "You must not come around the field of Adam's good fortune, for you do not recognize the secret of his innate disposition. No falcon of anyone's mind has sat upon the branch of Adam's good fortune! No eye of anyone's insight has grasped the beauty of Adam's limpid sun!"

Where did this eminence come from? From whence did this good fortune arise? It came from the fact that Adam was the oyster shell of the mysteries of lordhood and the treasury of the jewels of the empire. How many precious pearls and royal sparklers were placed in that oyster shell! Along with every pearl He arranged a black bead on the string. Along with the pearl of every prophet, He placed a black bead as its counterpart: With a pearl like Adam the Chosen was a bead like Satan the wretched; with a pearl like Abraham the bosom friend was a bead like Nimrod the rebellious; with a pearl like Moses of ʿImrān was a bead like Pharaoh the unaided; with a pearl like Jesus son of Mary was a bead like the tribe full of misguidance and transgression; with a pearl like Muṣṭafā the Arab was a bead like Abū Jahl full of ignorance.

When the angels heard this terrifying declaration, their stability and repose fled from them and the firmness of their intellects and patience departed. They all spoke up with questions and said, "*What, wilt Thou set therein one who will work corruption there and shed blood?* [2:30]. O Lord! O King! O Magnanimous! O Creator! This dust-dwelling Adam will stain the embroidered robe of proximity with disobedience. He will pull his head out from the collar of obedience. You have created us from holiness and declaring holy! You have adorned our breasts with reciting the formula of tawḥīd and glorifying! You have made all these our means!"

It is said that a fire appeared from the hidden affairs of the Unseen and incinerated a tribe of the angels. This declaration was made with the attribute of exaltedness: "*Surely I know what you do not know*" [2:30].

"You who are gazers, just keep on gazing! What do you have to do with the secret treasuries of the divinity? How can you intervene in the hidden affairs of Our unseen lordhood? It is We who know the preparations of Our divinity and the hidden affairs of the mysteries of Our lordhood. How can insignificant minds, the sciences and intellects of anyone other than Us, defective understandings and newly arrived insights, find a way to the mysteries of Our divinity? *With Him are the keys to the Unseen—none knows them but He* [6:59].

"In the Beginningless, We decreed that We would light the lamp of the realities of recognition in the breast of the dust-dweller Adam, turn over to him the edict of rulership, and plant the flag of the earthly empires in his soldierly heart.

"You who are the proximate angels of the Empire, be serving boys, spread the carpet in front of the throne of Adam's good fortune, and prostrate yourselves before him!

"You who circumambulate Our Throne, ask forgiveness for the not-yet-committed crimes of Adam's progeny, who have not yet come into existence! Ask for safety in their going forth, and say, 'Peace be upon them, peace be upon them,' so that when they come into existence, their feet will not slacken on the carpet of servanthood.

"You who are in charge of the veils, weep for the folk of heedlessness among Adam's progeny so that We may conceal their disobedience with Our forgiveness because of your weeping!

"You who are the folk of the cushions, take up this pure water whose waves are lapping around Our Throne with water bags of light and, on the Day of Resurrection, when they lift up their heads thirsty from the earth, provide water for them!

"You who are the sinless of the Lote Tree of the Final End, wait until the Greatest Fright appears at the resurrection, when awe and punishment's holding and grasping, taking and seizing, all come forth, and then give the faithful among them security from that Fright and convey to them Our greetings!

"We have commanded all this so that you angels may come to know the eminence of these dust-dwellers and make no protest at Our ruling."

There is a sound report that the Supreme Plenum and the proximate angels of the Court of Exaltation said, "O Lord, You have given the dust-dwellers the low world. Give us the high world, for we are the birds of the Presence and the peacocks of the Court."

The answer came to them, "I will not make the worthy progeny of him whom I created with My own two hands like those to whom I said, '*Be!*' and they came to be."

(*Kashf* 1:139–41)

Maybudī again compares the rank of Adam with that of the angels in his commentary on the verse "*We created you, then We formed you, then We said to the angels, 'Prostrate yourselves before Adam'*" (7:11).

The wise Lord is reminding the children of Adam of His favors. He is teaching them about His beautiful Godhood and His firmness in the Covenant. He is saying, "I created you, and I sculpted your beautiful faces. I drew your tall statures and gave you two seeing eyes, two listening ears, and a speaking tongue. I am the Lord who makes being from nonbeing, who brings forth what is from what was not, and who makes things newly from the outset. The painter of faces is I, the adorner of beauties is I, the one who pairs everything with its companion is I, the maker of every being in a fitting way is I. I created heaven, earth, and the inanimate things to manifest power. I created the angels, satans, and jinn to manifest awe. I created Adam and the Adamites to manifest forgiveness and mercy.

"For 700,000 years Gabriel, Michael, Seraphiel, the Cherubim, the Circlers, and the Row-keepers circumambulated the Kaabah of Invincibility, saying, 'The Glorified! The Holy!' They never gained access to or recognized My names of love, loving-kindness, and friendship. They never had the gall to claim friendship with Me, but I claimed friendship with the dust-dwellers: *We are your friends* [41:31]. *He loves them* [5:54]. I derived several of My names from My friendship and loving-kindness toward them: the Forgiving, the Loving, the Clement, the Ever-Merciful. To the angels, I showed only Severity and Invincibility. I kept them behind the veils of awe. To the dust-dwellers, I showed only clemency and mercy. I kept them on the carpet of expansiveness."

Among the angels, Gabriel was honored and foremost, and he was singled out for the specific favors of proximity. His name was Servitor of the All-Merciful. He was standing constantly on the carpet of justice with the attribute of awe. He had never seen the carpet of bounty and expansiveness. Before Adam the Chosen came, there was no separation or union, no rejection or acceptance. There was no talk of heart, sweetheart, and friendship. These wonders and storehouses all pertain to the register of passion. Other than Adam's heart, there was no oyster shell for the pearl of love. Everyone came by the road of creation, and he alone came by the road of love: *He loves them, and they love Him* [5:54].

From the angels there was nothing other than glorifying and hallowing—their work was one color. The wonders of service, the courteous acts of companionship, the storehouses of affection, the subtleties of love—all appeared with Adam, for he was the chameleon of predetermination.

Then We said to the angels, "Prostrate yourselves before Adam." The angels were commanded to prostrate themselves before Adam. The secret here is that the angels were looking at their own ceaseless worship with the eye of high regard and giving great weight to their own glorifying and hallowing. That is why they said, "*We glorify Thy praise and call Thee holy*" [2:30]. The Majesty of Unity, the Side of Invincibility, showed them Its exalted and endless unneediness toward the obedience of all the obedient and the worship of all the heaven-dwellers. It said, "Go, prostrate yourselves before Adam, and do not give your prostration any weight in the Exalted Presence. I still had

> not written out existence for the existent things when My majesty witnessed My beauty. In My own Selfhood, I was enough for Myself. Today that I have created the creatures, I am the same Exalted One I was. I have no need to join the faith and obedience of newly arrived things to My beginningless majesty."
>
> (*Kashf* 3:570–71)

Samʿānī frequently refers to God's rebuke of the angels after they protested at the creation of Adam. In the following passage, he explains that they were displaying their ignorance of God's wisdom and doubting His mercy and compassion. They were caught up in self-righteousness, like those who think they are doing God a favor by quoting the Qur'an and commanding people to be pious.

> *I am setting in the earth a vicegerent* [2:30]: "We will bring a sultan into existence. You who are servants, what do you say?"
>
> They said, "We cannot put up with their corruption."
>
> "Yes, if We were to send them to your threshold, you would reject them. If We offered to sell them to you, you would refuse to buy them. We will not place those who are disobedient and brokenhearted in the hands of stuffy-headed Qur'an-reciters. You blame them before they have sinned. Do you fear that their sinning will be greater than My mercy? Do you fear that My power will be incapable before their severity? Do you fear that their taintedness will stain My perfect holiness? My knowledge of their disobedience will not hold Me back from bringing them into existence. How can it hold Me back from having mercy on them?"
>
> (*Rawḥ* 620–21)

According to Samʿānī, one of the many marks of God's love for Adam was that He taught all the names to him alone. Other creatures have a limited capacity to receive and comprehend the divine attributes.

> When the spirit of that precious pearl Adam settled down in its lodging place at the command of the Faithful Spirit, the Real clothed him in the robe of knowledge, placed the crown of recognition on his head, put the bracelet of secrets on his wrist, and fastened the anklet of good fortune to his foot: *And He taught Adam the names, all of them* [2:31]. *Surely God chose Adam* [3:33].
>
> This is the way Adam had to be displayed to the adversary. Zulaykhā first adorned Joseph, then presented him to the women of Egypt. Zulaykhā adorned Joseph with clothing and jewelry, and God adorned Adam with pure knowledge. Like an adversary, He then said, "*Tell Me the names of these if you are truthful*" [2:31]. He did not say, "Tell Adam." He said, "Tell Me." They fell apart in awe at that address. Then He said to Adam, "*Tell them their names*" [2:33]. He said, "Tell them." He did not say, "Tell Me."

"Yes, your pride as angels lies in your works, and work is your attribute. Adam's pride lies in knowledge, and knowledge is My attribute."

He called Himself knower: *"The knower of the Unseen"* [34:3]. He also called us knowers: *"The possessors of knowledge"* [3:18].

"When I apportioned bearing witness, I said, 'It must not be done without beautiful friends: *God bears witness that there is no God but He, [and the angels, and the possessors of knowledge]* [3:18].'

"When I apportioned exaltedness, I said, 'The friends must have a share: *To God belongs the exaltedness, and to the Messenger, and to the faithful* [63:8].'

"When I apportioned the prayers of blessing, I said, 'The friends should take part: *It is He who blesses you, and His angels* [33:43].'

"O Muḥammad! On the day We praised your community and called you knowers, We saw those with long lives and all that obedience. On the day We created the bee and gave it honey, We saw those mighty falcons. On the day We gave silk to that little worm, We saw those awesome serpents. On the day We gave ambergris to the whale, We saw those tremendous elephants. On the day We gave pearls to the oyster, We saw those powerful crocodiles. On the day We gave sweet songs to the nightingale, We saw those decorated peacocks. On the day We praised and lauded Muḥammad's community, We saw those long-lived obedient ones. On the day We praised this handful of dust, We saw the angels lined up in rows of service."

> Before you asked I asked for you,
> all the world I adorned for you.
> Thousands in the city are in love with Me—
> live in joy, I rose up for you.

"Moses gazed over all the children of Israel and chose Aaron: *Make him a partner in my affair* [20:32]. I gazed from the Throne to the earth and chose you. Moses made Aaron a partner in prophethood. I made you a partner in bearing witness: *God bears witness that there is no God but He, and the angels, and the possessors of knowledge* [3:18]: O you who have faith! I say about Myself, 'God.' You also say about Me, 'God.'"

Tell them their names [2:33]. A man has a dear friend, and a new infant arrives. His family says to him, "What name should we give this child?"

He says, "Let us wait until that friend comes and see what he says. We will give him the name that he says."

He brought the existent things into existence, from the top of the Pleiades to the end of the earth. "Lord God, what are the names of these created things?"

The answer came, "I have a friend in the concealment of nonexistence. Wait until I bring him into the confines of existence. I will present all these existent things to him and see what he names them. O Adam! Whatever name you give, We have given."

(*Rawḥ* 625–26)

THE VIRTUES OF DUST

Adam was created of clay, a mixture of dust and water. Iblis was a jinn, created of fire. Before Adam, the commentators tell us, Iblis was so pious that he was placed among the angels. It is even said that God employed him as the angels' teacher. Then, when Iblis refused to prostrate himself before Adam, he was thrown out of paradise, and God said to Adam, "*Tell them their names*" (2:33). Thus Adam became the new teacher of the angels.

Iblis has sometimes been called "the first to use a syllogism"—clearly by those who had a dim view of philosophy—because of his response to God when He asked him why he had refused to prostrate himself: "*I am better than he: You created me of fire and You created him of clay*" (38:76). His conclusion is obviously based on the premise that fire is better than clay. But is it? Maybudī and Samʿānī, like other commentators, offer a variety of arguments to show that Iblis was mistaken. Maybudī explains that Adam was created from clay so that he would become aware of his own measure and recognize God's blessings when he saw them. He is commenting on the verse, "*O Adam, dwell you and your spouse in the Garden*" (7:19).

He was called Adam because he was created from the surface [*adīm*] of the earth, drawn from every region. Thus He said, "*We created man from an extraction of clay*" [23:12]. In other words, he was extracted from every region—sweet and briny, soft and hard. In Adam's clay were salty and sweet, coarse and soft, so the natures of his children have become diverse. Among them are both sweet-tempered and bad-tempered, open and closed, generous and stingy, easygoing and difficult, black and white.

Elsewhere He said, "*He created man from dried clay, like pottery*" [55:14]. Pottery is dried clay that gives off sound and is full of noise. In other words, the Adamite is noisy, his head full of tumult and turmoil, attached to talking.

Elsewhere He said, "*from clinging clay*" [37:11], from a clay that is sticky, clings to everything, and mixes with everyone.

Elsewhere He said, "*from fetid mud*" [15:26], a clay that is dark and black.

Thus He taught him his measure so that he would not transgress his stage. He was shown his own root so that if he should see generosity, he would not see it from himself. He would know that eminence lies in nurture [*tarbiya*], not in dirt [*turba*].

What arises from dirt? Wrongdoing, ignorance, and punishment. *Adam disobeyed his Lord* [20:121]. What arises from nurture? The generosity of guidance, the acceptance of repentance, and caresses. *Surely God chose Adam* [3:33]. The fruit of nurture is what He says: "*He loves them, and they love Him*" [5:54].

(*Kashf* 3:586–87)

Maybudī explains why dust is superior to fire in his commentary on a verse that tells people how to make ablutions if water is not available.

If you find no water, have recourse to goodly dust [5:6]. God connected purification to water or, at the time of necessity, to dust, and not to anything else. The wisdom here is that the Lord of the Worlds created Adam from water and dust, and human beings should always be aware of this. They should know that their own eminence lies therein and that they should give gratitude for this blessing.

Adam found eminence over Iblis because Iblis was from fire and Adam from dust, and dust is better than fire. Fire shows defects, and dust conceals them. Whenever you put something in fire, it shows its defects. It distinguishes genuine from false silver and adulterated from pure gold. Dust, however, conceals defects. It conceals whatever you give to it, so the defects do not show.

Fire is the cause of cutting off, and dust is the cause of joining. With fire there is cutting and burning, with dust there is joining and keeping. Iblis was from fire, so he broke off. Adam was from dust, so he joined.

Fire's nature is arrogance, so it seeks to be higher. Dust's nature is humility, so it seeks to be lower. Iblis brought higherness with his words, "*I am better*" [38:76]. Adam brought lowerness with his words, "*Our Lord, we have wronged ourselves*" [7:23].

Iblis said, "I and my substance." Adam said, "Not I, rather my God."

(*Kashf* 3:49–50).

Samʿānī often talks about the virtues of dust, not least Maybudī's last point here: dust is the least of things, so Adam's recognition of his own dust-nature prevents him from forgetting the fundamental truth of tawḥīd: "Not I, rather my God." By recognizing his own nothingness, Adam achieves the perfection for which he was created.

One of the common ways to express this ideal relationship between Lord and servant is to speak of annihilation (*fanāʾ*) and subsistence (*baqāʾ*). Man's perfection lies in seeing his own annihilation and nothingness relative to God, at which point the divine attributes that nurture him will shine forth in purity.

Man's essential nonbeing, says Samʿānī, helps explain why God said in the verse of the Trust, "*Surely he was a great wrongdoer, deeply ignorant.*" The failing was ontological, not moral; it grows up from the creative command, not the religious command.

O my spirit and world! The angels came, wearing the majestic satin of hallowing and the perfect shirt of glorification: *We are those in rows, We are the glorifiers* [37:165–66]. Adam the dust-dweller came, wearing the patched cloak of *deep ignorance* and the tattered coat of *great wrongdoing.* The angels recited the sermon of their own days: "*We are those in rows.*" God praised this handful of dust by Himself: "*And We honored the children of Adam* [17:70]. *We chose them, with a knowledge, above the worlds* [44:32]."

This is a secret. We are wounded by our own annihilation, and we receive bestowals from His subsistence. When we look at our own existence, we see only annihilation, but when we look at His uncaused munificence, we see only subsistence.

O dervish! Do not look at the form of dust. Look at the secret of the nurture. When you give a grain to dust, it gives it back many times over. Whatever you give to fire, it burns it away. They gave the grain of wheat—which carries the mystery of nourishment's capital—to the nursemaid, dust, so that she would nurture it at her side and breast. Then, in a short time, she gave back produce many times over, *in every ear a hundred grains* [2:261].

He sprinkled the grain of love and the unique seed of affection in the clay of dust's breast, for *He loves them, and they love Him* [5:54]. Then, with the hand of gentleness, He fermented the clay, for "He fermented Adam's clay in His hand for forty days."* He nurtured it with the north wind of bestowal and assisted it with the limpid water of bounty from the cloud of prosperity, for *He confirmed them with a spirit from Him* [58:22]. In the end, it received the secrets of the ear, and then came the springtime of connection and arrival. *A goodly word is like a goodly tree, its root established and its branch in heaven; it gives its fruit every season by the leave of its Lord* [14:24–25].

(*Rawḥ* 172–73)

O chevalier! Aloes has a secret. If you sniff it for a thousand years, it will never give off a scent. It needs fire to display its secret. Its face is black and its color dark. Its taste is bitter and its genus wood. It wants a hot fire to display the mystery in its heart.

There was a fire of seeking in Adam's breast, and its sparks looked on all the acts of worship and obedience and all the capital goods of the angels of the Sovereignty as nothing. He was a *great wrongdoer, deeply ignorant.* He was an incense that had to be thrown on the fire. From that incense a breeze became manifest. What was it? *He loves them, and they love Him.*

The chevalier's trials announce his nobility,
like fire the excellence of ambergris.

By God, you come to be in *He loves them,* and by God, you cease to be in *they love Him! He loves them* says, "Lift them all up." *They love Him* says, "Put them all down."

When you say, "*He loves them,*" your own shirt collar says, "You've got nothing over me." When you say, "*They love Him,*" the Throne comes before you and says, "I am your slave."

They said to a dervish, "Who are you?"

He said, "I'm the sultan. He's my agent."

Stand up, slave, pour the wine—
bring the cup for all these friends.
Outwardly I call you slave,
secretly I'm your slave.

Before Adam was brought into existence, there was a world full of existent things, creatures, formed things, determined things—all of it a tasteless stew. The salt of pain was missing. When that paragon walked out from the concealment of nonexistence into the space of existence, the star of love began to shine in the heaven of the breast of Adam's clay. The sun of loverhood began to burn in the sky of his secret core.

Suddenly I saw—
and the work began.

Who is this? A beginner in the road of creation, advanced in the road of limpidness. Who is this? The utmost in loveliness and beauty. Who is this? The sign of the gentleness of the Possessor of Majesty. Who is this? The one fermented by the mysteries of Our knowledge and wisdom, the one lifted up by Our choice and will.

When they brought Adam out, they brought him out in this garment. If you pile dust on dust for a million years so that something will come of it, nothing will happen. Look what happened to fire, a limpid substance, when His gaze was taken away from it. Since that happened to the subtle substance of fire, what hope can you have in gross dust?

(294–95)

The accursed one said, "*I am better than he: You created me of fire and You created him of clay* [38:76]. What is the wisdom that You tell light to prostrate itself before darkness?" Through these words he became an unbeliever.

"Do you think We make mistakes? Dust is better than fire. Dust sets things right, fire corrupts. If a father has two sons, he will give each of them some capital. If one of them spends the capital in the tavern and the other preserves it, what do you say? Which one is more to be praised and accepted?"

Also, dust in itself has no need for fire. But fire has need of trees, and trees are the result of dust.

Fire tells everyone, but dust conceals the mystery. If you want to know how dust keeps secrets, go to the cemetery and look at the tombs. You will see them all the same, but under the dust lie great differences. One is being caressed, another is being melted in fire. One is dreaming of lovely maidens, another of emaciated men.

Fire is for putting burdens on top, not for carrying them. When you put a burden on fire, it burns it, but when you put a burden on dust, it carries it and keeps silent.

Fire has force, but dust has good fortune. "Good fortune belongs to the Real, and force belongs to the unreal." The unreal shows itself, but it does not last.

"O accursed one! When they kill fire, they kill it with two things: dust and water. *He created you of dust, then from a sperm drop* [40:67].

"O accursed one! If you are proud and great because of fire, I give you to fire. Here is fire, and here are you. O Pharaoh! Are you proud of your rivers? Here is water, and here are you: *They were drowned, and made to enter a fire* [71:25]. O Korah! Are you proud of your treasures? Here are your possessions, and here are you: *We made the earth swallow him and his house* [28:81].

"O you who have faith! Are you proud of *God, the One, the Severe* [40:16]? Here I am, and here are you: *Faces on that day radiant, gazing on their Lord* [75:22–23]."

It is said that when Adam's body was placed between Mecca and Ta'if, the accursed one was passing by. He looked carefully, and awe entered his heart. He was afraid and said to himself, "I read in the Guarded Tablet that the court of the Real has an enemy whose name is Iblis. Perhaps this is that enemy."

You poor wretch! How should you know what is happening in the world?

Then Iblis said, "O angels! What will become of this body, for it does not have a heart?"

O dervish! Why would He show your heart to the enemy? "My mercy takes precedence over My wrath": My mercy toward Adam takes precedence over

My wrath towards Iblis. The newly arrived will never reach the Eternal. Wrath will never reach mercy.

(624–25)

On the day that He created Adam from dust, He made mercy incumbent on Himself by His generosity. He said, "*Your Lord has written mercy against Himself*" [6:54]. He wrote Adam's slip with the intermediary of others, but He wrote mercy against Himself without intermediary. After all, dust is the capital of incapacity and weakness. What can be shown to the weak except mercy?

Except those on whom your Lord has mercy, and for that He created them [11:118–19]. A group of the exegetes says that this means that He created them for mercy. He created you in order to have mercy on you. Dust in its makeup is humble and submissive, and people trample it underfoot and look down on it. In contrast, fire in its makeup considers itself elevated and great, and it keeps on trying to go up.

Water has a certain innate limpidness and a natural humility. Dust does not have that limpidness, but it does have humility. When Adam was brought into existence, he was brought from dust and water, so the foundation of his work was built on purity and submissiveness. Then this water and dust, which had become *fetid mud* [15:26] and *clinging clay* [37:11], was honored with the attribute of the hand. God said, "*What prevented you from prostrating yourself to him whom I created with My own two hands?*" [38:75]. But fire, which considered itself great, was made the object of severity through the attribute of the foot. "The Invincible will place His foot in the Fire, and it will say, 'Enough! Enough!'"*

The attribute of the hand imparts the sense of elevation, and the attribute of the foot gives the sense of debasing. Dust was debased by its own attribute, but it was elevated by His attribute. Fire was elevated by its own attribute, but it was debased by His attribute.

"O dust! O you who are put down by your attribute and lifted up by My attribute! O fire! O you who are lifted up by your attribute and put down by My attribute!"

Iblis performed many acts of obedience and worship, but all of them were accidental. His innate attribute was disobedience, for he was created of fire, and fire possesses the attribute of claiming greatness. Claiming greatness is the capital of the disobedient.

Adam slipped, and we disobeyed. But the attribute of disobedience is accidental, and the attribute of obedience original. After all, we were created from dust, and the attribute of dust is humility and submissiveness. Humility and submissiveness are the capital of the obedient. God looks at the foundation of the work and the point around which the compass turns. He does not look at uncommon things and accidents.

O dervish! On the day when Adam slipped, they beat the drum of good fortune for all the Adamites. God set down a foundation for Adam at the beginning of the work. He gave him capital from His own bounty.

The first example of bounty that He showed to Adam was that He placed him in paradise without any worthiness and without his asking. And the first example that Adam displayed of his own capital was his slip.

God made a contract with Adam at the beginning of this business. The stipulation of the contract was that whenever someone buys something or sells something, a taste must be given. Adam gave a taste of his capital when he disobeyed the command and ate the wheat. God gave a taste of the goblet of bounty when He pardoned that slip.

No sin is greater than the first sin. This is especially true when the person was nourished on beautiful-doing and nurtured through beneficence. The angels had to prostrate themselves before him—the chair of his good fortune was placed on the shoulders of those brought into proximity. He was taken into paradise without any worthiness. God gave him a home in the neighborhood of His own gentleness. Since He pardoned the first slip, this is proof that He will forgive all sins.

After all, we have a thousand times more excuses than Adam had. If we need the darkness of clay, we have it. If we need the frailty of dust, we have it. If we need the impurity of *fetid mud*, we have it. If we need some confused morsels, we have them. If the times should have become dark with injustice and corruption, we have that. If the accursed Iblis has to sit in wait for us, we have him. If caprice and appetite have to dominate over us, we have that. At the first slip, Adam was forgiven without any of these meanings. Since we have all these opacities, why should He not forgive us? In truth, He will forgive us.

(225–26)

Dear friends! Know in reality that were there no dust, there would not be all this burning nor any of this tumult. Were there no dust, there would be no happiness, and were there no dust, there would be no sorrow. Were there no dust, there would be none of this talk and none of these pains.

O chevalier! Dust is itself an expression of the pain and reality of love.

Hell with all its chains and punishments is the surplus of the sorrow of dust. Paradise with all its bounties and blessings is the excess of the secret caress of dust. Satan's accursedness is one of the traces of the perfection of the majesty of dust. Seraphiel's trumpet is prepared by the yearning of dust.

The resurrection is stirred up by the secrets of dust. The Scales are the result of the straight-seeing of dust. Munkar and Nakīr are deputies of love in the breast of dust. The reckoning and interrogation are among the lights of the truthful traveling of dust. The Narrow Path is one of the footsteps of dust. Mālik and the Zabāniya are the sword of the leftover remorse of dust. Riḍwān and the serving boys are the helpers of the joyful union reached by the footsteps of dust.

Beginningless prosperity is an inscription on dust. The Throne with all its tremendousness is eager for the lodging place of dust. The Footstool with all its elevation wishes to be struck by the footsteps of dust. The Unseen's request was prepared in the name of dust, the divine power is the master of the work of dust, the lordly artisanry is the hairdresser of the beauty of dust, the divine love is the food of the secrets of dust, the severity of exaltedness is the policeman of the tumult of dust, gentleness and mercy are entrusted specifically to the door of dust, the eternal attributes are the supplies and provisions for the road of dust, and the pure, holy, transcendent Essence is witnessed by the hearts of dust, *desiring His face* [6:52].

What I am talking about does not pertain to now. There was no dust, but there was gentleness toward this handful of dust.

He loves them is the gift of the Pure Unseen to dust, and *they love Him* is dust's gift to the Pure Unseen. *He loves them* went out ahead, and *they love Him* came behind. Supposing that *He loves them* had not gone before, *they love Him* would not have appeared.

Dust had not yet come, but pure gentleness had prepared a gift for dust. There was no mouth, but the wine was ready. There was no head, but the hat was shaped. There was no foot, but the road was paved. There was no heart, but the gaze was steady. There was no sin, but the storehouse was full of mercy. There was no obedience, but paradise was adorned. "Solicitude precedes water and clay."

(292–93)

THE WISDOM OF THE FALL

For Adam to be worthy of love, he had to bring all the divine names and attributes into actuality, not just the gentle and beautiful. In paradise, he was basking in beauty, mercy, and kindness, but they represent only one side of God's reality, albeit the precedent side. To recognize the other side, he had to leave paradise and encounter wrath and severity. The quickest way to do that was to disobey the command. In his commentary on the verse "*It is He who created you from clay*" (6:2), Maybudī explains that when Adam was in paradise, he was treated gently, like a child, but then he had to step out onto the path of manly lovers.

> When he was at rest in the highest paradises, he supposed that the same tent of safety would be pitched for him endlessly. Then he was addressed by the side of the Invincible and the court of the Exalted: "*What, one who is reared amidst ornaments?* [43:18]. O Adam, We want to make a man of you. You have become satisfied with color and scent like pretty brides!
>
> "O Adam! Pull your hands back from the neck of Eve, for you must use your hands for the neck of love's crocodile. You must become the drinking companion of the Shariah's lion. Pull back from the attributes of being, for you must travel with the feet of discipline and the boots of blame into the open horizons of poverty. Go, sit on the dust pile, and be content with a piece of bread, ragged clothes, and ruins so that you may become a man.
>
> "O Adam! Look carefully lest you be self-seeing. The angels who sang the song 'O Glorified! O Holy One!' to the melody of *We glorify Thy praise* [2:30] were self-seeing. They kept their eyes on their own beauty, so We emptied their inner selves of love for the sake of your eminence. We pulled you up from the depths of the sea of omnipotence so that you would sing the song of *Our Lord, we have wronged ourselves* [7:23] to the melody of your disobedience."
>
> (*Kashf* 3:298)

Samʿānī explains the wisdom behind Adam's fall in many contexts. Here are a few of his remarks:

> *Surely God chose Adam* [3:33] was the good news of a robe of honor. *Surely he was a great wrongdoer, deeply ignorant* [33:72] was an allusion to the robe's secret. *Surely God chose Adam* was his beautiful face. *Surely he was a great wrongdoer, deeply ignorant* was the mole on his face.
>
> O friend! They gave Adam the Chosen the majestic cape and beautiful shirt of *Surely God chose Adam* along with the patched cloak of *Surely he was a great wrongdoer, deeply ignorant* so that if the angels should wonder at the highness of his station, the loftiness of his steps, the elevation of his days, and the greatness of his name, He would show them the exalted robe and beautiful cape. But if Adam's makeup should lead him into self-admiration, He would show him the patched cloak of poverty so that he would hold himself back.
>
> (*Rawḥ* 133)
>
> The folk of the empire were commanded to serve Adam, but Iblis did not bow his head. He was struck with a blow. What was that blow? "*Leave it, for*

thou art an outcast!" [15:34]. When Adam saw the blow, fear and terror sat in his heart.

In the same way, when the teacher disciplines a child in grammar school, the fear of that blow works on the hearts of others. The nobler someone is, the more he fears. It may even be that he cannot bear it. He flees school and hides behind a wall. His kind father comes seeking him and sees him upset, tears dripping from his eyes. He puts him on his shoulders and takes him back to school. The whole way he instructs him: "If the teacher asks you where you were, you tell him that your relatives took you someplace."

He said, "Have you fled from Us, O Adam?" Adam fled because of that blow and wanted to hide, so He sent mercy to take him in its arms and provide him with an excuse: *But he forgot, and We found in him no resoluteness* [20:115].

(262)

O chevalier! Our interceder is our ignorance. Our leader is our negligence. Adam's greatest good fortune was that it was said about him, "*Surely he was a great wrongdoer, deeply ignorant*" [33:72].

"If I am a great wrongdoer and deeply ignorant, what is this Trust doing with me?"

They send a guard to the roof of the sultan's treasury to beat the clappers. But the sultan's greatness protects the treasury, not the guard's beating the clappers. *It is We who have sent down the Remembrance, and it is We who guard it* [15:9].

(562)

When Adam reached for that grain of wheat, it is not that he did not know what it was. On the contrary, he knew, but he made his own road short.

What a marvelous business! The wheat was put there in his name and made his nourishment, but it was forbidden to him: *Come not near this tree* [7:19]. Love took hold of his bridle. "The forbidden is enticing." He stretched his hand toward the tree. The tree said, "You were commanded not to eat of me." He paid no attention.

The moment the grain of wheat reached his throat, the call rose up from all over paradise, "*And Adam disobeyed*" [20:121]. The crown flew from his head, saying, "Peace be upon you—farewell, O Adam, for your sorrow will be drawn out." The chair said, "Get down from me, for I do not carry anyone who opposes Him."

O chevalier! This was an inner decree and a harsh command. The harsh command came outwardly, but when he looked at the inner decree, he looked at his secret core. "The worst of men is he who eats alone, beats his slave, and forbids supporting him."*

Yes, my spirit and world! The great ones have spoken about this and pierced the pearl of meaning with the diamond of thought. What was the wisdom in ejecting Adam from paradise?

Some say that the Exalted Lord wanted Adam's knowledge of Him to increase. First, He brought him into the garden of gentleness and sat him down on the chair of happiness. He gave him goblets of joy, one after another. Then He sent him away, weeping, burning, wailing. Just as he savored the goblet of gentleness at first, so also he tasted the drink of pure, unmixed severity at last—without any cause. O chevalier! God wrapped the edict of loftiness and transcendence in the exalted embroidery of "I do not care,"* and no one had the gall to protest.

Again, some say that the sapling of good fortune was planted with the hand of gentleness in the orchard of his covenant. It was watered with the effusion of lordly bounty until the tree became established—*its root established and its branch in heaven* [14:24]. He was the coffer of the wonders of power, within which were the secret drawers of creativity.

Or he was an ocean within which were both pearl and brick, night-brightening jewel and pitch-black bead, truth speaker and liar, sincere and heretic, enemy and friend, wretched and god-wary. Paradise was not the abode of enemies or the home of the wretched. The lordly wisdom required that he come into this world so that the goodly would be separated from the vile: *So that God may distinguish the vile from the goodly* [8:37].

It can also be said that Adam wanted from the tree to stay in paradise forever. So when his eyes fell on the tree, it was said, "The time has come for you to pack your bags. Do not let the limpidness of the moments delude you, for in between are the obscurities of blights. The shadows of the teeth appear between the favors."

O chevalier! Do not ever say that paradise was taken from Adam! Say rather that Adam was taken from paradise. A roasted heart will never be content with roast chicken.

(198–99)

What a marvelous business! When a porter lifts up a heavy burden, you say to him, "Well done!" What is the wisdom in *Surely he was a great wrongdoer, deeply ignorant* [33:72]? Indeed, in this case *great wrongdoer, deeply ignorant* is praise, not blame, for he carried it with his aspiration, not his capacity. This is like the words of the man who says to his companion when he carries a heavy burden, "Why are you carrying that? You will hurt yourself!"

O dervish! When the adversary admits the defects of his antagonist, the work turns easy. In the Beginningless, God called him *a great wrongdoer, deeply ignorant.* Then, despite His knowledge of his great wrongdoing and deep ignorance, He offered him the Trust. If he falls short, he will say, "*I have wronged myself*" [27:44]. The Exalted Lord will say, "I have forgiven you, and I do not care." He said, "*Surely man is a great wrongdoer, ungrateful*" [14:34]. Of Himself, He said, "*Surely I am All-Forgiving*" [20:82].

(380)

"O angels, do not look at the disloyalty of their deeds, look at the limpidness of My knowledge! O Iblis, do not look at the *fetid mud* [15:26], look at the robe of My attributes! Although My friends slip and their disobedience adulterates the coin of their practice, I hold before them the crucible of repentance—*the repenters, the worshipers* [9:112]. The wisdom of the slip is that when they look at themselves from that slip, they will bring forth poverty. If they were to look at Us from obedience, they would bring forth pride."

It is told that David said, "O Lord, why have You thrown me into sin?"

He answered, "Because, before you sinned, you used to enter in upon Me as kings enter in upon their servants, but now you enter in upon Me as servants enter in upon their king."

Self-admiration went to the head of that accursed one: *Shall I prostrate myself to someone whom You created of clay?* [17:61]. "O accursed one! Do you know what you are saying? You see the clay, but you do not see My activity in the clay."

(624)

They adorned that paragon with the varieties of good fortune and bounty and with the lights of perfection and beauty, and then they sent him into paradise. He wandered around, but he found nothing to cling to. He reached the tree known as the tree of trial [*balā*ʾ], though it is rather the tree of friendship [*walā*ʾ]. He saw it, so to speak, as a road-worthy steed. He did not hesitate a moment. When he reached it, he bridled it up. That nasty bridling was expressed as "*Adam disobeyed*" [20:121]. He lifted up his eyes to the tree and saw it as the secret companion for the road. And the tree also—it lifted the veil from its face and showed itself to him: "You cannot travel this road without me."

(236)

What a marvelous business! He said to Adam, "Do not go after the wheat!" Then, wherever they put Adam's chair, the wheat was there, disclosing itself like a bride. There is a secret in this. Yes, the people consider his greatness to be that he had chair, hat, crown, and belt, but that is wrong.

"O Adam, beware, beware! Do not go after this tree!" But the decree had gone out, and the decree had the upper hand. As soon as Adam put that morsel in his mouth, the greatness of those ornaments fell away from him. Adam was left naked, with only the crown of *Surely God chose Adam* [3:33] and the robe of *Then his Lord chose him* [20:122]. Thus people will come to know that authentic greatness has no need for those trappings.

(239)

O dervish! Adam was in paradise, but he caught the scent of something else. He said, "This world is adorned, but I have it in my heart to return one day to the nest of my sorrow. Even though the angels said, '*What, wilt Thou set therein one who will work corruption there?*' [2:30], I will go to a place where they will have to follow in my tracks."

The first attribute to shine in Adam's heart was the secret of faith. It said, "O Adam! Come into exile, for 'Islam began as an exile, and it will return as it began, an exile.'*"

He said, "Why should I come?"

Faith said, "To take care of things."

He said, "How can things be taken care of better than this? The eight paradises are at my command, Riḍwān is my servant and slave boy, and the angels of the Sovereignty are prostrating themselves before the presence of my majesty."

It said, "No, you must exchange the Abode of Peace for the Abode of Blame. You must remove the crown from your head and, in place of the crown, pour the dust of destitution on your head. You must replace the good name of *Surely God chose Adam* [3:33] with the blame of *And Adam disobeyed* [20:121], for love's good fortune lasts forever."

Adam said, "I will call out 'I do not care' to the world and plunder the good fortune of the house of vicegerency. Perhaps the Sultan of Love will say to me once, 'Peace be upon you!'"

(188)

HUMAN SINFULNESS

When God commanded Adam and Eve not to approach the tree, it was clearly a religious command, not a creative command, because they did approach the tree. The divine decree had already been issued that they would eat the wheat. Maybudī points out that God's foreknowledge of the sin is simply another manifestation of His mercy. He is commenting on the verse "*And eat from wherever you will, but come not near this tree*" (7:19).

> He forbade them to eat of it, and He concealed their eating of it in His unseen knowledge. Then He put the decree into effect over them so that they would know their own incapacity and weakness and see that protection from sin comes from the divine success-giving, not from the servant's effort.
>
> (*Kashf* 3:589)

Maybudī finds a reference to the inevitability of human sinfulness and the simultaneous inevitability of divine forgiveness in the verse "*Say: 'Each acts according to his own manner'*" (17:84).

> What comes from man other than disloyalty? What comes from water and clay other than error? What will be seen from the Lord's generosity other than loyalty?
>
> In the whole Qur'an, no verse offers more hope than this. He is saying, "Everyone does what comes from him, and from everyone comes what is worthy of him. The servant returns to sin, and the Lord returns to forgiveness."
>
> One of the revealed books tells us that God said, "O child of Adam! You keep on returning to sins, and I keep on returning to forgiveness."
>
> It was said to the abandoned one of the empire, the despairing Iblis, "Prostrate yourself before Adam!"
>
> He said, "I will not, for Adam is from dust, and I am from fire."
>
> It was said to him, "O unlucky one! No doubt everyone does what is worthy of him, and from everyone comes what is inside him. When fire dies down, it becomes ashes, which can never be renewed. Dust, even if it is old, is renewed by sprinkling water on it. O Iblis, O you who are of fire, you left aside one command, so you will die and never come to life! O Adam, O you who are of dust, you let one tear of regret fall from your eyes, so I have forgiven your sins and will caress you. O Iblis, what you did comes from fire. O Adam, what you saw is born of dust. *Say: 'Each acts according to his own manner.'*"
>
> (*Kashf* 5:626)

In discussing God's essentially forgiving nature, Maybudī cites, among others, the words of the Sufi teacher Yaḥyā ibn Muʿādh Rāzī (d. 872): "O God, I depend on sin, not obedience, for sincerity is necessary in obedience, but I do not have it. In disobedience, bounty is necessary, and You have that" (*Kashf* 7:250). In another passage, he amplifies on a saying of the great theologian, Sufi, and jurist Jaʿfar al-Ṣādiq (d. 765), the sixth Imam of the Shi'ites. He is commenting on the beginning of verse 5:1, "*O you who have faith!*"

It is narrated that Jaʿfar ibn Muḥammad said that these words have four traits through which the Lord of the Worlds honored and caressed the community. One is that they are a call, second an intimation, third an allusion, and fourth a witnessing. O is a call, *you* is an intimation, *who* is an allusion, and *have faith* is a witnessing. The call is an honor, the intimation is of mercy, the allusion is to love, and the witnessing is to recognition.

"He called to them before He made them appear, and He named them before He saw them." They were in the concealment of nonexistence when He called them to honor. They had not yet come into the circle of existence when He named them with a beautiful name: *He named you submitters from before* [22:78]. He saw the faults and He approved of the faults. He saw the offenses, and He bought the offenses. He saw the pure ones of the high world, and He chose the tainted ones of the low world, for "The sinner's sobs are more beloved to Me than the glorifier's murmur."

Given the beginningless solicitude of the Court of Unneediness toward the Adamite, his situation is like that of a child whose mother sews him new clothes. She says, "Beware, beware, O child! Do not let this fancy garment get dirty!"

The child goes outside and busies himself playing with the other children and dirties the clothes. He comes back home with dirty clothes, so he hides in a corner, distressed and bewildered. He keeps on saying, "Mother, I'm sleepy." The mother knows that the child is afraid of her rebuke. "Dearest," she says, "come. I sent you outside only after I had the soap and water in hand, for I knew what you would do."

The Adamite's state is like this. When that center-point of good fortune and chosen one of the kingdom was sent out from the concealment of nonexistence to the confines of existence, the pure spirits and holy ones began to shout, and they aimed arrows of denial at the world that God was bringing forth: "*Wilt Thou set therein one who will work corruption there?* [2:30]. You are creating a group who will blacken the garment of *Today I have perfected for you your religion* [5:3] with the smoke of disobedience and the dust of associating others with God. They will tear the veil of honor from the beautiful face of faith!"

He addressed them with the words, "Yes, I know what has been prepared in this oyster shell of mysteries. *We honored the children of Adam* [17:70]. The bounties of exaltation have made them exalted. I sent them out to the world of defilement wearing the garment of protection and the shawl of the

Trust only after I had in hand the water of forgiveness and the soap of mercy."

(*Kashf* 3:21–22)

Samʿānī often comes back to this same theme: God acts in a manner appropriate to His merciful and forgiving nature, and we act in a manner appropriate to our ignorant and disobedient natures.

Even if many great sins overcome you, the Creator's love will not leave you, for sin is your attribute, and love is His attribute. The attributes of the frail, insignificant, newly arrived thing detract nothing from the attributes of the Eternal, the Subtle, the Aware.

The Prophet said, narrating from his Lord, "My servant, if you encounter Me with offenses that nearly fill the earth, I will encounter you with the like of them in forgiveness, and I will not care."

Yaḥyā ibn Muʿādh said, "Even if the servant sins and does not care, he has a Lord who forgives and does not care."

"Tell My servants, 'Surely I am the Forgiving, the Ever-Merciful, and My chastisement is the painful chastisement' [15:49]: throw them between fear and hope!

"My servant, though you trade in disobedience, My attribute is forgiveness. You will not abandon your trade, so how could I abandon My attribute? *Tell My servants:* You may be disobedient, but you belong to Me. You may not obey Me, but I belong to you.

"O proximate angels, the Throne belongs to you! O cherubim, the Footstool belongs to you! O Gabriel, the Lote Tree belongs to you! O Riḍwān, paradise belongs to you! O worshipers and obedient servants, the houris, castles, rivers, and blossoms belong to you! O Mālik, hell belongs to you! O unbelievers and hypocrites, this world belongs to you! O destitute and sincere, I belong to you!"

At the time of sin, He called you deeply ignorant in order to pardon you, just as He said concerning Adam: "*Surely he was a great wrongdoer, deeply ignorant*" [33:72]. At the time of bearing witness, He called you knowers in order to accept you: "*God bears witness that there is no God but He, and the angels, and the possessors of knowledge*" [3:18]. At the time of obedience, He called you weak—"*And man was created weak*" [4:28]—in order to pardon your shortcoming.

"*Surely I am the Forgiving, the Ever-Merciful.* It is I who forgive disobedience, and it is you who disobey, for everyone does what comes from himself. If you wanted not to disobey, you would not be able to do so, because you are you. If I wanted not to show mercy, indeed it would never happen that I not show it, for I am I. I am the All-Merciful, the Ever-Merciful, the Clement, the Generous.

"When you throw something into water, it gets wet, not because of your command, but because of water's nature. When you throw something into fire, it burns, not because of your instruction, but because of fire's attribute. The sun and the moon give light, not out of kindness to you, but because that indeed is their work. I too—I forgive, not because of your excellence, but because that is My attribute."

Someone said to musk, "You have one defect: no matter whom you are with, you are still fragrant."

It said, "I do not look at the one I am with. I look at who I am."

(*Rawḥ* 337–38)

God's essential reality is love and mercy. This alone is sufficient to explain why He created the universe. Samʿānī explains that when the angels protested at Adam's creation, they did not know that blessing and good fortune are not rewards, but manifestations of mercy.

The recognizers say that the angels thought that they were being caressed because of their service and that opposition would be the cause of distance. Hence, they said: "We are obedient, and they are disobedient." God showed them something else: "Our caressing grows up from Our own bounty, not because of acts of obedience and worship."

He created Adam without his having a single act of obedience, while the angels had filled the seven heavens and the seven earths with obedience. He commanded the rich to prostrate themselves before him who had no capital goods.

He commanded the angels, whose faces were turned toward the Throne and who had bound the girdle of acquiescence, to turn their backs toward the Throne. He told them to take the best of all acts of service—which is prostration, because within it is the hope of proximity—to Adam. When they went forth according to the command, their turning away from the Throne and turning toward Adam brought no defect into the Empire. The Exalted Lord showed them this: "If the whole world turned away from worshiping Me, nothing would be taken away from My Presence, and if the whole world turned their faces toward serving Me, nothing would be added."

(*Rawḥ* 406)

O dervish! He created all existent things at the request of power, but He created Adam and the Adamites at the request of love. He created other things as the Powerful, but He created you as the Friend. First He spoke to you in the Beginningless: He mentioned you, then He named you, then He gave you recognition, then He made you appear.

The Exalted Lord wanted to clothe this speck of dust with the shirt of existence, sit him on the chair of vicegerency, bind the collar of finding on the neck of his eminence through His munificence, and string the gemstone of knowledge on the necklace of his felicity: *And He taught Adam the names, all of them* [2:31]. The angels of the Sovereignty said, "*What, wilt Thou set therein one who will work corruption there, and shed blood?*" [2:30].

The preacher of eternal gentleness came to the pulpit of the Will and gave them their answer: " 'There is no consultation in love.' What weight will your glorification have if I do not accept it? What harm will come to them from their sins if the cupbearer of gentleness places a goblet of pardon's limpid wine in their hands? *Those—God shall change their ugly deeds into beautiful deeds* [25:70]. Why do you look at the fact that they have remained in the opacity of slips? Look at the fact that the limpidness of My pardon belongs to them.

" 'If you did not sin, God would bring a people who did sin, and then He would forgive them':* Suppose that all of Adam's progeny put the ring of obedience in their ears, threw the mantle of acquiescence over their shoulders, and swept the filth of opposition from the courtyards of existence with the broom of struggle. If so, I would bring people into existence who sin and blacken their days with the smoke of disobedient acts, and I would forgive them. Then the creatures would know that My mercy comes as a gift, not at a price."

(223)

Those who speak of God's mercy and compassion toward sinners often have recourse to the verse "*O My servants who have been immoderate against yourselves, despair not of God's mercy—surely God forgives all sins*" (39:53). In explaining it, Maybudī reviews the basic difference between angels and humans:

Know that among God's creatures, perfect honor belongs to two groups: angels and Adamites. This is why He appointed prophets and messengers from among these two groups rather than any others. Their utmost eminence lies in two things: servanthood and love. Sheer servanthood is the attribute of the angels, and servanthood and love are both attributes of the Adamites.

He gave the angels sheer servanthood, which is the attribute of creation. Along with servanthood, He gave the Adamites the robe of love, which is the attribute of the Real. Thus He says concerning this community, "*He loves them, and they love Him*" [5:54]. He also gave the Adamites superiority over the angels in servanthood, for He said that servanthood is the angels' attribute, but without ascription to Himself: "*Nay, but they are honored servants*" [21:26]. He ascribed the servanthood of the Adamites to Himself: "*O My servants!*"

Then, according to the requirement of love, He completed His bounty on them. He concealed their defects and disobedient acts with the lights of love and did not tear away their curtain. Do you not see that He decreed slips for them, yet despite all those slips, He did not remove the name *servant* from them? Despite mentioning the slips and disobedience, He did not take away the eminence of ascription? He said, "*O My servants who have been immoderate against yourselves, despair not of God's mercy.*"

Then He kept the curtain over them and did not make the sins manifest, mentioning them instead in sum, with the lid on. He concealed them and said, "*who have been immoderate.*" They were immoderate, they were extravagant. But He desired to forgive them, so He did not tear away the curtain, nor did He throw away the name *servant*. Glory be to Him—how clement He is to His servants!

It is related that Moses said, "O God, You desire disobedience from the servants, but You hate it": the servants disobey because of Your desire, but then You hate it and You make the servant Your enemy because of the disobedience.

The Real said, "O Moses, that is the foundation of My pardon": that is to lay the foundation of My pardon and generosity. The treasury of My mercy is full. If no one is disobedient, it will go to waste.

The report has come: "If you did not sin, God would bring a people who did sin, and then He would forgive them."

Wait until tomorrow at the Resurrection. The command of the Real will come as a plaintiff against the servant, but the bounty of the Real will shelter him. The Shariah will seize his skirt, but mercy will intercede.

It is reported that the servant will be given his book in his hand and he will see his acts of disobedience. He will be ashamed to read them out. The Real will address him and say, "On the day when you were doing that and you had no shame, I did not disgrace you but instead concealed it. Today when you are ashamed, how could I disgrace you?" This is what the Prophet said: "God does not curtain a servant's sin in this world to reproach him with it on the Day of Resurrection."

(*Kashf* 8:439–40)

Those who sin and recognize their own sinfulness typically repent. More often than not, they slip again, so they need to renew their repentance. From the standpoint of the self-righteousness exemplified by the angels, this constant slipping and repenting demonstrates unforgivable weakness. Naturally enough, Samʿānī begs to differ. The Qur'an tells us that God loves people who repent, and God's love is eternal. As for Adamites, once-and-for-all repentance is hardly to be expected. They are not eternal—they are newly arriving, moment by moment, and each day brings new situations. What are they expected to do but slip? So, says Samʿānī, they should continue repenting, because "*Surely God loves the repenters*" (2:222). Their repentance, their asking forgiveness, and their love for Him are not even their own attributes, but rather God's presence within them. There is no lover and no seeker but God.

O dervish! The worth of the falcon lies in the fact that it comes and goes. "Surely God loves the tempted who repent."*

The unbelievers are like wild crows—they have no value. Dry-brained Qur'an-reciters are like chickens—they cost one dirham. But those who are tempted and repent are like falcons who come and go. Their value is a thousand dinars. *Surely God loves the repenters.*

"Our secret with you does not pertain to now. Our kindness with you does not pertain to today."

When there is talk of worship, speak of the heaven-dwellers. When there is talk of love, speak of the earth-dwellers.

Iblis, for one act of disobedience, was struck on the head so hard that he never came back to his senses. But here we have a hundred thousand who do not say their prayers or prostrate themselves, going instead to the taverns. Nonetheless, He forgives them, for Iblis was just a serving boy, but they are friends.

How can a bit of stinking water dare to claim love for Him who always was and always will be? Nonetheless, the lordly light that was deposited in the secret core of the friends began to seek. The seeker is the light, and the sought is the light. The gazer is the light, and the object of gaze is the light. When the light comes to the heart, it turns into love. When it comes to the secret core, it becomes unveiling. When it comes to the mind, it becomes union. When it comes to the tongue, it bears witness. When it comes to the limbs, it becomes practice. And when it comes into words, it becomes recognition.

The water is one, the spring is one, the tree is one. The water reaches one place and becomes bark, it reaches another and becomes trunk, it reaches another and becomes branch, it reaches another and becomes root, it reaches another and becomes blossom, it reaches another and becomes fruit.

(*Rawḥ* 539–40)

Samʿānī talks again about God's beginningless love in a passage that starts off by referring to a sound hadith that has come in several versions. Typically, it reads, "Our Lord descends to the heaven of this world every night and says, 'Are there any repenters? Are there any supplicators? Are there any who ask forgiveness?' "

How long will there be this heedlessness and indolence? The sweetbriar of intimacy has grown in the garden of holiness, and the heart-caressing roses have bloomed. The command's gentleness continues to address you with "Are there any sinners?"

The hand of exaltedness has appeared from the pavilion of love, and the tongue of the Reality calls out, "Are there any turning this way?"

The messengers of affection and the edicts of invitation have appeared with the proclamations and marks of the Reality, and the caller of generosity is saying, "Are there any Qur'an-reciters?"

The spirit-nurturing words and holy, purified verses come with the address "Are there any listeners?"

The paths of guidance have come forth with the serving boy of kind favor: "Are there any wayfarers?"

The gems of subtlety and pearls of generosity have come into the open from the shells of gentleness: "Are there any gazers?"

The Kaabah of felicity discloses itself in the precinct of His desire: "Are there any strivers?"

The ocean of the Unseen, replete with the pearls of faith and beautiful-doing, has boiled forth: "Are there any divers?"

The perfect beauty of "Surely God is beautiful and He loves beauty"* has promised union, saying, "Are there any lovers?"

"Come to My threshold so that I may do what your father and mother never did. What did your mother do? She gratified her desires. What did your father do? He satisfied his appetite. The work of mothers and fathers is built on appetite and taking shares, but I have no appetite and no share.

"Your mother and father pertain to now, but My work with you has no beginning. My work with you is not accidental, here one day and gone the next. My work is the clashing waves of the ocean of the unseen secrets, the flashing suns of the spheres of the beginningless decrees. My Godhood has no need for servants that I should say, '*Am I not your Lord?*' [7:172]. I have no necessity to say, '*Whose is the kingdom today?*' [40:16]. Even so, the former declaration opened the doors of the gentle favors of the commands, and the latter is the precursor to what was desired by the decrees."

There were a thousand thousand who were bowing and prostrating, a thousand thousand distracted and ecstatic, a thousand thousand burning at

His threshold—all of them wearing the girdle of sinlessness, the shirt of service, and the waistcoat of veneration. All were doing pious deeds, glorifying Him and reciting the words of tawḥīd, revering and extolling. Yet He created an impudent group and chose them over all the obedient, even though they had no precedent service or any intervening intercession. He said, "O handful of dust! *Am I not your Lord?* Am I not yours?"

The folk of heaven, with their obedience and service, were looking on. The Exalted Lord showed them to themselves in a handful of dust: *And when We said to the angels, "Prostrate yourselves before Adam!"* [2:34].

This was not because of any intervention, virtue, merchandise, reverence, or worship. "What was your excellence? What was your instrument, intervention, virtue, merchandise, service, servanthood? Answer Me! You do not know. I know: *Say: 'In the bounty of God'* [10:58]. *Say: 'Surely the bounty is in God's hand'* [3:73]. *Say: 'All is from God'* [4:78]."

"All our fear and dread lies in the fact that without intervention and virtue, You said, 'Come!' What if without sin, offense, and fault, You say, 'Go!' Where will we go?"

"O My friends, go, and have no fear, for We will not send away those whom We have called. We will not reject Our friends."

(*Rawḥ* 423–24)

THE ROLE OF IBLIS

Just as God appointed the prophets to guide mankind, so also He appointed Satan to lead them astray. Theologians list the Guide (*hādī*) as one of the most beautiful divine names, and some of them also mention its complement, the Misguider (*muḍill*), though the Qur'an does not use the name for God. Nonetheless, in most of the sixty-some instances in which the Qur'an employs the verb *misguide*, God is the subject. In one verse, it calls Satan a misguider (28:15).

The Qur'anic accounts of Satan make clear that he is no loose cannon. He does what he does as a creature of God created for a specific purpose. Without Satan, there would be no misguidance, and without misguidance, there would be no guidance and no human freedom. If there were only gentleness, no one would be treated with severity. If there were only beauty, nothing could be ugly. By definition, however, a universe calls for multiplicity, diversity, difference, contrast, and contradiction.

In one of his discussions of Satan's role in creation, Samʿānī begins by reminding his readers of tawḥīd, then launches a verbal assault on ignorant theologians, philosophers, and scientists who think that they have found rational explanations for sin and forgiveness. He points out that Adam's fall was not caused by his eating the forbidden fruit, but by divine foreknowledge. No matter what the Adamites do, their defects will be outweighed by God's love.

> Know that in verified truth the realm of being is nothing more than an image in the mirror of His majesty. Anyone who consigns something to himself independently is attached to an absurdity. Concerning this station, God's messenger Muḥammad reported like this: "I was sent as an inviter, and nothing of guidance comes back to me. Satan was sent as an embellisher, and nothing of misguidance goes back to him." O dervish, if that miserable fellow had been able to throw someone into error, he would have kept guidance for himself.
>
> The masters of uninformed intellects think that they can gain precedence over the roaring, cold wind by riding on the backs of little goats. They think that with a tiny bit of power mixed with incapacity they can enter into the field of disputing with the decrees of Majesty and show that the secrets becoming manifest from the curtains of the Unseen can be consigned to our mortal nature.
>
> They are like ants, weak in composition and small in makeup, walking on a piece of paper. Suppose an ant sees a black line appearing on the paper. It will imagine that that is the work of the pen. Its aspiration will not reach the writer's knowledge and power. Those who see the outward causes and shut their eyes to the celestial apportionings have a state like this.
>
> Dear friend, Adam had still not eaten the wheat when they sewed the hat of his election. Iblis had still not rebelled when they moistened the arrow of the curse with the poison of severity.
>
> Iblis says, "Even though You commanded me to prostrate myself to Adam and I did not, You also commanded Adam not to eat the wheat and he did. One for one!"
>
> "O expelled from the Threshold! Don't you know that the slips of friends are not counted against them, and the obedient acts of enemies are not counted for them?"
>
> When the beloved comes with one sin,
> her beauty brings a thousand interceders.
>
> (*Rawḥ* 163)

The Qur'an tells us that Satan led Adam and Eve astray, so they ate the forbidden fruit. At face value, Satan's misguidance seems to be a manifestation of divine wrath and severity. Fine, but "God's mercy takes precedence over His wrath," which is often interpreted to mean that His wrath does the work of His mercy, despite appearances. In his commentary on the verse "*Then Satan whispered to the two of them to show them what was hidden from them of their shameful parts*" (7:20), Maybudī explains that Satan's whispering was a divine mercy. After all, human beings, created weak and forgetful, could not avoid sin, but God put the blame on Satan.

> This verse is also a mark of solicitude and a proof of generosity, for they sinned, but He turned the sin over to Satan's whispering. Then He increased the solicitude, for He said, "*to show them what was hidden from them of their shameful parts.*" He said: "He made their pudenda appear to them, but not to others."
>
> They say that afterward, Adam and Iblis met. Adam said, "You wretch! Do you know what you did to me and what dust you stirred up in my road?"
>
> Iblis said, "O Adam, I take it that I took you from the road. Tell me then, who took me from the road?"
>
> They also say that both of them turned away from the command, but there is a difference between the two. Adam slipped because of appetite, and Iblis slipped because of pride. Being prideful is worse than gratifying an appetite. When a sin arises from appetite, there is room for pardon. When a sin arises from pride, faith gets lost in it. The report has come, "Pridefulness is My cloak and tremendousness My shawl—if anyone contends with Me in either, I will smash him."
>
> (*Kashf* 3:589)

Maybudī explains more of the wisdom and mercy concealed in Satan's activity in his commentary on the verse "*Then Satan made them slip therefrom*" (2:36). Like Samʿānī, he uses the imagery of a royal marriage. Samʿānī called the king's daughter the veiled virgin of love, and Maybudī calls her the veiled virgin of recognition (*maʿrifa*). It is this quality, unique to human beings, that gives them the capacity to love God.

> Look at this wonder: First He caressed the servant and put all his little jobs in order, then He sent him into turmoil and overthrew what He had done for him, and then He rebuked him.
>
> The Pir of the Tariqah said, "O God, You show your friends to the enemies, and You turn the poor ones over to heartache and grief. You make them ill, and then You take care of them Yourself. You make them helpless, and then You heal them Yourself.
>
> "You made Adam out of dust, and then You acted so beautifully toward him. You placed his happiness at the top of the ledger and made him the

guest in paradise. You sat him in the garden of Riḍwān, You made a compact with him not to eat the wheat, and in Your unseen knowledge, You hid the fact that he would in fact eat the wheat. Then You put him in prison, and You made him weep for years. Your tyranny does the work of tyrants, Your lordhood does the work of lords. All Your rebukes and war are aimed at Your friends."

The Pir of the Tariqah was asked, "What do you say: was Adam more complete in this world or in paradise?"

He said, "He was more complete in this world, for in paradise he fell into suspicion because of himself, but in this world he fell into suspicion because of passion."

The Pir of the Tariqah said, "Be careful not to think that Adam was taken out of paradise because of his lowliness. It was not that. Rather, it was because of the grandeur of his aspiration. The petitioner of passion came to the door of Adam's breast and said, 'O Adam, the beauty of meaning has been unveiled, but you have stayed in the abode of peace.' Adam saw an infinite beauty, next to which the beauty of the eight paradises was nothing. His great aspiration tightened its belt and said: 'If you ever want to fall in love, you must fall in love with that.'"

If there's no escape from feeding passion to the spirit
I'll suffer passion's grief for the likes of You.

The command came: "Adam, now that you have stepped into the lane of passion, leave paradise, for it is the house of ease. What do the passionate have to do with the safety of the Abode of Peace?" May the throats of the passionate always be caught in the noose of trial!

Your passion came to my door and began to knock.
I didn't open it, so it burned it down.

Adam himself did not go—he was taken. Adam himself did not want—he was wanted.

The command came: "The veiled virgin of recognition wants a mate to be her fiancé." They sifted the eighteen thousand worlds in looking for a mate without finding one, for the majestic Qur'an gives news that "*Nothing is as His likeness*" [42:11].

The cherubim and the proximate angels lifted up their heads at the Exalted Threshold, hoping that this crown would be placed on their heads and that the veiled virgin of recognition would become their fiancé. The call went out, "You are the sinless and the pure of the Presence. You are the glorifiers of the Exalted Threshold. If I make you the fiancé, you will say that it is because you match her in holiness and purity. Far be it from the Unity that it should have a match or an equal! *He does not give birth, nor was He given birth to, nor does He have any equal* [112:3–4]."

The Throne with its tremendousness, paradise with its adornment, heaven with its elevation—each fell to wishing, but to no avail. The call came: "Since the veiled virgin of recognition has no match, We in Our bountifulness will lift up the thrown-down dust and make it her fiancé." *He fastened to them the word of godwariness, to which they have more right and of which they are worthy* [48:26].

This is like a king who has a daughter and can find no match for her in his empire. He raises up one of his slaves and bestows on him possessions, position, and exaltedness and appoints him to be the commander and leader of the army. Then he gives his daughter to him. Thus his generosity will appear, and the slave will have the worthiness for union.

The likeness of Adam the dust-dweller is exactly this. God made him the target of His arrow from the first. He fired one arrow of eminence from the bow of election with the hand of the attributes. The target of that arrow was Adam's makeup.

> Take an arrow from the quiver in my name,
>   then place it in Your mighty bow.
> If You need a target, here's my heart.
>   Yours—a strong shot. Mine—a sweet sigh.

The arrow reached the target. Hence, Muṣṭafā reported this judgment to the world: "God created Adam in His form; his length was sixty cubits." It is a sound report that the Lord of the worlds took a handful of dust with which He sculpted Adam. Adam's boldness and nearness reached the place that when He told him to travel from paradise to the earth, he said, "O Lord, travelers don't go without supplies. What supplies will You give me for the road?"

He said, "O Adam, your supplies in the land of exile will be My remembrance. After that, on the day of Return, I promise you will see Me."

(*Kashf* 1:161–63)

BETWEEN A ROCK AND A HARD PLACE

God creates the universe by issuing the creative command. All things, not least prophets and satans, obey it by coming into existence. From this standpoint, the prophets make manifest the activity of God's beautiful and gentle names, and Satan displays the effects of His majestic and severe names. The

Qur'an pluralizes the word *satan* (*shayṭān*), and hadiths suggest that every human being has a satan assigned to him or her.

The prophets invite people to truth and guidance, and the satans call them to falsehood and loss. Prophetic messages convey commands and prohibitions: "Do this, don't do that." Satans urge people to ignore the prophets and follow their own feelings and opinions. For their part, people have sufficient freedom to assume responsibility for obeying or disobeying.

The creative and religious commands often appear to be at odds. This was obvious to everyone, and it led theologians to engage in endless debates over issues like free will and predestination. If we pay close attention to tawḥīd and the creative command, all is predetermined. If we look at the religious command, people can choose whether to follow prophetic guidance. Typically, theologians concluded that human beings are neither totally constrained nor completely free. Everything goes back to God, but people have some responsibility for their own actions. Inasmuch as they are responsible, they will be called to account in the next world.

Both Samʿānī and Maybudī talk about the tension between the two commands. Sometimes they contrast the two by calling the religious command "the command," and the creative command "the decree" (*ḥukm*). When God commands activities and people disobey, it shows that His decree has overridden His command. Although this can sound like a rather nasty form of coercion, no Muslim theologian has seen it that way. For Maybudī and Samʿānī, the contrast between the two commands shows the workings of God's creative love. He knows perfectly well that His human servants will not do a good job of obeying the religious command, even if they do not reject it out of hand. Part of the reason He issued the religious command in the first place was to show them that they are incapable of putting their own lives in order. He commands them to do this and that, but He pulls the strings, so they fall apart. In the end, He gives them infinitely more than they deserve. If they had not fallen apart, they would have imagined that they were worthy of God's love.

Samʿānī points out that disobedience to God's command shows God's hidden mercy, for He cannot call them to account if He Himself issued the decree that overrode the command. He explains that although God commands people to act in certain ways, the decree issued by beginningless love nullifies the command's effects. He concludes by pointing out that to speak of tawḥīd is to take the standpoint of the creative command, but to speak of prophecy is to assume the standpoint of the religious command. Since these two standpoints are the two basic axioms of Islamic thought, and since they often contradict each other, the creed of the community asserts neither free will nor predestination. It demands rather that the two be combined, despite the attempts of overly rationalistic types to exclude the middle ground.

> O chevalier! The commanded is one thing, the decreed something else. The position of the Folk of the Sunnah and the Congregation is that it is indeed permitted for the commanded to be one thing and the decreed something else. What was commanded in the case of Abū Jahl, Abū Lahab, Pharaoh, and Nimrod was one thing, but what was decreed was something else. The command was coming, striking with the whip of the call, but the decree was coming, pulling back on the reins. It is permitted that the servant's act be different from what is commanded, but it is not permitted for it to be different from what is decreed.
>
> All proofs rise up from the world of the command, and all excuses rise up from the world of the decree. When someone is to be shown bounty, the command's tongue is silenced and the decree is allowed to speak. When someone is to be shown justice, the decree's tongue is silenced and the command is allowed to speak. When you hear talk of mercy, that is nothing but His instructions to the army of His decree's authority. When you hear talk of punishment, that is nothing but His instructions to the army of the command.
>
> When He wanted to raise Adam up and put the crown of chosen-ness on his head, He brought His decree into words. When He wanted to blacken the face of Iblis with the smoke of the curse, He let His command do the talking: "*What prevented you from prostrating yourself before him whom I created with My own two hands?*" [38:75].
>
> Adam had not yet slipped when the tailor of gentleness sewed the waistcoat of repentance. Iblis had not yet disobeyed when the pharmacist of severity mixed the draft of poison: *Upon you shall be My curse* [38:78].
>
> O chevalier! Our position is neither predestination nor free will. The free-willers want to take away "There is no god but God." The predestinarians want to quarrel with "Muḥammad is God's Messenger."
>
> "There is no god but God" negates the creed of free will, and "Muḥammad is God's Messenger" erases the slate of predestination. It is not free will and the decree that put faith in order, it is confession, speech, acquisition, and acting. Then, when something goes back to lordhood, we accept it with veneration, and when something goes back to servanthood, we confess to our own incapacity.
>
> Jaʿfar al-Ṣādiq was asked, "Did God predestine the servants in their activity?"
>
> He said, "He is more just than that He would predestine them, then punish them."

> It was said, "Does He then disregard them?"
> He said, "He is more wise than that He would disregard them."
>
> (*Rawḥ* 70–71)

In another passage, Samʿānī contrasts the standpoint of prophecy with that of tawḥīd to show that in the last analysis, tawḥīd is in charge. He refers to God's solicitude toward the first and last prophets, and then points out that God Himself mentions their nothingness in face of His reality. He also explains to laymen the notion of acquisition (*kasb*), a term that the Ash'arite theologians used when trying to clarify how people can be both predestined and free at the same time. God creates human beings and their activities, they said, but human beings acquire the acts as their own through their own free choices.

> He gave Adam knowledge: *And He taught Adam the names* [2:31]. He gave Muṣṭafā strength and aid: "I was aided by their terror." Then He said about Adam, "*Surely he was a great wrongdoer, deeply ignorant*" [33:72]. What is this? "It is the demand of My perfect knowledge." He said to Muṣṭafā, "*Thou hast nothing of the affair*" [3:128]. What is this? "My perfect, never-ending power."
>
> "Knowledge belongs to Me, power belongs to Me, the Beginningless belongs to Me, the Endless belongs to Me, this world belongs to Me, the next world belongs to Me. No one has the gall to take a step outside the script of My permission.
>
> "When they bring a child to grammar school, he does not know how to write. The teacher writes a script on the tablet so that the child may follow after him. I recorded the secrets of your being and nonbeing on the tablet of Desire with the pen of Will. Then I put the pen of acquisition in your hand, but you cannot put in the dots without My knowledge and decree."
>
> This is the secret of their words "Tawḥīd belongs to the Real, and the creatures are intruders."
>
> (*Rawḥ* 607–8)

Those who stress the creative command point out that God in His unneediness cannot be affected by human acts. People will not achieve paradise because of good deeds, nor will they be put into hell because of disobedience. God issues the religious command, but people have no power to enact it or reject it. Samʿānī quotes from Abū Bakr al-Wāsiṭī, remarking that "no one in the Tariqah has spoken words of more purity": "'I would not worship a Lord who distances because of disobedience and brings near because of obedience.'

I would not worship a Lord who works on the basis of causality" (*Rawḥ* 531). In another passage, Samʿānī unpacks the meaning of Wāsiṭī's saying by pointing out that God acts in a manner appropriate to Godhood, irrespective of human beings. To think that created things can act upon God, causing Him to do one thing rather than another, is absurd. He imagines God speaking as follows:

> "O My unique knowledge, O you who were there in beginningless eternity! For a few days give a turn to commands and prohibitions. One hundred twenty-some thousand pearl divers in the oceans of the Sanctum entered the vast plain. Books and messages came one after another, but no one discharged what is rightfully due to Me. 'What do water and clay have to do with talk of the Lord of the Worlds? What does the vicegerent have to do with the Reality?'
>
> "O commands and prohibitions! Give the turn back to knowledge, for My knowledge does the work. From east to west, whenever dust was scattered on a skirt, they shook the skirt. My knowledge remained pure, and My decree bitter."
>
> Tomorrow He will say to His dear ones, "In that world, you did a few little jobs. Outwardly, you freely chose to follow the Law's prescription. In reality, you acted under constraint because of My decree. Your choice to follow the Shariah was a curtain over the form of My decree.
>
> "Today, I do not look at the curtain of your choice, I look at the form of My decree. The unbelievers will be addressed by the command, and the friends by the decree. The command will be the plaintiff against the strangers, and the decree will intercede for the friends. The strangers will go forth beaten and pounded by the command's severity to the place of the command's vengeance. The friends will go forth escorted by the intercession of the decree to the resting place of the decree's gentleness."
>
> (*Rawḥ* 516–17)

Samʿānī comes back to human helplessness constantly. In doing so, he stresses tawḥīd, the creative command, and the literal truth of the Qur'anic verse "*O people, you are the poor toward God, and God is the Unneedy, the Praiseworthy*" (35:15). He acknowledges the standpoint of the religious command, but he tells us that people have no ability to observe it on their own. Whether or not they do, they are in the hands of God's mercy.

> This is a rare business. He brought these hapless ones into existence from *vile water* [77:20] and *fetid mud* [15:26]—the weak from the weak from the weak,

dust from dust from dust, the bewildered from the bewildered from the bewildered, the incapable from the incapable from the incapable, the indigent from the indigent from the indigent. Then He took them by the collar and placed them without hope in the battlefield of the brave—a battlefield in which the command pulls in one direction and the decree in another. The beauty of the Threshold calls out, "O friend, pass by My road," and the beginningless majesty addresses them from the pavilion of Exaltedness, "Hapless one—beware, beware!"

(*Rawḥ* 48)

He made everyone drunk with the wine of *Am I not your Lord?* [7:172]. He created this world of ups and downs, then He sprinkled them with the water of commands and prohibitions. He sent these drunkards into this world of ups and downs. Then He set forth His will: "Try for it." No one had the gall to say a thing.

You take me to the well's edge and you push—
you say, "Refuge in God!," and then you push!

Yes, the road is dangerous like this, with many ups and downs, but the man is drunk. Then the address comes, "*So go straight to Him, and ask forgiveness of Him*" [41:6]: "Hey, you drunkard, walk straight!"

There is a lame mosquito, missing a wing, a leg, and an eye, the other eye shut. They throw it into an ocean of fire or an ocean of water. The address comes, "Hey you, don't burn your wings, don't get wet!"

The king said to me, "Drink wine, but don't get drunk!"
O king, everyone who drinks wine gets drunk.

(495)

Samʿānī sometimes contrasts the religious and creative commands by talking of the difference between the Shariah and the Haqiqah (*ḥaqīqa*), that is, the revealed religion on the one hand and the Divine Reality on the other. From the standpoint of the Shariah, people are commanded to act in certain ways. From the standpoint of the Haqiqah, people will act as God decrees. The Shariah pulls in one direction, but the Haqiqah may be pulling elsewhere. In the following, he begins by reminding us that no one truly knows God but God.

The Sufis say, "The wonder is not that someone does not recognize Him—the wonder is that some people do recognize Him." Everything that enters your perception is like you, and everything that fits into your heart has your measure. The recognition of the recognizer does not perceive the Real, the knowledge of the knower does not reach the Real: *Eyesights perceive Him not, and He perceives the eyesights. And He is the subtle, the aware* [6:103].

The ocean comes into a cup, the fish falls into a trap. The Shariah says, "O intelligent adult, shake the chain on the door of recognition!" The Haqiqah says, "O woebegone beggar, take the bags of your misfortune away from the threshold of My majesty."

Indeed, whenever something comes to hand with the Shariah, the sultan of the Haqiqah charges forth and plunders it. The preacher of the Shariah calls out from the pulpit of bounty, "Have faith and declare tawḥīd lest you be deprived of paradise!"

Then the sultan of Majesty comes into the field of exaltation on the steed of the Haqiqah and shouts out to the whole universe, "No one loves Him but He, no one seeks Him but He. *They measured not God with the rightful due of His measure* [22:74]. *They do not encompass Him in knowledge* [20:110]. What do creatures have to do with the Haqiqah? What do water and clay have to do with talk of the Lord of the Worlds?"

My pretty has never shown her face—
all this talk and debate is foolish.

When the Real comes with something too subtle for understanding, do not seek judgment from your speck of intellect.

The cupbearer of listening was sent with a thousand thousand heavy drinks to the presence of the heart's sultan, but intellect was a stranger to all of them. In the world of bewilderment, it was like a prisoner saying, "Woe is me!" The eyes gazed but did not reach those how-less attributes. The heart scattered a handful of dust in the eyes, and everyone turned away blind and embarrassed.

The scholars stood up and said, "We know such and such." The astronomers said, "We measure the spheres degree by degree." The philosophers said, "We have established the Prime Matter and the First Cause." The merchants stood up and said, "We made this transaction and made this much profit. We crossed over those mountains and deserts, we crossed seas without end."

The majesty of exaltedness answers, "This affair is not accomplished in partnership. O naturalists, look at My power! O Kalam experts, look at My desire! O merchants, look at My apportioning! Power says, 'Here is error for you!' Desire says, 'Here are mistakes for you!' Apportioning says, 'Here is folly for you!'"

On the day in the Beginningless when they beat the drum for the falcon of the mystery, this is how they beat it: "Annihilation for creation, and His subsistence! Nonexistence for creation, and His existence!"

O dervishes, accept this advice in His road: turn existence entirely over to Him!

O chevalier! In respect of the divine command, the entire universe has seeking, existence, and free choice. But, in respect of the lordly power, the house has no inhabitants.

(*Rawḥ* 184–85)

Maybudī takes help from a passage in Samʿānī (*Rawḥ* 53–54) to distinguish between the two commands. He is commenting on the verse "*So be wary of God as much as you are able*" (64:16). In Qur'anic language, godwariness (*taqwā*) designates the exalted virtue of being aware of God's majesty and magnificence in all situations and acting accordingly. Maybudī begins his explanation by citing another verse: "*Be wary of God as is the rightful due of His wariness*" (3:102). He then explains that the first of these verses abrogates the second, for no one can be wary of God as is His rightful due (ḥaqq). In effect, the religious command addresses human weakness and incapacity, telling people to do as best they can. It pertains only to the realm of prescription (*taklīf*), that is, this world, in which people are commanded to follow the Shariah. In the next world, people will be exposed to the infinite mercy of the creative command.

One of these verses is the abrogater, the other the abrogated. One alludes to what is incumbent by the command, the other alludes to what is incumbent by rightful due. What is incumbent by the command came and abrogated what is incumbent by rightful due. This is because when the Real calls the servants to account, He does so by what the command makes incumbent so that He may then pardon their acts. If He were to take them to task for what is incumbent by rightful due, then a thousand years of obedience would have the same color as a thousand years of disobedience. If all the prophets, the saints, and the limpid, and all the recognizers and lovers, came together, which of them would have the capacity to undertake His rightful due or to answer to His rightful due?

His command is finite, but His rightful due is infinite. This is because the command subsists as long as prescription subsists, but prescription pertains to this world, which is the abode of prescription. The rightful due subsists through the subsistence of the Essence, and the Essence is infinite. Hence, the subsistence of the rightful due is infinite. What is incumbent by the command will disappear, but what is incumbent by rightful due will never disappear. This world will pass away, and the turn of the command will pass away along with it. But the turn of the rightful due will never pass away.

Today everyone has a mad fervor in his head because he is looking at the command. The prophets and messengers look at their own prophethood and messengerhood, and the angels look at their own obedience and worship. The tawḥīd-voicers, the strugglers, the faithful, and the sincere look at their own tawḥīd, faith, and sincerity.

Tomorrow, when the pavilions of the lordly rightful due are thrown open, the prophets, despite the perfection of their state, will put away talk of their own knowledge: "*We have no knowledge*" [5:109]. The angels of the Sovereignty will strike fire to the monasteries of their obedience, saying, "We have not worshiped You with the rightful due of Your worship." The recognizers and tawḥīd-voicers will say, "We have not recognized You with the rightful due of Your recognition." And God knows best what is correct.

(*Kashf* 10:135)

DIVINE FORGIVENESS

God created the Adamites out of love and mercy, attributes that designate His essential reality. In the final encounter, all will go back to those attributes. In Maybudī's remarks on the verse "*He has written mercy against Himself*" (6:12), he reminds us that mercy has the first and final say.

Before He began to create the newly arrived things and to originate the engendered things, He struck the coin of mercy in the mint of the Unseen as the hard cash of the servants' states and works: *Surely it is I who am God; there is no god but I* [20:14]. "My mercy takes precedence over My wrath."

Tomorrow on the Day of Mustering, the Messenger will call out at the top of the bazaar of the resurrection: "O King, here is a handful of the disobedient. Let me be instructed to clothe them in the shirt of Your mercy, for You have said, '*We sent thee only as a mercy to the worlds*' [21:107]. O Lord, it is the day of the bazaar for these beggars. I was catching them with the lasso of the call, so I made them many promises. O Lord, do not shame Muḥammad in this gathering of the multitudes! Turn Your promise of mercy and generosity into reality, for You Yourself said, '*O My servants who have been immoderate against yourselves, despair not of God's mercy*' [39:53]."

From the Court of Majesty will come the call of generosity and mercy: "O Muḥammad! The work of your community is not outside of three: Either they are people of faith, or they are recognizers, or they are disobedient. If they have faith and are hoping for paradise, here then is My paradise. If they are the disobedient hoping for My forgiveness, here then is My mercy and forgiveness. If they are the recognizers hoping for vision, here then is My vision."

Thus, the road of the servants is to open their mouths in praise and laudation. In the state of brokenness, they should continue saying with the attribute of pleading and poverty, "O nearer to us than ourselves! O more lovingly kind to us than ourselves! O caresser of us without us through Your generosity—not because of our worthiness, not because of our works. The burden is outside our capacity, the practice not proper to us, the favor not within our ability. Whatever we have done has damaged us, whatever You have done subsists for us. Whatever You have done in our place, You have done by Yourself, not for our sake."

(*Kashf* 3:310–11)

To explain the return to mercy, Maybudī cites two earlier teachers in the midst of his commentary on the verse "*To Him is your returning place, all together—God's promise, in truth*" (10:4). The first paragraph is from Qushayrī's *Subtle Allusions.*

It has been said, "Promised to the obedient are the highest paradises, and promised to the disobedient are mercy and good pleasure. The Garden is the Real's gentleness, and mercy is the Real's description. Gentleness is an act that was not, then came to be, but the description is an attribute that always was."

Abū Bakr al-Wāsiṭī said, "The obedient are porters, and porters have nothing but burdens, but this is the threshold of Him who has no needs. The disobedient are destitute, and the destitute have nothing but destitution, and this is the carpet of the destitute.

"O owners of obedience, I do not say, 'Do not obey!' lest you think there is error in the Qur'an. As much as you can and as much as you have the capacity, bring forth acts of obedience! Then let them go, for they are nonbeing. The obedient person and the obedient act are two, but this is the carpet of oneness.

"O owners of slips! Do not constrict your hearts, for this burden of disobedience is also His burden, just as obedience is His burden. But, obedience is something that is put in place, and disobedience is something that is lifted away. Putting in place is your act, and lifting away is His act."

(*Kashf* 4:255)

Maybudī, like Samʿānī and many others, understands the notion of disobedience (*maʿṣiya*)—the most common term for sin—in the context of God's eternal forgiveness. Forgiveness in Arabic is *maghfira*, which derives from a root whose basic meaning is to conceal and protect (hence *mighfar*, "helmet"). God forgives by concealing sin and protecting people from its negative consequences. He forgives because it is His nature to forgive, and He is merciful because He can be nothing else. We go our way, He goes His. Maybudī speaks of God's forgiving nature in his commentary on the verse *"And We outspread the clouds to overshadow you"* (2:57). The verse discusses God's kindness to Moses and his people when they were wandering in the wilderness.

> This is an allusion to the Lord's gentleness and generosity. His loving-kindness toward the servants is such that the Lord of the Worlds says, "O hapless child of Adam! Why do you not love Me? For I am worthy of love. Why do you not trade with Me? For I am munificent and bounteous. Why do you not engage in transactions with Me? For I am a bestower who is ample in bestowal. My mercy is not tight, nor do I hold back blessings from anyone.
>
> "Look at what I did with the Children of Israel, how many blessings I poured down upon them, how much I caressed them in that empty desert! After they had turned away and disobeyed My command, I did not let them go to ruin. I commanded the mist to cast a shadow over them, I commanded the wind to place roasted birds in their hands, I commanded the clouds to rain down manna and honey on them, I commanded the pillar of light to give them brightness on the nights when there was no moon. When a child came into existence from its mother in that empty desert, it came into existence with the set of clothes that it needed. Then, as the child grew up, those clothes never became too old for it, nor did they become dirty. In the state of that person's life, the clothes were his ornament, and in the state of his death, his shroud. What blessing was there that I did not pour down upon them? In what manner did I fail to caress them? Yet they did not know My measure, nor did they show gratitude for the blessings.
>
> "O hapless one! No one wants you the way I want you. When you come, no one will buy you the way I buy. When you sell yourself, others will buy only the faultless, but I buy the faulty. Others call out for the loyal, but I call out for the disloyal. If you come in old age, I will adorn the whole empire to honor you, and if you talk to Me in the fullness of youth, I will take you into My shelter tomorrow on the Day of Resurrection."
>
> People disobey for a lifetime, then return in shame—
> We say to them, "Welcome, be at ease, greetings!"
>
> (*Kashf* 1:208–9)

Maybudī connects the return to God's mercy with a mother's love for her children in his commentary on the verse "*Mothers shall suckle their children two years completely*" (2:233).

The example given of utmost mercy is the mercy of mothers, but God's mercy toward His servants is more than that, and His love is not like their love. Do you not see that He commands mothers to give milk to their children for two complete years, He urges them to nurture them, and He counsels them to take care of them? He does not confine Himself to the love of mothers and leave it at that. This is so that you will know that God is more lovingly kind to the servant than a mother is to her child.

Once Muṣṭafā was passing by when a woman with a child in her arms was baking bread. They had told her that God's Messenger would be passing. She came forward and said, "O Messenger of God! We have heard you say that the God of the world's inhabitants is more lovingly kind to His servants than a mother to her child."

The Messenger said, "Yes, that is so."

That woman became happy and said, "O Messenger of God! A mother would never toss her child into this oven."

Muṣṭafā wept. Then he said, "God chastises in the Fire only those who refuse to say, 'There is no god but God.'"

Kaʿb ʿUjara said that one day God's Messenger said to his companions, "What do you say about a man slain in God's path?"

They said, "God and His Messenger know best."

He said, "He is in the Garden." Then he said, "What do you say about a man concerning whom two just men have said that they knew nothing of him but good?"

They said, "God and His Messenger know best."

He said, "He is in the Garden." Then he said, "What do you say about a dead man concerning whom two just witnesses say that they never saw any good from him?"

The Companions said, "He is in the Fire."

The Messenger said, "How badly you have spoken—a sinful servant and a forgiving Lord! *Say: 'Each acts according to his own manner'* [17:84]."

Part of His complete mercy and generosity to His servants is that tomorrow at the resurrection, a group will be taken and made to pass easily by the Scales, the Narrow Path, and the bridge over hell. They will arrive at the door of paradise and be told to halt. Then a letter will arrive from the Exalted Presence, a letter whose title is "The Eternal Love." From beginning to end it will be rebuke and war with the friends. He will rebuke the servants as is appropriate to their state.

The letter will say, "My servants! Did I not create you without recompense and sculpt you in a beautiful form? Did I not stretch out your stature? You were infants and did not know the road to your mother's breast. I showed you. I brought forth pure milk as your food from the midst of blood. I made your mother and father kind to you and had them nurture you. I preserved you from water, wind, and fire. I conveyed you from infancy to youth, and from youth to old age. I adorned you with understanding and excellence. I decorated you with knowledge and recognition. I sculpted you with hearing and eyesight. I had you obey and serve Me. At the door of death, I kept My name on your tongue and My recognition in your spirit. Then I put you on the pillow of safety. I who am Beginningless and Endless—I did all these beautiful things for you. What did you do for Me? Did you ever give a dirham to a beggar for My sake? Did you ever give water to a thirsty dog for Me? Did you ever move an ant from the path out of mercy?

"My servant! You did what you did, but I am ashamed to chastise you as you deserve. Instead I will do what is worthy of Me. Go: I have forgiven you so that you will know that I am I and you are you."

Indeed, if a beggar goes before a king, they do not ask him what he has brought. They ask him what he wants.

O God, what could come from a beggar that would be worthy of You if it were not that You are worthy of what comes from a beggar?

One of the pirs of the Tariqah said, "How can He not caress, when He is the most generous of the generous? How can He not forgive, when He is the most merciful of the merciful? How can He not pardon, when several times in the Qur'an He commands people to pardon? *So pardon them* [3:159], *Let them pardon and forbear* [24:22], *Take the pardon* [7:199]."

(*Kashf* 1:639–41)

Maybudī talks again of God's unlimited forgiveness in his commentary on the verse "*Our Lord, let not our hearts go astray after Thou hast guided us, and give us mercy from Thee!*" (3:8).

The meaning of this supplication is this: "O God, keep our hearts far from confusion and straying and make us firm on the carpet of service with the stipulation of the Sunnah."

And give us mercy from Thee: And give what you give, O Lord, as Your bounty and mercy, not as the recompense for our works or the compensation for our acts of obedience! Our acts of obedience are not worthy for the

Presence of Your Majesty, so the only thing to do is to efface them and ignore them.

One of the pirs of the Tariqah said, "The gallbladders of the travelers and the obedient servants burst in fear at the verse '*We shall advance upon what work they have done and make it scattered dust*' [25:23]. But of all the Qur'an's verses, I find this the sweetest."

He was asked, "What does it mean?"

He said, "We will finally be released from these unadmirable works and unworthy acts of obedience and attach our hearts totally to His bounty and mercy."

(*Kashf* 2:25)

In his commentary on the verse just cited, Maybudī offers a different version of this saying of the unnamed pir, and then he attributes more words to him. In fact, the additional words are a conflation of two passages by Samʿānī, specifically the two that will be cited shortly. The original saying mentioned here, in the commentary on 2:25, cannot be by Samʿānī, because Maybudī does not start quoting from him until much later in the book.

We shall advance on what work they have done and make it scattered dust [25:23]. One of the pirs of the Tariqah recited this verse and said, "Of all the Qur'an's verses, this is the sweetest. When He throws these tainted works of ours to the wind of unneediness, He will act toward us with bounty alone. What He does with His bounty will be worthy of His generosity. What is worthy of His generosity is better than what is worthy of our works."

Then he said, "He has rights against us, like obedience and worship, but we in our makeup are destitute, and He has decreed our destitution. When the decreer decrees that someone be destitute, the plaintiff can have nothing against him. 'If he has suffered hardship, that has comfort in view.'

"Whenever someone is destitute, it is incumbent to give him respite so that he may acquire some capital. But we will never acquire capital until we reach that world, when He will pour down the treasure of His bounty on our heads. We are not wealthy through our own being—we are wealthy through His attributes. Nothing comes from us or our works. When an affair is opened up for us, it opens up from His bounty.

"When He accepts us, He does not accept us because of the form of our practice. He accepts us because of the readiness that He gazed upon in His beginningless knowledge. Whatever there may be in the world follows upon that readiness. Wait until tomorrow, when He makes that readiness apparent and opens the doors of the treasuries. He will give the treasury of mercy to the disobedient and the treasury of bounty to the destitute so that they may discharge what is rightfully due to Him from His treasury, for the servants cannot discharge His right from what belongs to them."

The Pir of the Tariqah said, "O God, whatever I counted as a mark curtained me, and whatever I considered a resource was foolish. O God, lift up this curtain from me totally, remove from me the defect of my being, and do not leave me in the hand of striving! O God, let none of our deeds circle around us! Lift us up from our loss! O Beautiful-Doer, straighten out what You made without us! Entrust us not to what You can endure!"

(*Kashf* 7:40–41)

In the first of the two passages from which Maybudī has just drawn, Samʿānī reminds his readers of the distinction between the two commands. The creative command, rooted in love and mercy, brings all things into being. Once the Adamites come to exist, the religious command tells them that they should act in keeping with God's mercy and justice, though God knows full well that they will fail in this task. None can fulfill His rightful due but He. Why then does He bother issuing instructions? So that, having failed to follow the prophets adequately, people will recognize their own incapacity, acknowledge God's mercy, and love Him all the more. The passage belongs to Samʿānī's commentary on the divine name *tawwāb*, the "Ever-Turning," from the same root as *tawba*, "repentance," a word that literally means "to turn."

It is He who has given the success of repentance. *Then He turned toward them so that they might turn* [9:118]. When you repent through His giving success, He Himself praises you, saying, "*the repenters, the worshipers*" [9:112]. He Himself wrote your name on the scroll of His love: "*Surely God loves the repenters, and He loves those who purify themselves*" [2:222]—those who repent of disobedience, who purify themselves of the blights of obedience; those who repent of love for this world, who purify themselves of love for the next world and cling fast to love for the High, the Highest.

The repentance of the common people is from sins and ugly deeds, the repentance of the elect is from faults and blights, and the repentance of the most elect is from seeing beautiful deeds and paying attention to acts of obedience.

The great ones of the religion have said, "It may happen that sin becomes the cause of reaching God. Do you not see that the hoopoe reached conversation with Solomon through that?"

It often happens that sin is the cause of reaching God's approval. The disobedient find regret in their hearts and weep tears from their eyes and sigh in remorse. It is said to them, "Today weeping, tomorrow looking; today a step, tomorrow a message; today remorse, tomorrow vision; today a sigh, tomorrow shelter; today a stride forward, tomorrow a private audience."

O Muslims! This happiness will be completed on the day they lift up the veil and give the longtime hope of the hearts to the hearts. O friends, a sound report has reached us from Muṣṭafā that tomorrow, when the faithful go into paradise, there will be extra room in paradise. "So God will configure another creation." He will create new creatures and give them those places.

O dervish! Think carefully! It is fitting for Him in His generosity to create creatures who have never worshiped or toiled and to give them houris, palaces, slaves, and children. Will He then send away from the door a people who have taken some trouble, done some deeds, and had some hopes, who were His longtime slave boys and first servants? In truth, He will not do that.

O dervish! He sends someone to Byzantium, India, and Turkistan to bring the ones who have not yet come. Why would He drive away the ones who have already come?

"The demand of My knowledge attached itself to your makeup before the demand of your deeds attached itself to My mercy. Your heart had not yet thought of repenting when I wrote your name in the register of *the repenters*. You had not yet stepped onto the threshold of the world of existence when I recorded your name in the register of *the worshipers*.

"If I were to let you go free, to whom would I give you? If I did not want you, to whom would I leave you? Even if you become weary of My gentleness, I will not become weary of your disobedience. Even if you cannot carry My burden, my great mercy will buy you, along with all your offenses.

"Have patience for a few days. Today, commands and prohibitions do not accord with your desire. Tomorrow, everything will follow your desire. If today you see the wonders of the commands and prohibitions, wait until tomorrow, when you will see the marvels of knowledge and clemency. If today I make you suffer through power, tomorrow I will send you ease by the decree. If today the Law is prescribed for you by wisdom, tomorrow it will be lightened by bounty.

When Sultan Maḥmūd sat on the throne of kingship and held court, he would make Ayāz stand at the edge of the carpet, his hands folded before him. At night when they were alone together, Ayāz became Maḥmūd, Maḥmūd Ayāz.

Today, the work revolves around *Am I not your Lord?* [7:172]. Tomorrow, the work will rest on *He loves them, and they love Him* [5:54]. Today the carpet of *Am I not your Lord?* has been unrolled, so prayer, fasting, hajj, and struggle have come out into the open. Tomorrow you will be mustered in that world, and the carpet of *He loves them, and they love Him* will be spread. There will be no fasting and no prayer—only love and joy.

"In the Beginningless all is My beautiful-doing, at the present moment all is My bestowal of blessing, and in the Endless all is bounteousness. When My bestowal arrives, distinctions disappear.

"O intellects! Be dazzled by My artisanry. When I call to account, I take to task iota by iota. When I act with indulgence, I overlook mountain upon mountain."

In the end, *He loves them* will take our hands. The faithful will lift their heads from dust, and He will call out, "Welcome! May your coming be blessed!" When He accepts you, He will not accept you because of the form of your practice. He will accept you because of the readiness that He gazed upon in His beginningless knowledge. Whatever there may be in the world follows upon that readiness.

(*Rawḥ* 546–48)

In the second passage, the source of most of Maybudī's quotation, Samʿānī keeps tawḥīd in view while explaining that human beings possess nothing in face of God, so good works and evil deeds cannot have the slightest impact on His decree. This is good news, for justice does not allow asking the poverty stricken for payment, and mercy can only give of itself.

He has many rights against us, like obedience and worship, but we ourselves, in our own makeup, are destitute. He has decreed that we be destitute. When the decreer decrees that someone be destitute, the plaintiff has nothing against him. "If he has suffered hardship, that has comfort in view."

Whenever someone is destitute, it is incumbent to give him respite so that he may acquire some capital. But, we will never acquire capital until that world, when He will pour down the treasure of His bounty on our heads. We are not wealthy through our own being—we are wealthy through His attributes. Nothing comes from us or our works. When an affair is opened up for us, it opens up from His bounty.

In this world, we have the attribute of love and are the paragon of the world. In that world, we will have the attribute of love and will be the sultan of the world. The parasol of exaltedness will be raised over our heads, and we will open the hands of plundering and take the capital goods of the world's folk as plunder. Gabriel will not escape our hands, nor Michael, nor the bearers of the Throne.

He has no use for treasuries and no need for anything. Whatever He has, He has for us. Tomorrow He will give the treasury of bounty to the disobedient, the treasury of mercy to the sinners, the treasury of forgiveness to the helpless. Then we will be able to discharge what is rightfully due to Him from His treasuries, for we cannot discharge His rightful due from our treasuries. When a beggar is given the sultan's daughter, he does not have a dower worthy of her. From his own treasury, the sultan will send the dower so that the beggar may give it to the princess from his treasury.

(*Rawḥ* 540–41)

3

Spiritual Psychology

Philosophers and Sufis paid a great deal of attention to analyzing the nature of the human self. Avicenna and others wrote books on psychology, in Arabic *ʿilm al-nafs*, "knowledge of the soul." Given the routes that modern psychology has taken, it would be more appropriate to translate this term as "spiritual psychology," for its whole purpose was to help souls attach themselves to the realm of the spirit. As for Sufi teachers, they were typically spiritual psychotherapists. They taught disciples how to conform themselves to the models of human perfection set down by the prophets, taking Muḥammad's Sunnah as the template for transformation by love. In their reading, the Sunnah embraces not only the Prophet's outward and inward practices, but also the various dimensions of his self—his character traits, virtues, understanding, wisdom, love, and realization.

In Arabic, the word *nafs*, "soul," also means "self." In saying "the thing itself" or "God Himself," one uses the same word, *nafs*. The philosophers employed it to designate any kind of awareness and consciousness, any sort of interiority short of the full actualization of the intellect (*ʿaql*). Following in the footsteps of the Greeks, they held that there are different sorts of souls, arranged hierarchically, and that these can be discerned by analyzing the faculties that become manifest through the activities of living things. The Arabic word for faculty, *quwwa*, means "strength, power, potency, potentiality." We can talk about vegetal, animal, and human souls because in each case, specific potencies appear to us that we cannot discern at a lower level. Plants are differentiated by certain potencies not found in minerals, such as growth and reproduction. Animal souls possess additional faculties, such as volitional movement. Human beings add speech and reason.

Philosophers sometimes used the word *nafs* interchangeably with *quwwa*. They would then speak of the animal potency, meaning the animal soul, for the soul is simply the sum total of a being's inner potencies. The animal soul includes the potencies of plants but falls short of human potency. The basic understanding was that little by little, as potencies intensify, so also do awareness and consciousness, leading finally to the summum bonum of the human state, which philosophers often called the actual intellect (*al-ʿaql biʾl-fiʿl*). They described it as the achievement of conjunction (*ittiṣāl*) with the active, or agent, intellect (*al-ʿaql al-faʿʿāl*). This they understood to be a universal, cosmic awareness, the first manifestation of the Divine Reality. Historians of philosophy recognize it as the nous of Plotinus, the first emanation of the One. One can see another parallel in the notion of purusha in the Samkhya school of Hindu philosophy.

It is not too difficult to see that as people gradually ascend toward perfect intelligence and awareness, it becomes ever more difficult to explain what is going on. Inanimate things can be analyzed endlessly, but the moment we try to pin down exactly what defines life, we start running into puzzles, a fact especially obvious in medicine. Science meets inscrutability as soon as it tries to get inside living things, especially human beings. Despite the proliferation of sciences and ologies in modern times, the human self remains as much a mystery as ever.

The Muslim philosophers maintained that once full human potential is realized—as in the case of the great prophets—the soul is no longer a soul but rather an actual intellect. This does not imply that the intellect has lost the faculties and powers of the vegetal, animal, and human souls, but rather that those have now come to be fully realized. The philosophers called the soul's realization of its potential by a variety of names, including deiformity and theomorphism (*taʾalluh*, from the same root as *allāh*). They understood it to mean the actualization of the divine form in which man was created.

Early Sufi writings made no attempt to engage in systematic analyses of the soul, preferring instead to meditate on its nature, in keeping with various Qur'anic verses and prophetic hadiths. In talking about the soul, they used several words besides *nafs*, including heart (*qalb*), spirit (*rūḥ*), and intellect (ʿaql). At the beginning of Book 21 of *Giving Life*, which is devoted to explaining the marvels of the heart, Muḥammad Ghazālī says that those four words denote the same reality, that is, the human subtlety (*al-laṭīfat al-insāniyya*), but in each case from a different standpoint.

The attribute *laṭīf*, "subtle," is employed to designate invisible, impalpable realities pertaining to the spiritual realm. It is contrasted with gross or dense (*kathīf*), meaning the dark, heavy, concrete things of the sensory realm. As a divine name, laṭīf means not only subtle and, hence, beyond any of the densities and imperfections of the created realms, but also gentle, mild, forgiving, merciful. God's gentleness has ontological precedence over the multiplicities and distinctions that appear when things emerge from subtlety and enter into density and darkness.

By using the word *subtlety* to name the inner reality of the self, authors are saying that whatever the human subtlety may be, it cannot be pinned down by definitions, much less analyses of biological or physiological causality. The human subtlety does not derive from the dense elements found in the corporeal realm, quite the contrary. Physical things are sediments or shadows of the subtle realities that lie beyond. "As above, so below," as the ancient maxim put it. The philosophical notion of hylomorphism—that all things are compounded of matter (*mādda*) and form (*ṣūra*)—goes back to the self-evident fact (for Muslim philosophers and theologians, at least) that all perceived qualities, characteristics, traits, and attributes pertain not to the matter of things, but rather to their forms, which are subtle forces that employ matter as loci of manifestation. Ultimately, all forms go back to God, whom the Qur'an calls the Form-Giver (*muṣawwir*) and the philosophers called the Bestower of Forms (*wāhib al-ṣuwar*).

The best way to gain an understanding of the words that designate the human subtlety—words whose semantic fields often overlap or coincide—is to see how they are used in context. There is no agreement on definitions, but there are common themes, such as the distinction between the corporeal and the spiritual or the multilayered-ness of the noncorporeal realm.

THE HUMAN MICROCOSM

Sufis and philosophers use standard notions about the nature of things when discussing the self. Among these ideas is the intimate correlation between the universe as a whole, the macrocosm, and the human individual, the microcosm. If we like, we can trace this discussion back to Greek sources and find parallel ideas in the Indian and Chinese worlds, though Muslim theologians find plenty of references to it in the Qur'an. For example, they often understood the verse that says that God taught Adam all the names (2:31) to mean that knowledge of the entire cosmos is latent in the human self. The path of becoming truly human, which demands the full actualization of intelligence, depends upon realizing our innate knowledge of all things. In the midst of a long discussion of the human microcosm, Samʿānī points to God's wisdom in placing this potential in the human soul.

> The Adamite is an all-comprehensive city. His essence is a container for all the meanings of the cosmos. The wisdom in this is as follows: the Exalted Lord wanted to instill the treasuries of knowledge into this wondrous shape and to allow him to witness all the meanings of the cosmos, but the cosmos is too vast, and the face of the earth too extensive. There was no way that mortal nature could travel around the cosmos in its entirety, given its short lifespan and its incapacity in affairs. Hence, the divine wisdom required and requested from the divine power that an abridged transcription be made of the root of the macrocosm. This was then written out in the microcosm. He placed this abridged tablet before the child, the intellect, and He made him bear witness to it: *He made them bear witness against their own souls: "Am I not your Lord?" They said, "Yes indeed, we bear witness"* [7:172].
>
> (*Rawḥ* 177)

In the continuation of this passage, Samʿānī provides a list of correspondences between the microcosm and macrocosm, showing how they help explain the tremendous variety of human qualities and character traits. He reminds us that if we do not come to recognize the true reality of our selves, we will wander lost and distracted inside our own abridgment of the universe.

> This is why the great ones have said, "Everything is found in the Adamite, but the Adamite is not found in anything." Sometimes he is courageous like a lion, sometimes timid like a rabbit, stingy like a dog, savage like a leopard, tame like a pigeon, scheming like a fox, simple like a sheep, hurried like a gazelle, heavy like a bear, overbearing like an elephant, leading like a camel, strutting like a peacock, auspicious like a parakeet, inauspicious like an owl, guiding like a grouse, dumb like a fish, talking like a nightingale, changing like a wolf, avaricious like a pig, lost like an ostrich, beneficial like a bee, harmful like a rat, blessed like a phoenix.
>
> O dervish! When someone claims to have recognition of things but is ignorant of himself, he is like someone who gives food to others but is himself hungry, or someone who shows others the way but is himself lost. In reality, until a man connects with the assistance of the divine success-giving, he will not gain recognition of himself.
>
> (*Rawḥ* 178–79)

Maybudī explains that the diversity of the human makeup provides evidence for the immensity of the divine blessings and reminds us that we are nothing but dust, all else coming by way of mercy and kindness. He is commenting on a verse that is often taken as a reference to both the macrocosm (*the horizons*) and the microcosm (*their souls*): "*We shall show them Our signs on the horizons and in their souls*" (41:53). A good bit of this is drawn from Samʿānī (*Rawḥ* 63–64).

> It is said that the Lord's religion, which is the cause of the deliverance of the servants and the foundation of their familiarity with Him, is built on two things: one is showing on the part of the Real, and the other traveling on the part of the servant. Showing is what He said: "*We shall show them Our signs on the horizons.*" Traveling is what He said: "*Whoso does a worthy deed, it is for himself*" [41:46]. As long as there is no showing on the Real's part, there will be no traveling on the servant's part.
>
> Showing takes place in both the signs of the horizons and the signs of the souls. In the signs of the horizons, it is what He said: "*Have they not gazed upon the sovereignty of the heavens and the earth?*" [7:185]. In the signs of the souls, it is what He said: "*And in your souls; what, do you not see?*" [51:21]. He is saying, "Do you not look at yourself, and do you not think about your own makeup?"
>
> This is because the Lord of the Worlds has written out many fine points of wisdom and many realities of artisanry with the pen of eternal gentleness on the tablet of this makeup. He has inscribed on it the lights of fabrication and the traces of honoring. He made the round head—the pavilion of intellect and the gathering place of knowledge—a monastery for the senses. Whatever worth has been acquired by this hollow makeup and composite person has been acquired from intellect and knowledge. The worth of the Adamite lies in intellect and his respectability in knowledge, his perfection in intellect and his beauty in knowledge.
>
> God created his forehead like a bar of silver. He strung the two bows of his eyebrows with pure musk. He deposited the two dots of his eye's light into two figures of darkness. He made a hundred thousand red roses grow up in the garden of his two cheeks. He concealed thirty-two teeth like pearls in the oyster shell of his mouth. He sealed his mouth with glistening agate. From the beginning of his lips to the end of his throat, He created twenty-nine way stations, making them the places of articulation for the twenty-nine letters. From his heart, He brought a sultan into existence, from his breast a field, from his aspiration a fleet-footed mount, from his thinking a swift messenger. He created two taking hands and two running feet.
>
> All the aforementioned is but the robe of creation and the beauty of outwardness. Beyond this are the perfection and beauty of inwardness. For a moment, ponder the Lord's subtleties and kindnesses and the traces of the divine solicitude and kind favor that have arranged this handful of dust. Look at the different kinds of generosity and the special favors of proximity that He has placed within human beings.

> He created the whole cosmos, but He never looked at any creature with the eye of love. He sent no messenger to any existent thing and gave no message to any creature until it was the turn of the Adamites. They were pulled up by gentleness, caressed by bounty, and turned into quarries of light. He made their secret cores the locus of His own gaze, He sent them prophets, He set angels over them as watchers, He placed the burn of passion in their hearts, and one after another He sent them incitements to yearn and motivations to desire.
>
> (*Kashf* 8:545–46)

NAMES OF THE HUMAN SUBTLETY

Nowadays, we typically refer to the outward, visible realm of the macrocosm as the material world. The Qur'an often calls it the earth. It embraces anything that can be perceived by the five senses, directly or indirectly. In contrast, the inward, invisible realm is that of heaven, which is a domain of subtlety, awareness, consciousness, and intelligible light. Similarly, the human microcosm has two basic realms, body and spirit. In the mythic language of the Qur'an, God molded the clay of Adam's body with His own two hands. Having done so, God tells us, "*I blew into him of My spirit*" (15:29). Once Adam came into being, body and spirit were his outwardness and inwardness, but Adam was now Adam *himself.* Hence, the Qur'an uses *al-nafs*, the soul or self, to designate Adam as the human individual.

Authors sometimes distinguish between spirit and soul and sometimes do not. For many of those who make a distinction, the soul is colored by its ambiguity. It is the product of the union of spirit and clay, but in itself it is neither spiritual nor bodily. It is something new, born of the marriage of light and darkness, subtlety and density, awareness and unconsciousness. In its development, the soul will sometimes display the color of spirit, sometimes that of clay. It is constantly pulled in two directions, upward toward subtle luminosity and downward toward gross inanimateness.

The upper realm is that of heaven, angels, and spirits, who dwell in relative proximity to God. The lower realm is that of earth, minerals, plants, and animals, which dwell in relative distance from God. To the extent that people immerse themselves in the lower realm, they become characterized by dispersion, multiplicity, and darkness. Adam forgot because he gazed on this lower, outward realm. The cure for forgetfulness is *dhikr*, "remembrance," which means focusing on the upper realm of togetherness, unity, and light. The spur to remembrance is designated by the same Arabic word, *dhikr,* though now it is typically translated as "reminder." The Qur'an uses it in this sense to designate the content of the prophetic messages.

God's wisdom and mercy placed the soul in its ambiguous situation. By creating the universe, with its unlimited deployment, both vertical and horizontal, God set up contrasting forces, which pull simultaneously in different directions. Perhaps the key Qur'anic passage describing the soul's ambiguity is this: "*By the soul and That which shaped it, and inspired it to its depravity and its godwariness! Prosperous is he who purifies it, and failed is he who buries it*" (91:7–10). Here we see that God inspired the soul to move both downward and upward. It can bury itself in the lower realm or purify itself from dispersion and forgetfulness. By way of purification, it can achieve godwariness, a designation for the sum total of praiseworthy human attributes.

The philosophers used the word *nafs,* "soul-self," in a generic sense, without any moral connotations. The Sufis, however, often used it with a strong negative color, in which case they meant our ordinary, everyday forgetfulness, overcome by darkness and dispersion. Some of them used the word to designate as well the human self generally, and frequently they describe types of souls based on Qur'anic references. For example, it is often said that there are three levels of the soul: the soul that commands to ugliness, the blaming soul, and the peaceful soul.

According to traditional accounts, when God finished molding Adam's clay, He placed it on the earth near Mecca to ferment (like adobe). After forty years, He blew something of His own spirit into it. Maybudī alludes to these accounts in his explanation of the verse "*O Adam, dwell you and your spouse in the Garden*" (7:19).

> The reports say that He created Adam's body from clay and put it between Mecca and Ta'if for forty years. Every time Iblis passed by, he would say, "Why have you been created?"
>
> The Exalted Lord was saying to the angels, "When I have blown into him of My spirit, prostrate yourselves before him." So when the spirit came into his secret core, Adam opened his eyes and saw that his body was all clay. Here the wisdom was that he would know his own root, recognize his soul, not be deceived by himself, and see the subtleties that he saw as coming from the Real.
>
> When the spirit reached his breast, it saw darkness. Some say that this was the darkness of the slip. Others say that it was the darkness of the dust, for the root of dust is darkness, and the root of the spirit is light. When the spirit

wanted to go back, its breeze reached Adam's nostrils and he sneezed. Adam said, "The praise belongs to God," and the Exalted Lord said, "May your Lord have mercy on you!"

The spirit heard the mention of the Real's praise and mercy and took up residence. It said, "If this is worthy of God's praise and mercy, it is worthy to be my place."

When the spirit reached the navel, appetite for food appeared in Adam. He saw the fruit of paradise and wished for it. He wanted to stand but was not able to. The Exalted Lord said, "*Man was created of haste*" [21:37].

(*Kashf* 3:587–88)

In his commentary on the verse "*It is He who created you from clay*" (6:2), Maybudī points out that Adam's reality brought together the properties of the two macrocosmic worlds, the Unseen and the Visible, often called the World of the Command and the World of the Creation.

Adam was two things: clay and spirituality. His clay pertained to the World of the Creation, and his spirituality to the World of the Command. What pertains to creation is "He fermented Adam's clay in His hand." What pertains to the command is *I blew into him of My spirit* [15:29]. *Surely God chose Adam* [3:33] pertains to the beauty of the command, and *Adam disobeyed* [20:121] to the taint of creation.

In Adam were both rose garden and field of clay, so the clay was the place of roses. Every rose, however, has a thorn. A rose like the bosom friend Abraham had a thorn like the rebellious Nimrod. A rose like Moses had thorns like Pharaoh and Haman. A rose like Jesus had thorns like those impure Jews. A rose like Muḥammad the Arab had a thorn like Abū Jahl the wretched.

Who knows the secret of Adam's innate disposition? Who recognizes Adam's good fortune and rank? No eagle of anyone's mind has alighted on the branch of the tree of Adam's good fortune. No eye of anyone's insight has perceived the beauty of the sun of Adam's limpidness.

(*Kashf* 3:297–98)

Maybudī provides a typical explanation of the difference between body and spirit in his commentary on the verse "*From it We created you and to it We return you*" (20:55). The pronoun *it* refers to earth (*arḍ*), the realm of dust and clay.

Know that the Adamite is two things: spirit and body. The spirit is from light, and light is celestial. The body is from dust, and dust is terrestrial. The spirit wants to go up because it is celestial. The body wants to go down because it is terrestrial. In the perfection of His power, the King bound the two together. The spirit was bound to the body, and the body was bound to the spirit, so both are in bonds. The spirit and the body settled down together.

On the day of death, when the life of the servant comes to an end and the moment of death arrives, the bonds are loosened, as when a bird comes out of its cage. The spirit rises up from the body and goes skyward to its nest. The body takes the road of the earth to its center. The spirit is put into a lantern of light, which is hung from the tree of Ṭūbā. The body is wrapped in a shroud and entrusted to the earth.

(*Kashf* 6:149–50)

Samʿānī, like Muḥammad Ghazālī and others, sometimes compares the compound nature of human beings to a mounted rider. He alludes to the common notion that human spirits are identical in substance with angels, but different because angels do not govern bodies. Notice that here Samʿānī uses the word *soul* with a negative connotation, meaning the self as it is immersed in the darkness and dispersion of bodily nature. The Shaykh al-Islām from whom he quotes at the end is probably his father.

Glory be to God! How many pure subtleties has this mote of dust! The Adamite is a mount and a rider. The mount is the soul, and the rider the spirit. As for the angels, they travel without mounts.

Those who have no mounts always follow the road, for they do not have the means to go by other than the road. The one who is mounted sometimes goes by the road and sometimes by other than the road. The rider always aims for the road, but the mount aspires to the roadless road. "What I want and what the horse wants are two different things."

When the aim of the mount overcomes the aim of the rider, he takes the roadless road, but when the aim of the rider overcomes the aim of the mount, he takes the road. When the spirit overcomes the soul, then the jonquil of obedience, the hyacinth of chieftainship, and the iris of felicity grow up, but when the soul overcomes the spirit, only disobedience rises from the salt marsh of its distracted disposition.

In reality, the road out there is for the Adamites. The angels are feathered birds, *having wings two, three, and four* [35:1]. As for you, O dervish, do not look at the height of the birds, look at the wiles of the hunters.

The angels *are asking forgiveness for those who have faith* [40:7]. They were created from sheer spirit, and human beings from the subtlety of spirit and the heaviness of dust. From these two things God took two praiseworthy attributes—subtlety from the spirit and heaviness from the dust. From them

He compounded, arranged, and put together an individual, whom He called Adam. The density remained with the bodies and bodily things, and the lightness with the angels.

O dervish! It was an infinite felicity that you were brought into existence from these two meanings that abide through these two essences. Had He not made you into an individual by taking lightness from the spirit and denseness from the dust, you would have been a bad example for the two worlds.

The Shaykh al-Islām said, "There was a man who had an ugly face but a beautiful disposition. His wife had a beautiful face but an ugly disposition. The man said, 'Wife, let us cohabit so that we will have a child with your face and my disposition.' As it happened a child came forth with the father's face and the mother's disposition. About him they said, 'O bad substance, O you who combine the disgraces of your parents!' "

(*Rawḥ* 298)

In another passage, Samʿānī retells a well-known story about Adam's creation from clay and explains that God was concealing the real situation from Satan.

First Gabriel was sent to take a handful of dust from the earth. Gabriel came to take it, and the earth sought aid against him, for the earth was like a jewel box. Inside the jewel box of that handful of dust was the shell for the pearl of Adam's secret. It sought aid because its capital was being plundered. Gabriel went back. Then He sent Seraphiel, and again it sought aid, so he went back. Then He sent Michael, and it shouted for help, so he went back. Finally He sent Azrael. It sought aid: "I seek refuge in God from you."

Azrael replied, "I seek refuge in God lest I return to Him without having accomplished His command." He took a handful of dust with severity, without the approval of the earth, but he promised that he would bring the handful back to it.

What is the wisdom in this handful? Yes, the subtle secrets of the Unseen must be deposited in a container. The dust was taken by severity, and the spirit was deposited within it by severity, for the two were opposites. Had there been only spirit, the days would have been free of stain, and the acts without adulteration. But pure acts are not appropriate for this world, and from the beginning Adam was created to be the housemaster in *this* world.

God combined dust with the secrets. Something was needed within which the secrets would stay well guarded. The secrets were brought together with dust so that they would shine within it and the antagonist would not follow in their tracks. The dust was so that the folk of outwardness would be thrown off. The army of the uncaused Will prepared an ambush from Adam's dust so that Iblis would look at the dust, protest, and become accursed.

Iblis had been created of fire. He did not know that fire raises up its head, being proud of itself. "O accursed one, are you proud of fire? You belong to fire, and fire belongs to you. O Korah, are you proud of treasures? You belong to your treasures, and they belong to you. O Pharaoh, are you proud of the Nile? You belong to the Nile, and the Nile belongs to you! O tawḥīd-voicers, are you proud of Me? You belong to Me, and I belong to you."

He wanted to place a hundred thousand secrets in Adam's makeup. He gazed and saw no one in the world trustworthier than dust, so He placed the secrets in the dust. He did not give them to fire, for fire burns and acts treacherously. Deposits are not given over to the treacherous, but to the trustworthy. The secrets were the locus of exaltation, for they were the veiled virgins of the Unseen Presence, and the curtained ones are kept concealed. Nothing was like dust in concealment, so dust was made the curtain of the secrets. The privy would look at the secrets, and the nonprivy would look at the dust. (*Rawḥ* 420)

What exactly were the secrets deposited in dust? They were, of course, the divine attributes in the form of which Adam was created. In the following passage, Samʿānī reminds us that when God said, "*He loves them*," He was saying that He loves human beings because they manifest His own beauty. In effect, He loves Himself, for there is none beautiful but He. As Muḥammad Ghazālī put it in his chapter on love, "When someone loves only himself, his acts, and his compositions, his love does not transgress his essence and the concomitants of his essence, since they are connected to his essence. Thus, God loves only Himself" (*Iḥyāʾ* 4:474). Avicenna had already made a similar point in his metaphysics: "He is the lover of His own Essence. Since His Essence is an origin, It is the origin of all order and all good. Hence, the order of the good comes to be an object of His love accidentally" (*Ilāhiyyāt*, 292).

O chevalier! They made Adam a cup of poison from *Adam disobeyed* [20:121]. At once they sent in its tracks the antidote of gentleness: *If guidance comes to you from Me* [2:38]. "With one hand you're stingy, with the other you soothe."

They placed so many jeweled crowns of leadership on the felicitous head of Adam the dust-dweller that, had they not clothed him in the patched cloak of the severity of *Surely he was a great wrongdoer, deeply ignorant* [33:72] and had they not buttoned it up with *Adam disobeyed*, there would have been fear of many things.

What a marvelous business! He made apparent the secrets of His lordhood in places where the imaginative wings of intellect's phoenix could not fly. He took a handful of dust in the grasp of perfect power and kept it for forty years in the sunlight of His gaze until the dampness of being left it. Then He commanded the angels of the Sovereignty, "Go to the gate of this wondrous form, marvelous shape, and subtle guise and kiss the threshold of its majesty, which is beyond these seven heavens. *Fall before him in prostration!* [15:29]."

O dervish! He said to the angels, "Prostrate yourselves before Adam," but this level, distinction, rank, and status did not belong to water and clay. It belonged rather to the sultan of the heart. In the core of Adam's heart was deposited one of the divine subtleties, royal secrets, and unseen meanings, a secret concealed by the curtain of *Say: "The spirit is of the command of my Lord"* [17:85]. God gave back a hidden mark of this secret on the purified tongue of Muṣṭafā with the words, "He created Adam in His form"—not by way of declaring likeness and similarity.

When the angels of the Higher Plenum saw his greatness and elevation, they threw their spirits down before this impudent dust. But when the accursed one, that bat of the era, was placed in front of Adam's sunlight, he rubbed his eyes in utmost misery and saw nothing of good fortune.

Adam's essence was the depository of the secrets of the Unseen. Otherwise, how could a handful of dust have such worthiness that the residents of the precincts of holiness and the preachers of the pulpits of intimacy should prostrate themselves before him? Is a handful of worthless clay and water given such respect that it should be said to trustworthy Gabriel, unshakeable Michael, and stable Seraphiel, "Prostrate yourselves before him"? No, no—that handful of clay had a jewel box in the secret core of the heart.

O chevalier! All the intellectuals of the world are biting the fingers of wonder with the teeth of bewilderment: "Why is it that He loves this handful of dust and clay?" By the rightful due of the Real! He loves only Himself, for everyone who loves his own artisanry loves himself.

(*Rawḥ* 164)

What a marvelous business! He concealed a pearl in an oyster shell and stored a jewel in a box. With water and dust He prepared a citadel. Its spires of eminence could not be reached by the imagination of the others, so they talk only about the citadel's door. They knock on the clay and do not suspect. He made it of a clay of that sort so that they would lose their nerve by looking at it. Which pearl was it? The pearl of love.

(599)

In another passage, Samʿānī describes the qualities pertaining to the frames (*qawālib*), that is, the outer, bodily forms, as contrasted with those that pertain to the hearts (*qulūb*), the inner, spiritual essences. He points out that the body needs to observe the Shariah and perform the commanded acts of obedience, but the heart must devote itself solely to God. The passage follows a discussion of the love established by the Covenant of Alast, which made clear to God's servants that they should be loyal to the Covenant. The body is loyal through servanthood, and the spirit through love.

> The first shoot He planted in the garden of your hearing was the shoot of His lordhood. He watered it with gentleness and it sent down roots. Then the branch of loyalty grew up: *Those who are loyal to their covenant when they make a covenant* [2:177]. The leaf of good pleasure grew: *God is well pleased with them, and they are well pleased with Him* [5:119]. The flower of praise and laudation bloomed: "Those who praise God in every state." The fruit of union and encounter took shape: *Faces on that day radiant, gazing at their Lord* [75:22–23]. He recorded the book of the Covenant of Lordhood on the tablets of the spirits with the ink of succor and the pen of eternal gentleness: *Those—He wrote faith in their hearts and confirmed them with a spirit from Him* [58:22].
>
> To the bodily frames He spoke of lordhood, and to the spirits He spoke of love.
>
> "O frames, I am God! O hearts, I am the Friend!
>
> "O frames, you belong to Me! O hearts, I belong to you!
>
> "O frames, toil! That is what lordhood requires from servanthood. O hearts, rejoice! Have joy in Me and sing of Me in remembrance. That is what unqualified love demands.
>
> "O frames, yours are the realities of struggle! O hearts, yours are the gardens of contemplation!
>
> "O frames, yours is the discipline of practice! O hearts, yours is the rose garden of beginningless gentleness!
>
> "O frames, yours is asking! O hearts, yours is bestowal!
>
> "O frames, yours is need! O hearts, yours is joy!
>
> "O frames, yours is doing! O hearts, yours is pain!
>
> "O frames, do not let go of obedience! O hearts, obey none but Me!
>
> "O frames, yours is suffering! O hearts, yours is the treasure!
>
> "O frames, be like the knocker on a door! O hearts, ascend beyond the Splendorous Throne!
>
> "O frames, surrender the body on credit! O hearts, deal only in hard cash!"
>
> Do you not see that when there is talk of the bodily frame, promises are made? [*But as for him who feared the station of his Lord*] *and forbade the soul its caprice, surely the Garden shall be the refuge* [79:40–41]. But when there is talk of the heart, there is talk of hard cash: "I sit with him who remembers Me." "I am with My servant's thoughts of Me." *He is with you wherever you are* [57:4].
>
> (*Rawḥ* 154–55)

THE HEART'S FLUCTUATION

The Qur'an depicts the heart as the center of awareness and selfhood. In more than fifty verses, it urges people to ponder the signs of God and to use their intelligence (ʿaql) and understanding (*fiqh*) to decipher them. When it localizes intelligence, it places it in the heart, not the brain. It is worth remarking that there is nothing strange about this; parallel ideas are found in other premodern civilizations. The most salient example is perhaps from China, though scholars have typically translated the Chinese word for *heart, xin,* as "mind."

As a verb, the word for *heart, qalb,* means to fluctuate and change. In some of the hadiths that refer to this verbal meaning, the Prophet addresses God as Fluctuater of Hearts (*muqallib al-qulūb*). One of his wives said that he used to make the supplication, "O Fluctuater of Hearts! Fix my heart in Thy religion!" When she asked him about it, he replied, "O Umm Salama, there is no child of Adam whose heart does not lie between two of God's fingers. When He wants, He makes a person go straight, and when He wants, He makes him swerve."

In Sufi writings, two themes are highlighted in discussions of the heart. One is that the heart fluctuates because it is caught between soul and spirit. The soul—in the negative sense of the term—is immersed in bodily desires, and the spirit inclines to its source, the divine breath, so the heart is pulled back and forth between those two. As Samʿānī puts it, "The spirit is luminous and heavenly, the soul terrestrial and dark, so the heart fluctuates and is bewildered. The attribute of the spirit is all conformity, the attribute of the soul is all opposition, and the heart fluctuates in the midst" (*Rawḥ* 396).

The second theme is that the heart is the place of intimate conjunction between God and man. God gazes on the heart, and the heart gazes on God. Maybudī, citing Anṣārī, calls this vision by the unusual Persian word *hamdīdārī,* "mutual seeing," which he uses as a synonym for the common Arabic word *muʿāyana* (from the same root as *ʿayn,* "eye"), meaning eye-to-eye or face-to-face vision. A sound hadith reads, "God gazes not on your bodies or your forms, but He gazes on your hearts." According to a frequently cited divine saying, not found in the standard books on Hadith, "Neither the heavens nor the earth embraces Me, but the heart of My faithful servant does embrace Me."

Sufi discussions of the heart often resemble philosophical discussions of the rational, or talking, soul (*al-nafs al-nāṭiqa*). The heart is what makes human beings human. The potencies that people share with other living things are precisely shared, not specific to the human state. Samʿānī explains this in the midst of a long discussion of the heart's role in the human subtlety.

It is known that the specific characteristic of man's heart is knowledge and wisdom, that the perfect state of his clay lies in knowledge, and that the eminence of his road lies in wisdom. When someone keeps back from knowledge and wisdom and steps into the road of ignorance and foolishness, he is a beast in reality, though an Adamite in form.

In a similar way, the horse has the specific characteristic of pomp and pride and shares the strength to carry burdens with the donkey. If people do not find that pomp and pride in it, they make saddlebags for it and bring it down to the rank of a donkey. So also if the Adamite does not put his specific characteristic to work, he will be brought down to the beasts: *They are like cattle. No, they are farther astray* [7:179]. This is because the specific characteristic of the human substance does not lie in feeding and procreation, for plants have the same thing. Nor does it lie in the senses and movement, for animals have that too. Nor does it lie in the beautiful form, for the same thing is found on walls. Its specific characteristic lies in knowledge and recognition.

(*Rawḥ* 177)

God created the universe so that He would be recognized, and since only human beings have the capacity to recognize Him, He created everything else as the means and context for recognition. Given that the heart is the actualized human essence, one can say, as Samʿānī does, that God created all things for the sake of the heart:

When He created heaven and earth, the wisdom in creating them was to create a heart. He created this world so that they would know, and He created paradise so that they would see. Then He adorns paradise with the friends, He adorns the friends with the heart, and He adorns the heart with Himself. "Neither the heavens nor the earth embraces Me, but the heart of My faithful servant does embrace Me."

(*Rawḥ* 377–78)

The heart is the locus of intelligence and recognition, so it plays the role of king and commander in the human microcosm. Samʿānī begins a long disquisition on the structure of the microcosm and its relationship with the macrocosm with these words:

O dervish, as long as Adam had not come, the Throne was hungry, the Footstool naked, the Pen thirsty. When Adam came out, he made everyone happy. He sipped from the goblet of love's covenant—for *We made covenant with Adam before* [20:115]. Drunk with the covenant's wine, he took a dip in the ocean of at-ness. This was expressed with the words "*in a seat of truthfulness at an Omnipotent King*" [54:55].

"O Gabriel, Iblis did not prostrate himself. How is it that you have taken on the job of messenger boy?"

He answered, "I see the characteristics of the breast, not the form of the clay."

There are many way stations and stages separating the characteristics of the breast from the form of the clay. When the angels of the Sovereignty prostrated themselves before Adam the Chosen, they did so because the pearl of the heart had not been placed inside the jewel box of their own existence, but Adam had a heart. In reality, all the treasuries of the secrets and meanings have a road into this drop of blood. "Deeds are judged by intentions"* is an allusion to this secret.

As long as this drop in the ocean of your innate disposition does not carry the banner of good fortune and does not take the lead, you will not be taken to the world of contemplation and struggle. It must stand in front of the steed of your aspiration and shout, "Make way! Make way!" Beware—do not look at it with the eye of contempt, for the robe of chieftainship was placed on its shoulders.

In His munificence, the Exalted Lord gave existence to this fortified fortress, which is the locus of adornment and beautification. He scattered over it the effusion of bounties from the clouds of tenderness, making it a faultless mortal and a well-proportioned body. He sat the spirit king on the royal seat, for *I blew into him of My spirit* [15:29]. Then He gave the reins of rulership over this compound being into the hands of the heart, which is the king in the celestial sphere of the body's world. "There is a lump of flesh in the body. When it is worthy, the whole body is worthy, and when it is corrupt, the whole body is corrupt. Indeed, it is the heart."*

(*Rawḥ* 189)

Angels and spirits dwell in a realm of permanence and stillness, bathed in the light of God and drenched in His gentleness and mercy. God created Adam with His "two hands," and as many commentators remark, these are beauty and majesty, mercy and wrath, bounty and justice. Samʿānī explains that the heart alone embraces these two sides of the divine reality, so when God created it, He kept it for Himself.

The Exalted Lord created the Throne and put it on the shoulders of the proximate angels. He created paradise and gave it to Riḍwān. He created hell and gave it to Mālik. When He created the heart of the person of faith, Riḍwān said, "Give it to me, for within it are found the fine wine of intimacy and the drink of holiness."

Mālik said, "Give it to me, for within it are found the flames of yearning and the fire of passion."

The proximate angels said, "Give it to us, for it is the elevated throne of love and the wide plain of affection."

Others said, "Give it to us, for it is an adorned heaven, its passing thoughts like shooting stars."

The Exalted Lord dismissed them all and said, "The hearts are between two fingers of the All-Merciful." By these are meant bounty and justice. Sometimes the breeze of bounty blows over the heart, and it becomes joyful. Sometimes the hot wind of severity strikes against it, and it melts. It is confounded between these two attributes, senseless between these two states.

(*Rawḥ* 180–81)

When Adam was in paradise, he encountered mercy and gentleness. To actualize the perfect manifestation of the beautiful divine form, he had to enter the earthly realm, where severity rules. Only by suffering separation's severity could he yearn for union's gentleness. This yearning for union is precisely the description of love. According to Samʿānī, the difference between the spirit, which was blown into the body by the divine breath, and the heart, which fluctuates between two of God's fingers, is that the spirit remains unmoving in proximity's gentleness, but the heart is overcome by the change and alteration characteristic of all created things, caught in the contrasting forces of mercy and wrath.

O chevalier! He placed the burden of His severity only on a handful of dust. "'Neither the heavens nor the earth embraces Me, but the heart of My faithful servant does embrace Me.' The Splendorous Throne cannot support the gaze of My majesty, and the Footstool cannot carry My beginningless prosperity. It is the secret core of the heart of Adam and the Adamites that carries the burden of contemplating Me."

The heart was named *qalb* because of its fluctuation. The attribute of the heart is to be without rest. Why does it keep on fluctuating? Because the brand of severity's ruling power has been placed upon it. It is impossible to put a fiery brand on an unbroken colt and command it to be still. Yes, spirits are in repose itself, but hearts have the attribute of motion. He placed bonds on the spirit so that they would stay still, but He let the hearts move.

The butcher throws down the sheep and ties together its two front legs and one back leg, leaving one leg free. He says, "It would be wrong to bind all four. Putting the blade on the throat and not letting the sheep move would be a great wrongdoing, for then it would taste the wound of the blade while being still. Nothing is lost by letting it move."

Tying together the three legs is the butcher's severity, and leaving one leg free is his gentleness—a gentleness in severity, a severity in gentleness. The latter does not remove the former, nor the former the latter.

(*Rawḥ* 105–6)

O chevalier! You must wait many years if a tree is to bear fruit, and then one day you may have some. If you want it to bear earlier and better fruit, you must take a graft from another tree. Glory be to God! How many blessings are found in cutting!

Many thousands of years before Adam came forth, the angels were walking around and performing acts of obedience, but they did not reach the station, level, degree, and rank that Adam reached at first. Yes, they were trees full of fruit. But they did not have a graft from another branch.

On the circle of engendering, He drew this individual of clay, destined to remain in this world for only a short time. At once the Unseen Presence prepared a subtlety in the spirit and grafted it to the tree of his existence. Thus, what others would not reach in a long time, he would reach in a short time. He received no help from his own makeup, but rather from the solicitude of the Teacher. May the evil eye stay far away—for He made him very beautiful!

Once the body cohabited with the spirit, a heart appeared between the two, called the point of limpidness. No other created thing has a heart. The heart is not that lump of flesh that, if you threw ten of them to a dog, would not satisfy it. That is simply an outward target so that thoughts and understandings may gain some courtesy. The heart's meaning is purified of that.

From the spirit, the heart took subtlety, and from the dust, heaviness. It came to be praised and approved by both sides, and then it became the locus for the gaze of the Unseen. It is neither spirit nor bodily frame; or, it is both spirit and frame. If it is spirit, where does this embodiment come from? And if it is frame, why does it have subtlety? It is neither that nor this, but it is both that and this.

When the heart came into existence from these two meanings, the disparity of states and the diversity of steps appeared. The spirit does one work, the soul does another, and the heart is a prisoner in between, having read from the slate of poverty. If it inclines toward the spiritual foundation, the work of the spirit becomes manifest. If it leans toward the corporeal foundation, the work of the body appears. This is why the Master of the Two Worlds, the Messenger to the Two Weighty Ones, said in this station, "The heart is like a feather in a desert. The winds make it fluctuate from side to side."

(298–99)

Maybudī distinguishes between soul and heart in his explanation of the allusions found in the verse "*God has bought from the faithful their souls and their possessions*" (9:111). He explains why the verse employs terminology related to buying and selling—typically, a juridical discussion—and suggests why it talks about souls rather than hearts.

This verse is a generous felicitation from a generous Lord, who is generous in Essence, generous in attributes, generous in love, generous in caressing, and generous in bestowal.

The servant himself is bestowed by His bounty, and then He buys back what He Himself bestowed. He makes the transaction, but He bestows all the profit on the servant and accepts the loss for Himself. This is beautiful-doing and generosity, loving-kindness and gentleness.

In the Torah of Moses, God said, "The Garden is My Garden, and the possessions are My possessions. Buy My Garden with My possessions! If you profit, that is yours, and if you lose, that is Mine. O children of Adam, I did not create you to profit from you. I created you only so that you would profit from Me."

In the Beginningless, before the servant's existence, the Lord of the Worlds bought him. He was the seller and the buyer. He Himself sold and He Himself bought.

In the Shariah of Muṣṭafā, it is not permitted for the buyer and seller to be the same, unless it is a father, for whom it is permitted on condition of tenderness, negation of suspicion, perfect loving-kindness, and fatherly love. What then do you say about someone who is more clement and merciful toward the servant than a father, a God whose loving-kindness has no bounds and whose love is greater? Given that it is permitted for a father, it is more appropriate and more complete in the case of the loving Creator.

Moreover, the Exalted Lord knew that the servants are bad-tempered, disloyal breakers of the Covenant. He knew that when they reached maturity, they would protest. He shut down the road of protest by buying souls full of fault and blight in exchange for a paradise full of joy and blessing. He bought souls full of appetite and trial in exchange for a paradise that has the levels and degrees of proximity to the Real. According to the Shari'ite rules on transactions, when the price given for the bought object is more than it is worth, there is no way to protest.

Also, He bought the soul, not the heart. This is because the heart is an endowment [*waqf*] dedicated to the Real's love and affection, and it is not permitted to buy or sell endowments.

Moreover, one of the conditions in transactions is delivery. When something cannot be delivered, the Shariah does not permit it to be bought and

> sold. Birds in the sky and fish in the sea cannot be sold, because they cannot be delivered. The state of the servant's heart is exactly the same, and surrendering it is impossible. Thus the Exalted Lord says, "*He comes between a man and his heart*" [8:24]. Naṣrābādī said, "He buys your attributes from you, but the heart is one of His attributes, so it cannot be bought and sold."
>
> The Prophet said, "The heart of Adam's child is between two fingers of the All-Merciful."
>
> It is also said that the soul is the heart's doorman, standing like a serving boy, a subject serving its lord. As for the heart, it has the place of witnessing. Carrying lordhood like a sultan, it governs the kingdom. So if the value of the soul, which is the serving boy, is paradise, with its treasuries of blessings, what do you say about the heart, with all its nearness and proximity? What is its value other than the neighborhood of the Exalted Presence and the continuity of contemplation and vision?
>
> (*Kashf* 4:228–29)

THE HEART'S VISION

God created the heart for Himself. As the innermost core of the human reality, it gazes on God and is gazed on by Him. The goal of love is togetherness and union, and this is achieved in the heart. It alone is able to embrace God, so the quest for Him involves cultivating the heart and preparing it for vision. The heart needs to be purified, which means emptied of everything other than God. Samʿānī explains this while briefly reviewing the structure of the microcosm in fairly standard terms. As the seat of the intellect, the heart is like a king in relation to a kingdom. Among the chief animal potencies that it governs are appetite (*shahwa*) and wrath (*ghaḍab*), known in the Western tradition as concupiscence and irascibility. If the kingdom of the soul is to be put in order, both of those must be brought under intellect's dictates.

> O chevalier, this heart, which is the sultan in the castle of your breast, has soldiers arranged in ranks. Some of them are seen by the eyes and some are not. The soldiers seen by the eyes are the outward bodily members. The proof that these members are the heart's soldiers is that when it commands the eye to look, it looks, and when it says not to look, it does not look. So also are the other members. Just as the angels are subjected to the command of the Exalted Lord, so also these members are subjected to the heart. But there is one difference, namely, that these members are subjected and unaware, but the angels of the Sovereignty are subjected and aware.

The soldiers not seen by the eyes are like wrath, appetite, knowledge, and wisdom. Appetite is like an ill-mannered slave, deceptive and bad acting, who presents himself in the form of a sincere advisor. His custom is to quarrel with the vizier, who is intellect. Wrath is like the chief of police, known as the superintendent. The chief of police must observe the stipulations of the Shariah. He himself will observe the Shariah's stipulations only when he has been taught courtesy by the intellect's whip.

Once you come to know this, you should also know that all animals share with the Adamites in appetite, wrath, and the outward senses. What is specific to the substance of the Adamic heart is knowledge and recognition, both of which are beyond the level of sensory things. The allusion to this secret in the tongue of the lords of the heart is this: "Knowledge is a light that God throws into the heart of any of His servants as He wills." They have also said, "Recognition is the heart's life with God."

My father used to say that two living things must become companions in order to produce a child. One is a life that comes with the help of the Unseen: *So also We revealed to you a spirit from Our command* [42:52]. The other is a life that is inborn: *I blew into him of My spirit* [15:29]. When these two lives become companions, another life is born from the two, called "recognition." This is expressed in these terms: "Recognition is the heart's life with God."

Let me offer one more likeness for the heart, then I will return to the discussion: hearts are like containers within which is the fine wine of the realization of the meanings. The Commander of the Faithful ʿAlī said, "God has containers in His earth, and they indeed are the hearts. Of them, the most beloved to Him is the most tender, the most limpid, and the most solid." Then he said, "The most solid in the religion, the most limpid in certainty, and the most tender toward brethren."

This container was first clay, suitable for neither food nor drink. It had to be passed over a fire to make it into a cup for drink and a bowl for food. Now the stipulation is that you must pass the heart over the fire of passion so that it will be worthy for the food of proximity and suitable for the drink of love. Then you will be given the drink of good fortune in the cup of the heart. This is expressed like this: "*And their Lord will pour for them a pure drink*" [76:21].

O dervish! The heart is like a container, but a container that is full of water does not have any air. In the same way, when the heart is preoccupied with other than the Real, talk of the Unseen does not enter into it: "The preoccupied will not be diverted."

(*Rawḥ* 175–76)

In his commentary on the verse "*Then He sat on the Throne*" (7:54), Maybudī explains that God's Throne in the microcosm is the heart. In Islamic cosmology, the Throne is often identified with the starless sphere, which encloses the Footstool, also known as the sphere of the fixed stars. Sitting on the macrocosmic Throne, *God encompasses everything* (4:126), but sitting on the microcosmic throne, He dwells at the core of the human self.

> His Throne in heaven is well known. His Throne in earth is the heart of the friends. He said about the Throne in heaven, "*Upon that day eight shall carry above them the Throne of your Lord*" [69:17]. The angels will lift it up. He said about the Throne in earth, "*We carried them on land and sea* [17:70]. We Ourselves will carry it. We will not give it over to the angels."
>
> The angels gaze on the throne of heaven, but the God of the universe gazes on the throne of earth. Concerning the throne of heaven, He said, "*The All-Merciful sat on the Throne*" [20:5]. Concerning the throne of earth, He said, "I am with those whose hearts are broken." "The heart of the person of faith is between two fingers of the All-Merciful."
>
> (*Kashf* 3:639–40)

The true heart, then, is that which is not preoccupied with others, but is totally immersed in the vision of God. Maybudī explains this in his remarks on the verse "*Have they not seen how many generations We destroyed before them?*" (36:31). Notice the way in which he takes the notion of "seeing" in its widest possible sense. The fact that seeing is far more than the work of the physical eyes is taken for granted in a worldview that looks upon both the universe and the self as multilayered.

> Do they not look with the eyes of the head to see the wonders of the artifacts? Do they not look with the eyes of the secret core to see the subtleties of the obligations?
>
> Do they not look with the eyes of the head to see the signs of the horizons? Do they not look with the eyes of the secret core to see the signs of the souls?
>
> Do they not look with the eyes of the heart to see the lights of guidance? Do they not look with the eyes of the spirit to see the secrets of solicitude? Do they not look with the eyes of witnessing to see the Presence of the Witnessed? Do they not look with the eyes of ecstasy [*wajd*] to see the banner of finding [*wujūd*]? Do they not look with the eyes of selflessness to see the Friend face-to-face? Do they not look with the eyes of annihilation to see a world without shore?
>
> O poor wretch! How long will you look at the artifacts? Look once at the Artisan! How long will you be distracted by wonders? Look once at the

Wonder- Worker! How long will you be a man of every door? A man of every door will never see well-being and deliverance: "Be not a weathercock, lest you perish."* Tearing up a thousand bronze fortresses from the ground is easier than bringing a man of every door back to one door.

Abū Yazīd Basṭāmī was asked about the heart. He said, "The heart is that which does not contain the measure of one speck of desire for the creatures."

(*Kashf* 8:231–32)

Maybudī elaborates on the significance of the heart as part of his commentary on the verse *"And know that God comes between a man and his heart"* (8:24).

Revelation came to David the prophet: " 'O David, purify for Me a house in which I may reside!' O David, purify a house fitting to be the field of union with Me, and turn away from the others toward Me."

David said, "O Lord, which house can be fitting for Your majesty and tremendousness?"

He said, "The heart of the faithful servant. O David! I am with fevered hearts. Wherever you see someone in the path of searching for Me whose harvest has been burned by the fire of passion in seeking Me, take that as the mark. The pavilion of My holiness is set up only when the heart of the burnt is annihilated. The heart of the faithful servant is the treasury of My bazaar, the domicile of looking upon Me, the prayer niche of union with Me, the tent of yearning for Me, the lodging place of speaking with Me, the treasure-house of My secrets, the quarry of seeing Me."

When something is burnt, it loses value, but when a heart is burnt, it gains value. Muṣṭafā said, "The hearts are God's containers in the earth. The most beloved of the containers to God is the most limpid, the most tender, and the most solid." He said that the hearts of this community's lovers are cups for the wine of love for the Lord. Any heart that is more purified of engendered things and more merciful toward the faithful is more exalted in the Presence of Exaltation.

Beware—consider the heart exalted! Protect its face from the opacities of caprice and appetite, for it is a lordly subtlety and the gazing place of the Glorified. Muṣṭafā said, "Surely God gazes not on your forms or your acts, but He gazes on your hearts." He said: Do not adorn your faces, for the adornment of faces has no honor with the Exalted Presence. Do not curl your hair, for curled and knotted hair is of no account in that Court. Do not be proud of your forms, for the form has no measure or worth. The only thing of any use is a heart full of pain.

The Pir of the Tariqah said, "For this work, a man is needed with a heart full of pain. Alas that no pain remains in the world, nor in the hearts!"

Concerning His words "*God comes between a man and his heart,*" one of the realizers said, "He is alluding to the hearts of His lovers, the fact that He takes the hearts away from them, protects them for them, and makes them fluctuate through His attributes, as the Prophet said: 'The heart of Adam's child is between two fingers of the All-Merciful—He makes it fluctuate as He will.' Then He seals it with the seal of recognition and impresses it with the imprint of yearning."

(*Kashf* 4:37–38)

Samʿānī waxes poetic on the exalted stature of the heart in relation to "this talk," that is, the story of love, in the following passage. His basic point is simply that the heart was created to love God. If there were no such thing as love for God, there would be no such thing as a heart. Theologically, the point is clear: God created the universe so that He would be recognized and loved. The appropriate response to a merciful, compassionate, and loving God is to love Him, and the place of love is the center of awareness and consciousness, the heart. Hence, the heart was created for love. Having explained that point, Samʿānī comes back to the refrain of tawḥīd: it is His love and His love alone that gets the work done.

In truth and in truth! If this talk had no affinity with the heart, the heart itself would not be the heart. If the sun of this talk did not rise from the horizon of the souls, the Adamite would be just like other existent things. At first there was this talk, in the middle is this talk, at the end will be this talk. Today there is this talk, in the grave this talk, and tomorrow this talk. What is this? A mystery in an intimation, an intimation in a mystery, a gentleness in a severity, an unveiling in a veil, a light in a heart, a gaze toward a heart. What indeed came from this heart that gained worthiness for this gaze? The wealthy gaze on the poor, kings gaze on beggars, and beautiful ornaments are placed on the ugly.

He created this world so that people may know, and He created the afterworld so that people may see. Today they know what they will see tomorrow, and tomorrow they will see what they know today.

"We adorn paradise with Our friends, We adorn Our friends with the heart, and We adorn the heart with Our own beauty.

"You had to come into being so that the world would have light. You had to enter into existence so that lordhood would become manifest. When the prophets became prophets, it was because of your burning. When the angels became angels, it was because of your love. When We brought the noble Qur'an out from the curtain of jealousy into the open plain of exaltation, it was for the ease of your hearts. Moses at Mount Sinai was a trace of your hearts' pull. Muḥammad's *two bows' length* [53:9] was the fruit of your breasts' love.

"If you bring an act of obedience, do not look to the reward, for you are discharging the rightful due of *they love Him*. If I bestow a gift, I will not look at your acts, for I am discharging the rightful due of *He loves them*."

O dervish! When He accepts someone, He wants from him no capital goods. And when He rejects someone, He accepts from him no capital goods. When He takes you from this world, He takes you without capital. When He takes the folk of Islam to that world, He takes them without capital. And when He takes the folk of unbelief, He takes them without capital. Tomorrow when they lift their heads from the dust, the Islam of the Muslims will not be their capital, and the unbelief of the unbelievers will not be their capital.

The words of the angels, "We have not worshiped You with the rightful due of Your worship," throws their capital to the wind. The words of the Adamites, "We have not recognized You with the rightful due of Your recognition," strikes fire in the haystack of their capital. The words of the messengers, "*We have no knowledge*" [5:109], plunders what they knew.

Whatever He straightens, He straightens by His own means. Nothing of your deeds is worthy of joining with His deeds. If it were permissible for your obedience to join with His mercy, He would not rightly be a God. And if it were permissible for your disobedience to join with His punishment, your servanthood would be equal to His lordhood. If He shows mercy, He does so by His generosity, not because of your obedience. If He punishes, He does so by His justice, not because of your disobedience.

Here all things are mixed, but at the Court of Exaltedness there is only unmixed purity. For an incurable pain, nothing profits but unmixed purity. From you He takes the heart, He takes the spirit, He takes possessions. You come to have no known thing and no capital. All the joinings fall away from His acts. "O act of Mine! If you need a joining, here is My desire. O decree of Mine! If you need help, here is My will."

(*Rawḥ* 595–96)

THE COMMANDING SOUL

It was noted that philosophers use the word *nafs*, "soul-self," in a neutral sense to designate the invisible dimension of a being's life and awareness. Although some Sufi authors use *nafs* in this sense, more commonly they employ it to designate the soul's negative tendencies, which turn people away from the heart and spirit. They talk also about ascending levels of soul, and that discussion runs parallel to the philosophical division of souls into an ascending hierarchy of types, leading finally to the soul that is transmuted into an actual intellect. In the Sufi discussion, the lowest level is typically called the commanding soul (*al-nafs al-ammāra*), that is, the soul that commands ugliness (*sūʾ*).

Maybudī talks about four levels of soul in his commentary on the verse that mentions the commanding soul, that is, Zulaykhā's explanation why she tried to tempt Joseph: "*I do not acquit my soul; surely the soul commands ugliness*" (12:53). He cites various references to the commanding soul in the Qur'an and Hadith, including the famous saying in which the Prophet speaks of *al-jihād al-akbar*, "the greater struggle." Then he describes three other sorts of souls: deceiving (*makkāra*), sorcerous (*saḥḥāra*), and peaceful (*muṭmaʾinna*). I quote his description of the first and last levels, which are often discussed in contrast to the middle two, which are rarely encountered.

> The commanding soul has not been placed in the crucible of discipline, nor has the skin of its existence been taken to the tanner. In dealing with God's creatures, it rises up with antagonism and keeps the attributes of a predator. It constantly speaks ill of people, preaches only for its own benefit, and always takes steps in its own desires. It grazes in the world of mortal nature and drinks water from the spring of caprice. It knows nothing other than eating, sleeping, and gratifying its desires.
>
> Concerning the owners of this soul, the Exalted Lord says, "*Leave them to eat, enjoy, and be diverted by hopes—they will soon know*" [15:3]. Their form has a human color, but their attribute is satanic. This is why He says, "*satans of jinn and men*" [6:112].
>
> This soul is a tremendous veil and the disrupter of the religion, a quarry for every sort of ungodliness and the center of evils. If a person is able to escape from it, he will escape by opposing it, for the Splendorous Qur'an reports like this: "*As for him who feared the station of his Lord and forbade the soul its caprice, surely the Garden shall be the refuge*" [79:40–41]. All the prophets and messengers commanded the people to act with severity and to struggle against this soul. Muṣṭafā said, "We have returned from the lesser struggle to the greater struggle." "The most arduous struggle is the struggle against the soul."
>
> *Struggle in God, as is the rightful due of His struggle* [22:78]. The rightful due of struggle is that you do not nurture the attributes of the commanding soul—such as avarice, appetite, greed, rancor, pride, enmity, and hatred—but you hold them in check. Whenever they stick up their heads, you keep them away from yourself with the stone of struggle, just as that chevalier said:
>
> The serpent-soul is coiled around the treasure of your heart—
> strike it with the stone of struggle for the covenant of the heart!

> If you are ill in spirit and fear the jests of the Wheel's turning,
> pour a draft on your spirit from the cup of effort. . . .

> The peaceful soul is the soul of the prophets and the friends of God. It has the bond of protection from sin and the curtain of kind favor. The prophets are inside protection's pavilion, and the friends inside the curtain of guarding and kind favor. If for one instant the bond of protection were to be taken away from the prophets, the same thing would appear from them that appeared from Pharaoh and Haman. If for one moment the guarding, preservation, and kind favor were to be cut off from the friends, all of them would put on the sash of unbelief. If the Arab Prophet had gone forth for a thousand years, and if there had not been *Then he drew close, so He came down* [53:8], where would he have gotten to?
>
> The Pir of the Tariqah said, "O God, I am happy that at first I was not but You were. The fire of finding was mixed with the light of recognizing You, and You stirred up the breeze of proximity from the garden of union. You poured down the rain of solitariness on the dust of mortal nature and burned water and clay with the fire of friendship, thus teaching the recognizer's eyes how to see You."
>
> (*Kashf* 5:92–94)

In his commentary on a plea by Solomon, "*My Lord, forgive me and give me a kingdom such as no one after me may have*" (38:35), Maybudī talks about the correlation between the soul and this world (*al-dunyā*), which the Qur'an typically contrasts with the next world (*al-ākhira*), as in the verse "*No, you prefer the life of this world, but the next world is better and more subsistent*" (87:16–17). Caprice (hawā), derived from the same root as wind (*hawā'*), is a Qur'anic designation for the desires that pull the soul this way and that—any way but toward its true Beloved. The Qur'an says, "*Who is more misguided than he who follows his own caprice without guidance from God?*" (28:50).

> Solomon did not seek the outward kingdom. Rather, he desired only to be king over his own soul, for the king in truth is he who is king over his own soul. Whoever is king over his own soul will not follow his caprice.
>
> Solomon said, "Lord God, just as You put the world's creatures under my hand, so also put this soul under my hand so that I will not be obedient to it and will not go after its caprice. Obeying the soul and obeying the Real are opposites, and opposites do not come together." That chevalier said it beautifully:
>
> With two kiblahs you cannot walk straight on the road of tawḥīd—
> either the Friend's good pleasure, or your own caprice.

Muṣṭafā always used to say, "O God, do not entrust us to our souls for the blink of an eye, or less than that." All sorts of trials reached Joseph the Truthful from the well, the prison, and so on, but he never began to lament as he did from the commanding soul, when it was said, "*Surely the soul commands to ugliness, except as my Lord has mercy*" [12:53]. When Joseph said, "*Take me to Thyself as one submitted*" [12:101], he said so in fear of the commanding soul, not in fear of Satan. For although Satan is the adversary, he wants disobedience from the person of faith, not unbelief. It is the soul that wants unbelief, so it strives for it and calls him to all sorts of caprice and innovation, trying to pull him into unbelief.

In the Qur'an, the Lord of the Worlds mentions two things without saying what they are. He mentions the soul, but He does not say what it is. He mentions this world, but He does not say what it is. The ulama of the religion explain this world with these words: "What blocks you from your Protector—that is your 'this world.'" Whatever holds you back from God is this world. If you do not have tonight's bread but you admire yourself, your self-admiration is this world. If you possess the kingdom of the East and the West and are occupied with God, that is not this world, but rather the afterworld.

As for the soul, it is what Muṣṭafā said: "Your worst enemy is your soul between your two sides." The soul wants caprice, and the heart wants trial. The soul is Satan's gazing place, the heart the All-Merciful's gazing place. The soul is the devil's bench, the heart the storehouse of recognition. He placed the storehouse of recognition next to the enemy, but He kept it under His own guard and preserved it from the enemy.

He brought forth Moses and the Children of Israel and preserved them such that no one's skirt became wet. He put Abraham into the fire, but it did not burn one thread of his robe. In the same way, He placed the heart, which is the storehouse of recognition, next to the soul. Then He guarded and favored it so that the enemy could not touch it.

(*Kashf* 8:361–62)

Maybudī finds reference to the commanding soul in many verses. For example, he interprets God's words to Moses "*I shall show you the abode of the ungodly*" (7:145) in this way:

In the tongue of the folk of recognition, *the abode of the ungodly* alludes to the commanding soul and the ruined heart. The commanding soul is the source of appetites, and the ruined heart is the quarry of heedlessness. Just as no one sits and takes ease in a ruined house, so also obedience does not dwell in a ruined heart, nor does any good settle down there, nor does any

> worship come forth from it. We seek refuge in God from the depths of wretchedness!
>
> (*Kashf* 3:749)

Concerning the verse "O *you who have faith! Look after your own souls. He who is misguided cannot hurt you if you are guided*" (5:105), Maybudī explains that the folk of allusions understand this to mean "Subjugate your own soul before it subjugates you. Busy it with obedience before it busies you with disobedience." Then he goes on to cite sayings about the soul's characteristics.

> The nature of the soul is always to be at rest with this world and to hurry toward disobedience. It counts disobedience as a small thing and is lazy in obedience. It is conceited and acts with eye-service toward the creatures. Within it are found associating others with God, eye-service, and hypocrisy. It is said, "The soul is duplicitous in all its states, hypocritical in most of its states, and an associater in some of its states."
>
> Abū Yazīd Basṭāmī said, "If in that world the Lord says to me, 'Make a wish,' I will ask permission to enter hell to punish this soul, for in this world it has always made me writhe and suffer."
>
> Muṣṭafā said, "Your worst enemy is your soul between your two sides." He said this because when you get along with an enemy, you become secure from his evil, but when you get along with your own soul, you will perish. When you act well toward someone, he will thank you at the resurrection, and if you act badly, he will complain. The state of the soul is the opposite: when you act well toward it in this house, it will be your antagonist in that house, and if you act badly toward it in this house, it will thank you in that house.
>
> (*Kashf* 3:257–58)

In the Qur'anic context, the word *struggle, jihād,* means exerting effort in the path of God, wherever that path may take you. Then, in keeping with various hadiths, we have the greater, or inner, struggle, which targets the commanding soul, and the lesser, or outer, struggle, which is the fight against unbelievers in battle. In Stage Two of his commentary, Maybudī explains the following verse as a legal ruling about booty taken in the struggle against unbelievers. In Stage Three, he explains the difference between the outer and inner struggles.

> *And know that whatever booty you take, one-fifth of it is God's* [8:41]. Booty is the property of unbelievers that Muslims capture in the time of battle and struggle.

> It is said that struggle is of two sorts: the outer struggle and the inner struggle. The outer struggle is against the unbelievers with the sword, and the inner struggle is against the soul with severity. . . .
>
> He who struggles against the unbelievers becomes rich by possessing the booty. He who struggles against the soul becomes rich in the heart. When someone is rich in property, the property is either permitted and a tribulation, or forbidden and a curse. When someone is rich in the heart, his aspiration is greater than this world, and his desire greater than the afterworld.
>
> Muṣṭafā called struggle against the soul more magnificent and greater. He said: "We have returned from the lesser struggle to the greater struggle." This is because you can avoid the enemy, but you cannot avoid the soul. When you get along with an enemy, you will be secure from his evil. If you get along with the soul, you will see your own destruction.
>
> One of the misfortunes of the soul is what Muṣṭafā said: "God gazes not on your forms or your acts, but He gazes on your hearts." He said that He gazes on the heart, but He does not gaze on the soul. It is well known that gazing is the result of love, and not gazing the result of hatred. If the Real did not consider the soul an enemy, He would gaze on it just as He gazes on the heart. This makes it incumbent to consider the soul an enemy.
>
> One must conform with the Real and not gaze on the soul with kindness and love. In the battlefield of struggle, one must act against it severely with the sword of discipline. One must sew shut the eye of its desires with the needle of solitariness and disengagement. This is why Muṣṭafā said, "When someone detests his own soul in God's Essence, God will keep him secure from chastisement on the Day of Resurrection."
>
> (*Kashf* 4:59–60)

Maybudī finds allusions to the soul in the verse "*Your women are your tillage, so come to your tillage as you like*" (2:223). He points out that the verse addresses the desires of the soul, but the desires of the heart are something different. The heart's gaze remains on God, but the soul looks at others (*ghayr*), so God's jealousy (*ghayra*) keeps it away from vision.

> The servant has a soul and a heart. The soul is from the low world, and its root is water and dust. The heart is from the high world, that is, the lordly subtlety, and its stuff is pure light. The soul's station is absence, and the heart's station is witnessing. Muṣṭafā alluded to this with his words "There is no heart that is not between two fingers of God."
>
> God gave the soul, which stays absent, the same living quarters as its similars, and He made this a favor. He said, "*Your women are your tillage, so come to your tillage as you like.*" In another place He said, "*Marry the women who*

> *seem goodly to you"* [4:3]. In another place He said, *"That you may rest in them, and He placed between you love and mercy"* [30:21].
>
> Finding one's portions and inclining toward similars in this manner is the share of the soul, which remains in the lowland of jealousy. As for the heart, it has the station of contemplation, so it is forbidden to incline toward any others or to come down to any creature. Until it cuts itself off from creation and purifies its own secret core from other than the Real, it will not come under these words: *"He loves those who purify themselves"* [2:222]. The Lord of the Worlds loves those who are pure in this manner. He calls them men when He says, *"In it are men who love to purify themselves, and God loves those who purify themselves"* [9:108].
>
> (*Kashf* 1:605)

SELF-ADMIRATION

Discussions of the commanding soul focus on the bad qualities of the self and the necessity of eliminating them by discipline, even if authors acknowledge that nothing will be accomplished without God's grace and solicitude. One of the worst of the soul's bad qualities is to be pleased with itself. As long as we think we are fine, we will never get out of the rut. Especially dangerous is the soul's tendency to think that it is doing God a favor when it obeys His commands. Even worse are the qualities of eye-service (*riyā'*, literally "showing oneself") and hypocrisy (*nifāq*, "selling oneself"), which belong to those who obey the Shariah in order to achieve the desires of their own souls, such as respect and standing in the community.

In the story of Adam's creation, the Qur'an blames two sorts of creatures: the angels and Iblis. It criticizes the angels much more gently, but it does blame them for thinking that they themselves had merit because of their obedient acts. Their self-admiration drove them to question God about Adam's creation and to praise themselves: *"We glorify Thy praise and call Thee holy"* (2:30). As for Iblis, he is clearly the prototype of the self-admiring soul, convinced of his own superiority. His motto is simple: *"I am better than he"* (38:76).

The path of purification involves erasing the soul's forgetfulness and affirming the reality of God and His religious command. Maybudī explains, however, that two things are going on simultaneously. Inasmuch as someone is God's servant, he must assert himself by striving to observe the commands and prohibitions of the Shariah. Inasmuch as he is traveling on the inner path to God, the Tariqah, he must annihilate himself in order to reach the goal, which is the Haqiqah, the Reality Itself. The negative qualities that he is trying to overcome are precisely those tied up with the soul's self-assertion. If one's intention is not pure, undertaking the practices of the Shariah can build up the ego rather than wear it down. Hence, one must have "sincerity" (*ikhlāṣ*, from *khulūṣ*, "purity"), which is keeping the heart pure of others and acting solely for the sake of God. It is to put tawḥīd into practice by eliminating everything but God from the heart. Here Maybudī is commenting on the verse "*That is the last abode—We appoint it for those who do not desire elevation in the earth, nor corruption*" (28:83).

> Tomorrow in the house of the afterworld, those residing in the *seat of truthfulness* [54:55] and those in proximity to the Invincible Presence will be a group who in this world did not seek to be higher and greater than others. Here they considered themselves lesser and smaller than others and never looked upon themselves with the eye of approval. Thus, that chevalier of the Tariqah was returning from the halting place of Arafat. It was said to him, "How did you see the folk of the standing place?"
>
> He replied, "I saw a people whom I would have hoped, had it not been for the fact that I was among them, God would forgive."
>
> O chevalier! Do not look at yourself with the eye of approval! Do not go into the road of "I," for no one has ever seen any benefit from I-ness. What happened to Iblis happened because of I-ness, for he said, "*I am better*" [38:6].
>
> One of the great ones of the religion saw Iblis. He said, "Give me some advice."
>
> He said, "Do not say 'I,' lest you become like me."
>
> This indeed is the road of the wayfarers on the Tariqah and the chevaliers of the Haqiqah. Nonetheless, it is not permissible to throw away I-ness in the road of the Shariah, because things in the Shariah have been turned over to you, and that continues.
>
> Shaykh Abū ʿAbdallāh Khafīf said, "Throwing away I-ness in the Shariah is heresy, and affirming I-ness in the Haqiqah is associating others with God. When you are in the station of the Shariah, say 'I.' When you are on the road of the Haqiqah, say 'He.' Indeed, all is He. The Shariah is the acts, the Haqiqah the states. The acts abide through you, the states are arranged by Him."
>
> (*Kashf* 7:359)

The Qur'an depicts Pharaoh as the worst of men, an Iblis in human form, not least because he made the claim "*I am your Lord the Most High*" (79:24). According to Samʿānī, however, "It is the consensus of the folk of the Tariqah that anyone who sees himself as superior to Pharaoh is worse than Pharaoh" (*Rawḥ* 131). The Pir of the Tariqah put it this way:

> No one is more unworthy on the face of the earth than he who thinks himself worthy, and no one is more impure than he who thinks he is washed. Two things are necessary: need on your part and help from Him. The needy are not rejected, and there is no deception behind the wall of need. Exalted is he who is wounded by Him, and walking on the right road is he who goes with His lamp!
>
> (*Kashf* 7:92, on verse 26:5).

In the hadith literature, being pleased with one's own religiosity is often called "self-admiration" or "considering oneself wonderful" (*ʿujb*). Maybudī defines it in his commentary on a verse that mentions the Muslims' defeat at the battle of Hunain: "*God has already helped you in many homesteads, and on the Day of Hunain, when you admired your own multitude, but it availed you naught*" (9:25).

> Self-admiration is the ghoul of the road. It is the blight of religion, the cause of the disappearance of blessings, the key to separation, and the stuff of heedlessness. You admire yourself when you consider your own obedience important, you consider yourself the source of your service, and you look upon your service with the eye of approval. By the decree of the reports and the fatwa of prophethood, the obedience of such a person will never go any further than his own head.
>
> The Pir of the Tariqah said, "O God, I am trying to avoid two claims, and from each I ask the help of Your bounty: fancying that I have something of my own and fancying that I have a right against You.
>
> "O God, I have risen up from where I was, but I have not yet reached where I want to go.
>
> "O God, anyone who has not yet been killed by selflessness is a corpse. When someone's share of friendship is talk, he has been defrauded. When someone's religion is not the road of spirit and heart, what business has he with the Friend?"
>
> Muṣṭafā said, "If you did not sin, I would be afraid that you would have something worse than sin: self-admiration, self-admiration!"
>
> (*Kashf* 4:122)

Maybudī goes into more detail on the blight of self-admiration in his commentary on the verse "*They recognize God's blessings, then they deny them*" (16:83).

Some people say that this concerns the Muslims. For a time, they occupy themselves with obedience and undertake the path of discipline and struggle according to the Shariah. But in the end, self-admiration comes and ambushes them, destroying their obedience. Their self-admiration is that they consider their obedience and worship as service pleasing to God, and this brings them to exultation and happiness. They think, "This is my attribute and my strength." They remain heedless that it is God's blessings and bounty toward them. Then they do not fear the disappearance of the blessings, and they go forth feeling secure.

Muṣṭafā said, "A man's destruction lies in three things: One is niggardliness that he obeys, another is the soul's caprice that he follows, and the third is admiring himself."

(*Kashf* 5:434)

In his commentary on the allusions contained in the verse "*God desires only to put filth away from you, O folk of the house, and to purify you*" (33:33), Maybudī explains that *filth* alludes to vile acts and base character traits, like niggardliness and avarice, and *putting away* refers to God's activity of replacing vices with the corresponding virtues, like generosity and contentment. Then he says:

And to purify you means to keep you pure from admiring yourself, or considering yourselves pointers to God's door, or gazing upon your own obedience and works.

The Pir of the Tariqah said, "The gaze is two, the human gaze and the All-Merciful gaze. With the human gaze, you look at yourself. With the All-Merciful gaze, the Real looks at you. As long the human gaze does not pack its bags from your makeup, the All-Merciful gaze will not descend into your heart."

Poor wretch, why do you look at your own tainted obedience? How can you measure that against the threshold of His utter lack of needs? Are you unaware that if you gather the good works of all the sincerely truthful in the earth and the obedient acts of all the holy beings in heaven, these will not have the weight of a mosquito's wing in the scales of the majesty of the Majestic? But He, in His unneediness, approves servanthood in the servants and shows them the road. *God is gentle to His servants* [42:19]. He says, "Look at My gentleness, consider mercy as coming from Me, and ask for blessings from Me. *And ask God of His bounty* [4:32]."

(*Kashf* 8:57)

Samʿānī has no use for self-admiration and pious ostentation, which are nothing but eye-service and hypocrisy. Moving forward on the path to God depends on realization (*taḥqīq*), which is to gaze on the Real (ḥaqq) and to perform every act in keeping with His rightful due (ḥaqq).

> I wonder at the empty-headed Qur'an-reciter who makes two cycles of prayer at night and the next day knits the knot of self-seeing on his brow and thinks that his being has bestowed a favor on heaven and earth. All the dust motes of existence say to him, "What a simpleton you are! It is here that they make a Kaabah into an idol temple, turn someone who worshiped for seven hundred thousand years into the forever accursed Satan, and bind Balaam son of Beor—who had God's greatest name in his breast and whose every prayer was answered—in a kennel for dogs."
>
> O clueless of the passing world!
> You little drunkard—you don't know Me.
>
> What is needed is a realizing man, not an unmanly Qur'an-reciter. Anyone who speaks about his own works and looks at them for a single day will not achieve what we are talking about. The unmanly Qur'an-reciter is he who performs two cycles of prayer at night and the next day wants the whole world to hear about it. As for the man of realization, he fills the East and the West with prostrations of sincerity and throws them into the water of unneediness.
>
> A great man said, "I examined all my days, and in my whole life I had not committed more than forty sins. I repented of each sin 300,000 times, but I still walk in danger."
>
> If you could attach nothing to yourself, you would be fine.
>
> Abu'l-Ḥasan Kharaqānī has some magnificent words. He said, "If tomorrow He raises me from the earth and makes all the creatures present in that standing place, I will go to the Ocean of Unity and dive into that ocean so that the One may be, and Abu'l-Ḥasan may not be."
>
> Strive so that you may be angry with yourself for one day, morning until night, and see what the day will bring! The men who came into this path fought a war against themselves, a war that had no way to peace, for they found that the soul is the opposite of the religion. How can a man of the religion make peace with its opposite?
>
> Sometimes they described the soul as a dumb beast, sometimes a serpent, sometimes a dog, sometimes a pig. Every picture they painted was correct—except the picture of religion.
>
> O vile soul, you are lost and deranged—
> whatever touchstone I use, you come up false.

You must see your own obedient acts in the color of disobedience and count all your own meanings as empty claims. You must make your own spirit a broom for the dustbin and see mangy dogs as better than yourself. You must sweep the doorstep of the infidels with your virtues and walk a thousand thousand deserts of disappointment to the end. Otherwise you are simply a knocker on the door. Dust must belong to dust and stay pure from all claims!

God has men who, from the first day of their existence, placed their heads on the threshold of nonexistence in the attribute of poverty and indigence. They never lifted their heads from that threshold. They will rise up from the earth, come to the resurrection, pass over the Narrow Path, and go on to paradise without ever having lifted their heads.

O chevalier! In the daytime someone puts on clothes and comes to the market, and at night he goes back home and takes them off. But what can he do with his skin? If they put a thousand kingly crowns on your head and a thousand royal belts on your waist, what will you do with your own beggarly face and poverty-stricken color?

Tomorrow, the dear ones who had news of these words will be made present in the private chamber of the elect. They will be given flagons of lordly gentleness one after another, and the breeze of union will blow against them from the direction of prosperity. But these dear ones themselves will be saying, "I am the same beggar that I was on the first day."

O dervish! Poverty, indigence, abasement, and lowliness are the fundamental attributes of dust and clay. True, dust sits on the face and can be washed with water, but water cannot take away the color of your face.

Yaḥyā ibn Muʿādh Rāzī said, "My proof is my need, my provision indigence."

No gaze causes greater loss than a gaze that rises up from you and falls back on you. Such a gaze is the foundation of all loss. As for the gaze that goes far from you, that is the foundation of all gain.

(*Rawḥ* 88–90)

The word *dervish* (*darwīsh*), the Persian translation of the Arabic *faqīr*, means poor. The expression derives from Qur'anic verses that say that human beings are utterly in need of God, while He has no need for them. The Sufis called themselves fakirs or dervishes to acknowledge their own nothingness. Maybudī, drawing some of his remarks from Samʿānī's commentary on the divine name Unneedy, explains the meaning of poverty in his explanation of the verse "*And God is the Unneedy, and you are the poor*" (47:38).

God has no need for your obedience, and you are the poor toward His mercy. God is the Unneedy and has no need for anyone. He is One and has no associate or partner. He is the Invincible, and no one has the color of union with Him. He is the Owner of the Kingdom, and no matter what He does, no one has the gall to protest or the means to fight back.

If you were to gather all the good works of the sincerely truthful among the folk of the earth and all the obedient acts of the holy ones of heaven, they would not have the weight of a mosquito's wing in the scales of the majesty of the Possessor of Majesty. Beware! Never look at your own distracted works or your own tiny intellect with the eye of self-admiration. When you seek Him, seek Him through His bounty, not your intellect and knowledge. *Were it not for God's bounty toward you, and His mercy, none of you would ever have become pure* [24:21].

O chevalier! Exaltedness is His attribute, and unneediness His description. How can knowledge, understanding, and intellect have the gall to open up before His exaltedness? Bounty is His attribute, and exaltedness His attribute. Who opens up before His attributes? It is His attributes themselves that open up. When someone seeks refuge in intellect, the attribute of exaltedness comes forth and sends him back in despair. When someone seeks refuge in bounty, it escorts him to the highest of the High Chambers.

When someone leans on his own works, he will be left to himself. When someone clings to His bounty and mercy, he will be taken beyond the Gardens of Bliss to the *seat of truthfulness at an Omnipotent King* [54:55].

The Prophet said, "None of you will be saved by his deeds."

They said, "Not even you, O Messenger of God?"

He said, "Not even I, unless God envelops me with His mercy."

(*Kashf* 9:201–2)

ASCENDING LEVELS OF SELF

The simplest way to conceive of a human being is dualistically: body and spirit (or body and heart). Many authors talk this way, but many offer subtler analyses as well, typically speaking of ascending levels in a manner similar to philosophical analyses of the several levels of soul. Clearly, the spirit is "above" the body, because it derives from the luminous divine breath, whereas the body derives from dark clay. As for the commanding soul, it is tightly bound up with the body. Here are typical passages in which Maybudī describes three levels of self:

They ask you about the spirit [17:85]. Man is body, heart, and spirit. The body is the place of the Trust, the heart is the threshold of being addressed, and the spirit is the center-point of contemplation. All blessings are scattered on the body; its nourishment is food and drink. All favors are gifts for the heart;

its nourishment is remembering and mentioning the Friend. All vision and contemplation are the share of the spirit; its nourishment is seeing the Friend. The body is under the severity of power, the heart in the grasp of the attributes, and the spirit in the embrace of exaltedness—the carpet of intimacy spread, the candle of sympathy lit, the beginningless Friend having lifted the veil.

(*Kashf* 5:626)

Who sees you when you stand up [26:218]: "I see My friends constantly, and nothing of them is veiled from Me. Were something to be veiled, they would not stay alive."

O chevaliers! Know that the soul lives by serving Him, the heart lives by gazing on Him, and the spirit lives by loving Him. The soul that does not live by serving Him is idle, the heart that does not live by gazing on Him is carrion, the spirit that does not live by loving Him is captive to death.

(7:174)

Blessed is He in whose hand is the kingdom [67:1]. The kingdom of human nature is one thing, the kingdom of the heart another thing, and the kingdom of the spirit still another. Human nature runs the kingdom in this world, the heart runs the kingdom in the next world, and the spirit runs the kingdom in the World of the Haqiqah.

The kingdom of human nature is this: *Surely the life of this world is but play, diversion, and adornment* [57:20]. The kingdom of the heart is this: *He loves them, and they love Him* [5:54]. The kingdom of the spirit is this: *Faces on that day radiant, gazing on their Lord* [75:22–23].

(10:179)

Authors commonly speak of a fourth and deeper level of self, the secret (*sirr*), which in this meaning I translate as "secret core." Anṣārī defines it as "man's quintessence with the Real": "It can never be expressed with the tongue, nor can anyone recount it of himself" (*Maydān* 321). ʿAlī ibn ʿUthmān Hujwīrī (d. ca. 1077), author of one of the earliest Persian books on Sufism, *The Unveiling of the Veiled* (*Kashf al-maḥjūb*), provides a good example of how the word was used in a mythic account of love's origin translated from a lost Arabic *Book of Love* (*Kitāb al-maḥabba*) by the Sufi teacher ʿAmr ibn ʿUthmān Makkī (d. 903–4). The passage belongs to a relatively short discussion of love, which is situated in the midst of a chapter on the ritual prayer (*ṣalāt*).

In *The Book of Love*, ʿAmr ibn ʿUthmān al-Makkī wrote that God created the hearts seven thousand years before the bodies and kept them in the station

> of proximity. He created the spirits seven thousand years before the hearts and kept them in the garden of intimacy. He created the secret cores seven thousand years before the spirits and kept them in the degree of union. Every day He disclosed His beauty three hundred sixty times to the secret cores, He gazed upon the spirits three hundred sixty times, making them hear words of love, and He made manifest three hundred sixty subtleties to the hearts.
>
> Then the three of them looked at the realm of being and saw no one more honored than themselves, so vanity and exultation appeared in them. Because of this, the Real tested them. He jailed the secret core in the spirit, He imprisoned the spirit in the heart, and He restrained the heart in this body. Then He compounded them with intellect, He sent the prophets, and He gave commandments. They all started seeking their own stations. The Real commanded them to pray. When the body began to pray, the heart joined with love, the spirit reached proximity, and the secret core settled down in union.
>
> (*Kashf al-maḥjūb*, 453)

Still other levels are often added to the self's structure, especially from the fourteenth century onward in discussions of the "seven subtleties." A typical list gives body, soul, spirit, heart, secret core, hidden (*khafī*), and most hidden (*akhfā*). In the following, Maybudī comments on the Qur'anic source of two of these terms, the verse "*If you speak aloud, yet surely He knows the secret [core] and the most hidden*" (20:7). The first paragraph is taken from Qushayrī's *Subtle Allusions*, and the rest is Maybudī's free translation and commentary.

> The soul is not informed of what is inside the heart, the heart is not informed of the secrets of the spirit, and the spirit has no access to the realities of the secret core. As for that which is most hidden, no one is aware of it but the Real.
>
> What does the soul know about what is placed in the treasure-house of the heart? What does the heart know about the subtleties inside the sanctuary of the spirit? What does the spirit know about the deposits in the pavilion of the secret core? What does the secret core know about the realities in the most hidden?
>
> The heart is the house of recognition, the spirit is the target of contemplation, and the secret core is the place where love puts down its saddlebags. As for the most hidden, the Real knows what it is—people's imaginations and understanding are empty of knowing it.
>
> (*Kashf* 6:112)

One of God's names is Provider (*razzāq*), the one who gives everything its daily bread and conveys to each level of the human self appropriate nourishment. We have seen that God inspires the soul *to its depravity and its godwariness* (91:8). He alone knows what sort of inspiration will reach souls, hearts, and spirits. He provides, but He does not provide the same things to each person. Maybudī explains in his commentary on the verse "*And God has preferred some of you over others in provision*" (16:71).

> The provision of the soul is one thing, the provision of the heart another, and the provision of the spirit still another. For some the provision of the soul is the success of obedience, and for some it is abandonment to disobedience. For some the provision of the heart is the heart's presence with constant remembrance, and for some it is the attribute of heedlessness with constant hardness. For some the provision of the spirit is the perfection of recognition and the limpidness of love, and for some it is love for this world and occupation with attachments.
>
> (*Kashf* 5:423)

Given that God's provision goes back to the beginningless divine knowledge, no one can say how He will inspire a human self, nor how His inspiration will change, for nothing in the universe stays fixed in one situation. The interaction between the complementary divine attributes—majesty and beauty, gentleness and severity—demands that souls undergo fluctuation "between two fingers of the All-Merciful." In his commentary on the just-mentioned verse that speaks of God inspiring the soul with depravity and godwariness, Maybudī refers to the bewilderment that arises from the constant flux of life and awareness. He begins by describing the human microcosm.

> The poor Adamite who does not recognize his own exaltation and eminence! Of this dust-dwelling frame he finds access only to a name, a body, a trace. He does not know what secret lies in His words "*And We honored the children of Adam*" [17:70], what wisdom is found in His words "*And He created you in stages*" [71:14], what explication is seen in *the most beautiful stature* [95:4], what face-to-face vision is found in *He formed you, so He made your forms beautiful* [40:64].
>
> O chevalier! Of the human makeup and the Adamic individual, first think about the form. What artisanry the Lord of the worlds has shown to a drop of spilled water! What diverse paintings were achieved by "*Be!*" *and it comes to be* [36:82]! Mutually similar limbs, opposites like unto each other—each one He has made in its own scale.

He has adorned each limb with one sort of beauty, no more than its limit, no less than its measure. To each He gave an attribute, in each He placed a potency: the senses in the brain, splendor on the forehead, beauty in the nose, sorcery in the eye, sauciness on the lips, comeliness in the cheek, perfect loveliness in the hair. It is not clear whether the artisanry of the natures is more beautiful, or whether the governance of form giving is sweeter. He has created so many marvels and wonders from a drop of water! The intelligent man gazes on His artisanry, but the heedless man is asleep.

Once you have looked with the outward eye on the marks that bear witness to His power, look also with the inward eye on the subtleties of His wisdom. Then you will see the proofs of love and the traces of solicitude. The Adamic nature is the world of form, but the heart is the world of the attributes. The Adamic nature is the heart's shell, but the heart is the shell of the secret core's center-point.

Just as the orbs and bodies of the cosmos are bewildered by the form of the Adamic nature, so also the Adamic nature is bewildered by the form of the heart, the heart is bewildered by the secret core's center-point, and the secret core stays on the edge between annihilation and subsistence. Sometimes it dwells in the courtyard of annihilation, sometimes in the robe of subsistence. When in annihilation, it has nothing but burning and need. When in subsistence, it has nothing but caresses and mysteries. When in annihilation, it says, "Who is more miserable than I?" When in subsistence, it says, "Who is greater than I?"

When my gaze falls on my clay,
  I see nothing worse in the world.
When I pass beyond my attributes,
  I look at myself from the Throne.

(*Kashf* 10:508–9)

Part Two

The Life of Love

4

The Search

In the worldview of tawḥīd, everything comes from God and goes back where it came from. The unique status of human beings has to do with the fact that they have a certain freedom of choice in going back.

The creative command is timeless, which is to say that it is always being issued. The universe—defined as "everything other than God," including paradise and hell—goes on forever, even if our world disappears. All things in the cosmos come into existence by the creative command, for nothing has any being of its own. Once something comes to exist, it either disappears or is renewed by the command. The Ash'arite theologians offered a version of this teaching that historians have labeled occasionalism or atomism. In the Ash'arite view, true causality is vertical. Horizontal causality—the efficient causality that is the focus of modern science—is simply an appearance. Much more sophisticated theories of causality, taking both the vertical and horizontal sorts into account, were offered by later thinkers such as Ibn al-ʿArabī and Mullā Ṣadrā.

Scholars of Neoplatonism and medieval Christianity are familiar with the doctrine of *exitus* and *reditus*, the notion that everything comes from the One and returns to It. As noted in Chapter 1, the Islamic version is often called the Origin and Return (*mabdaʾ wa maʿād*). Both the coming and the going are driven by the creative command, because creatures receive their existence and reality from the Creator. In human beings, however, another factor enters the picture: the religious command, the moral imperative. God commands people to act in certain ways.

Traditional philosophers have deduced the necessity of right activity by analyzing the structure of the universe and the self. The resulting natural law has long been part of the Western tradition—not to speak of the Indian or Chinese—and is reflected in the Enlightenment urge to build a perfect society based on "self-evident truths." For Muslim scholars, the only self-evident truth is tawḥīd: the Ultimate Reality is one, everything derives from It, and everything goes back to It.

What is certainly not self-evident is the thingness of the things: What exactly is a thing? How exactly does it come forth from God? When it comes into existence, what pertains to its own, inherent thingness, making it distinct from every other thing? Philosophers addressed these questions by investigating the reality of being qua being and distinguishing between the Necessary Being and contingent things. Sufi theologians talked rather of the divine names and attributes. The issue of being per se did not become prominent in Sufi thought until Ibn al-ʿArabī.

Back to the human situation: we are addressed by the moral imperative, first in the form of prophetic messages, and second in the form of our own innate intelligence. As infants and children, we cannot grasp the significance of the moral commandments, so we are not held responsible for our actions. Once we reach young adulthood, however, the ability to discern between right and wrong comes into play, as does the presence of the prophetic messages. The Origin brought us into being, and we are now headed back to It with a newly acquired freedom of choice. To the extent that we are free, we are responsible. How free we are remains an open question. As for what we should do with whatever freedom we do have, the religious command responds, "*Say: 'If you love God, follow me; God will love you'*" (3:31). Prophetic guidance provides the only sure path to salvation.

THE MIʿRĀJ

Authors who talk about traveling the path to God recognize that outward activity is a reflection of an inner journey, an ascent that goes by way of soul, spirit, heart, secret core, and beyond. The paradigm of the journey is provided by the Prophet's miʿrāj, a word that literally means "ascending ladder."

Some of the philosophers, like Avicenna, were inclined to interpret the miʿrāj as a symbol or a metaphor, that is, as an imagistic way to represent the soul's realization of its potential and its transformation into an actual intellect.[1] Theologians and Sufis tended to take the literal truth of the ascent for granted. Muḥammad provided the model to be emulated, for he was the Logos embodied, the one who actualized all possible perfections. He traveled up through the spheres of the macrocosm while simultaneously plumbing the depths of his own secret core. Scholars in later times who described the ascending levels of the self as seven subtleties did so not least because the Prophet climbed through the seven spheres in his journey to God.

The Qur'an talks of all the prophets as models to be emulated, not simply Muḥammad. The theme is treated extensively by authors such as Maybudī and Samʿānī and provides, for example, the backdrop to the most influential books of Ibn al-ʿArabī: *The Ringstones of Wisdom* (*Fuṣūṣ al-ḥikam*) and *The Meccan Openings* (*al-Futūḥāt al-makkiyya*). Samʿānī explains why the Qur'an recounts the tales of the prophets:

> What wisdom is there in His speaking to you of Adam, Noah, Abraham, Moses, and Jesus? He is warming up the place of your hopes in Him and fanning the fire in the chamber of your patience. When someone sits down in front of a hungry man and eats delicious food, his mouth starts to water. "O friend! Though My goods are expensive and the poor can't buy them, well, there's no law against hoping."
>
> (*Rawḥ* 137)

From one standpoint, Muḥammad's ascent to God fulfills the promise of the Qur'an's descent from God. The Book was sent down so that people could climb up. Muḥammad forged the path, and others follow. When teachers describe the ascending stations on the path, they are mapping out the levels through which the soul must pass in its voluntary journey back to the One.

In one long passage of *Repose of the Spirits*, Samʿānī comments on the verses of Surah Najm that are taken as referring to the miʿrāj. He offers several interpretations for each verse, highlighting the nature of Muḥammad's entrance into the Divine Presence. Like many others, he understands the verse "*The eyesight did not swerve*" (53:17) as a reference to the Prophet's perfect love for God, which prevented him from gazing on the others (*aghyār*), the obstacles to one-pointed vision. Here is an excerpt:

> *He stood upright when he was on the highest horizon* [53:6–7]. His soul stood up straight in conformity with his heart, his heart stood up straight in conformity with his secret core, and his secret core stood up straight in conformity with the Real. There is no way to be the companion of something straight without straightness.
>
> "If his soul had not stood up straight with his heart, We would not have given that heart to that soul. If his heart had not stood up straight with his secret core, We would not have given that secret core to that heart. And if his secret core had not stood up straight with Us, We would not have become the companion of that secret core." . . .

Concerning the verse "*Then he drew close, so He came down, until he was two bows' length away, or closer*" [53:8–9], Jaʿfar al-Ṣādiq said, "When the beloved Prophet approached in utmost nearness, the utmost awe overcame him, so his Lord was gentle with the utmost gentleness, for the utmost awe can be endured only with the utmost gentleness."

God says, "*God warns you of Himself*" [3:30]. This is a word of awe. Then God says, "*And He is clement toward the servants*" [3:30]. This is a word of gentleness. In the same way, He says, "*In the name of God,*" a word of awe, and then at once He says, "*the All-Merciful, the Ever-Merciful,*" which are words of clemency and mercy, giving subsistence to souls and spirits. In the same way, when God said to Moses, "*Surely I am your Lord*" [20:12], Moses's heart was awestruck. But when He said, "*Take off your shoes*" [20:12], his spirit relaxed and his mind quieted.

That paragon reached the way station of *Then he drew close.* Then he stepped onto the carpet of *so He came down* [53:8]. He went up to the *two bows' length* of proximity and leaned back on the exalted cushion of *or closer* [53:9]. He heard the mystery, tasted the wine, reached contemplation, fled from the two worlds, and took ease with the Friend. *Then He revealed to His servant what He revealed* [53:10].

O dervish! Whoever takes along the gift of *the eyesight did not swerve* [53:17] will bring back the bestowal of *He revealed to His servant what He revealed.* In other words, there was what there was, and there happened what happened, and no one is aware of those mysteries. "The breasts of the free are the treasuries of the secrets."

(*Rawḥ* 212–13)

If, in one respect, Muḥammad's ascent delineates the stages of the path to God, in another respect it is the counterpart of Adam's fall. God sent Adam down into the world so that he and his children could rise up. Adam's creation marks the beginning of the story of love, and Muḥammad's miʿrāj its culmination. He created human beings because He loves them and wants them to love Him in return. He created Adam in *the most beautiful stature* (95:4) as the prototype for all his children. He created Muḥammad as the *beautiful exemplar* (33:21) for his community to follow. He made the last prophet actualize the fullness of human perfection by placing within him the individual perfections scattered throughout all previous prophets. The mark of his perfection is that during the miʿrāj, he reached the station of *two bows' length, or closer* (53:9). Samʿānī explains the relationship between Adam's descent and Muḥammad's ascent:

O dervish! Paradise was the steed of union and the pavilion of proximity. The enviers set out to upset the bliss and, perhaps, to drive Adam out with trickery.

The gentleness of the Presence said, "Wait and see. We will cut the roots of doubt and eliminate the substance of the enviers' envy. We will take Adam the Chosen to the world of transactions on the pretext of a slip. Then it will be spread about in the world that he is in prison and bondage there, in separation and distance. We will set up the pavilion of secrets, secret to secret, without the intrusion of others. We will bring the goblets of gentle favors, one after another, and root out the intrusion of the enemies' accusations. We will give his outwardness over to the policeman of *Fall down!* [2:36] and bring his inwardness into the exalted encampment of bounty. We will give him this goblet of joy moment by moment: *If guidance comes to you from Me, then those who follow My guidance, no fear shall be upon them* [2:38]."

This is a marvelous story. It was said to Adam, "*Fall down!*" It was said to Muṣṭafā, "Ascend!": "O Adam! Go to the earth so that the world of dust may settle down in the awesome majesty of your sultanate. O Muḥammad! Come up to heaven so that the summit of the spheres may be adorned by the beauty of your contemplation. The secret here is that I said, '*Fall down!*' to your father so that I could say, 'Ascend!' to you. Sit on the steed of aspiration and take the top of the spheres as the dust on the carpet beneath your blessed feet. Travel away from the corporeal and the spiritual. Gaze on Me without yourself."

(*Rawḥ* 206)

In the context of tawḥīd, the Real alone is truly real—all else partakes of unreality. Talking about an encounter with the Real may appear to contradict His utter transcendence and incomparability. This does not slow down the Qur'an, however, for it mentions man's meeting with God in many contexts, such as the verse "*O Man! You are toiling toward your Lord with toil, and you shall encounter Him*" (84:6).

If we take God's transcendence into account, creation is nothing compared to His reality—nothing is real but the Real. If we take God's immanence, mercy, and compassion into account, creation has a certain reality. In fact, all created things hang between existence and nonexistence. If we look at things without regard to God, they appear to exist, at least for the time being. When we compare them to the infinity of the Divine Being, they have no existence whatsoever.

As for the encounter with God, it is driven by the necessities of tawḥīd—the Origin and the Return. No one claims that a created, temporal, newly arrived thing will reach the Eternal. The Eternal remains forever eternal and transcendent, and the newly arrived remains forever newly arriving. Creatures can have no being of their own, so they depend on the creative command to exist. If people can encounter God, it is because He in His mercy bestows one bounty after another. The miʿrāj was a gift, from start to finish. In no way does it represent an accomplishment of the Prophet. So, too, everything that we have and can have is a gift. In Himself, God stays in His transcendence, but through His immanence, He bestows blessings on His creatures, on some more than others. Even Muḥammad, the greatest human being, is nothing compared to God. Compared to us, however, he is *a mercy to the worlds* (21:107), *a light-giving lamp* (33:46), a manifestation of God's guidance. With him, as with all creatures, one must take into account the simultaneous influence of mercy and wrath, gentleness and severity. Samʿānī explains:

> When you look at the Real's power, all nonexistent things take on the color of existence. When you look at the Real's exaltedness, all existent things take on the color of nonexistence.
>
> You should not suppose that whatever He knew, He said; whatever He could do, He did; and whatever He had, He showed. The existent things and the created things are a sample of His power. The revelations and inspirations are an iota of His knowledge. He sent you a few rulings of His knowledge, but your knowledge does not reach Him. In the same way, He put together a few clods of earth, but His power did not reach its end. He showed you a bit of yellow and red, but His treasury did not cease to be. If He were to create a thousand thousand Thrones, Footstools, heavens, and earths, He would not have made apparent an iota of His power. "Your power is a petitioner, My power transcendent. Your time is finite, My road infinite."
>
> On the night of the miʿrāj, the Messenger went to *two bows' length*. But for perfection, majesty, and tremendousness, *two bows' length* is the same as the bottom of the earth.
>
> When you look from the community toward Muṣṭafā, he shows you this face: "I am the master of Adam's children." When you look from the Real's majesty toward Muḥammad, he shows you this face: "I am the son of a woman of Quraysh who used to eat jerky."
>
> In the road of the Real's bounty, he reached *two bows' length*, but in the road of the Real's exaltedness, he was the lowest of the low. When His caresses arrive, the bottom of the earth has the same color as the highest of the high. When His majesty charges forth, *two bows' length* is like the bottom of the earth.
>
> (*Rawḥ* 515–16)

THE PRACTICE OF TAWḤĪD

The Qur'an tells people that if they love God, they should follow Muḥammad. Part of following him entails both climbing up the ladder and coming back down into the world. At its most practical level, the miʿrāj appears to the faithful as his Sunnah, which has clear, outward forms. The jurists have always busied themselves with codifying the forms and activities, frequently imagining that it is enough to follow the rules in order to live a life completely pleasing to God. Generally, however, scholars trained in the Islamic sciences knew that the rules deal strictly with activity. The difficult part of the Sunnah pertains to the internalization of the Prophet's character traits. The rules are set down in the Shariah, but the path of internalization is set down by the Tariqah. Both *Shariah* and *Tariqah* mean "path" or "road."

From around the twelfth century, it became common for authors to describe the Islamic tradition as having three basic dimensions: the Shariah (the broad avenue), the Tariqah (the narrow path), and the Haqiqah (the Divine Reality). In the eleventh century, the scheme was not so clear, nor does one encounter the purported hadith "The Shariah is my words, the Tariqah my acts, and the Haqiqah my states." Nonetheless, the terminology is used, not least because it provides a simple scheme with which to separate the dimensions of human concern as depicted in the Qur'an and the Sunnah.

One of the many verses referring to Muḥammad's role as the model to be followed is this: "*Whatever the Messenger gives you, take. Whatever he forbids you, forgo*" (59:7). Maybudī comments:

> The command came from the Real: "Whatever drink comes to you from the auspicious hand of Muḥammad the Arab, the Hashimite prophet, take, for your life lies in that. Read the tablet that he writes, learn servanthood from his character traits, take seeking from his aspiration, put his Sunnah to work, walk behind him in all states. The final goal of the traveling of the servants and the perfection of their states is My love, and My love lies in following the Sunnah and conduct of your prophet. Whoever walks straight in his tracks is in reality My friend. *Say: 'If you love God, follow me; God will love you'* [3:31]."
>
> (*Kashf* 10:42)

Following Muḥammad means putting tawḥīd into practice on the three levels of the Shariah, the Tariqah, and the Haqiqah. The goal is to undergo a transformation of the soul that leads to the one-pointed focus on the Haqiqah described in the verse "*The eyesight did not swerve*" (53:17). Discussions of the

Tariqah address the manner of passing beyond the world's multiplicity and the soul's darkness in order to find the spirit's light and the secret core's unity. Authors use a variety of terms to designate the desired state of one-pointedness. Among them is solitariness (*tafrīd*), which is often taken as a virtual synonym for the practice of tawḥīd. Maybudī defines it as "making the aspiration one-pointed in both remembering and gazing" (*Kashf* 5:475). Samʿānī calls it "becoming solitary [*fard*] for the Real" (*Rawḥ* 346). Another common term for one-pointedness is "togetherness" (*jamʿ*), which is contrasted with "dispersion" (*farq*), our normal state of consciousness. Maybudī uses these terms to explain the meaning of the verse "*Say 'God,' then leave them playing in their plunging*" (6:91). He and others see the admonition as an explicit command to put tawḥīd into practice.

> This is an eloquent allusion to the reality of solitariness, the center-point of togetherness, making the aspiration one-pointed, recognizing the Real as one, and turning away from others toward Him. *Say "God," then leave them:* Keep the heart turned toward Him and leave aside the others. What does someone seized by His love have to do with others? In this work, this world and the next are like a wall, and for the recognizer, talking about the two is nothing but defect and shame.
>
> (*Kashf* 3:425)

It is commonly said that tawḥīd has levels, the lowest of which is saying the first Shahadah, that is, voicing the words "No god but God," and the highest of which is to be one with the Real. A good example is provided by Muḥammad Ghazālī, who talks of four levels in "The Book on Tawḥīd and Trust," the thirty-fifth chapter of *Giving Life*. The passage illustrates Ghazālī's typical explanation of the proper role of Kalam, which was, after all, a discipline aimed at defining and defending right belief. By calling belief (*iʿtiqād*) a knot (*ʿuqda*) on the heart, Ghazālī is referring to the word's etymology. To believe in a doctrine is to tie one's heart and thoughts to a given formulation of truth. Note that Ghazālī is not talking about faith (*īmān*), which will be discussed in the next chapter, but rather the dogmas that color one's understanding of the objects of faith.[2]

> The first level of tawḥīd is that a man says with his tongue, "There is no god but God" while his heart is heedless of that, or he denies it, as in the case of the tawḥīd of the hypocrites.
>
> The second is that his heart assents to the truth of the words, just as the commonality of Muslims assent to its truth.

The third is that he witnesses it by way of the unveiling of the Real's light. This is the station of those given proximity. It is that they see many things, but despite their many-ness, they see them emerging from the One, the Severe.

The fourth is that he sees nothing in existence but One. This is the witnessing of the sincerely truthful. The Sufis call it annihilation in tawḥīd, for since he sees nothing but One, he does not see himself either. He does not see himself because he is immersed in tawḥīd, so he is annihilated from himself in tawḥīd, meaning that he is annihilated from seeing himself and creation.

The first level is tawḥīd by the tongue alone. In this world, it protects its possessor from sword and spear.

The second level is tawḥīd voiced by someone who believes in his heart what is understood from the words, so his heart is empty of giving the lie to it. This is because of the manner in which his heart has been tied in a knot, within which there is no expansiveness or spaciousness. Nonetheless, if he is loyal to it, it will guard him against chastisement in the next world—so long as the knot is not weakened by disobedient acts.

There are various stratagems that aim at weakening and undoing the knot, and these are known as innovation [*bid'a*]. There are also stratagems with which undoing and weakening may be prevented and which aim to firm up and strengthen the heart's knot. These are called Kalam, and the person who recognizes these is called a Kalam expert [*mutakallim*]. He is the opposite of the innovator. His goal is to prevent the innovator from undoing the knot in the hearts of the common people.

The Kalam expert may be singled out for the name *tawḥīd-voicer* in respect of the fact that his Kalam defends the understanding of the word *tawḥīd* for the hearts of the common people so that their knot will not be untied.

The third tawḥīd is voiced by someone who witnesses only one Actor, for the Real is unveiled to him as He is, so he sees that in reality there is no actor but One. The Haqiqah has been unveiled to him as It is. It is not that he has burdened his heart by knotting it with what is understood from the word *Haqiqah*, for that is the level of the common people and the Kalam experts. There is no difference between the Kalam experts and the common man in belief, only in the art of putting words together to prevent the stratagems of the innovator from undoing the knot.

The fourth is a tawḥīd voiced by someone in the sense that nothing is present in his witnessing other than the One. He does not see the all in the respect that it is many but rather in the respect that it is one. This is the furthest limit in tawḥīd.

(*Iḥyā'* 4:359–60)

Anṣārī often speaks of tawḥīd as having three levels. In *One Hundred Fields*, he makes it the sixty-ninth stage of the path to God, and he divides it into three sorts: saying that there is One, knowing the One, and seeing the One. In *Way Stations of the Travelers*, he places it at the very end of the path, the one-hundredth way station.

> The Chapter on Tawḥīd [100]. God says, "*God bears witness that there is no god but He*" [3:18]. Tawḥīd is to declare God incomparable with new arrival. In this path, the ulama have said what they have said, and the realizers have made the allusions that they have made, only with the intention of rectifying tawḥīd. All other states and stations are accompanied by defects.
>
> Tawḥīd has three faces. The first face is the tawḥīd of the common people, which is rectified by the marks that bear witness. The second face is the tawḥīd of the elect, which becomes firm through the realities. The third face is the tawḥīd that abides through eternity; it is the tawḥīd of the elect of the elect.
>
> The first tawḥīd is to bear witness that there is no god but God alone, without associate, the One, the Sanctum, who *does not give birth, nor was He given birth to, nor does He have any equal* [112:3–4]. This is the manifest, open tawḥīd that negates the greatest associationism. Upon it, the kiblah is set up, blame becomes obligatory, blood and property are spared, the abode of submission becomes separate from the abode of unbelief, and the creed of the common people is rectified. Even if they do not undertake the rightful due of inference after having become safe from confusion and bewilderment by truthfully bearing witness, their creed is rectified by the heart's acceptance. This is the tawḥīd of the common people, which is rectified by the marks bearing witness, which are the Message and God's artisanries. It becomes obligatory through hearing, it is found through the Real's showing, and it grows through contemplation of the marks bearing witness.
>
> The second tawḥīd becomes firm through the realities. It is to eliminate outward causes and to rise beyond the contentions of intellects and attachment to the marks bearing witness. It is that you bear witness to tawḥīd with evidence, not because of trust, nor as a means of approaching salvation; that you witness the precedence of the Real in His decree and His knowledge, His putting things in their places, His attaching them to their times, His concealing them in their traces; and that you realize the recognition of defects and travel on the path of eliminating new arrival. This is the tawḥīd of the elect, and is rectified by the knowledge of annihilation. It becomes limpid in the knowledge of togetherness, and it attracts to the tawḥīd of the lords of togetherness.
>
> As for the third tawḥīd, it is the tawḥīd that the Real has singled out for Himself and considered worthy of His own measure. He has lit up a flash of

it in the secret cores of some of His limpid ones, silenced them in describing it, and made them incapable of disseminating it. The allusions of the tongues of the alluders say that it is the elimination of new arrival and the affirmation of eternity, even though in this tawḥīd the intimation itself is a defect that must be eliminated for tawḥīd to be rectified.

It is this tawḥīd around which revolve the allusions of the tongues of the ulama on this path. Though they have embellished this tawḥīd with descriptions and divided it into divisions, expressing it increases its concealment, describing it increases estrangement, and expanding upon it increases difficulty. It is this tawḥīd toward which the folk of discipline and the lords of the states rise up; it is this that is intended by the folk of reverence and is meant by those who speak from within togetherness itself. With it, allusions are cut away. No tongue then speaks of it, and no expression alludes to it, for this tawḥīd is beyond that to which any engendered being alludes, or any time touches, or any cause conveys.

In times past, a questioner asked me about the tawḥīd of the Sufis. I answered with these three lines:

No one has voiced the unity of the One,
  for everyone who voices it denies it.
The tawḥīd of those who talk of its description
  is a loan voided by the One.
His tawḥīd is His voicing unity—
  its describer's description deviates.

(*Manāzil* 110–13)

Maybudī often discusses tawḥīd, usually speaking of three levels and sometimes two. In one long passage, he distinguishes between the general tawḥīd of Muslim belief and the specific tawḥīd of the recognizers. Then he provides a description of God and His attributes on the basis of transmitted reports. Finally, he turns to the realization of tawḥīd through presence with the Real. He is commenting on the verse "*Worship God, and associate nothing with Him*" (4:36). He takes it as an assertion of tawḥīd because associating others with God, *shirk*, is the opposite of tawḥīd. Negating the notion that God has partners is to affirm tawḥīd.

This verse begins by mentioning tawḥīd, which is the root of the sciences, the secret of the recognitions, the substance of the religion, the foundation of the submission, and the partition between enemy and friend. Any act of obedience without tawḥīd has no value or weight, and its outcome will be nothing but darkness and captivity. Any act of disobedience along with tawḥīd will yield nothing other than familiarity and brightness.

Tawḥīd is that you say that God is One and that you be one for Him. Saying One is the submitters' tawḥīd, and being one is the stuff of the recognizers' tawḥīd. The submitters' tawḥīd drives away the devil, washes away sin, and opens up the heart. The recognizers' tawḥīd cuts away attachments, washes away the creatures, and brings forth the realities.

The submitters' tawḥīd takes advice, opens the door, and gives fruit. The recognizers' tawḥīd effaces the customs of human nature and burns away the veil of mortal nature so that the breeze of familiarity may blow, the beginningless reminder may arrive, and the friend may gaze upon the Friend.

The submitters' tawḥīd is that you bear witness to God's one Essence, pure attributes, and beginningless names and marks. He is the God other than whom there is no god, the Creator of heaven and earth other than whom there is no other actor. No one has loyalty like Him in the whole cosmos. He is a Lord who is above all in measure, beyond all in Essence and attributes. From the Beginningless to the Endless He is the greatest Lord. When intellect holds that something is impossible, God has perfect power over it. His power makes no use of contrivance, and His self-standing has no change of state. In the kingdom, He is safe from disappearance, and in Essence and attributes, He is transcendent.

You will never see any created thing without marks of deficiency and faultiness, but the Eternal Actor is pure of deficiency, incomparable with faultiness, free of blights. He does not eat or sleep, nor is He the locus for newly arrived things or changing states. He is not new in attribute, nor does He accept alteration. He stands before "when," acts before activity, creates before creation, and is powerful before the artisanries.

In His Essence, attributes, and perfection
He has always been just as He is now.

Shaykh al-Islam Anṣārī said, "The tawḥīd of the Muslims amounts to three words: affirmation of attributes without excess, negation of similarity without declaring ineffectuality, and going forward according to the outward sense without mixing."

The reality of affirmation is that you acknowledge and surrender to whatever God said in explanation and whatever Muṣṭafā said plainly about Him. You stand firm in the outward sense, you offer no likenesses for it, you do not turn it away from its formulation, and you do not imagine things about it, for God comes into knowledge but not imagination. You avoid thinking about how it can be so, and you do not seek any forced explanation or interpretation. You do not turn away from saying it or listening to it. You know that, in reality, whatever creatures know about God's attributes is only the name. To perceive it is to accept it. The stipulation is surrender, and the commentary is to remember.

You should know that God's Essence accords with His measure, outside the artifice of creatures. He is a Being that is one, outside of imagination and apart from qualification. Whatever He wants, He does, not because of need, for He needs nothing. Rather, He puts things straight by want, pure knowledge, precedent wisdom, and penetrating power. His speech is true, His promise correct, and His Messenger trustworthy. His speech exists in the earth in reality, always joined with Him. His argument stands through it, His decree is irrevocable, His commands and prohibitions firm. *Surely His are the creation and the command. Blessed is God, the Lord of the Worlds!* [7:54].

This is tawḥīd as transmitted and recognition as reported. Through this tawḥīd, people reach paradise, escape from hell, and stay free from the Real's anger. The opposite of this tawḥīd is the great associationism. Whoever is held back from this transmitted tawḥīd remains in the great associationism, far from God's forgiveness.

The other tawḥīd is the tawḥīd of the recognizers and the adornment of the sincerely truthful. Speaking of this tawḥīd is not the work of water and clay, nor is it the place of tongue and heart. What will the tawḥīd-voicer say here with the tongue? His state is itself tongue. How can he express this tawḥīd? Putting it into expression is calumny itself. This tawḥīd is not from creation, for it is a mark from the Real. It is the resurrection of the heart and the plundering of the spirit.

The Pir of the Tariqah said, "O God, the recognizer knows You through Your light and cannot express the radiance of finding. The tawḥīd-voicer recognizes You through the light of proximity and burns in the fire of love without turning away from joy. O Lord, he seeks to find You in his finding because he is drowned in bewilderment. He does not know seeking from finding."

The poor wretch who recognizes Him through the artisanry! The poor man who seeks Him through the evidence! From the artisanry, you must seek whatever finds room, and from the evidence, you must ask for what is fitting.

How can the reality of tawḥīd cling to the tongue of reports? This is not tawḥīd reached by inference and effort, nor that which is proved by evidence and artisanry, nor that realized by any means whatsoever. It is found in the midst of heedlessness, it comes without asking, and it busies the servant with itself. Lit up by contemplation of the Near and observation of togetherness, the servant reaps the benefit of beginningless love and loses the two worlds.

> If seeing You brings loss to the spirit,
> then I'll buy the spirit's loss with the spirit.

The Pir of the Tariqah said, "O God, the mark of this work has taken the world away from me and concealed me even from the mark. Seeing You has left me without spirit. Love for You took away benefit, and I lost the two worlds.

"O God, do You know what makes me happy? I did not fall to You by myself. You wanted—it was not I who wanted. I saw the Friend at my pillow when I woke up from sleep."

Her love came to me before I knew love—
it came across a carefree heart and took possession.

Moses had gone in search of fire when he found *I made you for Myself* [20:41]. He was unaware when the sun of good fortune rose over him.

Muḥammad was asleep when the good news came: "Come and see Me, for I am buying you. How long will you sit without Me?"

Moses was not wanting conversation, nor was Muḥammad wanting vision. Finding comes in heedlessness. Do not suppose anything but this.

The Pir of the Tariqah said, "O God, the splendor of Your exaltedness left no room for allusions, the majesty of Your unity took away the road of ascription—I lost all that I had in hand, and all my fancies turned to nothing. O God, Yours kept on increasing and mine decreasing until at last there remained only what was there at first."

Tribulation lies only in the makeup of water and clay.
What was there before clay and heart? That is what I will be.

With the first tawḥīd, the servant escapes from hell and reaches paradise. With the second tawḥīd, he escapes from self and reaches the Friend.

(*Kashf* 2:506–9)

THE STAGES OF THE JOURNEY

Following the Sunnah means observing both the Shariah and the Tariqah, the goal being to reach the Haqiqah. Often the journey is said to begin with "emigration" (*hijra*), the term that is used to designate the Prophet's move to Medina, where the Islamic community became firmly established. In his commentary on a verse that praises *those who emigrate* (2:218), Maybudī explains that emigration is of two sorts: outward and inward. Outward emigration is to set off in the world in search of knowledge, and inward emigration is to set off inside the self in search of God. The inner journey goes by way of the subtleties and correlates with the basic dimensions of the tradition: submission or practice (islām), faith (īmān), recognition (maʿrifa), and tawḥīd. The tawḥīd that is the final goal is often called subsistence (baqāʾ), which, as noted earlier, is preceded by annihilation of self (fanāʾ). It is clear that Maybudī has this in mind, because he has taken the clause after the dash in the second paragraph from Anṣārī's description of subsistence, the one-hundredth of the one hundred fields.

> Inward emigration is that you go from the soul to the heart, from the heart to the secret core, from the secret core to the spirit, and from the spirit to the Real. The soul is the way station of submission, the heart the way station of faith, the secret core the way station of recognition, and the spirit the way station of tawḥīd.
>
> In the traveling of the wayfarers one must emigrate from submission to faith, from faith to recognition, and from recognition to tawḥīd. This is not the tawḥīd of the common people. On the contrary, this tawḥīd is pure of water and dust, purified of Adam and Eve—attachments cut, causes dissolved, traces nullified, limits voided, allusions ended, expressions negated, chronicles transformed.
>
> One day the master, Imām Abū ʿAlī Daqqāq, was drowned in the ocean of love and speaking of tawḥīd. He said, "If you see one of the honored pearls placing his foot in the lane of making claims and talking about tawḥīd, be careful not to be deceived. Know that tawḥīd's meaning is pure of water and dust, for it is the beauty of Unity that went into the field of the Beginningless to gaze on the majesty of the Sanctum. It spoke mysteries to Itself in the attribute of inaccessibility."
>
> (*Kashf* 1:581–82)

In his remarks on the verse that begins "*Whoso emigrates in the path of God*" (4:100), Maybudī explains that people who emigrate are of three basic sorts: the common people, who set out in search of this world; the renunciants (*zāhid*), who set out in search of the next world; and the recognizers (*ʿārif*), who set out in search of God.

> In this verse the Lord of the Worlds, the God of the worldlings, the keeper of all, the knowing and lovingly kind, gives a mark of His mercy and shows His gentleness to the servants. He invites the faithful to emigrate and praises those who do.
>
> The emigrants are of three sorts: one sort emigrates for the sake of this world. They undertake trade or the search for livelihood. Even though this is allowed in the Shariah, it is not clear where it will lay down its head at the end and what its outcome will be. Muṣṭafā said, "Love for this world is the beginning of every offense." He also said, "Do not take a landed estate, lest you become eager for this world."

This sort of emigrant is always undergoing suffering and hardship, caught in the hands of thieves and on the verge of destruction. Hoping to gain something that is allowed, he leaves aside something obligatory. Then he burns, and he loses the substance of both. God says, *"You desire the chance goods of this life, and God desires the afterworld"* [8:67].

The second sort is the renunciants. Their emigration is for the sake of the afterworld, and their traveling goes by way of meanings. They pass over the way stations of obedient acts and traverse the stages of worship on the feet of aspiration. Sometimes they make the hajj, go off to battle, struggle, make pilgrimages, perform the prayers, remember God's name, and meditate on God's blessings. Concerning them, God's Messenger said, "Travel! The solitary will take precedence."

They said, "O Messenger of God! Who are the solitary?"

He said, "The engrossed—those who are engrossed in the remembrance of God. Remembrance lifts away their loads, and they come forth unburdened on the Day of Resurrection."

The Exalted Lord says about them, *"Whoever desires the next world and strives after it with proper striving while having faith—those, their striving shall be thanked"* [17:19].

The third sort is the recognizers, whose emigration is for the sake of the Protector. They emigrate within their own makeup. They emigrate inside the curtains of the soul until they reach the heart, they emigrate inside the curtains of the heart until they reach the spirit, and they emigrate inside the curtains of the spirit until they reach union with the Beloved.

> I said, "Where should I search for You, O heart-stealing moon?"
> He said, "My resting place is the spirit of the friends."

A man came before Abū Yazīd Basṭāmī and said, "Why do you not emigrate and travel to benefit the people?"

He said, "My Friend has settled down and I am busy with Him."

The man said, "When water stays in one place for a long time, it becomes stagnant."

Abū Yazīd said, "You should be the ocean, and then you will never become stagnant." Then he recited the verses,

> I see the hajjis urging on their steeds,
> but here I am, urging on the steed of yearning.
> Their goal in pilgrimage is the Kaabah—
> my kiblah is Your face, my pilgrimage to You.

(*Kashf* 2:662–63)

In commenting on still another verse that refers to emigration (16:110), Maybudī describes the transformative journey that those who aspire to the path are called to undertake.

> The reality of emigration is that you emigrate from your own makeup, you abandon yourself and your desires, and you place the foot of nonbeing on top of your own attributes. Beginningless love may then lift the curtain, and endless passion may show its beauty. How well that chevalier spoke!
>
> Endless passion has nothing to do with a heart
> that stays firm in its own attributes.
>
> That paragon of the world and master of Adam's children, that goal of the existent things and center-point of the circle of the beings, always used to recite this supplication: "O God, do not entrust us to our own souls for the blink of an eye, or less than that!" Lord God! Remove from before us this makeup stamped by createdness and the relationships of opposition! Lift the burden of our souls away from us so that we may travel in the world of tawḥīd!
> (*Kashf* 5:473–74)

The journey to God has stopping places typically called stations (*maqāmāt*) or way stations (*manāzil*), ancient terms that were used for the stages of caravans. As noted in the introduction, the most famous Arabic book on the topic is Anṣārī's *Way Stations of the Travelers.* In less than one hundred pages of lapidary prose, it describes one hundred stations on the path, each station subdivided into three degrees. In the book's introduction, Anṣārī explains that a group of dervishes in Herat asked him to explain the Tariqah's stages. At first he thought he would explicate a saying of Abū Bakr al-Kattānī (d. 934), "Surely between the servant and the Real are one thousand stations of light and darkness." Then he decided that this would be too much for both him and them (it was not too much for Rūzbihān Baqlī a century later; his *Mashrab al-arwāḥ*, "The Drinking Place of the Spirits," describes 1,001 stations). So he turned to a saying of Abū 'Ubayd al-Busrī (ninth century), "God has servants whose ends He shows to them at their beginnings." After explaining why he settled on one hundred stations, he says that travelers on the path have three basic degrees: taking up the journey, entering into exile, and contemplation. The last pulls them into utter tawḥīd by way of annihilation.

Anṣārī then provides details on the chain of authorities of three hadiths that allude to the three levels. He finds a reference to the first level in the hadith that we just saw Maybudī quoting: "Travel! The solitary will take precedence." The second level is mentioned in the hadith "Seeking the Real is exile." As for the third level, he says it is designated by the description of iḥsān ("doing the beautiful") in the Hadith of Gabriel: "Doing the beautiful is that you worship God as if you see Him, for if you do not see Him, surely He sees you."

Anṣārī's Persian book on the same topic, *One Hundred Fields,* is about the same length as the Arabic, but provides an altogether different list of stations. Many of the names are the same, but not the order or the explanations. The Arabic was written about twenty-five years after the Persian, and Anṣārī clearly had different audiences in view. In any case, it is not unusual for a single author to give a variety of descriptions for the same stage on the path, even within a single book. The aim was to help people understand for themselves, not to provide scholarly classifications.

Anṣārī's introduction to *One Hundred Fields* provides a good summary of the manner in which he and others understood the notion of stages. Notice that he begins by saying that the book is based on a series of sermons in which he explained the meaning of the second of the two most often cited Qur'anic verses on love.

> This is the mention of what was said at the beginning of Muḥarram 448 [March 1056], in sessions on the creed concerning His words "*Say: 'If you love God, follow me; God will love you'*" [3:31].
>
> It has been mentioned that Khiḍr said, "Between the servant and his Protector are one thousand stations." The same thing was said by Dhu'l-Nūn al-Miṣrī, Abū Yazīd al-Basṭāmī, Junayd, and Abū Bakr al-Kattānī. Dhu'l-Nūn said "one thousand knowledges," Abū Yazīd and Junayd said "one thousand castles," and Kattānī said "one thousand stations."
>
> God says, "*Is he who follows God's good pleasure like him who is laden with the burden of God's anger, whose refuge is Gehenna? An evil homecoming! They are degrees with God*" [3:162–63]. The degrees mentioned in this verse are the one thousand stations.
>
> A sound hadith has come that Gabriel asked God's Messenger, "What is doing the beautiful?" He replied, "That you worship God as if you see Him, for if you do not see Him, surely He sees you."
>
> The one thousand stations have way stations, for the travelers to the Real have both way stations and stations. Thus, the servant may be taken degree by degree and made eminent by the Real's acceptance and proximity. Or the servant himself may traverse the way stations until he reaches the last, which is the station of proximity. Then, proximity itself has way stations.
>
> The "station" is where the traveler is kept back, just like the angels in heaven. God says [in the voice of the angels], "*None of us there is but has a known station*" [37:164]. "*Those [angels] whom they call upon are themselves*

seeking the means to approach their Lord, which of them shall be nearer" [17:57].

Each of these one thousand way stations is a way station for the traveler and a station for the stander.

Those who speak of this are three men: The realizer [*muḥaqqiq*] speaks on the basis of finding [*yāft*], and light appears from his words. The second man is empty of listening, and estrangement appears from his words. The third man is a pretender, and disrespect and alienation appear from his words.

Mastery of this knowledge belongs to finding; the mark of its rightness is the final outcome.

The one thousand stations have no escape from six things: reverence for the command, fear of deception, clinging to apology, service according to the Sunnah, living in kindness, and tenderness toward God's creatures.

Even though all the Shariah is the Haqiqah, and all the Haqiqah is the Shariah, the Haqiqah is built on the Shariah. Without the Haqiqah, the Shariah is useless, and without the Shariah, the Haqiqah is useless. Anyone who does not act with both is useless.

(*Maydān* 255–57)

Neither Samʿānī nor Maybudī provides a systematic description of the stations and stages on the path, but both take the notion of stations for granted. In his commentary on the verse *"Say: 'The praise belongs to God'"* (27:59), Maybudī wants to explain that praise is one of the stations, and in order to do so, he first summarizes the general discussion:

Know that the stations of the religion's road are of two sorts: one sort is called the preliminaries, for they are not the goal in themselves. These include repentance, patience, fear, abstinence, poverty, and self-examination, all of which are the means of approach to something beyond themselves.

The second sort is called the destinations or the ends, for they are the goal in themselves. These include love, yearning, contentment, tawḥīd, and trust, all of which are goals in themselves. They are not needed as the means of approach to something else. Praise of God and thanking and lauding Him are of this sort, for they are goals in themselves. Anything that is a goal in itself will remain at the resurrection and will never be cut off in paradise.

Praise pertains to this category because the Exalted Lord says about the attribute of the paradise-dwellers, *"And the last of their call is 'Praise belongs to God, the Lord of the worlds'"* (10:10); *"Praise belongs to God, who has put away sorrow from us"* [35:34]; *"Praise belongs to God, who was truthful in His promise to us"* [39:74].

(*Kashf* 7:245–46)

In his commentary on the verse "*And I have approved the submission as your religion*" (5:3), Maybudī compares the submission, *al-islām*, to a house that has gates and bridges leading to it, and in doing so he uses the typical language of stations.

> The submission is like a house that is reached by four gates, beyond which are four bridges, with degrees and levels beyond the bridges. If people do not pass through the gates and over the bridges, they will not reach the degrees and levels.
>
> The first gate of the traveler is to perform the obligations, the second is to avoid forbidden things, the third is to have confidence in God's assurance, and the fourth is to have patience in trials and sufferings.
>
> When you have passed through these gates, the bridges appear. The first bridge is contentment—being content with God's decree, placing it on your neck, and leaving aside the road of protest. The second bridge is trust in God—relying on God, taking Him as your support and refuge, and recognizing Him as your trustee. The third bridge is gratitude—recognizing God's blessings on you and putting them to work in obedience to Him. The fourth bridge is sincerity in the practices, the Shahadah, service, and recognition—the Shahadah in submission, service in faith, and recognition in the Haqiqah.
>
> Once you have passed over these bridges, there are degrees and levels for which each person is worthy as God wants. This is why the Lord of the Worlds says, "*They have degrees with their Lord, and forgiveness, and a generous provision*" [8:4].
>
> (*Kashf* 3:28)

Authors sometimes describe the path to God as having three basic stages: purification (*tazkiya*), or the elimination of ugly character traits; adornment (*taḥliya*), or the acquisition of beautiful traits; and disclosure (*tajliya*), or passing beyond selfhood altogether and being immersed in the divine attributes. In other words, to reach God one must eliminate bad qualities, acquire good qualities, and become one with the source of good. The first two stages are often linked with the two halves of the formula of tawḥīd: *no god*, known as the negation (*nafy*), and *but God*, known as the affirmation (*ithbāt*). By putting the negation into practice, one purifies oneself of everything other than God, and by putting the affirmation into practice, one recognizes that all belongs to God. In explaining the verse "*If you show something or you hide it, surely God knows everything*" (33:54), Maybudī talks about these as the first two stages of the path.

> Since you know that the Real is aware of your acts and states, that He knows and sees both what you hide and what you show, well then, always be at His

threshold. Keep your activity rectified by following knowledge, eating permitted food, and constant worship. Discipline your words by recitation of the Qur'an, constant apology, and giving good advice. Keep your character traits pure from everything that is dust on the religion's road or blockage of the well-trodden path of the Tariqah, such as niggardliness, eye-service, rancor, avarice, and covetousness.

A great man was asked, "What is the precondition of servanthood?"

He said, "Purity and truthfulness. Purity from every stain, and truthfulness in every adornment."

The defilements are niggardliness, eye-service, and craving. The adornments are generosity, trust, and contentment. The sentence "*No god but God*" includes both statements. *No god* is the negation of defilement, *but God* is the affirmation of adornment. When the servant says, "*No god*," he uproots every defilement and every veil of the road. Then the beauty of the words *but God* shows its face and adorns the servant with the attributes of adornment. Then he is taken, adorned, and trimmed before Muṣṭafā so that he may receive him with "My community!"

If the influence of *No god* does not appear to Muṣṭafā, and if he does not see the beauty of the robe of *but God*, he will not receive him with "My community!" Rather, he will say, "Away with you, away!"

(*Kashf* 8:97)

In his commentary on the verse "*Not equal are the two oceans, this one sweet, delicious to drink, that one salty, bitter*" (35:12), Maybudī talks about purification and adornment in different terms:

This verse alludes to the two states of turning toward God and turning away from God. Those who turn toward God are occupied with obeying Him and recognizing Him. Those who turn away from Him are shut off from worshiping Him and protest against His apportioning and decree. The former is the cause of union, the latter the cause of deprivation and separation.

These are two different oceans, one delicious and the other bitter, standing between the servant and God. One is the ocean of perdition, the other the ocean of salvation. This is their likeness:

Five ships are traveling in the ocean of perdition: avarice, eye-service, persistence in acts of disobedience, heedlessness, and despair. Whoever sits in the ship of avarice will reach the shore of love for this world. Whoever sits in the ship of eye-service will reach the shore of hypocrisy. Whoever sits in the ship of persistence in acts of disobedience will reach the shore of wretchedness. Whoever sits in the ship of heedlessness will reach the shore of remorse. Whoever sits in the ship of despair will reach the shore of unbelief.

As for the ocean of salvation, five ships are traveling on it: fear, hope, renunciation, recognition, and tawḥīd. Whoever sits in the ship of fear will reach the shore of security. Whoever sits in the ship of hope will reach the shore of bestowal. Whoever sits in the ship of renunciation will reach the shore of proximity. Whoever sits in the ship of recognition will reach the shore of intimacy. Whoever sits in the ship of tawḥīd will reach the shore of contemplation.

The Pir of the Tariqah gave an eloquent admonition to his companions and friends. He said, "Dear friends, it is time to seek salvation from this ocean of perdition and rise up from this pit of lassitude. Do not sell subsistent bliss for this evanescent house!

"A soul without service is estranged. Do not nurture the estranged! A heart without wakefulness is a ghoul. Do not be the companion of a ghoul! A soul without awareness is wind. Do not live in the wind! Do not be satisfied with name and description in place of meaning and reality! Do not feel secure from hidden deception! Always be careful about the outcome of the work at the last breath!"

(*Kashf* 8:178–79)

In another typical discussion of eliminating ugly character traits and replacing them with beautiful traits, Maybudī reminds us that it is God's pull that gets the work done, not human effort. He is commenting on the verse "*He effaces what He wants, and He affirms*" (13:39).

Know that the highway of the Real's religion is three things: submission, the Sunnah, and sincerity. In submission be fearful, in the Sunnah be hopeful, and in sincerity be a lover. Submission has no escape from fear, the Sunnah must have hope, and sincerity is nothing but the substance of the lover.

To the fearful, it is said, "Be afraid!" To the hopeful, it is said, "Keep on seeking!" To the lover, it is said, "Keep on burning!"

In the end, the address will come to the fearful, "*Fear not!* [41:30]. Do not fear, for the days of fear have come to an end." To the hopeful, it will be said, "*Grieve not!* [41:30]. Have no sorrow, for your hope has been reached and the tree of joy has grown." To the lover, it will be said, "*Rejoice!* [41:30]. Be happy, for the night of separation has ended and the morning of union has come."

Each of these things has its own path of effacement and affirmation in the world. From the heart of the fearful He erases eye-service and deposits certainty, He erases stinginess and deposits generosity, He erases avarice and deposits contentment, He erases envy and deposits kindness, He erases innovation and deposits the Sunnah, He erases fright and deposits security.

From the heart of the hopeful He erases free choice and deposits surrender, He erases dispersion and deposits togetherness, He erases perplexity and deposits the precedent light.

From the heart of the lover He erases the customs of human nature and deposits the marks bearing witness to the Haqiqah, He decreases the marks bearing witness to the servant and increases the marks bearing witness to Himself. Then, just as He was at first, so also He will be at last.

(*Kashf* 5:218)

Probably the best-known depiction of the stages of the Sufi path in the West is that by Farīd al-Dīn ʿAṭṭār in *The Language of the Birds* (*Manṭiq al-ṭayr*). The book describes a flock of many different kinds of birds who flew over seven mountains until thirty of them reached union with their king. ʿAṭṭār names the mountains seeking, passion, recognition, unneediness, tawḥīd, bewilderment, and poverty. In the following, Maybudī employs the same archetypal number to describe seven oceans over which the traveler must sail in order to reach the goal.

None of us there is but has a known station [37:164]. In the tongue of the Tariqah, this verse alludes to the states of encounter and the unveilings of the masters of the Haqiqah. These occur in gratitude for ecstasies, the lightning of unveiling, the bewilderment of witnessing, the light of proximity, the friendship of finding, the splendor of togetherness, and the reality of solitariness.

These are seven oceans placed at the top of tawḥīd's lane. As long as the traveler in the road does not pass over these seven oceans, he will not be allowed to reach the end of the lane. He must seek water from these oceans through the seven thresholds of the Qur'an, about which Muṣṭafā reported: "The Qur'an was sent down according to seven letters, each of which is a sufficiency and a healing. Each verse has an outward sense and an inward sense, and each letter has a limit and an overview."

The sincerely truthful and the wayfarers on the road have said that you must pass over these oceans to reach tawḥīd. Concerning these seven oceans, the commandment has come: "Pass through the gate of the message brought by that paragon of the world. From every wave, take a proclamation from his Shariah, and from every drop, seek the help of his covenant. Then you will be worthy of the way stations of Our friends."

This is what the Pir of the Tariqah is intimating with his words "When any reality sticks up its head from the recognizer's breast, it is not acceptable to the Real until two witnesses from the Shariah bear witness to its correctness."

(*Kashf* 8:315)

The Qur'an puts the verse just explained by Maybudī, "*None of us there is but has a known station*" (37:164), into the mouth of the angels. In citing the same verse, Ibn al-ʿArabī says that it applies to all created things except human beings. By exercising their free choice, people are constantly moving on their journey to God, and every journey has stages and stopping places. No one comes to a complete halt until death, at which point his or her station will be fixed, just like that of the angels and other creatures. Those who travel on the path to God are following in the footsteps of the Prophet. What then was his station? How was it that his station allowed him to be the guide not only of his own community, but also, as the Logos, of all prophets and all creatures? According to Ibn al-ʿArabī, he could be such a guide because he stood in the station of no station (*maqām lā maqām*). He explains that if the Prophet had stood in one specific station, his guidance could have led only to that station. He, however, was the perfect manifestation of the Divine Reality, which has no station, for It is Infinite Being, embracing all names and attributes, all realities, all stations, all beings.[3] Samʿānī explains the logic of having no station:

> Here there is a secret—for whoever may be worthy: pain and remedy, sorrow and happiness, poverty and riches—all are attributes, way stations, and stations. Way stations are in the road. The man who has arrived has no station and no way station, no spirit and no heart, no present moment and no state, no fear of separation and no hope for union.
>
> A farmer waters the field until the expected time arrives. When the field ripens, he holds back the water. Watering a ripened field is an error.
>
> (*Rawḥ* 562–63)

Elsewhere, Samʿānī describes the stages of the path by analyzing a supplication of the Prophet: "O God, I seek refuge in Thy approval from Thy anger, I seek refuge in Thy pardon from Thy punishment, I seek refuge in Thee from Thee. I do not number Thy laudations. Thou art as Thou hast lauded Thyself." He designates the final stage by the Persian-Arabic compound *bī-maqāmī*, "stationlessness."

> On the night of the miʿrāj, Muṣṭafā was made to pass over all the stations so that he would be higher than everyone else. Thus, they would all be seeking his station, and he would be fleeing from their stations. When he was taken through all the stations, nothing was left but stationlessness, and that is the attribute of the Real. He pulled up the ropes of his secret core's tent, so he was gazing at the Real, not at the station. All the creatures were gazing at the station, but he was gazing at the Real.

This is the meaning of the reported saying of Muṣṭafā, "I seek refuge in Thy pardon from Thy punishment." The first station on the road is fear and hope. Fear arises from gazing at punishment, and hope from gazing at pardon. Pardon and punishment are two acts, and their traces are paradise and hell. Muṣṭafā was shown that there is nothing in the hands of paradise and hell. If fire burned by its own essence, it would have burned Abraham. If paradise caressed by itself, it would have caressed Adam. "What burns is not fire, it is My wrath. What caresses is not paradise, it is My approval. If I pour the water of approval on a fire, it will turn into a scented garden, and if I strike the fire of wrath into a scented garden, it will become hell itself."

He passed beyond that station. He said, "I seek refuge in Thy approval from Thy anger." When he saw that paradise abides through approval, which is beneficence, and hell abides through anger, which is punishment, he said, "I seek refuge in Thy approval from Thy anger."

Then he also passed beyond that station, for approval and anger are attributes, and attributes do not act. Rather, that which is described by the attributes acts. When he saw this, he put aside attachment to acts and seeking aid from attributes. He said, "I seek refuge in Thee from Thee." I seek aid in You from You, for if trial were from other than You, I would seek aid in You. Since it is from You, how can I seek aid in other than You?

Complaint is of three sorts: Either complaining of the Friend to other than the Friend, or complaining of other than the Friend to the Friend, or complaining of the Friend to the Friend Himself.

Complaining of the Friend to other than the Friend is to declare oneself quit of the Friend, for until one is fed up with the Friend, one does not lament to other than the Friend.

Lamenting to the Friend about other than the Friend is associationism, for unless one sees other than the Friend, how does one lament to the Friend? Seeing other than the Friend is associationism.

Lamenting to the Friend about the Friend is tawḥīd itself. Outwardly it is complaint, but inwardly it is to show gratitude: "Since I have none but You, to whom should I speak?"

People imagine that the lover is complaining, but in fact his words display sincerity in love. God reported the lamentation of Job: *"Harm has touched me"* [21:83]. Despite his lamenting, God called him patient: *"Surely We found him patient—how excellent a servant he was!"* [38:44]. How is it that he was patient while complaining?

Here the Exalted Lord is saying this: "Complaining is to lament to other than Me. When he laments to Me, that is not a complaint. Job did not say, 'O people, *harm has touched me.*' He said, 'My Lord, *harm has touched me.*' Thus he took his own incapacity before the Strong, he displayed his own lowliness to the Unneedy. This is not complaining."

Then Muṣṭafā also passed beyond this station. He said, "I do not number Thy laudations": You Yourself should praise Yourself, for You know.

Look at this incapacity! Everybody learns the Friend's laudation from Muṣṭafā, but he admits to his own incapacity in laudation. How can this be? "Yes, when I am with the people, next to my knowledge their knowledge is ignorance. Their stipulation is to stay silent, and my stipulation is to speak. Then, when I talk to You, next to Your knowledge my knowledge and the knowledge of all beings, and a thousand thousand times more knowledge, is ignorance. Here I remain silent."

He was made to pass beyond that station also, for saying "I do not number" is an admission of incapacity, just as saying "I seek refuge in Thee from Thee" reports of power. Incapacity is your attribute, just as power is the Real's attribute. "O Muḥammad, you are still gazing at your own attributes. As long as you do not lift up your gaze to the pure attributes, you will not see Me."

He said, "Thou art as Thou hast lauded Thyself." Describing You is something You are able to do. "I do not number" is disengagement. "Thou art as Thou hast lauded" is solitariness. As long as the servant does not become disengaged from other than the Real, he will not become solitary for the Real.

(*Rawḥ* 344–46)

Maybudī too says that those who stand beyond all stations are the most perfect of human beings. He is commenting on a verse that begins, "*Shall I tell you of something better than that? For those who are godwary there shall be gardens*" (3:15).

After talking about the enemies, describing their life, and explaining their furthest goal, God in this verse comes back to the story of the friends. Tomorrow, the final outcome of those whose watchword today is godwariness will be paradise and approval. He said, "*For those who are godwary there shall be gardens.*"

Just as godwariness has levels, so also paradise has degrees. The first degree is the Garden of the Shelter, and the first level of godwariness is to avoid forbidden things and the soul's caprice. The Splendorous Qur'an ties the two together in its words "*As for him who feared the station of his Lord and forbade the soul its caprice, surely the Garden shall be the refuge*" [79:40–41].

The highest degree is the Garden of Eden, and better than the Garden of Eden is the Greater Approval. So the furthest goal of the paradise-dwellers is the Greater Approval, just as the Lord of the Worlds says: "*And goodly dwellings in the gardens of Eden; and approval from God is greater*" [9:72].

The Greater Approval belongs to those who reach the utmost godwariness. The utmost godwariness is that someone takes whatever has the scar of new arrival and the mark of creation as his own enemy, as Abraham said: "*Surely they are an enemy to me, save the Lord of the Worlds*" [26:77]. You must turn away from all things and, with detached heart, busy yourself with the suffering of passion for the Haqiqah. You must know for certain that the intrusion of others finds no room in passion's suffering. You must cut off your heart and spirit from all things.

> The heart is Your garden—take it all, for this heart
> has room either for my intrusion or Your image.
> In gratitude I'll send my spirit to You—
> a whiff of union does what a hundred spirits cannot.

Tomorrow, all will be taken to the furthest limit of their goals and aspirations. Here someone who hopes for the Garden of the Refuge is told, "Flee from the unlawful and be just, and that will not be held back from you." Someone who hopes for the Garden of Everlastingness is told, "Avoid the doubtful and be a renunciant, and that will not be held back from you." Someone who desires Firdaws is told, "Keep back from the lawful and be a recognizer, and that will not be held back from you."

A group remains that has no hopes and no desires. They desire what the Beloved desires and choose what the Beloved chooses. The paradises are presented to them, and the maidens and serving boys are made to sit on the turrets, scattering precious gifts for them, but they are detached from it all and turn their faces away. They say, "If we must give our heart to someone, well, let us give it to someone who will enslave it."

> Suddenly I gave my heart to the one with the tulip face.
> She was worthy of my heart—that is why I gave it.

(*Kashf* 2:42–43)

ASPIRATION, SEEKING, AND FINDING

In writing about tawḥīd per se, theologians stress the creative command along with God's foreknowledge of all things, His decree (*qaḍā'*, *ḥukm*), and His measuring out (*qadar*), that is, His predetermination of all that exists. God knows all things in His eternal knowledge, and He simply says *Be!* to what He knows. The same authors, however, generally spend more time looking at the religious command, which demands that people put tawḥīd into practice. If people can say yes or no to a given commandment, they will be called to account. The fact that God knew what they were going to say beforehand and simply said *Be!* to their words is irrelevant. They do not know their response until they make it. As far as they can see, they freely choose to respond as they respond.

From God's point of view, all is over and done with. From the human point of view, things have yet to work themselves out. Even though God knows the result, He puts people to the test in order to let them freely choose to act in certain ways. It is they who come to know how they will respond to the religious decree, since He already knows. People will then be called to account in the measure in which they were free, no more and no less. This, for our authors, is good news indeed, since God's mercy takes precedence over His wrath, and the All-Merciful pulls the strings.

On the practical level, the human dilemma comes down to achieving the right balance between the standpoints of the creative and the religious commands. Do we simply say, "What will be will be," and sit in idleness, waiting for events to unfold? This is an option, but it is self-contradictory, because not acting is itself a form of action. Moreover, to claim to be submitting to God's creative command while ignoring His prescriptive command is to forget that the prescriptive command itself derives from the creative command and calls on people to act in certain ways.

Jurists qua jurists understood the religious command in strictly legal terms: "Do this! Avoid that!" Guides to the Tariqah typically maintained that the rules and regulations of the Shariah perform the function of providing a stable personal and social framework for the real work, which takes place inside the self. Teachers addressed those who either understood this point or had the potential to understand it. They accepted the fact of the creative command but also acknowledged the existential reality of the religious command, which calls on individuals to engage in shaping their own destinies. In *Forty-Two Chapters*, Anṣārī explains the fallacy of thinking that because God already knows our final end, it makes no difference what we do.

> Abū Hurayra said, "I heard God's Messenger saying, 'No one will enter the Garden because of his deeds.'
>
> "It was said to him, 'Not even you, O Messenger of God?'
>
> "He said, 'Not even I, unless God envelops me with His bounty and mercy. So, be guided and seek proximity! And let none of you wish for death! If you are a beautiful-doer, perhaps you will be increased in good; and if you are an ugly-doer, perhaps you will seek help."
>
> The Allusion. The meaning is that a man may seek death because of impatience. If you are seeking Him, then He is what you should seek. If you are

seeking increase, elevation, and reward, that is the place for deeds. Or you may flee from the work or the burden. But the work is the cause of good fortune, and the burden the cause of elevation.

The time of your death will not be pushed back or brought forward by your wish. But when you seek death while fleeing from the work or the burden, that will be recorded to your account. Death will find you fleeing from the work and the burden, rather than being eager for increase, patient in trial, and content with the decree.

So, O servant, put aside wishing for death and strive to increase the work and the burden, for death will come on its own. When it comes, at that moment you should be in a state that welcomes the decree of the Real and yearns for the vision of the Friend. You should not be fleeing from the work.

Know that if you are a beautiful-doer in this world, then your life will be spent in increasing your elevation. If you are an ugly-doer, it may be that repentance will find you and purify you of alienating things by means of remorse and regret. Then it will not be necessary for you to be purified tomorrow in the Fire.

O servant, wish for the death of disobedience, not the death of obedience. The men of this road store away so much good fortune with every breath that their lack of need for the eight paradises is one drop of the ocean. What is this ocean of God? One of its drops swallows down the land and sea of the two worlds, as if a typhoon of mercy has risen up. It seems as if an ocean opens up in every particle of the cosmos, and no mark remains of the two worlds' land and sea. What a Blessings-Giver! What a Fount of Bounty!

You cannot enter paradise by means of good deeds, for deeds are accepted along with faith, and people do not gain faith without His bounty and mercy. This world and the afterworld, faith and submission—all come from His bounty.

Knowledge without deeds is sickly, and deeds without knowledge are barren. Knowledge along with deeds is a precious pearl. Knowledge that today does not hold you back from disobedient acts and does not bring you into obedience will not hold you back tomorrow from the fire of hell.

So strive in deeds and gaze on the bounty in the deeds. The beauty of His bounty can be seen in the mirror of beautiful deeds. The more the mirror becomes limpid, wide, and tall, the clearer and greater the beauty seen within.

This hadith does not suggest that you should be slack in deeds. Rather, it suggests that you should lose yourself in His bounty and mercy through this path. Eliminate the ugliness of your deeds with the beauty of good deeds, for you must not eliminate it with the fire of hell. Then the beauty of bounty and mercy will appear in the beauty of the deeds, and the road of paradise will be opened up to you. By seeing that you are immersed in His bounty, you will enter paradise, which is the home of the folk of bounty and mercy.

Work on your own makeup so that you may become a mirror for this work! Then what you are seeking will appear to you. Your only path is to become a mirror. You are the road, where are you going? You are the veil, of whom do you complain? You are the block, against whom do you speak? You are the mirror, where are you looking?

(*Chihil* 131–33)

In explaining the diversity of responses to the two commands, authors often address the question of aspiration (*himma*). They make the point that every person has a unique configuration of attributes, in keeping with the creative command, but each is called upon to strive and struggle in the path to God. To seek out a goal, people need to aspire to it. To reach the final goal of the Tariqah, they need to slice away all others with the sword of tawḥīd and focus on the One. The basic message is that God will give you what you ask for, so you should set your sight as high as you can. Otherwise, you will fall short of the human substance, created in the form of the Creator. Your worth as a human individual is defined by your aspiration. In Maybudī's commentary on the verse "*He adds to creation as He wills*" (35:1), he draws from Anṣārī's *One Hundred Fields* in explaining the importance of aspiration.

The Folk of Realization say that He means the highness of aspiration. He gives a high aspiration to whomsoever He wants.

The possessors of aspiration are three: the aspiration of one is this world—it is the furthest limit of his hope and the spindle of his effort's mill. According to the report, "When someone comes to the point where this world is his greatest aspiration, he does not belong to God. His heart will be inseparable from four traits: an aspiration that will never be cut off from him, an occupation in which he will never take comfort, a poverty in which he will never attain wealth, and a hope that will never reach its object."

On the night of the miʿrāj, Muṣṭafā saw a person adorned in the form of a bride. He said, "Gabriel, who is that?"

He said, "This world, which adorns herself for the eyes of those with low aspiration. Of your community, only one in 70,000 will buy back his spirit from love of her beauty by seeking God."

When someone's aspiration is only this world, the scent of severance comes from him. We seek refuge in God from him!

The aspiration of the second reaches the afterworld. The gardens and meadows, the bliss of the colorful things, the houris and palaces, the serving boys, the *good and comely* [55:70], keep on attracting his heart, as is shown by his passing days. This is the state of the wage earner who stays attached to the reward and is held back from the realities of the unveilings and the seclusion of whispered prayer.

The third person has a high aspiration and a hidden mystery in the heart. His heart is captive to love and his spirit drowned in face-to-face vision. He has no news of this world and no mark of the afterworld. With the tongue of bewilderment, he continues to say, "O Solitary, O Alone eternally and forever, O One and Unique in name and mark! Bring me to life with the life of the friends! Keep me alive in togetherness itself! Make me flourish in the light of proximity! Lift up duality from the midst! Settle me down with the proximate in the station of tawḥīd!"

(*Kashf* 8:168–69)

Samʿānī frequently encourages his readers to aim as high as they can, as in the following:

Gamble away desire, movement and rest, words and talk, ecstasy and states, patched cloak and pot, in the circle of the wine of Unity. Perhaps a draft will become your pain's share. Whenever someone takes up the road of tawḥīd, he sees that the Throne and the Footstool, paradise and hell, the Lote Tree of the Final End and *two bows' length*, are the road, not the destination. His goal and the object of his search is something else.

Tomorrow a group will be rebuked: "Did you have no more aspiration in the world but to perform a few cycles of prayer? You breathed some mouthfuls of air only to grab something to eat?" If this is what you do, let go of it and let it out of your sight so that it will not be a loss for you.

A man must call out from on high. Aspiration is a bird that hunts only on high. Supposing Solomon's kingdom is given over to someone and he gazes on it—by God, he would be a man of mean aspiration! There are not enough capital goods from the East to the West for an idol worshiper. Nimrod was given this world, but he was not pleased with it, so he lifted his bow and arrows and turned his face toward heaven.

Why do you look at the fact that the kingdom of this world was given to Solomon? Look at the fact that he put himself among the beggars.

O dervishes! Know for certain that the sultans, in their gold-embroidered tunics and jewel-studded caps, seek the ease of your life.

(*Rawḥ* 608–9)

In aspiring for something, people are seeking it. Both the Qur'an and the Sunnah make clear that seeking knowledge is an obligation. The goal of the seeker is to find the object of his search. Bookish knowledge, though a useful preliminary, does not count as finding, nor does knowing God in a scriptural or theological sort of way. The raison d'être of the religion is to take seekers from where they are to where they should be. Where they should be is where they began, that is, with God. The Return circles back to the Origin. Then seekers become finders, and the distinction between finders and Found loses its significance, for no one truly finds God but God.

Sufi authors repeatedly come back to the fact that we can do nothing on our own. As the Pir of the Tariqah put it, "It is not the acting of the servant that does the work—it is God's wish that does the work. How can the servant deliver himself with his own effort?" (*Kashf* 5:395, on verse 16:44). This is why our authors like to say that seeking comes from finding, not the other way around. You seek because you have found something bestowed on you by the creative command. Nonetheless, from the standpoint of the religious command, people have the duty to strive and seek. In his commentary on the verse "*And my success is only through God*" (11:88), Maybudī cites Anṣārī to describe the necessity of seeking despite being pulled back and forth between the two commands:

> The Pir of the Tariqah said, "As long as the spirit is in the body, breath is passing the lips, and awareness is present, there is no escape from servanthood. It is true that obedience comes from being given success, but that is no reason to stop trying. It is true that disobedience comes from abandonment, but there is no stipulation to put down roots. To suppose that you have the ability not to sin stands at the head of all sin. To fancy that these words excuse the sinner is also a sin.
>
> "O God, I have bowed my head to Your exaltedness and I sacrifice my spirit to Your ruling. You say to me, 'Don't do it!' and then You throw me into it. You say to me, 'Do it!' but then You do not let me do it. My place is antagonism and Yours exaltedness. What remains for me but bowing my head in obedience?"
>
> (*Kashf* 4:441–42)

Bowing one's head in obedience is to surrender oneself to the divine mercy, which, after all, has the first and final say. Maybudī explains this in his commentary on the verse "*Your Lord has written mercy against Himself*" (6:54). The first paragraph is taken from Qushayrī's *Subtle Allusions*.

> Although He has turned you over to the angel who writes your slips against you, He Himself has undertaken to write mercy for you. His writing for you is

beginningless, and that writing against you is temporal. The temporal does not nullify the beginningless.

Wāsiṭī said, "By His mercy they arrived at worshiping Him. It is not that by worshiping Him they arrived at His mercy. By His mercy they attained what is with Him, not by their acts, for the Prophet said, 'Not even I, unless God envelops me with His mercy.'"

(*Kashf* 3:374)

Maybudī often quotes Anṣārī to the effect that seeking comes from having found, as in this passage:

Shaykh al-Islam Anṣārī said, "He is not found by seeking, but the seeker will find Him. As long as the seeker does not find Him, he will not seek. Whatever can be found by seeking has little worth. The servant finds the Real before the seeking, but for him the seeking is the first step.

"The recognizer finds seeking from finding, not finding from seeking. In the same way, the obedient person finds obedience from sincerity, not sincerity from obedience; he finds the cause from the meaning, not the meaning from the cause.

"O God, Your finding is before seeking and seeker, so I seek and am overwhelmed by unsettledness. The seeker is seeking and the Sought is obtained before the seeking. This is a marvelous business! What is more marvelous is that finding is already at hand when seeking has not yet begun. Though the Real is seen, the curtain of exaltation is in place."

(*Kashf* 2:496–97, on verse 4:32)

God is the Provider of all things, and there is no provider but He. This does not mean, however, that people should not bother to seek their daily provision. The fact that He is the All-Merciful and that there is none merciful but He does not mean that they should not exert effort in opening themselves up to mercy. In any case, He is also the Speaker and the Commander, and His speech commands seeking. People should set their aspirations as high as they can and then work as hard as they can to achieve them. In Maybudī's commentary on the verse "*Say: 'Who has forbidden the ornament of God?'*" (7:32), he explains some of these points by referring to the levels of selfhood.

The ornament of the tongue is remembrance and the ornament of the heart is reflective thought.

Everything has an adornment. The soul is adorned by beautiful practice, along with the attribute of struggle. The heart is adorned by the continuity of union at the moment of contemplation. The secret core is adorned by the realities of proximity in the field of eyewitnessing.

What the Exalted Lord says here—"*Who has forbidden the ornament of God?*"—alludes to the fact that these adornments are not kept back from the seekers or prohibited to those whose hearts are present. The treasure-house of blessings is full of blessings—it wants seekers. The tablecloth of gentleness and mercy is set and ready—it wants eaters.

The Pir of the Tariqah said in whispered prayer: "O seekers, hurry, for the hard cash is near! O night travelers, sleep not, for the morning is near! O hurriers, be happy, for the abode is near! O thirsty ones, be patient, for the wellspring is near! O strangers, be joyful, for hospitality is near! O seekers of the Friend, be glad, for response is near!

"O Opener of my heart! What harm if You open my heart and place Your balm on my spirit? How can I search for gain when my hands are empty of capital? What if Your bounty threw me into good fortune?"

(*Kashf* 3:610)

Samʿānī expands on the situation that results from being commanded to seek while having no real power to do so:

Whatever the ulama have said is a report and whatever the shaykhs have said is a tradition. The reality of the Real is beyond reports and traditions.

A field has been placed before the creatures and the call has gone out, "O folk of the world! Step into this field and walk on the road. Go in the veil. Know not where you go, and know not whence you are coming. Set out from the threshold of Our knowledge and settle down at the threshold of Our decree."

"Lord God, what is the wisdom?"

"Indeed. If you were to know, you would be a partner in Our lordhood."

"Then what should we do?"

"Bind your belts to serve Us, gaze upon Our will, and be prepared for Our power, either for pardon and forgiveness, or for severity and punishment. 'The power of the Powerful suspends every contrivance.' "

(*Rawḥ* 575)

A man gets up in the morning and prays. He says, "Praise belongs to God for giving success." The secret of the Sunnah is this, and anything beyond this is dualism.

"I deposited light in your breast so that you would accept faith. I put strength in your tongue so that you would say the Shahadah. I prepared a secret in your makeup so that you would perform worthy deeds. You cannot come to My Presence with your own strength. A sweeper who comes from the toilet will not be placed on the sultan's throne.

"Wait until I dress you in a robe of success before you come into My Presence. Then, when I see you, I will see you with My own robe. Without Me, all your deeds are unreal, but all My deeds are real. I will not make your capital from the unreal; I will make it from the real, for when the real appears, the unreal vanishes. Nothing will remain in your hands. *We shall advance upon what work they have done and make it scattered dust* [25:23].

"We have made your capital from Our success-giving, confirmation, and help. Then, when the real that is Ours appears—*That day, the kingdom, the real, shall belong to the All-Merciful* [25:26]—Our real will come to meet it. Then you will have something in the midst."

Glory be to God! How many gentle divine favors were given to this handful of impudent dust! God brought the universe into existence with His own power, without any defect whatsoever. Nonetheless, the Will had the reins, and it itself was the requester. A seeker rose up from Power and girded its loins because of the existence of the requester. The seeker that was Power gazed at its own requester, and Adam appeared in the midst. It gave forth this mark of his station: "*I am setting in the earth a vicegerent*" [2:30]. From clay a heart, from dried clay a conjunction, from stinking sperm a friend and a servant.

In reality, our sperm drop's capital was not our finding and seeking. It was His giving. In the Beginningless, He made a contract between His bestowal and our asking, between His response and our supplication, between His forgiveness and our apology. So the capital in this contract is not our deeds, it is His bounty. *God is the Unneedy, and you are the poor* [47:38]. The man of wealth has capital and pays cash. But the poor, indigent man pays after a delay. (363)

O chevalier! He who seeks nearness to the King by sitting in a corner of his room doing his prayers is mocking himself. The unfortunate fellow who stands or sits in the hut of his own misfortune and thinks that, because of that standing and sitting, he is doing a favor for the King of the age heads up the world's madmen. All the acts of obedience and worship, good works, deeds, words, and states issuing from the children of Adam from the beginning of existence to the end of the age, when placed next to the perfection of the divine beauty, are the noise of an old woman's spindle. Beware—do not think that you are doing Him any favors!

Had He in His generosity and bounty not invited this handful of worthless, dirt-dwelling dust to the court of His eternity and spread out the carpet of bold expansiveness in the house of guidance, how could this woebegone of existence, this speck of impure dust, have the courage to put its foot on the edge of the carpet of the King of kings? But, "There is no consultation in love."

Some perform acts of obedience and desire the rewards; others disobey and sketch the line of asking pardon in the tablet of the heart. Still others don't have the gall to lift up their heads because of shame for their own existence.

The stories tell about an afflicted man who was walking along the road when an extremely beautiful woman passed by. His eyes fell on her perfect beauty, and his heart became her prey. He set off in her tracks. When she reached the door to her house, she turned around and saw the afflicted man behind her. "What do you want?" she said.

He said, "The ruling power of your beauty has exercised its authority over my feeble makeup and pulled it by the harness of its severity. My claim is that I want to make love to you, and this claim is no metaphor."

That woman had the adornment of perfect intellect on the dress of beauty. She said, "I will answer you tomorrow and solve this problem."

The next day, the afflicted man was sitting in wait, his eyes open: When would the perfect beauty of his goal appear? When would what had happened to him be resolved? The woman came, behind her a maid with a mirror in hand. She said, "Maid, hold the mirror before him. With that head and face, does he want to make love to *me*? He desires to reach union with *me*?

"You want to have a hidden secret with *me*?
You find in yourself a need for *me*?
In truth, black crow, you're a fine bird—
you want to mate with a white falcon!"

(17–18)

THE DESIRER AND THE DESIRED

In the technical language of Sufism, traveling on the path to God is called wayfaring (*sulūk*), a term that is contrasted with attraction (*jadhba*). It is often said that people go forward on the path through their own efforts and that at a certain point attraction takes over. But this is to take the standpoint of human effort. From the standpoint of divine grace and solicitude (*ʿināya*), it is God who attracts people to the path and pulls them toward Himself, so attraction is always in charge of wayfaring. The Sought pulls the seeker.

The closer we look at the implications of tawḥīd, the clearer it becomes that no one travels on God's path without His help. Effort alone cannot take the servant anywhere, least of all to the Divine Presence. If anyone is to reach God, the divine attraction must take over completely. Maybudī explains this in his commentary on one of the verses of the Fātiḥa, the Opening of the Qur'an that is recited in every cycle of the ritual prayer.

> *Guide us on the Straight Path* [1:6]. This is the essence of worship and the marrow of obedience. It is supplication, request, pleading, and imploring by the faithful. It is seeking straightness and firmness in the religion. It means: "Lead us to this path, make us travel on it, and keep us firm in it."
>
> The faithful are saying, "O God, show us Your road, then make us go forth on the road, then take us from traveling to being pulled." These are the three great roots: first showing, then traveling, then being pulled.
>
> Showing is what the Exalted Lord says in "*He shows you His signs*" [40:13]. Traveling is what He says in "*You shall surely ride stage after stage*" [84:19]. Being pulled is what He says in "*We brought him near as a confidant*" [19:52].
>
> Muḥammad asked God for showing. He said, "O God, show us things as they are!" About traveling, he said, "Travel! The solitary will take precedence." About being pulled, he said, "One attraction of the Real is equal to the works of jinn and men."
>
> In this verse, the faithful request all three of these from God, for not everyone who sees the road travels the road, and not everyone who travels the road reaches the destination. Many there are who hear but do not see, many there are who see but do not recognize, and many there are who recognize but do not find.
>
> (*Kashf* 1:35)

A person who enters the Tariqah is commonly called a *murīd*, a word typically translated as "disciple." It designates someone who has been accepted as a student by a spiritual master, who is typically called a shaykh or pir or *murshid*. In theory, the shaykh is qualified to be the master because he has traversed the path to God and because God has therefore given him the task of guiding others by the same route. The route is that set down by the Prophet, and wayfaring is to follow in the Prophet's footsteps.

Literally, the word *murīd* means "desirer." It is an active participle from the noun *irāda*, "desire," one of the primary divine names. It is therefore virtually identical with the creative love that is the source of the universe: "*His only command, when He <u>desires</u> a thing, is to say to it 'Be!' and it comes to be*" (36:82). Qur'an translators often translate *irāda* as "desire" when human beings are the subject, but as "will" or "intention" when God is the subject, no doubt thinking that God is beyond such lowly human attributes. Drawing such a distinction between divine and creaturely desire, however, is not supported by the Qur'an or Arabic usage. The Qur'an uses the same verb for God, people, and Satan, and in no way does it suggest that the meaning is different in each case. By introducing the distinction, translators obscure the fact that the human attribute of desire is a reflection of the divine attribute. Just as both God and human beings are lovers, so also both are desirers. In the last analysis, there no desirer but God.

In the technical language of classical Sufism, a desirer is someone who desires God. He or she is a seeker who, as an expression of desire and love, has undertaken to follow a teacher. The teacher has achieved whatever he has achieved by following his own teacher in a chain of teachers that goes back to the Prophet. In this sense of the word, desirer is then contrasted with desired (*murād*). One might expect desired to designate God (though it is not a divine name). In fact, what is meant is the shaykh. This does not imply that the disciple desires the shaykh. Rather, it means that the shaykh has reached the stage of divine attraction and has been snatched away (*rubūda*). Only someone whose human failings have been eliminated by God can be worthy of guiding others on the path.

Maybudī sums up the difference between desirer and desired in his commentary on the verse "*O you who have faith, respond to God and His Messenger when He calls you to that which will give you life*" (8:24).

> In the tongue of the folk of allusion, response is of two sorts: one is the response of tawḥīd, and the other the response of realization. Tawḥīd is that the faithful say "One," and realization is that the recognizers be one. Tawḥīd is the attribute of the travelers, and realization is the state of those snatched away. The first is the attribute of Abraham, the second the attribute of Muḥammad.
>
> Abraham was a traveler and stood before the Exalted Threshold in the station of service: *Surely I have turned my face toward Him who originated the heavens and the earth, unswerving* [6:79]. Muḥammad was snatched away, sitting in reverence at the top of good fortune. The Beginningless Presence addressed him, "Peace be upon thee, O Prophet, and God's mercy and His blessing."
>
> The traveling of the wayfarers lies in the outward response of following the Messenger. The attraction of the snatched away lies in the secret core's response of contemplating the Knower of Unseen Things.
>
> (*Kashf* 4:35–36)

Maybudī describes three levels of human desire in his commentary on the verse "*And do not drive away those who call upon their Lord, desiring His face*"

(6:52). He is elaborating on Anṣārī's description of desire as the fifth of the one hundred fields.

> Abū Yaʿqūb Nahrjūrī was asked, "What is the attribute of the desirer?"
>
> He recited the verse *"Those who call upon their Lord morning and evening, desiring His face"* [18:28]. Then he said, "They wake up and have nothing to ask from this world of theirs, nor any request for their afterworld. Their only aspiration is to talk with their Protector. When they become disengaged for God, the Real's solicitude devotes itself to them and undertakes to speak for them. Hence He said, '*And do not drive* them *away,* O Muḥammad!' "
>
> *Desiring His face.* The meaning of desire is a man's wanting when he travels the road. It is of three sorts: one is desiring only this world, another is desiring only the next world, and the third is desiring only the Real.
>
> Desiring this world is what He says: "*You desire the chance goods of this life* [8:67]. *Whoever desires this hasty world* [17:18]. *Whoever desires the tillage of this world* [42:20]. *If you desire the life of this world and its adornment* [33:28]." The mark of desiring this world is two things: contentment with increase in this world by means of decrease in the religion, and turning away from the poor among the Muslims.
>
> Desiring the afterworld is what He said: "*Whoever desires the next world* [17:19]. *Whoever desires the tillage of the next world* [42:20]." Its mark is two things: contentment with the safety of the religion by decreasing in this world, and intimate friendship with the poor.
>
> Desiring the Real is what God said: "*Desiring His face* [6:52]. *If you desire God and His Messenger* [33:29]." Its mark is stepping beyond the two worlds, becoming free of the creatures, and escaping oneself.
>
> (*Kashf* 3:372–73)

In several passages of Maybudī's commentary, he explains how the desirer turns into the desired:

> *It is He who makes you journey on land and sea* [10:22]. In the tongue of the folk of allusion, the journey on land is taking the road to the drinking places of the Shariah through inference by means of the message. The journey on the sea is the overwhelming force of the Real, which, at the moment of ecstasy, pulls the reins of the servant's steed without intermediaries through the way stations of the Haqiqah to the places of contemplating holiness.
>
> Just as on the sea you make a one-month journey in one day, so also in this field the chevalier traverses the distance of a whole lifetime with one divine attraction. This is why they say, "One attraction of the Real is equal to the works of jinn and men."

The journey on land is the journey of the worshipers and renunciants in the desert of struggle on the steed of discipline with the guidance of the Shariah. Their goal is the Paradise of Approval and everlasting blessings.

The journey on the sea is the journey of the recognizers and the sincerely truthful in the ship of kind favor, which is driven by the wind of solicitude in the sea of contemplation. Their goal is the Kaabah of union and the mystery of the Blessings-giver.

(*Kashf* 4:278–79)

So set thy face to the religion, unswerving [30:30]. "O paragon of the world! O master of Adam's children! Entrust yourself entirely to Me! Keep your intention and aspiration on Me! Turn your heart away from the creatures toward Me! Cease your requesting and forget about the two worlds as is worthy of Me!"

By virtue of this exalted proclamation to that paragon of the world, he stepped forth on the night of the miʿrāj from the Lote Tree of the Final End into the desert of Invincibility and turned his face toward his own specific kaabah, wearing as his beautiful cloak all the capital goods of the first and the last folk and putting them into His road. He passed on and showed no favor to anything. Finally, from the side of Invincibility came the call "*The eyesight did not swerve*" [53:17]. He kept his eyes in courtesy and did not gaze upon anything other than the Real. *Nor did it trespass* [53:17]. He did not covet anything beyond that limit.

Moses stepped on the mountain and went several paces beyond the limit of the Children of Israel. His mind was boiling in the hope of *Show me, that I may gaze upon Thee!* [7:143], so he had to be taught courtesy with the whip of *Thou shalt not see Me!* The paragon of the world, however, was taken to a station where the dust under his feet became the ointment for Gabriel's eyes. His attribute was this: *The eyesight did not swerve.* This is because Moses was traveling, but the paragon of the world was snatched away: *who took His servant by night* [17:1]. The one who comes can never be like the one who is brought.

Blessed is he who travels as the Real's companion, for in one breath he covers a thousand-year journey! "On the night when We take you, you will go farther than you could in a thousand months of going by yourself." To this He alludes with His words "*The night of power is better than a thousand months*" [97:3].

"When you go by yourself, you will fall farther behind with every step you take. When you go with Us, your every step will make you more passionate. When you go by yourself, the highwaymen will ambush you on the road. When We take you, the bandits will carry your banner."

(7:458)

And know that God comes between a man and his heart [8:24]. The wayfarers on the road of the Haqiqah are two groups: the knowers and the recognizers. The knowers find their hearts in keeping with the verse "*Surely in that is a remembrance for him who has a heart*" [50:37]. The recognizers lose their hearts in keeping with the verse "*And know that God comes between a man and his heart.*"

This is a strange intimation and a marvelous allusion: the heart is the road, and the Friend is the homeland. When someone arrives at the homeland, he no longer walks on the road. At the beginning there is no escape from the heart, but at the end, the heart is a veil.

As long as someone stays with the heart, he is the desirer. The one without a heart is the desired. At first the heart is needed because one cannot traverse the road of the Shariah without the heart. Thus He said, "*a remembrance for him who has a heart.*" At the end, remaining with the heart is duality, and duality is distance from the Real. Hence He said, "*He comes between a man and his heart.*"

(4:36–37)

Set thy face to the religion [10:105]. He says: Cleanse your religion from the contamination of eye-service and fix your intention on seeking the alchemy of the Haqiqah—your heart cut off from attachments, your belt tightened, and the ring of service on the ear of loyalty. Let your wants be sacrificed to the beginningless want, your soul to contentment, your heart to loyalty, your eyes to subsistence.

My soul wants life for union with You,
  my spirit wants ease for joining with You.
My ears want hearing to listen to You,
  my eyes want vision to yearn for Your beauty.

From here the light of the Haqiqah begins, the falcon of love flies in the air of solitariness, and the divine attraction arrives. It takes the servant away from the hand of self-determination. None of the intrusive dust of hoping for paradise settles on his present moment, no dread of hell blocks his path. With the tongue of his state, he says,

In the road of passion the passionate
  must not remember hell or paradise.

Up until this point, the servant was seeking, but now he is sought. He was the lover, but now he is beloved. He was desiring, but now he is desired. He saw the carpet of oneness and hurried until he found the proximity of the Friend. Reports turned into face-to-face vision. The obscure became clear. The servant arrived at himself when he reached the Friend. He did not see himself, for he saw the Friend.

The Pir of the Tariqah said, "O God, when I learned what was to be learned, I burned all the learning. I overthrew the collected and collected the overthrown. I sold nonbeing to illuminate being. O God, when I recognized oneness, I melted in the hope of happiness. When will I be able to say, 'I threw away the cup, I turned away from attachments, I gambled away all my being'?"

(4:346–47)

Samʿānī discusses the difference between the desirer and the desired while explaining that servanthood is the highest station anyone can reach. As Ibn al-ʿArabī likes to say, the perfect human being (*al-insān al-kāmil*) is the universal or unqualified servant. Having achieved the station beyond all stations, he stands in perfect receptivity toward God in both His transcendence and immanence, so he makes manifest all the divine attributes.[4]

Know that the miʿrāj was not built on intellect, for this gold coin was struck outside intellect's house. It was built rather on the divine power and the imperial wisdom: *God does as He wills* [14:27] and *decrees what He desires* [5:1]. Concerning Moses, He said, "*When Moses came to Our appointed time*" [7:143]. Concerning Muṣṭafā, He said, "*Glory be to Him who took His servant by night!*" [17:1]. He ascribed Moses's name to the sea and to the bush, but He ascribed Muṣṭafā's name to Himself.

O dervish! If there were any robe of honor better than servanthood, it would have been given to Muṣṭafā on the night of the miʿrāj. Jesus said in the cradle, "*Surely I am the servant of God*" [19:30]. But the Real, without intermediary, said concerning Muṣṭafā, "*His servant.*"

When He mentioned the proximity of Moses, He praised Moses. When He mentioned the proximity of Muṣṭafā, He praised Himself. He said, "*Glory be to Him who took by night.*" This indicates that Moses was subsisting in the attributes of Moses and that Muṣṭafā had been annihilated from his own attributes in the attributes of the Real. Thus ʿĀ'isha said, "His character was the Qur'an." He arrived where he arrived through the attributes of the Real.

This is "taking," but not with his own attributes, for that would be "coming." The one who comes is the seeker, and the one taken is the sought. He who comes is the desirer, and the one taken is the desired. He who comes is the rememberer, and the one taken is the remembered. The seeker is never like the sought, nor the desirer like the desired.

He who comes is absent. Once he comes, he is present. The taken one is not absent from the Taker for one moment.

Coming is a general attribute, and bringing a specific attribute. "The one who wants Me has no escape from coming. The one I want I bring Myself. When someone comes by himself, he may or may not find the road. The one I take cannot not find the road."

Moses came by himself, so the brand of *Thou shalt not see Me* [7:143] was put on his liver. Muṣṭafā was taken, so the crown of *Dost thou not see thy Lord?* [25:45] was placed on his head. In the same way, when Moses saw the mountain and the Real's self-disclosure to the mountain, he was thunderstruck, just as the Exalted Lord said in the clear text of the revelation: "*And Moses fell down thunderstruck*" [7:143]. This is because coming is the attribute of the comer. Anyone who abides through his own attribute can be overcome by someone else. The attributes of the Real cannot be overcome.

As for Muṣṭafā, he saw all the stations of the prophets. He also saw the highest paradises and the gardens, the serving boys and servants, the houris and palaces, the rivers and trees, hell and the varieties of punishment, the Tablet and the Pen, and the decree and apportioning in all of that, but he did not budge in the slightest from his place. This is because he was taken, and taking is the attribute of the Real. The attribute of the Real cannot be overcome. Again, since Moses was abiding through his own attributes, he was overcome, but Muṣṭafā was abiding through the Real's attributes, so he overcame.

What is strange is that Gabriel brought the verse "*Glory be to Him who took His servant by night.*" He came and said, "Get up so that I may take you."

"If you are the taker, what then is *Glory be to Him?* And if He is the taker, what are you doing in the midst? O Gabriel! You were not sent to take me, for the taker, the bringer, and the keeper is the Exalted Lord. Rather, a cape of the spirit's repose was placed on you, but the cape needed an embroidery, for a garment is not complete without an embroidery. Service at the doorstep of my prophethood was made the exalted embroidery of your cape."

Gabriel said, "Get up so that I may take you."

"If you yourself brought yourself, then you take me."

"*We descend not save by the command of thy Lord*" [19:64].

"Since you have no way to take a step without the command, the one who takes me is not you."

(*Rawḥ* 207–8)

In another description of the Prophet's exalted station, Samʿānī points out that all stages on the path to God recapitulate his miʿrāj, for he began the ascent early in life. Samʿānī is reminding his readers that aspiration and seeking are rungs on their own personal ladders to God. At the beginning of the climb, they will meet their own need (*niyāz*), a synonym for "poverty" (*faqr, darwīshī*), the foundation of love's path. To be in poverty is to be empty of all things and receptive toward God.

In this road, you must have truthful need, hot seeking, and unsettled pain. The first way station in the road of seeking is need. The great ones of the religion have said that need is the Real's messenger to the servant. Once the kernel of need is planted in the servant's breast, his reins will be pulled to the Presence.

The passing days make the beginners on the road familiar with need. When, for a time, they take painful steps on the road of need, need turns into aspiration. Earlier, they had been the owners of need, and now they are the possessors of aspiration. The pirs of the road agree that when love comes out from the Unseen Pavilion, it finds no home except in the chamber of the desirer's aspiration.

When they travel for a time on the road of aspiration and tramp on the path with footsteps of seriousness, aspiration turns into seeking. Just as the sperm drop becomes a blood clot, the blood clot becomes a lump of flesh, and the lump of flesh is then dressed in human nature, so also need turns into aspiration, aspiration becomes seeking, and seeking is pulled into the highway of the realities of *No god but God.* This drum of good fortune is beaten at the court of the sultanate: "He who seeks Me shall find Me."

The call then goes out: "O everything high! O everything low! O paradise and hell, Throne, and Footstool—get out of the way of My seekers, for they are My prey, and I am what they are seeking and aiming for. If they should tramp on you, nothing of you will remain."

Know that these levels and degrees I have mentioned are a miʿrāj in this road. No one takes a step on this road without having a miʿrāj in the measure of his desire. The prophets had both an outward and an inward miʿrāj. God's friends have a miʿrāj in their inwardness.

Know that in reality Muṣṭafā's miʿrāj did not begin in Mecca or Medina. Rather, it began when, at the outset of his work, they called him "Muḥammad the trustworthy." From being Muḥammad the trustworthy, he was pulled to prophethood, and from prophethood he was pulled to messengerhood. Then he advanced in messengerhood until he reached poverty. Then he was made to advance further in poverty, and he reached indigence.

Poverty, want, need, and indigence were the embroidery on the mystery of his prophethood. Had there been a belt in the beginningless and endless house of good fortune more exalted than the belt of poverty and indigence, it would have been sent to Muṣṭafā so that he could bind it to the waist of the covenant of servanthood.

When the substance of God's messenger Muḥammad rose up and advanced on these steps and ladders, one attraction took his person by way of following from before the gate of the Kaabah to the place of Abraham's prostration. From the Furthest Mosque he was taken with one pull to *two bows' length*. Then the Lord's jealousy let down the exalted curtain before the virgin secrets and gave nothing out to the people save this: "*Then He revealed to His servant what He revealed*" [53:10]. All the fluent and eloquent speakers stayed empty of this story. Only that paragon of the empire knew the flavor of that wine.

For seventy thousand years the folk of the heavens were waiting to see when this man would show his head from the hiding place of the secret. What gift would he bring to the Exalted Presence? When the night arrived concerning which the Splendorous Book says, "*Glory be to Him who took His servant by night*" [17:1], the proximate angels and the cherubim of the Higher Plenum stuck out their heads from the gazing places of glorification and hallowing. How would that paragon stroll into the Majestic Presence? At the very first step he took in the Threshold, he said, "I do not number Thy laudations: Thou art as Thou hast lauded Thyself."

Inescapably, those who step into that paragon's road with the feet of following will have a miʿrāj in the measure of their own present moments. We said concerning their miʿrāj that they will reach aspiration by way of need and that they will reach seeking by way of aspiration. Then, when the aspiring man steps into the world of seeking, he will be addressed like this: "You cannot find Him with your own seeking, but if you do not seek, you will be an associater. And if you say, 'I will seek in order to find,' then too you will be an associater."

In certitude and verification, if the policeman's hat of the beginningless seeking had not appeared from the specific chamber of generosity, all the worldlings would be flapping in the wind of their own illusions. Seeking comes from finding, not finding from seeking.

The master Abū ʿAlī Daqqāq said, "In your view, you have no escape from provision, but in my view, your provision has no escape from you."

O dervish! Know that in reality nothing is more obligatory for you than seeking. If you go to the shop, seek Him. If you go to the mosque, seek Him. If you go to the tavern, seek Him.

I'm in the tavern, my Friend's in the tavern—
a cup of wine in hand I whisper in prayer.

Even if the angel of death comes to you, be careful not to stop seeking. Say to him, "You do your work, I'll do mine."

(*Rawḥ* 266–68)

5

The Path

The Qur'an and Hadith typically refer to people in terms of attributes: the faithful, the unbelievers, the knowers, the fearful, the ungrateful, the spiteful, and so on. Later sources offer numerous schemes for classifying human types. The most basic distinction is that between those who know and those who do not, or the faithful and the unbelievers. The faithful (*mu'min*) can then be ranked in ascending degrees. For example, there are the faithful in general, the friends (walī), the prophets (nabī), and the messengers (rasūl). In this sort of scheme, any higher category—or call it a station—includes in itself the good qualities of the lower categories. Thus, the friends have all the good qualities of the faithful, but not those of the prophets. The prophets have faith and friendship, but they are not messengers. Each of the categories is susceptible of subdivision. The subdivisions can then be arranged as ascending stages on the path to God.

When we put aside the stages of prophethood and messengerhood, which came to an end with Muḥammad, human beings can be divided into three broad categories: those who reject the prophetic message (the unbelievers), those who attempt to follow it (the faithful), and those who make significant progress on the path (the friends). The criterion for judgment is proximity to God, which is achieved as seekers gradually actualize the divine form in which Adam was created. Distance from God results from the creative command itself. It is sustained by forgetfulness and heedlessness, the predominant characteristics of normal human beings.

We need to keep in mind that authors who engage in these sorts of discussions are providing a way to think about the human situation, especially our own. They are not suggesting that we have a right to judge others, given that real knowledge of human subtle reality is God's domain, not that of creatures.

The only thing of which we can be sure is that there are different human types. Everyone knows this, and in practice we judge people and put them into categories all the time.

In classifying people into types, the Qur'an and the Hadith praise those who live up to the virtues and beautiful character traits and criticize those who do not. The purpose is to provide standards by which people can judge their own activities and intentions. The real enemy is the self, not anyone else. The soul that commands to evil will leave no one alone. Thinking that one has conquered it is the worst of illusions, and self-admiration is to be avoided at all costs. Maybudī quotes a saying of the Prophet directed at ʿAlī ibn Abī Ṭālib: "O ʿAlī! When you see people busy with the defects of others, busy yourself with the defects of your own soul. When you see people busy with cultivating this world, busy yourself with cultivating your heart" (*Kashf* 3:258).

In any case, no one will achieve nearness to the Creator without being called and pulled. The power that brings about proximity, as Muslim theologians never tire of stressing, can come only from God. *He loves them* is the necessary precondition for *they love Him*. God's love is expressed first in the act of creation, then in the invitation to return. The invitation comes in the form of scripture, which provides the framework for actualizing love: *Follow me; God will love you*. Only then can people climb the ascending ladder. The ladder's generic name is religion (dīn). This word is used to refer to all the paths established by God, to each of them individually and to what eventually came to be called Islam.

RELIGION

In his commentary on the verse "*And We gave David and Solomon a knowledge*" (27:15), Maybudī talks of the various sorts of knowledge that are embraced by the word *religion*, pointing out that it designates the knowledge and practice not only of all the prophets, but also of the angels.

> In this verse the Lord of the Worlds lays a favor on David and Solomon, for He taught them the knowledge of the religion. *Religion* is a comprehensive word that comprises submission, faith, the Sunnah, the community, performing obedient acts and worship, and avoiding unbelief and disobedience. This is the religion of the angels, by which they worship and obey God, and it is the religion of the prophets and messengers from Adam to Muḥammad. The prophets and messengers invited their communities to it, as the Lord of the Worlds says: "*He has set down for you as the religion that with which He counseled Noah, and what We have revealed to thee, and that with which We*

charged Abraham, Moses, and Jesus: Uphold the religion, and scatter not regarding it" [42:13].

This religion is extremely obvious and unveiled to the folk of felicity, but extremely hidden from the folk of wretchedness. The Real gives religion-recognizing eyesight only to the folk of felicity. Only the folk of this eyesight recognize the religion, as the Prophet said: "How is it that you are with your religion like the moon when it is full, but only the seeing see it?"

It is also narrated that he said, "I have brought you a white, immaculate splendor whose night is like its day. For those of you who live, a great diversity will be seen among you after me concerning my Sunnah and that of the rightly guided vicegerents, so hold fast to it."

The religion in its totality is built on two things: listening and following. Listening is that you accept with spirit and heart the revelation sent down on Muṣṭafā. Then you go straight by following him. That is His words "*Whatever the Messenger gives you, take*" [59:7].

(*Kashf* 7:195–96)

The religion is commonly described as having three basic parts or dimensions. The Prophet provided one of the best-known schemes in the Hadith of Gabriel, which was mentioned in connection with iḥsān. Gabriel came to him in human form while he was sitting with some of his Companions. He asked certain questions and the Prophet answered. After he left, the Prophet explained that that was Gabriel, who had come "to teach you your religion." On the basis of this hadith (along with ample support from the Qur'an), the religion can be understood to have three dimensions: islām, which is submission or practice; īmān, which is faith or understanding; and iḥsān, doing the beautiful, or virtue, or transformation by love. In other words, the religion—and indeed, any religion—addresses right activity (the body), rectification of consciousness (the soul), and realization of the inmost reality (the spirit).

Notice that I take īmān, faith, as a category that embraces understanding, in keeping with the general thrust of the texts. Faith is certainly not blind belief. In the Hadith of Gabriel, the Prophet describes it in terms of its objects: "Faith is that you have faith in God, His angels, His books, His messengers, and the Last Day, and that you have faith in the measuring out, both its good and its evil." Without objects, faith is empty, and without an understanding of the objects and their implications for human existence, it is superficial. Faith, in short, is to recognize the Real and to adopt the activity appropriate to this recognition. Maybudī refers to a well-known hadith pointing to this notion of faith in his interpretation of the verse "*Have you not seen how God has struck a similitude? A goodly word is like a goodly tree*" (14:24).

> The good words and true speech of a person of faith are like a good tree that gives forth good fruit. A good tree in fine soil and wholesome water gives forth only sweet fruit. This is why He says, *"And the goodly land—its plants come forth by the leave of its Lord"* [7:58].
>
> The good land is the soul of the person of faith, the good tree is the tree of recognition, the wholesome water is the water of regret, and the sweet fruit is the formula of tawḥīd. Just as a tree sends down roots into the earth, so also recognition and faith send down roots into the heart of the person of faith. Just as the branches bring forth fruit in the air, so also the tree of recognizing tawḥīd brings speech to the tongue and deeds to the limbs, and both rise up. This is why the Exalted Lord said, *"To Him ascend the goodly words, and He uplifts the worthy deed"* [35:10].
>
> A tree is sustained by three things: roots sent down into the earth, a trunk standing in place, and branches lifted in the air. The tree of recognition has three things perfectly: assenting to the truth in the heart, acting with the limbs, and speaking with the tongue. The Prophet said, "Faith is recognizing with the heart, attesting with the tongue, and acting with the body."
>
> (*Kashf* 5:261–62)

It was noted in the previous chapter that the definition of iḥsān found in the Hadith of Gabriel becomes prominent in descriptions of the Tariqah, not least because it points to the inner life and the vision of God that is the goal of the quest: "Doing the beautiful is that you worship God as if you see Him, for if you do not see Him, surely He sees you." This innermost dimension of the religion is often called sincerity (ikhlāṣ). The basic meaning of the Arabic word is "to purify." In this case, it means to purify awareness and consciousness by emptying it of everything other than God. It is to actualize tawḥīd in the core of the self by going through the three basic stages of the Path: purification of the soul, adornment with the virtues, and conformity with the One.

The opposite of sincerity is hypocrisy (nifāq). Just as pride deserves to be called the mother of all sins in Christianity, hypocrisy can claim the name in Islam. It is to perform the correct acts with the wrong intention, that is, for the sake of someone or something other than God. It is, for example, to go to the mosque on Fridays lest your neighbors think bad things about you. Both beautiful-doing and sincerity are closely allied with a third Qur'anic term, godwariness (taqwā), which is commonly used to designate the sum total of all virtues.

In his commentary on the fifth verse of the Fātiḥa, *"Thee alone we worship, and Thee alone we ask for help"* (1:5), Maybudī explains that the two halves of the verse refer to adornment and purification and that the verse in its entirety refers to the submission, faith, and sincerity that describe the religion as a whole.

> This alludes to the religion's two great pillars, around which revolves the traveling of the religious. The first is adornment of the soul by worship without eye-service and obedience without hypocrisy. The second is purification of the soul, keeping it cleansed of associationism and corruption, and not depending on one's own power and strength.
>
> Adornment alludes to everything in the Shariah that ought to be, and purification alludes to everything in the Shariah that ought not to be.
>
> Look carefully at these two short sentences. When someone's heart has familiarity and brightness, he will understand from the two all the Shari'ite rulings of the religion. The words of Muṣṭafā will be verified for him: "I was given the all-comprehensive words and my speech made very brief."
>
> *Thee alone we worship.* It has been said that this is sheer tawḥīd, which is the belief that nothing other than He is worthy of worship. It is knowing that lordhood is fitting only for God and that He is an object of worship without peer, for He is one and unique.
>
> *And Thee alone we ask for help.* This is an allusion to the recognition of the recognizers. It is recognizing that He alone performs all acts and that servants cannot get along by themselves without His help.
>
> The root of this tawḥīd and the stuff of this recognition are that you recognize the Real's being and oneness; then His power, knowledge, and kindness; then His beautiful-doing, love, and nearness. The first is the foundation of submission, the second the foundation of faith, the third the foundation of sincerity.
>
> (*Kashf* 1:34)

It needs to be kept in mind that the word submission (islām) may or may not designate the religion of Islam in any given context. It can designate the universal submission of all things to the creative command, as in the verse, "*Whatsoever is in the heavens and the earth is <u>submitted</u> to Him, willingly or unwillingly, and to Him they shall be returned*" (3:83). It can designate, as it does in the Hadith of Gabriel, the practices of the religion as contrasted with the more inner dimensions, faith and beautiful-doing. It can designate the voluntary submission of any prophet or any follower of a prophet. Hence, the Qur'an calls Abraham and the apostles of Jesus among others Muslims. And it can designate Islam generally. In his commentary on the verse "*Have you seen him who cries lies to the religion?*" (107:1), Maybudī points to some of the common ground of the two words *religion* and *submission.* He has already explained in Stage Two that the exegetes try to give historical context to this verse by mentioning specific individuals to whom it may be referring. He connects his commentary on this verse with his explanation of the formula of consecration.

> In every letter of *In the name of God* are placed the secrets of the Beginningless and the Endless, but they are concealed by the veils of exaltation, lest the ears of the unworthy hear them or the nonprivy gain access. Not everything that reaches the outer ears is received by the spirit and heart. Outward hearing is one thing, and inner reception something else.
>
> One day Shiblī was with Junayd and said, "God!"
>
> Junayd said, "Is what you say the remembrance of the tongue or the remembrance of the spirit? If it is the remembrance of the spirit, then the tongue follows by itself. Otherwise, if it is simply the tongue, that is easy. Iblis says the same thing you do. How are you more excellent than he is?"
>
> This is the general threshold. Both friend and enemy, both familiar and stranger, enter the general threshold. There must also be those who find a place on the carpet of the king inside the curtain. Otherwise, everyone and every piece of straw reach the general threshold.
>
> How can just any straw find this path with color and words?
> It wants a curtain-burning pain and a man striding forth.
>
> The curtain-burning pain is the pain of the religion, and the man striding forth is the one who sticks to the religion.
>
> That miserable unbeliever cried lies to the religion and threw the submission behind his back. Look how the Lord addresses His beloved Muṣṭafā because of that miserable fellow, and look at the warning he gives to that unbeliever! "*Have you seen him who cries lies to the religion?* O Muḥammad! Have you seen that wretched man, that stupid Walīd and that ignorant Abū Jahl? They refuse the religion of the submission and deny your prophethood and miracles!
>
> "O Muḥammad! How will the religion be harmed if they do not accept it? What defect will the religion suffer from their nonacceptance? Surely this religion is firm, without fissures. It is the middle path and the most reliable handhold."
>
> In the tongue of the folk of the Haqiqah, the religion is that you set forth on the road of servanthood, you undertake complete acquiescence, and you turn your face away from every gate. You seek refuge in Him and flee to Him.
>
> One of the scholars of the Tariqah said, "The meaning of *Surely the religion with God is the submission* [3:19] is that you put aside everything but the Real for His sake, and you do not put aside what is rightfully due to Him for any reason whatsoever."

In a sound report, God's Messenger said, "The religion is ease." The religion is all ease because in the end it is that which conveys to ease.

(*Kashf* 10:633–34)

In his commentary on the verse "*God is the light of the heavens and the earth*" (24:35), Maybudī explains that there are both outer and inner lights. In describing the latter, he relates the religion's three dimensions to virtues and character traits and maintains that all three are necessary for common believers, who should be following the basics of the Sunnah. As for those who are advancing on the path of the Tariqah, much more is needed.

In reality, light is that which illuminates other than itself. Whatever does not illuminate another is not called light. The sun is light, the moon is light, and the lamp is light—not in the sense that they are bright in themselves, but in the sense that they illuminate others. Mirrors, water, jewels, and the like are not called light, even if they are bright by their own essences, for they do not illuminate others.

Now that this reality is known, know that *God is the light of the heavens and the earth:* it is God who is the brightener of the heavens and the earths for the faithful and the friends. It is He who gives form to bodies and illuminates spirits. All lights come forth from Him and abide through Him, some manifest and some nonmanifest. Concerning the manifest, He said, "*And We appointed a blazing lamp*" [78:13]. Concerning the nonmanifest, He said, "*Is he whose breast God has expanded for the submission so that he is upon a light from his Lord?*" [39:22].

Although the manifest light is bright and beautiful, it is subordinate to and a servant of the nonmanifest light. The manifest light is the light of sun and moon; the nonmanifest light is the light of tawḥīd and recognition.

The light of sun and moon is lovely and bright, but at the end of the day it will be eclipsed and occulted. Tomorrow at the resurrection, it will be opaque and rolled up—according to His words "*When the sun is enwrapped*" [81:1]. As for the sun of recognition and the light of tawḥīd, these rise up from the hearts of the faithful and will never be eclipsed or occulted, nor will they be overcome and rolled up. They are a rising without setting, an unveiling without eclipse, and a radiance from the station of yearning. A poet has said,

Surely the noonday sun sets at night,
but the heart's sun never disappears.

Know also that the nonmanifest lights are diverse in their levels. The first is the light of submission and, along with submission, the light of sincerity. The second is the light of faith and, along with faith, the light of truthfulness.

The third is the light of beautiful-doing and, along with beautiful-doing, the light of certainty.

The brightness of submission is found in the light of sincerity, the brightness of faith in the light of truthfulness, and the brightness of beautiful-doing in the light of certainty. These are the way stations of the Shariah's road and the stations of the common people among the faithful.

Then the folk of the Haqiqah and the chevaliers of the Tariqah have another light and another state. They have the light of perspicacity and, along with it, the light of unveiling; the light of straightness and, along with it, the light of contemplation; and the light of tawḥīd and, along with it, the light of proximity in the Presence of At-ness.

As long as the servant is within the stations, he is bound by his own traveling. It is here that the Real's pulling begins. The divine attraction joins with him, and the lights take each others' hands—the light of tremendousness and majesty, the light of gentleness and beauty, the light of awesomeness, the light of jealousy, the light of proximity, the light of divinity, the light of the He-ness. This is why the Lord of the Worlds said, "*Light upon light*" [24:35].

The situation reaches the point where servanthood disappears in the light of lordhood. But no one in the whole world has ever had these lights or this proximity to the Possessor of Majesty perfectly save Muṣṭafā the Arab. Everyone has part of it, and he has the whole, for he is the whole of perfection, the totality of beauty, and the kiblah of prosperity.

(*Kashf* 6:542–43)

In still another explanation of the religion, Maybudī refers to its three dimensions as stations. This is part of his interpretation of the verses "*He created man. He taught him the explication*" (55:3–4).

Some people say that *He created man* means all people generally—faithful and unbeliever, sincere and hypocrite, truthful and heretic. Whoever is human is included in this address. They say that He created everyone and taught them all explication. In other words, He gave everyone intellect, understanding, and upbringing so that they would find the road to their own best interests and discern between good and bad. He gave everyone language so that they would know each other's desires—in every region a language; or rather, in every city a language; or rather, in every neighborhood a language. He specified human beings for this and separated them out from other animals with this specification and bestowal of eminence.

It is also said that *He created man* means all the faithful of Muḥammad's community. *He taught him the explication* means the road of the Real, the pure Shariah, the unswerving religion. He taught it to them and showed its road to them: *Say: "This is my path. I call to God"* [12:108]. *Call to the way of thy Lord with wisdom!* [16:125].

He set this road up in three stations: first, recognition of the outward Shariah; second, recognition of the inward struggle and discipline; third, talk of the heart and its Beloved and the story of the friends.

Then He turned this over to three groups and taught the people on the tongues of these three groups: "Ask the ulama, mix with the possessors of wisdom, and sit with the great ones."* Learn the science of the Shariah from the ulama, the science of discipline from the possessors of wisdom, and the science of recognition from the great ones.

(*Kashf* 9:419)

THE BEAUTY OF DEIFORMITY

The Qur'an mentions many traits of character, both beautiful and ugly. Beautiful traits display the divine form in which people were created, and ugly traits obscure the original human substance. The Book and the Sunnah encourage people to do certain things and to avoid others and advise them to become qualified by virtues and to eliminate vices. The literature that discusses virtues and vices does not pertain to jurisprudence, which by nature addresses activity alone. Nor does it belong to Kalam, whose business is to analyze right and wrong beliefs. It was mainly authors associated with Sufism who turned the Qur'anic discussion of human qualities into a structured approach to avoiding ugliness and achieving beauty. The philosophers too had a good deal to say about these issues, employing a more abstract language and drawing inspiration from the ethical teachings of the Greeks.

If we read the verse "*He loves them, and they love Him*" as a statement of the creative command, then both God and man are lover and beloved by definition. Then we can read the verse of following, "*Say: 'If you love God, follow me; God will love you,'*" as a statement of the religious command. People who recognize their love for God should follow the Prophet with the goal of actualizing God's love for them. Although God already loves human beings, they can become the objects of a second sort of love by following the perfect exemplar.

Wherever there is love, there are lover and beloved. What attracts the lover to the beloved is, in one word, beauty. Here the literature employs *jamāl* and *ḥusn* interchangeably. The locus classicus for the word *jamāl* is the Prophet's well-known saying "God is beautiful, and He loves beauty." *Ḥusn* and its derivatives are used repeatedly in the Qur'an. Qur'an translators typically translate these as "beautiful" or "good," depending on their understanding of the context. If the

English *good* had the same connotations as Plato's Good, good would be an appropriate choice. But given this word's modern debasement and the fact that it is needed to translate *khayr,* the opposite of *sharr,* "evil," I consistently translate *ḥusn* and its derivatives as "beauty" and "beautiful," and their opposites, *sū'* and its derivatives, as "ugliness" and "ugly."

When we ask the question "Why does God love human beings?" the answer boils down to one word: beauty. From the perspective of ontology—the creative command—God loves human beings because they are the manifestations of His own beauty. In His beginningless knowledge, He knows them in their beauty, and when He gives existence to their beautiful forms, they come into temporal existence.

From the perspective of morality and ethics—the religious command—God may or may not love human beings, for He does not love the ugly. Inasmuch as people are beautiful, He loves them, but inasmuch as they are ugly, He does not. Moreover, He loves some people more than others, for beauty has degrees. The intensity of His love depends on the intensity of their beauty.

There can be no such thing as inherent human beauty, just as there can be such thing as inherent human existence. Existence is the fruit of the word *Be!* and beauty was instilled into us when God *taught Adam the names, all of them* (2:30). Whatever beauty we may have has come as a trust from God, not a permanent possession.

The hadith "God created Adam in His form" was interpreted in two basic ways. Jurists, Kalam experts, and all those who stressed God's absolute transcendence liked to insist that it means "God created Adam in *his* form," not "in *His* form." In other words, God created Adam in the fullness of his adult form. This interpretation is perfectly plausible, but it does not contradict the second interpretation, which says that God's form is that which is designated by His own names and attributes. It is these that He instilled into Adam when He created Him.

The Qur'an speaks of God's names as most beautiful: "*To Him belong the most beautiful names, so call Him by them*" (7:180). One of these names is Form-Giver (muṣawwir, 59:24). God says to human beings, "*He formed you, so He made your forms beautiful*" (40:64). He Himself is "*the most beautiful of creators*" (23:14), and He created man "*in the most beautiful stature*" (95:4). These and many other verses provide ample Qur'anic support for the notion that human beings, in their original created nature (*fiṭra*), are beautiful. The Beautiful created them in His own form, which is described by the most beautiful names, and He loves them because He loves beauty.

Although the creative command bestowed beauty on human beings, the religious command leaves it up to them whether they will actualize their beauty. As for why they do not retain their beauty as a matter of course, this is fairly obvious—look at what people do when you give them free rein. The Qur'an sees forgetfulness as the root of their perennial failure to live up to their own innate beauty. When *he forgot* (20:115), Adam sowed a seed that sprouts in each of his children. Adam himself remembered after having forgotten, but they may or may not remember. When they do, the first step they should take is to follow the religious command: *Follow me; God will love you.*

When the Qur'an specifies those whom God loves, it mentions them according to their virtues. When it describes those whom God does *not* love, it mentions them according to their vices. These virtues are much discussed in Islamic literature generally, along with many others that the Qur'an mentions in other contexts. There is less attention paid to the vices, but they also are given thorough treatment. Those whom the Qur'an mentions specifically as objects of God's love are the beautiful-doers, the just, the godwary, the self-purifying, the trusting, the patient, and the repentant. Those whom it names as *not* being the objects of His love are the transgressors, the wrongdoers, the ungrateful, the unbelievers, the sinners, the pompous, the boastful, the treacherous, the immoderate, the proud, and the exultant.

Keeping these beautiful and ugly traits in mind, we can see that the path of following the Prophet and becoming worthy of God's love can be described as that of eliminating vices and acquiring virtues. This is the process of negation and affirmation, or purification and adornment: negating human attributes and affirming divine attributes, getting rid of the ugly in order to make room for the beautiful, annihilation and subsistence. The science of ethics (*ʿilm al-akhlāq*), much developed by both philosophers and Sufis, is based precisely on this two-sided process.

The word *akhlāq*, "ethics," is the plural of *khuluq*, "character" or "character trait." In the normal, unvoweled Arabic script, it is written exactly the same as *khalq*, "creation," so it is only the context that tells us which is meant. The common root of the two words shows that character traits are the inner qualities of a person's created nature. A khuluq is not necessarily ethical, because the word is used for both beautiful and ugly traits. God created people's characters, and He made them diverse. In the case of the Prophet, the Qur'an says, "*Surely thou hast a magnificent character*" (68:4). This can be interpreted to mean that he, more than any other creature, brings together the attributes designated by the most beautiful names, for it is he whom God created most perfectly in His form. Just as he dwelt in the Station of No Station, because he embraced all stations but was not fixed by any one of them, so also his character encompassed all the beautiful traits of the human soul, heart, and spirit.

God is beautiful, and all beauty is created by Him. All virtues are His creations and can be traced back to the beautiful divine attributes, sometimes called *akhlāq allāh*, God's character traits. In the human case, virtues (*faḍā'il*) are also called beautiful or noble character traits (*maḥāsin al-akhlāq, makārim al-akhlāq*). Vices (*radhā'il*) are ugly or base character traits (*masāwi' al-akhlāq, safsāf al-akhlāq*). God's character traits are all beautiful, so the process of beautifying human character traits is often called *takhalluq bi-akhlāq allāh*, "becoming characterized by God's character traits." This is to say that a person gradually becomes beautiful in keeping with the original beauty of the human character, created in the divine form. To achieve this, one must follow in the footsteps of the one who possessed the *magnificent character.*

Several hadiths speak of the importance of keeping one's character traits beautiful. In one of his supplications, the Prophet says, "O God, Thou hast made my creation beautiful, so make my character beautiful too." He is alluding to the verse "*We created man in the most beautiful stature*" (95:4). Another supplication, often recited at the beginning of the ritual prayer, includes the sentence "Guide me to the most beautiful character traits—no one guides to the most beautiful of them but Thou." Notice that the second clause of this sentence is simply a restatement of the formula of tawḥīd, "There is no guide but God."

Maybudī illustrates the relationship between creation and character in his commentary on the verse "*Leave aside the outward sin and the inward*" (6:120).

> Know that the Exalted Lord created the creatures with His majestic power and perfect exaltation and arranged them in keeping with His subtle artisanry, wise gaze, and limitless generosity. He completed their limitless blessings both outwardly and inwardly. He said, "*He has lavished on you His blessings, outward and inward*" [31:20]. Then He asked the servants to be grateful for the blessings: "*And be grateful for the blessings of God, if it is He whom you worship*" [16:114].
>
> If you want to show what is stipulated for servanthood, then display gratitude for His blessings and do not employ the blessings of your Lord in opposing Him, whether outwardly or inwardly. This is why He said, "*Leave aside the outward sin and the inward.*"
>
> Just as He made blessings two sorts, the outward and the inward, so also He made opposition two sorts, the outward and the inward.

The outward blessing is the perfection of creation, and the inward blessing is the beauty of character. The counterparts of these are outward sin, which is opposition that enters the outward bodily parts, and inward sin, which is love for disobedience that enters the heart. This is why Sahl Tustarī said concerning the meaning of this verse, "Abandon bodily acts of disobedience and also the heart's love for those acts."

It is said too that outward sin is seeking this world and inward sin is seeking paradise. Even though seeking paradise is not disobedience in the tongue of knowledge, in the path of the chevaliers and the tasting of the recognizers, seeking paradise is to seek blessings. When someone seeks blessings, he is held back from the mystery of the Blessings-Giver and the joy of the Presence. They count anything that holds you back from that mystery and joy as associationism and disobedience, even if, for some people, it is obedience and worship. In this meaning, they sang,

> Whatever talk keeps you back from the road—
> let it be unbelief or faith!
> Whatever picture holds you back from the Friend—
> let it be ugly or beautiful! [Sanā'ī]

(*Kashf* 3:483)

Commentators find numerous insights into the nature of love and beauty in the Qur'an's retelling of the story of Joseph. Maybudī provides an example in his commentary on the verse "*They sold him for a small price*" (12:20).

It is not surprising that Joseph's brothers sold him for a small price. What is surprising is the work of those travelers, who acquired someone like Joseph for twenty dirhams! It is not surprising that people should sell subsistent paradise for this small world. What is surprising is that they gain such a magnificent paradise and tremendous kingdom with a loaf of bread given to a poor man! Indeed, good fortune does not have a price, and the Real's generosity is nothing but a gift.

If what Joseph possessed in himself—the characteristics of sinlessness, the realities of proximity, and the subtleties of knowledge and wisdom—had been unveiled to his brothers, they would not have sold him for that small price, nor would they have called him a slave. A single speck of those characteristics and subtleties was unveiled to the governor of Egypt and Zulaykhā. Look how they bestowed their kingdom on his work and what value they placed on him! So also, when the women of Egypt saw his beauty, they said, "*This is no mortal! This is none but a noble angel*" [12:31]. Yes, it is showing that does the job, not seeing. Muṣṭafā said, "O God, show us things as they are!"

Ibn 'Aṭā' said, "Beauty is of two sorts, outward beauty and inward beauty. Outward beauty is an adorned creation and a lovely form. Inward beauty is perfect character and fine conduct."

The Lord of the Worlds showed Joseph's outward beauty to his brothers. They saw nothing more, even though in God's eyes the outward has no importance. Hence they sold him for a small price. A trace of the inner beauty was shown to the governor of Egypt, so he said to his wife, "*Give him generous lodging*" [12:21]. This is so that the world's folk may know that in God's eyes, importance and worth belong to inner beauty, not outward. Muṣṭafā said, "God gazes not on your forms or your possessions, but He gazes on your hearts and your activities."

It is said that one day Joseph looked in a mirror and gazed on himself. He saw perfect beauty and said, "If I were a slave, what would my price be!? Who would be able to pay it?" The Lord of the Worlds did not let that pass, not until Joseph had tasted the punishment of gazing on himself. He was made a slave, and his price was twenty dirhams.

The Pir of the Tariqah said, "Do not look at yourself, for self-seeing has no worth! Do not adorn yourself, for self-adornment has no value! Do not approve of yourself, for self-approval has no support!"

> Quit being the companion of self-nurturing habit worshipers!
> Kiss the dust beneath the feet of those disgusted with self! [Sanā'ī]

"Do not adorn yourself," and let the Real adorn you: *And He adorned it in their hearts* [49:7]. "Do not approve of yourself," and let the Real approve of you: *God is well pleased with them* [5:119]. Do not belong to yourself, and let the Real belong to you: *And you did not throw when you threw* [8:17].

On the night of the mi'rāj, He said to Muṣṭafā, "Belong to Me as you always were, and I will belong to you as I have always been."

(*Kashf* 5:42–43)

In his commentary on the verse "*We sent thee only as a mercy to the worlds*" (21:107), Maybudī sums up the depiction of the Prophet as the possessor of beautiful character traits. In mentioning the character of the Qur'an, he has in mind the saying of 'Ā'isha "His character was the Qur'an."

He was a man who came out from under the cloak of 'Abdallāh ibn 'Abd al-Muṭṭalib. He passed by mortal loins, but he received help from the Unseen. God transformed his states and words: *Surely thou hast a magnificent character* [68:4]. The character of mortal nature was removed, and the character of the Qur'an put in its place. The speech of mortal nature was taken, and pure revelation was given: *He does not speak out of caprice. It is naught but a revelation revealed* [53:3–4]. Hence he came speaking of the Shariah, traveling to the Real, and moving in accordance with the command.

(*Kashf* 6:323–24)

The underlying issue in Sufi discussions of ethics was how to become characterized by the character traits of God, a process the philosophers often called gaining similarity to God (*al-tashabbuh bi'l-ilāh*), or deiformity (*ta'alluh*). Muḥammad Ghazālī and others explained that people should meditate on the meaning of the divine names precisely because salvation is found in conforming oneself to God's character traits.[1] In explaining the verse "*Be you lordly ones!*" (3:79), Maybudī cites two hadiths to stress that the goal of following the Sunnah is to become characterized by the divine traits.

In other words: be one of those singled out for God, those who are described by His words "When I love him, I am his hearing with which he hears and his eyesight with which he sees."

In keeping with the tasting of the folk of recognition, *the lordly ones* are those who become one for God with disengaged intention, sound trust, and intimacy's breeze. They step beyond the two worlds and seize hold of the gentleness of the Protector's love. They say the prayer of the dead for their own attributes.

When someone steps into the field of passion for the beautiful,
night and day will recite for him the prayer of the dead. [Sanā'ī]

They have souls undergoing annihilation and hearts full of thirst. They have burnt souls, secret cores lit by passion, and spirits hanging in hope.

I want a heart for choosing only You,
a spirit for breathing the pain of Your passion,
A body for desiring only Your love,
an eye for seeing You and only You.

Their aspiration goes beyond this world, their desire beyond paradise, their repose beyond heaven and earth. They are waiting: when will the sun of love rise, when will the moon of good fortune come forth, when will the breeze of felicity blow, when will the beginningless remembrance bear fruit?

When will I throw off this cage
and build a nest in the divine garden!?

It is also said that *the lordly ones* are those singled out for God. Through this they are ascribed to Him, described by His attributes, and come forth with His character traits as long as their servanthood lasts and their makeup stays in place. This view is taken from a saying of Muṣṭafā, "Become characterized by the character traits of God!" He also said, "God has a number of character traits. Whoever becomes characterized by one of them will enter the Garden."

The folk of knowledge have said that the exegesis of these character traits is the meaning of the ninety-nine names of God. In his traveling, the servant must pass by way of those meanings to reach union with God.

The Pir of Khurasan, Abu'l-Qāsim Kurragānī, said, "As long as the servant is acquiring these meanings and bringing together these descriptions, he is still in the path and has not yet reached the goal. He is traveling on his own and has not yet received God's attraction. As long as he stays in recognition, he is held back from the Recognized. As long as he is seeking love, he is unaware of the Beloved."

> Hurry to passion and don't sit in attachment,
> take a few steps beyond passion and being passionate!

A great man was asked, "When does the servant reach the Protector?"

He said, "When he reaches himself."

They asked, "How does he reach himself?"

He said, "Seeking becomes lost in the Sought and recognition in the Recognized."

They said, "Explain more."

He said, "Of the body, the tongue remains, and that is it. Of the heart, the mark remains, and that is it. Of the spirit, face-to-face vision remains, and that is it. Hearing goes, the Heard remains, and that is it. The heart goes, the Shown remains, and that is it. The spirit goes, the Found remains, and that is it."

(*Kashf* 2:185–87)

The "great man" just mentioned is probably Anṣārī, whose chapter on annihilation in *One Hundred Fields* makes similar points. In *Forty-Two Chapters*, Anṣārī speaks of the transformation of character while commenting on a saying by Abu'l-Ḥasan Bunān (d. 930): "Avoid base character traits just as you avoid forbidden things and sins." In his explanation, he alludes to the Prophet's saying "I was sent to complete the noble character traits" or, in another version, "the beautiful character traits."

The Intimation. The wayfarers on this road and the proximate to this threshold nurture the root of their own makeup with beautiful character traits, just as they nurture beautiful character traits with beautiful deeds.

Make the Shariah the sultan of your acts and the Tariqah the sultan of your character traits! Then you may complete the noble character traits with the Tariqah of the Men and arrange the character traits of both submission and faith by observing the Shariah.

After that you may reap the fruit of the road of the chevaliers. You will come out of the whirlpool of the soul's being, find the taste of the hidden non-being, and open the eye of the heart toward the Fluctuater of the Hearts. You will see majesty, beauty, and magnificence that you cannot perceive with the intellect.

(*Chihil* 22)

The soul needs to be purified of ugly traits so that it can be adorned by their beautiful counterparts. In the following, Maybudī explains that blameworthy traits pertain to the soul that commands to the ugly, and praiseworthy traits to the heart.

Repel the ugly with what is more beautiful [23:96]. In this verse the generous Lord, the wise and renowned Creator, commands Muṣṭafā to noble character traits and beautiful habits—a bright face, mild words, a soft heart, and a pleasant character; pardoning the bad-doers, hiding the defects of the defective, and doing good in place of bad.

In the tongue of the Tariqah, the *more beautiful* is for the heart to give fatwas by the Real's dictation. The *ugly* is for the soul to issue commandments by its own caprice. He is saying, "O Master, repel what the soul commands by means of what the Real shows: *Repel the ugly with what is more beautiful.*"

The Prophet always used to say, "Our Lord, do not entrust us to our souls for the blink of an eye, or less than that."

O God, lift up this curtain of self from before our heart so that the bird of the heart may be completely delivered from the cage of the soul and fly in the air of the Protector's approval! O God, this burden of soul is the burden of selfhood. Lift this burden of selfhood away from us so we may be released from self and turn to You!

(*Kashf* 6:474–75)

From one standpoint, the task of transforming character lies outside our hands, for as the Prophet said, "God has finished with creation and character." This, however, is the standpoint of the creative command. The religious command replies that people must try as best they can to act correctly, think rightly, and imitate the character traits of the prophets. The Qur'an itself is a book of instruction, telling them how to carry out this task—even if God's mercy and grace alone can provide the aspiration and strength to follow its guidance.

Samʿānī explains that God's loving-kindness in the Qur'an opens up four doors to His servants and that even if they shut these doors to themselves, His love and mercy will send them the keys.

> In His perfect generosity and munificence, the Exalted Lord opened four doors to you: the door of beautiful-doing, the door of blessings, the door of obedience, and the door of gentleness.
>
> He opened the door of beautiful-doing and munificence to you. You came forward with ugly-doing and shut the door to yourself. The Real sent the messenger of generosity with the key of forbearance and pardon: He said: "I will curtain your ugly-doing with My mercy, for I am a gentle Master and you are a weak servant. *It is He who accepts repentance from His servants and pardons the ugly deeds* [42:25]. *As for those to whom the most beautiful preceded from Us* [21:101]."
>
> He opened the door of blessings to you. You came forward with ingratitude and shut the door to yourself by shortcoming in giving thanks. *When We bless man, he turns away and pulls aside* [17:83]. He sent the messenger of bounty with the key of favor and said, "Though you fall short in giving thanks to Me, every day I will increase the blessing of My mercy. *Say: 'In the bounty of God, and His mercy [in that let them rejoice]'* [10:58]."
>
> He opened the door of obedience to you. You came forward with shortcoming and wanted to shut the door with disobedience. The Real sent the messenger of forgiveness with the key of repentance: "When you sin and do not care, I will forgive you and will not care. *O My servants who have been immoderate against yourselves, despair not of God's mercy—surely God forgives all sins* [39:53]."
>
> He opened the door of love to you. You came forward with disloyalty and shut the door to yourself with impudence. He sent the messenger of clemency with the key of curtaining. He said, "My servant, if you are bold toward Me with ugly deeds, I will pass over that, for I am your Lover and I am the Most Merciful of the merciful."
>
> (*Rawḥ* 390–91)

DOING THE BEAUTIFUL

When the religion is understood as having three dimensions—islām, or submission; īmān, or faith; and iḥsān, or beautiful-doing—the first two are seen as necessary preparations for the third. From the perspective of religious learning, submission is the domain of the jurists, faith that of theologians, and beautiful-doing that of Sufi teachers. As Anṣārī remarked in *Way Stations*, the description of iḥsān provided in the Hadith of Gabriel "is an all-comprehensive allusion to the position of this group" (*Manāzil* 6), that is, the recognizers and chevaliers. Discussions of iḥsān are always tightly bound up with the issue of perfecting the soul and becoming characterized by the divine character traits. The ultimate goal is for God to love the servant and to become "his hearing with which he hears and his eyesight with which he sees."

The fact that iḥsān pertains to "this group" does not imply that islām and īmān are ignored. Authors who discuss these issues make clear that everyone who truly has faith is also a submitter, but not every submitter has faith, since one can submit to the Shariah for a variety of social or political reasons. So also, every beautiful-doer has faith, but not everyone with faith is a beautiful-doer. The stations of islām and īmān are embraced by the station of iḥsān, in which love for God and being loved by Him reach their fruition. It did not go unnoticed by Sufi teachers that God mentions that He loves the beautiful-doers five times in the Qur'an, but not once does He say that He loves the submitters or the faithful, even if He is the friend (walī) of the faithful. Neither submission nor faith is sufficient to actualize beauty of soul.

God Himself is the Beautiful-Doer (*muḥsin*), one of the divine names. Moreover, *"He made beautiful all that He created"* (32:7). By encouraging people to act beautifully, God is encouraging them to bring themselves into harmony with the divine form in which they were created. Samʿānī explains that the value of servanthood, which is found in the actualization of submission and faith, lies in achieving the station of beautiful-doing. He is commenting on the divine name *ḥamīd*, the Praiseworthy, and he turns to an analysis of the meaning of the seven verses of the Fātiḥa, the second of which is *Praise belongs to God.* He sums up the meaning of the fifth verse in these terms:

> So *Thee alone we worship* is to carry out servanthood, and *Thee alone we ask for help* is to see God. The measure and worth of discharging servanthood lies in seeing God. This is the meaning of Muṣṭafā's words in answer to Gabriel when he asked, "What is doing the beautiful?" He said, "It is that you worship God as if you see Him, for if you do not see Him, surely He sees you." *They were commanded only to worship God, to be sincere in the religion for Him, to be unswerving, and to perform the prayer and pay the alms tax. That is the upright religion* [98:5].
>
> (*Rawḥ* 470)

Given the number of times that the Beautiful-Doer, beautiful-doing, and beautiful-doers are mentioned in the Qur'an, it is not surprising that commentators like Maybudī discuss iḥsān frequently and typically connect it to the highest goal of the religion. In the first of the following passages, Maybudī ties it back to being loyal to the oath that was sworn at the Covenant of Alast.

And do what is beautiful! Surely God loves the beautiful-doers [2:195]. Muṣṭafā said, "Doing the beautiful is that you worship God as if you see Him, for if you do not see Him, surely He sees you." Doing the beautiful is that you worship God in wakefulness and awareness as if you are gazing upon Him, and you serve Him as if you are seeing Him.

This hadith is an allusion to the heart's encounter with the Real, the secret core's convergence with the Unseen, and the spirit's contemplation of the Protector. It is an incitement to sincerity in acts, letting go of wishes, and loyalty to what was accepted on the First Day.

What was accepted on the First Day? Hearing *Am I not your Lord* and saying *Yes indeed* [7:172]. What is loyalty to what was accepted? Serving the Protector. How does one let go of wishes? In "As if you see Him." Where is sincerity in acts? In "He sees you."

When an eye has seen Him, how can it busy itself with glancing at others? When a spirit has found companionship with Him, how will it make do with water and dust? The word "*Return!*" [89:28] is addressed to the pure spirit. How will it make its home in the frame of water and dust? When someone has become accustomed to that Presence, how long will he put up with the abasement of the veil? How can the ruler of a city pass his life in exile?

The attribute of the spirit is subsistence, and water and dust undergo annihilation. He who lives in the Real is not like him who lives in this world. The realizer is aware of the secret of the Real: the Real is seeable. "As if you see Him" in the report bears witness to this.

(*Kashf* 1:522)

And those who pardon people. And God loves the beautiful-doers [3:134]. *'Afw* [pardon] has two meanings: One is to efface, as the Arabs say, "The winds pardoned the tracks." The other is bounty, as God says, "*Take the pardon*" [7:199], that is, take the bounty of their property.

Here He alludes to the fact that *those who pardon people* are those who pass over and efface the sins of people, but they do not limit themselves to that. Rather, they caress them and bestow upon them something of the bounty of what they own. This is the attribute of the beautiful-doers, and God is their friend. He says, "*And God loves the beautiful-doers.*"

In dealing with the Real, beautiful-doing is "to worship God as if you see Him." In dealing with people, it is that when someone is bad toward you,

you are good toward him; and when someone does not act worthily toward you, you act worthily toward him. This is why God commanded, "*Take the pardon*," that is, take the excellent and beautiful things from among the character traits, and then pardon those who wrong you, join with those who cut off from you, and act with beauty toward those who act with ugliness toward you.

(2:283–84)

Surely God is with those who are godwary and those who do what is beautiful [16:128]. This is one of the all-comprehensive verses of the Qur'an. All God's caressing of His servant in the two worlds, the rewards and the generous gifts, are included in what He says: "*Surely God is with.*" Every sort of service, every type of obedience, and all the roots of worship that the servant performs for God come under the word "*those who are godwary.*" All the rights that the servants have against each either, the various sorts of interaction, come under "*those who do what is beautiful.*"

In reality, the godwary and the beautiful-doers are such that the scent of love's breeze comes from the dust beneath their feet. If the tears of their eyes were to fall on the ground, the narcissus of desire would bloom. If the disclosure of their present moment were to fall on a stone, it would turn into a carnelian. If it were to fall on water, it would become wine. If the fire of their yearning were to flame up, the world would burn. If the light of their recognition were to shine, the universe would be radiant. They have no station in the cities, no ease with the people.

The common people have two festivals in the year, but they have a festival with every breath. The common people have festivals because of seeing the moon, but they have their festival because of contemplating God. The common people have festivals because of the turning of the year, but they have their festival because of the bounteousness of the Possessor of Majesty.

(5:476–77)

Among the several verses that command people to act beautifully is "*Act beautifully toward parents and kinsfolk, toward orphans and the indigent, toward the neighbor who is of kin and the neighbor who is not of kin, toward the companion at your side and the traveler, and toward those whom your right hands own*" (4:36). As part of his commentary on the verse, Maybudī points out that there are several sorts of neighbors. The obvious sorts are those who live next door to you. But you are not simply a bodily person living in a house. You are also a soul, a heart, and a spirit, and each of these has its own neighbors. In every case, the neighbor has a right or rightful due (ḥaqq), in keeping with the prophetic saying

"Your soul has a right against you, your Lord has a right against you, your guest has a right against you, and your spouse has a right against you; so give to each that has a right its right." The nearest of your neighbors is the Real, who is nearer than the jugular vein (50:16). His right is that you rectify your character. You must actualize love to such a degree that His character traits come to replace your own.

The neighbors are many, and their rights are in the measure of their proximity. There is the neighbor of the house, the neighbor of the soul, the neighbor of the heart, and the neighbor of the spirit. The neighbor of the house is the human being; the neighbor of the soul is the angel; the neighbor of the heart is the tranquility of recognition; and the neighbor of the spirit is the Real—majestic is His majesty!

He called the neighbor of the house "*the neighbor who is of kin*" [4:36]. About the neighbor of the soul, He said, "*Over you are guardians*" [82:10]. Concerning the neighbor of the heart, He said, "*It is He who sent down tranquility into the hearts of the faithful*" [48:4]. About the neighbor of the spirit, He said, "*He is with you wherever you are*" [57:4].

The right of the neighbors of the house is that you never leave aside taking them into consideration. By caring for them, you should always keep them thankful to you and at ease with you.

The right of the neighbors of the soul is that you keep them happy with your obedience and do not make them suffer by disobedient acts. Then, when they turn away from you, they will turn away satisfied and grateful.

The right of the neighbor of the heart is that you keep your own recognition pure of the stains of innovation and the defilement of bewilderment and that you adorn it with the garment of the Sunnah and the ornament of wisdom.

The right of the neighbor of the spirit is that you rectify your character traits. You observe courtesy to all sides, you fill your mind with reverence, you step beyond the two worlds, you escape from yourself, and you become one for the Real.

It has been reported that God said, "O Muḥammad! Belong to Me as you always were, and I will belong to you as I have always been."

> If you are with yourself, how can you sit with Me?
>   How far it is from you to Me!
> You will not reach Me until you become one:
>   either you'll find room in love's road, or I.

(*Kashf* 2:510–11)

THE SHARIAH, THE TARIQAH, AND THE HAQIQAH

When the Shariah and the Tariqah are contrasted with each other, the Shariah means the path of all Muslims, namely, the activities and beliefs that lead to paradise, and the Tariqah is the path of the few, those who dedicate themselves solely to God. Those who follow the Shariah without entering the Tariqah may then be called the common people (*ʿāmm*), and those who follow the Tariqah in addition to the Shariah the elect (*khāṣṣ*). The goal of both the Shariah and the Tariqah is the Haqiqah. Those who reach it may then be called the elect of the elect (*khāṣṣ al-khāṣṣ*), a designation that belongs to the prophets and a tiny portion of those who follow in their footsteps. In explaining the verse "*We raise in degree whomsoever We will*" (12:76), Maybudī talks about the structure of the religion in terms of these three levels.

> First there is going straight, then unveiling, then contemplation: "We give whomsoever We want a high standing, and We lift up his degrees: first the success of obedience, then the realization of recompense; first the sincerity of deeds, then the purification of states; first the resoluteness of service in the station of the Shariah, then the finding of contemplation in the Haqiqah itself."
>
> Going straight alludes to the Shariah, unveiling alludes to the Tariqah, and contemplation alludes to the Haqiqah itself. The Shariah is servanthood, the Tariqah is selflessness, and the Haqiqah is freedom in the midst of both.
>
> (*Kashf* 5:118)

Maybudī sometimes talks about the three levels together, but he often simply contrasts the Shariah with the Haqiqah. In the following, he is distinguishing between the Qur'anic message that is addressed to everyone and the parts of the message that can be understood and put into practice by only a few. This belongs to his commentary on the verse "*It is He who has sent down upon you the Book wherein are firm verses, which are the mother of the Book, and others ambiguous*" (3:7). This verse attracted a great deal of attention from theologians and jurists, for they wanted to distinguish between verses that are firm and clear and those in which there may be ambiguity. There has certainly never been anything like a consensus about which verses belong to which category.

> These are the two great divisions of the Qur'an, one apparent and clear, the other abstruse and difficult. The apparent belongs to the majesty of the Shariah, and the difficult belongs to the beauty of the Haqiqah. The apparent is so that the common people may reach joy and blessings by perceiving it and putting it into practice. The difficult is so that the elect may reach the mystery of the Blessings-Giver by surrendering and assenting to it.

From the place of blessings and joy to the place of intimacy and mystery are numerous ups and downs. Given the exaltedness of this state and the eminence of this work, He did not lift up the curtain of abstruseness and ambiguity, lest any of the nonprivy walk into this lane, for not everyone is worthy to know the secrets of kings.

Go, don't wander round the pavilion of secrets!
Why try? You're no man for this battle.
A man must cut himself off from both worlds
and drink down the dregs of the lovers' draft.

(*Kashf* 2:24)

Maybudī draws a similar distinction between the Shariah and the Haqiqah in his remarks on the verse *"For every one of you [prophets] We have appointed an avenue and a method"* (5:48). Notice that his description of the Haqiqah here could just as well apply to the Tariqah.

The avenue is the Shariah, and the method is the Haqiqah. The avenue is the customs of the Shariah, and the method is the road toward the Real. The avenue is what Muṣṭafā brought, and the method is a lamp that the Real holds next to the heart. The avenue is following the Shariah, and the method is finding access to the light of that lamp. The avenue is the message that you heard from the Messenger, and the method is the light that you find in the secret core. The Shariah belongs to everyone, and the Haqiqah belongs to some rather than others.

(*Kashf* 3:140)

The notion that the religion has ascending degrees is tightly bound up with the self-evident fact that understanding has different levels. A yawning gulf separates memorization of the Qur'an from actually grasping the realities that the Book discloses. In the first passage below, Maybudī talks about three levels of knowledge. In the second, he describes three levels of the religion in similar terms:

Whomsoever God desires to guide, He expands his breast to the submission [6:125]. The mark of this expansion is that at three moments He throws three lights into the heart of the servant: the light of intellect at the beginning, the light of learning in the middle, and the light of recognition at the end. Then, with the sum total of these lights, all his difficulties are solved and he begins to see something of the Unseen. Muṣṭafā said, "Be wary of the perspicacity of the man of faith, for he gazes with the light of God."

With the light of the beginning, he knows his own defects; with the light of the middle, he recognizes his own loss; and with the light of the end, he perceives his own nonbeing. With the light of the beginning, he escapes from associationism; with the light of the middle, he escapes from opposition; and with the light of the end, he escapes from himself.

(*Kashf* 3:485)

Those who are firmly rooted in knowledge [4:162]. The firmly rooted in knowledge are those who have obtained the varieties of knowledge: the knowledge of the Shariah, the knowledge of the Tariqah, and the knowledge of the Haqiqah.

The knowledge of the Shariah can be learned, the knowledge of the Tariqah comes through practice, and the knowledge of the Haqiqah comes by finding.

Concerning the knowledge of the Shariah, He says, "*Ask the folk of the remembrance*" [16:43]. Concerning the knowledge of the Tariqah, He says, "*Seek the means of approach to Him*" [5:35]. Concerning the knowledge of the Haqiqah, He says, "*We taught him knowledge from Us*" [18:65].

He turned the knowledge of the Shariah over to a teacher, He turned the knowledge of the Tariqah over to a pir, and He turned the knowledge of the Haqiqah over to Himself.

Whoever fancies that he has no use for the intermediary of a teacher in knowledge of the Shariah is a heretic. Whoever claims that knowledge of the Tariqah is possible without a pir is a tempter. Whoever says that the teacher of knowledge of the Haqiqah is other than the Real is deluded.

It has been said that those firmly rooted in knowledge are those who learn the knowledge of the Shariah and then put it into practice with sincerity to the point that they perceive the knowledge of the Haqiqah in their secret core. Thus Muṣṭafā said, "When someone acts on what he knows, God will bequeath him knowledge of what he does not know." When someone does not put the knowledge of the Shariah into practice, he has wasted his knowledge and it becomes an argument against him. When someone puts it into practice, his outward knowledge becomes an argument to his benefit and he receives the knowledge of the Haqiqah as a gift.

(2:774–75)

Maybudī describes three basic human types in his commentary on the verse "*God promises those of you who have faith and do worthy deeds that He will surely make you vicegerents in the earth*" (24:55). Notice that, like Muḥammad Ghazālī, he places the scholars of the religion, who are the experts in the Shariah and Kalam, among the common people, for they have not yet gone beyond rote learning and are still immersed in their own souls. The next group is the recognizers, the elect who are well advanced on the Tariqah. Although they are undergoing the process of becoming characterized by God's character traits, they still have a sense of themselves. Only the elect of the elect have reached the Haqiqah (called here "the realities of tawḥīd"). They have escaped totally from their own existence.

Know that the vicegerents in the earth to whom the Exalted Lord alludes in this verse are three groups. Each group has a known station in tawḥīd and a defined limit in making servanthood manifest.

The first are the ulama of the religion of submission and the jurists of the Shariah, the guardians of the creed and the counselors of the community. Their limit in making servanthood manifest goes no further than hoping to recognize the Real and fearing punishment. The fruit of their tawḥīd is confined to safety in this world and well-being in the next world. Their submission and faith are the Real's gentle favors and succor, but these are mixed with the contaminants of personal motives and the marks bearing witness to the soul's own shares. Their innate disposition has been overcome by the attributes of mortal nature, and their life put under the sway of habits and customs. In the world of servanthood, they are called those who mimic the folk of *No god but God*. They are veiled from the world of realities by the attributes of mortal nature. They are headed for paradise, but their state is as Junayd said to Nūrī: "These are the stuffing of the Garden, which has companions other than these. The stuffing of the Garden are its prisoners, and the companions of the Garden are its commanders."

The next group is called the elect of the empire. They abide through sincerity in obedience, soundness of desire, and truthfulness in poverty and intention. They are far from the contaminants of personal motives and the soul's shares, and are protected from lassitude and backsliding, but the hand of mortal nature displays the mirror of their attributes to their eyes, so they see that they abide on the carpet of tawḥīd by the Real's succor. Their seeing of their own present moment in the mirror of limpidness keeps them on the carpet of being. They have an excuse, but they are far from the world of nonbeing. Their vision of truthfulness and their observation of the marks bearing witness to sincerity block them from the world of nonbeing. Until someone reaches the world of nonbeing, the realities of tawḥīd will not show their face to him.

The third group is the elect of the elect. They abide through the Real's making them abide, not through their own abiding. They live through the opening that disengages, not the spirit that mobilizes. They have been emancipated from their own power and strength and disengaged from their own

> desires and aims. They do not remain in the circle of their own acts and states, nor are they captive to self-determination and free choice. They do not read the edict of felicity and wretchedness. They are not brought out from the pavilion of the Unseen, nor are they recorded in the registers of effacement and affirmation. In face of the severity of lordhood, they are like balls in the bend of the sultan's polo stick. They say, "We must stay in the bend of the sultan's polo stick, whether he sends the ball right or left."
>
> The first group is the sincere, who see that all is from Him. The second group is the recognizers, who see that all is in Him. The third group is the tawḥīd-voicers, who see that all is He.
>
> The first two groups dwell in the marks bearing witness to service and have not been released from the intrusions of dispersion. The third group is in companionship itself. They have reached the center-point of togetherness. One breath as His companion is better than a thousand years of living in service.
>
> (*Kashf* 6:574–75)

It is worth noting that the penultimate paragraph of this passage prefigures a famous controversy that arose five hundred years later with the Persian writings of Shaykh Aḥmad Sirhindī (d. 1624), who criticized Ibn al-ʿArabī by ascribing to him—on the basis of received wisdom and without textual justification—the notion of *waḥdat al-wujūd*, "the oneness of existence." He claimed that the correct position was *waḥdat al-shuhūd*, "the oneness of witnessing." In defining those two terms, Sirhindī said that *waḥdat al-wujūd* means "All is He" (*hama ūst*) and that *waḥdat al-shuhūd* means "All is from Him" (*hama az ūst*) or "All is in Him" (*hama bi-ūst*).[2] As we just saw, Maybudī understands these three statements as designating three ascending levels of tawḥīd (as he does in his commentary on 6:19, translated toward the end of Chapter 6).

In explaining the verse "*And Lot, when he said to his people, 'What, do you commit indecency?'*" (7:80), Maybudī provides still another classification of human types:

> Each person's indecency is appropriate to his days and states. Look at a man's station in traversing the road. Where is he located? His indecency follows the measure of his mortal nature right there.
>
> The world's creatures are no more than three groups: the common people, the elect, and the elect of the elect.
>
> The indecency of the common people is explained by the tongue of the Shariah, and its penalty is either the whip or stoning.
>
> The indecency of the elect is to look at the pleasures and appetites of this world with the eye of the head, to see their enjoyment and adornment, and to give them access to themselves, even if they are permitted and far from

ambiguity. For in the case of the elect, the blight of the permitted bliss of this world is more than the blight of the forbidden in the case of the common people. In the tongue of the Master of the Shariah, the penalty of this indecency is what he said: "Lower your eyes and hold back your hands."

The indecency of the elect of the elect is that they should gaze at other than the Real with the heart's awareness despite the fact that this declaration has come from the Real: "*Say 'God,' then leave them*" [6:91]. He is saying, "My servant, do not gaze at yourself—see everything as My act. Do not think that you are doing Me a favor with your activity—look at My success-giving. Flee from your own marks—see only My love." What does someone seized by His love have to do with others? Keep the heart turned toward Him and let the others go.

All this tumult comes from talk of you and me—
give up *me* and the world will be your garden.

(*Kashf* 3:680–81)

In his comments on the verse "*O you who have faith, have faith in God and His Messenger*" (4:136), Maybudī offers another explanation of the difference between the Shariah and the Haqiqah.

Faith is two sorts, one based on demonstration, the other on face-to-face vision. Faith by demonstration is the road of inference, and faith by face-to-face vision is finding the day of union. Faith by demonstration is to employ the evidence of intellects, and faith by vision is to reach the degrees of arrival. He says: "O you who have acquired faith by demonstration, strive to acquire faith by face-to-face vision!"

What is faith by face-to-face vision? Gazing with the eye of response on the Responder, gazing with the eye of solitariness on the Solitary, gazing with the eye of presence on the Present, being near to God's nearness by being far from self, being present with His generosity by being absent from self. He—majestic is His majesty!—is not far from the strivers nor absent from the desirers. He says, "*We are nearer to him than the jugular vein*" [50:16].

The Pir of the Tariqah said, "O Lord! You are found by the souls of the chevaliers, You are present to the hearts of the rememberers. They give marks of You up close, but You are far beyond that. They fancy You from afar, but You are closer than the spirit."

Lovely idol! Are you then my beloved?
Now that I look close, You are my spirit.

It is also said that the meaning of the verse is this: *O you who have faith* by assenting, *have faith* by realizing! You have accepted the Shariah, now accept the Haqiqah.

What is the Shariah? What the Haqiqah? The Shariah is a lamp, the Haqiqah a burn. The Shariah is a bond, the Haqiqah advice. The Shariah is need, the Haqiqah joy. The Shariah is the outer pillars, the Haqiqah the inner pillars. The Shariah is not having evil, the Haqiqah is not having self. The Shariah is service based on conditions, the Haqiqah exile based on witnessing. The Shariah is by intermediaries, the Haqiqah by unveiling.

The folk of the Shariah keep obedience and leave aside disobedience, the folk of the Haqiqah flee from themselves and take joy in oneness. The folk of the Shariah hope for everlastingness and subsistent bliss, the folk of the Haqiqah audaciously busy themselves with the Cupbearer.

The Haqiqah begins when He appears. The longing that overcomes you makes the wide world too narrow for you and turns the inside of your shirt into a prison. It strikes fire in your spirit and throws thirst into your heart. You see the burning, but not the Burner. You see the tumult, but not Him who stirs it up. There is no one to assist you, no one with whom to speak, no sympathizer with whom you can sit for a while.

> Isolated from friends in every land—
> the greater the sought, the fewer the helpers.

In the end, this chevalier lets out a sigh in his longing and bewilderment: "O God, my tree has been burnt by thirst. How long will it take before You tend to it? O Generous One! I am weeping over You! It is not beneath You to answer. Pour water once on my field!

"O God, if I am not worthy for what I desire, how can I love with a heart plucked of its feathers? If the hand of my need will not reach the branch of hope, how can I get on my feet? If You do not give me access to Yourself, how can I flee to You? O Generous One, give me access so that I may weep at Your threshold and rejoice in hope mixed with fear. Receive me, O Gentle One, so that I may busy myself with You. Gaze upon me once so that I may throw the two worlds into the ocean."

The Majestic Lord caresses the traveler with the attribute of generosity: "Fear not! Not every bite is poisoned. When a mother bites her child, she does so because of love."

(*Kashf* 2:739–41)

Among the many Qur'anic passages pointing to human diversity are seven verses saying that God puts a burden on souls only in the measure of their capacity. The word "to burden" is *taklīf.* As a technical term in the Islamic sciences, it came to mean the prescription of the Shariah. This is why many authors call the religious command the prescriptive command, meaning the God-imposed burden of following the religion. Here is Maybudī's commentary on one of these verses:

> *We burden no soul save to its capacity* [23:62]. The highway of the religion has a beginning and an end. The beginning belongs to the folk of the Shariah, and the end to the lords of the Haqiqah. The practice of the folk of the Shariah is service according to the Shariah, and the attribute of the lords of the Haqiqah is exile in contemplation.
>
> The foundation of the folk of the Shariah was built with easiness. Muṣṭafā said, "I was sent out with easy and indulgent unswervingness." The weak and the folk of concessions do not have the capacity for heavy burdens. The Exalted Lord put concessions into the Shariah for their sake and set aside heavy burdens: *We burden no soul save to its capacity.* This is the same as saying, "*He did not place upon you any hardship in the religion* [22:78]. *God desires for you ease and does not desire for you hardship* [2:185]."
>
> As for the traveling of the lords of the Haqiqah, God founded that on discipline and difficulty. They are addressed by the words "*Struggle in God as is the rightful due of His struggle* [22:78]. *Be wary of God, as is the rightful due of His wariness* [3:102]. *Whether you bring what is within your souls or you conceal it, God will call you to account for it* [2:284]."
>
> (*Kashf* 6:462)

Maybudī speaks of the nature of godwariness, the three levels of the religion, and the multilayered reality of the human self in his commentary on the verse "*O you who have faith, be wary of God and let each soul consider what it has sent ahead for tomorrow, and be wary of God*" (59:18).

> In this one verse, He mentions godwariness twice. First is the godwariness of the common people, namely, the avoidance of forbidden things. Second is the godwariness of the elect, namely, the avoidance of everything other than the Real.
>
> It is also said that the first alludes to the root of godwariness, and the second to the perfection of godwariness. No one can pass over the steep road of the resurrection without the perfection of godwariness. One must be detached from all objects of desire, one must seize on not reaching one's desires, and one must consider all sweet drinks as poison. When someone's feet reach this point, he has reached the perfection of godwariness.

Wāsiṭī said, "When the folk of godwariness act proudly toward the sons of this world, they are making claims in godwariness." For if this world had no impact on their hearts, they would not be proud about turning away from it.

A great one said, "This world is a shard of pottery seen in a dream. The next world is a pearl found in wakefulness. The man is not someone who is wary of a shard in a dream—the manly man is he who is wary of a pearl found in wakefulness."

In short, know that the steps of the travelers in the road of godwariness are three: The step of the Shariah illuminates the door of the bodily frame. The step of the Tariqah illuminates the door of the heart. The step of the Haqiqah illuminates the door of the spirit. When those who travel in the bodily frame arrive, the hospitality of *Surely the godwary shall dwell in gardens and a river* [54:54] will be brought for them. When those who travel in the heart arrive, the hospitality of *a seat of truthfulness* [54:55] will be brought for them. When those who travel in the spirit arrive, the hospitality of *at an Omnipotent King* [54:55] will be brought for them.

(*Kashf* 10:61–62)

In discussing the Shariah and the Haqiqah, Samʿānī stresses that the first pertains to the outward realm of bodily activity, and the second to the inward realm of vision and contemplation. Here are some of his comments:

O dervishes! Enter this road to see the caressing of servants! Enter to see the melting of lovers! You must devote your outwardness to the Shariah and your inwardness to the Haqiqah. You must take night and day as two steeds and throw out the carpet of all others. You must step outside your own desires, lest your name be written on ice.

(*Rawḥ* 168)

When a man has been given kingship over the world of holiness, why would he allow himself to come back and watch over the world of the senses? By God the Tremendous! If you step forth with seriousness and striving in the world of obedient acts and practices, if you adorn your outwardness with the duties of the Shariah, and if you trim your inwardness with the realities of the Haqiqah, then your feet will pass beyond the foremost feathers of Gabriel's wing.

Have you not seen how a mulberry leaf travels from its own makeup, passes beyond its form, and, because of its transformed attributes, becomes the emperor's robe and the king's garment? "If you desire the station of the saints, you must transform your attributes."

(332)

A great work has fallen upon us. We want to yearn, but we do not give yearning its rightful due. We want to love, but we do not give love its rightful due. We want familiarity, but we do not stay loyal to familiarity. We want to be lovers, but we have been routed by cold wind and breath.

If you have passion you'll be brought low,
or else you'll leave passion's path.

You want the station of the great ones, you want the standing of the truthful, you want the placement of the lovers—but you have not yet undertaken their perils. "He who does not put up with perils will not reach the goal."

You want the breath of Adam, you want the answered prayers of Noah, you want the station of Abraham, you want the pain of Muḥammad, but you have not taken one step outside your own desires, you have not taken one breath except in your own appetite. Have you not heard these heart-melting words? "The religion does not pertain to wishfulness and living well."

"If you desire the station of the saints, you must transform your states." After all, is it permissible for the top of the dustbin, which is the nest of crows, to be the bench of kings?

Nonetheless, there are intermediaries. If you want to reach someplace and become someone, you must rise up from where you are—your existence and your distracted, tainted, worn-out makeup. You must make a crown from the Shariah and a belt from the Haqiqah. You must put a stop to your own talk, narrative, and tales.

(23–24)

KNOWLEDGE AND LEARNING

Sufi literature commonly distinguishes between the knowers and the recognizers. As Maybudī put it in a passage already cited, the knowers devote themselves to knowledge of the religion and "find their hearts," but the recognizers "lose their hearts" (*Kashf* 4:36–37). The knowers strive to improve themselves by adding to their learning, but the recognizers strive to negate themselves by wiping away all acquired knowledge and making the heart empty for the One. Samʿānī has this sort of distinction in mind when he explains why Adam chose the wheat: he was following the Tariqah and aiming for the Haqiqah. That required annihilation of self. If he had simply followed the Shariah, he would have obeyed the command not to approach the tree.

When they brought that paragon into the world, he was addressed with the words "The whole of paradise is given over to you. But beware, do not go near that tree." At the same time, it was said to the tree, "Do not be anyplace except before the eyes of Adam, for We have secrets in this path."

"O Adam! You have come into paradise and sat down at the tablecloth of Riḍwān. This is indeed fine, but you should invite some of your progeny for whom provision has not been stipulated."

Every food he tasted in the highest paradise grabbed his skirt and said, "Be with us!" Except wheat. It said, "O paragon, detach your heart from these existent things, for He will not leave you here."

When he came out, he said, "I need the nourishment of wheat, because the others just flirted with me. It was the one who spoke the truth to me."

The Shariah was saying, "*Come not near this tree!*" [7:19]. The Tariqah was saying, "*Fall down out of it!*" [2:38]. The Shariah was saying, "Keep your hands away!" The Haqiqah was saying, "Strike fire to everything!"

From the day that paragon stepped forth from that world into this world, the eight paradises have burned in separation from his feet.

(*Rawḥ* 187–88)

The grain of wheat, whose breast had been wounded by the sword of need, was sent out from the concealment of the Unseen on the steed of severity. With goblets of poison it attacked the caravan of Adam's majesty and the camels of his beauty. It snatched away the shawl of his chosen-ness and put the cane of *Adam disobeyed* in his hand. It clothed him in the patched cloak of *But he forgot, and We found in him no resoluteness* [20:115]. It gave him the poor man's pot of *Our Lord, we have wronged ourselves* [7:23]. Then it placed before him the man-eating desert of passion. It is no abasement to travel on the Tariqah, and in the road of the Haqiqah there is no way station save the heart.

(133)

The generic word for knowledge in Islamic texts is *ʿilm*. It is often translated as "science," especially in the sense of a branch of learning, as in the science of the soul or psychology (ʿilm al-nafs). The word denotes knowing, coming to know, learning, and what is known (*maʿlūm*). Early on, it had no plural form, but the plural became necessary when the varieties of knowledge were classified, giving us learnings, sciences, or bodies of knowledge. The word's basic meaning is "the very act of knowing itself." The underlying truth about knowledge is the truth of tawḥīd: no one truly knows but God. Any knowledge possessed by anything else can only be a divine bestowal. As the Qur'an puts it, "*They encompass nothing of His knowledge save as He wills*" (2:255). The fact that all knowledge comes from God, directly or indirectly, was elaborated upon extensively by philosophers like Mullā Ṣadrā. Maybudī speaks of it in his commentary on the verses “*The All-Merciful. He taught the Qur’an. He created man. He taught him the explication*” (55:1–4).

> As much as teachers strive in teaching, masters inculcate, and memorizers keep classes going, all of these are secondary causes, and the teacher in reality is God. Whenever someone comes to be taught, He is the teacher. Whenever someone lights up, He is the light giver. Whenever someone burns, He is the burner. Whenever something is made, He is the maker.
>
> He taught Adam the knowledge of the names: *And He taught Adam the names, all of them* [2:31]. He taught David chain-mail making: *And We taught him the artisanry of garments for you* [21:80]. He taught Jesus the science of medicine: *And We will teach him the book and the wisdom* [3:48]. He taught Khiḍr the science of recognition: *We taught him knowledge from Us* [18:65]. He taught Muṣṭafā the secrets of the divinity: *He taught thee what thou didst not know* [4:113]. He taught the folk of the world explication: *He created man. He taught him the explication.*
>
> (*Kashf* 9:418–19)

Philosophers and many Sufi theologians were careful to differentiate among the various sorts of knowledge. Sometimes they classified knowledge into two basic kinds, transmitted (*naqlī*) and intellectual (*ʿaqlī*). Transmitted knowledge is learned by *taqlīd*, which means imitation or accepting someone else’s word for it. Most knowledge is of this sort, since we know the vast bulk of what we know (or think we know) on the basis of transmission from our cultural ambience, schools, books, the media, and so on. In contrast, intellectual knowledge is known by taḥqīq, which means verification or realization. The word is derived from the same root as *ḥaqq* (real, true, right, appropriate) and *ḥaqīqa* (reality, truth). It means to know the reality of a thing, or the Haqiqah per se, without intermediary. Early philosophers tended to talk about realization as actualization of the intellect through conjunction with the Agent Intellect, the first emanation from the One.

When knowledge is divided into these two sorts, the only real and true knowledge is what we know in ourselves and by ourselves. Anything we quote from others—no matter what or who the others may be, whether scripture, prophets, saints, philosophers, lawyers, scientists—is transmitted, which is to say that it is hearsay. When authors like Maybudī distinguish between knowers and recognizers, they are employing one of the most common ways of distinguishing between transmitted, imitative knowledge, and intellectual, realized knowledge.

There are many ways of dividing up the sorts of knowledge, but in both philosophy and Sufism, most classifications put realization of the Real, or recognition (maʿrifa) of the Haqiqah, at the highest level. In his commentary on the verse *"Say: 'Are they equal, those who know and those who know not?'"* (39:9), Maybudī describes three ascending levels of knowledge, the first of which is transmitted knowledge, and the next two of which pertain to advanced stages of the Tariqah. Beyond all this is God's knowledge of Himself, the true knowledge that is the source of all other knowledge.

> Knowledge is three: reported knowledge, inspired knowledge, and knowledge of the Unseen. Reported knowledge is heard by ears, inspired knowledge is heard by hearts, and knowledge of the Unseen is heard by spirits.
>
> Reported knowledge comes to outwardness so that the tongue may speak of it, inspired knowledge comes to the heart so that explication may speak of it, and knowledge of the Unseen comes to the spirit so that the present moment may speak of it. Reported knowledge comes from narration, inspired knowledge comes from guidance, and knowledge of the Unseen comes from solicitude.
>
> Concerning reported knowledge, He said, "*Know that there is no god but God*" [47:19]. Concerning inspired knowledge, He said, "*Surely those who were given knowledge before it*" [17:107]. Concerning knowledge of the Unseen, He said, "*We taught him knowledge from Us*" [18:65].
>
> Beyond all these is a knowledge never reached by the Adamite's imagination or grasped by his understanding. It is God's knowledge of Himself, in keeping with His reality. God says, "*They do not encompass Him in knowledge*" [20:110].
>
> (*Kashf* 8:399)

In explaining one meaning of the verse "*And We gave David and Solomon a knowledge*" (27:15), Maybudī refers to realized knowledge as understanding (*fahm*) and explains it as knowledge of the Haqiqah, which itself has stages.

> In the tongue of the folk of recognition and the tasting of the lords of finding, this is the knowledge of understanding.
>
> The knowledge of understanding is the knowledge of the Haqiqah.
>
> Junayd was asked, "What is the knowledge of the Haqiqah?"
>
> He said, "The God-given, lordly knowledge—the attributes gone, the Haqiqah staying."
>
> The state of the recognizer is exactly that: the attributes gone, the Haqiqah staying. The common people are in a station in which the attributes are apparent and the Haqiqah is concealed. As for the folk of election, the attributes have ceased to be and the Haqiqah stays. That chevalier has said this beautifully in the line

Endless passion has nothing to do with a heart
that stays firm in its own attributes.

First there is the knowledge of the Haqiqah, above this the eye of the Haqiqah, and beyond that the truth of the Haqiqah. The knowledge of the Haqiqah is recognition, the eye of the Haqiqah is finding, and the truth of the Haqiqah is annihilation.

The knowledge of the Haqiqah is what you have of the Real. The eye of the Haqiqah is the Real through which you are. The truth of the Haqiqah is your dissolution in the Real.

Recognition means *shinākht* [in Persian], and finding [wujūd] means *yāft*. Between recognition and finding are more than a thousand valleys. Junayd said, "This group did not come down from the Protector for the sake of recognition—they seek so as to find." Poor man, how will you find Him when you are incapable of recognition?

It is also Junayd who was asked, "How is it that one finds Him?" He did not answer, but stood up from his place. In other words, this answer is given by the heart, not the tongue. He who has it knows.

The Pir of the Tariqah said, "The light of faith comes from finding God. It is not that finding God comes from the light of faith."

Ḥallāj said, "When someone seeks God with the light of faith, that is like seeking the sun with a star's light. He, however, stands in His measure and abides in His exaltedness. He is far in His exaltedness and near in His gentleness."

(*Kashf* 7:196)

RECOGNIZING THE REAL

Transmitted knowledge provides the foundation not only of religion but also of every human enterprise. Nonetheless, it is the specific variety of knowledge known as recognition, maʿrifa, that takes the travelers forward on the path to God. The Arabic word designates both the basis of faith and the goal of the seeker, which is to say that it has many degrees. The word itself implies that we already have the knowledge, but it has slipped our minds. When we recognize it, we recall and recollect what we already know. The similarity to Plato's notion of anamnesis is obvious. It ties in nicely as well with the typical understanding of fiṭra, original disposition, the notion that all human beings are innately disposed toward tawḥīd, though they need prophetic reminders (*dhikr, tadhkira*) to come back to their senses.

As noted, the generic word for knowledge, *ʿilm*, connotes transmitted learning. The possessors of knowledge, the ulama (*ʿulamāʾ*), are the learned scholars of the community. They have mastered the transmitted sources, memorized the Qur'an and numerous hadiths, and gained competence in the science of jurisprudence, which demands knowledge of the commands and prohibitions. Most often their knowledge is, as it were, downloadable from their memories or their books. It is not something that wells up from recognizing the truth and reality of things.

One of the most famous sayings cited in support of recognition's centrality in the search for the Real is usually called a prophetic hadith, though it is more likely by ʿAlī: "He who recognizes his soul [or "himself"] recognizes his Lord." Most scholars translate the verb here as "know," but this loses the connotations of maʿrifa. What is implied is that the seeker recognizes his own true nature, directly, without intermediary, by reconnecting with the divine spirit blown into the body at creation. Only such self-recognition can allow recognition of God's actual reality, not least because no one can know for you, just as no one can love for you.

Historians and translators (myself included) have typically rendered maʿrifa (and its grammatical synonym, *ʿirfān*) as "gnosis," because gnosis implies direct rather than mediated knowledge.[3] Those who have achieved gnosis are then the gnostics (ʿārif). This makes the point easily enough—so long as we do not start thinking that the reference is to the Gnostics of antiquity. Despite the precedents for translating the words like this, there are major drawbacks. One is that the texts, not least the Qur'an and the Hadith, use *maʿrifa* in verbal form, but we have no English verb from gnosis, so one cannot be consistent in translation. If we translate the noun as "gnosis," we then have to translate the verb as "to know" or "to recognize" ("to gnosticize" simply does not work). As soon as we have two translations, the consistent use of this highly important term is lost to sight. Moreover, the word is used in the Qur'an and in everyday language precisely in the meaning of recognition, and it would be absurd to start translating these instances as gnosis—an abstruse, esoteric word that raises eyebrows in English. Authors use the same word for every sort of recognition, and to draw a line between recognition and gnosis can only be an artificial imposition on the texts.

The Qur'an and the Hadith say that everyone should strive for recognition, not just some specific group. Certainly, there are degrees of recognition, but even at its most basic level, recognition implies a firsthand participation in knowing that cannot come from rote learning. In Sufi texts, the recognizers are those who have achieved consciousness of their own true selves and of God. In no way do they depend on knowledge received from others. They know what they know without intermediary. One of Abū Yazīd Basṭāmī's sayings makes the point nicely: "You take your knowledge dead from the dead, but I take my knowledge from the Living who does not die."

In his commentary on the verse "*When they hear what has been sent down to the Messenger, thou seest their eyes overflow with tears because of the truth that they recognize*" (5:83), Maybudī differentiates between two sorts of recognition. Having explained that the verse mentions five characteristics of faith—hearing, seeing, recognizing, speaking, and doing—he focuses on the meaning of recognition:

> The Pir of the Tariqah said, "Recognition is two: the recognition of the common people and the recognition of the elect. The recognition of the common people is by hearsay, and the recognition of the elect is by face-to-face vision. The recognition of the common people comes from the Source of munificence, but the recognition of the elect comes from what they find."
>
> Concerning the recognition of the common people, He said, "*When they hear what has been sent down to the Messenger.*" Concerning the recognition of the elect, He said, "*He shall show you His signs, and you shall recognize them*" [27:93].
>
> *When they hear* is praise of the folk of the Shariah, and *He shall show you His signs* is a felicitation for the folk of the Haqiqah. When someone speaks of the Shariah and turns his back in any respect, he becomes a heretic. When someone speaks of the Haqiqah and looks at himself in any respect, he becomes an associater.
>
> (*Kashf* 3:215)

Maybudī provides a bit more explanation of what is meant by true recognition in his commentary on the verse "*Whatever mercy God opens to people*" (35:2). Notice that the verb here, *to open* (*futūḥ*), is used as a technical term to designate God's opening up of the heart, giving it access to the Haqiqah without intermediary. The title of Ibn al-ʿArabī's enormous book *The Meccan Openings* (*al-Futūḥāt al-makkiyya*) uses the word in precisely this sense. As Ibn al-ʿArabī tells us in several places, his book records what God opened up to him, not what he learned from teachers or books.[4]

> For understanding in the tongue of the Tariqah, this verse alludes to the opening of the folk of faith and recognition. Opening is a name for what comes from the Unseen unsought and unasked for. It is of two sorts: One is the influxes of provision and delightful life, unsought and unearned. The other is God-given knowledge, unlearned, conforming to the Shariah, never before heard, but familiar to the heart.

> The Pir of the Tariqah said, "Alas for this unlearnt knowledge! Sometimes I'm drowned in it, sometimes burnt by it."
>
> In respect of this knowledge, the speaker is the ocean, sometimes in flow, sometimes in ebb. When he stands in the station of expansiveness, he fills the world with limpidness. When he stands in the station of awe, he fills the world with human nature.
>
> (*Kashf* 8:169)

The Qur'an recounts that God was showing Abraham the signs of heaven and earth. When a star rose, he said, "*This is my Lord*" (6:76), but then it set. The moon rose and then the sun, but they both set. Finally, Abraham turned his face to God and said that he was not one of the associaters. This story is often taken as a reference to the ascending stages of knowledge leading to pure tawḥīd. Here is Maybudī's explanation:

> First He showed him the sovereignty of heaven and earth so that he would derive evidence of the existence of the Artisan by way of inference. He looked at the stars and said, "*This is my Lord*," that is, "evidence of my Lord, for my Lord has no beginning or end, but this has set." He said, "*I love not those that set*." At last the beauty of the Haqiqah showed its face to him. By means of inference and proofs he went back to witnessing and face-to-face vision. He turned away from everything and said, "*Surely they are an enemy to me, save the Lord of the Worlds*" [26:77]. He said to Gabriel, "As for turning toward you, no." First he was like a knower, then he became like a recognizer.
>
> Wāsiṭī said, "The world's creatures are going to Him, but the recognizers are coming from Him."
>
> He said also, "If someone says, 'I recognized God through the evidence,' ask him how he recognized the evidence.'"
>
> True, at the beginning there is no escape from evidence, as was the beginning of Abraham's path. All that evidence came into Abraham's path—the star, the moon, the sun. When he reached each piece of evidence, he would cling to it and say, "*This is my Lord*." When he passed beyond the degrees of the evidence, he saw the beauty of tawḥīd with the eye of face-to-face vision. He said, "*O my people, I am quit of what you associate*" [6:78], that is, I am quit of inference from the creatures to the Creator, for there is no evidence for Him save Himself.
>
> This is the same as that great one of the religion said: "I recognized God through God, and I recognized that which is beneath God through God's light." This is alluded to in His words "*The earth shall shine with the light of its Lord*" [39:69].

Here a chevalier of the Tariqah made an exalted point and clarified the traveling of the travelers and the pull that takes those who are snatched away. He said, "When the caress of *And God took Abraham as a bosom friend* [4:125] reached Abraham from the court of Unity in the attribute of clemency and mercy, the command came, 'O Abraham, there is no stipulation that you stand still in the road of bosom friendship. Go higher than the way station of *I submit to the Lord of the Worlds* [2:131]. Make the journey that is called the journey of solitariness. 'Travel! The solitary will take precedence.' "

Abraham was a fast-going seeker, looking for the reminder of the Beginningless. He put the sandals of intention on the feet of his aspiration and went forth on the journey of *I am going to my Lord* [37:99]. The treasuries of exaltedness were opened up from the hiding place of the Unseen, and many pearls of the Unseen and wonders of the treasuries were strewn in the road of *I am going.*

Abraham was still a traveler and became attached to *I am going.* He had not yet reached the center-point of togetherness. He looked back and saw plunder, so he busied himself with the plunder. The beauty of tawḥīd unveiled itself to him: "Why did you look back?" Finally, he asked forgiveness with *I love not those that set* [6:76].

He still saw those pearls of the Unseen, and he stood back: "*This is my Lord, this is my Lord,*" for those pearls of the Unseen were so heart-deceiving and distracting.

It was said to him, "O Abraham, you should not have halted like this. Why did you go forth on the road of *I am going to my Lord* and then look back at the plunder and treasures? Why did you not turn the eye of aspiration away from that? Why did you not put to use the Sunnah of *the eyesight did not swerve, nor did it trespass* [53:17]?"

This is the Sunnah of that paragon of the world and the characteristic of that master of Adam's children. On the night of nearness and familiarity, *the greatest signs* [53:18] disclosed themselves in his road and he remained in this courtesy: *The eyesight did not swerve, nor did it trespass.*

"O Abraham! When someone is searching for the reminder of the Beginningless and the mystery of the Blessings-Giver, what use has he for plunder and treasures?"

When a serpent bites a man's liver,
they give him the antidote, not candy.

Abraham pulled the hand of disengagement from the sleeve of solitariness and turned away from the secondary causes: *Surely I have turned my face to-*

> *ward Him who originated the heavens and the earth, unswerving, and I am not of the associaters* [6:79]. In other words: "I aim solely for God, I have purified myself of ties to anything but God, I have preserved my covenant in God for God, I have purged my finding through God. I belong to God in God, or rather, I am effaced in God, and God is God."
>
> (*Kashf* 3:409–11)

The basic sorts of knowing are often described in terms of three levels of certainty (*yaqīn*): knowledge, eye (ʿayn), and truth or rightful due (ḥaqq). Maybudī does this in his commentary on the verses that mention the first two of these terms (the third is mentioned in 56:95 and 69:51): *"Did you but know with the knowledge of certainty, you would see the Blaze, then you would see it with the eye of certainty"* (102:5–7).

> It is said that certainty has three pillars: the knowledge of certainty, the eye of certainty, and the truth of certainty. The knowledge of certainty settles down in the breast, the eye of certainty settles down in the secret core, and the truth of certainty settles down in the spirit.
>
> The knowledge of certainty discourses on faith, the eye of certainty gives marks of sincerity, and the truth of certainty throws one into the rightful due of recognition.
>
> Blessedness belongs to him who walks in the world of certainty's knowledge! Nearness belongs to him who sees a trace of the face-to-face vision of certainty's eye! The most beautiful belongs to him who finds awareness of the reality of certainty's truth!
>
> (*Kashf* 10:603)

When Sufis and philosophers insisted that transmitted knowledge, no matter who or what the source may be, can serve only as a preparation for the real work, they were very much aware that scholars and academics tend to get caught up with their own learning. Historians cannot help but note that there has always been tension and conflict between scholars of the formal Islamic sciences, such as exegesis, Hadith, jurisprudence, and Kalam, and teachers of Sufism and philosophy. This has much to do with the fact that learning can quickly become an end in itself or a means to gain prestige and standing. If Sufi teachers constantly stress the importance of love, this is partly because love cannot be explained, as everyone who has tasted it knows. Academic theorizing about love gets us nowhere. The only way to understand love is to become a lover, and the only way to become a recognizer is to recognize. Sufi teachers accepted that tawḥīd in the basic form of attesting to the creed is the foundation of the path to God, but they considered this the bare beginning. The goal of the path is for the soul to be burned away by the fire of love, leaving only the Beloved. Samʿānī points to the tension between scholars and realizers in many passages, of which this is sweeter than most:

> Ashʿath the Covetous was passing by a tray maker's shop. He said, "Make these trays you're making bigger! Maybe someone will give me something on one of them."
>
> Here we have your own breast full of wishes! Here we have your own worthless heart!
>
> It is said that there were three hundred sixty idols placed in the Kaabah. If all the accountants in the world came to record the number of idols in your breast, they would not be able to do so.
>
> In our times it is not necessary for Azar to carve idols, for everywhere in the world there's someone with unwashed face, an Azari idol in his breast. "The soul is the greatest idol."*
>
> In the city, a Zoroastrian is walking with his cap on his head, and you are walking with the turban of tawḥīd on top of your head and a fanciful notion of tawḥīd inside it. If turban and robe make someone a Muslim, then bravo, O leader of the sincerely truthful! And if Zoroastrianism means to attach your heart to two, well, you know what needs to be done.
>
> In short, know that nothing is given out on the basis of talk!
>
> Abu'l-Qāsim Mudhakkir lived in Nishapur, though he was originally from Merv. He was a sweet-tongued preacher. Once he was holding a session and speaking fine words. A man stood up and said, "If the work is completed with talk, you have gone to the place of honor. But if this pot needs some seasoning, you can't settle down on the basis of words."
>
> There was a singer who used to go to the house of a noble. Whenever he sang a song, the noble would say, "Well done!" He would sing another song, and again he would say, "Well done!" The singer was also a poet. One day he said,
>
> Every time I sing, you say, "Well done, sing another!"
> But you can't buy any flour with "Well done."
>
> In the bazaar, you can't buy anything with "Well done." They want pure gold and unalloyed silver.
>
> O respected man! In this road they want a burnt liver, they want a heart full of pain, they want footsteps with truthfulness, they want a spirit with passion, they want togetherness without dispersion. If you have the hard cash, the work is yours.

Indeed, the first trial that faces you is the trial of your own being. Gather your being and hand it over to the Sultan of tawḥīd so that He may destroy it, for nothing can bring together a dispersed man except tawḥīd. "Tawḥīd is to isolate the Eternal from the newly arrived." Tawḥīd is assaying: discarding the specious newly arrived and selecting the authentic eternal.

One of them said, "Tawḥīd, the tawḥīd-voicer, and the One. This makes Him '*the third of three*' [5:73]."[5]

Everyone in the world is attached to giving one and taking two. These men are attached to giving all and taking one.

(*Rawḥ* 197–98)

6

The States of the Travelers

Sufi teachers distinguish in many ways between the majority of Muslims, who simply follow the Shariah, and a minority who have reached advanced stages of the Tariqah. One way is simply to contrast the recognizers with the faithful in general, or with various groups among the faithful, such as worshipers (*ʿābid*), renunciants (zāhid), and wage earners (*ajīr, muzdūr*), as in these passages from Maybudī:

Whatever is in the heavens and the earth asks of Him [55:29]. The faithful are two: worshiper and recognizer. The asking of each is in the measure of his aspiration, and the caressing of each is suited to his capacity. The worshiper wants everything from Him, the recognizer wants Him Himself.

(*Kashf* 9:421)

Piety is not that you turn your faces east and west [2:177]. You have learned what the Shariah stipulates regarding the outward meaning of this verse. Now listen to the inner meaning in the tongue of allusion and recognize the signs of the Haqiqah, for the Haqiqah is to the Shariah as the spirit is to the body. What is a body without a spirit? Such is the Shariah without the Haqiqah.

The Shariah is the house of the servitors. All the people are gathered there. They keep it flourishing with service and worship.

The Haqiqah is the house of the sanctuary. The recognizers are gathered there. They keep it flourishing with veneration and contemplation.

The distance from service and worship to veneration and contemplation is the same as that from familiarity to love. Familiarity is the attribute of wage earners, and love is the attribute of recognizers.

The wage earner brings all the varieties of piety mentioned in the verse. Then he says, "Oh, if the wind blows against it, or something of it is taken away, I will lose the wage for that." The recognizer performs all of it according to its stipulations. Then he says, "Oh, if any of it remains, I will be held back from good fortune."

(1:468)

They ask you what they should spend [2:215]. Throwing away money in the path of the Shariah is beautiful, but it is not like throwing away the spirit in the field of the Haqiqah and becoming separate from all others at the moment of contemplation.

Keeping to the stipulation of loyalty is beautiful, but not as much as becoming separate from self and stepping onto the carpet of limpidness.

Someone asks, "What should we do with our property? How should we spend it?"

The Shariah answers, "From 200 dirhams, 5 dirhams; from 20 dinars, one-half dinar."

Someone else asks and the Haqiqah answers, "You will not be with Him along with your body and spirit."

Yes, the story of the wage earners is one thing, the story of the recognizers something else. The wage earner's recognition reaches recognizing the spirit, but the recognizer's recognition reaches throwing away the spirit.

(1:580)

I ask you for no wage for this; surely my wage falls on God, the Lord of the Worlds [26:109]. This is a report about each of the prophets. Each of them said, "*I ask you for no wage for this.*" Thus, everyone who acts for God's sake will know that it is not appropriate to seek wages from other than God.

If one day someone takes a step in God's road and desires a reward or requests a need, let him never desire it from other than Him! To Moses it was revealed, "Lift up your need to Me! Whatever you ask for, ask from Me, even the salt for your dough or the straw for your sheep."

This indeed is the degree of the wage earners, for they act with an eye to the recompense. The recognizers have another state and another work. When they act, they do not act for the sake of recompense. They consider recompense a freckle on the face of the act.

The Pir of the Tariqah said, "In any case, calling to account will be for the wage earners. What calling to account could there be for the recognizers? The recognizer is indeed a guest. The wage of the wage earner befits the wage earner, but the feast of the guest befits the host. The substance of the wage earner is bewilderment, but the substance of the recognizer is face-to-face vision.

"The recognizer's spirit is radiant with His love; his spirit is all eye, his secret core all tongue. His eye and tongue are helpless in the light of face-to-face vision.

"The wage earner's heart has the shining light of hope, but the recognizer's spirit has face-to-face vision. The wage earner wanders in the midst of blessings, but the recognizer cannot fit into expression."

The worth of the recognizer's spirit is not apparent. Do you know why? Because his spirit is not separate from the Presence. His bodily frame is like a shell, and his soul is like a pearl that originated from the Presence and returned to the Presence. If the soul had come from here, it would be egocentric, and if it were egocentric, the veil of dispersion would not have been incinerated. The fire of hell does not burn like the fire that burns in the recognizer's soul, for his fire is lit by friendship.

The lover's heart has the fire of craving,
hotter than the hottest fire of hell.

(7:152)

RECOGNITION AND LOVE

When Maybudī classifies the faithful into two groups, he often says that recognizers can be called the passionate (*ʿāshiq*), the lovers (*muḥibb*), or the friends (dūst), for the recognizers love what they recognize, and the lovers recognize what they love. He provides an example in his commentary on the verse "A*s for those who do devotions throughout the night, prostrating themselves and standing*" (39:9).

It has been said that putting God's commandments into practice is of two sorts, one according to the property of servanthood, the other according to the property of love. The property of love is higher than the property of servanthood, because the lover's constant wish is for the Friend to command a service. Hence all his service is voluntary, and nothing of it is coerced. He acknowledges the favors done to him, and he never thinks that he is doing God a favor, nor does he look for recompense.

In contrast, a service that is done because of servanthood has both free choice and coercion. The person is seeking a reward and expecting recompense.

The latter is the station of the worshipers and the common faithful, and the former is the attribute of the recognizers and the sincerely truthful. The

> two groups can never be equal. The worshipers are satisfied with the blessings and held back from the Blessings-Giver, but the recognizers have reached the Presence and take ease in contemplating the Friend.
>
> The Pir of the Tariqah said, "How should I have known that reward is a freckle on the face of love? I always thought that the greatest robe of honor was the reward. Now that I've found love, I've found that all found things are nothing."
>
> (*Kashf* 8:398)

In distinguishing among various sorts of the faithful, there is no suggestion that those called by one name necessarily lack the attributes of those called by another name. Just as recognizers are also lovers, they are also worshipers, because they perform the acts and possess the character traits that define a worshiper. The difference lies in the fact that a worshiper stops short of recognition. Lying behind this way of thinking is the notion of ascending rungs on the ladder to God. Actualization of the level designated by a rung depends on reaching the previous rung. In his commentary on the verse "*Those who do not hope for Our encounter*" (10:7), Maybudī describes the manner in which the positive attributes of the soul are tightly bound together. Each must be actualized, but some need to be acquired before others, such as recognition before love. Maybudī's second paragraph is translated from Qushayrī's *Subtle Allusions*, and the third quotes part of Qushayrī's explanation.

> The unbelievers do not hope for the vision of the Real, for they deny it. Inescapably, they will never reach it. The faithful have faith in the vision of the Real and hope that they will reach it. Inescapably, they will reach it. This is the same as what Muṣṭafā said: "When someone hears of the Real's generosity"—that is, he hears a report that the Real is generous toward the servant and will caress him with the vision of Him—"but does not accept the report and does not have faith in the vision, he will never reach that generosity."
>
> It is said that they do not hope to see the Real because they have not yearned, they do not yearn because they have not loved, they do not love because they have not recognized, they do not recognize because they have not sought, and they do not seek because the Real has not brought them into seeking and has shut the door of seeking. So all is from God and according to His desire and will. God says, "*Surely the final end is unto thy Lord*" [53:42].
>
> Had He desired that they seek Him, they would have sought Him. Had they sought, they would have recognized. Had they recognized, they would have loved. Had they loved, they would have yearned. Had they yearned for Him, they would have hoped for His encounter. Had they hoped for His encounter, they would have seen Him. God says, "*Had We willed, We would*

> *have given every soul its guidance*" [32:13]. As for those who do not hope for His encounter, their home will be chastisement and separation. This declaration shows that the final goal of those who hope for His encounter is union, encounter, and nearness.
>
> (*Kashf* 4:255–56)

Samʿānī often discusses the distinction between love and service. In the following, he correlates it with the difference between angels and humans. The Qur'an praises the angels for their service and criticizes human beings for theirs, but it also points out that God loves the Adamites, saying nothing of the sort about the angels.

> When the Adamite was created, shortcoming was made his attribute. A tree was placed in his outwardness, and a tree was planted in his inwardness. The outward tree was called "the prescription of the Law," and the inward tree was called "the bestowal of recognition." The fruit of the outward tree is service, and the fruit of the tree that bestows recognition is love.
>
> "Then I set down the custom that the tree of the Law's prescription, whose fruit is service, may be struck by a blight, but the tree that bestows recognition, which is expressed in the words '*its root established and its branch in heaven*' [14:24], will not be touched by any blight. Outwardly, a man is in the tavern, but the reins of passionate love are on high. He is truthful in his love but falls short in its rightful due."
>
> The man afflicted with shortcoming in his practice flees to the Threshold and cries out that the tree of the Law's prescription is not giving fruit. From the Exalted Presence comes the call: "God gazes not on your forms."
>
> Since there is no escape from friendship, well, you might as well love Him, for whoever is killed in the name of the Real will not become carrion.
>
> If I cannot escape passion's nurturing my spirit,
> let me then drink down the sorrow of passion for You.
>
> (*Rawḥ* 623)
>
> The beauty of the two worlds lies in two things: servanthood and love. Servanthood, however, is the attribute of creation, and love the attribute of the Real. The perfection of servanthood belongs to the angels, and the robe of friendship belongs to Adamites with faith. Among the faithful, it belongs to the elect.
>
> Concerning the angels, the Exalted Lord says, "*Nay, but they are honored servants*" [21:26]. He says, "*Over them are harsh, terrible angels, who do not*

> *disobey God in what He commands them and who do as they are commanded* [66:6]. They are servants who obey Our commandment and put it into effect. They do not disobey Us for the blink of an eye."
>
> Then, concerning the attribute of this community, He says, "*He loves them, and they love Him*" [5:54]. He also calls this community servants, but when He calls the angels servants, He does so without attribution—*servants*. He calls this community servants with attribution—*My servants* [15:42]. With this, He completed His bounty on this community. Despite their great boldness, impudence, sinfulness, and offense, He made apparent the lights of His love, without the precedence of service or the intermediary of obedience. This then is the attribute of love, and that is the attribute of obedience.
>
> People talk in secret to friends, not to servants. The servants are there for the friends, not the friends for the servants. This is the secret of the divine words "*He has subjected to you whatsoever is in the heavens and whatsoever is in the earth, all of it, from Him* [45:13]: Whatever We have, We have made your servant. Now, you be the servant of your Master, and the masters will serve you."
>
> (469)

Those who criticize the attitude of servants and wage earners do so because it is based on a failure to understand the meaning of tawḥīd: there is no beloved but the True Beloved. If one serves God for the sake of the reward, one loves the reward instead of God or along with God. This is shirk, associationism, though God forgives it because He knows He is dealing with weak and heedless creatures. Avicenna explains the reasoning here in his well-known book *Allusions and Remarks* (*al-Ishārāt wa'l-tanbīhāt*):

> The recognizer desires the First Real only for His sake, not for the sake of anything else. There is nothing he prefers to recognition of Him. His worship is directed only toward Him because He is worthy of worship and because worship is an eminent relationship with Him.
>
> The recognizer has neither desire nor fear. Were he to have them, the object of his desire or fear would be his motive, and that would be his goal. Then the Real would not be his goal but rather the means to something else, less than the Real, which would be his goal and object.
>
> The person who considers it proper to make the Real a means partakes of mercy in a certain respect. Since he has not been given to taste the joy of bliss in Him, he does not seek to taste it. He is acquainted only with imperfect joys, so he yearns for them and remains heedless of what lies beyond.
>
> (3:227)

Samʿānī makes the same point by saying that love based on bribery is not love, because people are attracted by the bribes rather than the beloved. If you love someone for what you can get from him or her—status, wealth, sex—you do not love the person, but the reward for service. Love based on tawḥīd aims only at the One Beloved. It demands disengagement (*tajrīd*) from everything other than God, and solitariness (tafrīd) with the Solitary.

> Friendship based on bribery comes into existence only from those who are mean and low in aspiration.
>
> He gives one group ten, He gives another twenty, He gives another fifty, and He gives another *manifold and multiplied* [3:130]. Then there is another group who stand up for God, sit down for God, love in God, and hate for His sake.
>
> He says, "I have great wealth in the treasury."
>
> They say, "What are treasuries to us?"
>
> He says, "This world and the next world belong to Me."
>
> They say, "What are this world and the next world to us?"
>
> A man had a small child in his house. In the morning he gave him some little broken thing. That night a dervish came. He saw that the father had nothing in his hands. He said to the child, "Come, dear child, lend that broken thing to your father so that tomorrow he will give you ten times more."
>
> What is "ten times"? Deception for children. They promise a child ten for one. To the intelligent man, they say, "Every loan that attracts profit is usury." If you lend a dirham and you receive back a dirham plus one grain, that is nothing but usury. "Ten for one" is permitted for children, but for adults, only one for one is permitted.
>
> *Who shall lend God a beautiful loan, which He shall multiply for him many times?* [2:245]. For whom is this? For those who have been driven mad by love for this world. As for the intelligent man, "I take one and I give one, and the one is I."
>
> *Did We not place in him two eyes, one tongue, and two lips?* [90:8–9]. *God did not place two hearts in the breast of any man* [33:4]. The heart is one, the tongue is one. The tongue with which you assert faith in Him is one, and the heart with which you love Him is one. "And I am one. Thus 'one for one' will be known to you."
>
> The spirits' king is passion's servant,
> all his children passion's army.
> Pure wisdom is the draft of pain,
> intellect's bond passion's anchor.
> A pure gambler, free of himself—

such was our paragon, passion's trainee.
His tears were the ink of mystery's book,
his color the expression of passion's register.

The secret of this road will show its face to you only at the center-point of disengagement. "Disengagement is that your outwardness becomes disengaged from motivations, and your inwardness from compensations." Becoming disengaged from inwardness is that you do not seek compensation for that from which you disengage your outwardness, neither at the present moment nor in the future. This is because if someone lets go of something in the present state while seeking something else as compensation, he is a merchant, not disengaged.

(*Rawḥ* 606)

THE LIFE OF REMEMBRANCE

The Qur'an talks a good deal about life and death. It affirms that life is strictly an attribute of God, *the Living who does not die* (25:58), and it reminds its readers that everything other than God dies and disappears. *It is death that you are fleeing, but it will meet you* (62:8). God alone is Life-Giver (*muḥyī*), and He alone is Death-Giver (*mumīt*). The Qur'an stresses that true life will come after death, whether a person ends up in paradise or hell. At the same time, it uses the words *life* and *death* to symbolize knowledge and ignorance.

Much of the discussion of life and death in Sufi literature focuses on voluntary death, which is to surrender the soul to God by submitting to His religious command. Rūmī and others frequently cite the purported hadith "Die before you die!" They also cite the well-known hadith of the two jihāds, the lesser struggle and the greater struggle. The lesser struggle aims to slay the enemies in battle, and the greater aims to slay the enemy in the breast. Maybudī explains the difference between physical, compulsory death and the voluntary death of the soul in his commentary on the verse "*When We decreed death for him*" (34:14).

Death is of two sorts: outward death and inward death. Outward death is obvious to everyone. Friend and enemy follow the road that leads to it; the common people and the elect are the same in it. *Every soul shall taste death* [3:185].

Inward death is that a man dies in himself from himself without himself and comes to life from the Real in the Real with the Real. It is the same as that chevalier said:

Die, O friend, before your death, if you want to live—
long ago, by such a death, Idris went up to paradise.

(*Kashf* 8:133–34)

In *One Hundred Fields*, Anṣārī mentions life as the seventy-third stage on the path to God and explains it by reference to three basic levels—fear, hope, and love.

What, is he who was dead, and We gave him life [6:122]. The life of the heart is three things. Any heart that does not have these three things is carrion: the life of fear along with knowledge, the life of hope along with knowledge, and the life of friendship along with knowledge.

The life of fear keeps a man's skirt pure of defilement, his eyes awake, his road straight. The life of hope keeps a man's steed quick, his traveling supplies complete, his road near. The life of friendship makes a man's measure great, his head free, his heart happy.

Fear without knowledge is the fear of the Kharijites, hope without knowledge is the hope of the Murji'ites, and friendship without knowledge is the friendship of the libertines.

This knowledge is knowledge of God. It is the precondition of fear and hope as well as of friendship.

(*Maydān* 312–13)

Samʿānī often identifies life with recognition, and death with ignorance:

God says, "*It is He who gives life and gives death*" [23:80].

Exalted is the man who dies in himself from his own selfhood and comes to life from the Real in the Real with the Real. In reality, life is what gives opening, not what comes with the spirit. Death is what snatches away faith, not what takes away the spirit.

If the spirits of all the world's folk were given to you and you did not have the spirit of faith's opening, you would be dead. And if a thousand years passed over your dust but the spirit of the All-Merciful's tawḥīd had grown up in your spirit's garden, you would be at the head of all the living.

Life is recognition, death ignorance. "Recognition is the heart's life with God." Exalted is the man who is taken all at once to the Water of Life and, like Khiḍr, washed therein and given endless life!

(*Rawḥ* 484)

The interplay of life and death, like that of all opposing and complementary qualities, goes back to the divine attributes. In explaining this, Samʿānī reminds us of the dangers of self-admiration.

Revelation came to David, "O David! Give good news to the sinners and warn the sincerely truthful!"

It is the habit of kings, when they want to poison someone, to look at him in order to make him feel more secure.

"When you have performed the hajj, done the prayers with sincerity, and fasted without ambiguity, then fear Me even more. Does anyone in the world have the gall to bring something to the Severe Threshold of the Invincible Presence?"

It was said to that paragon, "When you go before the people, go with the flag of rulership and the banner of prophethood. When you come to the Presence of My Exaltedness, come in the shirt of servanthood and the waistcoat of effacement."

Glory be to Him who took His servant by night! [17:1]. He did not say "His prophet."

"When there is talk of your prophethood and messengerhood, I swear an oath by your spirit: '*By thy life!*' [15:72]. When there is talk of My majesty and exaltedness, *thou wilt die* [39:30]."

Shaykh Abu'l-Ḥasan Kharaqānī said, "It is twenty years since my shroud was brought from heaven."

He said as well, "How marvelous that when I am with the people, He keeps me in the form of the living, even though He put on my shroud from His own Presence."

> Don't think about this talk, put on the shroud
> and clap your hands like a man.
> Say, "Either You or me in the city"—
> A realm with two chiefs is in turmoil.

One drop of sperm [*manī*] that comes from the inside establishes outward pollution, and one speck of I-ness [*manī*] that takes up residence inside makes inner pollution manifest. Outward pollution is taken away with water, but inner pollution will not disappear with all the world's oceans.

Whatever unbelief, misguidance, innovation, and hypocrisy may be in the world, all of it sticks up its head from the chamber of your own free choice. In the eighteen thousand worlds, no shadow is more inauspicious than imagining things. Sincerity alone puts imagination to flight.

Ibrāhīm Shaybān said, "I performed so many acts of discipline in the road that I slaughtered the soul with the knife of severity. Then I remained without me."

(*Rawḥ* 518–19)

Death is ignorance, life recognition. Recognition involves the recovery of a forgotten knowledge, so the meaning of the word overlaps with that of *dhikr,* "remembrance," "reminder," "mention." The Qur'an says that God sent the scriptures as reminders and that the proper human response is to remember. The jurists interpret the repeated Qur'anic instruction to remember God as commandments to perform the daily prayers and to recite the Qur'an, both of which the Qur'an calls remembrance. Sufis accept this interpretation, but the Qur'an says also, "*Remember the name of thy Lord!*" (73:8, 76:25). The Prophet encouraged his followers to keep their tongues moist with the mention of God's name. His wife ʿĀ'isha said about him, "He was remembering God at his every moment." From earliest times, Sufi teachers adopted the remembrance of God's name as their typical practice, and they encouraged their students to follow the Prophet's example by remembering God constantly and recognizing His presence in every state.

The importance of remembrance in the Qur'anic worldview is supported mythically by the story of Adam. He disobeyed the command not to approach the tree because *he forgot* (20:115). The cure for forgetfulness is remembrance, which can come only with God's help. The prophetic reminder, dhikr, must precede the human response, which is the dhikr of remembrance and mention. Maybudī makes this point in his account of the role played by Iblis in bringing about Adam's slip, part of his commentary on the verse "*Among the faithful are men truthful to the covenant they made with God*" (33:23).

> O chevalier! Listen to a point that is worth a thousand lives: When Adam and Eve were in paradise, the command came: "Do not be distracted from Me and do not be heedless of My remembrance, for Satan is a thief, and he is sitting in watch to ambush you on the road." For the blink of an eye, the strength of remembrance was held back from them, and the thief came and ambushed them.
>
> From the Invincible Threshold came the rebuke: "Adam, why did you forget My covenant?"
>
> Adam replied, "O Lord God, give me security! Grant me protection so that I may answer!"
>
> He was addressed with the words, "O Adam, I give you security. What do you want to say?"
>
> Adam said, "*Surely in that is a remembrance for him who has a heart* [50:37]. One can have remembrance only in the heart, but You took away my heart. The remembrance left the heart, and the house stayed empty. The thief came, and his hands were open. *Then Satan made them slip therefrom* [2:36]. O

> Lord, now that the work is done, You are the Generous. Be my host with Your generosity!"
>
> (*Kashf* 8:54)

Samʿānī reminds his readers that God's remembrance depends on His solicitude, guidance, and eternal mercy:

> The long and the short of it is that anyone who has heard His speech has done so through Him, and anyone who has remembered Him has done so through Him. Who in the eighteen thousand worlds would have the gall to speak of Him if this lofty proclamation had not come from the Exalted Presence on the hand of the messenger of confirmation? "*So remember Me, and I will remember you* [2:152]. *Call upon Me, I will answer you*" [40:60].
>
> (*Rawḥ* 500)

The practice of dhikr involves mentioning God's name, but the act itself is not sufficient. It needs to be accompanied by awareness of God's presence. Since people are diverse in this awareness, there are degrees of remembrance. Maybudī speaks of three degrees in his commentary on the verse "*And remember thy Lord often*" (3:41). His explanation is derived partly from Anṣārī's discussion of remembrance in *Way Stations*.

> It is said that remembrance of God has three degrees: The first is outward remembrance with the tongue of laudation and supplication. God says, "*And remember thy Lord often.*"
>
> Second is concealed remembrance in the heart. Thus God says, "*Or with more intense remembrance*" [2:200]. The Prophet said, "The best remembrance is the concealed, and the best provision the sufficient."
>
> Third is true remembrance, which is witnessing God's remembrance of you. That is His words "*And remember thy Lord when thou forgettest*" [18:24]. In other words, you should forget your own soul in your remembrance, then forget your remembrance in your remembrance, and then forget every remembrance in the Real's remembrance of you.
>
> The Pir of the Tariqah said, "O God, why should I remember when all I am is remembrance? I have given the haystack of my marks to the wind. Remembering is acquiring, and not forgetting is life. Life is beyond the two worlds, but acquisition is as You know.
>
> "O God, for a while I performed Your remembrance through acquisition, then for a while I delighted in my own remembrance of You. My eyes fell upon You, and I became busy with gazing. Now that I have recognized remembrance, I choose silence, for who am I to be worthy of this rank? I seek

> refuge from measured remembrance, temporal vision, familiarity through marks, and friendship by mail!"
>
> (*Kashf* 2:113)

Maybudī cites another saying of Anṣārī on remembrance in his comments on a verse that mentions the rightful due (ḥaqq) of the Qur'an's recitation (2:121). Once again his analysis is based on the multilayered structure of the human self.

> The rightful due of recitation is that you recite the Qur'an with burning need, limpid heart, and pure belief; with remembering tongue, believing heart, and limpid spirit—the tongue in remembrance, the heart in sorrow, the spirit in love; the tongue with loyalty, the heart with limpidness, the spirit with shame; the tongue in the work, the heart in whispered secrets, the spirit in joy.
>
> The Pir of the Tariqah said, "The servant reaches a place in remembrance where the tongue reaches the heart, the heart reaches the spirit, the spirit reaches the secret core, and the secret core reaches the Light. The heart says to the tongue, 'Silence!' The spirit says to the heart, 'Silence!' The secret core says to the spirit, 'Silence!' God says to the traveler, 'My servant, it has been a while since you have been speaking. Now I will speak, you listen.'"
>
> (*Kashf* 1:344)

In his commentary on the verse "*Who remember God, standing and sitting and on their sides*" (3:191), Maybudī classifies those who remember into three groups, taking his categories from a verse that mentions three sorts of reactions to God's messages: "*Some of them are wrongdoers to themselves, some are moderate, and some are front-runners in good works*" (35:32).

> Those who remember are three. One remembers God with the tongue and is heedless with the heart. This is the remembrance of the *wrongdoer*, who is aware neither of the remembrance nor of the Remembered.
>
> Another remembers Him with the tongue and is present with the heart. This is the remembrance of the *moderate* and the state of the wage earner. He is seeking reward and excused in his seeking.
>
> The third remembers Him with the heart; the heart is filled with Him, and his tongue is silent in remembrance. "When someone recognizes God, his tongue is mute." This is the remembrance of the *front-runner.* His tongue is lost in the remembrance, and the remembrance is lost in the Remembered. The heart is lost in love, and love in light. The spirit is lost in face-to-face vision, and face-to-face vision is far from explication.
>
> Remembrance set a trap whose bait was jealousy. The wage earner saw the trap and fled, the recognizer saw the bait and clung to the trap.

The Pir of the Tariqah said, "Remembrance is not simply what you have on the tongue. True remembrance is what you have in the midst of the spirit. Tawḥīd is not simply that you know that He is one. True tawḥīd is that you be one for Him and a stranger to other than Him."

(*Kashf* 2:396)

One of the verses commonly cited in discussions of love is "*So remember Me, and I will remember you*" (2:152). Although remembrance here is mutual, God's is contingent on that of the servant, like His love in the verse "*If you love God, follow me; God will love you.*" In both cases, God is responding to the servant's observance of the religious command. If we think rather of the creative command, we see that human love and remembrance must be a response to God. Here is Maybudī's interpretation of the verse of mutual remembrance.

This is to remember the lovingly kind Friend, the heartsease, and the spirit's food. Remembrance is the polo ball, and familiarity with Him the bat. Yearning for Him is the steed, and love for Him the field. Burning for Him is the rose, and recognizing Him the garden.

This remembrance makes the Real apparent. It is joined with the Haqiqah and separated from mortal nature. This remembrance is the watering place for the tree of tawḥīd, the fruit and produce of which is friendship with the Real. This is why the Lord of the Worlds said, "My servant does not cease remembering Me, nor I him, until he is passionate for Me and I passionate for him."*

This is not the remembrance of the tongue, which you know—this is inside the spirit. The time came when Abū Yazīd was remembering little with the tongue. When he was asked about that, he said, "I am in wonder at this remembrance of the tongue, and I am more in wonder at him who is a stranger. What would a stranger be doing in the midst? Remembrance of Him is in the midst of the spirit."

In the story of passion for You, many are the hardships.
I am with You, but many are the stations between us.

I wonder at him who says, "I remember my Lord."
Should I forget, then remember what I forgot?

That great man of his time said in a whispered prayer, "O Lord! How can I remember You when You Yourself are remembering and I am crying out from forgetfulness? You are the remembrance and the remembered. You are the help in finding Yourself.

"O Lord! When someone reaches You, his sorrows are finished; when someone sees You, his spirit laughs. Who has more joy in the two worlds than he who remembers You? Who is more worthy of happiness in You than the servant?"

O poor man, you are remembering yourself. What do you know about remembering Him? Not having traveled, what do you know about the way stations? Not having seen the Friend, how can you be aware of His name and mark?

> You are your own object of worship—you worship yourself:
> whatever you do, you do it for yourself.

If you pass into the spirit, you will gain dignity. If one day you pass by the lane of the Haqiqah and remember Him in your secret core, you will see "What no eye has seen, what no ear has heard, and what has never passed into the heart of mortal man."*

> Just once pass by Our lane
> and gaze on Our subtle artisanry.
> If you want roses, pass into the spirit
> and make the heart aware of union with Us.

It is written in one of God's scriptures, "'My servant! You will remember Me when you have tried out the others. I am better for you than anyone else.' My servant, when you have seen and tested others, then you will know My worth and recognize My rightful due. In other words, once you have seen their lack of loving-kindness and you have grasped My loving-kindness and loyalty, then you will know that I am more lovingly kind to you than anyone else and I am more useful.

"'My servant, did I not remember you before you remembered Me?' My servant, one mark of My loving-kindness is that I remembered you first, then you remembered Me.

"'Did I not love you before you loved Me?' First, I wanted you, then you wanted Me.

"'My servant, have you turned away from Me and toward another because you are ashamed to face Me? Where are you going? My door is open, My gifts are bestowed on you.'" This is as someone said:

> You have all your brightness from Me,
> you wander around, then you come back to Me.

By the exaltation of the Exalted! If you take one step in His path, a thousand generosities will reach you from Him. "From you a little service, from Him much blessing! From you a little obedience, from Him great mercy!"

> The Prophet alluded to this in recounting from God: "When someone remembers Me in himself, I remember him in Myself; and when someone remembers Me in an assembly, I remember him in an assembly better than his. When someone approaches Me by a span, I approach him by a cubit, and when someone comes to Me walking, I come to him rushing."
>
> (1:419–21)

CHANGING STATES

Travelers on the path are engaged in a struggle against the soul and all that distracts from God's remembrance, attempting to purify themselves of vices to make way for virtues. Each ascending degree of the soul's transformation is called a station, maqām, and is considered a permanent acquisition and an entrenched character trait. Stations are then contrasted with states (*ḥāl*). The root meaning of this word is "to change and alter." States are gifts from God that enter the heart but do not stay. They change quickly, and others take their place. Often, they are discussed as opposites—awe and intimacy, joy and sorrow, expansion and contraction, drunkenness and sobriety, annihilation and subsistence. According to the Sufi handbooks, states change and stations remain. Nonetheless, this terminology tends to be used loosely, not least because one person's state may be someone else's station.

Both states and stations are rooted in the divine, and authors often trace opposing pairs back to contrasting divine names. Thus fear (*khawf*) and awe (*hayba*) are said to be the human response to God's majesty and severity, and hope (*rajā'*) and intimacy (*uns*) to His beauty and gentleness. Maybudī describes the relationship between fear and hope in his commentary on the verse "*O people, be wary of your Lord!*" (22:1).

> *Be wary of your Lord* is two words, one severity, the other gentleness. *Be wary* is severity, which He brings about through His justice. *Your Lord* is gentleness, which He shows through His bounty. He keeps the servant between severity and gentleness so that he will live in fear and hope. When he is in fear, he looks at his own activity and weeps. When he is in hope, he looks at God's gentleness and is filled with joy.
>
> (*Kashf* 6:342)

In one passage, Samʿānī explains fear and hope through gender symbolism. Generally in Islamic texts, and for obvious reasons, masculinity is associated with the names of severity and majesty, and femininity with the names of gentleness and beauty. Both masculinity and femininity are present in any human soul, male or female, though at any given moment one predominates.[1]

> Sahl ibn ʿAbdallāh Tustarī said, "Fear is masculine and hope is feminine, and from the two are born the realities of faith."
>
> Fear and hope are each other's mates. When they come together in companionship, the beauty of faith will show itself, for hope has the attribute of femininity and fear the attribute of masculinity. This is because the domination of hope gives rise to lassitude and laziness, attributes of the female. The domination of fear gives rise to briskness and toughness, attributes of the male.
>
> Faith subsists through the subsistence of these two meanings. When these two meanings disappear, the result will be security or despair, both of which are attributes of unbelievers. People feel secure from those who are incapable, but to believe that He has the attribute of incapability is unbelief. People despair of the vile, but to believe that He has the attribute of vileness is associationism. One must prepare a confection and make an electuary combining hope and fear.
>
> When a lamp has no oil, it gives off no brightness. When there is oil but no fire, it gives off no illumination. When it has oil and fire but no wick to sacrifice its being to the fire's burning, the work will have no luster.
>
> Fear is like the burning fire, hope the replenishing oil, and faith the wick. The heart has the shape of a lamp holder. If there is only fear, this is like a lamp that has fire but no oil. If there is only hope, this is like a lamp that has oil but no fire. When fear and hope come together, a lamp appears that has both the oil that replenishes subsistence and the fire that is the basis of illumination. Faith takes help from both—subsistence from the one and illumination from the other. The person of faith travels with the escort of illumination and strides forth with the replenishment of subsistence.
>
> (*Rawḥ* 85)

Among the contrasting states commonly discussed in the texts are contraction (*qabḍ*) and expansion (*basṭ*). Nowadays we might call them depression and elation, but such terminology turns them into emotional vagaries, curable perhaps with a bit of chemical intervention. Islamic texts see the two as divine attributes, deposited in the soul by the creative command and reflecting two divine names, Contractor (*qābiḍ*) and Expander (*bāsiṭ*). At the beginning of his chapter on these names, Samʿānī writes,

> Contraction and expansion are the divine decree and royal determination. *He is not questioned about what He does, but they will be questioned* [21:23]. Sometimes He holds them in the grasp of His contraction so that the ruling

authority of majesty wreaks havoc on them, and sometimes He places them on the carpet of His expansion so that the ruling authority of beauty caresses them in bestowal.

It is the stipulation of the possessor of pain that he be in the grasp of power's contraction without protest and on the carpet of love's expansion without motive. A thousand thousand spirits be sacrificed to the forehead that has no creases of judgment!

That great man of the era said, "Contentment is to welcome the decrees with joy." Contentment is that you drink down goblets of pure poison without wailing and crying.

(*Rawḥ* 145)

In many passages, of which the following are typical, Maybudī explains the manner in which the shifting states of the travelers derive from the divine names. The quotation in the first paragraph is one of Qushayrī's fifteen interpretations of the mentioned verse in *Subtle Allusions*.

He effaces what He wants, and He affirms [13:39]. It has been said, "He effaces the recognizers by the unveiling of His majesty, and He affirms them by the gentleness of His beauty." Through the unveiling of majesty, intellects are eclipsed and swept away, and through the gentleness of beauty, spirits rejoice and are put at ease.

First He drowns the servants with the waves of astonishment in the ocean of unveiled majesty until, at the domination of intimacy with Him, they are freed from themselves through a state that the body cannot bear, the heart cannot understand, and discernment cannot view. Like drunkards, they turn to the valleys of astonishment, in thirst and bewilderment, sometimes weeping, sometimes laughing. They have no leisure to search out their frightened heart, no helper to whom to recount their portion. They continue saying with the tongue of brokenness in the attribute of poverty, "O God, today this burning of mine is mixed with pain—I have no capacity to bear it, no place to flee. O God, why is this blade so sharp?! There is no place for ease and no way to abstain. O Generous One, my home is so far away. The traveling companions have gone back, saying that this is the work of delusion. If my home is joy, this waiting is celebration, and this tribulation on top of tribulation is *light upon light* [24:35]."

Then, with the gaze of gentleness, He looks into the servants' spirits. The servants come back from intoxication to sobriety, take ease in the gentle favors of solicitude, and light up with the light of contemplation. They are released from self, freed from this world and the next, and live in the breeze of intimacy, seeing the beginningless reminder, having found everlasting happiness. They say, "O God, sometimes I spoke to You and sometimes I listened. Thinking of Your gentleness in the midst of my offenses, I suffered what I suffered. All became sweet when I heard the voice of acceptance."

(*Kashf* 5:219)

It is He who sends down the rain after they have despaired [42:28]. [Qushayrī writes,] "This verse alludes to the servant when the branches of his present moment have wilted, the limpidness of his love has turned opaque, the sun of his intimacy has been eclipsed, and the freshness of his covenant has become distant from the courtyards of proximity. At that point, it may happen that the Real will gaze upon him with the gaze of mercy and send mercy's rain to his secret core. Then the fresh twigs will return, and flowering roses will grow up in the places of witnessing intimacy."

The Pir of the Tariqah said, "Since the last of this work is so similar to the first of this work, the road to the Friend is a circle. It comes from Him and goes back to Him. The first of this work is like springtime and blossoms. A man is happy, fresh, and comfortable. Then he sees the downs and ups. Disappointments and dispersions come forth, for in worship there are both togetherness and dispersion, and in the stations there are light and darkness. In the darkness of dispersion, the servant sees so much concealment that he says, 'Oh, I tremble because I am worthless. What can I do other than burn until I rise up from this fallen-ness? What will happen then?'

"*He sends down the rain after they have despaired.* The clouds of munificence pour down with the rain of finding, the billows of bounteousness scatter the pearls of welcome, the rose of union blossoms in the garden of bestowal, and the last of the work goes back to the first. In joy and coquetry, the servant says, 'With reports, I went forth seeking certainty. Fear was my substance, hope my companion. The goal was hidden, and I was striving in the religion. All at once the lightning of self-disclosure flashed from ambush. With thought, they see like that; with the Friend, like this.'"

(9:34–35)

States change because of the contrasting divine names and God's never-ending reiteration of the creative command. They change also because servants look sometimes at themselves, sometimes at God. Maybudī finds a reference to this in the story of Joseph and Zulaykhā, when she offers her apology for having accused him wrongly:

When she said, "*That, so that he may know that I did not betray him secretly*" [12:52], Joseph saw the success-giving and protection of the Real. When she said, "*I do not acquit my soul; surely the soul commands to ugliness*" [12:53], she saw the shortcoming of her own service. The first clarifies gratitude for God's success-giving, the second clarifies apology for shortcoming.

The servant must always be passing back and forth between gratitude and apology. Whenever he looks at the Real, he should see blessings, take delight, and increase in gratitude. Whenever he looks at himself, he should see sin. He should burn and come forth in apology. Through gratitude, he becomes worthy of increase, and through apology he becomes deserving of forgiveness.

This is why the Pir of the Tariqah said, "O God, when I look at myself, I ask who is more miserable than I. When I look at You, I ask who is greater than I."

(*Kashf* 5:91)

In a manner that prefigures Ibn al-ʿArabī and his followers, Samʿānī says that God gave man two eyes so that with one eye he would see His beauty and majesty, and with the other he would see his own nothingness and abasement. A person's state at any moment depends on which eye predominates.[2]

O dervish, these men were given two eyes so that they would see the attributes of the soul's blights with one eye and the limpidness of God's generous gifts with the other. With one eye they see defects, with the other they see the gentleness of the Unseen. With one eye they see His bounty, with the other they see their own acts. When they look at the Real's bounty, they glory in it, and when they look at their own incapacity and weakness, they express their poverty. When they see the generosity of Pure Eternity, they become joyful, and when they see the footsteps of dust's nonexistence, they express their need.

That distracted man of Iraq [Shiblī], burnt by the fire of separation, used to say, "Would that I were fuel for the furnace and had not heard this tale!"

Sometimes he would say, "Where are the proximate angels and residents of the Holy Palisades?! Let them spread their carpets before the throne of my good fortune and the chair of my exaltedness!"

Sometimes my hands are full of silver, sometimes I'm poor.
Sometimes my heart's elated, sometimes wounded.
Sometimes I'm behind the people, sometimes ahead—
I indeed am the chameleon of the days.

That very Adam who struck the fire of passion into the merchandise of the Sovereignty's angels and was assigned all eight paradises as his own domain was given a cow. It was said to him: "Seek nourishment with the toil of your right hand and the sweat of your brow." Here we have a marvelous business! One moment of happiness followed by three hundred years of sorrow and grief!

(*Rawḥ* 130)

Fear is the human response to God's majesty, hope to His beauty. Maybudī sometimes says that these two belong to the common people, and the corresponding states in the travelers are contraction and expansion, or awe and intimacy.

> *They ask thee about the new moons* [2:189]. The waxing and waning of the moon and its increase and decrease are allusions to the contraction and expansion of the recognizers and the awe and intimacy of the lovers. The contraction and expansion of the elect are like the fear and hope of the common people. Contraction and expansion are higher than fear and hope, and so also awe and intimacy are higher than contraction and expansion. Fear and hope belong to the common people, contraction and expansion to the elect, and awe and intimacy to the elect of the elect.
>
> (*Kashf* 1:520)

> *Not equal are the two oceans, this one sweet, delicious to drink, that one salty, bitter* [35:12]. According to the tasting of the recognizers, these two oceans allude to the contraction and expansion of the wayfarers. The contraction and expansion of the advanced is like the fear and hope of the beginners.
>
> At the beginning of his desire during the moments of service, the desirer has no escape from fear and hope. In the same way, at the end of the state with perfect recognition, no one is empty of contraction and expansion.
>
> When someone is in fear and hope, his gaze is all toward the Endless: "What will be done with me tomorrow?" When someone is in contraction and expansion, his gaze is all towards the Beginningless: "What was done with me, what was decreed for me, in the Beginningless?"
>
> This is why the Pir of the Tariqah said, "Alas for the apportioning gone before! Alack for the words spoken by the Self-seer! I do not know if I should be happy or sad. My dread is what the Powerful said in the Beginningless."
>
> As long as the servant is in contraction, his sleep is like the sleep of the drowning, his food like the food of the ill, his life like the life of prisoners. He lives as is suited to his need. He follows the road in lowliness and misery and says with the tongue of abasement,
>
> "My two eyes full of tears, my liver full of fire,
> my hands full of wind, my head full of dust!"
>
> When his misery and lowliness reach their extreme and his abasement and incapacity become manifest, the Exalted Lord attends to his heart and opens the door of expansion and elation in his heart. His present moment becomes sweet, his heart is joined with the Protector, and his secret core is adorned

with awareness of the Real. He says with the tongue of gratitude, "O God, You were my tribulation, You became my good fortune! You were my sorrow, You became my ease! You were my burning brand, You became my lamp! You were my wound, You became my balm!"

(8:179–80)

Have they not seen how God originates creation, then makes it return? [29:19]. In the outward meaning, originating creation and making it return are this world and the next world. In the inner meaning, these allude to the changing of the moments and the recurrence of states for the possessors of hearts. Sometimes they are in contraction, sometimes expansion, sometimes in awe, sometimes intimacy. For a time absence dominates over them, for a time presence; for a time intoxication, for a time sobriety; for a time annihilation, for a time subsistence.

When the servant is in contraction and awe, he manifests servanthood by craving forgiveness and fearing punishment, just as the Exalted Lord said: "*They call upon Us eagerly and fearfully*" [21:90]. Then, when he steps into the world of expansion, he sees the marks bearing witness to intimacy. He is freed from his own power and strength and disengaged from his own desires and aims. He lives in the opening of disengagement, and his aspiration's goal and kiblah becomes *desiring His face* [6:52]. In this state, his soul will be like what Shiblī said because of drunkenness and selflessness: "At the resurrection, everyone will have an antagonist, and I will be Adam's. Why did he make my road steep so that I was held back by its mud?"

When he was in expansion, he spoke like that, and when he was in contraction, he used to say, "My abasement suspends the abasement of the Jews." Once again he would be so given over to expansion and intimacy that he said, "Where are the heavens and the earths that I may carry them on one of my eyelashes?"

This, then, is the meaning of the recurrence of the states alluded to by originating and making return. The proof text of this from the exalted Qur'an is His words "*You shall surely ride stage after stage*" [84:19], that is, state after state.

Part of the conduct and traveling of Muṣṭafā was that one day he would say, "I am the master of Adam's children." Then, in the state of contraction, he would say, "*I do not know what He will do with me or with you* [46:9]. Would that Muḥammad's Lord had not created Muḥammad!" Again, in the state of intimacy, he would say, "I am not like any of you—I spend the night with my Lord, and He gives me to eat and drink."

The Pir of the Tariqah gave out this meaning with a marvelous intimation: "O God, You made me pass over a thousand steeps, but one still remains. My

> heart is ashamed of so much calling on You. O God, You washed me with a thousand waters till You made me familiar with love, but one thing is still to be washed: wash me of me so that I may disappear from myself and You remain. O God, will I ever see a day without the tribulation of me? Will I ever open my eyes and not see myself?"
>
> (7:397–98)

DISPERSION AND TOGETHERNESS

In the realm of the Beginningless, all things were one with the One. Multiplicity appears when God issues the creative command. The initial state of oneness is sometimes called togetherness (jamʿ), and the fruit of the creative command is then dispersion (farq, *tafriqa*). In the path of the return, travelers undergo changes of state, sometimes basking in gentleness and sometimes burning in severity. Then togetherness can designate the proximity, or relative unity with God, brought about by gentleness, and dispersion can designate the relative separation from God demanded by severity. The goal of the path is then overcoming dispersion and achieving togetherness, or emerging from the dominating power of God's names of majesty and entering into the radiance of the names of beauty.

Maybudī explains that all that comes from God pulls the servant back toward togetherness, and all that comes from the servant pulls him into dispersion. This is one of several ways in which he explains the verse "*Say: 'If you love God, follow me; God will love you'*" (3:31).

> The beginning of this verse goes back to what the Folk of the Tariqah call togetherness and dispersion. *You love God* is dispersion, and *God will love you* is togetherness. *You love God* is to serve the Shariah, and *God will love you* is the generosity of the Haqiqah.
>
> Service on the part of the servant rises up to God. To this alludes the verse "*To Him ascend the goodly words*" [35:10]. Generosity on the part of God comes down to the servant. To this alludes the verse "*We fortified their hearts*" [18:14].
>
> Whatever comes from the servant is dispersion—defective in motive and joined with scatteredness. Whatever comes from God is togetherness—pure of motive and free of every defect.
>
> In the meaning of togetherness and dispersion, this verse is like the verse in which the Lord of the Worlds says, "*When Moses came to Our appointed time and his Lord spoke to him*" [7:143]. *Moses came* is the same as dispersion, and *His Lord spoke to him* is the same as togetherness.

Dispersion is the attribute of the folk of variegation [*talwīn*], and togetherness is the attribute of the folk of stability [*tamkīn*].

Moses was in the station of variegation. Do you not see that when God spoke to him, he went from state to state, changed, and was variegated? For no one could gaze on His face.

Muṣṭafā, one of the folk of stability, stood in togetherness itself. At the time of vision and conversation, he remained in the state of steadfastness and stability, not one hair of his body changing. The fruit of Moses's path in dispersion was this: "*And We brought him near as a confidant*" [19:52]. The fruit of Muṣṭafā's attraction in togetherness itself was this: "*Then he drew close, so He came down*" [53:8].

(*Kashf* 3:93)

On the ascending path back to God, dispersion and togetherness alternate in the travelers, so neither can be avoided. The two belong to the very constitution of reality itself, for dispersion displays the marks of majesty, and togetherness the traces of beauty. As Maybudī explains, both can be observed in the person of the Prophet and in the religion's two basic components, the Shariah and the Tariqah. The first paragraph in the first passage is taken from Qushayrī's *Subtle Allusions.*

He who made the Qur'an obligatory upon thee shall restore thee to a place of return [28:85]. Outwardly, the place of return is Mecca. The Prophet often used to say, "The homeland! The homeland!" and God made his request into reality. In secret and allusion, however, the meaning is this: "He appointed for you the attributes of dispersion so that you may convey the message and spread the Shariah. He will restore you to togetherness through your realization of annihilation from creation."

As long as Muṣṭafā was busy conveying the message, spreading the Shariah, and laying down the foundations of the religion, he was in the station of dispersion for the sake of the people's salvation. With this verse, he was taken from the narrow pass of dispersion to the vast plain of togetherness, the drinking place of His elect. Thus he said, "No one embraces me in my present moment save my Lord."

The Pir of the Tariqah said, "When someone's togetherness is sound, dispersion will not harm him. When someone's lineage is sound, recalcitrance will not cut him off. Speaking of togetherness is not the work of the tongue, and expressing its reality is calumny. How can the one destroyed by the ocean of trial explain? What mark has he who has drowned in annihilation itself? This is the talk of the heart's resurrection and the spirit's plundering. With the onslaught of union, what can be done by heart and eyes?"

(*Kashf* 7:359–60)

> *This is the path of thy Lord, straight* [6:126]. The straight path is to undertake servanthood while realizing lordhood. This is dispersion confirmed by togetherness, togetherness delimited by the Shariah. Dispersion without togetherness is the effort of the Mu'tazilites, who fell off the road and did not reach the station of the Haqiqah. Togetherness without dispersion is the path of the libertines, who let go of the Shariah and fancied a Haqiqah that was not.
>
> It is said that dispersion is the Shariah's place, and togetherness is the Haqiqah's place. If the Shariah is empty of the Haqiqah, this is deprivation, and if the Haqiqah is empty of the Shariah, this is abandonment.
>
> The Shariah is explication, the Haqiqah face-to-face vision. Muṣṭafā was possessor of both face-to-face vision and explication. If the Shariah and the Haqiqah are not brought together in the servant, the Abode of Peace will not be his place and home.
>
> (3:486)

In his two books on the path to God, Anṣārī describes dispersion as what needs to be overcome and togetherness as the station that needs to be achieved. In *Way Stations of the Travelers*, he makes togetherness the penultimate, ninety-ninth stage of the path, right before tawḥīd.

> God says, "*You did not throw when you threw, but God threw*" [8:17]. Togetherness is what eliminates dispersion, cuts away allusions, and rises beyond water and clay—after sound stability, quittance from variegation, deliverance from witnessing duality, incompatibility with sensing defectiveness, and purification of witnessing the witnessing of any of these.
>
> It has three degrees: togetherness of knowledge, togetherness of finding, and togetherness of Entity.
>
> Togetherness of knowledge is that all knowledges bearing witness come to naught in God-given knowledge, without mixing. Togetherness of finding is that the final end of conjunction comes to naught in finding itself, through effacement. Togetherness of Entity is that everything conveyed by allusions comes to naught in the Essence of the Real, in truth.
>
> Togetherness is the final end of the stations of the wayfarers, the shore of tawḥīd's ocean.
>
> (*Manāzil* 109)

In his *Book of Love*, Anṣārī provides another description of togetherness, this time clarifying its ontological roots:

> The reality of togetherness is the mark of unification, and unification is the mark of love. Dispersion is the mark of duality, and duality is the mark of estrangement.

> All the candle's brightness comes from togetherness. Wax without fire has no light, and fire without wax has no use in the session.
>
> This togetherness is the Tariqah, and beyond it is the Haqiqah, which is the nonbeing of mortal nature. As long as there is mortal nature, dispersion will appear. How then can lover and beloved be one? When created nature departs, the Real is suited for oneness. Togetherness like this is comely.
>
> The root is togetherness, dispersion an accident. When a man reaches maturity, he flees from himself and arrives at the Friend. Here he sees the reality of togetherness face-to-face, and dispersion is hidden within him. Then he may gaze and become all spirit until he is annihilated.
>
> (*Maḥabbat* 367)

Maybudī criticizes dispersion and praises togetherness in several passages, such as his commentary on the verse *"And be not like those who became dispersed and disagreed"* (3:105).

> Dispersion is the opposite of togetherness, and disagreement is the opposite of agreement. Dispersion is the scatteredness of the folk of the Tariqah, and disagreement is the scatteredness of the folk of the Shariah.
>
> Dispersion is that the servant desires one thing and the Real desires something else. Togetherness is that the servant's desire and the Real's desire are one. According to the report, "When someone makes his concerns one concern, God will spare him the concerns of this world and the next."
>
> It is said that dispersion is to gaze on the creatures and to see the secondary causes to such an extent that you are never relieved of suffering and creaturely antagonism. Togetherness is to gaze on the Real and to know that the Real is one, the work comes from one place, and the decree comes from this one door.
>
> (*Kashf* 2:241)

ANNIHILATION AND SUBSISTENCE

Western literature on Sufism has given a rather high profile to another set of terms employed to explain the nature of proximity to God: annihilation and subsistence. Some scholars suggest that annihilation is simply the Buddhist notion of nirvana brought back from India. Sufi literature itself sees it as one of several Qur'anic terms that can easily be understood as allusions to the death of the illusory self in the path to God. Typically, it and subsistence are described as two faces of the same coin. When one thing is annihilated, something else subsists. The two terms are paired because of the Qur'anic verse *"All that is upon it [the earth] undergoes annihilation, and there subsists the face of thy Lord, the Possessor of Majesty and Generous Giving*" (55:26–27). The verse is a clear expression of tawḥīd: "*All undergoes annihilation*" corresponds to the first half of the formula, the negation, "*No god.*" "*There subsists the face of thy Lord*" corresponds to the second half, the affirmation, "*but God.*"

Although the name *bāqī*, the Subsistent, is not mentioned in the Qur'an, it is typically listed among the ninety-nine names. In his chapter on this name in *Repose of the Spirits*, Samʿānī defines it like this:

> The meaning of *subsistent* is "everlasting." God says, "*All that is upon it undergoes annihilation*" [55:26]. So the Subsistent is He who has the same description in His endlessness as He does in His beginninglessness.
>
> (*Rawḥ* 611)

In *One Hundred Fields*, Anṣārī places annihilation and subsistence at the very end of the path, but in the later *Way Stations*, he makes them numbers ninety-three and ninety-four. The earlier book provides a clearer explanation of the meaning of the two terms.

> The ninety-ninth field is annihilation. God says, "*All is perishing but His face*" [28:88]. Annihilation is nonbeing. It is that three things cease to be in three things: seeking ceases to be in the Found, recognition ceases to be in the Recognized, and seeing ceases to be in the Seen.
>
> How can that which never was find anything of that which always is? How can the Subsistent Real join with the traces undergoing annihilation? How can the worthy bind itself to the unworthy?
>
> Everything other than He is among three things: yesterday's was-not, today's gone, and tomorrow's will-not-be. Everything but He is not, unless it is through Him. What is through Him has being.
>
> When rain arrives at the ocean, it arrives. Stars disappear in daytime. He who arrives at the Protector arrives at himself.
>
> The one-hundredth field is subsistence. *And God is better and more subsisting* [20:73]. God, and that is all: attachments cut, causes dissolved, traces nullified, limits voided, chronicles transmuted, allusions ended, expressions negated, reports effaced, and the Real subsisting in His own Selfhood.
>
> (*Maydān* 332–33)

Islamic texts typically refer to Abraham by the title *khalīl*, the "bosom friend," in keeping with the verse "*And God took Abraham as a bosom friend*" (4:125). His being a khalīl is often understood as the next-best thing to Muḥammad's being a ḥabīb, a beloved. Here is Maybudī's description of the annihilation achieved by Abraham. The word *enemy* (*ʿadū*) is the opposite of *friend* (walī), and we need to remember that *friend* is a synonym for *beloved*.

> "*Surely they are an enemy to me, save the Lord of the Worlds, who created me, so He is guiding me*" [26:77–78]. The mark of love is that when the lover comes to the description of the Beloved, he turns his heart away from others. He remembers only the Beloved and speaks only in laudation of the Beloved. He does not become sated by remembering Him, lauding Him, and thanking Him, nor can he remain silent. This was the case when Abraham began to remember and praise God. Look how he clung to much remembrance and laudation and made much supplication and request!
>
> What a difference between these two groups—the owners of requests and the companions of the realities! The owners of requests strive, bring forth obedience, and count out litanies, and then, after that, they present their requests. Their hearts are attached to the reward, and they implore by supplicating and requesting what they want. A report has come: "Surely God loves those who implore in their supplications." This is the station of the lords of the Shariah. Moses was in this station when he said, "*My Lord, open my breast and ease my task!*" [20:25–26], and so on.
>
> Above this is the station of the companions of the realities. In remembering and lauding the Beloved, they never turn to requesting what they want. Sometimes their tongues cling to laudation, and sometimes their hearts are mixed with contemplation, their secret cores having reached union. Annihilated from themselves, they subsist through the Real. This was the state of Abraham when he said, "*who created me, so He is guiding me.*" In other words: "He is guiding me from me to Him, for my existence has been effaced, and none but the Object of my worship guides me in myself."
>
> This is why the Pir of the Tariqah said, "O God, show me the road to Yourself and release me from the bonds of myself. O He who brings about arrival! Make me arrive at Yourself, for no one arrives by himself.
>
> "O God, remembering You is the delight of life, loving You celebration, recognizing You the kingdom, finding You joy, companionship with You the spirit's repose, proximity to You light. Your seeker is slain though alive, and finding You is the resurrection without the Trumpet."
>
> (*Kashf* 7:125)

When Samʿānī refers to annihilation and subsistence, he typically does so in the context of showing that annihilation is our created reality, since we are essentially nonexistent and only accidentally existent. It follows that it is foolish to cling to what is annihilated by nature. Rather, we should cling to the Subsistent. In the following, he refers to the formula *No god but God* and explains that only by embracing negation can a person enter into affirmation.

> This road wants a man whose aspiration aims high, whose goal is the highest station, and whose attributes have been swallowed down by the dragon of *No*, which is the doorkeeper of the world of *But*. His soul has become the precious pearl of the Shariah, his heart has mounted on the mule of seeking, his spirit is waiting for opening, and his secret core rejoices in God's subsistence.
>
> (*Rawḥ* 330)

In part of a long discussion of God's wisdom in taking Muḥammad on the miʿrāj, Samʿānī says that God wanted to show everyone that Muḥammad had left his soul behind. In effect, his soul had been transmuted into spirit. Part of his explanation touches on annihilation and subsistence and shows how the notions can be applied at each ascending level of selfhood.

> This is why the Real said, "*You did not throw when you threw, but God threw*" [8:17]. He negated him with *You did not throw*, and He affirmed him with *when you threw.*
>
> What a marvelous business! How can one thing be both affirmed and negated? What is the meaning? "O annihilated from your own attributes, O subsistent through My attributes!"
>
> The Real attracted his secret core, the secret core attracted the spirit, the spirit attracted the heart, and the heart attracted the soul.
>
> His soul reached a place where it was unaware of the two realms of being, his heart reached a place where it was unaware of the soul, his spirit reached a place where it was unaware of the heart, and his secret core reached a place where it was unaware of the spirit.
>
> His being began to seek his soul, his soul began to seek his heart, his heart began to seek his spirit, his spirit began to seek his secret core, and his secret core began to seek contemplation.
>
> The being said, "I have no rest without the soul." The soul said, "I have no rest without the heart." The heart said, "I have no rest without the spirit." The spirit said, "I have no rest without the secret core." The secret core said, "I have no rest without the contemplation of the Real."
>
> The being began to shout, "Where is the soul?" The soul began to shout, "Where is the heart?" The heart began to shout, "Where is the spirit?" The spirit began to shout, "Where is the secret core?" The secret core began to shout, "Where is contemplation?"

Then he drew close in his soul, *and He came down* into his heart, *until he was two bows' length away* inside his spirit *or closer* [53:8–9] in his secret core through contemplation.

The soul has the station of service, the heart the station of love, the spirit the station of proximity, and the secret core the station of contemplation.

If you take away the soul's strength to serve, it will perish. If you take away the heart's strength to love, it will cease to be. If you take away the spirit's strength to be in proximity, it will be finished. If you take away the secret core's strength to contemplate, it will be annihilated.

The nourishment of his soul was service, the nourishment of his heart was love, the nourishment of his spirit was proximity, and the nourishment of his secret core was contemplation. All creatures live through the spirit, and the spirit lives through the Real. "How far apart are those who live through their hearts and those who live through their Lord!"

(*Rawḥ* 319–20)

THE VISION OF GOD

Kalam experts rejected the notion of the vision (*ru'ya*) of God in this world, and among them the Mu'tazilites rejected the beatific vision in paradise. In contrast, Sufism takes the hadith of iḥsān—"It is that you worship God as if you see Him, for if you do not see Him, He sees you"—as a program of action that can, God willing, result in the vision of Him in this world.

What exactly does it mean, however, to see God? No one imagines that God can be seen in the same way that people and objects are seen. Moreover, no one says that God can be seen as He sees Himself. Rather, God can be seen to the extent that He discloses Himself to the servant. God's self-disclosure (*tajallī*), a word that scholars often translate as "theophany" or "epiphany," is His showing of Himself, and as Sufis maintained from early on, God's self-disclosure is always unique, just as He Himself is one and only one. In a long chapter on tawḥīd in *Food of the Hearts*, one of the first Arabic books to go into detail on the pithy sayings of early Muslims concerning the path to God, Abū Ṭālib Makkī explains that God's self-disclosure is never repeated.

God is beyond limits and standards, He precedes receptacles and measures, and He possesses attributes countless and infinite. He is not confined to any form, dependent on any attribute, judged by any judgment, or found by any cognizance. He does not disclose Himself twice in one description, nor does He become manifest in one form to two beings. No two words arrive from Him in one meaning. Each of His self-disclosures has a form, every servant has an attribute when He becomes manifest in him, every gaze has a speech, and every word gives understanding. There is no end to His self-disclosure, no limit to His descriptions, no exhaustion of His words, no termination of His bestowal of understanding, and no way to qualify these meanings of His, for tawḥīd has no "how," power has no quiddity, and creatures have no similarity to these attributes, for the Essence has no equal.

(*Qūt al-qulūb* 2:171)

In explaining the meaning of the verse *"They measured not God with the rightful due of His measure"* (22:74), Maybudī cites Wāsiṭī as one of the great Sufis who insisted on the impossibility of seeing God in God's measure. In the second passage, Samʿānī makes a similar point.

Wāsiṭī said, "Creatures do not recognize the rightful due of His measure—only the Real." No one knows His measure except Him. No one can recognize Him as is worthy of Him except Him. Intellects are confounded and understandings bewildered at the beginnings of the shining of His majesty. Prophets and messengers came back on the feet of incapacity from the threshold of the reality of recognizing Him.

(*Kashf* 6:409)

When He bestows upon you the vision of Himself, He gives it in the measure of your eyes' capacity, not in the measure of His majesty and beauty. This is why it has been said, "He spoke to Moses in respect of Moses. Had He spoken to Moses in respect of His tremendousness, Moses would have melted." When He spoke to Moses, He spoke in the measure of his hearing's capacity. Had He made manifest a speck of the world of His own majesty and tremendousness, Moses would have dissolved.

(*Rawḥ* 26–27)

Sufi teachers used a variety of words drawn from the Qur'an and the Hadith to designate varieties of suprarational understanding and vision, such as unveiling (*kashf, mukāshafa*), witnessing (*shuhūd*), contemplation (*mushāhada*), and face-to-face vision (*ʿiyān, muʿāyana*). Anṣārī and others offered differing definitions of each term. In reading the definitions, we need to keep in mind that we are not dealing with the desire of a philosopher or a Kalam expert to be precise. Rather, the Sufi teachers are spiritual guides, attempting to aid students in the task of achieving self-recognition and God-recognition. Thus, Anṣārī's descriptions of the way stations and fields are pointers designed to open the souls of the travelers, not to make sense to scholars or the curious. In both *Fields* and *Way Stations*, he mentions contemplation right before face-to-face vision. I cite *Way Stations*, which is somewhat easier to follow.

The Chapter on Contemplation. God says, "*Surely in that is a remembrance for him who has a heart or gives ear while he is contemplating*" [50:37]. Contemplation is the falling away of the veil once and for all. It is beyond unveiling, for unveiling is the realm of attributes within which traces subsist, but contemplation is the realm of the Entity and the Essence.

It has three degrees. The first degree is the contemplation of recognition, which flows beyond the definitions of knowledge within the tablets of the light of finding, kneeling in the courtyard of togetherness.

The second degree is the contemplation of face-to-face vision, which cuts away the ties bearing witness, puts on the descriptions of holiness, and silences the tongues of allusions.

The third degree is the contemplation of togetherness, which attracts to togetherness itself, possesses sound entrance, and embarks on the ocean of finding.

The Chapter on Face-to-Face Vision. God says, "*Dost thou not see thy Lord, that He stretched out the shadow?*" [25:45]. There are three face-to-face visions.

First is the face-to-face vision of eyesight.

Second is the face-to-face vision of the heart's eye. It is recognition of a thing according to its attributes, with a knowledge cut off from doubt and unsullied by bewilderment. This is a face-to-face vision of the marks bearing witness to knowledge.

The third face-to-face vision is the face-to-face vision of the spirit's eye. This is to see the Real utterly face-to-face. The spirits come to be purified and honored by subsistence so that they may whisper to the brilliance of the Presence and contemplate the splendor of exaltation and so that the hearts may be attracted to the courtyard of the Presence.

(*Manāzil* 93–94)

Anṣārī's whispered prayers, much more than his books on the stations of the path, employ the paradoxical language of those who tried to express the inexpressible. Maybudī quotes one of these prayers in his commentary on the verse "*When he entered upon the water of Midian*" (28:23), which refers to Moses's encounter with Shuʿayb (Jethro). He reads the story as the journey of the heart to the Real. The first paragraph is excerpted from Qushayrī's *Subtle Allusions*, and the second from the chapters on annihilation and subsistence in Anṣārī's *Fields*.

He entered the water of Midian with his outwardness, and he entered the influxes of familiarity with his heart. The influxes of familiarity are the courtyards of tawḥīd. When the servant enters the courtyards of tawḥīd, the lights of contemplation are unveiled for him and he becomes absent from his senses in his soul. Rulership, then, belongs to God alone, for there is no soul, no sense perception, no heart, no intimacy. This is dissolution in the Sanctum and total annihilation.

When the servant reaches the courtyards of tawḥīd, he is drowned in the light of contemplation, absent from himself, and present with the Real. Seeking ceases to be in the Found, recognition ceases to be in the Recognized, and seeing ceases to be in the Seen—attachments cut, causes dissolved, traces nullified, limits voided, allusions and expressions negated. When rain arrives at the ocean, it arrives. Stars disappear in daytime. He who arrives at the Protector arrives at himself.

The Pir of the Tariqah said, "O Found and Findable! What mark is given of a drunkard but selflessness? Everyone suffers tribulation because of distance, but this poor wretch because of nearness. Everyone is thirsty from not finding, but I from being quenched.

"O God, all love is between two, with no room for a third. In this love, all is You, with no room for me. If this work is from my side, I have nothing to do with it. If it is from Your side, all is You. What business have I to meddle and make claims?"

(*Kashf* 7:309–10)

In the following passages, Maybudī provides similar explications of the nature of finding God, at the same time pointing out that the multilayered reality of the human self will perceive the Real in a variety of modes simultaneously.

Perhaps you torment your soul that they are not of the faithful [26:3]. He is saying, "O master! They are a handful of the estranged, the objects of My harsh and forceful severity. Why do you occupy your heart with them? Why do you make yourself suffer because they will not believe? Turn them over to My decree and busy your heart with My love and companionship. Whenever a heart takes its ease in My love and companionship, it has no room for any other."

Sahl ʿAlī Marwazī was asked, "What is the greatest of God's generous gifts to the servant?"

He said, "That He empty his heart of everyone but Him."

Junayd was asked, "When is the heart happy?"

He said, "When He is inside the heart."

Shaykh al-Islām Anṣārī said, "He is not in the heart by His Essence. Rather the remembrance of Him is in the heart, love for Him in the secret core, and gazing upon Him in the spirit. In contemplation there is first the heart's vision, then the heart's proximity, then the heart's ecstatic finding, then the heart's seeing face-to-face, then proximity's mastery over the heart, then the heart's dissolution in face-to-face vision. Beyond that, nothing can be expressed."

(*Kashf* 7:91–92)

No, but whosoever submits his face to God, doing the beautiful, his wage is with his Lord, and no fear shall be upon them, neither shall they grieve [2:112]. The Shaykh al-Islām Anṣārī said, "Do you know when the realizer reaches the Real? When the flood of lordhood arrives and the dust of mortal nature disappears, when the Haqiqah increases and pretexts decrease. Body does not remain, nor heart, nor spirit. He stays limpid, released from water and clay. Light is not mixed with dust, nor dust with light—dust is with dust, and light with light. The tongue is lost in remembrance, remembrance in the Remembered. The heart is lost in love, love in light. The spirit is lost in face-to-face vision, and face-to-face vision cannot be explained."

If you hope for this day, come out of yourself like a snake from its skin. Abandon yourself, for it is not beautiful for you to be ascribed to yourself. This is exactly what that chevalier said:

> Endless passion has nothing to do with a heart
> that stays firm in its own attributes.
> No friend in passion's road has ever embraced
> the realm of meaning along with the realm of form.

(1:329)

Among the many words used to designate the higher stages of tawḥīd is the already mentioned *solitariness* (*tafrīd*). Its meaning is often explained as being "alone with the Alone" or "solitary (fard) with the Solitary." Maybudī writes,

You did not throw when you threw, but God threw [8:17]. This is an allusion to the reality of solitariness and the path of unification. He is saying: "Leave aside all other objects of desire. What does he who is seized by My love have to do with other than Me? O Muhammad, place no obligation on Me because of your activity, but look at My success-giving! Be not proud of your own remembrance—look at My inculcation! Flee from your own marks and see only My love!"

The path of unification is that of oneness and estrangement from self. Giving marks of "me" and "us" is duality, and duality is proof of estrangement. With duality there are today and tomorrow, but the tawḥīd-voicer is apart from today and tomorrow. As long as the tawḥīd-voicer has not found the shadow of the Sun of existence, he has not been released from self. As long as he has not been released from self, he has not found the Real.

(*Kashf* 4:24)

Another synonym for union with God and vision of the Real is *nearness* or *proximity* (*qurb*), which the Qur'an uses to designate the status of angels and paradise-dwellers. The Near (*qarīb*) is one of the divine names, as in the verse "*So ask forgiveness of Him and repent to Him. Surely my Lord is near, a responder*" (11:61). Maybudī discusses proximity in his commentary on a verse addressed to the Prophet, "*O thou encloaked one, stand up!*" (74:1–2).

> "O source of bounteousness, O rising place of beauty, O chosen by the Majestic! O you who have pulled the cloak of mortal nature over your head and covered yourself with the rug of human nature. If you want proximity to Me, *stand up* through Me and drop from yourself everything other than Me. Rise up from yourself and rise up from your own rising up! Flee to the sanctuary of My exaltedness! Lift off the cloak of mortal nature from yourself, remove the rug of human nature from the road of the heart so that the heart may be a vast plain! Let it fly like a bird in the world of desire on the air of seeking until it arrives at the nest of proximity."
>
> A great man was asked, "What is the meaning of proximity?"
>
> "If you mean the servant's proximity to the Real, expressing that is easy and alluding to it simple: it is service in seclusion, hidden from the people; the unveiling of the Haqiqah, hidden from the angels; immersion in companionship, hidden from oneself.
>
> "If you are talking about the Real's proximity to the servant, that cannot be put into words, nor do expression and allusion have any access to it. It is nothing but what He Himself says: '*Surely I am near* [2:186]: unsought, uncalled, unperceived, I am close. Compared to My closeness, the eye's blackness is distant from the eye's whiteness, for I am closer than that, and the breath is far from the lips, for I am closer than that. I am not close to your intellect's preserve, for I am close to My own attributes in the description of My own firstness.' "
>
> The Pir of the Tariqah said, "If people were to see the light of proximity in the recognizer, they would all be burned away, and if the recognizer were to see the light of proximity in himself, he would burn away. The knowledge of proximity does not fit into tongue and ear. It is a narrow road, and proximity disdains companionship with the tongue's water and clay. Whenever proximity shows its face, how can the universe and man wait around?"
>
> (*Kashf* 10:293–94)

Maybudī offers another explanation of proximity in his long commentary on the disconnected letter *qāf*, which is the first verse of Surah Qāf (50). Written out, the word *Qāf* is the name of a mythic, impassable mountain said to surround the world. Notice that in the last paragraph, Maybudī again borrows Anṣārī's description of subsistence from *One Hundred Fields*.

The chevaliers of the Tariqah and lords of recognition have voiced another secret in the meaning of qāf. They say that Mount Qāf, which is known to surround the world, is the work of the Qāf with which He has surrounded the hearts of the friends.

In this world, when someone wants to pass beyond Mount Qāf, his feet are held back and it is said to him, "There is no road beyond Qāf and no way to pass over it." In the same way, when someone has stepped into the province of the heart and the desert of the breast and wants to take one step outside the attributes of the heart and the world of the breast, his foot is held in the heart's station. It is said to him, "Where are you going? I am right here with you. 'I am with those whose hearts are broken for Me.'*"

The Pir of the Tariqah said, "O God, if I have, why don't I catch a scent? And if I don't, to whom shall I voice this longing? O God, when someone is given one look, his intellect takes flight. How can he who sees You constantly with the eye of the heart have any rest?"

This is a marvelous work—someone who gazes on Him and also seeks Him from Him. He is together with His seeker, so what use is seeking? This is why the Lord of the Worlds says, "*We are nearer to him than the jugular vein*" [50:16]. This verse alludes to the Real's proximity to the servant. As for the servant's proximity to the Real, that is as He says: "*Prostrate yourself and draw near*" [96:19].

Muṣṭafā said, reporting from the Real, "The servant never ceases drawing near to Me through supererogatory works until I love him." At first the servant's proximity to the Real is through faith and assenting to the truth, and at last it is through beautiful-doing and realization.

"Doing the beautiful is that you worship God as if you see Him, for if you do not see Him, He sees you." This report alludes to the heart's encounter with the Real, the secret core's convergence with the Unseen, and the spirit's contemplation during hidden, whispered prayer.

The Real's proximity to the servant is of two sorts. One is proximity with all creation through knowledge and power, as in His words "*And He is with you wherever you are*" [57:4]. The other is proximity with the elect of the Threshold through the characteristics of kindness and the marks bearing witness to gentleness, as in His words "*We are nearer to him.*"

First He gives the servant proximity to the Unseen so as to keep him back from the world. Then He gives him proximity through unveiling so as to keep him back from the world's folk. Then He gives him true proximity so as to keep him back from water and clay.

He decreases the marks bearing witness to the servant and increases the marks bearing witness to Himself so that just as He was at first, so also He is at last—attachments cut, causes dissolved, traces nullified, limits voided, allusions ended, expressions negated, reports effaced, the One Real subsisting in His rightful due. "*And God is better and more subsisting*" [20:73].

(*Kashf* 9:283–84)

In his commentary on the verse "*Say: 'What thing is greater in bearing witness?'*" (6:19), Maybudī illustrates something of the manner in which the higher levels of tawḥīd can be explained through notions like union, unification, contemplation, and vision. The word "bearing witness" here is *shahāda*, and Maybudī takes it to mean "bearing witness to God's unity."

There is no bearing witness more truthful than the Real's own bearing witness to what He witnessed at the first. That is, His words "*God bears witness that there is no god but He*" [3:18]. This is the Real's bearing witness that the Real is the Real.

On the first day, at the beginningless covenant, with true words and pure speech, He reported the unitary existence, the everlasting being, the endless majesty, the eternal beauty, the continuous Essence, and the abiding attributes.

Abū ʿAbdallāh Qurashī said, "This is a teaching for the servants and a directive for the seekers. With His own gentleness, He is teaching the servants to bear witness in their measure to His oneness and solitariness, just as He bears witness as is fitting for Him. Put aside the path of resistance, lest you fall into the pit like the abandoned Iblis."

One of them said, "God bears witness to His oneness, His unity, and His everlastingness. Others, like the angels and the possessors of knowledge, bear witness by assenting to the truth of that to which He bears witness concerning Himself."

He Himself bore witness to His lordhood, greatness, and oneness, for no one else was worthy of bearing witness. The creatures cannot reach the core of His majesty and tremendousness, and their bearing witness is nothing but assenting to the truth of the Real's bearing witness.

Jaʿfar ibn Muḥammad said, "The bearing witness of people is built on four pillars: first, following the commandments; second, avoiding prohibitions; third, contentment; and fourth, approval."

It is said that people's bearing witness is of three sorts: the bearing witness of the common people, the bearing witness of the elect, and the bearing witness of the elect of the elect. The bearing witness of the common people is to emerge from associationism. The bearing witness of the elect is to enter into contemplation. The bearing witness of the elect of the elect is the breeze of companionship from the side of proximity for the sake of union.

The person of sincerity sees that all is from Him, the recognizer sees that all is in Him, and the tawḥīd-voicer sees that all is He.

Every named being is a loan, and true being is He—the rest is defamation. *Say "God," then leave them* [6:91]. Oh, all is You, and that is all! How could anyone appear alongside You?

(*Kashf* 3:323)

In Surah 56, the Qur'an speaks of three sorts of people: the companions of the left, who go to hell; the companions of the right, who go to paradise; and the foremost, who are given proximity. Maybudī explains the meaning of their proximity in his commentary on verses that refer to the High Chambers (*ʿilliyyūn*), which will be witnessed by the third group in the next world.

A *book inscribed, witnessed by those given proximity* [83:20–21]. Those given proximity are the folk of proximity. I am not talking about the proximity of distance, but the proximity of friendship. Today they are near, and tomorrow they will be near, living above the Throne. It is not that today they are far and tomorrow they will be near, or that today they are absent and tomorrow they will be present. Today they are exactly what they will be tomorrow, and tomorrow they will be exactly what they are today.

He who is given proximity is he whose ears will not be distracted by the sound of the Trumpet, nor his eyes by paradise. When someone sees Him, what else will come into his eyes? When someone hears from Him, what else will enter his ears? When someone has found the good news of proximity with Him, how can he be happy with anything other than Him?

How can he who is given proximity be aware of the sound of the Trumpet, or be distracted by the terror of the Resurrection, or be touched by the smoke of hell, or cling to the bliss of paradise?

Today, everyone is with the people, but they are with the One. Tomorrow, all the people will be drowned in bliss, but they will still be with the One.

(*Kashf* 10:424)

Samʿānī agrees with Maybudī. Today the great friends of God have the vision that they will have after the resurrection. They do not worship God "as if" they see Him, but rather face-to-face. They take vision in hard cash, unlike those who are content to wait for paradise.

In truth, in truth, whatever He gives, He gives as hard cash. He does not hold back anything, for "The hearts of the free do not tolerate waiting." He holds back the form of paradise, but He hurries forward with the reality of paradise. When this talk came, it brought paradise along with it.

The master Abū ʿAlī Daqqāq said, "The ulama point you to the Garden, and that is real. I point you to such a meaning that were a whiff of it offered to the heavens and the earth, every single mote of them would become an exalted Garden."

They say, "The body surrenders itself for credit, but the heart deals only in hard cash."

Abu'l-Ḥasan Kharaqānī said, "People disagree whether they will see Him tomorrow. As for Abu'l-Ḥasan, he deals only in hard cash. When a beggar does not have his evening bread, he takes the scarf from his head and offers it at auction. He would never sell it for credit."

(*Rawḥ* 305)

Part Three

The Goal of Love

7

The Reality of Love

Early experts in Kalam typically paid little attention to the creative command, devoting their efforts instead to proving the necessity of following the religious command. In general, they understood God's love as the kindness displayed by that command, for it leads to salvation. As for human love for God, they understood it to mean obedience to the command. In contrast, both Sufis and philosophers paid a great deal of attention to the creative command and the very nature of things. They saw love as the dynamic force that brings the universe into existence, sustains it constantly, and drives all things back to the One. They understood the religious command in the context of the all-embracing divine love present in creation.

When we look at love as God's creative power, then what Lois Anita Giffen and others have called profane love—that is, the human experience of love for other human beings—can be only a metaphor (*majāz*), in the sense conveyed by the Arabic proverb "A metaphor is the bridge to the reality." The reality (ḥaqīqa) is precisely the Haqiqah, the origin and goal of the ephemeral and illusory realm that is the cosmos. Interpersonal human love is then a sign and mark of the presence of God's love in creation.

LOVE IN PHILOSOPHY

Although I have put aside most of the material on love that I gathered from philosophical writings for another occasion, it would be remiss of me to ignore the important role played by philosophy in the development of love theory among both Sufis and later Kalam experts. Historians of Islamic thought have usually drawn a sharp distinction between philosophy and Sufism, often labeling them rationalism and mysticism, respectively, the latter understood as irrational and emotive. In fact, the approaches of these two disciplines shared a great deal, more than either shared with Kalam. Both held that the goal of learning was to transform the soul and to achieve intellectual and spiritual perfection. Both saw the human self as an ascending hierarchy of awareness and intelligence. And both held that God, the Sheer Good, was the source of all love and the ultimate object of love. They also agreed that the practical guidelines codified by jurisprudence were not sufficient to guide seekers in returning to the One.

Al-Fārābī (d. 950), one of the greatest of the Muslim philosophers, explains why God is the final goal of love. At the end of the first chapter of his well-known *Principles of the Views of the Folk of the Virtuous City* (*Mabādiʾ ārāʾ ahl al-madīnat al-fāḍila*), he says that love, lover, and beloved are the exact same reality in God Himself; only in the realm of contingency can distinctions be drawn among them.

> In the First Cause, the lover is the same as the beloved, the admiring the same as the admired, and the passionate the same as the object of passion. This is the opposite of what we find in ourselves, for in us the beloved is virtue and beauty, but the lover is not beauty and virtue. Rather, the lover in us is another potency, and it is not the beloved. So the lover in us is not the same as the beloved. As for the First Cause, the passionate in It is the same as the object of passion, and the lover the same as the beloved. So It is the first beloved and the first object of passion, whether or not anyone else loves It and whether or not anyone else has passion for It.
>
> (88)

Al-Daylamī, a younger contemporary of al-Fārābī, drew from the philosophical literature in his *Treatise on Mystical Love* to make a similar point in language more congenial to that of the Sufi teachers:

> The root of love is that God is eternally described by love, which is one of His abiding attributes. He is always gazing upon Himself for Himself in Himself, just as He is always finding Himself for Himself in Himself. In the same way, He loves Himself for Himself in Himself. Here lover, beloved, and love are a single thing without division, for He is Unity Itself, and in Unity things are not distinct.
>
> (*Kitāb ʿaṭf al-alif*, 36–37)

The first widely read philosophical treatise devoted specifically to love was written by the tenth-century group of philosophers known as Ikhwān al-Ṣafāʾ, a name that is usually translated as Brethren of Purity. I would rather call them the Brethren of Limpidness. The word *ṣafā'*, the opposite of *kudūra*, "opacity," is used to designate the quality of a soul that has risen up from the darkness of forgetful nature and become transparent to the light of spirit and intellect. A few early authors derived the word *ṣūfī* from it, understanding a Sufi to be a limpid one, someone whose soul has been delivered from its natural opacity to become the locus of disclosure for the divine beauty.

The Brethren published forty treatises, largely with the goal of making the insights of Greek philosophy and mathematics available to the educated public. One of their works is called *On the Quiddity of Passion* (*Fī māhiyyat al-ʿishq*) or, as one might also translate it, "What Is Passion?" They use *ʿishq* as the generic word for *love* and at first employ it consistently, then start using it interchangeably with *maḥabba*.

At the beginning of the treatise, the Brethren point out that love is a topic of universal concern and that the Greek philosophers often discussed it. After reviewing some of the early definitions, they reject most of them as too focused on medical and psychological causality. The last definition they cite is "intense yearning for unification." They consider this the most adequate, yet acknowledge that love cannot be defined.

Next the Brethren turn to an analysis of love that uses the basic levels of soul, that is, the vegetal, animal, and rational. Each of the three souls has a love and a passion appropriate to its own nature. The passion of the vegetal soul, called shahwa, appetite or concupiscence, is love for food, drink, and reproduction. That of the animal soul, called ghaḍab, wrath or irascibility, is love for domination and control. That of the rational soul is love for recognizing the Real and acquiring the virtues.

The Brethren then apply their typology to the human situation. Every human being possesses all three souls, since each of us has the faculties and potencies of plants, animals, and humans. The enormous diversity of human types can be classified under three broad headings, depending on which of the three souls predominates in any given individual. The passion of people ruled by the vegetal, appetitive soul will lie in gratifying the senses. Those dominated by the animal, wrathful soul will love power and control. Those in whom the rational soul has the upper hand will search for knowledge, understanding, and virtue.

Next the Brethren sort the objects of people's love into general categories, such as sensory objects, children, leadership, craftsmanship, and knowledge. They explain that people are innately attracted to beauty and that human beauty is the pinnacle of created beauty and the cause of intense and passionate love. In what follows, I translate the last chapter of the treatise, which explains how love can bring about the ultimate perfection of the human soul.

Chapter. Next you should know that when someone is afflicted with passion for an individual, these tribulations and terrors pass over him, and states like this occur for him. If his soul does not awaken from its sleep of heedlessness, either he will console himself and come to his senses, or he will forget and become afflicted with passion for someone else, for his soul is drowning in its own blindness and intoxicated by its own ignorance.

Next you should know that among the people are the common and the elect. When the common people see beautiful artifacts or adorned individuals, their souls yearn to gaze upon them, or to achieve proximity, or to meditate upon them.

As for the elect, they are the wise. When they see well-made artisanry or an adorned individual, their souls yearn for the wise Artisan, the knowing Originator, the ever-merciful Form-Giver. They want to gain awareness of Him and achieve ease through Him. They strive to become similar to Him in their artisanries and to follow Him in their acts, words, deeds, knowledge, and practice.

Next, you should know that deficient souls have low aspirations. They love only *the adornment of the life of this world* [18:46]. They wish only to remain here everlastingly, for they recognize nothing else and do not conceive of anything else. In contrast, eminent, disciplined souls disdain longing for this world. They renounce it, and they desire and long for the afterworld. They wish to join up with their own kind and shape, namely, the angels. They yearn to rise up to the Sovereignty of Heaven and roam in the vast space of the spheres. This, however, is impossible before separation from the body, in keeping with defined conditions, as we mentioned in *The Treatise on the Uprising and the Resurrection*.

Know also that in their acts, recognitions, and character traits, the souls of the wise strive to become similar to the Universal Soul of the spheres and to join with it. The Universal Soul does the same, for it is similar to its Creator in governing the spheres, moving the stars, and bringing the engendered things into being. It does all this in obedience to its Creator, in worship of Him, and in yearning for Him. This is why the wise have said, "God is the first object of passion, and the spheres turn only in yearning for Him and in love for subsistence and extended continuity in the most complete state, the most perfect limit, and the most excellent end."

Then you should know that what incites the Universal Soul to govern the spheres and propel the stars is its yearning to make manifest the beautiful qualities, virtues, pleasures, and joys that are present in the World of Spirits but cannot be expressed by tongues, except tersely, as He said: "*Therein shall be whatever souls desire and gives pleasure to the eyes*" [43:71].

Next you should know that all these beautiful qualities, virtues, and good things come from God's effusion and the shining of His light upon the Universal Intellect. From the Universal Intellect, they fall on the Universal Soul, and from the Universal Soul on Prime Matter. These are the forms that the particular souls see in the World of Bodies on the outsides of the individuals and bodily things, from the circumference of the spheres down to the limit of the earth's center.

Know also that the pervading of these lights and beautiful qualities, from the first to the last, is like the pervading light and brightness on the night of the full moon, sent out by the orb of the moon's substance to the air. The light on the moon's orb is from the sun, that on the sun and the stars from the shining of the Universal Soul, that on the Universal Soul from the Universal Intellect, and that on the Universal Intellect from the effusion and shining of the Creator, just as God says: "*God is the light of the heavens and the earth*" [24:35].

It has now become clear from what we mentioned that God is the first object of passion, that existent things yearn for Him and aim for Him, *and to Him the affair will be returned, all of it* [11:123]. For in Him they have existence, abidance, subsistence, continuity, and perfection. This is because He is the Sheer Existent and has everlasting subsistence and continuity and never-ending completion and perfection. High indeed is God exalted beyond what the wrongdoers and the ignorant say!

May God convey you to Him, my brother, and complete your light as He promised His friends and chosen servants in His words "*The day you shall see the faithful men and women, their light running before them and on their right hands* [57:12]. *They shall be saying, 'Our Lord, complete our light for us and forgive us, surely Thou art powerful over everything!'*" [66:8].

May God bestow on you, us, and all the noble brothers the success to reach the path of propriety, and may He guide you, us, and all of our brothers on the road of right conduct! Surely He is clement to the servants.

(*Rasāʾil Ikhwān al-Ṣafāʾ* 3:284–86)

Avicenna is commonly considered the greatest philosopher of the Islamic world, even of the whole medieval period. He wrote numerous books on many topics. His most famous book is probably *The Healing* (*al-Shifāʾ*), a multivolume statement of the position of Peripatetic philosophy. In the volume on metaphysics, he often refers to love as a cosmic principle, approving, for example, of Aristotle's statement that the Unmoved Mover moves all things by being the object of their love, for, as Avicenna says, It is "the Good, the First Beloved" (*Ilāhiyyāt*, 316–17). He offers his most detailed and influential explanation of love in his short *Treatise on Love* (*Risāla fī'l-ʿishq*).

Like the Brethren, Avicenna uses *ʿishq* as the generic word, but unlike them, he never uses the word *maḥabba*, so I translate *ʿishq* as love. In the first chapter of his treatise, he explains that love pervades all life and consciousness. In chapters two through four, he describes how it makes itself manifest in inanimate things, plants, and animals. In the fifth chapter he explains why human souls fall in love with beautiful faces, in the sixth he talks of the love that pervades deiform souls, and in the seventh he offers concluding remarks. Unlike the Brethren, he writes for people trained in philosophy and makes little allowance for beginners.

Avicenna's concluding chapter provides a summary of his metaphysics of love. Much of the discussion focuses on the notion of tajallī, "self-disclosure," a word that we have encountered several times. As noted, it derives from the Qur'anic story of Moses and his request to see God: "*Then, when his Lord disclosed Himself to the mountain, He made it crumble to dust, and Moses fell down thunderstruck*" (7:143). Avicenna explains that all things come into existence by receiving the self-disclosure of the Good, and all things strive in the measure of their own capacities to become united with the Good, which is to say that they are driven by love for the Good and the Beautiful. As he remarks in his metaphysics, "All beauty, agreeableness, and perceived good is beloved, the object of passion" (*Ilāhiyyāt*, 297). He soon mentions the divine ones (*ilāhiyyūn*), those who are masters of metaphysics (*ilāhiyyāt*, the "divine things"). He has in mind those who have achieved the final goal of philosophy, which is deiformity (ta'alluh) or gaining similarity (*tashabbuh*) to God. In short, his treatise explains the manner in which all created things participate in God's self-disclosure, which is nothing other than the manifestation of the creative command.

> In this chapter we desire to clarify that each of the existent things loves the Absolute Good with an innate love, and that the Absolute Good discloses Itself to Its lovers. Their receptions of Its self-disclosure and their conjunctions with It, however, are disparate. The furthest limit of proximity to It is the reception of Its self-disclosure in reality, I mean, as perfectly as possible. This is what the Sufis call "unification." In Its munificence, the Good loves that Its self-disclosure is received. Then the things come into existence by means of Its self-disclosure.
>
> Thus we say: given that every existent thing innately loves its own perfection—for its perfection is the meaning through which it gains its own good—it is clear that the meaning through which things gain their good, wherever it may be found and however it may exist, must be loved by things seeking the good.

Next, there is no more appropriate way to gain the good than the First Cause of all things, so It is loved by all things. If, in fact, most things do not recognize It, this does not negate their innate love for their own perfections.

By Its Essence, the First Good is manifest and disclosed to all existent things. Were Its Essence essentially veiled from and not disclosed to all existent things, It would never be recognized, nor would anything be received from It.

If this manifestation and disclosure occurred essentially through the influence of others, then the Good's Essence, which transcends reception by others, would necessarily be influenced by others, but this is contradictory. Rather, Its Essence discloses Itself by Its own essence. It is veiled because of the incapacity of some essences to receive Its self-disclosure. So, in reality, there is no veil except in those who are veiled. The veil is inadequacy, weakness, and deficiency.

Moreover, the Good's self-disclosure is nothing but the reality of Its Essence, for nothing discloses itself by essence to Its Essence unless it is Its unmingled Essence, as the divine ones have clarified. Its generous Essence discloses Itself, and that is what the philosophers sometimes name the form of the Intellect.

The first recipient of Its self-disclosure is the divine angel named the Universal Intellect, for its substance gains Its self-disclosure like a form that falls into a mirror through the disclosure of the individual of whom it is the image. Near to this meaning is what has been said: "The Agent Intellect is Its image [*mithāl*], so you should avoid saying 'likeness' [*mithl*]."

The Agent Intellect receives the Good's self-disclosure without intermediary by perceiving its own essence along with all other intelligibles within and from its own essence, in actuality and fixity. The things assume form as intelligibles without vision or the aid of sense perception or imagination. Posterior things are intelligible to it through prior things, effects through causes, and vices through virtues.

Then the divine souls receive the self-disclosure, also without intermediary at the reception, even if they do so with the aid of the Agent Intellect, which brings things from potentiality into actuality and bestows on the forms the potencies of receiving, grasping, and resting.

Then the animal potency receives the self-disclosure, then the vegetal, then the natural. Whatever receives it yearns to gain similarity to the Good in keeping with its own capacity. For example, the natural bodies move with natural movements only to gain similarity to the Good in their final goal, which is subsistence in their most specific states, that is, when they reach these in their natural situations. This is despite the fact that in their origins, their movements have no similarity to the final goal.

So also are the animal and vegetal substances. They act out their specific activities so as to gain similarity to the Good in their final goals. These goals are the subsistence of the species or the individual, or the manifestation of a potency or a power or the like—even if they do not gain similarity at the origin of these goals, like copulation and taking nourishment.

So also are the human souls. They act out their intellective activities and good works in order to gain similarity to the Good in their final goals, which are to be just and intelligent, even if they also are dissimilar to It in the origins of these goals, like learning and the like.

The divine, angelic souls move in their movements and act in their activities in seeking to gain similarity to the Good in the continuity of generation and corruption, tillage and procreation.

Animal, vegetal, natural, and human potencies gain similarity to the Good in the final goals of their activities and not in their origins, because origins are only states of preparedness and potential, while the Absolute Good is incomparable with the admixture of states of preparedness and potential. Their final goals, however, are actualized perfections, and the First Cause is described by actual, absolute perfection. Thus it is permissible to gain similarity in the final perfections, but things cannot be similar to It in the originating preparednesses.

As for the angelic souls, they have received similarity to It in the forms of their essences by means of an endless reception, empty of potentiality, for they perceive It intelligibly without end. Because of what they perceive of It, they are in love with It without end. And because of what they love of It, they gain similarity to It without end. So much do they crave to perceive It and receive Its form—for this is the most excellent perception and form reception—that they are almost distracted from perceiving anything else or receiving the forms of any other intelligibles. In reality, however, recognizing It goes back to recognizing all existent things. They, as it were, receive Its form intentionally and receive the form of everything else following on that.

Thus, if the Absolute Good did not disclose Itself, nothing would be received from It. If nothing were received from It, nothing would exist. So if It did not disclose Itself, there would be no existence, for Its self-disclosure is the cause of every existence. And since, by Its very existence, It loves the existence of everything caused by It, It loves the reception of Its self-disclosure.

The love of the Most Excellent for Its own excellence is the most excellent love, so Its true beloved is the reception of Its self-disclosure. This is the reality of Its reception by deiform souls. This is why it may be said that they are

Its beloveds. To this refers what has been recounted in the reports from God that the servant does such and such "until he is passionate for Me and I passionate for him."*

Wisdom does not allow disregard for something that has any sort of excellence in its existence, even if it falls short of the utmost excellence. Thus in Its wisdom the Absolute Good loves that things receive from It, even if they do not reach the degree of perfection in that.

This is why the Most Tremendous King is pleased when things gain similarity to Him, whereas perishing kings become angry at those who become similar to them. No one can reach the final goal of what he wants in gaining similarity to the Most Tremendous King, but he can reach the extent of what he wants in becoming similar to perishing kings.

Now that we have arrived at this point, let us conclude the treatise, praising God and blessing all His prophets.

(*Risāla fi'l-ʿishq*, 82–88)

LOVE IN EARLY SUFISM

One of the more succinct early books on Sufi teachings is *Introduction to the School of Sufism* (*al-Taʿarruf li-madhhab al-taṣawwuf*), a 150-page Arabic treatise by Abū Bakr Kalābādhī (d. 990) that was translated into English by A. J. Arberry as *The Doctrine of the Sufis*. In seventy-five short chapters, it provides a compendium of the sayings of Sufi teachers on topics like tawḥīd, the divine attributes, the path to God, recognition, hope, fear, vision, and love. A few years after it appeared, a scholar named Abū Ibrāhīm Mustamlī Bukhārī, a contemporary of Avicenna who died about fifty years after Kalābādhī, wrote a long commentary (1,800 pages in its modern edition) on Kalābādhī's work; it is apparently the oldest book on Sufi teachings in the Persian language. By writing in Persian, Bukhārī opened up the text to those with little formal education. The original Arabic is in any case so allusive and bound up with technical terminology that even well-educated Arabic speakers would find it difficult to follow. Moreover, books like Kalābādhī's *Introduction* or Qushayrī's *Treatise*, which has a similar though much longer chapter on love, were not read the way we read books. They were studied carefully, line by line and word by word, at the feet of a teacher. Bukhārī's Persian commentary made a teacher less necessary.

In the typical fashion of the Sufi handbooks, Kalābādhī's two-page chapter on maḥabba cites sayings by well-known teachers but gives little or no explanation. Bukhārī's commentary translates each saying into Persian and provides detailed explanation. He begins the chapter on love with a little treatise that stands on its own, apparently the oldest surviving essay on love in Persian. It offers a concise picture of how love was being discussed in both Kalam and Sufism in the tenth and eleventh centuries (and later). When he mentions the Folk of the Principles, he means the Kalam experts. The Folk of Recognition are the Sufi teachers.

> Love is one of the attributes that is found between people and also between the servant and the Real. Every such attribute is an attribute of mutual similarity. Such attributes should not be ascribed to the Real unless they are found in the Shariah in both respects. The attribute of love has come in the Shariah, as when He said: *"He loves them, and they love Him"* [5:54]. In another place He said, *"Say: 'If you love God, follow me; God will love you'"* [3:31]. Elsewhere He said, *"Among the people are those who take to themselves peers, apart from God, loving them as God is loved. But those who have faith love God more intensely"* [2:165].
>
> Given what we have mentioned, there is no escape from knowing the interpretation of love. Then there will be a difference between the love that is an attribute of the Real and the love that is an attribute of the created things, for there is no meaning that has more similarity. Moreover, there is a love that is unbelief, and a love that is faith.
>
> Let us first explain the love that is found between the creatures. Then we will differentiate between newly arrived love and eternal love.
>
> As for the love that is between the creatures, its first degree is conformity [*muwāfaqa*] of nature. Someone sees or hears something that conforms to his nature, so his nature is at ease with that thing.
>
> After a period of conformity with his nature, he reaches the second degree, inclination [*mayl*]. Inclination belongs to the soul. The soul inclines to companionship with the person or thing and turns away from others. The more inclination increases, the more turning away increases.
>
> After some time in the second station, he reaches the third station, which is affection [*wudd*], that is, wishing and hungering. When he reaches this station, he loves the person and loves to see her, sit with her, and listen to her.
>
> After he spends some time in this third station, he reaches the fourth degree, which is love. Concerning the word, there is a great deal of talk. One group has said that its root is *maḥā* [he erased] and *batt* [he severed], that is, he erased from his secret core everything other than the beloved and cut off from his secret core everything but the beloved's remembrance.
>
> Another group said that it is derived from *ḥubb* [meaning "jar"]. When the jar is full, there is no room for anything else; likewise, when the heart is full of love, it has no room for other than the friend.

Another group said that love is derived from *ḥabb*, meaning "seed." In the word's original meaning, the *ḥabb* of something is its core and marrow, which is why the heart's core is called the seed of the heart. When friendship reaches the core, it is called love.

Once the person has passed some time in this station, he reaches the fifth degree, which is distraction [*walah*]. Distraction is bewilderment. He becomes perplexed and bewildered. Whatever he sees, he fancies that it is his friend. Whatever he hears, he fancies that it is the words of his friend, like a mother whose child is lost, so she is said to be distracted.

When he passes beyond this fifth station, he comes to the sixth station, which is called caprice [*hawā*]. This is said to be derived from the air [*hawā'*] that is between heaven and earth, in the sense that air is limpid and does not have any opacity. When he reaches this sixth station, his heart becomes so limpid for the friend that not a single dust mote finds a place in it.

One group has taken *hawā* in the sense of descending and falling, as when God said: "*By the star when it goes down* [*hawā*]" [53:1], that is, falls, plunges, descends, and leaves. If the derivation is from here, then the word means that all the objects of desire and everything other than the friend fall away from him.

Another group has said that *hawā* is derived from the desired object and inclination, as God has said, "*And forbade the soul its caprice*" [79:40]. According to this opinion, the meaning is that his every inclination and desire becomes what is desired by the friend.

Still another group said that the sense of the derivation of *hawā* is that the person becomes entirely preoccupied by the thing. He sees everything as it, and all its defects become virtues, as when God said, "*Have you seen him who has taken his caprice as his god?*" [25:43]. When the unbeliever inclines toward an idol and sees the defect of contingency, he becomes blind to seeing it and replaces it with the attribute of eternity, which is divinity. The Real calls this caprice.

Once he has spent some time in this sixth station, he passes on to the seventh station, which is the degree of passion. This is also love, but since it has passed beyond the limit, it is called passion. In the same way, when munificence passes beyond the limit, it is called extravagance.

'Ishq is said to be derived from *'ashaqa*, which is the plant that twists around a tree and begins to consume it, and the tree's color turns yellow. Then it loses its fruit, drops its leaves, and becomes dry, worthy of nothing but being felled and burned. Passion also, having reached perfection, overthrows the faculties, holds the senses back from their benefits, and impedes nature from its nourishment. It throws weariness between the lover and the

people, and he finds companionship with other than the friend tiresome. It pulls all meanings out of his soul. Either it will make him ill or drive him mad. It holds him back in this world until it destroys him.

The discussion that we just mentioned is not a stipulation of this book. By mentioning it, we desired two things: first, once this is known, we may describe love for the Real, and you will not confuse the two. Then faith will not turn into unbelief, nor will unbelief turn into faith.

The other goal was to describe briefly the love found between created things and to note that in the creatures, this is not a description that we perceive. Thus it will be known that if we do not perceive the reality of the love that occurs between the two sexes, how can we perceive the reality of the love that is between the servant and the Real? Whatever falls short of what is rightfully due to creation will fall even further short of what is rightfully due to God.

Now we turn back to the description of the love that is between the Real and the servant. The Folk of the Principles hold that the Real's love for the servant is a desire for the good, and the servant's love for the Real is obedience. Thus also in the visible world, when a servant is more obedient to his lord, people say that he is more loving toward his lord. And when a lord is kinder to his servant, they say that the lord is more loving toward the servant. In this meaning, the poet said,

> Were your love truthful, you would obey him—
> surely the lover obeys the one he loves.

This has been said because love from the lesser incites obedience and service. As much as love increases, lightness and elation in obedience increase. As is well known in the visible world, distraction in service comes from weariness and boredom with the one served, whereas elation and lightness in obedience and service come from intimacy with and love for the one served. So God's creatures have this.

Again, both the Real's love and His enmity are a desire, and desire is one attribute. The Real wills everything with this one desire. In the same way, He knows everything with one knowledge. The knowledge does not change, but the known things change. With the same eternal knowledge, He knows every known thing because it is a known thing. In the same way, He desires all desired things with one desire. Desire does not change, but the desired things change. Hence, with the same eternal desire He wants every desired thing because it is a desired thing.

So desire is one, and the desired things are different. God wants one person to receive bad for what he does, and He wants someone else to receive good for what he does. When He wants good, His desire is called love. When He wants evil, it is called enmity. The names become different because of adjacency. It is not that the Real's attributes of enmity and love are different or change into each other. This happens only with the attributes of created things, when enmity brings about a change so that someone no longer loves, or love brings about such a change in the lover that he no longer has enmity. The attributes of created things bring about changes in the created things, because it is permissible for their attributes to change.

Again, the Real's attributes do not bring about change in the Real, because He is eternal, and it is not permissible for His attributes to change. But His attributes influence created things. If we have enmity or love for someone, that brings about pain or ease in us. As for the Real's love and the Real's enmity, they bring about pain and ease, tribulation and beneficence, and chastisement and mercy in the creatures. The Real remains in the same attribute that He had in the Beginningless.

Let us turn to the words of the Folk of Recognition. The Folk of Recognition say that for them, love and enmity are not what the Folk of the Principles say. For it is permissible for the servant to be empty of obedience and at the same time not be empty of love, for being empty of love is unbelief. Thus, obedience is not love, but obedience is the influence of love. Moreover, if obedience were love, disobedience would be enmity. There is consensus among the people, however, that the disobedient person of faith is not an enemy through disobedience. Rather, as long as he is one of the faithful, he is a lover, even if he is disobedient. It follows that obedience is not love, but love incites obedience. A person's obedience is the influence of love and the evidence of love, not love itself.

As for the Real's love and the Real's enmity, the Folk of Islam agree that these are beginningless attributes. The good and evil that reach the servant are the influence of beginningless love and enmity. Wherever beginningless love exercises its influence, it makes conformity appear; and wherever beginningless enmity exercises its influence, it makes opposition appear. This is because the Beginningless exercises influence and brings about change, and the newly arrived changes and undergoes influence. The Beginningless influences the newly arrived, but the newly arrived does not influence the Beginningless. Undergoing influence is to change. It is permissible for the newly arrived to change, but not for the Eternal.

Now that you have come to know the difference between the two loves, you should know also that love is an attribute that people are incapable of describing. No one who has described love has reported about love itself. Rather, they talk about its attributes, its influences, and the lovers' acts.

This is because the describer is one of two: either he is a lover or he is not. If he is not a lover, how will he describe something he has not seen? And if he is a lover, he will be so preoccupied with love's burning that he will not have the opportunity to describe it. And if he does, but those who hear have no trace of this burning, his description will not be understood. Hence there is no use in describing it.

This is why all tongues have been dumb about love. They spoke of its influences, attributes, and acts. Someone who is not aware of love does not know what they are talking about, and someone who is under its influence sees what the description describes.

(*Sharḥ al-taʿarruf*, 1387–92)

Soon after Bukhārī completed his commentary, Hujwīrī wrote his 600-page *Unveiling the Veiled* (*Kashf al-maḥjūb*). R. A. Nicholson, who translated the book into English a hundred years ago on the basis of a rather faulty text, thought it was the first book on Sufism in Persian. The text devotes ten pages to love in the midst of a fifteen-page chapter on the ritual prayer (ṣalāt), which, Hujwīrī tells us, is the manifestation of love for God. Much of his discussion is devoted to the derivation of the word and the views of Kalam experts. In one passage, he tells us that the Sufi teachers agree that *Sufism* is simply another word for love.

Love is well known among every people. It is famous in every tongue and current in every language. No intelligent man of any sort is able to conceal it from himself. Among the shaykhs of this group, Samnūn al-Muḥibb has a specific school of thought. He says that love is the root and foundation of the road to the Real, and the states and stations are its way stations. Whatever place the seeker may have on the road may disappear, except love. As long as the road exists, love can never disappear. The other shaykhs all agreed with him in this meaning, but the name is too general and famous. They wanted to conceal love's properties from the people, so they changed the name. To verify the existence of love's meaning, they named its limpidness *ṣafwa*, and they called the lover a ṣūfī. A group of them named the lover's abandonment of his own choice and his affirmation of the Beloved's choice *poverty*, and they called the lover *a poor man*.

(*Kashf al-maḥjūb*, 451–52)

In *Way Stations of the Travelers*, Anṣārī mentions love as the sixty-first station, and this has led some modern scholars to suggest that he did not give much importance to it. As noted earlier, however, he talks about the central importance of iḥsān, doing the beautiful, in the introductions to both *Way Stations* and *One Hundred Fields*. In *Way Stations*, he calls iḥsān "an all-comprehensive allusion to the position of this group" (*Manāzil* 6). In other words, the path to God is bound up with achieving beauty of character, and beauty cannot be disengaged from love. Those who strive to achieve iḥsān are motivated by love for Him and for everything beautiful. In the chapter on love in *Way Stations*, Anṣārī says, "Love is the mark of the Tribe [the Sufis], the title of the Tariqah, and the seat of the relationship [with God]" (*Manāzil* 71). It is likely that he placed love in the middle of the path for the same reason that Ghazālī offers in *Giving Life*:

> Love for God is the furthest goal among the stations and the highest pinnacle of the degrees. After reaching love, later stations, like yearning, familiarity, and contentment, are among its fruits and consequences. All the stations before love—such as repentance, patience, and abstinence—are preliminaries to it.
>
> (*Iḥyā'* 4:427).

In his earlier *One Hundred Fields*, Anṣārī takes the same position as Hujwīrī, noting that the path to God is simply the path of love. Remember, he said at the very beginning that the book is based on a series of sermons in which he explains the meaning of the verse "*Say: 'If you love God, follow me; God will love you'*" (3:31). In other words, the one hundred fields are the ascending stages of the soul's journey in love as it follows in the footsteps of the Prophet. In the very last paragraph of the book, after having described the one hundred fields, Anṣārī returns to the theme of love:

> These one hundred fields are all drowned in the field of love. The one hundred-and-first field is love: "*He loves them, and they love Him*" [5:54]. "*Say: 'If you love God*'" [3:31]. Love is three stations: The first is truthfulness, the middle drunkenness, and the last nonbeing.
>
> (*Maydān* 333)

DESCRIPTIONS OF LOVE

Among the important themes highlighted by most discussions of love is its inexplicability. Anyone can be a lover, but no one can explain love, something that is fairly obvious from everyday experience. The texts rarely try to define love and choose instead to describe its qualities and characteristics. For example, in the first 450 pages of *Repose of the Spirits*, Samʿānī mentions love repeatedly before offering anything like a definition. Here is the closest he comes to explicating the two basic sorts of love—God's love for man and man's love for God. The passage pertains to his chapter on the divine name walī, the Friend.

A man was fishing, and a fish fell into his trap. The fish said, "I am a living being who glorifies God. Will you forbid me to glorify?"

Another fish answered him: "Are you doing God a favor by glorifying Him? What place is this for talk of glorification? You must give up your sweet life. Don't talk."

He sent a whiff of love's story into the world, and the whole world became distracted, but before reaching the outskirts of His majesty, they came to naught. The sword of severity was drawn, the garment of exaltedness was donned, and a hundred thousand friends and sincerely truthful were perplexed and pulled into the road. The seeker was lost in the seeking, and the searcher annihilated in the searching. The finder of ecstasy reached finding, ecstasy was lost in vision, and finding the Found turned into losing. The seer reached vision of Him, and His vision disappeared in the bewilderment of vision. No eye is worthy of seeing Him. No heart buys this story.

> My eyes want only to see You,
>   my ears want only Your words.
> They have high aspirations,
>   but they're not worthy of You.

He created the dust, and in it He prepared recognition. Then He handed recognition over to love. He removed the intermediaries and handed love over to proximity. He removed the marks of the road and handed proximity over to bewilderment. Bewilderment is beyond all the stations. "O Guide of the bewildered, increase me in bewilderment!"* Shiblī said, "These are the words of a bird in a cage. No matter where it sticks out its head, it cannot find the road."

The bewildered are those who dwell in the pavilion of divine jealousy. If they want to come out to the creatures for a moment, they cannot. Everything outside the curtain is loss of the road, and everything inside the curtain derives from the traces of the perfect divine majesty.

Anyone who cannot go from creation to the Real has lost the road, and anyone who cannot go from the Real to creation is bewildered. No matter how far he goes, he returns only to Him. This is like Moses and his people—though they went far, they were at the first step.

"I had pure attributes—so there had to be a recognizer. I had unqualified beauty—so there had to be a lover. I had an unconditioned Essence—so there had to be a seeker."

There were attributes, so there had to be a recognizer. There was beauty, so there had to be a lover. There was the sought, so there had to be a seeker. There was the intended, so there had to be an intender. There was the gaze, so there had to be an object of the gaze. There was reception, so there had to be something received. There was mercy, so there had to be an object of mercy. There was forgiveness, so there had to be an object of forgiveness.

The other created things had nothing to do with love, for they did not have high aspirations. The work of the angels was upright because there was no talk of love with them. All this up-and-downness, this above-and-beneathness, these drafts mixed with poison, these swords hanging over the heads of the Adamites—these are all because the talk of love was with them.

Orderly and arranged work belongs to those who know nothing of love. When a whiff of love's rose reaches the nostril's of someone's covenant, tell him to detach his heart from the rose, for "Love *scorches mortal man* [74:29]. *It spares not, nor leaves alone* [74:28]."

> Passion for You made me a tavern-goer like this—
> otherwise I was safe and orderly.

> By God, I do not know whether I should blame my soul
> for love, my unlucky eyes, or my heart.
> I blamed my soul, but it said the eyes had sinned.
> I blamed my eyes, but they said, "Blame the heart for sinning."

O chevalier! You hear all this talk of love, but what exactly is love? What is the servant's love for the Real? What is the Real's love for the servant? This is a tremendous root.

The Real's love for the servant is desire for a specific bounty and conjunction with a specific secret and kindness. This secret is beyond speech, and only lovers know what it is, for physicians know the measure of the pain of the ill. "Before the encounter, the lover's recompense is iniquity." No cause can prepare for this gentleness, and no contrivance can be its means.

The servant's love for the Real is that he finds in his heart a state whose outcome is that he conforms to the commandments. He chooses the commandment over what is chosen by the gambling, wine-drinking, commanding soul, whose love is built on the body's desires for its own shares. Anyone who seizes the belt of love detaches his heart from all shares whatsoever.

Love is curtained by the attributes of the states, for its roots are in the jewel box of curtaining. These are the states of the pious.

Love demands clinging to the gate of the Beloved. It is derived from *aḥabba'l-baʿīr*, that is, "the camel put its knees on the ground," so no matter how much you beat it, it did not move from its place.

All these words are reports and narratives. As for the reality, love is a state that cannot be expressed in words.

(*Rawḥ* 463–65)

Samʿānī talks in some detail about the meaning of love at the beginning of his commentary on the divine name wadūd, the Loving, and then ties the discussion back to the tale of God's creation of Adam.

O You who disclose Your love by caressing the servants, O You who love Your servants despite Your unneediness, O You who throw love between the servant and Yourself without any partner!

He says, *"He is the Forgiving, the Loving/Beloved"* [85:14]. And He says, *"Those who have faith and do worthy deeds—to them the All-Merciful shall assign love"* [19:96].

Wadūd is an intensive from *widād.* You can also say that *wadūd* means *mawdūd* [beloved]. In the verse, the *Forgiving* is He who has much forgiveness, and the *Loving/Beloved* is He who is intense in love. In other words: He has much forgiveness toward them because He loves them, and He has much forgiveness for them because they love Him.

The master Abu ʿAlī Daqqāq said, "He singled out Adam by creating him with His hand, He singled out Moses with His words, '*I made you for Myself*' [20:41], and He singled out us with His words '*He loves them, and they love Him*' [5:54]."

Explaining the road of love with the tongue is easy, but undertaking the stipulations of love is the work of Men.

Ḥārith Muḥāsibī said, "Love is that you incline toward something with your entirety; you prefer it over your soul, your spirit, and what belongs to you; you conform to it secretly and openly; and you know that you fall short in what is due to it."

The road of love is such that you must busy yourself with the Beloved totally. You must expend your spirit, heart, and body in His road. You must seek conformity with Him both secretly and openly. You should not give priority to your own share's evil eye. Rather, you must give priority to His share. And when you have done all this, you must know that you are thrown down by incapacity and you must recognize that you are broken by shortcoming.

Abu'l-Qāsim Naṣrābādī said, "Love is battling against solace in every state." Love is that whenever your heart talks of not having sorrow, you take up spear and sword and fight against your heart.

In the two worlds, no one dared talk of love. All at once, the roar of love's royal drum fell into the Sovereignty. The proximate angels said, "What happened? Why have our many thousand years of glorifying and hallowing been given to the wind?"

It was said, "Don't look at these forms, look at the deposit of Majesty: *He loves them, and they love Him.*"

Gabriel, Michael, and the other exalted ones had become satisfied and content with glorification and hallowing. All of a sudden, the footsteps of Adam came into the world. The ways were altered and the foods changed: "O Gabriel, bind up your waist and be a messenger! O Michael, prepare yourself to be the keeper of the treasury! O Azrael, make your heart happy with taking away worn-out clothing! O Seraphiel, submit yourself to giving out new clothing!

"First you must taste a draft so that the dust of your claim '*We glorify Thy praise*' [2:30] may depart from you."

"What must be done?"

"*Prostrate yourselves before Adam* [2:34]. You must go before this piece of clay and prostrate yourselves. That will be an increase in your road, not an increase in his, for he has already been accepted by election: *Surely God chose Adam* [3:33]. *I blew into him of My spirit* [15:29]. *Him whom I created with My own two hands* [38:75]."

(*Rawḥ* 408–9)

Maybudī offers one of his longer descriptions of love in explaining the verse of mutual love. He begins by pointing out that the verse contains a warning for those who turn away from God and good news for those who turn toward Him. Here is part of what he has to say:

The good news is that whoever does not turn back is counted among the friends, the folk of love and faith. Those who do not fall into the abyss of turning back have the good news that the name of love will fall upon them.

God says, "*Should any of you turn back on your religion, God will bring a people whom He loves and who love Him*" [5:54]. First He affirms His love, then the servants' love. Thus you know that so long as God does not love the servant, the servant will not love.

Wāsiṭī said, "Gehenna was nullified when He mentioned His love for them with His words '*He loves them, and they love Him.*' What do defective attributes have to do with beginningless and endless attributes?"

Ibn 'Aṭā' was asked what love is. He said, "Branches that grow in the heart and give fruit in the measure of intellect."

The Pir of the Tariqah said, "The sign of finding friendship's response is contentment, the water of friendship increases through loyalty, the substance of friendship's treasure is light, the fruit of friendship's tree is joy. Whoever fails to keep away from the two worlds is excused from friendship. Whoever seeks from the Friend something other than the Friend is ungrateful. Friendship is friendship for God, all the rest disquiet."

He loves them, and they love Him. A great work and a magnificent bazaar rose up in water and clay and became the kiblah of the Real's friendship and the target of union's arrow. How could the traveler not be delighted that friendship is the nearest way station to the Protector? The tree that produces only the fruit of joy is friendship, the soil that grows nothing but the flowers of intimacy is friendship, the cloud that rains nothing but light is friendship, the drink whose poison turns into honey is friendship, the road whose dust is musk and ambergris is friendship. Friendship's inscription is beginningless, and friendship's burning brand endless.

When the Friend's friendship is my habit and disposition,
I am all from the Friend, and all of me is the Friend.

Behold how long friendship's good fortune lasts! Listen how fitting is the tale of the friends! Friendship's field has the width of the heart, and the kingdom of paradise is one branch of friendship's tree. Those who drink friendship's wine are promised vision. Whoever is sincere will reach the goal.

God revealed to David, "O David, he who seeks Me will in truth find Me, but how can those who seek others find Me?

"O David, tell the people of the earth, 'Turn toward companionship and intimacy with Me! Become intimate with My remembrance! Then I will be your heart's intimate.'

"I have created the clay of my friends from the clay of My bosom friend Abraham, from the clay of My speaking companion Moses, and from the clay of My beloved Muḥammad.

"O David, I have created the hearts of those who yearn for Me from My own light and nurtured them with My own majesty. I have servants whom I love and who love Me: *He loves them, and they love Him.* They remember Me and I remember them: *So remember Me, and I will remember you* [2:152]. They are happy with Me and I am happy with them: *God is well pleased with them and they are well pleased with Him* [5:119]. They stay loyal to My covenant and I stay loyal to their covenant: *And be loyal to My covenant, and I shall be loyal to your covenant* [2:40]. They yearn for Me and I yearn for them: 'Surely the yearning of the pious to encounter Me has become protracted, but My yearning to encounter them is more intense.'*"

(*Kashf* 3:154–56)

In Stage Two of his commentary on the verse of following (3:31), Maybudī says that love has four marks, the first of which is to follow the Messenger. Then he writes:

In another place, He made hoping for death the mark of friendship: "*If you suppose that you are the friends of God, apart from the people, then hope for death, if you are truthful*" [62:6]. He says: If you speak in truth that you love God, hope for death, for friendship is the motivation for yearning, and when someone is overcome by yearning, he desires to see the Friend. When someone desires only to see the Friend, he is always hoping to reach the Friend, and death is the only way to reach Him. So why do you dislike death, when death causes arrival at the Friend?

It is said that for some, death is a comfort, and for others it is a blight. Some find it to be a comfort because "When someone loves meeting God, God loves meeting him." Others find it to be a blight because "When someone dislikes meeting God, God dislikes meeting him."*

It was said to a renunciant, "Do you love death?"

He paused. The questioner said, "If you were truthful in your renunciation, you would not dislike death."

The third mark of truthfulness in love is that the remembrance of the Beloved is always so fresh in the lover's heart and on his tongue that heedlessness and forgetfulness have no access to him. The Prophet said, "When someone loves something, he keeps on remembering it."

The fourth mark of loyalty in friendship is that he loves everything related to the Beloved, such as the Qur'an, which is His speech; the Kaabah, which is His house; Muṣṭafā, who is His Messenger; and the faithful, who are His friends. Muṣṭafā said, "Love God because of the blessings with which He nourishes you, love me because of God's love for me, and love the folk of my house because of love for me."

(*Kashf* 2:86)

Samʿānī describes the characteristics of lovers in a passage that begins by looking at the repercussions of God's beginningless love in the created realm. In the fourth paragraph, when he mentions "the beginningless dot," he has in mind the dot under the Arabic letter *bāʾ* in the word *ḥubb* (written *ḥb* in its unvoweled form). Aḥmad Ghazālī uses similar imagery in this passage: "Love's root grows in Eternity. The dot under the *bāʾ* in *He loves them* became a seed scattered in the ground of *they love Him*. Or rather, the dot was scattered in *them*, and *they love Him* grew up" (*Sawāniḥ* 44).

O dervish! The brand on you was put in the fire before your existence, and your robe was prepared before you came into being. "God created the spirits four thousand years before the bodies." He gave the spirits stations and way stations in which they were adorned with the jewels of generosity before creation, and then He put them into these bodies. He set down the spirit in the neighborhood of this unmanly soul so that the soul's stink would be remedied by the spirit's purity and fragrance. Beautifully done! In Your munificence, You prepared secret cores and sewed the robes of pious hearts before their existence!

O dervish! Were it not for the assistance of the Exalted Presence, no person of faith could safeguard his faith for one instant. He filled the world with assistance, He threw robes on His elect, and He placed robes on the others. The goal was the same. After all, when a sultan, out of friendship, commands someone to come somewhere for a feast, the goal is not the place, it is the friend. "My goal in your lane is your face."

I made the covenant of love not for dust
but for that wherein My beloved dwells.

Know that in reality no fragrant herb subtler than the herb of love grew in the meadow of lordhood and servanthood. It is love that conveys a man to the Beloved—everything else is a highway robber on the Tariqah. All the tawḥīd-voicers' attributes fall apart in tawḥīd, and all the lovers' attributes come to naught in love. Tawḥīd remains without description, and love remains without attribute.

All the lovers stood up and stepped forth in love. The beginningless dot in *He loves them* [5:54] came forth and welcomed them all. All of them fled because of their incapacity to show gratitude for that one dot. No one dared take a breath. They knew that even if the seven heavens and the seven earths were to become their instructors, they would not be able to ask for the subtle gifts that He gave them without their asking.

When the lovers gazed on their own incapacity and His exaltedness, He, in His gentleness, placed the gift of vision on top of that. If love's final end is not vision of the Beloved, then to speak of love is a metaphor.

Here, however, there is a rule: friendship for Him does not come together with scattered desires in the same heart. The obligation of the body is prayer and fasting, and that of the heart is friendship.

In friendship, the person of faith has no escape from three states: fear, hope, and love. Fear comes from gazing at wrath, hope from gazing at generosity, and love from gazing at the divinity. Whoever finds purity finds it through His glorifiedness, and whoever finds love finds it from His divinity. Whoever sees, recognizes; whoever recognizes, clings; and whoever clings, burns. Those who are burnt can no longer burn. Those who recognize

> Him recognize Him through Him, and those who love Him love Him through Him.
>
> (*Rawḥ* 461–62)

One of the more obvious marks of love is burning and fire. As Samʿānī says, "Love in its essence is fire, and every fire has a flame. The flame of love's fire is yearning. And what is yearning? The thirst of hearts to encounter the beloved" (*Rawḥ* 358). Maybudī describes some of the characteristics of love's fire in his commentary on the verse "*Surely your Lord is God, who created the heavens and the earth*" (7:54). He bases his discussion on the clear distinction between the meanings of the names Lord (rabb) and God (allāh). *Lord* designates God as the caretaker of servants (ʿabd), and *God* designates Him as the reality that embraces all names and attributes and simultaneously stands beyond all. Servants look to the Lord for help and guidance, and lovers look to God for absolutely everything. In the process, they forget themselves and pass beyond all thought of gain and loss.

> First He said *Lord* as the share of the common people, then He said *God* as the share of the recognizers and the sincerely truthful. *Lord* puts the hearts of good men at ease, *God* plunders the spirits of the recognizers. *Lord* bestows blessings on the askers, *God* throws love into the lovers' hearts. *Lord* pours the blessings of vision on the faithful, *God* lights up the lamp of love and vision in the recognizers.
>
> The Pir of the Tariqah said, "Love and vision met. Love said to vision, 'You are like light, for you brighten the world.'
>
> "Vision said to love, 'You are like fire, for you burn the world.' Then vision said, 'When I disclose myself, I pull suffering from the heart.'
>
> "Love said, 'Well, when I settle down in the heart, I plunder it.'
>
> "Vision said, 'I am a gift for those who are tested.'
>
> "Love said, 'I throw tumult into the world.'"
>
> Vision is the share of those who recognize Him in the artisanries. They reach Him on the basis of the artisanries—the engendered, determined, and newly arrived things, namely, the creation of the earth, the heavens, the sun, the moon, and the subjected stars. Love is the share of those who recognize Him through Him and who come from Him to the artisanries, not from the artisanries to Him.
>
> The Pir of the Tariqah said, "Miserable is he who recognizes Him through the artisanries! Wretched is he who loves Him for the sake of blessings! Foolish is he who searches for Him with his own effort!

> "He who recognizes Him through the artisanries worships Him in fear and want. He who loves Him for the sake of blessings turns away on the day of tribulation. He who seeks Him by himself fancies that the not-found will be found.
>
> "The recognizers recognize Him through His light, but no one can give expression to the radiance of finding. Burning in the fire of love, they never turn away from joy."
>
> (*Kashf* 3:638–39)

While commenting on the verses "*What will apprise you what the Crusher is? The lit-up fire of God!*" (104:5–6), Maybudī explains that love's fire burns away everything other than God.

> In the tongue of the folk of allusion and in keeping with the tasting of the folk of understanding, *the lit-up fire of God* is what the Pir of the Tariqah said: "It is a fire set by the limpidness of love that spoils the delights of life and strips away solace. Nothing can hold it back except the encounter."
>
> This is the state of that chevalier of the Tariqah, Ḥallāj, who said, "They struck *the lit-up fire of God* in my inwardness seventy years before it burned." Then the kindling of the present moment of "I am the Real" sent out sparks. The sparks fell on that burnt one and took flame, so nothing was left of him but sparks.
>
> (*Kashf* 10:612–13)

Samʿānī explains that the fire of love gradually burns away self-centeredness and prepares the lover for total annihilation. At first, the seeker's soul is like new cloth that will not burst into flame no matter how much you work on it with flint and steel. The soul is full of itself, its own shares and desires, its own virtues and vices. To catch fire, it must be singed and ready.

> Love is the talk of the burnt, not that of the self-made. Fire wants something already burnt in order to catch. That Orb of light, that Illuminator of the dark night, that Master of hospitality toward His speaking companion Moses, that Narcissus of the bosom friend Abraham—He wants the burnt!
>
> If you put a thousand precious silks before stone and iron, the fire will not catch, for they have the frivolity of color. If you bring new cloth, that will be of no use, for it has the smell of existence.
>
> Fire comes out from the curtain of concealment into the open and throws out sparks. When it does not see any confidant, it pulls back its head until it finds something already burnt. Then it catches and brightens the world.
>
> In the same way, the fire of love will never catch in any self-seeing man of wealth or any refractory sultan. Rather, it will catch in a person so burnt that

if you test him by poking your finger on a spot of his heart, it will fall to pieces.

So for the fire to get going, you need the burnt. If you try with Byzantine or Baghdadi silk, that won't do. If you use new cloth, the fire will hardly catch. You need a worn-out patch, halfway between existence and nonexistence—distraught and bewildered between effacement and affirmation.

First the patch is thrown to the edge of nonexistence, but the structure of its parts is kept together. Once it has been chastised by the passing of time and trampled underfoot by the days, you bring it and wash it clean. Then you strike fire in it so that its parts may be put to work and burn. Then you place a heavy burden on it and keep it in a solid cupboard. With the tongue of its state, the fire will say, "I have burned it, and a day will come when I will brighten it."

"O luminous fire, this burnt cloth is black and dark. What do you want with it?"

It said, "Yes, so it is, but it has my brand."

Today, the fire of *He loves them, and they love Him* has been struck in your heart and you have been burned by love. Just as they put a heavy burden on that burnt cloth, so also they will put the heavy burden of death on your parts and members. Then they will keep you in the cupboard of the grave, contemplating the gentleness of the One. After that, tomorrow, when the light of the King's gaze appears in the world, it will catch in you and give you a beauty such that next to you the full moon will be worthless. No longer will the moon have any standing, nor will the sun have any light. Where is this expressed? *Faces on that day radiant, gazing on their Lord* [75:22–23]. *And when you see, you will see bliss and a great kingdom* [76:20].

(*Rawḥ* 301–2)

In *Brides of Explication*, Rūzbihān Baqlī summarizes much of the discussion of love over the centuries while explaining the verse "*Say: 'If you love God, follow me; God will love you'*" (3:31).

For the recognizers and the lovers, the reality of love is the incineration of the heart in the fires of yearning, the repose of the spirit in the pleasure of passion, the drowning of the senses in the ocean of intimacy, the purification of the soul with the waters of holiness, the vision of the Beloved with the all-seeing eye, shutting the all-seeing eye toward the two worlds, flying with the secret core in the Unseen, and becoming characterized by the character traits of the Beloved. This is the root of love.

As for the branch of love, it is conformity with the Beloved in everything of which He approves, acceptance of His trial with the attribute of contentment, surrender to His decree and measuring out with the stipulation of loyalty, and following the Sunnah of Muṣṭafā.

As for the courtesies of the folk of love, these are severance from appetites and pleasures, hurrying to good deeds, stillness in seclusion and self-watchfulness, sniffing out the inblowings of the attributes, humility in whispered prayer, and entering into supererogatory works and worshipful acts. The goal is to become qualified by the Real's attributes and to be led by His light among the creatures. God says, "The servant never ceases drawing near to Me with supererogatory works until I am his hearing, eyesight, tongue, and hand."

There will be no unmixed love until the rational spirit, with the eye of the secret core, sees and contemplates the Real in the attribute of Beauty and the loveliness of Eternity, not with the attribute of bounties and blessings. For when love is born from seeing blessings, that is love with a cause. But the reality of love has no causes from the lover's side inasmuch as he is something other than the Beloved.

(*ʿArāʾis al-bayān*, 1:141)

CHOSEN BY LOVE

It is fairly obvious that love may come without any known reason. When it does, it cannot be repelled. Maybudī quotes a hemistich: "Love is what comes, not what is learned" (*Kashf* 10:400). More than once he cites a whispered prayer of Anṣārī to the same effect, as in the following passage, in which he is commenting on the verse "*And surely in the cattle there is a lesson for you: we give you to drink of what is in their bellies, between feces and blood, pure milk, sweet to the drinkers*" (16:66).

Two impurities came together, one feces and the other blood. God with His power made pure milk appear between the two. In the same way, two drops came together in the womb. God's determination and form giving made a form of such beauty appear from the two! *He formed you, so He made your forms beautiful* [40:64].

He brings together two difficult tasks for the servant, one the burden of disobedience, the other shortcoming in obedience. Then God's bounty makes mercy and forgiveness appear between the two: *He will set right your deeds for you and He will forgive you your sins* [33:71].

In what preceded all precedents and began all beginnings, the Pen wrote in the Tablet that the candle of the Shariah and the lamp of faith and certainty would light up in someone's breast. It does not matter whether he falls asleep. When he wakes up, he will see the lit candle next to his pillow.

The Pir of the Tariqah said, "O God, do You know what has made me happy? I did not fall to You by myself. You wanted—it was not I who wanted. I saw the Friend at my pillow when I woke up from sleep."

By way of allusion, God is saying, "I took milk, which is your nourishment and your share, and passed it over feces and blood, preserving it from both. As for tawḥīd, it is My rightful due, so it is much more deserving of being preserved by Me. It will pass over this world and the afterworld and not receive any trace. Were the trace of this world or the afterworld to sit on tawḥīd, it would not be worthy of Me. Tawḥīd is pure of this world and the afterworld. The light of tawḥīd is the destruction of water and dust. Turning the eye of the heart away from self is to perceive the finding of tawḥīd."

(*Kashf* 5:407–8)

To say that love has no cause (*ʿilla*) is to say that it has no cause outside God Himself, who "loved to be recognized, so He created the creatures." All the factors that seem to stir up love in people's hearts are in fact secondary causes (*sabab*) of love, not the primary cause. As long as we look for causality in this world, in the realm of efficient causality familiar to people nowadays, there can be no explanations, only correlations. Aḥmad Ghazālī writes:

Chapter [57]. When there is true love, it is the foundation of holiness, nothing but purity and cleanliness. It is far from accidents and causes, pure of portions. This is because its beginning is *He loves them.* With Him, of course, there is no possibility of cause or portion. Anything with the mark of cause or portion is outside the work, accidental, uninvited, and borrowed.

(*Sawāniḥ* 44)

Samʿānī often refers to the fact that people love God without any cause. In the first passage below, he does so by differentiating between what seekers on the path to God can do and what they cannot do. They can repent, pray, fast, and so on, because all these are activities, whether of the soul or the body. These things have causes related to the seekers, who can use their freedom of choice to put the causes into effect. But they cannot choose to love. Love comes on its own. In other words, people can try to obey the religious command, but they have nothing to say about the creative command. It is the creative command that throws love into the heart, and no one can help the lover by giving him good advice, for his free choice is not involved. Hence the Arabic saying that Samʿānī sometimes quotes, "There is no consultation in love."

Sometimes the ocean of trial begins to send up waves, and the lover no longer has the capacity to bear it. He believes that he can repent of love in order to be delivered from the trial of his caprice. But this belief is wrong. In the shariah of love, repentance is folly, for it is to seek a reprieve and to wish for a concession. "Sufism is constraint without peace and severity without mercy."

O you who speak to me with good advice,
 you tell me I should turn away from love.
On the Day of Mustering, God will not
 gather my bones without my love for Him.

O dervish! Repentance is something that you acquire, but love is neither acquired nor connected with any cause. It sometimes happens that the Beloved's beauty unveils to the lover the ruling properties of jealousy and guards the eyes against glancing and gazing, or rather, against thoughts and notions. Majesty demands that he abandon his own portions and desire. He must choose the Friend's desire over his own—in separation and severity, withholding and rejection, restraint and repulsion.

The burnt lover, willingly or unwillingly, repents of seeking for what he wants and looking at causes. Then He assigns the fancy of yearning and the ardor of burning to his heart and liver. The lover is unable to bear it. He cannot go forth with patience and self-restraint. What a wonder is the lover in this state! What harshness he suffers, with no mercy or favor! If he preserves his repentance, it is said, "Good for you, O weary man!" And if he breaks it, it is said, "Bravo, O covenant breaker!"

(*Rawḥ* 365)

Passion is not a matter of choice. What a lovely day when someone is walking on a road and all at once his feet fall on a treasure! The one entrusted with this talk comes down, throws the lasso of seeking around his neck, and pulls, whether to the gallows or the throne.

(400)

But who is "the one entrusted with this talk"? The word entrusted (*muwakkal*) is typically used to describe the angels, each of which has been given a specific task by God. Perhaps Samʿānī has in mind an angelic function, but in any case he means that love descends from on high, from the realm of the Unseen, and it has no true cause other than God. The creative force of *He loves them* instills in human beings the mystery of *they love Him*. This point has already been discussed with a stress on the divine side of things, but a few more selections from Samʿānī can help bring out how human love is implicit in divine love.

God held the beauty of His love before the hearts of the great ones, and the luminous traces of the beauty of unqualified love appeared in the mirror of their hearts. So our love abides through His love, not His love through our love.

The mirror image subsists through the beauty of the form, not through the subsistence of the mirror. If you take the form away, the image will go. If the sultan of *He loves them* should put on the shirt of exaltation and unneediness, nothing but wind would remain in the powerless hands of *they love Him*.

(*Rawḥ* 520)

Repentance substitutes for obedience just as dust substitutes for water [in ablutions]. The obedient person has obedience, but the disobedient person has repentance. The compensation for obedience is the Garden, and the compensation for repentance is love: "*Surely God loves the repenters*" [2:222].

"Love is My attribute. When there is talk of attributes, how can there be talk of the eight paradises—or rather, of a thousand thousand paradises? If I do not forgive you, who will forgive you? *Who forgives sins but God?* [3:135]. If the prince of Khurasan does not accept you, the prince of Iraq will accept you. But if I do not accept you, who will accept you?

"Abraham, who was the father of the creed and wore the robe of bosom friendship, I called a servant, and Isaac and Jacob, with all their struggle and contemplation, I called servants: *And remember Our servants Abraham and Isaac and Jacob* [38:45]. Job, with all his patience, I called a servant: *And remember Our servant Job* [38:41]. Solomon, with all his gratitude, I called a servant: *What a fine servant!* [38:30]. And you, with all your disloyalty and fault, I called a servant: *Tell My servants, 'Surely I am the Forgiving, the Ever-Merciful and that My chastisement is the painful chastisement'* [15:49]."

Say: "O My servants who have been immoderate against yourselves, despair not of God's mercy—surely God forgives all sins" [39:53]. This is nothing but the divine solicitude and the kingly kind favor. Surely God wrote a writing, and it is with Him on the Throne: "My mercy takes precedence over My wrath."

Already Our word has preceded [37:171]. *As for those to whom the most beautiful preceded from Us* [21:101]. All at once the precedence of mercy charges out from the concealment of the Unseen and unsettles a man. Love moves in his heart. Love becomes thought, thought becomes aspiration, aspiration becomes intention, intention becomes resolve, resolve becomes strength, strength becomes movement, and assistance comes with continuity. Then, in seriousness and effort, the man says, "God is greater."

In the middle of the night or at dawn, if disquiet appears for the truthful lover and sleep flees from his eyes, he will put aside his warm clothing, his sweet sleeping place, and his beautiful spouse. He will get up, make an ablution, and come in pleading to the Exalted Presence. Then the call will come from the Presence, "My servant, if indeed you have said farewell to sleep and ease, here then is My beauty and majesty. 'How beautiful in My eyes are those who make themselves beautiful for My sake!'"

When will an attraction of the Real be taken from the quiver of the Will and shot at the target of your heart's core? When you become the prey, you will turn away from this person and that.

"With one pull, We make an idol worshiper the possessor of a breast and We make a highway robber like Fuḍayl a traveler on the road. We do not need your deeds, but you need Our help. For the sake of your heart, We bring deeds into the midst for which We have no need. Will you remove from the midst the help that you need?

"There is an exalted secret in your deeds. The least thing is your acquisition, and the greatest thing is My decree. By virtue of love, We bring the least thing, which is your acquisition, into the midst. Do you approve of removing from the midst the most exalted thing, which is My success-giving?"

O dervish! When Muṣṭafā said, "There is no ritual prayer without the Fātiḥa of the Book," it is as if he said, "There is no prayer without God's help."

Do you suppose that obeying commands is idleness? Do you suppose that going to His threshold is a small job? You cannot go before a sultan who owns the name of sultanate metaphorically without permission. Can you come into the Exalted Presence, the threshold of that King who always was and always will be, without the edict of permission, the proclamation of leave, and the sigil of acceptance?

(511–12)

Samʿānī talks again about the divine origin of love in explaining the story of Jacob, whose love for Joseph became so intense that his eyes went blind because of weeping. He was cured when Joseph sent his shirt from Egypt.

You are surprised that when the scent of Joseph came from his shirt, Jacob said, "*Surely I smell Joseph's fragrance*" [12:94]. We smell the scent of the Josephs of the community from the corners of the churches and idol temples. When someone is descended from mortal loins, his covenant will hold that there is one Joseph. But when someone is descended from the loins of the Tariqah, then from Abyssinia there arises for him the Joseph of loveliness, from Persia the Joseph of beauty, from Byzantium the Joseph of good.

O dervish! From the lane of the Friend comes the fragrance of the Friend. After the fragrance comes the turn of the Friend's face. Jacob first smelled the fragrance, then reached contemplation.

It was said to someone, "Which is the best fragrance?"

He said, "The fragrance of the person you love or the child you have raised."

This is a rare business! The shirt was in the hands of Joseph's brothers, but they had no awareness of this work's secret. The attractions of passion had fallen into Jacob's heart and spirit, so he sent out his yearning in welcome, and Joseph sent his fragrance to the possessor of awareness. At a distance of eighty parasangs, the fragrance reached the yearning. The yearning became all fragrance, and the fragrance all yearning. Jacob's cry was heard from the House of Sorrows, "*Surely I smell Joseph's fragrance!*" What a masterful puff of air!

O dervish! First the station of Mount Sinai began to seek Moses, then Moses began to seek—otherwise, Moses was carefree. First the station of *two bows' length* began to yearn for Muḥammad's feet, then Burāq was sent to Muḥammad—otherwise, that paragon's work was all set. Joseph's beauty came seeking for Jacob's passion, then Jacob bound the belt of passion—otherwise, he would have been unaware of this story. First the request of the Beginningless set out to seek us, then we began to seek—otherwise, we knew nothing of passion's secret.

The Sought must begin to seek in order for the seeker to have seeking. Jacob continued trying to find Joseph with his own seeking, but until Joseph began to seek, Jacob gained nothing by sending his sons. . . .

O dear ones! Our seeking is our seeking, and His seeking His seeking. Jacob did not reach Joseph until Joseph sought. How will we reach the Pavilions of Majesty without the escort of His seeking? In truth, in truth, the seeking of the seekers is deception itself! The aimers' aiming and the worshipers' wayfaring and worship are simply form. If the peaked cap of seeking's policeman does not appear from the special chamber of generosity,

> You are nothing, nothing, and your empty words nothing—
> you won't take home morsels with the wind of caprice.

What a marvelous business! Jacob, who was God's Israel, pure and purified, a prophet and born of a prophet, was given over to the hand of passion's tumult: *Surely you are in your same old error* [12:95], that is, your same old passion.

He was remembering Joseph so much that one day when the shawl fell off his tunic, he asked for the tailor. He wanted to say, "Attach a shawl here," but what came from his tongue was "Attach a Joseph here."

"Passion is the illness of the generous."

"Passion is a divine madness."

"Passion is the Real's net through which He catches the hearts of the pure. At first it is madness and at last death, at first patience and at last the grave."

> Awfully strange is the road of the passionate—
> it begins and ends in pain.

How will a meddler see this road's mark?
  How will a fancier find way to the Marvelous?
Love without trial is most absurd—
  fresh dates never come without thorns.
How long will you turn lazily in all directions?
  The time has come to start seeking!
Hunger must become hard cash
  for flight to give birth to the secret of joy.

(*Rawḥ* 306–9)

ALLUSIONS TO LOVE

In the introduction to the *Book of Love,* Anṣārī tells the tale of the Hidden Treasure, the beginning of love, the creation of the universe, and the differentiation of the creatures. He also explains why love can never be expressed in words.

Know that every expression and allusion is a dispersion and a tale, but all togetherness is beyond speech and hearing. Love is the share of unification, and dispersion the share of bodies.

In those days, there was neither father nor mother; in those times, the children were missing. In what preceded all precedents, before the togetherness and difference that were hidden and not yet apparent, there was neither before nor after, neither wretchedness nor felicity.

There were no way stations or stations in love, no travelers on the road, no disparity in footsteps, none of the darkness of blight and distance, none of the clouds of presence and absence, no ascending traces or descending imagination. The bazaar of union was stagnant, and the edict of separation void, for there was no trace of the images of creation. The beauty of *He loves them* had no use for the mole of *they love Him.*

Her own face had itself as a moon,
  her own eye had itself as collyrium.

If I don't apply My light's collyrium to your eyes,
  how will you perceive My magnificent Presence?

He wanted to make apparent the hidden pearls of love's oyster and to pick out some of the gems. Thus it was that He made everyone's hard cash apparent and separated the elect from the commoners. The divine desire and glorious solicitude decreed that the sun of *He loves them* would shine and that the rose of *they love Him* would bloom. All beings would then seek refuge in the sun's brightness, and each would find the road to its own destination.

From the sphere of love, the sun of unification shone on the world of the realities and meanings. In conjunction with the sun, they saw the seeable. The folk of the attributes gazed at the sun with the eye of imagination. The sun's felicity had raised the banner of brightness and left nothing concealed. This was at the time when He said, "*And We made covenant with Adam before*" [20:115]. It was not yet the moment for the masters of allusion, nor yet the days for the lords of expression.

When the spirit became spirits and the individual individuals, some were commoners and some elect. The folk of the realities and meanings, who had the edict of friendship from that sun's effusion, were placed under the sun's guardianship. They took up residence in the field of face-to-face vision, far from union and separation.

The folk of attributes and forms, who saw that their eyes had insight because of that Presence, cut themselves off from seeing because of defective eyes. In the measure of their own eyesight, they cut away what surrounded them. Some drowned in the ocean, some burned in the fire, some yearned for the cup, some leaned on pleasure. So it is that everyone tells tales and narrates traditions.

(*Maḥabbat* 337–39)

Up to this point, I have been neglecting Aḥmad Ghazālī's *Apparitions*, considered by many the earliest and greatest classic on love in the Persian language. Part of the book's fame lies in its apparently simple but in fact elusive prose. Aḥmad knew full well that his text was hard to follow, not least because, so it seems, he was trying to express the inexpressible with the clearest possible expression. This leads to the reader's perplexity and bewilderment, qualities that are not unexpected in affairs of the heart. At the same time, Aḥmad maintains that lovers will understand his message, even if scholars and theoreticians will find a closed book. He gave his book the subtitle *Fi'l-ʿishq*, "On Passion." Although the text usually uses the term *ʿishq*, it also uses *maḥabba* and makes no attempt to distinguish between the two words.

In the first paragraph of the introduction, Aḥmad explains that love cannot be expressed directly and that only those who have tasted it will understand. The word tasting (*dhawq*) is commonly used to designate the perception of truths and realities that cannot be conveyed to others, just as you cannot explain the taste of a pomegranate. Once two of you have eaten the fruit, however, it can be discussed. Note that Aḥmad uses the word *meaning* (*maʿnā*) in both the ordinary sense—what is signified by a word—and in the technical Sufi sense, according to which it designates the unseen reality of which a form (ṣūra) is the visible appearance. The meanings are thus the multiple realities (*ḥaqāʾiq*) that pertain to the realm of the Haqiqah, the Reality in Itself.

> These words contain a few chapters connected with the meanings of love, even though talk of love does not enter into words or fit into sentences, for its meanings are virgin. The hand of words' compass does not reach the skirts of their private parts. Even though my work is to give the virgin meanings over to the penises of words in the seclusion of speech, expressing this talk is to allude to diverse meanings. Hence it is indistinct—only, however, for the person who has not tasted it.
>
> (*Sawāniḥ* 1)

In the first chapter, Aḥmad describes the origin of love, saying that it emerges in the universe along with the spirit blown into Adam's clay. By remarking that love is incomparable with directions, he is pointing to its identity with the Divine Reality, God in Himself, the Essence. God's love has no specific kiblah toward which it turns, because it is none other than the universal mercy of the All-Merciful, which gives rise to all that exists. In the same way, the Real Being is not one thing rather than another thing, but the germ of all things, so it gives rise to whatever may possibly come to be. Each thing has a specific thingness that makes it distinct from every other thing, but Being-Love-Mercy transcends thingness and bestows existence on all without discrimination.

Like Love in Itself, human love has no specific object, despite the fact that we think we love her or him, this or that. We cannot avoid loving, because *they love Him* follows necessarily upon *He loves them.* What we normally fail to perceive is that our love is directed precisely at *Him.* Muslim theologians agree that this pronoun *He* (*huwa*) points to the Essence, that is, God in Himself, since God as *He* stands beyond the specification of any individual name. *He* is neither this nor that, and *He is with you wherever you are* (57:4), no matter what or where you may be. *He is the First and the Last, the Outward and the Inward, and He is knower of everything* (57:3).

The creative command has brought us into existence loving *Him* alone. Our love becomes differentiated into love for this person and that because of our "(present) moment" (*waqt*). This technical term designates the manifestation of the Eternal within the seeker's awareness right now. We live neither in the past, which is gone, nor in the future, which has not yet come, but in the present moment, with *Him.* Since the heart is "between two fingers of the All-Merciful," our present moment undergoes constant fluctuation. Love is never absent from the heart, but the present moment turns the heart this way and that, so the object of the heart's attention, its kiblah, changes. The goal of the Tariqah is to achieve one-pointed concentration on the true Beloved in the present moment, the eternal now, in imitation of the Prophet, about whom the Qur'an says, "*The eyesight did not swerve, nor did it trespass*" (53:17).

Chapter [1]. God says, "*He loves them, and they love Him.*"

My steed set out from nonexistence with love,
  my night always bright with union's wine.
Of that wine not forbidden by my religion
  my lips will not stay dry till I am back in nonexistence.

Love came from nonbeing to existence for my sake—
  it was I whom love sought in the world.
I will not be cut off from You so long as fragrance comes from incense,
  night and day, year and month—despite the envious.

Her love came to me before I knew love—
  it came across a carefree heart and took possession.

When the spirit came from nonexistence into existence, love was waiting at the border of existence to take the spirit as its mount. I do not know what sort of mixture took place at the beginning of existence. If the spirit was the essence, then the essence's attribute was love. Love found the house empty and took over.

The disparity in love's kiblah is something accidental, for its reality is incomparable with directions. To be itself, love has no need to turn its face in any direction. But I do not know to which earth the acquiring hand of the present moment will take the water. When the groom sits on the sultan's steed, the steed does not belong to him. "Our words are allusions."

Sometimes they give potsherds or beads to an apprentice until he becomes a master. Sometimes they give the preparation of precious gems and sparkling pearls to his unskillful hands even though the skilled hand of the master does not have the nerve to touch them, much less pierce them.

When the chameleon of the present moment strikes its deceiving marvels on the pages of the breaths, it leaves no tracks, for it walks on water; or rather, on air, for breaths are nothing but air.

(*Sawāniḥ* 3–4)

In this passage, Aḥmad alludes to a point of doctrine that would have been obvious to his readers but gets obscured in translation, and that is the distinction between essence (dhāt) and attribute (*ṣifa*), standard in Islamic thought. A thing's essence is the thing in itself, and its attributes are its qualities and descriptions. Here Aḥmad says, "If the spirit was the essence, then the essence's attribute was love." The spirit would be the essence because it came into existence by means of the divine inblowing: "*I blew into him of My spirit*" (15:29). The Qur'an mentions *My spirit* only in this context, so this spirit was called the ascribed spirit, that is, the spirit ascribed to God by the pronoun. If the spirit is considered man's essence, the spirit's attribute will be the love for the sake of which it was created.

Aḥmad much prefers poetical imagery to philosophical elaboration. When he wrote, "If the spirit was the essence," the conditional *if* makes clear that the relationship between love and the human spirit can be discussed in many ways. Any number of formulations can throw light on its nature, at least for those who have tasted something of its reality. In the following, by *effacement* (*maḥw*) he means the annihilation achieved by the lovers who dwell with the Haqiqah, that is, within the reality of *He loves them;* in that station, they affirm His love, not their own. Those who have not reached this stage partake of *they love Him*, so they affirm their own love.

> Chapter [3]. Sometimes the spirit is like love's earth, from which the tree of love may grow. Sometimes it is like the essence through which love's attributes may abide. Sometimes it is like a partner in a house, the two taking turns residing there.
>
> Sometimes love is the essence, and the spirit the attribute, so the spirit abides through it. But not everyone understands this, for this pertains to the world of the second affirmation, after effacement. It appears crooked to the folk of affirmation before effacement.
>
> When You formed my water and clay
> my spirit was accident, Your love substance.
> When destiny and decree wet the Pen
> my love sat next to Your beauty.
>
> Sometimes love is heaven, and the spirit earth: what rain will fall in the present moment? Sometimes love is the seed, and the spirit the earth: what plant will grow? Sometimes love is a jewel, and the spirit the mine: what jewel will come forth and what sort of mine will it be? Sometimes it is the sun in the spirit's heaven: how will it shine? Sometimes it is a flame in the spirit's air: what exactly will burn? Sometimes it is the saddle on the spirit's horse: who will mount up? Sometimes it is the bridle on the head of the spirit's recalcitrance: in which direction will it be taken?
>
> Sometimes the spirit is bound by the chains of severity in the Beloved's glance. Sometimes unmixed poison is placed in the mouth of the present moment's severity: whom will it bite and whom destroy? Someone said,
>
> I said, "Don't hide your face from me—
> let me take a share of your beauty."

She said, "Fear for your heart and liver,
for love's tribulation will draw its blade."

All these are the present moment's display in the shine of knowledge, the edge of which is the shore of the ocean. Knowledge has no way into the depths of this work, for love's majesty is far from its descriptions, explications, and perceptions. Someone said,

Love is concealed—no one has ever seen it face-to-face.
How long will these lovers make their foolish claims?
Everyone boasts of love with his own fancy.
Love is empty of fancy and of this and that.

The being of the dust motes is perceived in the air, yet it is clear that no one can find them. Both they and finding are in hock to the shining of the sun.

You are the sun, and we the dust motes—
without Your face how will we show our faces?
How long will You stay in mask and curtain? Just once
rise up from behind the mountain and let us rise.

If He does not give of Himself, it is not only because of greatness and transcendence, but also because of subtlety and excessive proximity.

The furthest limit of knowledge is the shore of love. If someone is at the shore, he will have a portion of this talk. If he steps forth, he will drown. How then will he report? How can someone drowned have knowledge?

Your beauty is greater than my seeing,
Your mystery outside my knowing.
My aloneness in loving You is a crowd,
my strength in describing You a weakness.

No, rather, knowledge is love's moth. Knowing is outside the work. Inside it, knowledge is the first to burn. How then can it report?

(*Sawāniḥ* 5–7)

In another passage, Aḥmad speaks of the beginning of love, its reality, and the fact that the distinction between lover and beloved is not at all clear. After all, the verse of mutual love affirms that God is both lover and beloved, and it also tells us that man is both lover and beloved. Given that there is no true love but the love that is God, the distinction between lover and beloved gets lost in love.

Chapter [21]. The beginning of love is that the hand of contemplation throws the seed of beauty into the earth of the heart's seclusion. Then He nurtures it with the shining of the gaze, though this does not have one color.

It may happen that throwing the seed and taking the fruit are one. Hence someone said,

At root every love starts with looking—
when the eye sees, the work begins.
How many birds have fallen into wanting's trap!
The moth wanted light and fell into fire.

The reality of love is the conjunction of two hearts. But the lover's love for the beloved is one thing, and the beloved's love for the lover something else. The lover's love is the reality, and the beloved's love is the reflection of the lover's love shining in his mirror.

Since there is conjunction in contemplation, the lover's love inevitably requires abasement, toleration, lowliness, and surrender in all things, and the beloved's love tyranny, pride, and inaccessibility.

In the place of our Heart-taker's beauty and loveliness,
we are not suited for Him—He is suited for us.

But I do not know which is lover and which beloved. This is a great mystery, for it may be that at first it was His pull, and then this result. Here the realities are reversed. *You will not will unless God wills* [76:30]. Inescapably, *He loves them* comes before *they love Him*.

Abū Yazīd said, "For a long time I fancied that I wanted Him. In fact, He first wanted me."

(*Sawāniḥ* 21–22)

Aḥmad reminds his readers that God's love for man has no beginning or end, for the Beginningless and the Endless are the same in God's eternal reality. Only in the realm of new arrivals and present moments can we look back to the Beginningless and ahead to the Endless. Notice that he refers to the circle of existence, the *two bows* that designate the descending arc from God and the ascending arc back to Him. The unity of the two, which is the oneness of the Beginningless and the Endless, can be perceived only at the present moment.

Chapter [8]. Is it not enough for the Adamite that his specific characteristic is to be a beloved before being a lover? Is this a small distinction? *He loves them* offered so much hospitality to the beggar before he ever showed up that he will drink it down forever without end, with some still left over.

O chevalier! When the Beginningless offers hospitality, how can it be fully received except in the Endless? Or rather, once the Eternal puts out hospitality in the Beginningless, how can the newly arrived receive it fully even in the Endless? *No soul knows what delight of the eyes is hidden away for it* [32:17].

O chevalier! The Beginningless has reached here, but the Endless cannot reach a furthest limit. The hospitality will never be received in full.

If you ever come to see with the secret core of your own present moment, you will know that the *two bows' length*—that of the Beginningless and the Endless—is your heart and your moment.

(*Sawāniḥ* 12)

Given that love is the Divine Essence, it can never manifest itself fully, nor can the newly arrived lovers ever reach the Eternal. They will attain their everlasting happiness by taking up the Trust given to their father Adam and discarding the pretense of knowledge and learning. Scholars and thinkers have no entrance into this realm unless they also become lovers.

Chapter [9]. Love will never fully show its face to anyone. The secret here is that it is the bird of the Beginningless. Now that it has come here, it is traveling to the Endless. Here it does not show its face to the eyes of newly arrived things, for not every house is worthy of being its nest—its nest is the majesty of the Beginningless. Every once in a while, it flies back to the Beginningless and puts on the mask of its own curtain of majesty and inaccessibility. It has never shown the face of perfect beauty to the eyes of knowledge, and it never will.

Because of this secret, if the lover for one moment should see the centerpoint of His Trust, he will at once be released from the attachments and barriers of here-ness and freed from the fancy of knowledge, the measures of intuition, the philosophizing of imagination, and the spying of the senses.

(*Sawāniḥ* 12–13)

Many of the seventy-seven chapters of *Apparitions* include a few lines of poetry, perhaps the favorite vehicle of lovers in their attempts to express the inexpressible. In some chapters, Aḥmad provides hints about how poetic imagery and symbolism should be read. Notice that in the following, he mentions the World of Imagination (*ʿālam-i khayāl*). One hundred and fifty years later Rūmī would explain in some detail how the lover's consciousness comes to be infused with images descending from the imaginal world, which lies beyond the visible world but beneath the spiritual world.[1] As Henry Corbin and others have explained, the imaginal is by no means the imaginary. It designates a realm that is far more real than this world and all it contains. The travelers on the path of love enter into its mysteries as they go deeper and deeper into the heart.

> Chapter [37]. The reality of love will mount only on the steed of the spirit. The heart is the locus of its attributes, but love itself stays inaccessible in the veils of exaltedness. What does anyone know of its essence and attributes?
>
> One of its fine points may show its face to the eye of knowledge, but no more explanation or mark of it can be given to the tablet of the heart. When it does show its face in the World of Imagination, sometimes it has a specific mark, and sometimes it does not.
>
> Chapter [38]. Sometimes the mark is the tress, sometimes the cheek, sometimes the mole, sometimes the stature, sometimes the eyes, sometimes the eyebrow, sometimes the glance, sometimes the Beloved's laughter, sometimes rebuke.
>
> Each of these meanings has a mark coming from the place of the lover's seeking. When the mark of someone's love is the eyes of the Beloved, he feeds on the Beloved's gaze and is further from defects, for the eye is the precious pearl of heart and spirit. When love gives forth the mark of the Beloved's eyes in the World of Imagination, that is evidence that the seeking of the lover's spirit and heart is far from bodily defects.
>
> If it is the eyebrows, that is his spirit's seeking, but the vanguard of awe stands in front of the seeking, for the eyebrows belong to the eyes.
>
> In the same way, the path of love's perspicacity finds in each of these marks the explanation of a spiritual or corporeal seeking in the lover, or a defect, or a fault. This is because love has a mark in every one of the inner curtains, and these meanings are its marks on the curtain of imagination. Hence, its marks explain the level of love.
>
> (*Sawāniḥ* 31–32)

In his chapter on the two divine names Downletter (*khāfiḍ*) and Uplifter (*rāfiʿ*), Samʿānī explains why lovers couch their language in allusions, pointers, and symbols. They are jealous (ghayra) for the virgin brides, which are the secret meanings they have glimpsed in their quest to know God. They do not want the others (ghayr) to gaze on the brides. The others are the unworthy, those who still dwell in the realm of multiplicity, far from annihilation in love's unity.

> Ḥudhayfa ibn al-Yamān asked the Messenger of God about knowledge of inwardness. He said, "It is a knowledge between God and His friends of which no proximate angel or any of His creatures is aware."
>
> The great ones have said, "Our secrets are virgin, not grasped by any imaginer. So protect the secrets from the others!"

All who catch this meaning's scent are jealous—
you might say they have neither tongue nor speech.
If they talk, their jealousy for the meaning
keeps their words to the tracks and traces of the tents.

The lords of the orchards of realities and the seekers of the wine of severed attachments have perfect jealousy for the beauty of the exalted meanings, so they bind them in a thousand thousand curtains. Then perhaps they can conceal the virgin brides of the meanings inside a veil—namely, the breast of a dregs-drinking possessor of pain—without the intrusion of the others' accusations. "The breasts of the free are the graves of the secrets." "He who has no secret is insistent." "One of the characteristics of the free is keeping secrets from the others."

Sometimes they give out this talk as the locks and mole of Laylā, sometimes as the distractedness of Majnūn's state; sometimes as intoxication, sometimes sobriety; sometimes annihilation, sometimes subsistence; sometimes ecstasy, sometimes finding. These words, expressions, and letters are the containers for the fine wine of realizing the meanings. Those in the ranks of lovers are busy with the wine itself. The unworthy are in bondage to the cup.

The understanding of these Men in the secrets of the Sunnah and the Book has reached an inviolable sanctuary around which the imagination of the lords of outward meanings does not have the gall to circle. From each letter they have a station, from each word a message, from each verse a ruling power, from every chapter a burning. . . .

In their road, threats are promises, and promises hard cash. In their road, paradise and hell are way stations, and everything beneath the Real is unreal. "Is not everything less than God unreal?"

In the desert of their present moment, this world and the next are two miles, and love's road is their hearts and spirits. In their road, day and night are two steeds, and the trailing skirts of their states are pure of the stains of others. By day they dwell in the lodging place of secret whispering, by night in the litter of joy. By day they gaze on the artifacts, by night they contemplate the beauty of the Artisan. By day they dwell in good character with the people, by night with the Real in the *firm footing* [10:2]. By day they are busy with the work, by night with drunkenness. By day they seek the road, by night they speak of the mysteries.

Your face puts my night in forenoon sun—
darkness belongs only to the sky.
The people are in the darkness of their night,
I in the brightness of Your face.

They have burnt the soul in the crucible of breath, raised the torch of passion in the road of truthfulness, lifted the head of aspiration beyond the spheres, and dumped the caprice of the refractory soul into the pit. They have stirred up their makeup from the sleep of heedlessness and, with the ear of passion, heard the call "*Am I not your Lord?*" [7:172]. They have reached the standing of free men and have not attended to their own rights. They have gone down into the Zamzam of holy intimacy and cleansed themselves of the pollution of deep ignorance.

On the prayer carpet of the Covenant of the Presence, they sit in wait for the call to prayer of "*Whose is the kingdom today?*" [40:16]. They have traveled a long road on the stallion of need, cut the throat of appetite with the blade of sincere truthfulness, escaped from the trap of the two worlds, and gained release from the dragon of caprice.

"In earth they are ascribed to heaven, and in heaven to the Lord. Their bodies are earthly, but their hearts pertain to heaven, rather to the Throne, rather to Unity, rather to the Sanctum. They are *neither of the East nor of the West* [24:35]; rather of Majesty, rather of the Unseen Beauty."

They have pulled rags over the moons of the secrets. "Patched cloaks are the curtains of pearls." They have concealed the secret pearl of ruling the world in the shell of their cloaks.

(*Rawḥ* 171–72)

STAGES OF LOVE

The path of love is one of purification by stages. From early times, authors differentiated among various degrees of love, as we saw in Bukhārī's commentary on Kalābādhī's *Introduction to the School of Sufism*. When the secret of *He loves them* becomes manifest, human love gradually intensifies, and little by little *they love Him* can reach its goal. Maybudī reminds us that the stages of love, which, from the traveler's standpoint, are the way stations of seeking and finding, are in fact the stages of God's attraction and solicitude. The seeker's seeking proves that He is seeking the seeker, for no one can seek without His bestowal of the power to seek.

Is he whose breast God has expanded for the submission so that he is upon a light from his Lord? [39:22]. Know that the human heart has four curtains. The first curtain is the breast, the lodging place of the submission's covenant, in accordance with His words "*Is he whose breast God has expanded for the submission?*" The second curtain is the heart, which is the locus of the light of faith, in accordance with His words "*He wrote faith in their hearts*" [58:22]. The third curtain is the mindful heart, the pavilion of contemplating the Real, in accordance with His words "*His mindful heart did not lie about what he saw*" [53:11]. The fourth curtain is the smitten heart, the place of putting down the saddlebags of love, in accordance with His words "*He smote her heart with love*" [12:30].

Each of these four curtains has a characteristic, and the Real gazes upon each. When the Lord of the Worlds desires to pull someone who has fled from Him with the lasso of gentleness into the road of His religion, He first gazes upon his breast, so that it may become pure of caprice and innovation and so that his feet may go straight on the avenue of the Sunnah.

Then He turns His gaze to his heart so that it may become pure of this world's defilements and of blameworthy character traits, such as self-admiration, envy, pride, eye-service, greed, enmity, and frivolity. Then he may go forth on the road of scrupulosity [*wara*ʿ].

Then He gazes on his mindful heart and keeps him back from attachments and created things. He opens the fountainhead of knowledge and wisdom in his heart. He bestows the light of guidance on his heart's centerpoint, as He said, "*so that he is upon a light from his Lord.*"

Then He gazes on his smitten heart—a gaze, and what a gaze! A gaze that embellishes the spirit, brings the tree of joy to fruit, and awakens the eye of revelry; a gaze that is a tree whose shadow is companionship with the Friend, a gaze that is a wine whose cup is the recognizer's heart.

When this gaze reaches the smitten heart, it lifts it up from water and clay and the lover steps into the lane of annihilation. Three things cease to be in three things: seeking ceases to be in the Found, recognition ceases to be in the Recognized, and friendship ceases to be in the Friend.

The Pir of the Tariqah said, "The two worlds were lost in friendship, and friendship was lost in the Friend. Now I dare not say that I am, nor can I say that He is."

All of my eye it filled with the form of the Friend.
  Happy am I with the eye so long as the Friend is within it.
Separating the eye from the Friend is not good—
  either He's in the place of the eye, or the eye itself is He.

(*Kashf* 8:411–12)

In *Way Stations*, Anṣārī describes three degrees of love, the first pertaining to the beginners, the second to the travelers, and the third to those who have arrived.

The Chapter on Love [61]. God says, *"Should any of you turn back on your religion, God will bring a people whom He loves, and who love Him"* [5:54].

Love is the attachment of the solitary heart between aspiration and intimacy in both bestowal and withholding.

Love is the first valley of annihilation, the steep pathway that goes down to the way stations of effacement. It is the last way station in which the vanguard of the common people encounters the rearguard of the elect. Everything beneath it is individual desires for the sake of compensation.

Love is the mark of the Tribe, the title of the Tariqah, and the seat of the relationship [with God]. It has three degrees:

The first degree is a love that cuts off disquieting thoughts, makes service enjoyable, and offers solace in afflictions. This love grows up from examining favors, becomes fixed by following the Sunnah, and grows into responding with indigence.

The second degree is a love that incites preferring the Real to all else, elicits remembrance on the tongue, and attaches the heart to witnessing Him. This is a love that becomes manifest from examining the attributes, gazing upon the signs, and undergoing the discipline of the stations.

The third degree is a dazzling love that cuts off expression, makes allusions subtle, and does not reach description. This love is the pivot of this business, and all loves beneath it are called for by tongues, claimed by creatures, and made obligatory by rational faculties.

(*Manāzil* 71–72)

Anṣārī also divides love into three sorts in *The Book of Love*, but from a different standpoint. One sort depends on the causes and conditions with which all of us are familiar, a second pertains to the creative command, and the third pertains to the Divine Reality Itself, the Haqiqah. Notice that he says that the way stations are set down by the Shariah. He means the Qur'an and the Sunnah, not the law delineated by the jurists.

Yes, my dear, the province of love cannot be visited or expressed. The feet of procrastination and prescription have no access to this lane, nor are the folk of form aware of these words.

The way stations in this lane are tremendously disparate. Though set down by the Shariah, they are not found in the traditions. This wine is to be drunk, not heard. This station is to be reached, not asked about.

Love is three: a love pertaining to causes, a love pertaining to creation, and a love pertaining to the Haqiqah. The caused is caprice, the creational is decreed, and that of the Haqiqah is bestowed.

Love that rises up from causes descends into the soul and lays it low. Creational love aims for that side. The Haqiqah's love bestows being.

The love that arises from created nature enters the heart and makes it cease to be. The love that arises from the Haqiqah settles down in the spirit so as to make it cease to be and to give it being from itself.

The mark of love is that the lover is drowned in the beauty of the Beloved.

You must not sit before the Friend by virtue of your own being. No one sees the Friend except through the Friend.

> I turned away from all that was mine
> to recognize all that was the Friend's.
> I melted in the fire of passion for Him,
> I burned more than I was able to bear.

This love comes from the Unqualified Presence. It is the text of *they love Him,* by which the creatures are captivated.

> It was I who said *He loves them* without your being,
> I too strung the pearl of your *they love Him.*
> Apart from Me no one else was there—I heard, I spoke.
> It was I who was, I who heard, I who spoke.

(*Maḥabbat* 341–42)

Maybudī classifies love into three sorts in his commentary on the verse of loving God and following the Prophet (3:31). Using the Persian *dūstī* as the generic term, he says that friendship has three basic levels: caprice, love, and passion. Having made the distinction, he throws out hints and allusions as to the nature of the final stage.

> Friendship has three way stations: caprice is the attribute of the body, love the attribute of the heart, and passion the attribute of the spirit. Caprice abides through the soul, love abides through the heart, and passion abides through the spirit. The soul is not empty of caprice, the heart not empty of love, and the spirit not empty of passion.
>
> Passion is the home of the passionate, and the passionate the home of trial. Passion is the chastisement of the passionate, and the passionate the chastisement of trial.
>
> In passion for You I will be a pure fire worshiper—
> I will be burnt in heart, roasted in spirit!
> I will dwell in hot fire and water,
> night and day I will be chastised!

The passion that is the spirit's attribute has three sorts: first is truthfulness, second drunkenness, third nonbeing. Truthfulness belongs to the recognizers, drunkenness to the distracted, nonbeing to the selfless.

Truthfulness is that what you say, you do; what you show, you have; and whence you call out, you are.

Drunkenness is being unsettled and distracted. When the gaze of the Protector becomes constant, the heart is distracted. When the bestowal becomes great, it passes the capacity for reception.

Drunkenness belongs to the soul, the heart, and the spirit. When the wine overcomes the intellect, the soul becomes drunk. When familiarity overcomes awareness, the heart becomes drunk. When unveiling overcomes intimacy, the spirit becomes drunk. When the Cupbearer discloses Himself, He bestows being. Then drunkenness turns into sobriety.

O Sweetheart, I am not, make me be!
Pour me a draft of union's wine!
Sit with me alone and make me drunk!
When You are tired of me, flatten me with a fine point.

Nonbeing is that you become lost in friendship—you appear neither in this world, nor in that world. The two worlds become lost in friendship, and friendship becomes lost in the Friend. Now I cannot say that I am, nor can I say that He is.

Separating the eye from the Friend is not good—
either He's in the place of the eye, or the eye itself is He.

The Pir of the Tariqah said: "O Lord! I seek the Found, I say to the Seen, 'What do I have, what do I seek, what do I see, what do I say?' I am entranced by this seeking, I am seized by this speaking.

"O Lord! I did it myself, I bought it myself—I lit myself on fire. I called out from friendship, I gave my heart and spirit to joy.

"O Kind One! Now that I am in the whirlpool, take my hand, for I have fallen hard."

From now on, Sanāʾī, don't speak of passion's pain—
many like you are lost in passion's world.
Take some advice: Don't try so hard for passion,
for passion's pain stirs up dust from running water.

(*Kashf* 2:94–96)

Manṣūr ibn Ardashīr ʿAbbādī (d. 1152), a scholar and preacher from Merv and a compatriot and younger contemporary of Samʿānī, wrote several books, most of which seem to have been lost, but we do have his Persian *Making Limpid: On the States of the Sufis* (*al-Taṣfiya fī aḥwāl al-ṣūfiyya*). Written in a sober and systematic style, it reflects the author's training in the Islamic sciences, not least philosophy. In four sections, it discusses the path to God, both the Shariah and the Tariqah; the basic way stations (beginning, intermediate, and advanced); the outer and inner states; and technical terms. In the section on inner states, ʿAbbādī mentions maḥabba as the fourth of seven levels, though he uses the Persian *dūstī* in the actual discussion. His description of love presents a fine summary of the picture drawn by the literature:

> God says, "*God will bring a people whom He loves, and who love Him*" [5:54]. Know that the cause of all seeking is love.
>
> Whoever has love in perfect friendship must become pure and empty of blights, changes, contaminations, opacities, and all personal motives.
>
> As long as he finds in friendship the motivation of caprice, the search for union, or the wish for the soul's share, his friendship is not worthy of being called love, rather caprice.
>
> When the heart becomes agitated for something absent, this is called yearning. When the recognition of the person is confirmed, this is called affection. When someone is chosen for friendship, this is called bosom friendship. When friendship is emptied of blights and devoted utterly to seeking the Friend's approval, this is called love. When he melts in the crucible of tribulation and turns his face toward annihilation, this is called passion.
>
> Each of these levels of friendship was realized by a group among the prophets, the friends, and the faithful.
>
> Whenever friendship is attached to created things, it is a metaphor. This sort of friendship gives birth to blights, falling in the end into various sorts of ruin and corruption.
>
> The first seeking of all seekers comes from yearning. Recognition becomes manifest through bosom friendship and through the followers' seeking to become similar to the one followed. When the faithful obey the command of Him who is worshiped, this derives from love. When the lovers are purified of their own share of union and separation in the crucible of friendship, this derives from passion.
>
> It is not appropriate to ascribe passion to the Creator, nor is anyone permitted to call friendship for the Lord passion. This is because the Qur'an and the reports speak of love and bosom friendship. Love is the furthest limit of bosom friendship and is more eminent than bosom friendship. God made apparent that He gave bosom friendship to Abraham and love to Muḥammad—upon both of them be blessings and peace!—and Muḥammad is greater than all the prophets.

In the past reports from the Exalted Presence spread by the revelations, it is transmitted as follows: "Abraham is My bosom friend, Moses is my chosen one, and Muḥammad is My beloved. By My exalted majesty, I have chosen the beloved over the bosom friend and the chosen one!"

Since Muḥammad is the greatest of the prophets, love is the most eminent level in friendship. Concerning Moses, the Lord mentioned love: "*I cast upon you love from Me*" [20:39]. Concerning the faithful, He mentioned love for Him: "*Those who have faith love God more intensely*" [2:165]. He also reported about His love for the faithful and the faithful's love for Him: "*God will bring a people whom He loves, and who love Him.*"

The Lord's love is His mercy, welcome, acceptance, generosity, and gentleness. The love of the faithful is seeking the approval of the Real, following the command of the Shariah, and turning away from all created things. In love for Him the person of faith becomes purified of all contaminations. He comes to prefer love for the Lord to all the loves of the two worlds.

Moreover, when the servant takes the Lord as his Friend, the Lord takes the servant as His friend. From love for the Real come forth various sorts of assistance to the servant's senses, thoughts, intellect, and heart. Then the servant's property in worship becomes the same as the Patron's property in lordhood, as He reported: "I am for him hearing, eyesight, and confirmation."

The divine love is the root, and the servants' love is born from this divine love. Just as the life of created things comes from the assistance of the Creator, so also the love of the existent things comes from the assistance of the divine love. In the perfection of His solicitude, the King made love appear in all creation—from here, where all is dark dust, to there, the place of the Guarded Tablet. With the assistance of this love, all creatures draw near to one another and seek the levels of one another. Because of becoming similar and drawing near, transitions occur, and because of these transitions, the world subsists. When the moment for the world's disappearance arrives, He will strip away the love, and everything will disappear.

Hence, the assistance of the seekers in their seeking, the light of the eyes of the wayfarers, the abiding subsistence of the lords of the Tariqah, and the fixity and constancy of the possessors of insight derive from love and bosom friendship. Whoever has more love has a greater share of the mysteries and a greater portion of the perfection of state.

The faithful carry the burden of this world's tribulation with the assistance of love. They consume the blessings of the next world through the excellence of love. They see the divine beauty through the light of love. They find the lordly approval by means of love. They reach everlasting life with the strength of love. They find the fruit of love on the tree of love, and they recognize the reality of Existence in the midst of love.

So the beginner must have yearning, the intermediate person must have bosom friendship, and the advanced must have love. If anyone reaches perfect passion, he will see what he sees, for the reality of passion cannot be recounted. May God make our hearts the quarries of His love! May He empty our hearts of love for this world! May He always make love the inscription on our heart's ring stone! Surely He is the Loving, the Responding.

(*Taṣfiya* 170–73)

In the fourth section of his book, ʿAbbādī explains Sufi terminology concerning knowledge, states, character traits, and courteous acts. In the section on states, he talks about passion in a manner reminiscent of the treatises of both the Brethren of Limpidness and Avicenna, though the philosophers would no doubt criticize him for massive oversimplification, especially in his description of the ascending levels of being. Nonetheless, the basic thrust of his argument provides a good summary of love's overall role in the universe as understood by philosophers and Sufi teachers. The word *final goal* (*ghāya*), mentioned at the outset, was used to designate the final cause, or telos, of Aristotle, that is, a thing's perfection (*kamāl*), that for the sake of which it comes to exist. All things, as Avicenna explained, are lovers, striving to reach their own perfections. Only by understanding the final goal can we perceive why things are what they are and why they continue striving to become fully themselves.

Question: What is passion?
Answer: Know that everything has a final goal. When it reaches it, it receives a name that it did not have before. It cannot go beyond its own final goal and perfection unless it turns away from perfection and goes toward deficiency.

For example, from the beginning of infancy the state of human nature is directed toward advancing. Once human nature reaches the final goal of its life span's balance and finds the perfection of its state, it turns toward deficiency and falls into old age. In the same way, at the beginning of its growth a plant looks toward increase and seeks its own perfection, which is to produce fruit. When it reaches that point, it turns toward diminution and lassitude and dries up.

So also, the rational soul comes to be joined with a specific individual so as to take benefit, and it seeks the perfection of its own felicity. By learning and inquiring about the Real, it reaches the final goal of knowledge and the perfection of recognition. Then it leaves aside nurturing the specific individual and turns entirely away from the individual's end. In its next-worldly states, the soul will see what it did and saw at first.

In the same way, from the first gaze that attaches to the beauty of the object of passion, the state of friendship increases by striving for more and seeking the perfection and final goal of friendship. When the soul reaches the end where there can be no more increase, it becomes free of the contaminations of appetite and disengaged from its own attachments. In the final goal and perfection of friendship, it becomes detached from separation and union, suffering and ease, proximity and distance. From there, it turns toward destruction and abandons its own shares. This final goal and perfection of friendship is called passion.

When the soul reaches knowledge of endless felicity, the result of this perfection is death. When the human life span reaches the ultimate limit of balance, it turns to inactivity, old age, and brokenness. So also with the perfection of animals—it turns to weakness and incapacity.

Passion is the final end, goal, and perfection of friendship. Its result is the destruction of the attributes of the one who is passionate. His own cravings are completely nullified, and he is not able to undertake the things desired by passion. Just as the plant called ʿashaqa wraps itself around a fruit-bearing tree and completely dries it out, so also when the state of passion reaches the human soul, it completely dries out the ramifications of the appetites and the excess branches that are the shelter of human nature's beasts, cattle, predators, wild animals, and birds, all of which seek disparate shares from the existence of the object of passion. Follies are nullified, attachments disappear, and, in extreme friendship, the person turns his face away from what he is seeking and goes back to voluntary separation. Then, in the purity of the state, he is annihilated in the sorrow of passion without remedy or suspicion. The Lawgiver has given this sort of passionate person the property of martyrdom, as he said: "He who has passion, conceals, stays chaste, and dies, dies a martyr."

In the same way, mineral substances have final ends in their seeking. When emeralds and lapis lazuli are freed from that, they join with plants. Grapes, dates, and plants in general also have causes through which they join with animals such as elephants, wolves, sheep, and other animals with large organs.

The completion of the rank of animals is that they should know how to talk and gain selfhood, thereby reaching human nature. The final end of the Adamites is prophecy and messengerhood, through which they gain similarity to the first intellects and the Universal Substance. When they reach that point, they turn totally away from the province of bodily things and take on nothing but the properties of spiritual substance. All this holds for individuals.

In speech there is the same thing, for it advances level by level. For a time it may voice rhymes, for a time proverbs, for a time wisdom, for a time admonition. When it reaches its final end, which is revelation, it falls outside limits and takes on the robe of eternity, for then the speech of God is heard.

So also is the case with activities. From habit they go to nature, then become expression, then gain the property of sincerity by means of truthful intention. Finally they emigrate from the empire of movement, take on the name religion, and become ascribed to the Object of worship: *Does not the pure religion belong to God?* [39:3].

In the same way, a man falls into the state of familiarity called recognition, then is taken to a state called friendship. When love and bosom friendship aim for perfection, he passes beyond all accidents and becomes one of the passionate. When he receives the name passion, he leaves the province of imagination and fantasy and receives names such as divine light.

So the name passion is given to the final end of the traveler's friendship. All at once he falls into lamentation, and is described as having gained similarity to the divinity.

Since he worships, he is called worshiper; since he knows, he is called intelligent; since he recognizes, he is called recognizer. When he avoids everything but Him, he is called renunciant. When he seeks Him through truthful intention, he is called sincere. When he steps into friendship for Him, he is called yearning. When he throws away all created things in contentment, he is called bosom friend. When he gives up his own existence by witnessing Him, he is called beloved. When he is such that he destroys his own annihilation and subsistence in the existence of the Friend and seeks no cause or pretext for his friendship—rather, he is immersed and overcome by having gained similarity to the sheer Essence of the Beloved—he is called passionate.

This passion is the cause of the spirit's separation from the body so that it is severed from the world of terrestrial things and becomes elevated completely into the province of celestial things. Such passion is born from the light of witnessing the Friend. It comes like lightning, puts light into the eyes, sound into the ears, speed into movement, and shunning creation into attributes. If the person attends to some work, this is not because of a motivation or his own share. Rather, he does so because that work is ascribed to passion or to the Friend. His good and evil reach others without his volition. Because of his passion, he pays no attention to anything and has no leisure to do so.

The same thing is manifest from the state of heaven and the heaven-dwellers. They have so much passion for the Object of Worship that they move constantly in seeking. From their movement, traces and diverse lights appear in this world's realm—good and evil, auspiciousness and misfortune—without their intention or volition. For in their passion for the Object of Worship, the heaven-dwellers do not have any leisure time for themselves or others. Rather, the intensity of their passion keeps them in their work, and traces arrive from the work. Then when they reach the goal of their passion, the stuff of passion that is the root of their movement will become the stuff of stillness. They will suddenly become still, and then the resurrection will take place.

On this earth, passion in the spirit of the passionate will do the same thing that it will do in heaven. Thus, in name and meaning the passionate man does not enter the province of making claims. Passion has nothing of the worlds of new arrival or eternity. It is the reflection of a radiance that falls into the window of the heart from behind the curtain of the Unseen. It strikes the thunderbolt of the Befalling[2] in every direction and takes the passionate away from all things and all places, sacrificing him in the chamber of the Beloved. For "The first of passion is disquiet, and the last of it is destitution."

We have explained passion in other books with more analysis, even though passion cannot be known through explication and demonstration. This is enough answer for you.

(*Taṣfiya* 208–11)

HUMAN FRIENDSHIP

At the beginning of the just-quoted discussion of maḥabba, after mentioning the verse of mutual love, ʿAbbādī wrote, "Know that the cause of all seeking is love." This sums up the role of love in the universe: God's love and mercy for everything that may possibly exist drive all things to seek their own perfections. By making this point, teachers are reminding people that they will love, willy-nilly, and that they will taste the consequences. Since they have no escape from love, they need to get it right, and getting it right has everything to do with giving it its rightful due (ḥaqq). This in turn is clarified by the formula of tawḥīd: "There is no true beloved but God." This does not mean that love for others is illegitimate—quite the contrary. It means that in loving God, man must love what God loves, for love demands conformity with the beloved.

To say that we have no choice but to love means that we are ruled by the creative command. To say that we will taste love's consequences means that we have a certain freedom in love and will be held responsible to that extent. The creative command demands that we love, and the religious command calls us to direct our love toward its worthy objects. Maybudī explains this in his commentary on a verse that refers to the Day of Resurrection, when veils will be lifted and people will see the realities face to face: "*Bo-*

som friends on that day will be enemies of one another, except the godwary" (43:67).

> Know that in reality God alone deserves friendship, no one else. This is because perfect beauty and never-ending majesty belong to Him, the beginningless Essence and everlasting attributes belong to Him, limitless existence and infinite munificence belong to Him, and noninstrumental knowledge and uncontrived power belong to Him.
>
> Abū Bakr Ṣiddīq said, "When someone tastes of unmixed love for God, that prevents him from seeking this world and alienates him from all mankind." Whenever the limpidness of the Real's love settles down in someone's heart, the opacity of seeking this world and people's acceptance packs its bags from his heart. If he then loves anyone among the creatures, it is because that person has an attachment to the Real or an affinity with the Real through His friendship. Whenever anyone has a friend, in reality he also loves his abode, lane, and neighborhood. This is why He says of the friendship of the godwary and pious [for the Kaabah], *"Its friends are only the godwary"* [8:34]. Friendship for God's Messenger is what he himself says: "Love me because of God's love!"
>
> So the final end of all loves is the perfection of the beauty of the Divine Presence. To this He alludes with His words *"Surely the final end is unto thy Lord"* [53:42].
>
> (*Kashf* 9:88)

Ontologically—from the perspective of the creative command—people love things other than God because they perceive His beauty in creation. In their normal state of forgetfulness, they do not have the discernment to recognize that all beauty is the radiance of God's names and attributes. Hence, they love those in whom beauty appears. Morally and spiritually—from the perspective of the religious command—they are called upon to love those whose beauty conforms to God's beautiful character traits. Just as God loves those who do what is beautiful and those who are sincere, so also should human beings. Love for others, then, is a corollary of love for God. In the same way, people should hate what God hates. When God says that He does not love ugliness and hypocrisy, they also should not love them. It goes against love's nature to direct it at the ugly rather than the beautiful.

Maybudī talks about friendship with other than God in many passages of his commentary, for the Qur'an repeatedly instructs people to treat others with compassion, love, and beautiful-doing. Here are some of his explanations.

> *Let not the faithful take the unbelievers as friends rather than the faithful* [3:28]. The reality of the servant's faith and the final goal of his going forth on

the path of tawḥīd take him back to God's friendship. The reality of friendship is conformity, that is, being a friend of His friend and an enemy of His enemy. The master of the Shariah alluded to this with his words "The most reliable handhold of faith is love in God and hate in God."

The traditions say that the Lord of the Worlds sent a revelation to one of the former prophets: "Say to the servants, 'In this world you have taken up renunciation in order to hurry to your own comfort and be relieved of this world's suffering. With your obedience and worship, you have sought your own exaltation and your own good name. Now look: What have you done for Me? Have you ever loved My friends? Have you ever taken My enemies as your enemies?"

This is exactly what He said to Jesus: "O Jesus, if the worship of all the inhabitants of heaven and earth accompanies you in the path of the religion, but you have no love for My friends and no enmity for My enemies, then your worship has been useless and without profit."

It is reported that Abū Idrīs Khawlānī said to Muʿādh, "I love you in the path of God."

Muʿādh said, "Let it be good news! I heard God's Messenger say that on the Day of Resurrection, God will place seats around the Splendorous Throne for a group whose faces will be like the full moon. Everyone will be fearful because of the awe of the resurrection, but they will be secure. Everyone will be in dread, but they will be still. It was said, 'O Messenger of God! Which group is this?'

"He said, 'Those who love each other in God.'"

It has been related as well that God says, "I have obligated My love on those who love each other in Me, sit with each other in Me, visit each other in Me, and spend freely on each other in Me."

Mujāhid said, "When God's friends smile in each other's faces, their sins fall away like leaves from a tree. They will reach God pure, and He will take them into His protection and security at the resurrection."

(*Kashf* 2:83)

Hah! There you are: You love them, but they do not love you [3:119]. The faithful had limpid hearts and generous natures, and they did not keep tenderness and mercy back from the estranged. They wanted good for them and attached their hearts to their submission. They wanted their salvation and did not hold back God's mercy from them—whether they were acquaintances or strangers. This continued to cross their minds:

Bring the sweetmeat, for it is the heart's beloved,
suited for both the elect and the common.

This is the same tenderness that Muḥammad showed to the estranged. He said, "O God, guide my people, for they do not know."

As for the unbelievers, those who had no limpidness in their hearts or loyalty in their natures, they never wanted good for the people of faith, nor did they love them. They grieved at the good that reached them and became happy at the bad. God says, "*If something beautiful touches you, it vexes them, and if something ugly strikes you, they rejoice at it*" [3:120].

Indeed, everyone does what is fitting for him, for "The pot pours what is inside it." The person of faith is generous and lovingly kind, for what is fitting for faith is generosity and chivalry. The unbeliever is vile and bad-wanting, for what is fitting for unbelief is vileness and unseemliness. The person of faith calls God's creatures to salvation and deliverance. The unbeliever calls them to the Fire and captivity. To this He alludes with His words "*O my people! What is it with me that I call you to salvation and you call me to the Fire?*" [40:41].

(2:262)

No good is there in much of their whispering, except for him who bids to charity, or the approved, or setting things right among the people [4:114]. The best activities of the servants are the three things in this verse: charity, the approved, and setting things right among the people. The goodness in this verse is not specified for one individual, but rather its profit reaches others. The wonder is not that you should open a door for yourself; the wonder and chivalry are that you should open a door to yourself for another.

Pir Bū ʿAlī Siyāh said, "So what if you make yourself happy? The work is done by making someone else happy."

Muṣṭafā alluded to this: "The worst of men is he who eats alone."

As for charity, it is of three sorts: with possessions, with the body, and with the heart. Charity with possessions is giving comfort to the poor by expending blessings. Charity with the body is undertaking for them the duty of service. Charity with the heart is being loyal to beautiful intention and firm aspiration. This is charity toward the poor.

There is also charity toward the rich. It is that you act with munificence toward them and do not expose your need to them; you take back your hope from their charitable gifts and do not covet anything from them.

When charity, the approved, and setting things right come together in someone, from head to foot he becomes veneration itself, the oyster shell for the mysteries of lordhood, and he is accepted by those who bear witness to the divinity. His name is given out as sincerely truthful, and tomorrow he will be gathered up along with the sincerely truthful. This is the magnificent wage that the Exalted Lord has promised: "*We shall give him a mighty wage*" [4:114].

(2:695)

The faithful indeed are brothers [49:10]. The faithful are those caressed by the Lord of the Worlds in the Beginningless, when brotherhood was established among them. This is a brotherhood that will never be cut off, a kinship that will never be broken, a lineage that will be joined with the Endless. It is to this that the report refers: "Every tie and lineage will be cut on the Day of Resurrection, save My tie and My lineage." What is meant by this is the lineage of the religion and godwariness, not the lineage of water and clay. If it were the lineage of water and clay, Abū Lahab and Abū Jahl would have a share of it. It is this to which He alludes with the words "*Surely the most noble of you with God is the most godwary*" [49:13].

O chevalier! You know that all the faithful are your brothers and kinsmen in the lineage of faith and godwariness. Attend to the rightful due of brotherhood and the stipulations of kinship. Live in agreeableness with them, choose the road of preferring others and chivalry, and serve them without recompense. If they sin, excuse them. If they are ill, visit them. Put your own share entirely off to the side and increase their portion. This is the rightful due of brotherhood. If you have the head for it, then enter. Otherwise, emigrate.

Dhu'l-Nūn was asked, "With whom should we be companions, and with whom should we come and go?"

He said, "With him who does not possess, who does not censure any state of yours, and who does not change when you change."

He is saying, "Be the companion of someone who owns nothing." In other words, whatever wealth and property he has, he does not consider it his own right. He recognizes his brothers' right to it more than his own right. Wherever there is antagonism in the world, it rises up from you-ness and I-ness. When you remove you-ness and I-ness from the road, agreement comes and antagonism leaves.

He said also that you should be a companion of someone who will never censure you and who, if he sees a defect from you, will not turn away from you. He knows that the Adamite is not empty of defect and that being pure and without defects is the attribute of the Holy Lord alone.

A man had a wife and acted well toward her in the work of passion. The woman had a white spot in her eye, and the man, because of his great passion, knew nothing of that defect. One day his passion for her diminished, and he said, "When did this white spot appear in your eye?"

She said, "From the moment your perfect passion diminished."

Muṣṭafā said, "Love for a thing makes you blind and deaf." A man's friendship blinds him to seeing the defects of the beloved and makes him deaf to hearing blame.

> Dhu'l-Nūn's third description was "he does not change when you change." With these words, he cut him off from companionship with creatures. He is saying, "When you are a companion, be the companion of the Real, not creation, for creatures change when you change, but in the majesty of His unity and the perfection of His everlastingness, the Real never changes, even if creatures change."
>
> The Pir of the Tariqah said, "O God, You are the shelter of the faithful and await the strivers at the end of the road. Exalted is he whom You want. If he flees, You are in the road for him. Blessed is he to whom You belong—indeed will You ever be mine?"
>
> (9:268–69)

Several hadiths refer to the ugliness of cutting off the womb (*qaṭʿ al-raḥim*), meaning severing the ties of love and compassion established by blood relationship and lineage. These sayings suggest that the womb, as the human locus of creative mercy (raḥma), is intimately connected with God as the All-Merciful (raḥmān), whose mercy *embraces everything* (7:156). In one hadith, for example, the Prophet quotes God as saying, "I am God and I am the All-Merciful. I created the womb, and I gave it a name derived from My own name. If someone cuts off the womb, I will cut him off, and if someone joins the womb, I will join him to Me."

Anṣārī devotes Chapter 28 of *Forty-Two Chapters* to the womb. He begins by quoting two more hadiths about the womb, including "No one who cuts off the womb will enter the Garden." Then he points out that if human relationships take on such importance in the eyes of God, it follows that our relationship with God is even more important. To be sure, one must love one's neighbor as oneself, but this love must be based on love for God with all one's heart, mind, soul, and strength. By "this group," Anṣārī means the lovers of God, and by "this talk," the business of love.

> The Allusion. When someone cuts himself off from kinship, his state is like this. Consider him who cuts himself off from the Friend. What will his state be? When someone cuts himself off from friendship with the Friend, how will he be? And when he cuts himself off from His friends, how will he be?
>
> When someone cuts himself off from kinship, he is choosing to be far from mercy. When someone cuts himself off from this group, he is choosing to be far from God's elevation and proximity, for "*Surely God is with those who are godwary and those who do what is beautiful*" [16:128].
>
> Cut yourself off from yourself, not from the friends of the Friend! Join with this talk, not with other than the Friend!

> Establish your relation with this group through nonbeing, not with being. As long as you have being, you will be cut off from this group and joined with selfhood.
>
> The members of this group are related to one another in that they do not have one-anotherness with one another. They have kinship with one another in distance from their own selfhoods. This kinship was before water and clay, for "Spirits are mustered troops."* They are mirrors, not veils, for one another.
>
> You must cut off your relation with yourself so as to join with this group. You will see paradise as hard cash, life as everlasting, mercy as rain, the Ever-Merciful apparent, and the pretexts concealed.
>
> (*Chihil* 168–69)

In Chapter 32 of the same book, Anṣārī explains why it is important to love others as part of achieving love for God. He begins by citing a hadith saying that no matter how well or badly someone may perform his religious obligations, "A man will be with the one he loves." People will be judged, in other words, by their choice of friends. Notice that in parts of this passage, the word *friend, dūst,* is ambiguous, which is to say that it is not clear whether Anṣārī means a human friend who is also a friend of God, or God as the Friend. He seems to be saying that in every case, love is nothing but the love that energizes the universe. Distinctions need to be drawn among the objects of love, but not in love itself. To love is to actualize a divine attribute, however feebly. As Rūmī points out, all metaphorical love helps us learn how to love truly and worthily, that is, how to love the True, the Worthy, the Real.[3]

> The Allusion. A man is with his friend and goes forth on his path. Even if he cannot travel in the same way or as much as his friend does, he still travels in his path. He will be with him in effort, striving, seriousness, and seeking. Night and day he will cling to his skirt and attach himself to his saddle straps. He will throw down his prayer carpet along with his in order to conform to him. He will overthrow this world to prepare himself for his work and his command. He will throw away his home and family and gamble away his life for him.
>
> Even if he cannot be like him in inward presence, togetherness, and friendship with God, he will be with him in effort, seriousness, and worship, and he will desire his station. Hence he will be with him in what he is able to do with his steps and what he cannot reach with his breaths. In desire, love, and eagerness, he will be with him. He will reach what his own hands and capacity can reach, and through friendship and love he will reach what he himself cannot reach. Hence, he will be with the one he loves both today and tomorrow.

Happy is he who is wounded by the blow of the Friend! Joyful is the heart that is unsettled because of His friendship! Friendship is not in the heart, but in the spirit. It is not even in the spirit, but it points to it. Friendship is a robe of honor from on high, a heavenly gift. It is not I-ness and we-ness. Friendship is not something known that enters the pocket. Look at where this business is coming from and with whom it is! It is something spontaneous that comes from the Unseen.

Living with the friend is life. Being held back from the friend is to be held back from the living spirit. Everyone who loves someone knows this. Traversing the ocean and sleeping on razor blades are easier than being without the friend.

He who lives through the living spirit lives through water and bread, and he who lives through the Friend lives forever. Living without the Friend is the mark of the day of blindness. Living without the remembrance of the Friend, by God, is not living. So, O seeker, do not call empty fervor friendship, for the Friend is with him who is His friend, or He is with him in one skin.

One mark of friendship is that in every state the friend is with the friend, breathing the same breath in happiness and sorrow. Do you not see that when the Messenger migrated, those who were his Companions went with him? If he struck with a sword or was struck by one, they were with him. If his feet became swollen in prayer, they were with him. If he kicked this world behind himself, they were with him in every state that passed. If they were all in prayer, they were with him.

It is also true that He said to those who claimed friendship that if you want friendship with God, strive in following so that you may reach friendship: "*Say: 'If you love God, follow me; God will love you'*" [3:31]. He is saying that you should follow with your feet and not be satisfied with talk. The mark of following is to stride forth, not to be satisfied with talk. The mark of love is that you are with the friend wherever he goes.

Uways Qaranī was far from the Prophet in form, but when the Prophet's teeth were broken, he was with him. In seriousness, effort, service, and worship, he never chose to be distant for one instant. He never rested from effort, for his friendship did not allow him to be separate from his friend, for he heard from the Friend, "Be with the friend!"

One of the conditions of friendship is conformity. Separation from the friend is not a feigned tribulation, for separation is hardship itself. Whenever there is friendship, separation is the worst of all hardships.

The friend becomes corrupt with the corrupt, and the friend stays worthy with the worthy.

O worthy man! If you see in yourself an inclination to see a corrupt person and become his companion in himself or in his corruption, attend to that quickly and repel it. Do not let that inclination pull you into friendship with him, lest your friendship destroy you.

And O corrupt man! If you find an inclination toward the folk of worthiness and toward worthiness itself, quickly add to it so that it may pull you into friendship with the worthy and you may become the possessor of endless good fortune, for the friend will be with the friend.

Preserve respect for the friendship of the good by keeping away from badness and the bad. Do not give the friendship of the good to the bad, for companionship with bad brings forth bad opinions about the good. Disrespect for the good is the clearest sign of the misfortune of the misfortunate.

Balaam, with all his obedience, was brought down to the standing of a dog because of one disrespectful act toward a friend. *His likeness is as the likeness of a dog* [7:176]. And the dog of the Companions of the Cave had respect for His friends and came from the standing of a dog to that of the friends and the great ones. *And they will say, "Seven, and the eighth of them was their dog"* [18:22].

O seeker! If you see in yourself that your respect for the good and your eagerness to visit the good are weak, put on the garment of trial and affliction, for weakness is the mark of being deprived of endless good fortune. We seek refuge in God from abandonment!

The mark of proximity to the Patron is love, and the mark of love is drunkenness—the person is disgusted with his own being and free of self-worship. If you find this good fortune, you will have escaped and bound yourself to Him. Beware of the abasement of the veil and the whip of rebuke!

O God! Yours increased and mine decreased. At last there remained what was there at first. O God! Patience fled from me, and my ability to bear became weak. I sowed the seed of repose, and unsettledness grew! O God! You wanted, I did not want. I found the gaze of gentleness when I woke up from sleep.

(*Chihil* 192–94)

8

The Suffering of Love

The Qur'an says that faith will call down trial on those who claim it, and the hadith literature makes clear that prophets have suffered more affliction and trial than anyone else. Qushayrī explains why this should be so in *Subtle Allusions.*

> *Do the people reckon they will be left to say, "We have faith," and will not be tried?* [29:2]. Do the people reckon that they will be left simply to claim that they have faith without trial being demanded from them? This will never happen, for the worth of a man lies in his trial. When the measure of someone's meaning is greater, the measure of his trial will be greater.
>
> Souls will be tried by the demand to emerge from the homeland of indolence and to engage in the most beautiful activity. Hearts will be tried by seeking and truthful meditation while looking attentively at the proofs of tawḥīd and realizing knowledge. Spirits will be tried by disengagement from love for all things, solitariness apart from every cause, and distance from repose in any created thing. Secret cores will be tried by withdrawal to the witnessing places of unveiling and by patience with the traces of Self-disclosure until they are consumed by them.
>
> (*Laṭā'if* 5:86–87)

SEPARATION AND UNION

The story of love is a familiar one: boy meets girl, boy loses girl, boy finds girl. Its constant retelling no doubt has much to do with the fact that it resonates with something deep in the human soul. We know that we have lost something (myths of the primordial paradise are practically universal), and we know that to be happy, we need to recover what we have lost. Otherwise, why all the dissatisfaction, all the seeking and searching, all the hopes for better times and places, all the dreams of utopia?

Rūmī's six-volume epic on the ups and downs of love, the *Mathnawī*, begins with a verse announcing that he will be repeating the same old story: "Listen to the reed as it complains, / telling the tale of separations." The reed or flute is the soul, torn from its reed bed, moaning and yearning in pain. All its complaints boil down to one complaint: I don't have what I want. As Anṣārī put it in the passage quoted at the end of the previous chapter, "Whenever there is friendship, separation is the worst of all hardships." Maybudī makes the same point: "Whoever is veiled from the Friend is in trial itself, even if he has the keys to the kingdom's treasuries in his sleeve. Whoever is attracted by the Friend is in bestowal itself, even if he does not have his evening bread" (*Kashf* 7:40, on verse 25:22).

In short, the human soul dwells in separation (*firāq*) as a result of the creative command, so it longs for union (wiṣāl). Talk of union was anathema to many Kalam experts, who held that it was incompatible with God's transcendence. No doubt they also found the sexual connotations offensive. In no way, however, does the Arabic word for union imply a unity of substance or an identity of servant and Lord—any more than sexual union means that lover and beloved become literally one. Most of those who used the word understood it rather as the necessary complement of separation.

Separation and union are relative terms. There cannot be absolute union, because the One alone is absolute; nor can there be absolute separation, because *He is with you wherever you are* (57:4). There is no escape from God, so there is no escape from union. What keeps people separate from Him is their failure to recognize His presence. Moreover, recognition of His presence has degrees. True recognition demands realization, the actual attainment of the Divine Presence, reaching the Haqiqah by following the Shariah and the Tariqah.

Createdness and contingency separate creatures from what they love. It is impossible to dwell in the world and find lasting happiness in and from it, as most people know or will soon find out. Whatever comes, goes. *All is perishing but His face* (28:88). Only those who dwell in His face are fully content. But getting to His face demands effort, trial, and pain. Moreover, God in His mercy wants people to suffer. Otherwise they will stay lackadaisical and live beneath themselves. This is why Rūmī addresses aspiring lovers with the words, "Beware, do not sigh coldly in your indifference! / Seek pain! Seek pain, pain, pain!" (*Mathnawī* 6:4304).

In his commentary on the verse "*Indeed We sent to nations before thee, and We seized them with adversity and hardship*" (6:42), Maybudī cites a saying by one of the early Sufi teachers to explain why God afflicts people with pain and suffering.

> Ibn ʿAṭāʾ said, "We took away from them all the paths so that they would return to Us": I blocked all their roads so that they would turn away completely from the realm of being, busy themselves with My companionship, and put love for Me in their hearts.
>
> (*Kashf* 3:359)

In the realm of being, which is that of multiplicity, dispersion, and otherness, only the Adamites have the capacity to love God in Himself, because only they were taught all the names and given the ability to recognize Him for what He is. Pain and suffering enter the picture the moment they understand that they do not have what they want. All social and political movements, not to speak of human endeavors generally, bubble up from the recognition that things are not what they should be. Everyone is busy with the inalienable right to pursue happiness, but no one ever finds it for long. We Adamites alone see that we are out of kilter, and we alone have the freedom to change our state, to strive for nearness, to become characterized by the character traits of God Himself, and to achieve the union that can stop the craving. Samʿānī tells us that before Adam, no one had the requisite awareness of self and Lord to suffer. The Persian expression "to throw dust on the head" means to acknowledge the hopelessness of one's situation.

> O dervish! When an afflicted person reaches the limit in his affliction, he throws dust on his head. He who created you created you from dust itself, so your makeup is affliction itself. Other afflicted creatures throw dust on their heads because of you. The whole world was paradise as long as you had not come. The earth was all gardens and orchards before you came. When your blessings came into the world, kind sir, the orchard became a field of brambles, the garden a blemish, the roses thorns, and good fortune tribulation. It is you who have thrown yourself into distress, and the creatures have been thrown into distress by you. You do not know your cure, nor does anyone else know how to cure you.
>
> (*Rawḥ* 289)

From the perspective of the creative command, God's majesty and severity demand separation, while His beauty and gentleness call for union. God is both gentle and severe, merciful and wrathful, so people will always be hanging between separation and union, whether in this world or the next. Samʿānī traces the ups and downs of love back to the divine names in any number of passages. Here, for example, is the beginning of his commentary on the two divine names the Majestic, the Beautiful (*jalīl jamīl*), followed by other passages in which he explains why God's very reality demands that love be accompanied by the pain of separation.

> The Majestic, the Beautiful mean the magnificent, the beautiful-doer. He melts the hearts with His majesty and caresses the spirits with His beauty. With His majesty, He makes hearts *scattered dust* [25:23], and with His beauty, He makes spirits the source of happiness and joy. With His majesty, He links hearts with sorrow and grief, and with His beauty, He makes spirits happy and delighted.
>
> In the contemplation of His majesty, the recognizers breathe the sigh of "Woe is me!" In the contemplation of His beauty, the lovers drink down the wine of bestowal from the hand of good fortune's cupbearer. When you gaze at His majesty, it bloodies your liver, and when you gaze at His beauty, it comforts your heart.
>
> Oh, how many have been called to this road by the messenger of His beauty! Then, when their hope for union became strong, He appointed the sultan of majesty to plunder their capital and give them over to the wind.
>
> This is the foundation of love: At first it is all benevolence, at last it is all severity. At first it is all honey, then it is all poison.
>
> When they want to send a boy to school, they tie an amulet around his neck and give him new clothes to keep him still. But, when two days pass and he sees the teacher's strap, he knows that it was all a pretext. Now there is no way but patience.
>
> In passion for the pretty faces, what profits other than patience?
> Be firm-footed in passion—don't turn away from passion.
> O you who run after your heart in every direction—
> look for it where you lost it!
> In truth, passion's destitution is wealth—
> the destitute have won the ball in passion's field.
>
> He clothed us in the garment of love and said, "*He loves them, and they love Him* [5:54]. *Those who have faith love God more intensely*" [2:165]. Then He offered the Trust to us.
>
> A lover is someone who takes burdens on himself and carries them. He is long-suffering in the road. He comes forth to oppression by taking it on himself, to arrogation by being gracious, to pridefulness by self-abasement.
>
> Because of the burning of love's fire, we were the ones who lifted up the burden that heaven, earth, and the mountains were not able to carry, even

though we did not have the capacity to do so. Nonetheless, bewilderment is a great pillar in the shariah of love. Hence, we lifted up the burden and put aside refusal. But the address came: "*Surely he is a great wrongdoer, deeply ignorant*" [33:72].

(*Rawḥ* 361–62)

He disclosed His names and attributes to the universe so that lovers would get to work and yearners would seek for vision. By virtue of exaltedness, He let down the curtain of magnificence and set up the banner of tremendousness. He made the attribute of inaccessibility the pavilion of His own majesty so that the hearts of the dear ones would roast and the eyes of the lovers would pour with tears. As soon as they become agitated and begin to seek the mysteries, the call of Unity arrives from the curtains of the Sanctum's beauty: "Away with you, away with you! O handful of dust! How dare you circle around the courtyard of Solitariness!?"

Whenever they drink down the cup of despair, put on the shirt of destitution, pull their heads into the collar of bewilderment, and lose hope of finding, the call of gentleness comes from the pavilions of the divine beauty: "Patience, patience! Pass some days at the threshold of Our majesty in hope of contemplating Our beauty, and be happy in the midst of the fire. Though the night is dark, keep your heart strong, for sunrise is near."

He did not use the sword of severity against the angels, but He used it against you, for in reality life belongs to you: *And that He may try the faithful with a beautiful trial* [8:17].

(350)

By majesty's decree, a group remained in deprivation, and by beauty's decree, a group took benefit. In every command He gave you, He sought from you a servanthood. In every decree He enacted over you, He wanted an awareness inside your heart.

In one place, He struck the fire of severity in the hearts, saying, "*Do they feel secure from God's deception?*" [7:99]. In another place, He planted the herb of gentleness in the garden of bounty: "*Despair not of God's mercy!*" [39:53].

When a man becomes aware of this talk, he catches fire from head to toe. He looks at the vast plain of exaltedness and does not see any home. He wanders in the bloody tears of bewilderment, and tears of remorse pour down his face.

O dervish! The sword of severity becomes sharper every day, but these hapless ones fall more and more into passion.

(508)

When He said, *"Am I not your Lord?"* [7:172], that was the night of running the kingdom. When He said, *"He loves them, and they love Him,"* that was the time of caressing. In the religion of love, there must be both gentleness and severity, both caressing and melting, both attraction and killing, both making do and burning. There must be caresses so that a man may know the harshness of being taken to task, and there must be taking to task so that he may know the worth of caresses.

When His men carry the burden of caresses, they carry it while contemplating severity. When they carry the burden of severity, they carry it while seeing gentleness. Whenever anyone is nurtured in only one thing, he does not have the capacity to carry something else. If you put a dung beetle, which spends its days in stench, in the midst of roses, there is fear that it will be destroyed, for it has passed its days in stench and does not have the capital to carry the burden of fragrance.

The angels were nurtured in gentleness and never had the opportunity to carry the burden of severity. But the Adamites are the threshold of both gentleness and severity. "If You chastise me, I love You, and if You show mercy to me, I love You." That great man is saying: If You have mercy, I am Your lover, and if you appoint for me a hundred thousand heart-piercing, liver-burning arrows, I am still Your lover.

(513)

Separation is a foretaste of hellfire, and union a preview of paradise. Notice that Maybudī mentions this while explaining one of the verses concerning divorce.

O Prophet, when you divorce women, divorce them after the set period [65:1]. This explains the ruling on divorce. Although the Shariah permits divorce, God hates it, for it is the cause of separation. Muṣṭafā said, "Among the permitted things the most hateful to God is divorce."

He said also, "Take spouses and do not divorce, for the Throne shudders at divorce." And "Whenever a woman asks her husband for divorce, the ease of the Garden is forbidden to her." He said: Get married and do not seek divorce, for the Tremendous Throne trembles at divorce and separation. Any woman who seeks divorce from her husband without his having harmed her or made her suffer will never smell the scent of the eight paradises.

Marriage is the cause of joining, and God loves union. Divorce is the cause of parting, and God hates separation. The wall of separation's world is affliction, and the water of separation's ocean is the bloody tears of remorse.

The day of separation has no sun, and the night of severance no day. If there were any drink bitterer than separation, it would have been placed on that rejected one of the Threshold, Iblis. A bowl was prepared of curses, the drink of severance and separation was poured into it, and it was put in his hand. He drank it all down, not leaving a drop. That was expressed like this: "*Upon you shall be My curse until the Day of Doom*" [38:78].

The great ones of the religion have said that two goblets appeared from the Unseen. One was *And he was one of the unbelievers* [2:34] and the other was *He is Ever-Merciful toward the faithful* [33:43]. The cup of unbelief was full of the drink of separation, and the cup of mercy full of the drink of union. He sent the cup of mercy on the hand of welcome with the escort of bounty to the spirit of Muṣṭafā the Arab. God says, "*Surely God's bounty upon thee is magnificent*" [4:113]. The cup of unbelief was given by the hand of justice with the description of abasement to Iblis the abandoned. It was said, "*I shall surely fill Gehenna with thee and whosoever follows thee, all together*" [38:85].

Rābiʿa ʿAdawī said, "Unbelief has the flavor of separation, and faith has the pleasure of union. That flavor and this pleasure will appear tomorrow at the resurrection. In the plain of awe and the courtyard of harshness, it will be said to one group, 'Separation without union!' and to another group, 'Union without end!' "

(*Kashf* 10:148–49)

Although Rābiʿa's saying here represents a standard understanding of the nature of hell and paradise, it suggests a static situation in which all those who achieve salvation are wrapped in permanent, unchanging bliss. Samʿānī explains that the actual situation is much more complex, because separation and union remain relative situations even in the next world. People who achieve paradise will not stop their quest for union with the Real, even if the standard Shariah language says that after death, they will no longer be able to perform the acts through which God is sought, such as prayer, fasting, and pilgrimage. Samʿānī points out that this cannot mean that they stop seeking, for God in Himself will remain forever beyond their grasp. The finite will never reach the Infinite, so the Arc of Ascent will extend forever.

A mouthful has come that is not suited for your craw. The mouthful is that of elephants, and the craw that of sparrows. You have been brought into a tremendous road. The whole world is bewildered because the command came, "Seek Me!"

Man is so incapable that the Qur'an says, "*If a fly steals something from them, they cannot retrieve it*" [22:73]. If a man cannot bring to hand something snatched away by a fly, how can he bring to hand the majesty of the Beginningless? Nonetheless, in the measure of your capacity and strength, expend your effort, and He, from His world, will straighten out your work.

Know that in reality, this world and that world are both for the sake of seeking. If someone says that the next world is not the world of seeking, that is impossible. True, there will be no prayer and fasting, but there will be seeking. Tomorrow all the shariahs will be scratched out by the pen of abrogation, but two things will remain forever and without end: love for God and praise of God. These have no severance, dissolution, or lapsing. It is fitting that prayer, fasting, hajj, and struggle come to an end, but it is not fitting that seeking come to an end. It is permissible for prayer and fasting to be abrogated, but it is not fitting for the bond of love and the covenant of passion to be abrogated.

O dervish! In reality, you should believe that if you go to paradise, every day that passes will open you to a world of recognizing the Real that was not there before. This is a work that will never come to an end, and may it never come to an end!

The seeking of these Men has no cause such that it could disappear by a cause. If seeking, yearning, and love disappeared through contemplation, these would have a cause. If they had a cause, they would be inside a veil, and if they were veiled, they would be rejected.

This is a seeking that was put there by Him first and will be given by Him last. You are placed in the midst of the journey and given by Him. The Beginningless is what He put, and the Endless is what He gives. You are one of the travelers placed by Him and given by Him. First, you were put there without cause, and last, He will give to you without cause.

(*Rawḥ* 77–78)

In the usual dialectic of separation and union, the goal of lovers is to escape from self and reach the Beloved. This is how Maybudī talks in his commentary on the verse "*Say: 'My prayer and my sacrifice, my life and my death, belong to God*'" (6:162). The first paragraph is taken from Qushayrī's *Subtle Allusions.*

He who knows that he is in God knows that he belongs to God. When he knows that his soul belongs to God, no share of him remains for other than God. He surrenders to God's decree. He does not protest against God's predetermination, he does not oppose God's chosen ones, and he does not turn away from embracing God's command.

This verse about Muṣṭafā alludes to the station of union. Union is joining with the Real and being released from oneself. The mark of this work is a heart alive through meditation and a tongue loosed in remembrance. One becomes a loan to the creatures, a stranger to oneself, free from attachment, at rest with the Real.

The Pir of the Tariqah said, "O God, ever since You called me, I have been alone in the crowd. When You said 'Come!' my seven bodily parts heard. What comes forth from the Adamite? The Adamite's worth is clear: his purse is empty, he treads on air.

"This work was before Adam and Eve, a bestowal before fear and hope, but the Adamite undergoes trials because of seeing. He alone is joyful who is free of seeing causes and is disloyal toward his own self. Though the millwheel of the states is turning, so what? The pivot of His will is in place."

(*Kashf* 3:544)

THE TRIALS OF ADAM

Maybudī talks about trial and tribulation as sure signs of God's love. In one passage, he offers a mythic depiction of love's origin and explains that the role of suffering is to weed out the unqualified. He seems to be saying that all these events took place at the beginning, on the Day of Alast. In other words, God knew in His beginningless knowledge exactly what would unfold. Maybudī is explaining the inner meaning of a verse that outwardly refers to the siege of Medina and the Battle of the Ditch: "*There it was that the faithful were tried and shaken with intense shaking*" (33:11).

It is said that the Real divided Adam's progeny into one thousand kinds and let them look at the carpet of love. The desire for love rose up in all of them. Then He adorned this world and displayed it to them. When they saw its embellishments and splendors, they became drunk and entranced and remained with this world, except for one group, who stayed on love's carpet and stuck up their heads in their claim.

Then He divided this group into one thousand kinds and displayed the afterworld to them. When they saw the everlasting joy and bliss, the *spreading shade and pouring water* [56:30–31], the houris and the castles, they were entranced by it and stayed with it, except for one group who stayed on the carpet and sought the treasuries of recognizing Him.

The address came from the Invincible Court, the Exalted Threshold, "What are you seeking and why are you staying?"

They said, "*Surely Thou knowest what we desire* [11:79]. O Lord! You are the tongue of the tongueless. You are the knower of the secrets and the hidden. You Yourself know what we want."

We have a reckoning other than that of the worldlings,
we have an intoxicant other than wine.

The Exalted Lord took them to the top of the lane of trial and showed them its deserts and perils. That one kind became a thousand kinds, and they all turned away from the kiblah of trial, saying, "This is not our work. We do not have the capacity to carry this burden." One group, however, did not turn away and, like the passionate, entered the lane of trial. They did not think of trial or suffering. They said, "It is enough good fortune for us that we carry grief for You and that we suffer the sorrow of Your trial."

> Who am I to put on the cloak of loyalty to You,
>   or to have my eyes carry the burden of Your disloyalty?
> But if You issue the decree to my body, heart, and spirit,
>   I will pull all three dancing into Your love.

Only those who recognize Him know the measure of pain for Him. If someone does not recognize Him, how will he know the measure?

The Pir of the Tariqah said, "O God, in my pain I lament in fear that the pain will cease. Anyone who laments at the Friend's blows is unmanly in love for the Friend."

O chevalier, if you have the capacity and gall for this work, then set out on the road! Drink the wine of trial and call the Friend to witness. Otherwise, enjoy your well-being and stop talking. No one ever sacrificed himself by faintheartedness or distinguished himself by leaning on water and clay. You can't be a pearl diver when you fear for your life, and you can't distinguish yourself by leaning on water and clay. Either take no heed of life or don't tangle with yourself.

(*Kashf* 8:30–31)

Like many others, Samʿānī finds an allusion to the origin of trial, balāʾ, in the Covenant of Alast, when all the children of Adam responded with the word *balā*, "*Yes indeed.*" Though written in slightly different ways, the two words are pronounced the same in Persian. In one of his retellings of the story, Samʿānī contrasts God's question on the Day of Alast, "*Am I not your Lord?*" with a question He will ask on the Day of Resurrection. To the first question, the servants answered in the affirmative, thereby asserting their own realities, a prelude, as it were, to their entrance into the realm of being. On the Day of Resurrection, God will ask, "*Whose is the kingdom today?*" but the servants will remain silent, for their sojourn in this world will be over and they will see that they were passing shadows, with no reality of their own. Hence, God answers His own question: "*God's, the One, the Severe*" (40:16).

When your Lord took from the children of Adam [7:172]. The pearl diver of power was sent into the ocean of Adam's loins to bring out the night-brightening jewels and night-hued beads and to place them on the shore of existence—Pharaoh and Moses, Abraham and Nimrod, firm Muṣṭafā and accursed Abū Jahl. Just as He brought forth the friends, so also He brought forth the enemies. He offered them the drink of the Lord's address, and they all took it with the hand of *Yes indeed.* They drank it down and put the ring of servanthood on their ears. By answering the address of the Lord of lords, they appeared.

Then, at last, there will come the address of majesty, "*Whose is the kingdom today?*" No one will say a word. At the beginning, there was talk upon talk, but at the end there will be silence upon silence. Yes, beginners have a tongue and a talk, but enders have neither tongue nor talk.

At first, they were under the sway of the Shariah. The policeman of the Shariah was behind them, and the Shariah is an affirmation of man. Hence, they appeared with *Yes indeed.* But at last, they will be in the garb of the Haqiqah. The Haqiqah is the negation of man. Hence, they will not speak.

O dervish! You can buy a nightingale, which calls out night and day, for one dirham. But a falcon, which does not call out once in its lifetime, costs a thousand dinars.

At first they were in the road of sobriety and being, so they answered God's address. At last they will be in the road of effacement and nonbeing, so He, in the perfection of His gentleness, will make Himself their deputy. He will say, "*God's, the One, the Severe.*"

This is an exalted secret. If at first He Himself had answered the address and said "*Yes indeed,*" then all the blights would have been lifted from the road. In this world there would be neither synagogue nor church, neither cross nor crucifix. But this world is the house of blights, and the next world is the house without blights. Blights cannot be avoided here, but they cannot happen there.

The first address was the policeman of this world's road, and the last address will be the policeman of the next world's road. Anyone who finds life in this world finds it by virtue of the first address, "*Am I not your Lord?*" Anyone who finds subsistence in the next world will find it by virtue of the last address, "*Whose is the kingdom today?*"

Know that, in reality, if He had answered the first address, this world would never undergo annihilation. And if you were to answer the last address, the next world would never have subsistence. It is the blow of your answer that has come over this world and made it susceptible to annihilation. It is the ray of His answer's robe that will shine on the next world and give it the attribute of subsistence.

O chevalier! Know that in reality the Covenant was made with you on that day to see who would stick to it. Strive from the depths of your spirit not to lose the ring that you put on your own ear with your attestation on the day of the Covenant of Alast. Otherwise you will be hung by trial's snare.

Breaking off from the curly earlocks of the black-moled Beloved and then, in the end, breaking the Covenant—these are not the marks of manliness. If they cut off your head, if they bring out the two worlds against you, if they place the dagger of antagonism on the throat of your present moment—still, you must be solitary, you must be a man.

Be the man whose feet are on the ground
and whose head aspires to the Pleiades!

On the day of *Am I not your Lord?* a table of love was set up. By the decree of gentleness, they sat you down at the table and gave you a lawful morsel from the covenant of the lordly majesty. With the hand of *Yes indeed,* you placed that morsel in love's mouth. There is no morsel more appetizing than the morsel of tawḥīd in the mouth of love.

Beware! Beware! Do not throw away this morsel with the casting of dislike. If you do, you will remain forever in the trial [balā'] of your *Yes indeed* [balā]. (*Rawḥ* 153–54)

Another hint at the nature of love can be found in the spelling of the Arabic words for love (maḥabba) and tribulation (*miḥna*). In the normal, unvoweled Arabic script, the only difference between the two words is the placement of a single dot. Samʿānī finds the following allusion:

O dervish! When the phoenix of love flew from the nest of the Unseen, it reached the Throne and saw tremendousness, it reached the Footstool and saw embracingness, it reached heaven and saw elevation, it reached paradise and saw beneficence, it reached hell and saw punishment, it reached the angels and saw worship, it reached Adam and saw tribulation. It settled down with him. They said to it, "Why is it that you have settled down with Adam?"

It said, "The two of us have meanings, secrets, and realities that are compatible, though we have been differentiated by one dot. The outward man looks at the dot of form in order to differentiate, but the realizing man lifts his eyes from the dot and makes his spirit busy with the work of meaning." (*Rawḥ* 221)

As the first to carry the Trust, Adam was the first to suffer trial. His story illustrates the principle voiced by Samʿānī in a passage already quoted: "At first love is all benevolence, and at last it is all severity" (*Rawḥ* 361). Here are some of Samʿānī's explanations of why Adam had to leave paradise.

At the beginning, Adam was clothed in the robe of generosity and placed on the chair of majesty. The angels had to prostrate themselves before him, and the edict was written for the celebration of his vicegerency. In the second state, the address came: *"Fall down!"* [2:36].

The same angels who had prostrated themselves before his chair put their hands on his back, just as when someone is evicted and ejected from a house. Adam was biting the fingers of wonder with the teeth of bewilderment: "What is this? What happened?"

Unconditional love was saying, "O passionate man, seek, and have no fear!"

(*Rawḥ* 139)

This talk wants a ruined corner and a burnt heart. If you need a flourishing world, no place was more thoroughly set up than paradise. Mecca was a flourishing site, and Medina a ruins.

Paradise was the site of enjoyment, and this world is the site of anxiety and sorrow. At first, Adam's business was getting along with exaltation, joy, and whispered secrets. After a while, the dust of misfortune settled on his crown. He took a glance by way of passion at destitution's beauty and became entranced by it. Whatever joinings and bonds there were, he tossed them away. Like the disengaged, he came into the road of destitution.

This talk wants a burnt liver—someone who has lived seventy years without one thing turning out according to his desire, who has shot a thousand thousand arrows without one reaching the target, who has lived happily in the midst without obtaining one sought object while acknowledging a thousand thousand obligations.

(609)

What a marvelous business! God fastened a hundred thousand ornaments and fineries on Adam and then commanded the angels to prostrate themselves before his throne. This is a secret worth a thousand holy spirits.

As for you, He said, "Perform the prayer!" and then He turned your prayer over to a stone: "So that you may know that I have no needs."

He commanded the angels to prostrate themselves, then He turned their prostration over to dust: "So that they may know that I have no needs."

"O Adamites! Turn your faces toward a stone. O angels! Turn your faces toward dust."

The prostration of the angels was a trial, and turning your face toward a stone is a test. They were tried by a handful of dust, and you are tested by a stone: "I showed you the worth of your faces when I said, '*Turn your faces towards it*' [2:144]. Turn your faces toward a stone, for stones are suited for clods of earth, and clods are suited for stones. I placed the worth of your blood in your hands when I said, 'Go to war so that the unbelievers may shed your blood!'"

The point here is the first statement—that Adam's makeup was adorned with a hundred thousand ornaments and the garden of his loveliness and beauty was pruned. Love, which was the original bosom friend, drinking from the same cup and goblet, looked on from afar. The tree to which Adam stretched out his hand was named the tree of love. The love kneaded into Adam took his reins and pulled him straight to the tree.

> I said to her, my eyelids wounded,
>   wounded by their flowing tears,
> "No one is like me in rapture."
>   "So," she said, "you see me as having a likeness?"

"O sorrow of Jacob! Take the path of beauty, for Joseph's beauty is perfect beauty." At every moment Jacob's sorrow was increasing, at every instant Joseph's beauty advancing.

The tree of love was a stranger in paradise, and at the beginning of the era, Adam was also a stranger in paradise. "And every stranger is a kinsman to the stranger." The stranger fell back on the stranger. They took one hot breath. The heat of their love's fire burned the eight paradises. Now what could be done? They had to wrap their arms around each other's necks and turn their faces to the abode of the tested.

Adam was brought into the world of tribulation. Tribulation's rain, which is commands and prohibitions, poured down on his head from the cloud of the Law's prescription. Lowliness and tribulation make someone into a beggar. If he should pass up two pieces of bread, at night he will come home and turn the house upside down. There are many houses whose décor is nothing but hunger, the carpets of pennilessness spread, the curtains of hunger hung down, the cushions of lowliness put in place.

In the whole world there was no chamber more adorned than the chamber of God's messenger Muḥammad. The Splendorous Throne wanted to become that chamber's bed. The brocade, silk, and satin of paradise wanted to be its carpet. But it already had a bed of poverty, a cushion of hunger, a seat of want. Nonetheless, the Faithful Spirit was holding the banner at the door.

One night Muṣṭafā sent that piece of his own liver, Fāṭimat al-Zahrā, to the house of her husband. When they took a woman to her husband's house, the custom was to bring along a container for a fiber-filled pillow, a hand mill, and a rug. The people said, "These two dear ones will be sleeping with each other. They need a bed and a couch."

Muṣṭafā said, "Go out into the open and bring back some sand."

The house was low, its carpet threadbare. What was the robe of the folk of the house? *God desires only to put filth away from you, O folk of the house!* [33:33]. Peace!

(600–601)

The great ones have said, "A man does not find the sweetness of faith until trial comes to him from every direction."

> The passionate man has nothing
> in his spirit but suffering.
> When he finds the scent of his beloved,
> the spheres can no longer string his bow.

The first passionate man to write the ABCs of passion in the grammar school of existence was Adam. Look at what happened to him! No kindness was done to him with that grain of wheat. From the sheath of the Eternal Desire, they drew the sword of *Adam disobeyed* [20:121] and filled the cup of severity with the drink of poison. That same man who had been striking fire into the monasteries of the obedient with the brilliance of his lightning turned his face to this ruined tavern. He heard the call, *"Fall down out of it, all of you"* [2:38].

> Yesterday that man was talking fine points and abstruse words
> and today he has pawned his cloak in the tavern.
> Now that he has pawned his cloak,
> he had better forget the fine points and abstruse words.

O dervish! When a man is a gambler and tavern goer, the awards of sultans and the bestowals of kings have no luster. When he receives a gift, he takes it to the tavern and gambles it away. But since the sultan loves this tavern-going man, the more he goes to the tavern, the more he bestows robes of honor on him.

Adam the Chosen stepped into the place of slipping and received as wage the chamber of *Adam disobeyed.* But by virtue of the beginningless solicitude, the King gave him goblets of chosen-ness one after another and hamstrung the envy of the enviers.

O friend! If the sultan's award bestows luster, it does so for a perfectly judicious possessor of resoluteness. But the shawl of resoluteness was snatched away from the shoulders of that center-point of dust's existence, for *he forgot, and We found in him no resoluteness* [20:115].

Why do you look at the repentance of the judicious possessor of resoluteness? Look rather at the fact that the sultan gave him a robe of honor once in his life, but this cheerful, ineffectual fellow receives an uninterrupted bestowal of gentleness moment by moment.

O exalted Gabriel, O peacock of the angels! It is now several thousand years that you have been moving the pieces of resoluteness on the chessboard of obedience to the extent of your ability, but in your lifetime you have been given only one robe of honor. The work is done by this carefree scoundrel. With the needle of endless bounty, the tailor of beginningless gentleness sewed his cape of exaltedness in the measure of his worth and the stature of His blessings, for *He loves them, and they love Him* [5:54]. *God is the friend of those who have faith* [2:257].

The Splendorous Throne was given one robe of honor: *Then He sat on the Throne* [7:54]. The elevated heaven was sent one award, and that was the award of descent—though similarity and likeness are far from the road. Mount Sinai was given one drink with the hand of passion, and that was the drink of self-disclosure. The other existent things were all like this. Those who received robes of honor acknowledging their dignity kept the robes. When this impudent handful of dust was sent a robe, he took it down to the tavern of mortal nature and gambled it away for the dregs of pain and the wine from passion's cask.

Drinking dregs in the tavern is my habit,
  being ruined by drunkenness my creed,
The largest cup was made for me—
  not finding my desires is my good fortune.

(149–50)

THE TRIBULATION OF THE PROPHETS

According to Islamic theology, God protected all 124,000 prophets from sin. They led lives in complete obedience to God's command and guided their followers to the path of salvation. Beginning with Adam, they were as perfect as it is humanly possible to be. Some, especially those enamored of prosperity theology, might think that such good servants would have an easy time of it and that God would make life difficult for the sinners. In the religion of love, the opposite is true. The more perfect someone may be, the more he or she will suffer. The prophets suffered more than the faithful, and the faithful more than the unbelievers. The Gospel points in the same direction, as does the time-honored notion of taking up one's cross and following Jesus.

God tests people in the measure of their capacity. The prophets, as the greatest human beings, have the greatest capacity. All prophets are God's beloveds, which is to say that all of them are His lovers. So He tests them. As for the faithful, *they love God more intensely* (2:165) than the unbelievers, so they must suffer because of their love. Those who have no love in their hearts will have a relatively easy time of it, in this world at least, for there is no need to test their faith. Concerning the prophets as the role models for lovers, Samʿānī says,

> Yes, come into this path and see the remorse of Adam, hear the cries of Noah, see the disappointment of Abraham, hear the talk of Jacob's affliction, see the moonlike Joseph's well and prison, observe the saw on Zachariah's head and the blade on John's neck, and see the burnt liver and roasted heart of Muḥammad. A wound this severe, a love this sharp—the Beloved disdainful and inaccessible! Each moment He is more unneedy and more jealous of His own majesty and beauty. The more docile His burnt ones, the more refractory He is. The more abased His lovers, the more He kills them. The more tamed His yearning seekers, the more He thirsts for their blood.
>
> (*Rawḥ* 58)

When the wage-earning faithful follow the Shariah and seek the promised reward of paradise, God has mercy on them and eventually gives them what they want. Their seeking, however, is based on love for their own benefit and share (*ḥaẓẓ*). It is no doubt praiseworthy to observe the rules in order to avoid punishment and to win the prize, but this cannot be compared with surrendering to love and throwing away all thought of reward and punishment. According to Samʿānī, Moses provides an example of what happens when love takes over.

> The Prophet said, "I ask You for the Garden, for it is the final goal of the seekers." Beneath this is a subtle secret. The Prophet said that the Garden is the final goal of the seekers. As for those who have no seeking and no fleeing, God said about them, "*Surely the final end is unto thy Lord*" [53:42].
>
> *The lote tree of the final end* [53:14] is the station of one group, and *Surely the final end is unto thy Lord* is the station of another group.
>
> As long as the seeker's destination and goal is bounty and bounteousness, bestowal and gifts, the door of response is open and the sought object is linked to compliance. But when a man passes beyond that station with steps of seriousness, when he raises the banner of aspiration in the world of love, when he gives a place in his heart to yearning and longing for the station of witnessing and contemplation and the rank of unveiling and finding, then he becomes a sick man whom no one visits and a desirer not desired. Whatever he requests, whatever supplication he utters, whatever story he tells, whatever complaint he narrates, he meets the rejection of his seeking and the blockage of his road.

> Have you not heard the story of Moses? He was granted so many of his desires and goals, but when he talked about vision, it was said to him, "*Thou shalt not see Me*" [7:143]. Yes, such is the severity of beloveds, and upon this the work is built.
>
> (*Rawḥ* 349)

The Qur'an talks about the trials and tribulations of the prophets in many verses, and Maybudī frequently advises his readers to deal with their own suffering by following the prophetic examples. The moment people acknowledge their love for God, they have to expect harsh treatment. In commenting on a Qur'anic reference to Job (21:83), Maybudī says,

> When people choose someone for friendship, it is their habit to want every ease for their friend and not to let stormy winds blow over him. The divine custom is contrary to this. Whenever He chooses someone for friendship, He sends the drink of tribulation with the robe of love. When the rank of someone is higher in the station of love, his tribulation is greater. This is why Muṣṭafā said, "Surely the people most severely tried are the prophets, then the friends, then the next best, then the next best."
>
> (*Kashf* 6:294)

Samʿānī often explains that the prophetic tales offer guidance to lovers. This is how he reads the story of Abraham and the star, moon, and sun, Maybudī's commentary on which was quoted in the previous chapter. As part of his explanation, he cites a well-known saying of the Prophet according to which the Prophet and ʿAlī were walking together when a beautiful young woman passed. They glanced at her as she approached and then turned away. ʿAlī, however, took another look. The Prophet told him that the first glance was his to enjoy, but the second counted against him. Samʿānī sees here a universal principle of love. When the beloved shows herself, the vision is yours to enjoy. But when you try to see her, you are seeking your own share, your own pleasure in the vision, and that counts against you. Your share has become the goal in place of the beloved.

> This is one of their sayings: "Love is fire, recognition fire, and this talk fire upon fire." It never happens that something catches fire without tumult and burning.
>
> In my lane, how fine love's tumult and turmoil!
> In Your lane, how fine beauty's business and work!
>
> Know that in reality, as long as fire does not enter the heart, a man will not begin to seek. In the days of Abraham, all the fires were gathered inside

his breast. He was so hot in the road that he saw the goal everywhere he looked: *When night fell upon him he saw a star. He said, "This is my Lord"* [6:76]. He saw the star with the eye of his head, but he saw the Real with the eye of his secret core. Proximity and love's burning fire rushed ahead in his heart's witnessing and overcame the witnessing of his eyes. Abraham said, "*This is my Lord.*" He reported about his heart's vision, not his eyes' vision. Do you not see that when he looked again, he did not see the star? He said, "*I love not those that set*" [6:76].

In this road, a man is allowed one gaze. The first gaze belongs solely to your secret core. All other gazes are your own share and portion, not that of the secret core. "Do not follow your gaze with another gaze, for the first belongs to you, but the second counts against you."

Know that in reality—and these are exalted words—the lover is not seeking his share in the first gaze, but he is seeking it with the second. All the ambushes that appear for someone on the road come when he seeks his own share. This is why it is said, "Nothing will be put aright when you seek your own share."

It has also been said, "When someone loves you for the sake of something, he will hate you when it disappears." This is why it is correct for God to have the reality of love, but not anyone else. For when someone is helpless in his own work, he is seeking his own portion and share. But the Exalted Presence is incomparable with portion and share. *He loves them* came in the Beginningless, when He was pure of all shares. Then, since He was pure, He brought *they love Him* under His own protection. *They love Him* came into existence under the purified protection of the beginningless *He loves them.*

Like Abraham, you must come into the ranks of cutting away attributes. In manliness, you must shout out over the whole realm of being, "*Surely they are an enemy to me*" [26:77]. Then the crown of bosom friendship will be placed on your head, and the robe of love will be draped over your body.

You must draw the line of dismissal across the star of gazing on others, the moon of attention to occasions, and the sun of diverting yourself with causes. Then the stars of love, the moons of recognition, and the suns of limpidness will pitch the tents of their good fortune in the heaven of your heart.

(*Rawḥ* 351)

The Qur'an mentions Moses by name far more than any other prophet, and commentators have noted that this is a sure sign of God's love for him, sometimes citing the hadith, "When someone loves something, he keeps on mentioning it." Maybudī looks at practically every Qur'anic account of Moses as a sign of his love affair with God. In his commentary on the story in which Moses asks God to show Himself to him, he reviews some of the basic stages of love. He begins by reminding his readers that hurry in lovemaking is not good form.

And We promised Moses "thirty nights." Then We completed them with ten. So the promised time of his Lord was forty nights [7:142]. How exalted is making promises in friendship! How great is sitting in the promised place of friendship! How sweet is breaking promises in the religion of friendship!

Concerning the intimations of this verse, the Pir of the Tariqah said, "The promises of lovers, even if broken, show intimacy." Then he said,

"You put me off, You procrastinate,
You promise, but You don't come through."

It is not approved to put off the promised time or to add days before the promised moment except in the religion of friendship, for in friendship disloyalty is the same as loyalty, and disdain the same as friendship. Do you not see what the Lord of the Worlds did with Moses in this exchange? He promised him thirty days. When those passed, He added ten more. He added them because Moses was happy with that. Moses counted the thirty days as capital and the ten days as profit. He said, "Indeed, I heard the hard cash of the Real's speech for a second time when He added that."

In this journey, Moses waited thirty days without remembering food and drink or being aware of hunger, for he was carried by the Real in a journey of generosity, waiting for whispered conversation. The other time, when he was sent to Khiḍr on the first journey in search of knowledge, he did not have the capacity for a half day of hunger, so he said, "*Bring us our food*" [18:62]. This is because that was a journey of teaching and hardship. At the beginning of the traveling, he was carrying; he was not being carried. He was aware of his own suffering, for he was with himself. He saw the marks of hunger because he was in the road of creatures.

And Moses said to his brother Aaron, take my place among my people [7:142]. His intention was whispered conversation with the Real, so he left Aaron with the people and went alone, for there is no sharing in friendship. The friend's attribute in the path of friendship is nothing but aloneness and oneness.

If you're not busy and you're alone,
come to Me in loyalty—you're worthy of Me.

Then, when he was going to Pharaoh, he asked for Aaron's companionship: "*Make him a partner in my affair*" [29:32], for that was going to the creatures, and things having to do with the creatures bring aversion and dread. In carrying the burden of dread, no one flees from a kind companion and his companionship.

When Moses returned from whispered conversation and saw that the Children of Israel had left the circle of obedience and become calf worshipers, he rebuked Aaron, not them, so that you would know that not everyone who sins is deemed worthy of rebuke. Rebuke is appropriate when a person still has something of friendship. He who burns in fear of separation is the one who recognizes the exaltation of union:

> How can passion for the Beloved be suited for just anyone?
> Majnūn alone was worthy of love for Laylā.

When Moses came to Our appointed time [7:143]. Moses had two journeys: one was the journey of seeking, the other the journey of revelry. The journey of seeking was the night of the fire, as in His words, "*He observed a fire on the side of the mountain*" [28:29]. The journey of rejoicing was this one: *When Moses came to Our appointed time.*

Moses came, having become selfless to self, lost to himself in his own secret core. He had drunk the wine of love from the cup of holiness, so the pain of this talk's yearning was pressing into him and the wave of *Show me* was billowing up from the ocean of his passion. He wandered around the neighborhoods of the Children of Israel and gathered the words of their messages and goals so that he could draw out his words when he arrived at the Presence.

> I consider it forbidden to talk with others—
> when I talk to you, I draw out my words.

When he reached the presence of whispered conversation, he was drunk with the wine of yearning and burnt by listening to the Real's Speech. He forgot everything, and the hard cash of his state appeared like this: "*Show me, that I may gaze upon Thee!*" [7:143].

The angels threw the stones of blame at his desire: "O child of menstruating women! Do you hope to see the Exalted Lord? What does dust have to do with the Lord of lords?" How can a being made of dust and water talk to Eternity? How can someone who was not, then was, be worthy of seeking union with Him who always was and always will be?

In drunkenness and selflessness, Moses answered with the tongue of solitariness: "Accept my excuses, for I did not fall here by myself. First He wanted me—I did not want. I saw the Friend at my pillow when I woke up from sleep. I was seeking for fire, and making came forth: *I made you for Myself* [20:41]. I was not aware, and the sun of bringing near rose up—*And We brought him near as a confidant* [19:52].

"From the first You began passion's talk—
now make me worthy of You!"

The command came to the angels, "Leave Moses alone, for when someone drinks the wine of *I made you for Myself* from the cup of *I cast upon you love from Me* [20:39], he will make no less of an uproar than this."

In the realities of those unveilings, Moses tasted the wine of love from the storeroom of gentleness. His heart flew into the air of solitariness, and the breeze of union's intimacy blew on his spirit from the side of nearness. The fire of love shot up in flames, patience fled from his breast, and he lost all restraint. He said, "*Show me, that I may gaze upon Thee:* Please, at least a look!"

If sparks were to shoot from this burnt heart
no trace would remain of the Pleiades' circle.
There's danger when I stand before you, sweetheart—
at least lift separation's veil for a look.

The Pir of the Tariqah said, "Everyone has a hope, and the recognizer's hope is vision. Outside vision, the recognizer has no need for any wage, nor will he have anything to do with paradise. People are all passionate for life, so death for them is difficult. The recognizer wants death in hope of vision. Then his ears may enjoy the listening, the Real's lips will repay the debt of love, his eyes will be adorned with the day of vision, and his spirit will be drunk without giddiness from the wine of finding."

I want a heart for choosing only You,
a spirit for breathing the pain of Your passion,
A body for desiring only Your love,
an eye for seeing You and only You.

He said, "Thou shalt not see Me" [7:143]. They say that at the moment Moses heard "*Thou shalt not see Me,*" his station was higher than at the moment he said, "*Show me so that I may gaze upon Thee.*" At the former moment, he was in what the Real desired, and at the latter moment, he was in what he desired. Moses's being was more complete in what the Real desired than in what he desired, for the latter is dispersion, and the former is togetherness, and inescapably, togetherness is more complete.

He said, "Thou shalt not see Me, but look at the mountain." Moses received the blow of *Thou shalt not see Me.* At once, however, He applied the balm of *but.* He said, "O Moses, I struck the blow of *Thou shalt not see Me* and applied the balm of *but* so that you would know that this was not My severity, but rather an excuse."

Then, when his Lord disclosed Himself to the mountain [7:143]. When a sliver of the signs of majesty and a trace of the exaltedness of unity reached the mountain, it returned to the state of nonexistence and no mark of it remained. He said, "O king! If a black stone had the capacity for this talk, it would have accepted the Trust at the beginning of existence and bought it with spirit and heart." Here there is a subtle point: the mountain, with all its tremendousness, could not endure, but the hearts of the weak and the old women of Muḥammad's community could endure. God says, "*And they feared it, and man carried it*" [33:72].

And Moses fell down thunderstruck [7:143]. When Moses's existence disappeared in that strike and his mortal nature was thrown to the mountain, the self-disclosure fell on the true center-point: "Now, We are. When You disappear from the midst, it is We who are seen."

The Pir of the Tariqah said, "O God, I seek the Found. I say to the Seen, 'What do I have, what do I seek, what do I see, what do I say?' I am entranced by this seeking, I am seized by this speaking.

"O God, the splendor of Your exaltation left no room for allusion, the eternity of Your unity took away the road of ascription—I lost all that I had in hand, and everything I fancied came to naught.

"O God, Yours continued increasing and mine decreasing until at last there remained only what there was at first."

> You said, "Be less and less"—that was good and straight.
> You are Being enough, less and less is fine for Your servant.

When he recovered he said, Glory be to Thee! I repent to Thee! [7:143]. When he came back to his senses, he said, "O Lord, You are far too pure for any mortal to hope to reach Your Sanctum, or for anyone to seek You through himself, or for any heart or spirit to talk today about the vision of You. I repent."

It was said, "O Moses, do people put down the shield all at once the way you have? Do they wander off all at once the way you do? Have you turned back so soon and so easily?" The tongue of Moses's state was saying,

> I desire union with Him, He desires separation—
> I renounce what I desire for His desire.

"What should I do? I did not reach the goal. Well then, let me go back to the place of service and the station of servanthood's incapacity, and let me go to the beginning of the command."

When someone is perplexed in his own work,
he had best go back to the beginning of the thread.

When he went back to the place of service and the station of repentance, the Lord of the Worlds repaired his heart and spoke to him with benevolence: "*O Moses I have chosen you over the people with My messages and My speech*" [7:144].

(*Kashf* 3:730–34)

In his commentary on the verse "*Do the people reckon that they will be left to say, 'We have faith,' and will not be tried?*" (29:2), Maybudī explains again why the prophets and God's friends suffer more than others.

The Prophet said, "Surely the people most severely tried are the prophets, then the friends, then the next best, then the next best." He said also, "When God desires good for a people, He tries them."

The lordly likeness from the Presence of Lordhood is this: "Trial from Our threshold is a robe of honor for the friends. In the station of friendship, whoever seeks a level beyond others will smell more of tribulation's rose in the pleasure garden of the friends."

If you want to know this, then look at the state of the master of Adam's children, the one emulated by the folk of the Shariah, the foremost chieftain of the folk of the Haqiqah. When that paragon walked into this lane, he was not left without heartache and grief for an hour. If he sat cross-legged for a while, the address would come, "Sit like a servant!" If he put a ring on his finger once, the whip of rebuke would come down: "*What, did you reckon that We created you for frivolity?*" [23:115]. If just once he placed his foot boldly on the ground, the command would come, "*Walk not in the earth exultantly!*" [17:37]. If one day he said, "I love 'Ā'isha," he would see what he saw.[1]

When the words of the hypocrites pushed his trial to the extreme, he complained inwardly to God. He was addressed: "O paragon, when someone's heart and spirit witness Me, does he complain of trial?"

All the venom in the storehouses of the Unseen was poured into one cup and put in his hand, and then a curtain was lifted from his secret core. It was said, "O Muḥammad, drink down this venom while contemplating My beauty! *Be patient with thy Lord's decree, for surely thou art in Our eyes* [52:48]."

(*Kashf* 7:375–76)

Kalam experts and jurists, and nowadays political activists of every stripe, have often criticized the path of love as too otherworldly. Premodern scholars who objected to talk of love seemed to fear that Muslims would become impudent toward God and ignore the creed and the Shariah. Modern ideologues and activists, who place politics, reform, and utopian social engineering at the center of Islam, most likely fear that their own empty promises will be recognized for what they are. As Wilfred Cantwell Smith often pointed out, people devote themselves to a fanciful notion of "Christianity" or "Islam" and forget the engagement with God that was the founding impetus of the great revelations.

No doubt passages focusing exclusively on love for God can lead to a sense that these teachers were going overboard. Nonetheless, one needs to keep in mind that love demands observance of both the broad path of the Shariah and the narrow path of the Tariqah. In other words, it is based on the prophetic example: *Follow me; God will love you*. There is no other way to achieve the proximity to God that is the religion's goal. Both the Shariah and the Tariqah call for engagement with everyday life, but always with God as the focus and tawḥīd as the ruling vision. As our authors sometimes point out, the suffering inflicted on the prophets and their followers has a good deal to do with the fact that the path to God calls upon them to turn away from exclusive focus on the Real in order to obey the religious command. The Prophet's saying "There is no monasticism in Islam" was thus interpreted to mean that the discipline of living in the world with detachment is a far more efficacious means of achieving the goal. Here is Samʿānī's explanation of the suffering that is entailed by the necessity of following the religious command to engage with the world.

> It is told that once a king awakened to the path of the religion. The clouds of his grief rained down so many drops of regret on the earth of his face that his eyes went blind. They asked him, "All this effort and striving that you have—what has the Real given you for this struggle?"
>
> He said, "He has given me everything, for He has stripped me of what I desired and replaced it with desire only for what He desires."
>
> Abū Dharr said, "How beloved are the three hated things—illness, poverty, and death!"
>
> They knew that what the Real desires is for them not to reach their desires, so they threw away their desires for the sake of His desire. They said, "Let it all be what He wants, and let none of it be what we want."
>
> The short of it is that the blood of the friends' livers was mixed with the tears of their eyes to make the mortar for the bricks of passion's castle. Then they sent the crier of unneediness to the top of the castle to convey this call to the ears of the passionate: "This is nothing but throwing away the spirit. Otherwise, do not busy yourself with the nonsense of the Sufis."
>
> This is the road of need, not the road of kindness. The first thing He did with Muṣṭafā was to take away his father and mother so that he would not see the kindness of a mother or sit at the feet of a father's tenderness.

"*Surely We shall cast upon thee a heavy word* [73:5]: O Muḥammad, you have come to the cave of Ḥirā and made yourself a place of seclusion, but there is a steep climb ahead. You must go to the door of Abū Jahl, you must be joyful under camel's innards, you must sacrifice your teeth to the stone-hearted, you must strike your face against the blood of your own upright heart. You must take from Us, and you must convey to the people and keep an upright character in the midst. This is a marvelous business for you: companionship with the people, along with disengagement from the people. All of them will be seizing your skirt, but your heart must pay no regard to anyone."

O chevalier! The one who keeps his heart with God without people's companionship is not like him who keeps his heart with God along with people's companionship. He who keeps his heart with God in the mosque is not like him who keeps his heart with God in the bazaar.

It is said that a man of the path went into the desert and hunted a lion. He sat on its back, took a viper in his hand and made it into a whip, and then came back to town. He reached the door of a bakery, and the baker said to him, "Hey, you! What is this business? The work of a man is to sit between the two pans of a scale and make his heart one with God. God loves the strong person of faith."

O dervish! It is a great principle of the road that a person is allowed to open his eyes toward the creatures so long as he does not stop seeing the Real while seeing the creatures. But when someone loses sight of the Real by seeing the creatures, he is not allowed to look at them.

The burden of messengerhood is indeed a heavy burden—passing the days with creatures and being pure of them. Muḥammad came to the cave of Ḥirā without any burdens, his back straight. He returned with his back bent, his body trembling.

When Muḥammad returned from the mountain, he said to Khadīja, "Wrap me up! Wrap me up!" He drew up the blanket and pulled it over his bowed head. At once Gabriel came from the Presence of Majesty and said, "*O thou enwrapped one!* [73:1], *O thou encloaked one!* [74:1]: O you who have pulled your head under the blanket! You cannot be so fragile and delicate in My road."

(*Rawḥ* 112–14)

THE PATH OF FOLLOWING

Love demands following in the Prophet's footsteps. He suffered more than other prophets, so following his path will call down pain and tribulation. At the same time, God is merciful and compassionate: "*We burden no soul save to its capacity*" (23:62). He asks His lovers only for what they have, that is, for what

He has given them. Most people, however, are not willing to hand it over, for they think that it is theirs. Seeing others attracting their love, they give themselves over to them. They offer God little more than lip service, if any service at all. For those who have recognized the truth of tawḥīd, however, the path of love is that of burning away the others, and that hurts. Nonetheless, pain from Him is better than pleasure from anyone else. This is a constant theme, to which Samʿānī refers in the following.

O chevalier! The great ones have said that trial is needed in love like salt in the pot. Any possessor of beauty who does not play the coquette with her passionate lover will not have given beauty its rightful due. By the right of the Real! If tomorrow the address "Gaze upon Me!" should come, you should say, "Your beauty lies far beyond the gaze of my likes!"

O dervish! Had He not taken Adam to task for that grain of wheat, His majesty would not have been diminished. Had He shown His vision to Moses, His beauty would not have suffered loss. But the perfection of beauty demands that a thousand thousand of the passionate wail and moan, captive to the chains of His severity.

Adam was truthful in his passion and conforming in his love. He drank down all the poisonous drafts of disappointment and blows of severity that were given to him. He was saying with the tongue of his state, "If you send me a poisonous draft, I will welcome it with my spirit, and if you strike me with severity's blow, I will bear it in the midst of my heart.

"Don't drive me away, but if You burn me, that's fine.
What I want in all this is Your approval.
"When a heart's worthy of friendship for You,
You can put it in the hottest fire without harming it.

"Don't send me away, but if You do put me on the gallows, that is all right. Don't abandon me, but if You kill me, that is fine, for the good fortune of passion for You is subsistence. The more I drink severity's wine, the more I reap the fruit of awareness in spirit and heart. When I suffer blow after blow from the sword of Your majestic severity, I will find pleasure in life.

"As long as I fail to take passion to its end,
I will not reap the fruit of heart and spirit."

When someone dies in passion—so, let him die.
There's no good in passion without death.

"He who has passion, stays chaste, conceals, and dies, dies a martyr."

O dervish, if your head starts to ache some night, serve that ache with head and eyes, for a headache that He gives is not trivial.

It is said that revelation was sent to Ezra: "O Ezra, if I give you an apricot, then thank Me for the apricot. Do not look at the apricot's insignificance. Look at the fact that on the day when I was dividing up provisions, I remembered you."

My heart's name, O pretty one, is in Your book.
  I am happy that in any case I am part of Your army.
I am obedient, in short, to Your every command—
  all my bags are on Your donkey.

What is this talk? "A pain without remedy, a night without dawn, an ocean without shore, an illness without cure, a wound without physician, a trial without healing." *And that He may try the faithful with a beautiful trial* [8:17]. He sends a trial, and then He says: "Here's a beautiful trial for you." The trial is beautiful because it is from Him, and the trial is pleasant because He is in it.

At first love appears as need
  but when events drive
The young man into passion's path,
  things happen that old men can't bear.

On the day they spread love's carpet and set up passion's banner in the world of yearning, they set fire to all objects of desire. They scattered the seeds of not reaching desires in the ground of the hearts and drenched it with the water of remorse and the flood of bewilderment.

(*Rawḥ* 140–41)

In another passage about God's severity and the lovers' pain, Samʿānī reminds his readers of the saving power of mercy, which, after all, is always present.

Here there is an exalted secret: when a dervish claims love for the sultan, that becomes nothing but tribulation for him. But if the sultan begins with his own generosity and caresses the dervish with his own love, tribulation becomes nothing but ease for him.

It is He who began the talk of love: "*He loves them.* O dervishes! I love you. Even if you do not reach the pavilions of My exaltedness on the carcass of your own misfortune, you will reach Me on the welcoming Burāq of My unqualified love."

O dervish, in love you must have seeing and listening. Seeing is the heart's food, and listening the spirit's share. In this world, eyes have no seeing—it is the heart that sees. The spirit has listening, the heart seeing. At the beginning of the work, they gave the spirit one cup of listening to the words *"Am I not your Lord?"* Its head is still spinning from that cup's intoxication, for no one can give reports or marks of it. But the heart, from the moment it came into existence, has been receiving cup after cup of wine without cease—three hundred sixty cups every day. The cups are never emptied, nor is the thirst ever quenched.

(*Rawḥ* 599)

Samʿānī makes a similar point after mentioning two hadiths citing God's words concerning the weak and helpless. They have nothing with which to approach Him, so what can He do but approach them?

"I am with those whose hearts are broken for Me." "I am the sitting companion of those who remember Me."

He is saying, "We will never combine two things in you: burnt-heartedness and separation. When the poor, helpless lover is weak and emaciated, broken and wounded by the arrow of love, and when the Beloved is beautiful and tender, the lover does not have the capital to go to the Beloved's court. What can He do but trample the coquetry of beauty underfoot and come forth in compassion to the corner of the lover's sorrows?"

(*Rawḥ* 335–36)

Maybudī summarizes the affliction visited on the lovers in his commentary on the verse *"God is the friend of those who have faith"* (2:257).

The equal of this verse is where He says, *"That is because God is the protector of those who have faith, and the unbelievers have no protector"* [47:11]. He is the friend and caretaker of the faithful, not only in this world, but also in the next, as He says: *"We are your friends in this life and the next"* [41:31].

In the story of Joseph, He quotes his words *"Thou art my friend in this world and the next"* [12:101]. There is a great difference between these two verses—*We are your friends* and *Thou art my friend*—though anyone who does not have the eyes to see is excused.

We are your friends comes from togetherness itself, but *Thou art my friend* alludes to dispersion. This is not because the friend is superior to the prophet, for the end of the friend's work is but the beginning of the prophet's work. But the weak are shown greater benevolence, and the incapable are given more caresses, for they are not so bold as to claim familiarity. They see themselves as tainted, so they do not have the tongue to speak. Whoever is more helpless is closer to the Friend. Whoever is more broken is more worthy of love: "I am with those whose hearts are broken for Me."

It has been reported that on the Day of Resurrection, one of the broken and burnt will be taken to the Presence. God will say, "My servant, what do you have?"

He will say, "Two empty hands, a heart full of pain, and a spirit troubled and bewildered in the waves of grief and sorrow."

He will say, "Go straight ahead to the house of My friends, for I love the broken and grieving. 'The sinner's sobs are more beloved to Me than the glorifier's murmur.' "

I said, "What can I offer Your tresses
if You come close to Your servant?
I'll offer this miserable burnt liver—
burnt liver has a use for musk."

David said, "O God, I take it that I must wash my limbs with water so that they may be purified of defilement. With what shall I wash my heart so that it may be purified of other than You?"

The command came, "O David! Wash the heart with the water of regret and grief so that you may reach the greatest purification."

He said, "O God, where can I find this grief?"

He said, "We Ourselves will send the grief. The stipulation is that you bind yourself to the grieving and the broken."

He said, "O God, what is their mark?"

He said, "They wait all day for the sun to go down, then they pull down the curtain of night and begin to knock at the door of the isolated cell of *We are nearer* [50:16]. Burning, weeping, and sighing all night long, needy and melting, their heads on the ground, they call on Us with longing voice: 'O Lord, O Lord!' With the tongue of their state, they say,

"Let the night of separation pull the bow,
let the day shoot its arrow like Ārash.
On the night I am happy with You, O idol,
you would say that night has put its foot into the fire."

From the world's Compeller comes the call, "O Gabriel and Michael! Leave aside the murmur of glorification, for here comes the sound of someone burning. Though he has the burden of disobedience, he has the tree of faith in his heart. He was kneaded with the water and clay of love for Me.

"The proximate angels, from the day they came into existence until the Day of Resurrection, have kept their hands on the belt of serving Me. They place My commandment on their eyes and burn in hope for one glance.

Then they put the fingers of longing in the mouth of bewilderment—'What is this? We do the service, but the love goes there. We run and rush, but arrival and seeing are theirs!'"

The Exalted Unity answers them in the attribute of predetermination: "The work is done by burning and grief. They are the source of burning and the quarry of grief."

> Without perfect, burning pain, don't mention religion's name.
> Without the beauty of yearning for union, don't lean on faith.
> To the Beloved's spirit-catching, curling tresses on the day of union
> sacrifice only your wretched, bleeding heart!

(*Kashf* 1:709–11)

LIFE IN DEATH

Those who embrace the life of love reject the illusion of everyday life, the seemingly normal state of indifference to the Real. They put aside their aspirations for things and seek that which has no thingness. Not only do they abandon all the busyness and diversion that keep people entranced with families, friends, surroundings, and society, but they also abandon all hope for paradise and fear of hell. From the standpoint of those immersed in this world, embracing love is embracing death.

It was noted that death can be understood in two basic ways: physical death and death of the soul's desires. As often as not, the second sort of death is described as being slain by the Beloved. Lovers bare their necks and let the sword of *No god* lop off their heads, becoming martyrs to tawḥīd. Even books on profane love devote a good portion of their anecdotes and poetry to the martyrs of love—literally, the "witnesses" (*shahīd*), those who died in the sorrow of separation. Often they cite the hadith "He who has passion, stays chaste, conceals the secret, and dies, dies a martyr." In *Theory of Profane Love,* Giffen devotes half her analysis of theoretical issues to martyrdom. The word *witness* is not used in the sense of *martyr* in the Qur'an, but later authors connected the notion of martyrdom with verses declaring that those who are slain in the path of God are not dead, but alive with their Lord.

Maybudī frequently talks about lovers being slain in the path of love. Their shariah, he tells us, is different from the shariah of those who simply obey the Law. "In the outward shariah, all is gentleness, benevolence, blessing, and caressing. In love's shariah, all is severity, harshness, killing, and spilling blood" (*Kashf* 9:269, on verse 49:10).

In Islamic law, the punishment for unjust killing is retaliation. One of the several verses that refer to retaliation cites the Torah but also suggests that it would be better if people forgave those who trespassed against them: "*Therein We wrote for them, 'A life for a life, a nose for a nose, an ear for an ear, a tooth for a tooth, and retaliation for wounds,' but whosoever forgoes it as charity, that shall be an expiation for him*" (5:45). In the case of killing, the Shariah allows the payment of wergild (*diya*) to the relatives of the slain person. As for the Tariqah, it maintains that the wergild of a lover slain by the Beloved is subsistence in the One Being. Hence, a divine saying is sometimes quoted: "When someone loves Me, I kill him, and when I kill him, I am his wergild." As can be seen from Maybudī's citations of the saying, it probably goes back to Shiblī.

In the Qur'anic version of the story of the Golden Calf (compare Exodus 32:26–28), Moses says, "*My people, you have wronged your souls by taking the Calf. Now repent to your Creator and kill your souls. That is better for you with your Creator*" (2:54). In Stage Two of his commentary, Maybudī explains that Moses, at God's instruction, commanded those who had not worshiped the Calf to execute those who had. When he became deeply sorrowful at all the killing, God revealed to him, "Will you not be content that I am going to place both the killed and the killers in the Garden?" In Stage Three, Maybudī takes the verse as an allusion to the struggle against the commanding soul.

> *Kill your souls.* By way of the inner sense, this is addressed to the chevaliers of the Tariqah: "Cut off the heads of your souls with the sword of struggle so that you may reach Me. *Those who struggle in Us, We shall guide them on Our paths* [29:69]."
>
> Be careful not to say that killing the soul by way of struggle is easier than the killing that happened among the Children of Israel. Their killing was only once, and after that, everything was ease and repose. But these chevaliers have a killing at every hour and every moment.
>
> He who dies and reaches ease is not dead—
> the truly dead is dead among the living.
>
> What is strange is that the more they see the blows of trial's sickle, the more their passion increases day by day. Like a moth with the candle, every day they are more troubled by their trouble.
>
> You are my heart's light, though You pair me with fire,
> my head's crown, though You keep me in dust,
> As dear as the eye, though You keep me lowly—
> You make me happy, though You keep me mourning.

It is as if every hour the postman of the Presence sends a message of inspiration from the Court of Exaltation to the spirit of these dear ones: "O chevaliers, the beginning of this work is killing, and the end is joy. The outwardness of friendship is peril, and its inwardness mystery. 'When someone loves Me, I kill him, and when I kill him, I am his wergild.' "

(*Kashf* 1:197–98)

O you who have faith! Written for you is retaliation in the case of the slain [2:178]. He is addressing the body, heart, and spirit and saying, "O totality of the servant! If you want to step into the lane of friendship, first detach your heart from life and toss away everything you know about states and acts, for in the shariah of friendship, your life will be taken as retaliation, and everything you know will be the wergild, though more is needed. Such is the shariah of friendship. If you are the man for the work, enter! Otherwise, nothing will get done with self-love and defilement."

In the tracks of manliness, plane trees live long,
  in the tracks of defilement, jasmine goes fast.
Throw away your life, travel the road, live upright, and be a man!
  Then you will subsist—when you empty your skirt of these ruins.

Yes, it is a marvelous work, the work of friendship! It is a wonderful shariah, the shariah of friendship! Whenever someone is killed in the world, retaliation or wergild is mandatory against the killer. In the shariah of friendship, both retaliation and wergild are mandatory for the person killed.

The Pir of the Tariqah said, "How should I have known that there is retaliation for those killed by friendship? But when I looked, that was Your transaction with the elect. How should I have known that friendship is sheer resurrection and that those killed by friendship should ask for wergild? Glory be to God! What work is this, what work!? He burns some people, He kills some people, and no one burned has regrets, no one killed turns away."

How You kill us and how we love You!
  O marvel! How we love the killer!

May my eyes' light be the dust beneath Your feet!
  May my heart's rest be Your curly locks!
In passion for You, may Your cruelties be my justice!
  May my life be sacrificed in grief for You!

One person is burnt and left unsettled, another slain and perplexed in the field of solitariness. One is hanging on reports, another mixed with face-to-face vision. Who planted these seeds? Who stirred up this tumult? One is in a whirlpool, another wishing for water, but the drowned is not sated, the thirsty has no sleep.

(1:479–80)

The Pir of the Tariqah said, "Alas, the Friend who continues stirring up the dust of trial! Water is pouring from the springhead of my eyes! He is a fire who burns the spirit and heart, a teacher who teaches nothing but trial and iniquity. His hands are always bloody from killing the passionate, for His chamber is not found in the lane of safety. Wherever He takes up residence, He wants the spirit as repast. Safety is lost in trial, leisure in preoccupation."

(8:328–29, on verse 38:1)

And in the path of God fight those who fight against you, but do not transgress. God loves not the transgressors [2:190]. In the language of the recognizers and the path of the chevaliers, this killing and fighting is another way station of the travelers and another state of the lovers. As long as you have not been killed by the sword of struggle in the path of the Shariah and burned by the fire of love, you will not be allowed to enter by this gate.

Be careful not to believe that fire is simply the lamp that you know and nothing more; or that killing is simply the state that you know. Those killed by the Real are one thing, those killed by the throat something else. Being burned by the fire of punishment is one thing, being burned by the fire of love something else.

That great pir said, "How should I have known that this is the smoke of the burning brand's fire? I thought that wherever there is fire, there is a lamp. How should I have known that in friendship the sin belongs to the killed and that the judge gives refuge to the adversary!? How should I have known that the bewilderment of union with You is the path and that those drowned in You seek You all the more?"

One day Shiblī went into the desert. He saw forty men, distracted, impassioned, and overcome by this talk. Each of them had gone into the desert, a brick under his head, his life having reached the gullet. The tenderness of affinity appeared in Shiblī's breast, and he said, "O God, what do You want from them? You have placed the burden of pain on their hearts, You have struck fire in their haystacks. Will You now kill them all with the sword of jealousy?"

His secret core was addressed with the words, "I will kill them. Once I kill them, I will pay them the wergild."

Shiblī said, "What is their wergild?"

The address came, "When someone is killed by the sword of My majesty, his wergild is the vision of My beauty."

I will fight against Your passion's army
and be killed—someone killed has value.
The wergild of those killed by hand is dinars,
the wergild of those killed by passion is seeing.

(1:520–21)

Let there be one nation of you, calling to the good [3:104]. This is the description of a people who stand through the Real's making them stand and who have been freed from their own power and strength and disengaged from their own desires and aims. They are outside the circle of works and states, free of the captivity of choice and self-determination. They know God, they call upon God, and they strive in God's religion. They do not think about people or their blame. In their hearts, they have friendship for the Protector, and in their eyes, the collyrium of Self-disclosure. They see everything just as it is. Others look from the artisanry to the Artisan, but they look from the Artisan to the artisanry. They are the elect of the Presence, branded by the Empire.

Be the elect servant of the king—with his brand
you are safe from police by day and patrols by night.

They are the ones burnt by union and killed by love. Their blood has been spilled and their property destroyed, but their hearts are in His grasp, their spirits in His embrace. This is why they say,

You have a Heart-taker better than life.
Don't grieve—let go of life.

(2:240–41)

Samʿānī reminds his readers that true life is found in death at the beginning of his commentary on the divine name *muqīt*, the Nourisher.

Every creature has a nourishment from which it takes its strength. If you take that nourishment away, it perishes. Outwardness has a nourishment and inwardness has a nourishment, bodies have a nourishment and spirits have a nourishment, frames have a nourishment and hearts have a nourishment. *Each people now knew their drinking place* [2:60].

The nourishment of the hearts is the remembrance of Him who makes hearts fluctuate. *Surely hearts are at peace in the remembrance of God* [13:28].

What a wonder that anyone is given access to the Exalted Threshold! "When someone remembers Me in himself" then "I remember him in Myself"* puts down its bags in this alienated dustbin, which is annihilation within annihilation.

Nonetheless, it is impossible to treat stupidity. When someone goes mad, he can be brought back to the road with treatment. But when someone becomes a fool, there is no way to cure him. "I treated the blind and the leprous, and they all became well, but treating the stupid has thwarted me."

Kick the forms and the created things in the head and set up the tent of aspiration on top of the spheres! "All game is in the belly of the onager!"

Aim for the world of divinity! What sort of world? A world the throne of whose majesty tramples down everything, and the carpet of whose perfection was not woven by the spheres! "Tawḥīd belongs to the Real, and the creatures are intruders."

Today in extreme ignorance and with unworthy eyes, you see the rose bouquet of good fortune tied to the thorns of tribulation, for the jewel is beneath the road's dust, and your moon-faced Joseph at the bottom of the well. A day will come when this curtain of delusion will be thrown aside and the prince will be taken from the dog keeper and delivered from his hands. That is why the Prophet said, "The first gift of the faithful is death." "People are asleep, and when they die, they wake up."

How can a donkey know the worth of Jesus?
How can the deaf know the voice of David?

Leave the straw for the donkeys and the bones for the dogs and step forth into the world of eternity. Detach your heart completely from all others. *Devote yourself to Him devoutly* [73:8]. Let nothing remain of the others, great or small, until you are given access to this dome of proximity: "I have a moment with God embraced by no proximate angel or sent prophet."*

(*Rawḥ* 347–48)

In another passage, Samʿānī reminds us that we are mere pawns in the game of love. God loves us because He loves Himself. He created us with love, and love does the work.

"A hundred thousand were standing and supplicating, but no one paid attention to their supplication. To you, I say, 'I bestowed on you before you asked from Me, I responded to you before you called on Me, and I forgave you before you asked Me to forgive you.'"

When someone dwells in the majestic neighborhood of *No god but God*, no harm will come to him. "If I did not welcome you in the Beginningless, who would have looked at you? Like Jonah, go down so as not to see yourself. Like Muḥammad, go up so that when you see yourself, you will see in God.

"The surface of the earth obeys you, and its stomach is full of forgiveness for you. The seven heavens are the dome of your proximity, and the eight paradises are where you will put down the saddlebags of your journey. Do you suppose that on the night of the miʿrāj the Messenger went to *two bows' length* alone, without Me? No, I was always with him."

If we were worthy enough for the Real to speak to us in the Beginningless, at the beginning of the work and without intermediary, why will we not be worthy for the Messenger to take us along with him on the night of the miʿrāj? It is because of the exaltedness of your movement and rest that He did not overlook any movement and rest of yours. For each, He wrote down rejection or acceptance, reward or punishment, approval or anger. After all, the moon and the sun move in their spheres, but no one talks about them.

O chevalier! When someone loves someone, whatever he does for that person he does for himself.

"If I bestow by My own bounty, I will water the tree of friendship. If you look at heaven, it is your province. If you look at earth, it is your empire. If you look at the Throne, it has your name on it."

What is this? "In the Beginningless, I spoke words for your sake. I will finish them. On your part a supposition, on My part a world. On your part a step, on My part a universe. Though you have no power, 'I am with My servant's thoughts of Me.'* Though you have no strength to come forward, *He is with you wherever you are* [57:4]. Turn your face to the world and put aside the sword. I Myself will guard your back."

"With whom should I tangle?"

"Tangle with Iblis, for I kept him alive so that he would be killed at your hand. I will destroy the enemies at your hand until I remain, and you. Then I will kill you so that I alone remain. You will be a witness, martyred to your own beautiful Witness."

(*Rawḥ* 549–50)

THE MOTHER OF JOY

People who think about love in romantic terms may chalk up all this talk of death to some defect in the Islamic worldview. If one looks at Western literature, however, the association between love and death, *amor* and *mort*, has a long history, and so it must. To love someone unconditionally is to die to oneself.

As for the stress on pain, this is a matter of common experience. When lovers are apart, they suffer the sweet sorrow of separation. Love cannot be dissociated from either separation or union. Without separation's pain, there can never be union's joy. Maybudī often quotes Anṣārī to make the point, as in these passages:

> The Pir of the Tariqah said, "When it pleases Him to take a servant into His friendship and make him worthy for the Presence of Solicitude, first He places the burden of trial on him so that he will be tamed by its blows. Then the servant feeds on the reality of contentment. After that, he becomes such that he himself falls passionately in love with trial."
>
> (*Kashf* 4:382, on verse 11:25)

> The Pir of the Tariqah said something appropriate to this place: "O Lord, I have a heart full of pain and a spirit full of suffering. Exalted of the two worlds! What can this poor wretch do? O Lord, I am not helpless because of You, but helpless in You. Whenever I am absent, You say, 'Where are you?' But when I come to the Threshold, You do not open the door!
>
> "O Lord, in the outward submission, despair is deprivation, and in the Haqiqah itself, hope is no doubt a deficiency. What then is my remedy between this and that? In the Shariah, patience is a mark of being pleased, but in the Haqiqah, impatience is the very command. What proof then can I offer You between this and that?
>
> "O Lord, everyone has fire in the heart, and this poor wretch in the spirit, for everyone has rhyme and reason, but my poor self has nothing at all."
>
> (2:625, on verse 4:86)

> The Pir of the Tariqah said, "O God, sometimes I seem to be in the devil's grasp, so much curtaining do I see. Then at times a shining light makes all mortal nature disappear.
>
> "O God, since the eyes are still waiting for face-to-face vision, what is this trial of the heart? Since this path is all trial, why is there so much pleasure?
>
> "O God, sometimes I speak to You, sometimes I listen. In the midst of my offenses, I think of Your gentleness. I suffer what I suffer. All becomes sweet when I hear the voice of acceptance."
>
> (6:87, on verse 19:65)

> Shaykh al-Islam Anṣārī said, "How should I have known that suffering is the mother of joy and that beneath a single disappointment lie a thousand treasures? How should I have known what gate this is or what response is given to the story of friendship? How should I have known that companionship with You is the greatest resurrection and that the exaltation of union with You lies in the abasement of bewilderment?"
>
> (2:41, on verse 3:14)

Samʿānī sometimes explains that suffering is a consequence of the complementary divine names that bring the universe into existence. Unity is strictly a divine attribute, so created things can know, recognize, and experience only through multiplicity and diversity. There must be darkness for them to see light. They must know pain to experience joy. There will never be union without separation. The prophets and friends are those who embrace the pain now, knowing that union's joy will be all the greater.

The purified blood of the sincere was made a road
into which none step without losing their lives.

This is the work of the bold. O chevalier! Until you throw down the shield from your side and turn your breast toward the arrows, you will not gain the name of courage. As long as a man has a shield in hand, he has not detached his heart from life. When he throws down his shield, hamstrings his horse, draws his sword, and makes his feet firm on the ground, then you will know that he has detached his heart from life.

It is said that the pure-born John wept so much that the skin on his face came off and pits appeared on his cheeks. He kept weeping so constantly that blood came forth instead of tears. In pain, Zachariah looked at his son from afar. He would clean the blood from his eyes with a piece of cotton, which he would squeeze, and the blood would drip from the cotton. One day he said, "Lord God! Have mercy on this poor soul, for he has no ease or rest."

The address came, "O Zachariah! Keep your sympathy at a distance. You should not be so fragile at My threshold."

O dervish, here there is a secret, by God the tremendous! Suppose that there were none of these pains, trials, and tribulations and that you were brought into existence, taken by the hand, and put into paradise. You would not find an iota of pleasure. This is the reason Adam went and found no pleasure.

On the day you sit on the seat of good fortune in the highest paradise, you will cross your legs, take the tweezers of gentleness, and one by one pull out the thorns from your feet. You will say, "What a pity that these thorns went into my feet instead of my spirit!"

The travelers will find pleasure when they reach the *seat of truthfulness* [54:55] and the place of gentleness, where He Himself will call out, "O My friends, your little bits of suffering have arrived. The burdens you have carried for My sake are in My eyes and esteemed by Me. I saw the bits of suffering that reached you."

Then He will say to David, "Stand up and declare My splendor with your compassionate voice! Entertain My friends for a while with your sweet voice in the scented garden of gentleness at the table of the All-Merciful." Such a feast, such hospitality, such music, such acceptance! The canticles of intimacy in the compartments of holiness with assertions of praise and declarations of splendor!

The desirer will have reached the Desired—the water gone back to the reservoir, the bird hastened to its nest, the smoke gone, the dust settled. The work will have returned to this: the servant and the Lord, the Lord and the servant.

(*Rawḥ* 114–15)

I conclude this chapter with a celebration of pain taken from the beginning of Samʿānī's commentary on the divine name shahīd, Witness.

Some say that the meaning of this name is "knowing," and some say that it means "present." This is presence in the sense of knowledge, vision, and power. As for the presence that is worthy of mortal attributes, the Exalted Lord is incomparable with that. *Nothing is as His likeness, and He is the Hearing, the Seeing* [42:11].

When a truthful, tawḥīd-voicing person of faith believes with certainty that the various sorts of trials that pass over him and the cups of terrible loss that he drinks down occur in the presence of his Goal and that they are witnessed by the Object of his worship, then he will receive the trial with kisses and will not go back to weeping and wailing. Thus it is in the story of Abraham: when he was put in the ballista, he paid no attention to any others and had no concern for the punishment and the fire, for he had perfect realization and full acknowledgment.

He gave solace to all the roasted hearts when He said, "I am the witness of what happens to you."

And the unbelievers have an intense chastisement [42:26]. The reason for this is that the faithful have a chastisement [*ʿadhāb*] also, but it is not intense, it is sweet [*ʿadhib*], for it is built on contemplation.

Those who were friends had their stomachs torn apart, and those who were enemies had their teeth broken. The address came: "*Be patient with thy Lord's decree, for surely thou art in Our eyes*" [52:48].

This is why the paragon said, "This is a mountain that loves us and that we love": on the day the drink of severity was sent to me, my boon companion was Uḥud.

"Trial for friendship is like fire for gold." Love without trial is a pot without salt.

The stipulation of a man in this road is that he open up his spirit to abasement. Wherever he sees lowliness, he buys it with his life. Wherever he sees a slap, he puts forth his neck. Wherever he sees a drawn sword, he sends his own spirit to welcome it.

"It is not for the person of faith to abase himself."* But this does not contradict the words "Perfect exaltation is found in abasement before His gate."

What His Exaltedness does to this handful of dust! Do not put down your bags with "He who seeks Me shall find Me," for "Pridefulness is My cloak" lies beneath it.

Do not look at *He is with you wherever you are* [57:4], for *High indeed is God, the King, the Real* [20:114] comes along with it.

Do not put down the burden because of *Faces on that day radiant* [75:22], for *Eyesights perceive Him not* [6:103] has seized His reins.

Whatever is given by *He is the First* is snatched away by He is *the Last*. Whatever is shown by He is *the Outward* is effaced by He is *the Inward* [57:3].

What is all this? This is so that the person of faith and certainty will circle around the realms of hope along with the mysteries of fear. You cannot say that you will not find, for the Shariah disputes that. Nor can you can say that you will find, for the Exaltedness does not approve.

"O seekers! I am the Exalted. O strivers! I am the Magnificent. O wayfarers! I am the Invincible. O lovers, I am the God. Go down into the valley. Wherever you look, you will see little stones piled on top of one another. They mark the slain in My road."

"When someone is killed by His love, his wergild is his Lord." When someone is killed by love for Him, his wergild is His vision.

When the vanguard of the army of beneficence arrives, it seeks the threshold of strangers. When the vanguard of the army of tribulation arrives, it seeks the corner of the dear ones.

Love and tribulation have the same form in writing, so they are distinguished by the dot. When a dot-worshiping man reaches Him, he looks at the dot. When a meaning seeker reaches Him, he looks beyond the dot and throws his spirit into the work of meaning.

"O world keepers, have invitations and festivals! O exalted ones, have tribulation and tumult! One group is like that, one group like this.

"I give to everyone, but I do not give this trial and tribulation to just anyone. I gave the unfortunate Pharaoh four hundred years of kingship and well-being, and I did not disturb him. But if for one hour he had wanted the pain, burning, and hunger of Moses, I would not have given it to him.

"Look at the beneficence of this world—how far it goes! His head lifted high with one crown—give him a thousand! Then look at those addressed by My love—how far they have fallen! Kick them in the head!"

"The blows of the beloved do not hurt." If all the spirits of the seekers and lovers gathered together to thank Him for the sword of His severity, they would not be able to do so. Suppose you asked Zachariah what he wanted when the saw was placed on the crown of his head. The cries of yearning would have come forth from his parts and motes, saying, "I want them to saw me forever!"

On the day the dear ones of the Presence claimed love, they said farewell to safety and well-being. "Let those who love me, O folk of the house, put on armor for trial—trial reaches those who love me more quickly than a flood reaches its resting place."*

(*Rawḥ* 429–31)

9

THE REALIZATION OF TAWḤĪD

Historians of Sufism have sometimes distinguished among three paths to God—activity, love, and knowledge. Some have attempted to see these three as developing one after another, beginning with ascetic practices, gradually turning to expressions of love, then becoming theory and speculation. Although this sort of classification may be useful for heuristic purposes, it falls short when we look at the actual texts, not least because the Qur'an and the Hadith talk constantly about all three issues. Of course historical development takes place, but it is probably more useful to look for it in the manner in which the insistence on right activity gradually led to the codification of jurisprudence, the emphasis on right thought led to the schools of Kalam, and instructions concerning love and doing the beautiful led to spiritual psychology and Sufism.

Some have claimed that the Qur'an has little regard for love because it mentions the word relatively rarely, much less than words designating knowledge or activity. The issue, however, is not word count. Rather, what exactly is love all about? Enough has been said to show that talk of divine love addresses the relationship between the One and the many. This is precisely the question brought up by tawḥīd, the underlying theme of the Qur'an and the foundational axiom of Islamic thought. By talking about tawḥīd from the perspective of love, teachers shifted the focus from detailed instructions about right and wrong activity, or abstract debates about God's Essence and attributes, to the existential plight of human souls—the pain that people suffer because they do not have what they want. The only way for them to find what they want is to realize tawḥīd.

We should not argue about words. Wanting, willing, yearning, wishing, craving, longing, needing—all are love, and they are innate to the human substance. Everyone, not least our own consumer society, acknowledges this. The question then becomes, "What do we really love? What do we really want and really need?" To provide an adequate answer, we need to know who we really are, not who we imagine ourselves to be. The scientific knowledge that props up the modern worldview provides mountains of information on everything accessible to the senses and instruments, but it can never address my own awareness of myself. I alone can know me, and you alone can know you. Everything I know about you, all the information I acquire about anything whatsoever, is hearsay. The only thing I can know directly, without intermediary, is my own self, and even that is problematic. No amount of physics, chemistry, biology, psychology, and sociology—not even philosophy and theology—will allow me to wake up to the core of my own being.

In short, I can know only for myself, not for anyone else. And I can love only for myself, not for anyone else. Everyone knows that listening to stories about lovers or theories about love's nature is not the same as being in love. What seems to have been forgotten is that learning about what people have discovered or thought—that is, the hearsay knowledge that props up human society and culture—is not the same as knowing for oneself. When authors shift the focus from knowledge to love, they are no longer talking about theological and philosophical abstractions, but rather about the living awareness of free beings. The moment such beings gain a glimpse of tawḥīd, they are faced with two fundamental questions: How did they become separate from their Source? How can they go back where they came from? Or, in other terms, how is it that the lover finds himself separate from the Beloved? And given his separation, how can he overcome it?

The Qur'an answers the first question with the creative command, which demands that people come into existence wanting, wishing, craving, yearning—all because God loves them. It answers the second with the religious command: people must focus their wants and desires on what is worthy of love, not on passing fancies.

RECOGNITION OF POVERTY

The first step in grasping the real nature of the human situation is to understand the initial insight of tawḥīd: the distinction between the One and the many, the Real and the unreal, the Beloved and the lover. Once it is grasped that the One alone is one, it will be seen that the Real is utterly different from the unreal. If Islamic theology begins by asserting God's incomparability and transcendence, it is precisely because He alone is one and everything else is many, He alone is necessary and everything else is contingent.

The very fact of recognizing that the Real is the Real and that all else is unreal sets up the relationship between being and nonexistence. That which is and has always been determines the nature of that which is not and has somehow appeared. To say this is to talk of the creative command, the distinction between Creator and creatures, or between the Lord and compulsory servants. Talk of Lord and servants reminds us that there is also a religious command, which invites people to serve the Real not only by ontological compulsion, but also by free choice.

Understanding the distinction between the Real and the unreal asks for far more than knowledge of the creed, which anyone can learn by reading up on Islam. As understood by Muslim spiritual teachers, recognition of the distinction between the Real and the unreal demands grasping the essential unreality of the human situation and choosing to live appropriately. In other words, it is recognizing God as Lord and freely acting as servant.

We have already met the saying that is typically cited as a scriptural basis for the correlation between recognition of God and recognition of self: "He who recognizes himself recognizes his Lord." One of the many interpretations of this saying is precisely "He who recognizes himself" as a servant "recognizes his Lord" as a Lord. Anyone who does not attend to his own servanthood will never actualize a proper relationship with God's lordhood. If people do not act in keeping with who they really are, they will never find a happy relationship with the Real. To establish this relationship they need to put love into practice: "*If you love God, follow me; God will love you.*"

It was noted that the servant's ontological situation is commonly called poverty (faqr, darwīshī). Creatures have an absolute need (*iftiqār, niyāz*) for the Creator, since they have nothing of their own save nonexistence. Whatever their semblance of existence, it pertains to them accidentally, not essentially; metaphorically, not in reality. Love appropriate for the Absolutely Unneedy demands realization of absolute need.

It is worth repeating that in premodern times, Muslim seekers of God rarely called themselves Sufis, since the word was taken as designating a high stage of spiritual realization. Instead, they commonly referred to themselves as the poor, the dervishes, because doing so acknowledged one's own nothingness. Even so, the actual realization of poverty was considered a high station on the path; people are typically so caught up with themselves that they cannot begin to understand what their nothingness implies. The common refrain that the path demands annihilation of self refers precisely to overcoming the false sense of reality that pervades human consciousness. Samʿānī tells us that the first step on the path is to recognize one's own nonbeing, and the final step to actualize it.

> What we need is for the Sultan to have a good opinion of us.
>
> Tomorrow He will allow Muṣṭafā to intercede in order to display Muṣṭafā. Otherwise, no interceder will come forth for the state of the friends. His friendship has already interceded for them. Our work stays with Him, and His work with us stays with His own lordhood. What comes out of the house of beggars is worthy of beggars, and what comes out of the house of sultans is suited for sultans.
>
> "Today is fitting for your work with Me, and tomorrow will be fitting for My work with you. Today is your never-having-been, and tomorrow will be My always-having-been. Today you are wounded by your never-having-been, and tomorrow you will be lifted up by My always-having-been."
>
> When will they take away the mask
> and let us tell poison from sugar?
>
> When the turn of His justice arrives, the prophets seek a road of escape. When the turn of His bounty arrives, the tavern goers hold their heads high.
>
> David's heart became constricted, and he was ashamed at what he had done. He stayed in prostration for forty days: "O God, forgive me, though I have no excuse": I dare not say more. When someone does not have money for soap, why would they give him sugar?
>
> O dervish! As long as you have not confessed to your own destitution, nothing will come of you. Dervishes put on a hundred thousand patched cloaks hoping to find a whiff of destitution.
>
> You must not voice the tawḥīd of your own tawḥīd-voicing. You must voice the tawḥīd of His Oneness.
>
> Whoever is more a master is more naked. Muḥammad was the master of the whole world in both the Shariah and the Tariqah. It was for his sake that Gabriel was obedient for many thousands of years. Then, on the night of the miʿrāj, it was said to Gabriel, "You hold this man's banner, and that will be sufficient reward for your acts of obedience." But look how the Prophet was stripped naked: "*Thou hast nothing of the affair*" [3:128].
>
> (*Rawḥ* 517)

In his commentary on the verse "*O people, you are the poor toward God, and God is the Unneedy, the Praiseworthy*" (35:15), Maybudī explains that there are two basic sorts of poverty. The first is ontological, arising from the creative command, the fact that all things are in utter need of *Be!* The second is acknowledgment of one's own poverty and need by following the religious command.

Know that poverty is of two sorts: the poverty of created nature and the poverty of attributes. The poverty of created nature is general, belonging to every newly arrived thing that has come into existence from nonexistence. The meaning of poverty is need. Every created thing needs the Creator—first for creation and second for nurture. Thus, you know that God has no needs or requirements, and everything else has needs and requirements. This is why the Exalted Lord said, "*God is the Unneedy, and you are the poor*" [47:38].

As for the poverty of attributes, that is what the Lord of the Worlds said: "*the poor emigrants*" [59:8]. He specified the Messenger's Companions for this poverty and praised them for it, as He said: "*For the poor, who are constrained in the path of God*" [2:273]. He named them *poor* to disguise the wealth of their state and so that no one would know of their wealth. This is as they say: "Call me Arsalan so that no one will know who I am."

The Pir of the Tariqah said, "Friendship is built on disguise. The name *king* for Solomon is the disguise of poverty. *Disobedience* for Adam is the disguise of being chosen. The blessings that clothed Abraham disguised bosom friendship. This is because the stipulation of love is jealousy. Friends do not show their state to just anyone."

Someone without an iota of being, who never gazes on the two worlds and who always keeps God's gaze before his eyes is called poor, for he is indigent of everything and wealthy through the Real. One must have wealth in the breast, not in the storehouse. The poor man is he who sees no handhold in the two worlds other than the Real and does not gaze upon himself. He has recited the prayer of the dead over his own essence and attributes—as that chevalier said:

> Endless passion has nothing to do with a heart
>   that stays firm in its own attributes.
> When someone steps into the field of passion for the beautiful,
>   night and day will recite for him the prayer of the dead.
>
> (*Kashf* 8:180–81)

Maybudī quotes Anṣārī to explain that recognizing one's own poverty and neediness can become so intense that it burns away everything other than the Unneedy. Thus, need is nothing but the fire of love.

The Pir of the Tariqah said, "The reality of this work is all need. It is an endless longing, a congenital pain. In it there is both joy and melting, both hidden resurrection and everlasting life. It is the unsettledness of the hearts of the finders, the trial of the spirits of the proximate, and the bewilderment of the knowledge of the realizers. It is the incinerating passion of the recognizers, the enraptured striving of the friends, and the perplexity of the chevaliers. Their perplexity in this road is like someone who falls down a bottomless well. The more he goes down in the well, the more it becomes bottomless, so his feet never touch the ground. So also the travelers on this road are always traveling, falling and rising. They never come to a stop, nor have they any consolation in their grief, any bottom to this ocean, any end to this story."

(*Kashf* 4:358–59, on verse 11:1)

In his commentary on the verse that mentions "*the poor emigrants*" (59:8), Maybudī classifies poverty into two sorts in order to explain why the Prophet sometimes blamed poverty and sometimes praised it.

Know that poverty is two: The first is that from which God's Messenger sought refuge, saying, "I seek refuge in Thee from poverty." The other is that about which God's Messenger said, "Poverty is my pride." The former is close to unbelief and the latter close to the Real.

The poverty that is close to unbelief is poverty of the heart, which strips it of knowledge, wisdom, sincerity, patience, contentment, surrender, and trust. Like a ruined land, the heart becomes destitute of these ruling powers. When the heart is like ruins, it becomes the home of the satans. When Satan comes, his soldiers show their faces: appetite, wrath, envy, associationism, doubt, suspicion, and hypocrisy. The mark of this poverty is that whatever the poor man sees, he sees crooked. His ears hear superficially, his tongue speaks only in lying and backbiting, and he always steps into unworthy lanes. This is the poverty concerning which God's Messenger said, "Poverty is almost unbelief." "O God, I seek refuge in Thee from poverty and unbelief!"

As for the poverty about which he said, "Poverty is my pride," it is that a man becomes naked of this world and thereby close to the religion. According to the report, "Faith is naked, and its garment godwariness." This is what the Sufis call disengagement: a man becomes disengaged from the customs of human nature, just as a sword becomes disengaged from its scabbard. As long as the sword remains in its scabbard, its excellence does not become apparent, and no act appears from it. In the same way, as long as the heart remains in the scabbard of human nature, its excellence does not become apparent, and no work opens up from it. When it becomes naked of the scabbard of human nature, its forms and attributes display themselves within him.

(*Kashf* 10:58–59)

Samʿānī often points out that need for God is woven into human nature. In the following, he reminds us that the neediness of beggars gives luster to the rich. If philanthropists did not bestow their wealth, how could they show their goodwill? What is peculiar about the human situation is that need for God is infinite, because man was created in His form. The ontological poverty of non-human things is limited, for they were created to make manifest only some of God's attributes, not all of them. Recognition of infinite need is precisely the basis for loving God alone. "I was a Hidden Treasure, and I loved to be recognized."

> O dervish! The treasury of bestowers gains luster from the requests and neediness of requesters. No requester had greater need than dust. Heaven and earth, the Throne and the Footstool, were given to dust, but its need did not decrease by one iota. The eight paradises were given over exclusively to its work, but need seized its reins, for poverty was the host at the table of its existence: *Surely man was created grasping* [70:19].
>
> A grasping person is someone who never becomes full. He brought Adam into paradise and permitted him its bliss, but He said, "Don't go after that tree." Nonetheless, despite all the blissful things, Adam was seized by the tree. "The forbidden is enticing." Yes, He forbade it to him, but He did not purify his inwardness of wanting it. Indeed, every serving boy in the world is a serving boy of his own want.
>
> They say that in the Guarded Tablet it is written, "O Adam, do not eat the wheat." In the same place it is written that he ate it. *Surely man was created grasping.*
>
> The avarice of the Adamites goes back to the days of Adam himself. Whoever is not avaricious is not an Adamite. As much as someone eats, he needs more. If he eats something and says, "I'm full," he is lying. There is still more room, for the Adamite is never full. "Nothing will fill the stomach of Adam's child but dust."*
>
> (*Rawḥ* 155–56)

In another passage, Samʿānī cites a Sufi saying to make the point that Adam left paradise precisely because he recognized his need for the Infinite and the impossibility of fulfilling it in paradise.

> Shiblī said, "I have a need that seized my hand and brought me into this road."
>
> They said, "What need do you have?"
>
> He said, "It is a need such that the eight paradises were made into a mouthful and thrown into it, and not a mote of them appeared."
>
> By God the tremendous! Adam knew the worth of paradise when they put it in his hand.

> "O Adam, what is paradise worth?"
>
> He said, "When someone fears hell, he sees paradise as worth a thousand spirits. When someone fears You, he sees paradise as not worth a grain."
>
> (*Rawḥ* 198)

Aḥmad Ghazālī explains that the lover has no role other than to bring forth the attributes of the Beloved. The lover's need for the Hidden Treasure makes the Beloved's splendor manifest, and conversely, the Beloved's splendor demands the existence of the lover. At the beginning of this passage, he alludes to the fact that Love in Itself, the Divine Essence in respect of Its unity, set up the distinction between lover and Beloved by distributing the infinite jewels concealed in the Treasure. All the jewels—the contingent things—announce their need by their very existence.

> Chapter [41]. In love's apportioning, all exaltation, tyranny, unneediness, and magnificence became the attributes of the Beloved, and all abasement, weakness, lowliness, poverty, need, and helplessness became the portion of the lover. Thus, love's food is the lover's attributes, for love is the lord of the lover's passing days. What, then, will the lover's passing days bring forth? This changes with the present moment.
>
> As for the attributes of the Beloved, they become manifest only when their opposites become manifest in the lover. As long as the lover does not have need, the Beloved will not show His unneediness. In the same way, all attributes are suited for Him in this respect.
>
> Chapter [42]. Given that this is so, lover and Beloved are opposites. They do not come together except with the precondition of sacrifice and annihilation. This is why someone said,
>
> When that verdant sweetheart saw my yellow face
> she said, "Have no hope for union with me.
> "Seeing you is to see my opposite:
> yours the color of autumn, mine the color of spring."
>
> Chapter [43]. In every state, the Beloved is simply the Beloved, so His attribute is unneediness. In every state, the lover is the lover, so his attribute is poverty. The lover always needs the Beloved, so poverty is always his attribute. The Beloved needs nothing, for He always has Himself, so His attribute is unneediness.
>
> Every night my eyes shed blood in sorrow,
> my heart ambushed by separation.
> You have You, O sweetheart, that is why You are happy.
> How could You know what night is like without You?

You have always stolen hearts—You're excused.
  You have never tried out sorrow—You're excused.
I have spent a thousand nights in blood without You.
  You have never had a night without You—You're excused.

If you fall into the error of thinking that perhaps the lover can be the owner and the Beloved the servant and that He would then enter the lover's embrace through union, that indeed is a great error. The reality of love has placed the collar of the sultanate on the Beloved's neck and taken away the earring of servanthood.

The Beloved can never be someone's property. This is why those who speak of poverty toss away their spirits and hearts. They offer up the religion, this world, and their passing days. They do every work, they leave aside everything, they have no fear for their lives, they traverse the two worlds. But when they reach the center-point of love, they do not offer up the Beloved, nor can they do so. Property can be offered up, but not the owner. The Beloved is the owner.

The hand of freedom does not reach the skirt of love and loverhood. Just as every bond is untied there, that is, in the freedom of poverty, so also all untying becomes a bond here, that is, in the servanthood of love.

Once these realities are known, it seems that love's majesty will appear only when the lover harms his own being so as to put aside causes and be released from profit and loss.

(*Sawāniḥ* 35–37)

Aḥmad insists on the utter difference between the Real and the unreal, Being and nonbeing, the Necessary and the contingent, the Beloved and the lover. If the lover is ever to find a taste of union, it will be simply that—a taste bestowed by the Beloved's bounty.

Chapter [36]. The lover will never become familiar with the Beloved. When he thinks himself closer to Him, he is further away, for the sultanate belongs to Him and "The sultan has no friends."

The reality of familiarity is to be at the same level, but that would be absurd for lover and Beloved. The lover is wholly the earth of abasement, and the Beloved is wholly the heaven of inaccessibility and magnificence. If there is any familiarity, it will lie in the property of the instant and the present moment, but this is a loan.

I suffered grief in the measure of heaven and earth
  trying to grasp You and Your sugar lips.
A gazelle can become tame with people,
  but not You—I tried a thousand stratagems.

How can the tyranny of the Beloved come together with the abasement of the lover? How can the disdain of the Sought fall in with the need of the seeker?

That is the cure of this, and this has no cure but that. An ill person requires a remedy, but the remedy does not require the ill. Thus has it been said,

What can the lover do? His heart's not in his hand.
What can the destitute do? He has no means to be.
Your beauty gets no eminence from my bazaar.
What harm to the idol if there were no idol worshipers?

(*Sawāniḥ* 30)

Aḥmad explains that the Beloved with whom the lover achieves union can never be the Beloved per se, for the Eternal stands forever beyond the newly arrived. In fact, the lover achieves union with the Beloved's presence in his own spirit.

Chapter [65]. In verified truth, love is that the beloved's form becomes the weave of the lover's spirit so that the lover's spirit takes its food from this abiding form. This is why, though the beloved may be a thousand parasangs distant, the lover knows her to be present and counts her as closer than all close things. He feeds on the hard cash of his own awareness, the mirror that holds the beauty of the beloved's face.

Pour me wine and tell me it is wine—
don't pour in secret when you can pour openly.

Union with the Beloved is to feed on the awareness of the spirit's cash. It is not finding. As for the reality of union, that is unification itself. But this point is concealed from the eye of knowledge. When love reaches perfection, it feeds on itself. It has nothing to do with the outside.

(*Sawāniḥ* 48–49)

Toward the beginning of his commentary on the divine name *fattāḥ*, the All-Opening, Samʿānī explains that recognizing self depends on recognizing ontological poverty. This divine name means that no one opens doors but God. Those who recognize God as such will trust in Him completely and will sacrifice what freedom they have to the divine wisdom. Adam's glory lay precisely in his recognition of poverty, in contrast with the angels, who admired their own wealth and prowess.

O dervish, whenever the Real's measure descends into a heart, the measure of the whole world packs its bags. When the contemplation of the Real finds a place in the eyes, any other contemplation turns into nothing.

Intimate with Him, I have no other desire—
I fear only going astray and not seeing Him.

As long as a man has not reached the center of this work or become aware of the secret of this question, he grabs hold of every branch and becomes attached to every little thing. Once he reaches the treasury of the secrets and finds the quarry of the realities and the springhead of gentle favors, he falls back on the fountain of life that is the *goodly life* [16:97]. He sees creation's existence as nonexistence next to the Real's existence, he knows creation's subsistence to be annihilation next to the Real's subsistence, and he recognizes creation's exaltedness as abasement next to the Real's exaltedness.

Now he takes his little corner far from the homeland of mortal nature, the courtyard of Adamic nature, and the way station of human nature, and he puts it into the pavilions of majesty. He knows that it is impossible to seek wealth from poverty and that it is ignorance to take the capital of subsistence from the source of annihilation. He is consumed by contemplation itself and drowned in the ocean of unveiling. He becomes like a dust mote before the sun, appearing only when it witnesses the sun's beauty.

O dervish! Every star high on the dome of the celestial world has taken a ray of light in its mouth. In form, the stars are much more exalted than these dust motes in the terrestrial world, for they have light, radiance, splendor, and brilliance, and the motes are simply dust that have remained in the air in the footsteps of existence and without taking up space. But do not look at the highness, radiance, limpidness, and brilliance of the stars, nor at this nonbeing and tininess of the dust motes. Wait until the emperor of the stars and the chief of the planets raises its head. You will see those high in rank and elevated in degree disappear, losing name and mark, but those tiny shapes and insignificant makeups will come out of the confines of tininess into the vast plain of manifestation.

What is the divine wisdom and lordly secret in this? It is that stars, which are the stonings of the satans, are attached to the arrogance of appearance and the self-esteem of manifesting their own light, but the sun's empire does not accept the intrusion of duality.[1] "Two swords do not fit into one scabbard nor two lions into one thicket." When the sultan-sun sits on its steed of light, it charges forth on the field of exaltation. The stars conceal their faces with the veil of despair and the mask of shame. They declare themselves quit of the manifestation of their own light.

As for this dust mote, it is helpless, nurtured in the cradle of indigence, all imaginings having fallen away from it. It is the prisoner of the wind, not grasped by the hand or perceived by the glance. As soon as the world-adorning sun sticks up its head from the horizon of eminence, the mote comes forth in service to the sun in helplessness, lowliness, and abasement. The sun, by virtue of generosity, dresses it in a robe of its own light. The dust mote discloses itself to the eyes in the robe of the sun's brightness.

Now that this introduction has been made, you should know that in reality, His Men are the same in relation to the divine beauty and majesty. Those who, in imagining themselves to be existent, make the claims of self-seeing and rely on their own acts and states are like the stars that try to associate themselves with the sun in brightness. When the sun of the divine majesty rises from the constellation of the Sanctum, all of them pull their faces behind the mask of shame and put the finger of bewilderment in the mouth of remorse. They come to know that mortal man has nothing in his hands but wind.

As for those who are purified of appetite for reputation, disgusted with every claim, and naked of self-seeing, they have turned their eyes to the beauty of the Presence and sit in anticipation of the breaking of union's dawn. They are like the dust motes that, when the sun of majesty shows its head from the constellation of beauty, fall to the knees of abasement and pleading, needy for the Presence, poor toward the Exaltedness, helpless in the road, and fallen before the Threshold. They come forth in the garment of destitution, but the royal generosity and divine munificence bestow a robe of pure light on them. With this light they appear to the eyes.

You are the sun, I a dust mote—
they know me only as the sun's mote.

Here there is another secret. God says, "*We offered the Trust to the heavens and the earth and the mountains*" [33:72]. The sun of the Trust shone forth from the constellation of the divine offer. For several thousand years the angels of the Sovereignty had been in the gardens of declaring holy, grazing with the nostrils of acquiescence on the jasmine of glorification, the sweetbriar of praise, and the red rose of reciting tawḥīd. They were shouting out, "*We glorify Thy praise,*" and making the uproar of "*We call Thee holy*" [2:30]. Then, like the stars, they lifted the bags of poverty and confessed to their incapacity and brokenness: "*They refused to carry it*" [33:72]. They refused out of apprehension, not out of pride. But that fearless mote of dust pulled the hand of need from the sleeve of poverty and indigence and took the Trust to heart, not thinking at all about the two worlds.

(*Rawḥ* 117–19)

Although poverty is essential to the human makeup, recognizing it as such is about as far away from everyday awareness as can be. People are entranced by themselves, and the most difficult thing in the world is to leave the self behind. This is why Anṣārī, in the *Book of Love*, talks about the exceedingly elevated station of those who have reached the true station of poverty. People talk about it, but no one has ever seen it.

> Poverty is a phoenix of which there is only the name. No one has access to it.
>
> Poverty is sanity, and the poor man is mad. Poverty is the roof, and the poor man is the house. Poverty is the station of the road and the secret of "I have a moment with God."* Poverty is the red sulfur and the green elixir. Poverty is a nonbeing before which no one has any being. *God is the Unneedy, and you are the poor* [47:38]. Everything other than He is poor, and this station is before all.
>
> People follow what they hear, but this work lies in seeing. He who passes beyond this world is a renunciant, and he who passes beyond the next world is a striver. These are attributes of water and dust, and the poor man is pure of both.
>
> "Poverty is almost unbelief." It is not that the dervish has no religion, but that he has no self. The dervish sits nowhere and nothing makes him sit.
>
> First the man imitates what he hears, then he imitates what is shown. After hearing and showing, he busies himself with being. Then he puts being into nonbeing. Neither creatures nor himself remains for him, neither seeker nor something out in front to seek. This is the attribute of the dervish.
>
> Whatever comes to you in the two worlds,
> you worship it—you are no dervish.
>
> If you are a dervish, what is this bewilderment? If you are selfless, what is this thinking? If you are with yourself, then be someone who remembers. If you have the religion, then be someone who thinks. If you are selfless, then be present! Observe the words of the Master of the Shariah: "The meditation of one hour is better than sixty years of worship."
>
> (*Maḥabbat* 368–69)

In Chapter 28 of *Forty-Two Chapters*, Anṣārī provides a brief description of a shaykh of Cairo, Abū ʿAlī al-Ḥusayn ibn Muḥammad ibn al-Kātib (d. 951), and then cites one of his sayings. Notice that he offers a critique of the Mu'tazilite theologians, who are deservedly famous for their reliance on ʿaql, "intellect," or, in their case, their own standards of rationality. Anṣārī contrasts their reliance on intellect with the Sufis' reliance on ʿilm, "knowledge," by which he means the transmitted learning derived from the Qur'an and the Hadith.

Abū ʿAlī said, "The Mu'tazilites sought the Real's incomparability with their own intellects, so they fell into error. The Sufis sought it with knowledge, so they found the right road."

He means that the Sufis declared God's incomparability, but they spoke of His attributes in keeping with the instruction of the saying "I have faith in what God said as God desired it, and I have faith in what God's Messenger said as God's Messenger desired it." They spoke of His attributes in keeping with what He said about His attributes, and they negated unworthy attributes from Him, that is, whatever He negated from Himself.

Whatever the Mu'tazilites said accorded with intellect, and whatever the Sufis said agreed with knowledge. Those were in error, and these were correct. How is it possible for the newly arrived intellect to know anything about the Eternal Essence? It does not even know what it is itself or where it came from. How will it know the Artisan? And God is the guide.

The Intimation. Do not go in the tracks of selfhood when you have God's Book and the Messenger's Sunnah. When something brings you to you, hamstring it with knowledge. When something takes you away from you, attract it with spirit and heart. Find what can be known in this work by losing yourself. Then you may reach the goal.

If you want to reap the fruit of this work, do whatever you do so as not to remember yourself. If you are a buyer of this work, mix nothing with it. Turn your back toward everything else and flee from all, for this work is not done in association. If the two worlds are sent to serve you, pay no regard.

If you claim to be seeking this story, one of the work's stipulations is that you have no work outside this work, that you combine no work with seeking for this work. By occupying yourself with this work, you will become heedless of every work. Either melt in the sorrow of separation while free of the two worlds, or be joyful in union with the Friend while free of remembering yourself and all the world's creatures.

When someone finds the flavor of this work, he finds nothing in the two worlds but thorns. When someone tastes a draft of this cup, he no longer sees himself or the folk of the two worlds. He becomes forever drunk, never again to be sober. All sobrieties are sacrificed to this drunkard, and no one sober ever comes to know the secret of his drunkenness.

Does the sober man know what the drunkard sees? And how would the drunkard know that there is anyone other than the Friend to be seen? For drunkenness comes from friendship, and friendship is the name of those with no names and the mark of those with no marks. The desert of friendship is full of the blood of the dear ones. In truth, this is so—by God, it is so!

Do you know why friendship's story is so long? Because the Friend has no needs.

Do not attach your heart to creatures, lest you be wounded. Attach your heart to the Real and be released.

The Real created this world, adorned it for a group, and said, "This is the place of trial." He created the afterworld, adorned it for a group, and said, "This is the place of bestowal." He adorned His own Presence for a group—that is, He made them recognize Him—and He said, "O chevaliers! This world, the next world, and the two realms belong to you."

If you have feet, bind them to Him. If you have a head, tie it by His noose. The Friend is the ocean, the rest are streams. If you are seeking pearls, seek them from the ocean, not the streams.

You have the promise if you speak of Him, and you have the threat if you do not seek Him. Once you are released from the cage of this world, you will join with the gentleness of the One.

A dervish has no house and no place. You have heard *"Return unto thy Lord!"* [89:28]. Don't delay, stop talking, and come. Be as you appear, and appear as you are.

The spirit of the folk of meaning has become lost in yearning. This dervish's capacity bent in two when he began to yearn for Your Presence. There is no god but God, there is no god but He.

(*Chihil* 169–71)

In another passage of *Forty-Two Chapters*, Anṣārī again refers to the high station of poverty and offers instructions on how to reach it. His basic point comes up constantly in the texts: negate all others with the *No* of the formula of tawḥīd—*"No god but God"*—and affirm only God. Foremost among the others is the self.

What is poverty? An outwardness without color, an inwardness without war. The dervish has neither fame nor disgrace. He knows neither peace nor war.

The Shariah commands, "Keep your skirt clean!" The Haqiqah commands, "Be with Me!"

Scatter this world for the creatures, then live. Don't scratch anyone's heart, then be happy.

The wayfarers on this road have girded their waists to repel this world by following the Sunnah. If the kingdom of this world were offered to them, they would choose two days of starvation and a half day of not filling their stomachs, for fear of becoming wealthy.

O seeker! Strive to grasp these words and follow this road so as to go beyond yourself. Take to the dust and become dust with the attributes of dust. When you become dust, you will be pure.

Do not live in the description of water and dust, becoming a renunciant. Live rather in the attribute of the spirit and heart and become a recognizer.

Once you are not, all will be yours. As long as you are, you are beneath everything.

Your effort in seeking anything of this world is the writ of your servanthood to it. Your effort at becoming free of all things is the edict of desire for this work.

Strive for the nonbeing of your own being. Then you may do justice to the word *No.* Try to free yourself from the bonds of the others, requesting that *but God* be unveiled to you.

Your striving will be welcomed by the attraction of gentleness, and you will be snatched away from the two worlds. You will be emptied of your youness, and gentleness will do with you as it will. There is no god but God, there is no god but He.

(*Chihil* 65–66)

THE SWORD OF JEALOUSY

At the end of the passage just quoted, Anṣārī sums up the path that leads to the realization of tawḥīd with the words "Try to free yourself from the bonds of the others, requesting that *but God* be unveiled to you." Talk of the others, ghayr, brings up the issue of jealousy, ghayra, which is simply the word *ghayr* with an added vowel. The beloved's jealousy is stirred up when others intrude on the lover's love.

No doubt jealousy has a bad name in modern times, but perhaps this is because people understand it only in human terms, where it can easily destroy relationships. Indeed, the function of God's jealousy is precisely to destroy the soul's relationship with anything other than the One. Though not typically listed among the divine names, the Jealous (*ghayūr*) is mentioned in the hadith literature. Its close connection with tawḥīd is suggested by the Hebrew Bible: "For thou shalt worship no other god: for the Lord, whose name is Jealous, is a jealous God" (Exodus 34:14).

If jealousy is a recurring theme in the literature of love, it is simply because the Shariah and the Tariqah both aim at exclusive devotion to the One, leaving no room for others. Devoting oneself to others is associationism, the opposite of tawḥīd. As Maybudī puts it, "In the religion of friendship, seeing others in place of the Friend is nothing but associationism" (*Kashf* 5:130, on verse 12:84). When God's jealousy exercises its ruling property, it erases the others from the gaze and leaves only the One. According to Samʿānī, it was precisely God's jealousy that took Adam out of paradise and threw him into love.

> It was the sultan of solitariness and the army of tawḥīd that hunted Adam in paradise and snatched him away from all beings. When someone is plundered by the ruling power of God's jealousy, he no longer concerns himself with any others.
>
> (*Rawḥ* 200)

To concern oneself with others is to be their servant. This is why Anṣārī said in the passage just quoted, "Your effort in seeking anything of this world is the writ of your servanthood to it." His next sentence goes to the heart of the spiritual quest, in Islam as elsewhere: "Your effort at becoming free of all things is the edict of desire for this work." Remember that desire (irāda) is the attribute of the seeker on the path of the Shariah and the Tariqah, the person who desires God and who strives to follow the path to God as laid down by the Sunnah.

In the verse "*Everyone has a direction to which he turns*" (2:148), the Qur'an alludes to people's scattered devotions and their failure to find the One. Maybudī explains that the verse can be read as a reference to the different kiblahs toward which people turn in their prayers, such as Jerusalem or Mecca. In a more general sense, it simply means that everyone has an object other than God that he worships, whether he knows it or not. The point of putting tawḥīd into practice, after all, is precisely to rid oneself of devotion to others, to turn away from every direction and focus on the Directionless. Ibn al-ʿArabī would later talk of the same issue in terms of the god of belief (*al-ilāh al-muʿtaqad*), meaning not God in Himself, who is unknowable and beyond any form or formulation, but the specific object or objects of devotion that each human individual, even an atheist, takes as his point of orientation.[2]

> By allusion He says, "All the people have turned away from Me. Without Me, they have become familiar with others. They have taken a sweetheart other than Me. They have accepted the other as a beloved.
>
> "You who are the chevaliers of the Tariqah and claim to love Me, lift up your eyes from anything beneath Me, even if it be the highest paradise. Then you will go straight in following the Sunnah and the conduct of Muṣṭafā, and you will perform the rightful due of emulating that paragon of the world. For as the greatest of the prophets, his conduct was to turn his eyes away from all

beings and not to see any refuge nor to approve of any resting place other than the shelter of Unity."

When a man wears down his spirit in passion's road
he had best incline toward none but the Friend.
The passionate in passion's road
must not think of hell or paradise.

When someone puts himself right in following Muṣṭafā, the candle of friendship with the Real will be lit in his road and he will never fall away from friendship's highway. To this is the allusion in the verse *"Follow me; God will love you"* [3:31]. Whenever someone goes straight on friendship's highway, he will be secure from all the directions that are the kiblahs of the mimickers. One of the distracted said in this state,

So what if I don't have the world's kiblah—
my kiblah is the Beloved's lane, just that.
Take this world, that world, and all that exists—
the passionate have the Beloved's face, just that.

Ḥallāj alluded to the kiblahs of the mimickers when he said, "The desirers have been turned over to what they desire." Everyone has been sat down with his own beloved.

The truth of this work is that all creatures have claimed friendship with the Real, but there was no one who did not want to be someone in His court.

Whoever finds a name for himself finds it from that Court—
belong to Him, brother, and think of no one else.

Since all claim friendship with the Real, He strikes them with the touchstone of trial in order to show them to themselves without Him. He threw something into them and made it their kiblah, so they turned their faces to it. In one it was wealth, in another position, in another a spouse, in another a lovely face, in another pride, in another learning, in another renunciation, in another worship, in another fancy. He threw all these into the people, so they busied themselves with them and no one spoke of Him. They all stayed off the road of seeking Him.

This is why Abu Yazīd Basṭāmī said, "I passed by His gate, but I did not see any crowding there. The folk of this world were veiled by this world, the folk of the afterworld were veiled by the afterworld, and the Sufi claimants were veiled by eating, drinking, and begging. There were others among them of a higher level who were veiled by music and lovely faces. But the great leaders of the Sufis were not veiled by any of these. Rather, I saw that they were bewildered and intoxicated."

The Pir of the Tariqah said something with the taste of these words: "I recognize the drinking place, but I am not able to drink. My heart is thirsty, and I wail in hope of a drop. The fountain cannot fill me because I am seeking the ocean. I passed by a thousand springs and rivers in hopes of finding the ocean. Have you ever seen anyone drowning in fire? I am like that. Have you ever seen anyone thirsty in a lake? That is what I am. I am exactly like someone lost in the desert. I keep on saying, 'Help! I'm at wit's end! I have lost my heart!'"

(*Kashf* 1:412–13)

One of the most insidious of the others mentioned by the Qur'an is hawā, "caprice" or "misguided love." Maybudī explains some of its dangers in his commentary on the verse "*When Abraham said, 'My Lord, make this land secure, and keep me and my sons away from worshiping idols!'*" (14:35).

Whenever something holds you back from the Real, that is your idol. Whenever your heart inclines and looks to something other than the Real, that is your caprice. The Exalted Lord says, "*Have you seen him who has taken his caprice as his god?*" [25:43]. One person looks to property and trade, another to wife and children, another to position and respect. One person has remained in the bonds of venerating piety and self-restraint and has not taken a step beyond that. Another has made obedience and worship his kiblah—looking at it and leaning on it have become the veil of his road.

The Lord of the Worlds says, "*And repent all together to God, O you faithful! Perhaps you will prosper* [24:31]. O you who have faith, if you want Me to make your hearts the sanctuary of My gaze and to keep you secure from the veil of severance, turn your faces totally to Me and turn away from everything else!" Sometimes He calls to His road with the tongue of the artifacts to make people realize familiarity. Sometimes He calls to Himself with the tongue of unveiling to confirm friendship.

He says: "Turn away from yourself and totally to Him so as to recognize what is rightfully due to Him. Look beyond your own obedience and see His favor. Be released from your own existence and taste His friendship." This is what Abraham meant when he said, "*And keep me and my sons away from worshiping idols!*"

In explaining this verse, Jaʿfar al-Ṣādiq said, "Do not push me back to witnessing bosom friendship, and do not push my children back to witnessing prophethood." Lord God! You have given me bosom friendship. Turn my eyes away from it so that I will not see it from myself. You have given my children prophethood. Do not attach their eyes to seeing their own activities or themselves.

Ibn ʿAṭāʾ said, "He commanded Abraham to build the Kaabah. He built it as commanded, completed it, and then said, '*Our Lord, accept it from us!*' [2:127].

"A rebuke came: 'I commanded you to build the house, and then you lay a favor on Me for doing so? I gave you the success to do it. Are you not ashamed to lay a favor on Me and say, "*Accept it from us*"? You have forgotten My favor toward you and mentioned your own act and favor.'

"Because of the harshness of this rebuke Abraham supplicated, '*Keep me and my sons away from worshiping idols!* Lord God, in the road of my bosom friendship and my children's prophethood, seeing our own activity and ascribing it to ourselves are idols that lie in ambush for us. By Your gentleness, remove these idols from the road and remove our being from the midst! Keep on bestowing Your favor upon us!'"

(*Kashf* 5:281–82)

Even the Prophet was not exempt from the blows of God's jealousy. Maybudī provides an example in his commentary on the well-known episode of the slander against ʿĀʾisha. She was separated from a caravan, a man found her and brought her to camp, and then rumors began to fly that she had been alone with him and something had happened. Doubts entered the Prophet's heart, and it took a revelation to quell them. In his explanation, Maybudī quotes a few of Qushayrī's remarks from *Subtle Allusions*, translates others, and adds a great deal to the account.

Those who came with the slander are a band of you. Do not reckon it evil for you; rather, it is good for you. Against every man of them shall be the sin he has earned. Whosoever of them took most of it on himself will have a great chastisement [24:11]. Know, O chevalier, that the hearts of the Real's friends are inside the curtain of jealousy—today they listen inside the curtain of jealousy, and tomorrow they will see inside the curtain of jealousy.

The Real does not show your heart to anyone, for He keeps it inside the curtain of jealousy. In the grip of the attributes, it sees the Real face-to-face on the carpet of joy in the presence of witnessing and seclusion, and the Real gazes upon it. If the heart looks back at another, at once it will see the courtesy-teaching whip.

Thus it happened to a great one of his time. He was exceedingly happy in a tremendous desire for God. He had complete ecstasy, and his work was in total conformity with Him. Then once he heard the call of a bird, and he looked back toward the call. He went beneath the tree and was waiting for the bird to call again. A voice spoke to him, "You have dissolved God's bond! You have given away the key to My covenant, for you have become intimate with another!"

Muḥammad ibn Ḥassān said, "Once I was wandering in the mountain of Lebanon, hoping to see one of the friends of the Real, one of the great ones who take up residence there. I saw a young man come out from a corner. The hot wind of summer had blown against him, and he was burnt and bedraggled. When he saw me, he turned away and entered in among the chestnut trees to conceal himself. I followed him. I said, 'O chevalier! Give me the benefit of some words, for I came in hope of that.'

"He answered, 'Beware! He is jealous. He does not love to see other than Himself in the heart of His servant.'"

Adam the Chosen was the center-point of the compass of existence, the substance of the creation of mortal man, and the chosen of the empire. He turned his heart toward the bliss of paradise and gave himself over to it. From the Exalted Presence came jealousy's messenger: "Are you not ashamed to bring your aspiration down to Riḍwān's house of good fortune and to look back at something other than Me? Now that You have looked back at something else, take your bags and go down to the house of the decree. Throw down your head in incapacity and be broken by shortcoming in the quarry of trial, and wait for My decree!"

In the same way, Abraham's eyes looked back at Ishmael. He saw an exalted nobility and rectitude, the seed of bosom friendship, the oyster for the pearl of the chosen Muḥammad. His heart busied itself with him. The command came, "O My bosom friend! Did I keep you away from the Azari idols so that you could gaze on Ishmael's beauty? Now, take up knife and rope and sacrifice everything less than Me in the road. Two beloveds cannot fit into one heart."

In the same way, Muḥammad the Arab, the Master of Adam's children, the foremost of the prophets and messengers, had busied a corner of his heart with ʿĀʾisha, so much so that when he was asked, "Which of the people do you love most?" he said "ʿĀʾisha."

In one of the reports, it has come that ʿĀʾisha said, "O Messenger of God! I love you and I love being near to you!"

When they busied their hearts with love for each other, the ruling power of jealousy opened the curtain of exaltedness and, with the attribute of harshness, showed them a sliver of its authority. The satans of mankind and jinn joined hands, and the slanderous talk entered the midst. The lie fabricated by the hypocrites took flight. What is even more wondrous is that in those days the path of perspicacity was shut to Muṣṭafā lest the innocence of ʿĀʾisha should appear to him. He did not know the reality of that business until jealousy had driven home its severity and the turn of trial had come to an end.

The cause of this is that at the time of trial, God blocks the eyes of His friends' perspicacity in order to complete the trial. This is why Abraham did not distinguish and recognize the angels when he presented to them the *roasted calf* [11:69] and supposed them to be guests. Lot also did not recognize them as angels until they announced to him that they were angels.

Things reached the point that all the joy, whispered secrets, and gentleness that Muṣṭafā had with ʿĀʾisha came to a halt. Instead of calling her Ḥumayrā by way of endearment, he kept on saying, "How is your family?" ʿĀʾisha was kept away from nearness to Muṣṭafā at her father's house. She was ill, wailing, burning, weeping, her heart full of pain and her spirit full of remorse. She was looking at her own misery and abasement and saying, "I never imagined that anyone could suspect me of this or bring words like this to the tongue."

The friend, it seems, is unaware of my grief,
and sleep no longer comes my way.
Each moment my night becomes darker—
O Lord, it seems the night has no dawn!

Then, when the verses of exoneration came down and the turn of trial came to an end, God's Messenger gave ʿĀʾisha the good news: "God has revealed your innocence."

Her mother and father said to her, "O ʿĀʾisha, betake yourself to God's Messenger and praise him."

She said, "No, by God, I will not betake myself to him, nor will I praise him, nor will I praise you two. Rather, I will praise God, who revealed my innocence."

She had so given her heart to the Messenger's nearness and love that she had said, "I love you and I love being near to you." After being immersed in that, she gave everything over to love for the Unity and busied herself with serving the Divine Threshold. She always used to say, "By the praise of God, not your praise!"

O chevalier, if the accusers of ʿĀʾisha had not voiced that calumny, the verses declaring her eminence would not have descended from heaven. If the Christians had not said, "*The Messiah is the son of God*" [9:30], Jesus would not have been given the generosity of "*Surely I am the servant of God—He gave me the Book and made me a prophet*" [19:30]. If the man of faith did not sin, he would not have been honored with the address, "*Despair not of God's mercy*" [39:53].

> This is why, at the beginning of the story, He said, "*Do not count it as evil for you; no, it is good for you.* O ʿĀʾisha, do not imagine that what they said was bad for you. If it was bad, it was bad for them. Because of it, they became worthy of *great chastisement*. For you, it was all goodness and generosity, the perfection of reward and the elevation of rank."
>
> It has come in the stories that paradise has an outskirts, and tomorrow the Exalted Lord will gather the faithful in the outskirts, and before they go into paradise, He will host them in a perfect invitation, a fitting bestowal of eminence, a complete caressing. Then He will place a favor on Muṣṭafā: "O Muḥammad, this invitation is the banquet for your contract of marriage with Mary, daughter of ʿImrān, and Āsiya daughter of Muzāḥim. O Muḥammad, I kept Mary away from companionship with men and brought forth from her a child without a man for the sake of your honor and jealousy. I kept Āsiya next to Pharaoh, but I took away Pharaoh's manliness and never let him be alone with her. I conveyed her to you pure, without defect, no one's hand having touched her."
>
> Now listen to a subtle point: he honored Mary and Āsiya, who will be wives of Muṣṭafā tomorrow in the next world, and He praised them for purity and guarded them from the people. ʿĀʾisha the truthful, who was his wife in this world, who pleased him, who was his companion, whose love was in his heart, and who will be married to him tomorrow in paradise—what wonder that God honored her, sent Qur'anic verses and revelation exonerating her, and Himself gave witness to her purity and approved of her?
>
> (*Kashf* 6:512–15)

In Chapter 26 of *Forty-Two Chapters*, Anṣārī explains that God's friends and lovers will not be delivered from jealousy's afflictions until they pass beyond themselves. He is discussing the nature of the knowledge that people should seek to help them travel on the path. He begins by citing a saying of Abū Yaʿqūb Isḥāq Nahrjūrī: "The most excellent act of the desirer is that which accords with knowledge of the Haqiqah and has no suspicion or doubt in the Shariah." In his explanation, he refers to the two basic characteristics of Adam: being chosen by God and being a great wrongdoer and deeply ignorant. The process of walking on God's path involves turning away from ignorance, recovering the knowledge of the names taught to Adam, and becoming worthy for the state of chosen-ness and vicegerency.

> The Intimation. When someone is quickly taken to task, he will be quickly let go, but when someone is left alone, there is fear. When a servant sins and is quickly taken to task, that is the mark of acceptance. When he sins and is

not held to account, that is a sign that he has not been accepted, and he is in danger.

Practice must be built on knowledge, for such practice has value.

The jealousy of friendship does not allow a friend to breathe easy with other than the Friend. If you look back at others, that is blindness itself.

Being blinded by form is easy in this work. "Not seeing" is to see others and to fail to differentiate between seeing and not seeing. Ignorance is to depend on yourself, to act wrongly toward the Friend, and to settle down with yourself.

If you do not get rid of your attribute of great wrongdoing and your deep ignorance of the names, there is fear that you will be totally deprived of the inheritance of election and chosen-ness. As long as you do not get rid of this attribute, you will not find this meaning in yourself. You can never recover the beginning of the thread with this perplexed intellect. Your intellect is perplexed because it has turned its face toward you.

If solicitude provides guidance, intellect will turn back to the work, to the knowledge of the names, and to the attribute of election and chosen-ness. When intellect finds the inheritance of this work, it will catch a scent of this work and be released from all work.

The two worlds became manifest for the sake of affliction. When someone reaches chosen-ness, he will be released from affliction.

Trial has been put in charge of the friends. It drives them forth to take them to the Friend.

The trial of the common people is not to reach what they desire, and for them this is an expiation. The trial of this group is a fire that falls into them when they see others and burns away both themselves and the others.

Do not compare the trial of this group with the trial of every group, for the trial and blessing of every group is apparent, but this group stands apart from what keeps people busy.

Strive to find a taste of this work so that you may be relieved of the tribulation and ease of the two worlds, released from yourself through His gentleness and favor, and remain forever with Him.

(*Chihil* 159)

Despite the necessity of seeking knowledge in order to advance on the path, knowledge itself can become a dangerous idol. In Chapter 32 of *Forty-Two Chapters*, which begins with the hadith "A man will be with the one he loves," Anṣārī turns to a brief account of ʿAbdallāh ibn Muḥammad ibn ʿAbd al-Raḥmān al-Shaʿrānī al-Rāzī (d. 964). He cites one of his sayings and then explains that both knowledge and practice can become objects of love and divert seekers from tawḥīd.

ʿAbdallāh was asked, "Why is it that some people recognize their own defects but do not turn away from them or repent?"

He said, "It is because they are busy boasting of their learning and exulting in their knowledge. They take pride in it, but they do not put it into practice. They are occupied with outward shame, but not with inner acts of courtesy. In other words, they make their outwardness straight by talking and listening, but they do not perform the inner acts of courtesy. Hence, God blinds their hearts with correct knowledge and belief. He attaches their limbs to worship, but He holds them back from success in their work. For they know the reward of knowledge, but they are not able to act in keeping with it."

The Intimation. The scholar imagined that he was the friend of knowledge, but in fact he was the friend of boasting and bragging and made knowledge the means to it. Friendship with knowledge followed behind, and that is why he fell back.

When the cause of friendship with something is something else, then the friendship is with that root thing, and friendship with the branch follows after it. Even if the name is placed on the branch, that has no benefit, for love for the branch intrudes on something else. The Friend is He on whom all friendships are intruders and to whom all are sacrificed. So do not make the mistake of thinking that the scholar is an insightful critic!

Look at what your heart wants from knowledge: Status? Wealth? Boasting and pride? Gratifying desires? Self-restraint? Are you seeking to negate yourself or to affirm yourself? Are you striving to reject your caprice or to achieve its desires? Are you passionate for the name, message, and commandments of friendship, or are you passionate for your own name and pleasure? Are you expending yourself in the road of His approval or in following your own caprice?

Beware, lest you turn your own simpleminded patience into the lowest of the low! Listen to yourself in yourself! Do not conceal your own defects with other people's defects. Rather, conceal other people's defects with your defects!

Whenever you fail to see the bond of love and the mark of truthful friendship on any of your own bodily members, begin to lament: "Where did the key to friendship's treasury go?"

When anyone has patience to look at others for one moment, this is evidence that he knows nothing of the patience of lovers. If the lover falls in with other than his Friend, he is not able to bear separation from his Friend for one moment. Remembering others is worse for him than a cutting blade. Being cut off from Him is greater than hell, and joining with Him is sweeter than paradise.

When there is talk of friendship, life is the least of the least. Compared to one moment of separation's fire, hell is less than a lamp next to the seven depths of hell. How will our separation be, for separation gives off the scent of blood!

O God, You have the fire of separation. Of what use is the fire of hell?

O God, when I recognized three things, the terror of three things left me. As soon as I recognized the poison of distance from You, I forgot the bitterness of hell. As soon as I recognized the delight of mentioning and remembering You, I forgot the delights of paradise. As soon as I recognized the splendor of proximity to You, I forgot the terror of the resurrection.

When people do not know this, this is evidence that they have read the name of friendship and separation, but they have not found friendship, nor have they tasted separation. They drive forth in error, they simmer in their delusions, and they suppose that they have it. Wait until the curtain is lifted from this business!

They suppose that they belong to this group. Would that they knew this much: "A man is with him whom he loves."

Look! With whom are you? Where are you in showing friendship? Perhaps you may come out of your error and buy friendship with the nonbeing of your soul, heart, and spirit. Then you will be aware of this talk face-to-face. And God bless Muḥammad and His household, all of them!

(*Chihil* 195–96)

Given that Samʿānī explains each divine name as a different melody sung to the tune of tawḥīd, it is hardly surprising that he often discusses God's jealousy. His first explanation of its meaning comes in his commentary on the phrase "*No god but He*," which he lists as the third of God's ninety-nine names (after *He* and *God*).

No god but He will be discussed briefly and succinctly, God willing. In simple Persian, this statement means "There is no god but the one God"—majestic is His majesty!

No god is the policeman of negation's severity, seated on the steed of awe, the sword of the Lord's jealousy in its hand. Wherever there is any other, it lops off its head with jealousy's sword so that the sultan of *but God* may sit on the royal seat of the heart's kingdom and issue commandments to the serving boys, which are the limbs. If someone puts his head on the line of obedience and binds his waist with the belt of acquiescence, the robe of exaltation will be draped over the clothing of his secret core. But if someone twists his head away from the collar of servanthood, the brand of loss will be pressed on his face, and the collar of imprecation, repulsion, and rejection will be hung around his neck.

O chevalier! When a sultan is about to dismount at a house, there is a stipulation that first the chamberlain must come and sweep the house. He will take away the refuse and rubbish and put down the sultan's royal seat. When the sultan arrives, the work will be finished and the house ready. In the same way, when the exalted sultan of *but God* is about to dismount in a breast, the chamberlain of *no god* comes before. It sweeps the courtyard of the breast with the broom of disengagement and solitariness and destroys the refuse and rubbish of mortality, Adamic nature, satanity, and human nature. It sprinkles the water of contentment and spreads the carpet of loyalty. It lights up the sandalwood of limpidness in the incense burner of contentment. It puts down the royal throne of felicity and the seat of chieftainship. When the sultan of *but God* arrives, it leans back on the cushion of the secret core in the cradle of the Covenant.

There is another secret more exalted than this. It is that this *no* is a gallows erected at the crossroads of the Compeller's desire, over which He appointed the executioner of His will. If the meddlesome intellect does not pull back its feet in the measure of the rug—as they say, "Extend your feet in the measure of the cloth"—severity will hang it from the gallows of *no*. This will be a lesson for the eyes and a cause of wakefulness in the breast. *So take heed, O possessors of eyesight!* [59:2].

O dervish! Everyone who aims for the Presence of *but God* must pass by *no god*, which is severity's mouth, open like a crocodile's. The crocodile of severity must swallow down all his attributes, whether disobedient or obedient. Then he will arrive at the presence of *but God*'s good fortune, solitary and disengaged—no dust on the heart, no burden on the back, no reckoning with anyone, no commerce in the heart, no harm in the breast, no business with any created thing.

Thereby he will become disengaged through God and be His representative. He will have erased the dust of the others from the tablet of the heart, given his makeup to taste the poison of severity, and taken his aspiration beyond the peak of the Throne. He will have fled from the realm of being and found rest with the Friend, thrown the ball of revelry into the field of the quest, drawn the sword of severity from the scabbard of manliness, made do with the Friend in the midst of the soul, thrown the die of the heart on the board of passion, cast the hook of the quest into the ocean of good fortune, overthrown the whole house and family of human nature, cleansed the tablet of caprice, and torn away the cloak of disloyalty.

(*Rawḥ* 7–8)

In his commentary on the name *muhaymin*, the Overseer, Samʿānī talks of shame (*ḥayāʾ*) as a virtue that should guide both thought and activity. Shame is closely allied with beautiful-doing (iḥsān), which, as we know, the Prophet defined by saying, "It is that you worship God as if you see Him, for if you do not see Him, surely He sees you." As Samʿānī explains, "When the servant knows that the Real is watching his states and is near to him, he must put on the clothing of shame and be ashamed in the place where the Real is aware" (*Rawḥ* 38). He enumerates various sorts of shame that a person should have, illustrating each with Qur'anic verses, hadiths, and anecdotes. One of these has to do with eliminating self-admiration.

There is the shame that is the shame of the obedient for their obedience. Abū Bakr Warrāq said, "Sometimes I perform two cycles of prayer, and then, when I say the greeting and finish, I am embarrassed and ashamed at this obedience of mine, as if I were a thief." As long as a man does not arrive at this station, the pleasure of obedience will not reach the taste buds of his faith.

Sufyān Thawrī was sitting in a litter after having set off for the Kaabah. With him in the litter was a friend. Sufyān kept weeping and scattering the water of his eyes' ocean on the shores of his cheeks. His friend said, "O Sufyān, do you weep in fear of sin?"

Sufyān reached out and picked up a piece of straw. He said, "I have many sins, but for me my sins have not the measure of this piece of straw. I fear this: is this tawḥīd that I have brought real tawḥīd?"

These were people who had, but they showed themselves as not having. You do not have, but you show yourselves as having. They were the rich who fancied themselves indigent, front-runners who had the remorse of laggards. Now the situation has been reversed, and men have become obstinate in irreligion. They are indigent, but they fancy themselves rich. They are laggards but claim to be front-runners.

Are you a man—you who hope for chieftainship? The will must be your will, the want your want, and the desire your desire. But this business will not be completed in partnership.

An afflicted and wounded man, his soul come to the edge, had fallen beneath a thornbush, attacked by a hundred thousand trials, troubles, adversities, and hardships. All at once this cry rose up from him: "At least, for one moment, give me back to myself so that I may recover my own thread."

He heard a call, "This work will not be set straight in partnership. Either Me, or you."

The ship must be broken and the man drowned, leaving only you and the Goal, the Goal and you.

In my love for Buthayna I desired that we two
be alone on a raft in the ocean.

Smash all that is not named Friend,
lose all that is not named passion!

Everything other than the Goal is a crowd on the road to the Goal. The veiled lady of this talk is jealous. She will not show her beautiful face in the midst of the crowding of others. She will not lift the mask of exaltation. She is a dust mote in the sun of passion's world. If the sun fills the whole world, she will not show her face. She wants a place of seclusion, without the crowding of others, so that she may lift up the mask of jealousy.

Master Abu ʿAlī Daqqāq said, "Paradise has no business with me, and hell has nothing to do with me, for there is nothing in my heart but joy in the Real's subsistence."

When I became joyful in Your subsistence,
I scratched annihilation's line across myself.

Those who step into this road do so not for any cause, but rather for love. The petitioner does not come from the door, but rather from within the breast. They kick aside paradise and hell, and then they step forth on the road.

Looking for compensation in the road of obedience is a fatal poison. If you were to walk on this road for a thousand years and your obedience was not accepted, and then it occurred to your mind that it should have been accepted, you would have been a status seeker, not a road seeker. You will not be a realizer in this road until you abandon your status with both the Real and the creatures.

Someone says, "I don't want status with the creatures, I want status at the Threshold." Do not seek for status, either here or there! Bind up your waist and, like a man, find the broom of solitariness and disengagement. A thousand times a day sweep the threshold of your own dreadful existence. If it should happen that you stay at the threshold for a thousand years and then it is said to you, "Go, for you are not worthy of Me," you will have been given your due.

(*Rawḥ* 40–42)

God is gentle and severe, beautiful and majestic, life-giving and death-giving, creative and destructive. His munificence and power bring a universe into existence, but His jealousy takes it away. Human beings are caught in the midst of this give-and-take, affirmation and negation. This is the foundational truth of reality per se: *No god but God.* To live in harmony with reality, people must acknowledge the nonexistence of the others, beginning with themselves. They must negate others and affirm the One. *If you love God* and affirm His Reality, *follow me* by negating your own wishes and conforming to the Sunnah, which is the embodiment of the religious command. Samʿānī describes tawḥīd's dialectic by talking of the interplay of power and jealousy.

> These creatures that you see affirm Power and negate Jealousy. The sultan of majesty's Jealousy charges forth from the world of exaltation and perfection and snatches the hat from the head of the world's folk. "How can it be correct that you be existent and He be existent, that you have being and He have being? *God is the Unneedy, and you are the poor* [47:38]."
>
> If you say concerning an existence whose edges are open to nonexistence that it is existence, that is a metaphor. "An existence between two nonexistences is like no existence at all."
>
> Recite the verse of your own nonexistence from the tablet of His Eternity! Raise the flag of your own nonbeing in the world of His Being! From the cup of Sufism's covenant, drink the unmixed wine of negating self-determination in the flow of the decrees! Draw the line of erasure across the register of your days! Do not bring the dead donkey of your own miserable "was not" into the same line as the majestic Burāq of "He has no beginning and no end."
>
> In the world of the command, sit on the steed of existence so that you may perform the commandments! In the world of passionate love, sit on the steed of nonexistence so that you may receive the commandments! When the draft of the address arrives in the cup of the Sunnah and the Book, drink the wine of the command and become drunk with its beauty!
>
> Once you have drunk the wine of the command and put on the garment of compliance, then you will be confounded in nonexistence by the giddiness of passion, contemplating the Eternal Witness and unaware of awareness.
>
> In your bowing and prostrating, give being and existence to yourself and become existent in the majestic existence of *And He is God* [28:70]. But in reality, tear the cloak of metaphorical existence and look back to the Divine Beauty and the Royal Perfection. These creatures that you see are existent through His munificence and nonexistent through His existence. His munificence has tossed the cape of existence on the neck of the existent things, but His existence tosses all existent things into the concealment of nonexistence.
>
> (*Rawḥ* 165)

The path of love demands loyalty to the Covenant of Alast, which in turn demands emptying oneself of desire for others and being filled with desire for the One. As Samʿānī puts it:

O poor men who have no bread! O wealthy men toward whom the worldlings have turned their faces! Do not forget Him. He pardons everything except the sins and offenses of the heart. Nowhere did He say, "I love heaven," or "I love earth," or the Throne, the Footstool, the spheres, the angels. He said, "I love the Adamites." Loyalty is the stipulation of the road.

So what must be done? You must not let any others into your heart. "If you let creatures into your heart, your heart will be an offender, and We will not pardon it. If We were to pardon the offense of the heart, love's jealousy would go. If love's jealousy went, love itself would not remain."

When a heart does not carry the banner of passion, kick it in the head, for it is not a heart, but an intruder in the convocation of the passionate.

Tomorrow everyone will be gazing on his own heart's beloved. One will seize the skirt of paradise, another will hunt out the Garden of Eden, and still another will catch the highest of the High Chambers. But the day of the friends' good fortune will be the day when they look out and see that the field of Unity is empty of the intrusion of others. *Whose is the kingdom today? God's, the One, the Severe* [40:16].

"O Seraphiel! Blow into these spirits, then blow into your own spirit. Drive them away and go away with them!"

O dervish! If anyone thinks that paradise is adorned with the beauty of wide-eyed maidens, the jasmine scent of passion's covenant has not yet reached his nostrils. The lords of the heart know the meaning of these words.

These hapless creatures! For seventy years in this world, newly arrived things intrude upon them, and then they settle down in paradise with more newly arrived things!

By the ruling of the Shariah, this world is the road and paradise is the sought object. But by the fatwa of the Haqiqah, paradise is both road and thief, and the Real is the only goal.

(*Rawḥ* 608)

In another passage, Samʿānī describes God's jealousy in the various stages of Adam's creation. God created him in His form, taught him all the names, and brought the universe into existence as his playing field. But He created Adam for Himself, not for any of the secondary causes, so people are wrong to think that they have been put into the world to do as they please. If they devote themselves to the others—the things, desires, whims, people, idols, and gods that are laid out before them—they will fall into associationism. Their task is to focus on the One. As for God's jealousy, it will turn all their metaphorical loves into dust.

That paragon was sent into paradise as a requisite of munificence and generosity, and he was put on the couch of exaltedness. The whole of paradise was placed under his command. He looked it over, but he did not see a speck of sorrow or love's reality. He said, "Oil and water don't mix."

The stipulation of poverty is disengagement and solitariness. When a fruit ripens in the shade, it has no flavor. "The stipulation of Our road is a head hung down and a bed of ashes."

It was said, "O Adam! Since the state is like this, you must go back to the dustbin where you took the first step."

He said, "I will need an excuse for all these pretty faces."

It was said, "We will call out your excuse." The Qur'an expresses this with the words, "*And Adam disobeyed*" [20:121].

When he came out of paradise, he saw a black mark on his face. He said, "O Lord! What is this?"

He said, "O Adam! What you have chosen does not come with whiteness of face, for 'Poverty is blackness of face in the two worlds.'* Everything that has being has it for your sake, but you are more beautiful barefoot."

He created an individual. He threw the noose of subjection on the neck of all that was anything in heaven and earth and put it in Adam's hand. The sun was his torch holder and cook, the moon his color changer, the mountains his treasurers, heaven his roof, earth his carpet. He subjected to him the exalted angels, with their high degrees and ranks and their brilliant stations and honors. One of them drives the clouds, another brings the rain, a third provides daily bread, a fourth writes down works, a fifth asks forgiveness.

What a marvelous business! Someone sins, and dust comes to sit on the pages of his state. The Shariah proclaims to the spirit of living things that this man has slipped and disobedience has come into existence from him. But God wants to wash away the stain of that slip. "For his sake, We have written an edict to your spirits: 'Sacrifice your lives to him!'" He created everything for him, but He did not turn him over to anything. He gave him some names, but He did not turn him over to the names. He sat him on a throne and had the angels prostrate themselves before him, but He did not turn him over to that. He brought him into this world and made the great and small of it his kingdom, but He did not turn him over to this world.

First he had the cape of nonexistence, but He did not leave him in nonexistence. Then he put on the cape of existence, but He did not turn him over to that. He gave him attributes, but he did not let him loose with the attributes.

He created him, gave him beauty, and displayed that beauty to the world's inhabitants. A hundred thousand seekers began to seek. The Exalted Jealousy came out and did not turn him over to anyone.

"If you didn't want to sell, why did you give him to the broker?" All being took a share of his beauty, but He Himself kept the trailing skirts of his state free from those shares.

(*Rawḥ* 237–38)

Elsewhere Samʿānī explains that God's loved ones are never obvious, because His jealousy keeps them hidden from the prying eyes of others.

In one of the revealed books, it is written, "I created the whole world for you, and I created you for Me."

There was a man who had a repulsive face. One day he was looking in a mirror and thinking to himself in wonder, "What wisdom did God have in creating this ugly face?"

He heard a voice from the midst of the mirror: "My wisdom in creating you is the love that I kneaded into your secret core. The secret of that love was concealed by the jealousy of the Unseen so that the eyes of others might not fall upon you."

When the center-point of this dirt-dwelling dust put on the shirt of existence and the robe of generosity and munificence, the secret of love appeared: "I am the King, and I invite you to become kings. I am the Living, and I invite you to live."

O dervish! If He had not given you kingship, no recognition of Him would have come to you, for no one recognizes a king but a king. Where does the splendorous scripture allude to this good news? *"Then We made you vicegerents"* [10:14]. *"And He made you kings"* [5:20].

He made you a king and He gave you a kingship. That kingship is a tiny sample of the kingship of the Possessor of Majesty. A throne of passion was built from your spirit, and a footstool of truthfulness was set up as your heart. A tent was erected in the desert of your makeup as a dwelling-place for the cavalry of your imagination. Your brain was placed before you as a Guarded Tablet. Your five senses were turned into the angels of your heavenly sovereignty's makeup. Your intellect was made into a moon, and your knowledge a sun, shining on the sphere of your body. Through all of these you were made a king. In the tongue of prophecy, that was expressed in these terms: "Each of you is a shepherd, and each of you will be asked about his sheep."

O friends of the Real! Be careful not to look at yourselves with contempt, for this is not the place for the flying of your dignity's phoenix nor for the soaring of your secret core. Even if your outwardness is made of dust and you are accustomed to impudence, your inwardness comes from the world of purity. Who is equal to you in the two worlds? Even if the peacock of your existence did not fly in the meadow of the Beginningless, it will fly in the gardens of the Endless and reach union with the Friend, forever and ever. Even if the pearl of your inwardness was mixed at the beginning with bestial and predatory attributes, once it is sifted by the sieve of good fortune and struggle, and once the blood of this refractory soul is spilled from its nature, it will be worthy of the neighborhood of the Sultan's Presence. It is a heavenly pearl on the face of the earth. Where is this state expressed? "Recognition is radiant lights flashing in the heart and lifting it away from defects to the unseen things."

(*Rawḥ* 158–59)

Samʿānī again explains how God's jealousy focuses people's eyes on the reality of tawḥīd in the following passage. In the midst of it, he provides a typical interpretation of the story of Moses as a message to every human soul. As he says elsewhere, "Do not imagine that there is only one Mount Sinai in the world and one Moses. Your body is Mount Sinai, and your heart Moses. The food of your heart is *Surely it is I who am God* [20:14]. If He were not jealous of the heart, by God the heart would not be the heart!" (*Rawḥ* 614).

His love comes and burns away everything other than Him. When it comes, it strikes the fire of jealousy into the haystack of gazing on others. "A desolate heart, within it a shining lamp." Exalted is the heart in which there is no room for others!

A body is wanted tamed by the commandments. A heart is wanted contemplating the command. A spirit is wanted drunk with the wine of holiness in the session of intimacy. A secret core is wanted standing on the carpet of expansiveness, empty of every being. A radiance of the light of gentleness is wanted shining from the Mount Sinai of unveiling, snatching you, like Moses, away from all others and setting you down in the station of contemplation and the domicile of struggle. It will remove the *shoes* [20:12] of gazing on the two worlds from your feet, snatch the *staff* [20:18] of disobedience from your hand, and bring you to the *holy valley* [20:12] and the unqualified bush. It will make you drunk with spirit-mingled and repose-inducing wine, and at every moment it will call out to the hearing of your secret core, "*Surely it is I who am God* [20:14]: It is I who am I. If anyone says 'I am,' I will break his neck. Even if you are not jealous of your thoughts, aspiration, and resolution, I in My lordhood am jealous."

It has been said, "Jealousy is two: human jealousy and divine jealousy. Human jealousy is concerned with outward things, and divine jealousy is concerned with conscious thoughts."

Do you imagine that He is foolish to keep all these secrets under the protection of His own gaze? To the same degree that He is jealous of His own Unseen, He is jealous of your secret core. That is why He said, "*Surely I know what you do not know*" [2:30]. It is because He is keeping that for this, and He is nurturing this for that. It will be an exalted moment when the curtain is lifted from the midst. The secret core will gaze on the Unseen, and the Unseen will gaze on the secret core. What do you say about that time? Will forgiveness count for anything?

"We made the whole world the servant of your good fortune's presence. We addressed you, saying, 'Do not be the servant of any but Our Threshold: *Do not prostrate yourselves before the sun and the moon, but prostrate yourselves before God, who created them* [41:37]. *We created you, then We formed you, then We said to the angels, 'Prostrate yourselves before Adam'* [7:11]. O folk of the world! Prostrate yourselves before them. O handful of dust! Prostrate only to Him."

What is this? It is the divine jealousy toward the creation of dust. "I am jealous and Saʿd is jealous, but God is more jealous than we. Part of His jealousy is that He *forbade indecencies* [7:33]."*

He busied each of your motes with one of His secrets: "O hearing, be gathered in listening: *When the Qur'an is recited, listen to it* [7:204]. O eyesight, have insight and heedfulness: *Take heed, O possessors of eyesight!* [59:2]. O tongue, remember His beautiful-doing: *Remember God as you remember your fathers, or with more intense remembrance!* [2:200]. O nose, be disdainful of smelling the stench of others. O hands, be takers of the goblets of gentleness. O feet, be walkers in the gardens of discipline. *Say "God," then leave them!* [6:91]. *And devote yourselves to Him devoutly* [73:8]. *So take him as a Trustee* [73:9]."

If it were appropriate for one mote of you to belong to another, then what is the mission of the prophets? He sent one hundred twenty-some thousand pivots of messengerhood with limpid states, and the gist of their invitation was this: "O dust and clay, belong to Me from the depths of your spirit and heart! If you turn away from the road by one iota—the whips of punishment are in place. The commandments have been sent. If you turn away from the commandments—the reprimands are in place."

He calls with gentleness, and He brings back with harshness. He has filled the world with dread and blights: thorns with fresh dates, headaches with wine, troubles with treasures, tribulation with good fortune. You can never settle down, find intimacy and familiarity, or reach conformity with a single mote. Whether you like it or not, whether by compulsion or free choice, you will go back to the Threshold.

Muṣṭafā said, "Command children to pray when they are seven and, when they are ten, if they do it freely, good. Otherwise—the rod and the whip." This is a marvelous business! A frail compound, an insignificant makeup, a defective intellect, inadequate knowledge. Then the command of the Prophet comes: "Command him to pray!"

What is this prayer? Its meaning is that an invitation was offered to the heaven with its length and breadth, to the earth with its deployment and vastness, and to the towering, firm-rooted, lofty mountains, and they all refused. What a marvelous business! If the many-thousand-year-old heaven could not carry this burden, what is the secret here that the command of Majesty comes and places it on the head of a frail child? "Yes, give him a taste of this draft for the sake of getting used to it. Then he will know its flavor."

The long and short of it is this: "Be seven years old or seventy, the burden of My work will not pass by your door. Whatever color you have, you must carry My burden. Swallow the bitters without frowning! You must take on the job, despite Iblis." What a marvelous business! The sword is drawn, the draft prepared, the man frail.

O dervish! A request came out from the curtain of the Unseen to the vast plain of manifestation. It passed by the whole world and paid no attention to anyone. When it reached Adam's dust, it pulled back the reins of Majesty. It lifted the veil from its own heart-snatching beauty and said, "Peace be upon you! I have come for you. Are you ready for Me?"

(*Rawḥ* 201–2)

THE ONENESS OF LOVE

It was noted earlier that tawḥīd is commonly described as having levels. The lowest is uttering the formula *No god but God*, and the highest is oneness with the Real. It is worth reviewing these levels before looking closely at the final stage of tawḥīd, in which nothing remains but the One.

In a passage from *Giving Life* that was quoted in Chapter Four, Muḥammad Ghazālī speaks of four levels. The first is saying the words of the formula, the second believing in the words, the third seeing the One, and the fourth aloneness with the One. In his Persian summary of this passage, Ghazālī makes a point that he did not mention explicitly in the Arabic. This is that the second level is marred by imitation (taqlīd), that is, rote learning, blind acceptance, and the failure to achieve realization (taḥqīq).

The first degree of tawḥīd is that someone says with the tongue, "*No god but God*," but he does not believe it in the heart. This is the tawḥīd of the hypocrite.

The second degree is that someone believes its meaning in the heart, like the common man; or by some sort of evidence, like the Kalam expert.

The third degree is that someone sees, by way of witnessing, that everything comes forth from one root, that there is no more than one actor, and that no one else has any activity. A light appears in the heart, and witnessing occurs through this light. This is not like the belief of the common man or the Kalam expert, for their belief is a knot tied in the heart by means of imitation or evidence. This witnessing is an expansion of the heart that unties all knots.

There are differences between these three: one person convinces himself or believes that the master is in the house because so-and-so said he is in the house. This is the imitation of the common man, who heard it from his mother and father. Another person infers that the master is in the house because the horse and servants are standing by the doorway. This is like the belief of the Kalam expert. The third person sees him inside the house by way of witnessing. This is like the tawḥīd of the recognizers.

Although this third tawḥīd is great in degree, its possessor still sees creatures while he sees and knows the Creator, so there is a great deal of multiplicity. As long as he sees two, he stays in dispersion and does not have togetherness.

The perfection of tawḥīd is the fourth degree. The person sees only one, and he sees and recognizes all as one. Dispersion has no way into this. This is what the Sufis call annihilation in tawḥīd.

(*Kīmiyā-yi saʿādat*, 799–800)

Throughout his writings, even when he speaks openly of the degrees of unveiling achieved at the summit of the path to God, Muḥammad Ghazālī walks on a tightrope, careful not to fall into the scandalous formulations of which Sufi teachers were so often accused. His brother Aḥmad had no such reservations, nor did he show any interest, in *Apparitions* at least, in developing theoretical arguments to support tawḥīd. He speaks rather to those who are in the midst of realizing tawḥīd through love. At the furthest stages of this path, he tells us, nothing remains but love itself, which is God's very Essence, the Real per se. The lover's goal cannot be to achieve union with the Beloved, for that would mean that two can become one. On the contrary, when the lover returns to his own essential nonbeing, he ceases to be, and so also does the Beloved, for all relationships have been nullified.

In one of the longer chapters of *Apparitions*, Aḥmad speaks of three stages of tawḥīd that are more or less parallel with the three mentioned by his brother (after the utterance of the formula). But Aḥmad is talking about love, so he is careful to point out that it is God's jealousy that gets the work done. At the same time, he speaks of the role of blame (*malāma*), which every lover can expect to face. This is one of many issues discussed in Sufi texts that address the practical ethics of living in a conformist society. After all, family, neighbors, and the sanctimonious will always try to dissuade lovers, reminding them of their duty to parents, family, and society: "Get a job, marry, have children. Don't ruin your life." Some of those who came under such pressure adopted the path of the blameworthy (*malāmatiyya* or *malāmiyya*). They became blatant nonconformists, making themselves obnoxious and scandalous. As a rule, they did not disobey the clear commandments and prohibitions of the Shariah, but they did ignore various sides to the Sunnah that tended to get exaggerated by people caught up with appearances.

In any case, Sufi texts frequently explain that seekers should welcome the blame of family and society, because it can help them detach themselves from everything other than God. Judging from anecdotes handed down about Aḥmad Ghazālī, he adopted that path—quite in contrast with his brother Muḥammad. What is certain is that he discusses blame as essential to love in one of the longest chapters of *Apparitions*, defining it as the sword of jealousy. When it sets to work, it slices away all others in keeping with three stages of tawḥīd: first people and things, then the selves of the seekers, then the Beloved. In the final stage, love alone remains.

> Chapter [4]: On blame. Love's perfection is blame. Blame has three faces, one toward the creatures, one toward the lover, and the third toward the Beloved.
>
> The face toward the creatures is the sword of the Beloved's jealousy, wielded so that the lover will not look at others. The face toward the lover is the sword of the present moment's jealousy, wielded so that he will not look at himself. The face toward the Beloved is love's jealousy, wielded so that he will feed on love and not be tied to wanting, for he must not seek anything outside it.
>
> I seek nothing in the world but Your love—
> separation and union are the same for me.
> Existing without Your love would turn me upside down—
> if You want, bring union, if You want, separation!
>
> All three faces are jealousy's sword, cutting off the gaze from others, for this work reaches the point where the lover is the other, and the Beloved is also the other. This is the ruling power of love's shining, for the food of love's perfection comes from unification. In it there is no room for the distinction between lover and Beloved.
>
> When someone considers union to be a coming together and then feeds on that state, this is not the reality of love.

I would break the covenant and be empty of love
were I to say to You, "Come and help me!"
Bring union if You want, separation if You want.
I am free of both—Your love is enough for me.

Love must eat both. Once the reality of union is inside love's craw, the possibility of separation will disappear. But not everyone understands this.

When union is separation, separation is union itself. So being separated from oneself is the same as conjunction. Here food is having no food, being is nonbeing, finding is not finding, and one's portion is not having any portion.

Not everyone has access to this, for its origins are beyond the utmost ends. How could its utmost end fit into the courtyard of knowledge? How could it enter the field of imagination? This reality is a pearl in a shell, and the shell is at the bottom of the sea. Knowledge has access only to the shore. How could it reach here?

When knowledge is drowned, certainty turns into supposition. From knowledge and certainty a furtive thought arises; in the garment of the pretense of *I thought* [69:20], it goes to the threshold of this talk's exaltedness. *"Do you not have faith?' [Abraham] said, "I do, but [that my heart may be at rest]"* [2:260] alludes to something like this.

This is the same as "I am with My servant's thoughts of Me, so let him think of Me what he wants."* So the servant is conjoined with the thought, and the thought is conjoined with the Lord. The thought is the diver in the sea. It may happen that the pearl falls into its hand, or that it falls into the pearl's hand.

The reason for the blame of the creatures is that if a hair tip of the lover's inwardness should look outside, or if he should have any source of relief or any attachment outside, blame will cut it off. The booty will be found on the inside, so he will flee right there: "I seek refuge in Thee from Thee." His surfeit and hunger will be from there. "I am hungry some days, I am full some days."* He will have nothing to do with the outside.

This is the lane of blame and the field of destruction,
the road of gamblers who spend all that they have.
It needs a man, a scoundrel in tattered clothes,
passing by at night like a fearless thief.

He turns back from hoping for the work of others and brings himself to this work without fear.

Let them tear away my sheepskin cloak
  for Your sake, O nimble, thieving Friend!
Be solitary in love and don't fear the creatures:
  take the Beloved—and dust be on the world's head!

After that, the ruling power of the Beloved's jealousy will shine. It will shout against his safety and make him turn his face away from himself. He will become a blamer of himself. *Our Lord, we have wronged ourselves* [7:23] shows itself here.

Then love's jealousy will again shine and turn the lover's face away from the Beloved, for he had departed from himself by wanting the Beloved. It places a burning brand on his wanting—"Not creatures, not yourself, not the Beloved!"

Perfect disengagement shines on the solitariness of love. Tawḥīd belongs to love, and love belongs to tawḥīd. There is no room for others. As long as he is with love, he abides through it and feeds upon it. Both lover and Beloved are others to him, like strangers.

Knowledge has no awareness of this station, for it is reached neither by the allusions of knowledge nor by expression. Nonetheless, the allusions of recognition point to it, for one side of recognition lies in ruin—not like knowledge, whose sides all appear in sound construction. Here the waves of love's ocean clash, breaking against themselves and turning against themselves.

O moon, you rose and began to shine,
  you strolled around your sphere,
You saw yourself facing the spirit
  and at once you went down and hid.

Love is both the sun and the spheres, both heaven and earth. It is lover, beloved, and love, for lover and beloved are derived from love. When the accidents of derivation disappear, the work falls back on the oneness of its reality.

(*Sawāniḥ* 7–10)

In some chapters of his book, Aḥmad uses the language of annihilation and subsistence to talk about the mysteries of love's oneness. In the following, he is alluding to the hadith of God's becoming the servant's faculties, which designates the point at which the servant is delivered from the ruling power of the present moment. At that point it makes no sense to talk in the dualistic terms of separation and union.

Chapter [19]. As long as his own self is there, properties will pass over him: separation and union, acceptance and rejection, contraction and expansion, sorrow and happiness, and meanings of this sort. He will be a prisoner of the present moment. When the present moment comes over him, its property appears. He has to follow the property of the moment's color, and it makes him into its own color. The properties of the arrivals belong to the moment.

In the path of being annihilated from himself, these properties will be effaced and the opposite pairs will disappear, for they are the sitting place of want and causality.

When He brings the servant from himself to Himself, his road to himself comes from Him and by way of Him. Since his road to himself comes from Him and by way of Him, these properties do not pass over him. What would the properties of separation and union be doing here? How could acceptance and rejection seize his skirt? How could contraction and expansion or sorrow and happiness circle around the pavilion of his good fortune? This was said in the verses

> I saw the makeup of the universe and the root of the world,
> I passed beyond defect and disgrace with ease,
> The black light beyond the unmarked—
> that too I passed; neither this remained nor that.

Here he is the master of the present moment. When he descends to the heaven of this world, he enters in on the moment. The moment does not enter in on him. He is free of the moment.

Indeed, his existence is through Him and from Him. And this seems to be the "separation" of this state. His annihilation is from Him and in Him. This they call being hidden in the core of *but God* and becoming a hair in the Beloved's tresses. Thus has it been said,

> I suffered so much iniquity from Your tresses
> that I became one hair of those curls.
> After this what wonder if I am with You—
> what is one hair more or less in Your curls?

(*Sawāniḥ* 19–20)

Aḥmad devotes a good portion of *Apparitions* to love's trial and suffering. In fact, he says, love and trial are the same thing. This is because talk of love announces separation from the Beloved. To speak of love is to voice duality, and duality is the same as otherness. God's jealousy does not put up with otherness, so it burns it away. Lovers experience this burning as pain and suffering. Only at the end, in unification and unity, are otherness and suffering overcome.

> Chapter [16]. Love in reality is trial. In love, intimacy and ease are alien and borrowed. The verified truth is that separation in love is duality, and the verified truth is that union is oneness. All the rest is the fantasy of union, not the reality of union. This is why someone said,
>
> Love is trial—I am the one who won't avoid trial.
> When love is asleep, I am the one who stirs up misfortune.
> My friends say, "Avoid trial!"
> Trial is my heart. How can I avoid my heart?
> The tree of love is growing in my heart.
> When it needs water, I pour it from my eyes.
> Though love is sweet and sorrow not,
> how sweet it is to mix the two!
>
> (*Sawāniḥ* 17)

In short, the lover's very existence is the cause of suffering, as Aḥmad says in the following chapter. He may have wanted to call down a bit of blame on himself with it, because he seems to be saying that God, whose help is sought in every ritual prayer, is not the helper. What he is actually saying, however, is that love in itself—God's very Essence—cannot put up with duality. Love demands sheer oneness, so all those who continue to recognize themselves as one thing and their Beloved as something else will fall short in tawḥīd.

> Chapter [47]. Know that the lover is an antagonist, not a helper, and the Beloved is also an antagonist, not a helper. This is because help is tied to the effacement of the traces of both. As long as there is duality, each is himself for himself, and this is absolute antagonism. Help lies in unification.
>
> Thus the lover and the Beloved never help each other, for they will not find help. The suffering of love all derives from this: help never comes. By God, this is a marvelous work! Existence is intrusion. How can the attributes of existence find room here?
>
> Thus you have come to know that suffering in love is basic, and ease in love is borrowed. It is indeed impossible for it to be based on ease.
>
> (*Sawāniḥ* 39)

Aḥmad's insistence that love lies beyond the duality of lover and beloved is prefigured by several passages in Anṣārī's *Book of Love*. In the chapter devoted to ʿishq, for example, he says that this word designates the point where love alone remains.

> If you are caught by passion, seek no deliverance. If you are killed by passion, seek no retaliation, for passion is a burning fire and a shoreless ocean.

It is both the spirit and the spirit's spirit. It is a story without end and a pain without remedy. The intellect is bewildered in its perception, the heart unable to grasp it. It makes the hidden apparent and the apparent hidden. It is the ease of the spirit and the outset of openings. Though the spirit is the life of the bodies, passion is the life of the heart. When the man is silent, passion tears his heart to pieces and purifies it from everything but itself. When he shouts out, it turns him upside down and gives news of his story to city and lane.

Passion is both fire and water, both darkness and sun. It is not pain, but a bringer of pain, not affliction, but a bringer of affliction. Just as it causes life, so also it causes death. Just as it is the substance of ease, so also it is the means of blights.

Love burns the lover, but not the beloved. Passion burns both seeker and sought.

> Every heart that circles passion's burning incense
> will at last be burned by passion's sparks.
> This point was written out in passion's book:
> "The one busy with passion has no use for the Friend."
>
> When someone sees passion's beauty in himself,
> he will make the Beloved his target and be melted by passion.
> If you recognize passion, whom will you recognize?
> In passion the Beloved charges forth in passion.

(*Maḥabbat* 356–57)

NONBEING IN TAWḤĪD

Before water and clay was the Beginningless, and after water and clay will be the Endless. The goal of lovers is to return to the beginningless nonexistence from which they came, the beginningless and endless realm of love. Despite some of the imagery, this is not understood to mean the loss of individuality. It can better be understood as the reintegration of the metaphorical self with the true self. As Rūmī put it in a tale told to illustrate the Hidden Treasure, we were all fish swimming in the ocean, unaware of ourselves and the water. The ocean wanted to be recognized, so it threw us up on dry land, where we flip and flop and call it love. When we go back home, we will be the same fish that we always were, but now aware of our identity with the water.[3]

Samʿānī explains why beginningless love is both the same as and different from endless love:

In the Beginningless, the approval of *He loves them* was busy with *they love Him* without your intervention. Today you have being, but you are far from the midst.

By the right of the Real! The food of the hearts and souls is His Being. Otherwise, no one would ever find subsistence. Tomorrow, when all find subsistence in that abode, they will not find it through their own being. They will find it through the food of His Being. If someone in this abode were to reach the stage where his food is the contemplation of His Being, death would be forbidden to him.

> You are the soul's food. When You depart
> the soul that feeds on You does not remain.
>
> You are my spirit and world. Did I not see You,
> farewell to my spirit and world!

O dervish! In this road, life is bondage, the spirit a place of peril, and living a veil. Unless you come to lament of your own spirit in this road, nothing will come of you.

The spirit that you have is the cause of your annihilation. If we suppose that you did not have this spirit, then the angel of death would have no power over you. Seek a life that is not tainted by the spirit's intermediary. This life is expressed in these terms: "Recognition is the heart's life with God."

If a man is to be given access to the carpet of intimacy, he must be purified of his own attributes. Where can you achieve this purification? You must go to the ocean of the Glorified and swim in the depths of glorification. "The secret core swims in the oceans of lights and wins the pearls of tawḥīd, which are strung on the necklaces of faith and studded on the belts of union." Nothing comes of a polluted man or a menstruating woman.

Let us come back to the talk of the work that *He loves them* had with *they love Him* in the Beginningless, without you. Which day was that? There was still no garment of existence, no dust or clay, no universe or Adam. Was that proclamation made by your bounteousness and answered by your gentleness?

O dervish! A passion that appears in childhood will disappear in old age. It is black hair that has business with a moonlike face. What does this bit of blue sky have to do with it?

It is the custom of those who practice archery to set up a field. On one end is a target, and on the other end another target. There are two targets, and one archer. Where does He give a mark of the words I just said to you? "*He is the First and the Last*" [57:3]. Even more explicit is what He said to Muṣṭafā: "*You did not throw when you threw, but God threw*" [8:17].

O chevalier! When the scales of the Majestic Unity and the Perfect Divinity are brought forth, created nature does not weigh an iota, or half an iota. Know that in reality, "None carries the Real but the Real." You were wanted so that you could be a spectator.

(*Rawḥ* 534–35)

In one of his retellings of the story of Adam, Samʿānī refers to the report that God let Adam's clay ferment for forty years before He blew into him of His spirit. Where was Adam while this was going on? He was certainly not present in the lifeless clay. Rather, he was in the realm of nonbeing, the place of peace and joy to which he will return in the end.

Adam was kept between Mecca and Ta'if for forty years in the encampment of subtle recognitions. He Himself, without intermediary, placed the collar of the gaze on the neck of his tawḥīd. May a thousand thousand spirits be sacrificed to that era! What pleasure can a man have beyond the wine of that gaze when his being is not blended with it!? Unmixed wine, without self-determination, in the cup of the effacement of the Law's prescription!

When someone has put poison in the cup, how can there be pleasure in that? Today there is the gaze, but the gaze is mixed with your being. The true gaze is that which belonged to Adam in the era of "He fermented Adam's clay in His hand"—a pure gaze, without the intrusion of dust's free choice.

No wine is tastier than the beloved's gaze
smiling on the lover's face.

Know that in reality our true life was those forty years when we were in nonexistence and the gaze of the Eternal was taking care of our work without pens or steps. "O man, abandon your gaze! Here is My gaze." No one ever abandoned anything for God and in God without getting something better in return.

Ibn ʿAbbās narrated that God's Messenger was with Asmāʾ bint ʿUmays when he said, "And upon you be peace."

She said, "To whom were you returning the greeting?"

He said, "That was Jaʿfar ibn Abī Ṭālib. He just passed by with Gabriel and Michael."

Muṣṭafā had sent Jaʿfar into battle and made him the head of the army, so he held the banner of Islam in his hand. The unbelievers had attacked and cut off his hand, so he took up the banner with the other hand. They struck him again and cut off his other hand, and they struck him seventy-three times in the breast. Jaʿfar said, "God will give me two wings in place of hands, and with them I will fly in paradise wherever I want with Gabriel and Michael."

First a man becomes a speaker, then a knower, then a flier. Where is the likeness of this? In the story of Solomon, the Exalted Lord says, "*Then he fell to slashing their shanks and necks*" [38:33]. Solomon had beautiful horses, like birds without wings. Each of them had a huge body like an ocean wave, curls like an eagle, a tail like an ostrich, feet like the wind, hooves like ingots, faces like the moon, and eyes like the sun. When that tale of the prayer took place, he drew his sword and cut their necks.[4] It was said to him, "Now that you have done away with them, We will make the wind your mount."

"O Jaʿfar, you gave away your hands. Here are wings. O Solomon, you gave away your horses. Here is the wind, your porter on land and sea.

"O truthful lover, if you sacrifice your eyes and expend your hearing, then here: Our gentleness will be your eyes, Our bounty your hearing, Our generosity your lamp and candle: 'When I love him, I am his hearing, his eyesight, and his hand.' "

May a thousand thousand hearts and eyes be sacrificed to that first gaze!

O chevalier! There was no name or mark of Adam, there was no trace of dust, and the lordly gaze was debating with your antagonists: "*Surely I know what you do not know*" [2:30]. When He placed the cap of chosen-ness on Adam's head, it concealed all his defects. Why do you look at the fact that the child came forth ugly from its mother? Look at the mother's tenderness!

(*Rawḥ* 498–99)

To find God, the servant must lose himself. To reach union with the Beloved, the lover must surrender absolutely. To attain subsistence in God, the self must be annihilated. To reach *but God*, the seeker must submit to the sword of *no god*. To enter into eternal life, man must die before he dies. These are different versions of the same refrain, repeated constantly by the minstrels of love. Maybudī sings the same song in his commentary on the verse "*Seek the means of approach to Him!*" (5:35).

He is saying: O you who are worshipers, seek nearness to God with the virtues! O you who are knowers, with proofs! O you who are recognizers, with abandoning the means of approach!

What is the worshipers' means of approach? *The repenters, the worshipers, the praisers, the wayfarers, the bowers, the prostraters, the commanders to honor and forbidders of dishonor, the keepers of God's bounds* [9:112].

What is the knowers' means of approach? *Have they not gazed upon the sovereignty of the heavens and the earth?* [7:185].

What is the recognizers' means of approach? *Say "God," then leave them* [6:91].

The worshipers' means of approach is practice, the knowers' means of approach unveiling, and the recognizers' means of approach face-to-face vision.

The worshipers' means of approach is truthfulness, the knowers' means of approach friendship, and the recognizers' means of approach nonbeing.

The worshipers' means of approach is remembrance with need, the knowers' means of approach remembrance with joy, and the recognizers' means of approach remembrance with neither need nor joy. This story is long.

This is why the Pir of the Tariqah said, "O God, if anyone has found You by seeking, I have found You by fleeing. If anyone has found You by remembering, I have found You by forgetting. If anyone has found You by searching, I have found searching from You. O God, the means of approach to You is You. First were You, last are You. All is You, nothing else—the rest is folly."

(*Kashf* 3:121–22)

In a snippet of Persian text handed down from Anṣārī, he translates and explains the hadith of God's love for the servant and calls the person who reaches this station a "Sufi." Clearly, he does not have in mind the later meaning of the word, that is, a dervish or follower of the Tariqah. Rather, he has in view a well-known saying that suggests what happens when the traveler attains to the Haqiqah: "The Sufi is not created." In other words, such an individual, having returned to God already in this life, has gained awareness of his original status in the beginningless divine knowledge.

Abū Hurayra, Ibn ʿAbbās, Mālik, and ʿĀʾisha all narrated that the Messenger said, "God says, 'So much does My servant seek nearness to Me through supererogatory works that I love him. When I love him, I am his hearing, so he hears through Me; his eyesight, so he sees through Me; his tongue, so he speaks through Me; his feet, so he walks through Me; his hands, so he takes through Me; his heart, so he knows through Me.' "

The servant is a pretext in the midst, and the Real is one. The flood of lordhood arrives, and the dust of mortal nature disappears. The Haqiqah increases, and the pretext decreases. With the first breeze the body burns, with the next the heart. Then the spirit remains limpid, delivered from water and clay.

Light does not mix with dust, nor dust with light. Dust goes back to dust, light to light. The tongue becomes lost in remembrance, remembrance in the Remembered. The heart becomes lost in love, love in light. The spirit becomes lost in face-to-face vision, and face-to-face vision is far from explication.

> The Real's share reached the Real, and Adam's share reached Adam: water and dust to annihilation, duality to nonexistence, Adam and Eve gone. Invisible, the lightning of Oneness took the servant away from water and dust. He looked at himself: "It is I," but it was the Real. It was He who gave witness with "Who are you?"
>
> When someone is a mortal man, he is not a Sufi, for a Sufi is quit of mortal nature. He is not an Adamite. *You did not throw when you threw, but God threw* [8:17] makes clear who he is. *I blew into him of My spirit* [15:29] shows who he is.
>
> The Sufi is the spirit, and the spirit is the Sufi. The spirit stands through the Real, and the body through the spirit. When the Uncreated stands in the created, the Haqiqah becomes limpid. The created comes to naught in the Uncreated, for water and dust cease to be, and Adam and Eve go.
>
> When the Haqiqah becomes limpid, I-ness turns into a loan. What is I-ness? Saying "You and I, I and you." If you are with the Haqiqah, who is the Real? If He is the Real, the Real is one, not two. As long as there is duality, that is in relation to Adam and Eve. When duality disappears, the one is God. But not every eye has face-to-face vision.
>
> Listen with reverence, for it is the time of explication: who was there first? Today it is the same. The rays come from the sun, the sun is in heaven.
>
> (*Majmūʿa-yi rasāʾil-i fārsī*, 398–99)

In his commentary on the verse "*Who does greater wrong than he who bars God's places of prostration?*" (2:114), Maybudī tells us that *places of prostration* (*masājid*, plural of *masjid*, source of the English word *mosque*) alludes to a variety of things beyond the physical locations where the ritual prayer is performed. The soul is a place of worship that is ruined by appetite and caprice, the heart is a place of recognizing God that is ruined by attachment to things, and the spirit is a place of contemplating God that is ruined by glancing at others. Those who keep the homeland of the soul flourishing are renunciants, those who cultivate the heart are recognizers, and those who preserve the spirit's secret core are lovers. After recounting anecdotes about the first two stations, he illustrates the third with a report from Abū Yazīd.

> When someone has kept his secret core free from glancing at others, the homeland of contemplation flourishes and he becomes one of the friends. Thus Abū Yazīd turned the eyes of his aspiration totally away from all others, stuffed up the ears of effort, and kept the tongue of loss in the mouth of disappointment. He extracted the intrusion of the commanding soul, put himself in the ballista of meditation, shot himself into every valley, melted his

body with the fire of jealousy in all the crucibles, and drove the horse of seeking into the space of every desert. With the tongue of solitariness he was saying,

> People are wishing for repose and ease,
> but I, O Exalted One, wish to encounter You empty.
>
> Each has a prayer niche in some direction,
> but Sanāʾī's prayer niche is Your lane.

Abū Yazīd said, "When this claim appeared from my makeup, the Unity made me taste the blow of jealousy. He questioned me with awesomeness to show me how to come out of the furnace of testing. He said, '*Whose is the kingdom?*' [40:16].

"I said, 'Yours, O Lord.'

"He said, 'Whose is the free choice?'

"I said, 'Yours, O God.'

"When He saw and knew my weakness and need, He was aware that my attributes had reached His attributes. He said, 'O Abū Yazīd! Now that you have come to have nothing, you have everything. Now that you have come to have no tongue and no spirit, you have tongue and spirit.'"

> Other than this tongue, we have another tongue,
> other than hell and paradise, we have another place.
> Men of free lineage live with another spirit,
> their pure substance has another source.

"Then He gave me a tongue of eternal gentleness, a heart of light, and an eye of divine artisanry. If I speak, I speak with His assistance. I walk with His strength, I see with His light, I take with His power, and I sit in His session: 'I am his hearing, and he hears through Me. I am his eyesight, and he sees through Me.'

"When I reached this station, my tongue became the tongue of tawḥīd and my spirit the spirit of disengagement. I do not speak for myself, nor do I come back to myself. In reality the speaker is He, and I am a spokesman in the midst."

This is what the Unity said: "*You did not throw when you threw, but God threw*" [8:17]. This indeed is "I am his hand and he takes through Me"—if you can recognize it.

(*Kashf* 1:330–31)

Anṣārī describes the station of nonbeing in Chapter 18 of *Forty-Two Chapters*. He is commenting on a saying of Abū Ḥamza Khurāsānī, one of the companions of Junayd: "For many years I was in the state of ritual consecration. Whenever I came out of it, I would renew it. Every year I would make a journey of one thousand parasangs during which the sun would set on me and rise on me."

> The Intimation. It is difficult to find repose in lost-heartedness. When a man is unable to put up with it, he will wander around the world. If this inability falls into his attributes and his heart turns cold toward forms, then his traveling will be in the attributes, and his form will be still. If the attributes take assistance from the form, the inability will appear in both, and he will travel in both.
>
> One person will be still, stillness having been opened up to him. Another will set off in the opening of stillness to traverse the world's land and sea. One, taking no steps, will become the neighbor of nonexistence. Another, in the sanctuary of selflessness, will be the confidant of this breath, neither still nor traveling, neither attached to self nor belonging to the people. One will travel the world, and the other will have the world inside himself. One will be quit of both, the two worlds having become nothing in him while he is annihilated in himself.
>
> Glory be to God! Who has seen anything more amazing than this in the world!? Nonbeing hidden in being! The person is walking inside the shirt, but it is said that he is not he. The body is lost in the heart, the heart in the spirit, and the spirit is lost in that which lives forever.
>
> How can the tongue express something that does not come to the tongue? How can the spirit allude to something to which no one can allude? How can a mark be given of something that has no mark?
>
> There is a group in the world who are the world's kings. They are the dervishes. It is said that they are not they. If they are not they, who are they? If they are they, what is the evidence, the mark?
>
> What use is the denial of the deniers, for the shining water has already come. In their blindness, they are like moths in a ruin or ill-fortuned nightingales outside the garden. What need is there to mention with the tongue, unless there be a command? What can a stranger do in the midst, for the remembrance of the Friend is in the spirit.
>
> Blessed is he who has taken one step in this road, satisfied with the command, accepting the decree, praised by love, his veil lifted by solicitude, himself caressed by gentleness. There is no god but God, there is no god but He.
>
> (*Chihil* 110–11)

Anṣārī has a good deal more to say about passing beyond existence and nonexistence in several passages of *Forty-Two Chapters*. Take, for example, his commentary on a saying by Abu'l-ʿAbbās Sayyārī (d. 953): "No intelligent man enjoys the station of contemplation, for the contemplation of the Real is annihilation and dissolution, and there is no enjoyment in annihilation and destruction."

The Intimation. No one serves this group by habit, rather by abandoning habits. No one becomes a companion of this group by his own existence, rather by the annihilation of existence.

You will have patience with the commandments when you efface the choices of caprice.

Robes of honor were bestowed at dawn when you were asleep. Wakefulness rises up from knowledge and the sessions of the ulama, but you are distracted. Be drowned in need and reach joy!

All patience in the face of their patience takes flight. Pleasure in the face of their ease goes back to nonexistence. Happiness in the face of their delight is annihilated. Whatever people find of their tracks is lost.

Once the road of selflessness is found, all selfhood disappears. Blessed is he who is given this good fortune, for all good fortune disappears in this good fortune.

Next to their ease, the ease of the two worlds' folk is hell next to paradise. The eight paradises, which are His scented gardens, are reflections of the hearts of His friends. Paradise is within you, and the spirit is its treasury. Recognition of God is an ocean without shore.

If one iota of this work were to lift its head from its hiding place, it would take away the sorrow of the two worlds and desiccate all happiness. Blessed is he who is given a taste of one drop from this ocean! He is delivered from the disdain and need of the two worlds and taken to the Sought of all.

At this threshold, one should have the wailing of David, the weeping of Jacob, the seeking of Moses, the patience of Job. In this road, one should have the moaning of Noah and the crying of Majnūn—either a heart full of pain or a skirt full of blood. In this road, if you have not reached your desires, you are a man, and if you have no pain, you are dust.

O God! Though we are sinners, we are Muslims, and though we have done bad, we regret it. If You burn us, we are worthy of that, but if You forgive us, we are the place for that.

These words are collyrium for the eyes of those who see, elixir for the ears of those who hear. If you have the capacity to see and hear, welcome! Otherwise, be silent.

If you do not practice and tremble for something, in that you have no worth whatsoever.

O God, though the body is an offender, the heart is obedient. Though the servant is a sinner, Your generosity is the interceder.

O God, either do not place us next to offenses or pass over our offenses!

O God, I suffer because I am not of one color, as if I am at war with ill fortune. Sometimes I am the pride of the paradise-dwellers, sometimes the shame of the hell-dwellers.

If someone finds nothing of this work, no one will be able to grasp the immensity of his affliction. There is no god but God, there is no god but He.

(*Chihil* 183–85)

In the just-quoted passage, Anṣārī talks of the goal of the path and speaks as a seeker overcome by the constantly changing present moment. Hence he says, "O God, I suffer because I am not of one color." Colors are the specific attributes that define the body, soul, and heart of the seeker. At each instant, the seeker is thrown into a new state that colors him with specific attributes and qualities. His goal is to reach the Station of No Station, where all colors and qualities disappear in what Rūmī calls "the dying vat of *He*."[5] This is the station of one-coloredness (*yak-rangī*) or, even better, colorlessness. It is the spirit's secret core, where God encounters God and love's unity leaves no trace of lover and beloved. Maybudī explains that the Religion of Love is the path of escaping colors in his commentary on the verse "*Their greeting on the day they encounter Him shall be 'Peace!'*" (33:44).

Tomorrow this caress and rank, this endless good fortune, will be suited for someone who today is separate from the attributes of his own being. All attributes of selfhood are bonds, every bond is a color, and the chevaliers disdain every color.

He who painted a thousand worlds with color—
why would He buy my color or yours, O bankrupt man!

Why do you paint yourself, poor wretch! Self-painting has no worth. Why do you adorn yourself? Self-adornment has no value. Let it go so that *He adorned it in their hearts* [49:7] may adorn you without you. Let it go, and then *He loves them, and they love Him* [5:54] will approve of you without you.

The Pir of the Tariqah said, "Look from Him to Him, not from you to Him, for the eyes are with what they see at first, and the heart is with the first beloved. Everyone with a chamber in this lane knows that this is so. Seeing the Friend is the spirit's law, and throwing away life in the Shariah of Friendship is its religion."

(*Kashf* 8:75)

One of the Qur'anic sources for the notion of colorlessness is a verse that mentions *God's color* (2:138). In Stage Two of his commentary, Maybudī offers a standard explanation, according to which it refers to a Christian practice of baptism with colored water (hence the common translation of the expression as "the baptism of God"). He also points out that from early times some commentators understood God's color as a reference to the fiṭra, the original disposition that inclines innately toward tawḥīd. It is mentioned in the famous hadith "Every child is born according to the fiṭra. Then its parents make it into a Christian, a Jew, or a Zoroastrian." In this second interpretation, "God's color" designates the color of tawḥīd. In Stage Three, Maybudī focuses on this literal meaning of the word *color* or *dye* (Persian *rang*). "God's color" is then the color of colorlessness (*rang-i bī-rangī*)—what Samʿānī calls stationlessness.

> *If they have faith in the like of that in which you have faith, then they will have found guidance; but if they turn away, then they will have split from you. God will suffice you against them; He is the hearing, the knowing. God's color—and who is more beautiful in color than God?* [2:137–38]. "O master of the east and west and messenger to men and jinn! We have set down these tasks in your tracks and have commanded the world's folk to follow you. We wrote the Compact of Love for your servitors and brought them under Our gaze. We threw your opponents into the lowland of abasement and vileness. Whoever opposes you is on the side of the enemies, and whoever serves you on the side of the friends. When someone wants you, We want him and will give him access to Us. When someone turns away, We will burn him and throw him down. *Whoso obeys the Messenger has obeyed God* [4:80].
>
> "O paragon! Do not let your heart be tight because these estranged people have turned away and spoken ill. We will suffice you against their business, and We will remove their torment from you. *God will suffice you against them.*
>
> "Then We will bring a people who appear in the color of tawḥīd, who are adorned with the attribute of friendship, and who are clothed in *God's color*, which is colorlessness."
>
> Whoever is pure of the color of the color mixers is colored by *God's color.* When someone reaches *God's color* and falls back on Him, He colors him in His own color. In the same way, the elixir makes copper and iron the same color as itself, and they become precious. If the estranged fall back on Him, they become His familiars. If the disobedient fall back, they become obedient. (*Kashf* 1:387)

We should not forget that talk of reaching colorlessness is simply another way of conceptualizing the Tariqah, the process of eliminating ugly character traits and becoming characterized by the beautiful character traits of God. Maybudī reminds us of this in his commentary on a Qur'anic passage that recounts how Moses commanded the children of Israel to slaughter a cow. When they pushed him for details, he offered a description of its qualities. According to Maybudī, the cow's attributes—the qualities that make it worthy to be offered up to God—are precisely those of the perfected self.

> This story of the cow of the Children of Israel in these verses and the mention of its attributes is one of the subtle points of wisdom and exalted pearls of the Qur'an. The Qur'an itself is the all-encompassing ocean. Many are the kingly pearls and night-brightening gems found in the ocean's depths.
>
> You should read everything that the Exalted Lord said about the cow of the Children of Israel as an allusion to your own attributes. Then you will reach the station of worthiness to dive into this ocean, and He will give you access to its deposited wonders and unseen pearls.
>
> Altogether, the attributes that He clarified in these verses are three: first, *neither old nor virgin* [2:68]; second, *golden, bright her color* [2:69]; third, *not abased to plow the earth* [2:71].
>
> First, *neither old nor virgin.* He says it should not be broken down and old, nor newly born and immature. In other words, the feet of these chevaliers will become firm in the circle of the Tariqah when the intoxication and greediness of youth no longer veil them, and when the weakness of old age does not hinder them. Do you not see that revelation reached Muṣṭafā when he was not a newly born youngster, nor had his days reached *the worst state of life* [16:70]? If there had been a state more complete, revelation would have reached him at its time.
>
> Whenever desire for God pairs itself with the intoxication of youth, there is fear of the highwaymen. It is rare that a youngster in his new desire remains secure from the highwaymen. If it does happen in the empire, it seldom does. This is why Muṣṭafā said, "Your Lord marvels at a young man who has no youthful fervor."
>
> The second attribute is *golden, bright her color, gladdening the gazers.* When the chevaliers step into the field of the Tariqah in the state of the perfection of mortal nature and stand firm in it, the Unity will bring them into the color of love, and the color of love is colorlessness. It will wash them clean of anything mixed with colors—*We shall strip away all the rancor that is in their breasts* [7:43]. They will become pure spirit. Their makeup and their meanings will all take on one attribute. Any eye that gazes on them will be brightened, and any heart that ponders their work will feel familiarity.

Sufyān Thawrī became ill and was taken to a Christian physician. The Christian examined him and meditated. Then he said, "This is a wondrous state I see. This man's liver is bleeding because of his fear of God, and the blood is coming out with his water. The religion that he has can only be true. I bear witness that there is no god but God, and I bear witness that Muḥammad is His Messenger."

When that Christian physician looked at the evidence, he felt familiarity. When someone looks at the faces of the Real's friends with pure belief and meditates on their conduct, what will happen to the love in his heart? This is why He says, "*bright her color, gladdening the gazers.*" The color that makes lookers happy is the color of familiarity and friendship. Today He brings them forth in the color of familiarity and friendship, and what color is more beautiful than that? *Who is more beautiful in color than God?* [2:138]. Tomorrow He will color them with His own color. The Prophet said, "They will be colored with the light of the All-Merciful."

The third attribute is what He said: *not abased to plow the earth or to water the tillage, secure with no blemish on her.* They are pure, virtuous, fortunate, beautiful in conduct, increasing day by day. They have not been tainted by the defects of the mimickers, nor have they fallen to the station of those low in aspiration, nor have they been inscribed by friendship for the others or branded by the secondary causes. The sultan of mortal nature does not hold them in its hand, nor does the judge of appetites issue its rulings to them. They do not incline to likenesses and images, nor do they lean on their own choice and contrivance. Just as they recognize that He who is worshiped is one, so also they know that the Intended is one, the Witnessed one, the Found one.

Everyone is busy with his own affairs
and I aspire to the helping Friend.

Each has a prayer niche in some direction,
but Sanāʾī's prayer niche is Your lane.

(*Kashf* 1:229–30)

In the twenty-fourth chapter of the *Book of Love*, Anṣārī explains that union is achieved when the lover comes to be characterized by the Beloved's character traits, thereby reaching one-coloredness. Unlike the other chapters, which are named after well-known states and stations, this one is named after one of "their sayings," an aphorism handed down by the Sufi teachers.

A Chapter on their Saying, "I am Thou and Thou art I." These words allude to togetherness and are not fit for every ear. Outward listening does not have the capacity to hear them, nor does eyesight have the right form to be aware of their meanings. They need a man who is passion itself, whose passing days are the unbound elixir. Then the beauty of these words will shine upon him, and he will perceive the reality of this talk.

A dispersed man has nothing to do with these words, for these words have nothing to do with plurality and numbers. There must be one-coloredness and oneness before anyone may become familiar and luminous.

This saying is not outside of two states, and this meaning not more than this: If the man has His attributes, then both I's are worthy of Him. If the man is a dervish or has his own attributes, then both I's are the attribute of Eternity, without the defect of the man's thoughts or his participation.

As long as the man has the attribute of being, he says, "I am—I have no access to Me." When the man reaches the attribute of nonbeing, he says, "I am—no one is aware of Me; the state is aware and has not gone astray."

If a man comes to be killed by the Invincible, he will have much to say in this talk.

In my passion for You, happiness has had enough of me.
Sit, be happy—sorrow is my work.
You are seeking to kill me—that is easy.
I am seeking union with You—that is the rub.

(*Maḥabbat* 366–67)

In one passage of *Forty-Two Chapters*, Anṣārī invites his readers to enter into the work (*kār*), that is, the path of abandoning self with the goal of realizing the station of colorlessness. He speaks here for all the authors quoted in this book. None of them was simply a scholar trying to dissect love. All were lovers, doing their best to express the inexpressible and alert others to the joy of finding, urging them to get down to the job of seeking. Anṣārī is commenting here on a saying by ʿAlī ibn Ibrāhīm al-Ḥuṣrī (d. 981), a companion of Shiblī: "Whenever someone claims something of the Haqiqah, the marks bearing witness to testing will turn him into a liar."

The Intimation. Practice bears witness to the claim of knowledge, letting go of habits bears witness to desire, loyalty bears witness to love, and the state bears witness to the states of the secret core.

The one who speaks of this lane is he who is described as having no descriptions. If a scent of his being remains, he considers himself the greatest offender in the world.

This group seeks safety from the defect of selfhood and freedom from I-ness and we-ness. If one day you become free to enter this work, you will recognize in this freedom a whiff of that freedom. If one day you are healed of idleness, you will catch a whiff of the health of these seekers. Every breath you bring forth not in search of this work, even though you may excavate a mountain, will be ascribed only to idleness. An idler is a doer of nothing. When someone is busy with the unreal, he is worse than an idler. *And say: "The real has come, and the unreal has vanished away"* [17:81].

So, O man of faith, be not an idler or a worker of the unreal. Be like the men of this work, free of self and others. Be not a nonworker, and witness no others in the work. Purify your practice with the Sunnah and purify your seeing with recognition. Do not pull your hands back from the work, nor your eyes back from Him.

Gaze on Him, not on the practice, lest you be a nonworker or an idler—a seeker without the work, gazing on the work. By losing yourself in the work, you may join with the folk of the work and reach this vision and conduct.

What a marvelous work is this work! All the world is lost in this work. Arrival is found in this work. Something is found face-to-face that no report giver has ever reported and no intellect has ever perceived. Whoever arrives is lost in it, for no report comes back—like someone drowned in the ocean, of whom neither name nor mark remains.

O God, blood does not come from those You kill, nor smoke from those You burn. The one killed by You is happy in the killing, and the one burnt by You content with the burning.

O God, how can I seek You? In the empire I am less than a hair.

O God, when we gaze on You, we are kings wearing crowns, and when we gaze on ourselves, we are dust with dust on our heads.

There is no god but He, there is no god but God. And God bless Muḥammad and all his household!

(*Chihil* 245–46)

Notes

CHAPTER 1: THE THEOLOGICAL CONTEXT

1. I provide copious documentation concerning Ibn al-ʿArabī's critique of rationalizing abstraction in *Sufi Path of Knowledge.*
2. For more of Ibn al-ʿArabī's views on the relationship between rational thought and imagination, see Chittick, *Sufi Path of Knowledge,* especially Chapter 11.
3. See Chittick, *Ibn ʿArabi,* Chapter 9.
4. In *The Philosophy of the Kalam* (141), Harry Wolfson traces the theoretical formulation of the two commands back to the Mu'tazilite Abu'l-Hudhayl (d. ca. 841). Many authors investigated the implications of the distinction, such as the Hanbalite theologians studied by Joseph Bell in *Love Theory.* Ibn al-ʿArabī makes more use of it than most; see, for example, Chittick, *Sufi Path of Knowledge,* 291–94 and passim.
5. For example, see Chittick, *Sufi Path of Knowledge,* Chapter 5.
6. An early citation of this saying is found in a treatise of the Ikhwān al-Ṣafāʾ (tenth century), who say that it comes from "one of the reports about one of God's prophets" (*Rasāʾil* 3:356). I have not found an explicit attribution of this saying to the Prophet before Ibn al-ʿArabī. As a master of the science of Hadith, he knew perfectly well that it is not found in the standard books. He tells us that its authenticity was proved to him by visionary unveiling (*Futūḥāt* 2:399, line 28; see Chittick, *Sufi Path of Knowledge,* 391n14).
7. See, for example, Chittick, *Sufi Path of Knowledge,* 130.

CHAPTER 2: THE STORY OF LOVE

1. Chittick, *Me & Rūmī,* 156.
2. The reference is to two Qur'anic stories, that of the Companions of the Cave (the Seven Sleepers of Ephesus), whose faithful dog was counted as one of them, and Balaam Boer, a diviner whose prayers were always answered and who was asked by the king to pray against Moses and the Israelites (Numbers 22–24). The reference to

Balaam falling to the level of a dog is derived from commentaries on a brief reference to him in Qur'an 7:175–76.

CHAPTER 4: THE SEARCH

1. See Heath, *Allegory and Philosophy.*
2. For more on belief as a knotting of the heart, a point much discussed by Ibn al-ʿArabī, see Chittick, *Imaginal Worlds,* Chapter 10.
3. See Chittick, *Sufi Path of Knowledge,* 375–79.
4. See ibid., 371.

CHAPTER 5: THE PATH

1. For example, the title of the fourth chapter of the first section (*fann*) of Ghazālī's commentary on the divine names, *al-Maqṣad al-asnā,* is this: "Explaining that the servant's perfection and felicity is found in becoming characterized by the character traits of God and becoming adorned by His attributes and names in the measure in which that is conceivable for him."
2. See "A History of the Term *Waḥdat al-Wujūd,*" in Chittick, *In Search of the Lost Heart.* In Timurid Iran two centuries earlier, the Sufi teacher Zayn al-Dīn Khwāfī (d. 1435) had staunchly upheld the position "All is from Him" as a counter to waḥdat al-wujūd, which by then was generally associated with Ibn al-ʿArabī's name. Khwāfī was opposed by his contemporary Shāh Qāsim Anwār (d. 1433–34), who spoke for "All is He." See Bashir, *Sufi Bodies,* 99.
3. *ʿIlm* and *maʿrifa* can be used as synonyms. Thus, the plural form *maʿārif* is sometimes used in the same meaning as *ʿulūm,* the sciences, though usually *maʿārif* implies the intellectual, philosophical sciences, and *ʿulūm* the transmitted, religious sciences. The discussion is complicated by the fact that the word *ʿirfān,* a synonym for *maʿrifa* from the same root, came to be used in Iran in relatively recent times to designate theoretical Sufism, especially that of Ibn al-ʿArabī and his followers. Gerhard Böwering suggests translating this word as "theosophy," since as a general designation for an approach to the intellectual sciences, *ʿirfān* can be differentiated from Kalam and philosophy ("ʿErfān"). The word, however, is rarely used by our authors or even by Ibn al-ʿArabī and his early followers. When it is, its meaning cannot be distinguished from that of *maʿrifa.*
4. See Chittick, *Sufi Path of Knowledge,* introduction.
5. The full verse reads: "*Those are unbelievers who say that God is the third of three.*" The speaker is saying that tawḥīd cannot be realized along with the existence of the self. We saw Anṣārī make the same point in his discussion of the highest level of tawḥīd in *Way Stations of the Travelers.*

CHAPTER 6: THE STATES OF THE TRAVELERS

1. On gender symbolism in Islamic texts, see Murata, *Tao of Islam.*
2. On the meaning of the two eyes in Ibn al-ʿArabī, see Chittick, *Sufi Path of Knowledge,* Chapter 20.

CHAPTER 7: THE REALITY OF LOVE

1. See, for example, Rūmī, *Kulliyyāt*, verses 21,574–76, cited in Chittick, *Sufi Path of Love*, 279.
2. The word is *wāqiʿa*, one of several Qur'anic names for the events surrounding the Last Day. It is mentioned in the verses "*When the Befalling falls, none shall deny its falling*" (56:1–2). ʿAbbādī seems to have in mind what is often called the lesser resurrection (*qiyāmat-i ṣughrā*), that is, subsistence in God after the annihilation of the self.
3. On the difference between true and metaphorical (or derivative) love, see Chittick, *Sufi Path of Love*, 200–6.

CHAPTER 8: THE SUFFERING OF LOVE

1. Maybudī explains what he means here in his commentary on 24:11, quoted in the next chapter under the section on jealousy.

CHAPTER 9: THE REALIZATION OF TAWḤĪD

1. The allusion is to Qur'an 67:5, "*And We adorned the lower heaven with lamps, and We made them the stonings of the satans.*"
2. See Chittick, *Sufi Path of Knowledge*, Chapter 19.
3. Rūmī, *Majālis-i sabʿa*, 121–22. For a translation, see Chittick, *Sufi Path of Love*, 70–71.
4. Maybudī explains the tale of the prayer in Stage Two of *Unveiling the Secrets:* Solomon had hundreds of fine horses, and one day he had his servants bring them in for review. He became so entranced by their beauty that he forgot his afternoon prayer until the sun had set. He then slaughtered the horses because they were the cause of his forgetfulness. In his case God permitted this act, even though Islamic teachings would forbid it (*Kashf* 8:348–49).
5. Rūmī, *Mathnawī* 2, verse 1345.

Bibliography

ʿAbbādī, Manṣūr ibn Ardashīr. *al-Taṣfiya fī aḥwāl al-ṣūfiyya*. Edited by Ghulām Ḥusayn Yūsufī. Tehran: Bunyād-i Farhang-i Īrān, 1347/1968.

Abrahamov, Binyamin. *Divine Love in Islamic Mysticism: The Teachings of Al-Ghazālī and Al-Dabbāgh*. London: Routledge, 2003.

——. "Ibn al-ʿArabī on Divine Love." In *Tribute to Michael: Studies in Jewish and Muslim Thought Presented to Professor Michael Schwarz*, edited by Sarah Klein-Braslavy, Binyamin Abrahamov, and Joseph Sadan, 7–36. Tel Aviv: Tel Aviv University, 2009.

Addas, Claude. "The Experience and Doctrine of Love in Ibn ʿArabi." *Journal of the Muhyiddin ibn ʿArabi Society* 32 (2002): 25–44.

Anṣārī, ʿAbdallāh. *Chihil u daw faṣl*. In Anṣārī, *Majmūʿa*, 1–252.

——. *Maḥabbat-nāma*. In Anṣārī, *Majmūʿa*, 335–72.

——. *Majmūʿa-yi rasāʾil-i fārsī*. Edited by Muḥammad Sarwar Mawlāʾī. Tehran: Intishārāt-i Tūs, 1377/1998.

——. *Manāzil al-sāʾirīn/Les étapes des itinérants vers Dieu*. Text and translation by S. de Laugier de Beaurecueil. Cairo: Imprimerie de l'Institut Français d'Archéologie Orientale, 1962.

——. *Ṣad maydān*. In Anṣārī, *Majmūʿa*, 253–334.

——. *Ṭabaqāt al-ṣūfiyya*. Edited by Muḥammad Sarwar Mawlāʾī. Tehran: Intishārāt-i Tūs, 1386/2007.

ʿAṭṭār, Farīd al-Dīn. *Farīd al-Dīn ʿAṭṭār's Memorial of God's Friends*. Translated by Paul Losensky. Mahwah, N.J.: Paulist Press, 2009.

——. *Manṭiq al-ṭayr*. Edited by Muḥammad-riḍā Shafīʿī Kadkanī. Tehran: Intishārāt-i Sukhan, 1384/2005.

——. *The Speech of the Birds*. Translated by Peter Avery. London: Islamic Texts Society, 1998.

——. *Tadhkirat al-awliyāʾ*. Edited by Muḥammad Istiʿlāmī. Tehran: Zuwwār, 1346/1967.

Avicenna (Ibn Sīnā). *al-Ilāhiyyāt min al-shifāʾ/The Metaphysics of* The Healing. Text and translation by Michael E. Marmura. Provo, Utah: Brigham Young University Press, 2005.

———. *al-Ishārāt wa'l-tanbīhāt.* Edited by Sulaymān Dunyā. Cairo: Muṣṭafā al-Bābī al-Ḥalabī, 1947.

———. *Risāla fi'l-ʿishq.* Edited by Ḥusayn al-Ṣiddīq and Rāwiyya Jāmūs. Damascus: Dār al-Fikr, 2005.

———. "A Treatise on Love by Ibn Sina." Translated by Emil L. Fackenheim. *Medieval Studies* 7 (1945): 208–28.

ʿAyn al-Quḍāt Hamadānī. *Tamhīdāt.* Edited by ʿAfīf ʿUsayrān. Tehran: Dānishgāh, 1341/1962.

Bashir, Shahzad. *Sufi Bodies: Religion and Society in Medieval Islam.* New York: Columbia University Press, 2011.

Bell, Joseph Norment. *Love Theory in Later Hanbalite Islam.* Albany: State University of New York Press, 1979.

Beneito, Pablo. "On the Divine Love of Beauty." *Journal of the Muhyiddin ibn ʿArabi Society* 18 (1995): 1–22.

———. "The Servant of the Loving One: On the Adoption of the Character Traits of al-Wadud." *Journal of the Muhyiddin ibn ʿArabi Society* 32 (2002): 1–24.

Böwering, Gerhard. "ʿErfān." *Encyclopaedia Iranica* 8:551–54. http://www.iranicaonline.org/articles/erfan-1.

———. *The Mystical Vision of Existence in Classical Islam: The Quranic Hermeneutics of the Ṣūfī Sahl At-Tustarī (d. 283/896).* New York: de Gruyter, 1980.

Bruijn, J. T. P. de. *Of Piety and Poetry: The Interaction of Religion and Literature in the Life and Works of Ḥakīm Sanāʾī of Ghazna.* Leiden: Brill, 1983.

———. *Persian Sufi Poetry: An Introduction to the Mystical Use of Classical Poems.* Surrey, U.K.: Curzon, 1997.

Bukhārī, Abū Ibrāhīm Ismāʿīl ibn Muḥammad Mustamlī. *Sharḥ al-taʿarruf li madhhab al-taṣawwuf.* Edited by Muḥammad Rawshan. 4 vols. Tehran, 1363/1984.

Chittick, William C. "The Aesthetics of Islamic Ethics." In *Sharing Poetic Expressions: Beauty, Sublime, Mysticism in Islamic and Occidental Culture.* Edited by A.-T. Tymieniecka, 3–14. Dordrecht: Springer, 2011.

———. "The Anthropology of Compassion." *Journal of the Muhyiddin ibn ʿArabi Society* 48 (2010): 1–15.

———. "Divine and Human Love in Islam." In *Divine Love: Perspectives from the World's Religious Traditions.* Edited by Jeff Levin and Stephen G. Post, 163–200. West Conshohocken, Pa.: Templeton Press, 2010.

———. "The Divine Roots of Love." In Chittick, *Ibn ʿArabi: Heir to the Prophets,* 35–51. Oxford: Oneworld, 2005.

———. *Imaginal Worlds: Ibn al-ʿArabī and the Problem of Religious Diversity.* Albany: State University of New York Press, 1994.

———. *In Search of the Lost Heart: Explorations in Islamic Thought.* Edited by Mohammed Rustom, Atif Khalil, and Kazuyo Murata. Albany: State University of New York Press, 2012.

———. "Love as the Way to Truth." *Sacred Web* 15 (2005): 15–27.

———. *Me & Rūmī: The Autobiography of Shams-i Tabrizi.* Louisville, Ky.: Fons Vitae, 2004.

———. *The Sufi Path of Knowledge: Ibn al-ʿArabī's Metaphysics of Imagination.* Albany: State University of New York Press, 1989.

———. *The Sufi Path of Love: The Spiritual Teachings of Rumi.* Albany: State University of New York Press, 1983.

———. *Sufism: A Beginner's Guide.* Oxford: Oneworld, 2008.

———. "The Sword of *Lā* and the Fire of Love." *Mawlana Rumi Review* 2 (2011): 10–27.

Corbin, Henry. *Creative Imagination in the Sufism of Ibn ʿArabī.* Princeton, N.J.: Princeton University Press, 1969. Reissued as *Alone with the Alone,* 1998.

———. *Spiritual Body and Celestial Earth.* Princeton, N.J.: Princeton University Press, 1977.

Dakake, Maria M. "Guest of the Inmost Heart: Conceptions of the Divine Beloved among Early Sufi Women." *Comparative Islamic Studies* 2008:72–97.

Daylamī, Abu'l-Ḥasan al-. *Kitāb ʿaṭf al-alif al-ma'lūf ʿala'l-lām al-maʿṭūf.* Edited by J. C. Vadet. Cairo: Institut Français d'Archéologie Orientale, 1962.

———. *A Treatise on Mystical Love.* Translated by Joseph Norment Bell and Hasan Mahmood Abdul Latif Al Shafie. Edinburgh: Edinburgh University Press, 2006.

Derin, Suleyman. *Love in Sufism: From Rabia to Ibn al-Farid.* Istanbul: İnsan Publications, 2008.

Ernst, Carl. *Ruzbihan Baqli: Mysticism and the Rhetoric of Sainthood in Persian Sufism.* London: RoutledgeCurzon, 1996.

———. "The Stages of Love in Early Persian Sufism, from Rābiʿa to Rūzbihān." In *The Heritage of Sufism.* Vol. 1, *Classical Persian Sufism from its Origins to Rumi (700–1300),* edited by Leonard Lewisohn, 435–55. Oxford: Oneworld, 1999.

Fārābī, Abū Naṣr al-. *Mabādi' ārā' ahl al-madīnat al-fāḍila/On the Perfect State.* Text and translation by Richard Walzer. Chicago: Kazi Publications, 1998.

Ghazālī, Aḥmad. *Sawāniḥ.* Edited by Nasrollah Pourjavady. Tehran: Instishārāt-i Bunyād-i Farhang-i Īrān, 1359/1980.

———. *Sawāniḥ: Inspirations from the World of Pure Spirits.* Translated by Nasrollah Pourjavady. London: KPI, 1986.

Ghazālī, Muḥammad. *The Alchemy of Happiness.* Translated by Jay R. Crook. Chicago: Kazi Publications, 2002.

———. *Iḥyā' ʿulūm al-dīn.* 4 vols. Beirut: Dār al-Hādī, 1993.

———. *Kīmiyā-yi saʿādat.* Edited by Aḥmad Ārām. Tehran: Markazī, 1345/1966.

———. *Love, Longing, Intimacy, and Contentment/Kitāb al-maḥabba wa'l-shawq wa'l-uns wa'l-riḍā: Book 36 of* The Revival of the Religious Sciences. Translated by Eric Ormsby. Cambridge: Islamic Texts Society, 2011.

———. *al-Maqṣad al-asnā.* Edited by F. A. Shehadi. Beirut: Dar el-Machreq, 1971.

———. *The Marvels of the Heart/Kitāb ʿajā'ib al-qalb: Book 21 of* The Revival of the Religious Sciences. Translated by Walter James Skellie. Louisville, Ky.: Fons Vitae, 2010.

Ghazi bin Muhammad. *Love in the Holy Quran.* Chicago: Kazi Publications, 2011.

Giffen, Lois Anita. *Theory of Profane Love Among the Arabs: The Development of the Genre.* New York: New York University Press, 1971.

Heath, Peter. *Allegory and Philosophy in Avicenna (Ibn Sīnā), with a Translation of the Book of the Prophet Muḥammad's Ascent to Heaven.* Philadelphia: University of Pennsylvania Press, 1992.

Homerin, Th. Emil. *The Wine of Love and Life: Ibn al-Fāriḍ's* al-Khamrīyah *and al-Qayṣarī's Quest for Meaning.* Chicago: Middle East Documentation Center, 2005.

Hujwīrī, ʿAlī ibn ʿUthmān. *Kashf al-maḥjūb.* Edited by Maḥmūd ʿĀbidī. Tehran: Surūsh, 1383/2004.

——. *The Kashf al-Mahjúb: The Oldest Persian Treatise on Sufiism.* Translated by R. A. Nicholson. London: 1911.

Ibn al-ʿArabī, Muḥyī al-Dīn. *al-Futūḥāt al-makkiyya.* 4 vols. Cairo: 1911.

——. *Traité de l'amour.* Translated by Maurice Gloton. Paris: Albin Michel, 1986.

Ibn Dabbāgh. *Kitāb Mashāriq anwār al-qulūb wa mafātiḥ asrār al-ghuyūb.* Edited by Hellmut Ritter. Beirut: Dār Ṣādir, 1959.

Ibn al-Fāriḍ. *Dīwān.* Translated by Th. Emil Homerin as *ʿUmar Ibn al-Fāriḍ: Sufi Verse, Saintly Life.* Mahwah, N.J.: Paulist Press, 2001.

Ibn Qayyim al-Jawziyya. *Rawḍat al-muḥibbīn.* Aleppo: Dār al-Shawʿī, 1397/1977.

Ibn Sīnā. *See* Avicenna.

Ikhwān al-Ṣafāʾ. *Rasāʾil Ikhwān al-Ṣafāʾ.* 4 vols. Beirut: Dār Ṣādir, 1957.

ʿIrāqī, Fakhr al-Dīn. *Fakhruddin ʿIraqi: Divine Flashes.* Translated by William C. Chittick and Peter Lamborn Wilson. New York: Paulist Press, 1971.

——. *Lamaʿāt.* Edited by Jawād Nūrbakhsh. Tehran: Intishārāt-i Khānaqāh-i Niʿmatullāhī, 1353/1974.

Kalābādhī, Abū Bakr al-. *The Doctrine of the Sufis.* Translated by A. J. Arberry. Lahore: Sh. Muhammad Ashraf, 1966.

——. *al-Taʿarruf li madhhab al-taṣawwuf.* Edited by ʿAbd al-Ḥalīm Maḥmūd and Ṭāhā ʿAbd al-Bāqī Surūr. Cairo, 1960.

Karamustafa, Ahmet T. *Sufism: The Formative Period.* Edinburgh: Edinburgh University Press, 2007.

Keeler, Annabel. *Sufi Hermeneutics: The Qur'an Commentary of Rashīd al-Dīn Maybudī.* Oxford: Oxford University Press, 2006.

Knysh, Alexander. *Islamic Mysticism: A Short History.* Leiden: Brill, 2000.

Landolt, Hermann. "Walāya." *Encyclopedia of Religion.* New York: MacMillan, 1987.

Laugier de Beaurecueil, Serge de. *Khwādja ʿAbdullāh Anṣārī (396–481 H./1006–1089): Mystique hanbalite.* Beirut: Institut de Lettres orientales, 1965.

Lewis, Franklin. *Rumi: Past and Present, East and West.* Oxford: Oneworld, 2000.

Lewisohn, Leonard, ed. *ʿAṭṭār and the Persian Sufi Tradition: The Art of Spiritual Flight.* London: Tauris, 2006.

——, ed. *Hafiz and the Religion of Love in Classical Persian Poetry.* London: Tauris, 2010.

——, ed. *The Heritage of Sufism: Classical Persian Sufism from its Origins to Rumi (700–1300).* Oxford: Oneworld, 1999.

Lumbard, Joseph Edward Barbour. "Aḥmad al-Ghazālī and the Metaphysics of Love." PhD diss., Yale University, 2003.

——. "From *Ḥubb* to *ʿIshq*: The Development of Love in Early Sufism." *Journal of Islamic Studies* 18 (2007): 345–85.

Makkī, Abū Ṭālib al-. *Qūt al-qulūb.* 2 vols. Cairo: Muṣṭafā al-Bābī al-Ḥalabī, 1961.

Maybudī, Rashīd al-Dīn. *Kashf al-asrār wa ʿuddat al-abrār.* Edited by ʿAlī Aṣghar Ḥikmat. 10 vols. Tehran: Dānishgāh, 1331–39/1952–60.

Mojaddedi, Jawid. *Rumi's Teachings on Friendship with God and Early Sufi Theories.* New York: Oxford University Press, 2012.

Morris, James. "Ibn 'Arabī's 'Short Course' on Love." *Journal of the Muhyiddin ibn 'Arabi Society* 50 (2011): 1–22.

Murata, Sachiko. *The Tao of Islam: A Sourcebook on Gender Relationships in Islamic Thought.* Albany: State University of New York Press, 1992.

Qushayrī, Abu'l-Qāsim. *Laṭā'if al-ishārāt.* Edited by Ibrāhīm Basyūnī. 6 vols. Cairo: Dār al-Kātib li'l-Ṭibā'a wa'l-nashr, n.d. [1971].

——. *Al-Qushayrī's Epistle on Sufism.* Translated by Alexander D. Knysh. Reading, U.K.: Garnet, 2007.

——. *Al-Risāla.* Edited by 'Abd al-Ḥalīm Maḥmūd and Maḥmūd ibn al-Sharīf. Cairo: Dār al-Kutub al-Ḥadītha, 1972–74.

Rawan Farhadi, A. G. *Abdullah Ansari of Herat (1006–1089 CE): An Early Sufi Master.* Richmond, U.K.: Curzon Press, 1996.

Ritter, Hellmut. *The Ocean of the Soul: Man, the World, and God in the Stories of Farīd al-Dīn 'Aṭṭār.* Translated by John O'Kane and Bernt Radtke. Leiden: Brill, 2003.

Rosenthal, Franz. *Knowledge Triumphant: The Concept of Knowledge in Medieval Islam.* Leiden: Brill, 1970.

Rūmī, Jalāl al-Dīn. *Kulliyyāt-i Shams yā dīwān-i kabīr.* Edited by B. Furūzānfar. 10 vols. Tehran: Dānishgāh, 1336–46/1957–67.

——. *Majālis-i sab'a.* Edited by Tawfīq Subḥānī. Tehran: Intishārāt-i Kayhān, 1379/2000.

——. *The Mathnawī.* Edited by R. A. Nicholson. 8 vols. London: Luzac, 1925–40.

Rūzbihān Baqlī. *'Abhar al-'āshiqīn/Le Jasmin des Fidèles d'Amour.* Edited by Henry Corbin and M. Mu'īn. Tehran: Institut Franco-Iranien, 1958.

——. *'Arā'is al-bayān fī ḥaqā'iq al-Qur'ān.* Edited by Aḥmad Farīd al-Mizyadī. 3 vols. Beirut: Dār al-Kutub al-'Ilmiyya, 2008.

Sam'ānī, Aḥmad. *Rawḥ al-arwāḥ fī sharḥ asmā' al-malik al-fattāḥ.* Edited by Najīb Māyil Hirawī. Tehran: Shirkat-i Intishārāt-i 'Ilmī wa Farhangī, 1368/1989.

Sanā'ī, Abu'l-Majd. *Dīwān.* Edited by Mudarris Raḍawī. Tehran: Ibn Sīnā, 1341/1962.

——. *Ḥadīqat al-ḥaqīqa wa sharī'at al-ṭarīqa.* Edited by Maryam Ḥusaynī. Tehran: Markaz-i Nashr-i Dānishgāhī, 1382/2003.

Schimmel, Annemarie. *And Muhammad Is His Messenger: The Veneration of the Prophet in Islamic Piety.* Chapel Hill: University of North Carolina Press, 1985.

——. *Mystical Dimensions of Islam.* Chapel Hill: University of North Carolina Press, 1975.

Smith, Wilfred Cantwell. *The Meaning and End of Religion.* Minneapolis: Fortress Press, 1990.

Suhrawardī, Shihāb al-Dīn. *Fī ḥaqīqat al-'ishq/On the Reality of Love.* In *The Philosophical Allegories and Mystical Treatises,* translated by Wheeler Thackston, 58–76. Costa Mesa, Calif.: Mazda, 1999.

Takeshita, Masataka. "Continuity and Change in the Tradition of Shirazi Love Mysticism: A Comparison between Daylamī's *'Aṭf al-Alif* and Rūzbihān Baqlī's *'Abhar al-'Āshiqīn.*" *Orient* 23 (1987): 113–31.

Wolfson, Harry. *The Philosophy of the Kalam.* Cambridge, Mass.: Harvard University Press, 1976.

Index of Qur'anic Verses

Page numbers in italics indicate commentary on the specific verse.

Index of Hadiths and Sayings

Sources are identified minimally. In the case of Hadith, I have limited myself to the six major Sunni collections (those of Bukhārī, Muslim, Nasā'ī, Abū Dāwūd, Tirmidhī, and Ibn Māja), plus Aḥmad ibn Ḥanbal (*al-Musnad*), Suyūṭī (*al-Jāmi' al-ṣaghīr*), and al-Ghazālī (*Iḥyā'*). NF means that I did not find the saying in any of these books.

Index of Names and Terms

Proper names are identified briefly unless discussed in the text. Figures given a biography in Qushayri's *Epistle* are marked by "Q" followed by a page reference to the Knysh translation. Page numbers in italics indicate key discussions of the specific term.